Childhood in America

Childhood in America

EDITED BY

Paula S. Fass and Mary Ann Mason

New York University Press

NEW YORK AND LONDON

NEW YORK UNIVERSITY PRESS
New York and London

Library of Congress Cataloging-in-Publication Data
Childhood in America / edited by Paula S. Fass and Mary Ann Mason.
p. cm.
Includes bibliographical references and index.
ISBN 0-8147-2692-5 (alk. paper) — ISBN 0-8147-2693-3 (pbk. : alk. paper)
1. Children—United States—History.   2. Children—United States—History—Sources.   3.
Youth—United States—History.   4. Youth—United States—History—Sources.   5.
Adolescence—United States—History.   6. Adolescence—United States—History—Sources.
I. Fass, Paula S. II. Mason, Mary Ann.
HQ792.U5 C4199 1999
305.23'0973 21—dc21

99-045125

New York University Press books are printed on acid-free paper,
and their binding materials are chosen for strength and durability.

Manufactured in the United States of America

For our students

Contents

Acknowledgments   xxi

Introduction: Childhood in America: Past and Present   1
Paula S. Fass and Mary Ann Mason

PART 1. Childbirth and Infancy   9

1. Before the Birth of One of Her Children   11
   Anne Bradstreet

2. Women as Childbearers, 1650–1750   12
   Catherine M. Scholten

3. Brought to Bed: Childbearing in America   16
   Judith Walzer Leavitt

4. Mothers' Sacred Duty: Breast-Feeding Patterns among
      Middle- and Upper-Class Women in the
      Antebellum South   20
   Sally McMillen

5. Reconstructing Motherhood: The La Leche League in
      Postwar America   23
   Lynn Y. Weiner

6. Amazing Births: Medical History in "Miracle" Births   29
   Charles Petit

7. Woman Gives Birth to Baby Conceived outside the Body   32
   New York Times

8. The Eggs, Embryos, and I   35
   Melissa Moore Bodin

9. The Egg Women   38
   Margaret Talbot

10. Choosing Childlessness   41
     Newsweek

11. Thoughts on Child Rearing   44
     Anne Bradstreet

12. The Use of Reason in Child Rearing   45
     John Locke

13. Toys   49
     Maria Edgeworth

14. The Cry   52
     L. Emmett Holt

15. Too Much Mother Love   54
     John B. Watson

16. The Mother-Child Dyad Revisited: Perceptions of Mothers
     and Children in Twentieth-Century Child-Rearing
     Manuals   56
     Nancy Pottishman Weiss

17. Child Science and the Rise of the Experts   61
     Joseph M. Hawes

18. The Construction of Reality in the Child   64
     Jean Piaget

19. Understanding the Infant   67
     Jerome Kagan

20. Mothers and Fathers Working and Rearing Children   72
     T. Berry Brazelton

PART 2. Boys and Girls   77

21. In Reference to Her Children, 23 June, 1659   79
     Anne Bradstreet

22. Breeching Little Ffrank   82
     A. North

23. Suits and Frocks 83
Karin Calvert

24. American Girlhood in the Nineteenth Century 87
Anne Scott MacLeod

25. Nineteenth-Century Boys' Literature 90
Daniel T. Rodgers

26. Briar Rose 95
The Brothers Grimm

27. Little Women 98
Louisa May Alcott

28. Nancy Drew and the Secret of the Old Clock 100
Carolyn Keene

29. The Sexual Life of the Child 102
Sigmund Freud

30. Feminine Psychology 104
Karen Horney

31. Male and Female: Sex and Temperament 108
Margaret Mead

32. Infantile Sexuality 110
Erik H. Erikson

33. Moral Reasoning in Girls and Boys 116
Carol Gilligan

34. How Schools Shortchange Girls 119
American Association of University Women Report

PART 3. Adolescence and Youth 123

35. Courtship and Gender Differences 125
Ellen K. Rothman

36. Children's Voices from the Civil War 129
Emmy E. Werner

37. Adolescence in Historical Perspective   132
     John Demos and Virginia Demos

38. The Physiology and Psychology of Adolescence   139
     G. Stanley Hall

39. Compulsory Schooling and Parent-Adolescent Relations   142
     Stephen A. Lassonde

40. The Natural History of the Gang   146
     Frederic M. Thrasher

41. Adolescent Girls in Samoa and America   149
     Margaret Mead

42. Identity, Youth, and Crisis   153
     Erik H. Erikson

43. Anorexia Nervosa in the 1980s   161
     Joan Jacobs Brumberg

44. Reviving Ophelia: Saving the Selves of Adolescent Girls   166
     Mary Pipher

45. Families Started by Teenagers   169
     Jane Mauldon

46. Why the Young Kill   177
     Sharon Begley

47   Petting   181
     F. Scott Fitzgerald

48. The Member of the Wedding   183
     Carson McCullers

49. Manchild in the Promised Land   187
     Claude Brown

50. Becoming a Man: Half a Life Story   191
     Paul Monette

51. Adulthood? Later, Dude!   196
     D. James Romero

PART 4. Discipline   201

52. Family Life in Plymouth Colony   203
     John Demos

53. Protecting Children from Abusing Masters   206
     Colonial Documents

54. Inculcating Self-Discipline   208
     John Locke

55. Introducing Children into the Social Order   211
     Carl N. Degler

56. A Milder and Warmer Family Government   216
     Horace Bushnell

57. Learning Self-Control   218
     Louisa May Alcott

58. The Life of a Slave Child   221
     James W. C. Pennington

59. Managing Young Children   223
     Benjamin Spock

60. Corporal Punishment   227
     North Carolina Middle District Court

61. Cracking Down on Kids   229
     Annette Fuentes

PART 5. Working Children   235

62. Fathers/Masters: Children/Servants   237
     Mary Ann Mason

63. Children's Involuntary Labor   241
     Colonial Documents

64. Apprentices, Servants, and Child Labor   244
     Colonial Documents

65. Children and Manufactures   248
     Alexander Hamilton

66. Choosing a Trade   249
     Benjamin Franklin

67. Children in the Mills   251
     August Kohn

68. Children at Work in the City   253
     David Nasaw

69. A Child Worker in the Garment Industry   256
     Rose Cohen

70. The Changing Social Value of Children   260
     Viviana A. Zelizer

71. Coming of Age in Mississippi   263
     Anne Moody

72. Children and the New Deal   265
     Paula S. Fass

73. American Children in the Second World War   269
     Robert William Kirk

74. Child Labor and the Law   272
     U.S. Supreme Court

75. Working Children in Contemporary Chinatown   275
     Samuel G. Freedman

PART 6. Learning   281

76. Education and the Concept of Childhood   283
     Philippe Ariès

77. Family Instruction in Early Massachusetts   286
     Colonial Document

78. A Puritan Education   288
     Edmund S. Morgan

79. Émile 292
Jean-Jacques Rousseau

80. Moral Education for Citizenship 294
Carl F. Kaestle

81. The Education of Mary Anna Longstreth 296
Harvey J. Graff

82. Tom Sawyer's Examination Day 298
Mark Twain

83. The Child and the Curriculum 303
John Dewey

84. Testing the IQ of Children 307
Paula S. Fass

85. For the Love of Books 313
Richard Wright

86. School Desegregation 318
U.S. Supreme Court

87. Education in the Post-Sputnik Era 321
Diane Ravitch

88. Children of Crisis 326
Robert Coles

89. Hunger of Memory: The Education of Richard Rodriguez 331
Richard Rodriguez

90. The Quest for Clarity 333
Jerome S. Bruner

91. Children and the Individuals with Disabilities
Education Act 337
Albert Shanker

92. The Theory of Multiple Intelligences 339
Howard Gardner

93. Mother's Little Helper: Ritalin and Attention
     Deficit Disorder   243
     LynNell Hancock, Pat Wingert, Mary Hager, Claudia Kalb,
     Karen Springen, and Dante Chinni

PART 7. Children without Parents   347

94. Kidnapping and White Servitude   349
     Abbot Emerson Smith

95. Orphans' Court   352
     Lois Green Carr

96. Abraham Lincoln and Sarah Bush Lincoln   355
     David Herbert Donald

97. A Childhood in Slavery   357
     Frederick Douglass

98. Placing Orphan Children with Farm Families   359
     Charles Loring Brace and His Critics

99. Huckleberry Finn   367
     Mark Twain

100. Shadow of the Plantation: Separation and Adoption   371
     Charles S. Johnson

101. Surviving the Breakup: How Children Respond to
     Divorce   374
     Judith S. Wallerstein and Joan Berlin Kelly

102. Solomon's Children: The New Biologism, Psychological
     Parenthood, Attachment Theory, and the Best
     Interests Standard   381
     Arlene Skolnick

103. Fit to Be a Parent?   387
     Mary Ann Mason

104. Lesbian Parents in Custody Disputes   391
     California Court of Appeal

104. Surrogacy and Child Custody   395
     California Supreme Court

106. Teenage Voices from Foster Care   399
     Autobiographical Documents

107. Foster Care and the Politics of Compassion   404
     Nanette Schorr

108. Orphanage Revival Gains Ground   410
     Katharine Q. Seelye

PART 8. The Vulnerable Child   415

109. Waifs of the City's Slums   417
     Jacob A. Riis

110. Preserving the Home   422
     Conference Document

111. The Mothers' Aid Movement   424
     Documents from the Child Welfare Movement

112. Infant Mortality   427
     Charles R. King

113. Polio   432
     U.S. News & World Report

114. "Welcome to Willowbrook"   436
     Geraldo Rivera

115. Kidnapping in Contemporary America   438
     Paula S. Fass

116. The Last Frontier in Child Abuse   444
     Suzanne M. Sgroi

117. By Silence Betrayed: The Sexual Abuse of Children in
        America   449
     John Crewdson

118. Miscounting Social Ills   453
     Neil Gilbert

119. Psychiatric Hospitals for Juveniles?   456
      Sylvia Ann Hewlett

120. Couple Held in Beating of Daughter   459
      Todd S. Purdum

121. A Glimpse into a Hell for Helpless Infants   462
      New York Times

122. An Infant's Death, an Ancient "Why?"   466
      Jan Hoffman

123. Media Violence and Children   469
      Hillary Rodham Clinton

124. A Teenage Voice from Foster Care   473
      Autobiographical Document

PART 9. Sexuality   479

125. The Turn of the Screw   481
      Henry James

126. Child-Loving: The Erotic Child and Victorian Culture   488
      James R. Kincaid

127. Polymorphous Perversity   491
      Sigmund Freud

128. Delinquent Daughters: The Age-of-Consent Campaign   494
      Mary E. Odem

129. Coming of Age in Samoa   499
      Margaret Mead

130. Preadolescent Sexuality   500
      Kinsey Institute for Sex Research

131. Lolita   511
      Vladimir Nabokov

132. The Disappearance of Childhood: The Total Disclosure
            Medium   515
      Neil Postman

133. The Assault on Truth: Freud's Suppression of the
      Seduction Theory   518
      Jeffrey Moussaieff Masson

134. The Unraveling of a Monstrous Secret   521
      Marla Williams and Dee Norton

135. On Prison Computer, Files to Make Parents Shiver   524
      Nina Bernstein

136. The Politics of Parental Notification   530
      Maris A. Vinovskis

PART 10. The Child and the State   535

137. The Family in the Social Order   537
      Colonial Document

138. The Child-Saving Movement   539
      Jacob A. Riis

139. The Progressive-Era Transformation of Child Protection,
      1900–1920   543
      Linda Gordon

140. The State as Superparent   549
      Mary Ann Mason

141. The Children's Bureau   555
      Government Documents

142. The Establishment of Juvenile Courts   559
      Susan Tiffin

143. Juvenile Court and the Artistry of Approach   566
      Ben B. Lindsey and Rube Borough

144. The Children's Charter   570
      White House Conference Document

145. The First Amendment in School   573
      U.S. Supreme Court

146.   Juveniles' Right to Due Process   578
       U.S. Supreme Court

147.   Punishing Very Young Criminals   585
       Peter Fimrite

148.   Vote for Eighteen-Year-Olds: What Justices Said on
              Both Sides   587
       U.S. News & World Report

149.   The Right to Vote   591
       U.S. Constitution

150.   Now That the Voting Age Is Lower . . .   592
       U.S. News & World Report

151.   Contraception   594
       U.S. Supreme Court

152.   Abortion   596
       U.S. Supreme Court

153.   Mental Health and the Rights of the Child   599
       U.S. Supreme Court

154.   Visitation Rights   603
       Illinois Appellate Court

155.   A Voice for the Child?   609
       Mary Ann Mason

156.   United Nations Convention on the Rights of the Child   612
       UN Document

PART 11. The Child's World   617

157.   The Material Culture of Early Childhood: The Upright
              Child   619
       Karin Calvert

158.   My Life in the South   625
       Jacob Stroyer

159. A Russian Jewish Girlhood on the Lower East Side   627
      Rose Cohen

160. Quiet Odyssey: A Pioneer Korean Woman in America   632
      Mary Paik Lee

161. Call It Sleep   637
      Henry Roth

162. Young Lonigan   642
      James T. Farrell

163. Growing Up Native American: The Language We Know   646
      Simon Ortiz

164. Down These Mean Streets   649
      Piri Thomas

165. I Know Why the Caged Bird Sings   653
      Maya Angelou

166. China Boy   657
      Gus Lee

167. Talking to High Monks in the Snow: An Asian American
          Odyssey   663
      Lydia Yuri Minatoya

168. The Adventures of Tom Sawyer   666
      Mark Twain

169. The Days Gone By   669
      James Whitcomb Riley

170. The Wizard of Oz   670
      L. Frank Baum

171. Anne of Green Gables   673
      L. M. Montgomery

172. The Sneetches   676
      Dr. Seuss

173.   Snozzcumbers   679
       Roald Dahl

174.   American Children and Their Books   684
       Gillian Avery

175.   Children in Fiction and Fact   690
       Anne Scott MacLeod

176.   Kids' Stuff: Toys and the Changing World of American
          Childhood   694
       Gary Cross

177.   What Makes Nick Tick: Nickelodeon Is a Sensibility,
          a World, an All-Empowering Club. It's CNN
          for Children   697
       Don Steinberg

178.   Children's Literary Voices   700
       Merlyn's Pen

       Sources   704

       Index   715

       About the Editors   725

Acknowledgments

This anthology grew (and grew) as two colleagues and friends began to imagine an anthology on the topic of childhood, broadly conceived and inclusive, that would assist us in teaching a new course and defining a new field. As we proceeded to make it happen, our dependence on help from others also grew (and grew). We are especially indebted to the University of California at Berkeley and New York University Press, two institutions whose support has been crucial to the completion of this project. We were able to afford to publish this book because of money that was made available to us from the Hewlett Foundation and the University of California at Berkeley Office of the Dean of Undergraduate Affairs, who understand the importance of innovative, collaborative, and interdisciplinary undergraduate teaching. As dean, Carolyn Porter made things possible that would likely not have happened without her help.

At Berkeley two extraordinary graduate students, Laura Mihailoff and Samantha Barbas, provided the energy, intelligence, and commitment to bring together the many little pieces assembled here. We also would like to thank Jennifer Di Bara, Diana Selig, Jan Greenough, Rachel Hope Sinnreich, and Laura Curran, who assisted us at various points, Melissa Trafton, who brought us our wonderful jacket illustration, and our many undergraduate and graduate students from whom we have learned as we have been developing children's history as a lively arena for research and learning. Over the years our colleagues Steve Sugarman, Jane Mauldon, David Kirp, Neil Gilbert, Judy Stacey, Judy Wallerstein, Phil Cowan, Caroline Pape Cowan, Joan Hollinger, Arlene Skolnick, Rick Barth, Agnès Fine, and Claire Neirinck have made huge contributions to our understanding of childhood as we explored family issues together. Martha Minow and Barbara Katz Rothman have offered valuable suggestions that helped us think about the book more effectively. Mia Reiser, Gail Phillips, and Nadine Ghammache provided invaluable and generous assistance with bookkeeping and secretarial matters throughout.

At New York University Press Tim Bartlett, now at Basic Books, first gave this book his attention. Ever since, Niko Pfund has been its guardian angel. He has been kind, stimulating, attentive, and encouraging—everything a good editor should be. In addition, he has been an inspiration, something that can be said only of the very best. At New York University Press too, Daisy Hernandez and Despina Papazoglou Gimbel have ushered the book through to completion with attention and care.

We also want to thank our families. Bibi and Charlie made suggestions about children's literature and each also went to work finding passages that we have included. Eve reminded her mother of important children's issues and the Supreme Court's rulings on them. Jack and Paul have put up with a lot but since they love children as we do, we hope they find that it has been worthwhile.

Introduction
Childhood in America: Past and Present

Paula S. Fass and Mary Ann Mason

Valuing Children

Children are constantly on our minds. They are convenient symbols for our better selves, and we use them to make points, make laws, win elections. But children have also become a necessity in new ways. For many adults in the second half of the twentieth century, the parent-child relationship has replaced marriage as their primary social and emotional connection. Adults can no longer count on husbands and wives for lifelong emotional support and affection as statistics prove the unreliability of marriage. Only with children, many adults are coming to believe, can one hope to find long-term emotional ties. Without children, one often has difficulty finding comfort even in the secondary web of human connections: neighborhoods and civic institutions. Children provide the links to neighbors and school activities that tie the adult to the community. Indeed, the recent boom in medically assisted reproduction reflects this need. The urgent desire to parent has created a rich industry based in new technological interventions that allow infertile or gay or lesbian couples to circumvent each stage of the usual procedure of insemination, conception, pregnancy, and childbirth (see part 1). These interventions raise basic questions about the biological essence of motherhood and fatherhood. More important, they attest to the pressing centrality of children in the lives of adults. When children are not born naturally, adults must invent them in new ways.

Children have always been critically important for parents as well as communities, but not always for the same reasons. For most of our history, until the twentieth century, the social worth of children was understood primarily in terms of economic rather than emotional value. From early settlement in the first half of the seventeenth century until well into the nineteenth, the family was an interdependent unit in which children played an integral part. From the earliest age when a child could hold a spinning card, she was likely engaged in household industry. By the age of twelve or so most children were treated as adult producers (see part 5). For most Americans, childhood as we have come to know it in modern times did not exist.

Beginning in the eighteenth century, children's personalities became an important philosophical matter and the subject of artistic representation, but the value of children was still measured in terms of the services they performed. Even in the nineteenth century, when sentimental images of children and childhood innocence were treasured in public language and culture, most children were firmly part of a family economy and their contribution was viewed in those terms. Individual children may have been loved and even spoiled, but most parents depended on their labor for family survival.

Children worked from an early age, and learned as they worked to become adults, under the supervision of their fathers if they were boys, of their mothers if they were girls. The father, as head of the household, held almost complete power of custody and control over children; the mother was a distant second in command. Orphans, defined as children who had no fathers, and children born out of wedlock were apprenticed at an early age (by means of a legal contract) to masters who included them in the household with their own children, teaching them a trade in return for their services (part 7). Still another class of children— children born into slavery—came under the control of the masters of the household. When the War for Independence began in 1776, about one in five American children were slaves. These children were not only early put to hard physical labor, but they were legally considered chattel who could be freely bought and sold by their masters.

In the middle of the nineteenth century the family, one might say, was stood on its head. In middle-class households, at least, mothers replaced fathers in supervising their children. With industrialization and the growth of cities, the economic production that had been central to the household moved out, leaving behind a largely domestic space. As a result of these dramatic changes in nineteenth-century social life, mothers took over most aspects of child nurture. Where earlier the father had controlled the everyday activities of children beyond infancy, the mother now became preeminent. Mothers supervised even boys beyond early childhood at home in the father's absence and at school, where women rather than men began to dominate as teachers. In law and in social attitudes mothers were elevated as the nurturers and caretakers of children. Children in turn were viewed as tender innocents in need of gentle moral nurture. The Victorian mother and child came to dominate sentimental representations of family life.

By the second half of the nineteenth century, the first wave of feminism also enlarged women's legal rights to their children as women struggled for more public roles. For the first time, a mother could be granted custody in the event of separation or divorce and a father could not bequeath his children to a guardian other than the mother in the event of the father's death.

Despite the new child consciousness and sentimentalization of children and mothers in nineteenth-century culture, it was not until the end of the nineteenth century and the beginning of the twentieth that children began to be widely valued primarily in emotional rather than economic terms. As a result of new laws prohibiting child labor and enforcing extended periods of schooling, children were transformed into emotional rather than economic assets. Parents had fewer children and were directed to put more effort into raising them rather than receiving the services of many children, as had earlier generations. Society invested in institutions designed to extend the period of leisured growth and development, especially schools and institutions that emphasized play. It was in this context that what we have come to know as modern childhood began.

It is important to remember that even in this new environment in which children were cherished and their development sheltered, not all children were given the freedom to play and to learn. With the reduced role of children as economic producers children who had no parents, or whose parents were too poor to raise them, were increasingly placed in institutions, mostly orphanages, which held them to a strict work routine. Some children, usually the homeless children found begging on city streets, were "placed out" to farms where child labor was still needed. Poor parents were rarely given help to raise children in their own homes. Poverty, for the most part, was considered a defect of character from which children should be protected by removal. And while slave children were freed as a consequence of the Civil War, most of them shared in the hard toil their parents came to know as southern sharecroppers. Some serious efforts were initially made toward schooling this newly freed class of children, but little of the life of modern childhood with its focus on play and learning was allotted them.

The early part of the twentieth century ushered in a new social awareness of the welfare of children that attempted to bring the lives of the poorest children into line with the developing perspectives of childhood, but the results were often ambiguous as child labor laws and mandatory school attendance interfered with the rights of parents to raise their children as they saw fit. Immigrant parents, in particular, had depended on their children's labor in Europe, Latin America, and Asia and resisted what they perceived as an oppressive and unfair usurpation of their authority. Some of the newer interventions, however, helped families stay together. For the first time, the state worked with private charities to create mothers' pensions and private stipends to keep poor children with their families. Adoption and foster care were promoted as family-centered alternatives to orphanages for children without parents.

During the early twentieth century children's lives were increasingly routinized around school, not work, and augmented with more varied forms of play and entertainment (part 11). Then as now, children were valued almost exclusively in emotional terms, or as investments in a brighter future, not as the working constituents of the economy. By then too, psychologists were deluging mothers with advice on how to rear their children according to the latest and best scientific theories, while doctors had taken over the delivery process and were helping the young to weather the most dangerous periods of infancy and childhood. Science and technology were transforming childhood into the object of new specialized attention that required that children become ever more the precious focus of parental solicitude. A scientifically raised child would become, it was believed, a predictably successful (and later, a happy, well-adjusted) adult.

On the other hand if parents, mothers especially, failed to apply proper child-raising techniques, the adult would fail and the mother would be to blame.

Today the emotional value of children has soared despite, and perhaps because of, the breakdown of marriage. For many, parenthood now serves as a replacement for marriage bonds. But most children are no longer part of a traditional family structure. Among the surest signs of this change is the erosion of the centrality of Victorian motherhood as an anchor of child life. Today more than half of all mothers return to work outside the home during the first year following their child's birth. Children increasingly spend their days outside the home, in day care and other institutions. At the same time, divorce and the sharp increase in out-of-wedlock births are transforming family relationships. The household, too, has been reconfigured as natural parents are replaced by step-parents, and half-siblings and stepchildren are added to the roster of household members. Fewer than half of all children will be raised in a family with their two natural parents.

Amidst this vast institutional transformation, we no longer imagine that our children will help to support the family with their labor, and as the conventional family is transformed we are losing confidence in scientific parenthood. We look instead to children for the bonds and personal ties they provide over a lifetime. Not all children are well cared for or treasured, but our expectation of children has changed radically, along with our own feelings about our right to expect love. We now need children more than ever before.

Reinventing Children

Just as each generation writes its own history, each writes a prescription for a new perception of children to meet its changing needs. Children who were valued for their services were perceived very differently than they are today, when they are looked to for a complex range of emotional supports and human ties. A child who was expected to perform serious farming tasks at age ten must early on be shaped to adult patterns of responsibility. The notion of an emotionally stormy adolescence, a nearly universal expectation in the twentieth-century West, could not be entertained in a work-oriented environment (see part 3). Puritan parents may have loved their children, as the poet Anne Bradstreet attests, but their culture ultimately defined all unredeemed children in terms of sin and animalistic corruption, and work (often in the households of others) provided the discipline to keep children in line and parents from overindulging them. When the Enlightenment invented the new child of the eighteenth century, he brought with him a rational and malleable nature that could be brought up systematically to adulthood, while schooling trained him for work, citizenship, and responsibility. The more romantic notions of the early nineteenth century became the basis for the sentimentalization of childhood, in which sweetly innocent children were made newly lovable and vulnerable, and opened up play as a whole new arena for child life. Starting with the views of John Locke, the great

English philosopher of the Enlightenment, all of these images left some residue in our understanding of childhood, but it was ultimately the view of the child as a separate being whose nature was not pre-adult, but non-adult, and for whom play rather than work was the defining environment, that was most indelibly inscribed in modern views of childhood.

Despite these intellectual and conceptual antecedents, the modern child, whose importance to parents and others is defined by her emotional value, was a creation of the late nineteenth century, a social creation strongly supported by a newly visible and potent state. It was the innocent child the state stepped in to protect at the turn of the century. The concept behind the formation of the juvenile court was to remove children from abusive parents and to save still malleable children who were leaning toward a life of crime. The state would offer comfort and rehabilitation, not punishment. And increasingly, children were to be raised by families, not institutions, as foster homes and adoption substituted for orphanages and as mothers' pensions provided support to the unfortunate (see part 10).

In recent times the state has started to focus on children in a new way, no longer perceiving them as tender innocents, but rather as young adults ready to take on responsibilities and punishment. Partly because families are less stable and parental authority less clear, the state has begun to give children rights independent of their parents (part 10). These newly gained rights allow children limited civil liberties, the right to some reproductive choices, and greater due process rights for juvenile offenders in the courtroom. But this also means that playful irresponsibility is cut off for many children. Ironically, but not altogether coincidentally, as children are being given the rights of adults they are also being newly held to adult standards. Children as young as thirteen can now be tried as adults for some crimes. The fate of the juvenile court, which emerged at the turn of the twentieth century to protect the separateness of childhood, is in doubt—one indication among others of the profound changes now under way.

While childhood experience changed slowly in the past, the vast acceleration of social change in the last century and especially the last twenty-five years has led to major reevaluations of many of the essential components of our earlier vision of childhood. We may well be in the midst of a new invention of childhood to meet our radically changing social lives and circumstances. The changes in the family are surely one of these. But so are many broader social changes, whose effects we are only now beginning to evaluate. Among the most prominent of these has been the enormous expansion of that domain that our nineteenth-century ancestors called play and we today define as entertainment. New commercial toys and especially electronic media like television, video games, and computers have profoundly altered the world of childhood (part 11). So have the accelerated demands for skills in today's world that have placed schools so often at the top of our list of complaints and so fundamentally at the center of all discussions of the reforms required for a more adequate modern childhood (part 6). But the new demands that schools adequately prepare children for adult skills can often ignore the childhood spaces they occupy. Where schools were initially expanded in order to substitute a longer childhood for the rush to work, they are today being increasingly tied to the work world.

This book will look back over the last four hundred years to consider how children have been defined and redefined by the adults who depend on them. We have tended to emphasize changes in the last two hundred years, when childhood has been most clearly set apart, and have given special attention to documents about the last twenty-five because they seem to tell us something we need to know as we pass into the next century.

In considering children we must always keep in mind that in every era there are wide social variations within the population. For most of our history, for example, a high percentage of children lived as slaves. Throughout the twentieth century, race and immigrant status as well as economic standing and membership in an ethnic community have had a marked effect on how children were viewed and treated and the kinds of lives they could be expected to lead. We have tried to maintain this awareness of difference without losing sight of a common thread.

Childhood is like a many-faceted prism, whose light is both reflected and distorted in the eyes of the beholder. We will be looking at the many facets of childhood through the eyes of many witnesses, turning the prism from childbirth through adolescence, from the angles of sexuality, learning, and gender, and from the perspective of the growing supervision provided by the state. The book is divided into eleven parts, each of which usually proceeds through time, but mixes different kinds of accounts—court cases and autobiographies, historical analyses and psychological theories, poems and social reports. The story in each section moves from past to present, but because we have juxtaposed contemporary observations with historical analyses, items are not necessarily in chronological order. Our aim is to capture how children in the modern world have penetrated into every aspect of culture and how our understanding of them has changed over time. It is also designed to capture the multiple realities that coexist today and in the past in the lived experience of children themselves. This is, of course, the most daunting challenge, since children are the most elusive witnesses. They are rarely asked to reflect on their experiences in writing (even when they can write), and when they are, what they have to say is all too often not saved. Where possible, we use material provided by children or at least written from the child's-eye view (part 11).

We hope this anthology will make clear that children's impact on institutions, politics, and social thought is much greater than we usually realize. The means we devise to teach, socialize, and protect children define who we think we are as human beings and as a society. And they provide significant markers of how we have changed. Child-rearing advice and approaches to discipline (parts 1 and 4), which have been changing since the eighteenth century, but never so quickly as in the twentieth, are good illustrations of this. So is our (usually) troubled approach to sexuality in children or with children (part 9). Our views of gender have tended to be much more stable, but here too, the last twenty-five years have introduced new ideas and demands for greater similarity in the treatment of girls and boys (part 2). It may be too grand to say that we define ourselves by the way we think of our children and how we manage their growth, but it is not that far from the truth.

In addition to obvious practical and logistical restrictions involving length and cost, this anthology is by definition unfinished because the definition of our subject is ever in flux. In the twentieth century definitions of childhood's end have been progressively extended first into the once "new" realm of adolescence (see part 3) and then beyond, as schooling has expanded into college and graduate training. As one article, "Adulthood? Later Dude!" makes clear, we are today at a loss to say when we are grown-up, or we prefer not to admit it. In the other direction, some of what had previously been constituted as the essence of childhood, sexual innocence, for one example, has been attenuated, and younger children know much more than they did in the past. We may well be at a point when the life cycle and its parts are being radically reconfigured and with them the scope, meaning, and value of childhood. What all this means to our conceptions of children, their emotional value to adults, and the quality of their lives it seems too soon to know, though not too soon to ask about. This, then, is an especially good time to learn where we've been in order to better understand where we might be going, not because it is all completely clear, but because it is germinating. So bearing in mind its great variety and its historical limitations, we hope that this collection will allow the reader to begin discovering childhood in America.

A NOTE FOR THE READER

This book is intended first and foremost as a pedagogical text and a panoramic introduction for the general reader. The editors have accordingly excised all notes in the excerpts contained herein, so as to better streamline the text and engage the reader. We encourage all those interested in learning more about any particular excerpt to consult the original text; full citations are provided in the "Sources" section.

Baby in Red Chair (artist unknown), c. 1810. Courtesy of the Abby Aldrich Rockefeller Folk Art Collection, Williamsburg, VA.

Part One

Childbirth and Infancy

Although they would seem to be the most biological and "natural," childbirth and infancy, like other aspects of childhood, have changed radically over time. They have been heavily influenced by changing technologies, beliefs about human nature, and attitudes about learning. The first selections in part 1 discuss childbirth and infant care: what it means to give birth, the pains and hazards of labor, changing attitudes about breast-feeding, and the role of modern birth technologies in redefining conception and reinventing childbirth. The rest of part 1 is devoted to a series of child-rearing theorists, from John Locke to T. Berry Brazelton. The views of Benjamin Spock, unquestionably the most influential child-rearing expert of the twentieth century, are included in a later section on discipline (part 4). What is most apparent from this set of readings is the strong trend toward scientific intervention in all phases of the conception, birthing, and infancy cycle. This began in the late nineteenth century and has grown rapidly ever since. The readings also make clear that women (and men too) have in various ways desired, resisted, and compromised with the new technologies and expertise-driven developments.

The hazards of childbearing in the seventeenth century are poignantly evoked by the Puritan poet Anne Bradstreet in this poem written as she anticipates the possibility of her death in childbirth. Writing to her husband, Bradstreet takes special care not only to express her love, but to plead that her "babes" be cared for and protected from "step Dames injury," a painful reminder that children in earlier times were frequently raised by stepparents.

Before the Birth of One of Her Children

Anne Bradstreet

All things within this fading world hath end,
Adversity doth still our joyes attend;
No tyes so strong, no friends so clear and sweet,
But with deaths parting blow is sure to meet.
The sentence past is most irrevocable,
A common thing, yet oh inevitable;
How soon, my Dear, death may my steps attend,
How soon't may be thy Lot to lose thy friend,
We both are ignorant, yet love bids me
These farewell lines to recommend to thee,
That when that knot's unty'd that made us one,
I may seem thine, who in effect am none.
And if I see not half my dayes that's due,
What nature would, God grant to yours and you;
The many faults that well you know I have,
Let be interr'd in my oblivious grave;
If any worth or virtue were in me,
Let that live freshly in thy memory
And when thou feel'st no grief, as I no harms,
Yet love thy dead, who long lay in thine arms:
And when thy loss shall be repaid with gains
Look to my little babes my dear remains.
And if thou love thy self, or loved'st me
These O protect from step Dames injury.
And if chance to thine eyes shall bring this verse,
With some sad sighs honour my absent Herse;
And kiss this paper for thy loves dear sake,
Who with salt tears this last Farewel did take.

The historian Catherine M. Scholten introduces us to the general demographic picture of the colonies in the seventeenth and eighteenth centuries, when American families were prolific and the birthrate higher than in Europe and much higher than it is today. Scholten reviews the usual explanations for this phenomenon — the need for labor and the availability of land — and underscores how the high mortality rate of children and the role of women influenced childbearing decisions (1985).

Women as Childbearers, 1650–1750

Catherine M. Scholten

Travelers to America in the colonial period were impressed with the large numbers of children they saw. One visitor remarked that even "Women from other Places who have been long Married and without Children" became "joyfull Mothers" in America, and colonial braggarts proclaimed, "Our Land free, our Men honest, and our Women fruitful." Benjamin Franklin's more analytical mind discerned, about 1751, that the American population doubled approximately every twenty years, independent of immigration. Thomas Malthus, who derived his principle of population from observation of the British North American colonies, calculated the same rate of growth and termed it "probably without parallel in history."

The estimates of each woman's contribution to population growth were, until recently, based on impressions. Historian Arthur Calhoun, relying on randomly gathered genealogies, considered that families of ten to twelve children were "very common" and that families of twenty to twenty-five children were "not rare enough to call forth expressions of wonder." Subsequent statistical studies of colonial communities show that Calhoun's estimates were exaggerated, but even so, the average woman gave birth to about eight children between her twentieth and fortieth years. This was the highest average rate of birth in American history and was, as Franklin and Malthus correctly observed, higher than contemporary European birthrates.

Why did colonial American women have so many more children than their European contemporaries, or American women in more recent times? Franklin and Malthus—and many others since—attributed the high birthrate to distinct American patterns of land and labor distribution, which lowered the age of marriage. Cheap land and a political system favorable to property ownership meant that no part of the society could have any fears about providing amply for a family by farming. American marriages, Franklin thought, took place earlier than European ones because there was no need for most males to endure a prolonged period of servitude before accumulating the means to support a family. And, by increasing the years of a woman's sexual activity, early marriage increased the number of children she bore.

In general, these explanations are persuasive, although in nineteenth-century America there is reason to doubt a direct correlation between free land and high birthrates. Historians who have compared urban and rural fertility have discovered that the decline in the American birthrate began about 1810, before the United States was statistically an urban nation, and urban and rural fertility declined simultaneously. Independent of conditions in the nineteenth century, statistics do bear out the old assumption that colonial women married early, at the age of twenty-one or twenty-two, which was indeed younger than women in contemporary English agriculture communities.

The corollary to the classic argument that American fertility was related to land use is that children were an asset in the labor-scarce colonies. As one pamphleteer observed, children increased so well in America that they would soon supply the lack of servants. Certainly child labor was "a social fact, not a social problem," and six- and seven-year-old children performed chores of household manufacturing and farming in their own families or as apprentices.

Whether colonial American women and their husbands *consciously* bore children for these reasons is doubtful, however. Certainly they understood the value of children as laborers, and parents also hoped that children would support them in their age or infirmity. The New England Puritans who outlined the reciprocal duties of parent and child termed children "comforts in age" and "a Safe-guard and Protection to us as they grow up." Within this context, the high incidence of child death through accident and disease probably also encouraged procreation. Entries such as William Allason's fill journals throughout the colonial period. My wife "brought me a fine Boy," wrote Allason in 1774, "but poor fellow he stayed only 26 days with us, and made an Exchange much for the better." Mortality rates for children under age ten approached 50 percent throughout the colonies during the middle of the eighteenth century. In his essay on population Benjamin Franklin performed the elementary arithmetic: if a marriage produced eight children, four would grow up.

But it is clear that there are no simple correlations between material conditions and population growth. The availability of land, sustenance, and labor, and the incidence of wealth and mortality do not alone explain the frequency of childbearing, especially in the American case. We must consider too the power of abstractions, in particular those social values that encouraged childbearing in the face of maternal exhaustion.

A range of social values potentially affecting fertility suggests itself—political goals, personal hopes for social and economic improvement, limited concern for women and children as individuals, religious conviction that procreation was God's will. The status of women has ultimate significance, however. Without question, the burden of fecundity fell on colonial women. In a situation where there was little political or economic reason to restrain birth, the high rate of birth reflects the limits of social concern for women and is evidence of the pervasive assumption that frequent childbearing was woman's natural lot and her primary social contribution.

In colonial society all moral authorities agreed that procreation was a divine command. Like their European counterparts, the authors of American sermons and manuals on domestic relations invested the command to multiply with layers of meaning. Childbearing did not continue the species in a mere biological sense; it also meant that there would be a legitimate succession of men created in God's image, and of his commonwealth. Children were his blessings, "among the Choice Favours and Gifts of Providence," and instruments of his design. Ministers stressed the folly of presuming that any birth occurred independently of divine will. Each child was a servant of Christ, perhaps destined to perform a unique task. "Who knows but that this child may be an eminent instrument to God's glory, a vessel of use in his generation, and a blessing to the whole family?" ran the rhetorical question. The person who attempted to control child-bearing tampered dangerously with the divine plan. Those who carried them-selves "graciously" if their house filled with children served the Lord.

Women, theologians argued, especially ought to welcome pregnancy as a "merciful visit" of the Lord, a sign of his blessing, and an opportunity to coop-erate in their own redemption. In sermons to women, ministers reconciled the two seemingly disparate revelations that childbearing was at once an honor and a curse. It was the "first privilege of the Sex" to carry the "living soul" of the child. Cotton Mather suggested that women derived "more than a little" of their dignity from maternity, for "the Redeemer was *Borne* of a woman"; and Benja-min Colman called pregnancy the "Honour of our first Mother Eve."

Although ministers saluted mothers in their congregations with "Blessed are you among women," they also depicted the pains of childbirth as the appropriate special curse of "the Travailing Daughters of Eve." Women inherited the punish-ment for Eve's transgression. If the sorrows of childbirth were evidence of sin, the New Testament indicated that they might also be a means of salvation. Ministers followed Paul's word that woman "shall be saved in childbearing if she continued also in faith and charity." They also thought that women's fear of death in childbirth was a mercy, because the "excesses of Piety" that followed "secures for them Eternal Blessedness."

These formal religious explications are the most elegant expression of a men-tality that perceived frequent childbearing as woman's ordained lot. Cotton Mather might puzzle through scripture and, with doctrinal precision, tell women that it was "unnatural in you to complain of a state, whereunto the Laws of Nature, established by God, have brought you." Lesser minds bypassed the intricate reasoning and took scripture plainly. Thus, a popular medical manual explained simply that women bring forth children in pain because of God's curse on Eve and reminded readers that the prime purpose of the sacrament of mar-riage was the production of offspring. Whatever mixture of faith and reason led people to accept scripture literally, the social consequences for women were constant. Their expectations and their behavior were limited. "I do believe women have nothing in the general in view but the breeding contests at home," Virginia gentleman Landon Carter wrote in 1772. "It began with poor Eve and ever since then has been so much of the devil in woman."

Understandably, women viewed the matter in different perspective. Although they accepted frequent childbearing as inevitable, few went so far as to embrace the statement of some ministers that they should welcome childbirth as their divinely ordained mission. On the contrary, some indicated that childbearing sapped them; and well it did, since the average woman spent about six years of her life pregnant, and eight more years nursing infants if they survived. The weariness of Mary Clap, wife of Thomas Clap, president of Yale College, surfaces even through the ritual phrases of her elegy. "She always went thro the Difficulties of Childbearing with a Remarkable Steadiness Faith Patience and Decency, She Had Calm and Humble Resignation to the Divine will," her husband remembered. "Indeed She would Sometimes Say to me that Bearing tending and Burying Children was Hard work, and that She Had Done a great Deal of it for one of Her Age (She Had 6 Children whereof she buried 4 and Dyed in ye 24 year of Her age.)" President Clap missed the point after his wife's death, as he had during her life, for he continued, "Yet [she] would Say it was the work She was made for, and what god in his providence Had Called Her to." Elizabeth Drinker, a Philadelphia Quaker, probably echoed the sentiments of most women when she reflected, "I have often thought that women who live to get over the time of Child-bareing, if other things are favourable to them, experience more comfort and satisfaction than at any other period of their lives."

3

The birthing room was originally a woman's domain. The historian Judith Walzer Leavitt describes how male physicians were at first carefully introduced into this female-centered space; later their authority increased as the delivery site shifted from home to hospital (1986).

Brought to Bed
Childbearing in America

Judith Walzer Leavitt

The women's network that developed at least in part through the strong attachments formed across the childbirth bed had long-lasting effects on women's lives. When women suffered the agonies of watching their friends die, when they had helped a friend recover from a difficult delivery, or when they had participated in a successful birthing, they developed a closeness that often lasted their lifetime. Surviving life's traumas together made the crises bearable and produced important bonds that continued to sustain other parts of women's lives. "It was as if," Marilyn Clohessy wrote, "mothers were members of a sorority and the initiation was to become a mother." Nannie Jackson's female support network offers one example of the importance of good friends. Her diary, which survives only for the year 1890–91, is a litany of friends helping one another. Her best friend was Fannie, who lived half a mile away; Nannie visited her daily, and sometimes two, three, and four times a day. Once, during the eighth month of her third pregnancy, she visited Fannie three times in one evening, and her husband got angry. But, Nannie noted, "I just talk to Fannie & tell her my troubles because it seems to help me to bear it better when she knows about it. I shall tell her whenever I feel like it." Indeed, in this diary fragment from 1890, there is evidence of significant rebellion against her husband's wishes and her strong reliance on her relationship with Fannie. During her confinement, Fannie came and stayed for four days and nights. But Fannie was only the most important in a long list of close friends. Nannie, who was white, visited daily with many other women, both white and black, cooking special things for them, sharing the limited family resources, helping them with sewing projects, sitting up with them when they were sick, helping out at births, arranging funerals. Nannie and her friends, whose economically limited lives left nothing for outside entertainment or expense, found rich resources within their own group.

The psychological dimension of the women's network played a significant role in making women's hard lives bearable and in sustaining them during difficult times. Perhaps more significant to these women, however, was the practical assistance friends could provide during the times of crisis. During labor and delivery, when a woman might not be able to stand up for herself, she could rely on her women friends to do her talking for her. The women gathered around the birthing bed made decisions about when and if to call physicians to births that midwives were attending; they gave or withheld permission for physicians' procedures; and they created the atmosphere of female support in a room that might have contained both men and women.

In the colonial period, a birthing woman "called her women together" when she went into labor. Midwives and other attendants assessed the situation and managed the birth as long as events progressed relatively normally. If they judged the situation to be abnormal, they advised calling in a physician. In these situations, the physician entered the room as an expert, but an expert who had a nasty duty to perform. The "learned man" would use his instruments to force delivery, either by fetal manipulation and live delivery or, much to be dreaded, by fetal dismemberment and extraction. As historian Laurel Thatcher Ulrich concluded, "In a moment of extreme peril the traditional experience of the midwife gave way to the book-learning and professional aura of the minister-physician." But for most of the colonial period only at the beckoning of the attending women and as a last resort would birth procedures incorporate male activity.

Not until the last half of the eighteenth century did some urban women begin calling in physicians early in normal labor as the major attendants. Yet even then, and throughout the nineteenth century, those women who asked physicians to attend them continued to call their women friends and relatives to help them and relied on the advice of the women along with the advice of the physician. Sometimes the women, usually called first, advised that no medical attendant be called. As one doctor realized, "A certain amount of inconvenience is anticipated [by the birthing woman], and so long as this supposed limit is not passed, the patient contrives, with the advice of her female friends, to dispense with a medical attendant." At other times, the attending women suggested additional help. Many physicians attributed their obstetric calls to midwives or to neighbor women who were already present at a progressing labor. Dr. John Meachem, struggling to establish himself after graduating from medical school, recorded a successful first case: "Mrs. Doolittle was present, and I always thought that she had a good deal to do with engineering this call. At least I gave her the credit." In Michigan, Ellen Regal, who had come to Ypsilanti to attend her sister's con-finement in 1872, disapproved of her sister's choice of birth attendant. She wrote to her brother, "the more we hear of the doctors here the more we all feel as though we could not trust any of them." Ellen took it upon herself to travel home to Ann Arbor to enlist the help of a trusted family doctor.

Physicians found themselves increasingly called to attend women in labor in the nineteenth century, but frequently in the company of midwives and women friends. While midwives were probably not invited into the homes of the "privileged" group . . . the middle-class women who asked physicians to attend them oftentimes included the neighborhood midwife in their list of birthing-room companions. These various attendants exhibited some tensions about having to work with each other, but on the whole they learned to get along together. . . .

When male physicians began attending normal labor and deliveries, and standards of excellence began to change in eighteenth- and nineteenth-century America, birthing women faced a dilemma. Women who were accustomed to female birth attendants had to decide whether to retain their traditional female attendants or to increase their chances of survival and future health, as they saw it, by inviting men into their birthing rooms. We have already seen that some urban, advantaged women made this decision quite easily and chose male attendants. Modesty being less important for them than safety, they opted for the physicians who represented science because they believed that medicine held out promises for increased safety. But even the Drinkers, the Philadelphia family who welcomed William Shippen and his colleagues into their birthing rooms, noted with relief, when a new attendant was brought in to relieve a protracted labor by bloodletting, "he is a married man." Strange men witnessing intimate female events produced, at the least, a fear of loss of female modesty. Willing to accept the new ways, women were not always comfortable with them.

Indeed, some women continued to prefer female attendants even though they may have thought that male medicine provided the best birth methods. As one physician realized, "Confidence in her physician is of the greatest moment, but at once all the innate modesty of the young girl rebels against the appearance of a stranger—and male, too—in the most delicate position. A shock of startled modesty at once takes the place of all that reliance, trust and confidence that should exist." To this physician, such "adverse circumstances" threatened successful delivery.

As the nineteenth century progressed and physician-directed obstetrics became increasingly acceptable among those Americans who could afford medical services, the decision for those women who were concerned about modesty remained difficult. Especially after physicians introduced anesthesia into obstetric practices and could promise relief from the worst pains of labor, women who wanted female attendants felt their choices increasingly limited. Some women rationalized that keeping birth a domestic event monitored by women made it all right to have male attendants. Most of the nineteenth-century births that physicians attended (and these were at most half of America's births) also continued to be attended by women whom the birthing women selected and trusted and to be governed at least in part by decisions those women made together. Into this still female environment many women found it possible to invite male practitioners.

But for other women in the nineteenth century, and especially for most immigrant women, who retained the traditions of the old world, delivery by a male physician remained unthinkable. Only in the most dire of circumstances would these women consider consulting a man. As Dr. Josephine Baker realized early in the twentieth century when she addressed the problem of regulating obstetrics practice in New York City, "If deprived of midwives, [immigrant] women would rather have amateur assistance from the janitor's wife or the woman across the hall than to submit to this outlandish American custom of having a male doctor for a confinement." Baker claimed that what she called "inherent racial prejudice and the even greater prejudice of their husbands" encouraged immigrant women to choose only female attendants. . . .

From the birthing women's perspective, the greatest contribution nineteenth-century obstetrics achieved was in providing pain relief during labor and delivery. Women feared their confinements in the nineteenth century and, like their grandmothers before them, eagerly sought new birth procedures, especially those that might make them more comfortable during the long hours of their travail. By the middle of the century middle-class women had become accustomed to male birth attendants, although a large segment of the population—probably growing as immigration soared in the latter part of the century—remained faithful to female midwives and traditional birth procedures. Advantaged native-born urban women sought every obstetric improvement that male physicians could offer because they continued to fear childbirth and its attendant discomforts and because they had the financial ability to alter their traditional experiences. Next to the fear of death, pain was probably the single part of birth most hated by birthing women. Fanny Longfellow's exuberant description of her childbirth under ether in 1847, the first in the United States, demonstrates just how ready women were to alleviate the pain of childbirth. "I never was better or got through a confinement so comfortably," she wrote her sister-in-law:

> Two other ladies, I know, have since followed my example successfully, and I feel proud to be the pioneer to less suffering for poor, weak womankind. This is certainly the greatest blessing of this age, and I am glad to have lived at the time of its coming and in the country which gives it to the world.

Women who experienced their childbirths as the hour in which they "touched the hand of death" eagerly sought relief from the frightful event. Ether and chloroform, anesthetic agents of different chemical properties that blocked the perceptions of pain, promised such relief. At the middle of the nineteenth century, when the two drugs were introduced, women like Longfellow embraced anesthesia enthusiastically. One of Walter Channing's patients told him after her etherized birth "how wonderful it was that she should have got through without the least suffering, and how grateful she was."

4

By the nineteenth century alternatives to breast-feeding were available to some women. According to the historian Sally McMillen, white women in the antebellum South chose to breast-feed their children for a variety of reasons, including the influence of tradition and a concern for the health of the children (1985).

Mothers' Sacred Duty
Breast-Feeding Patterns among Middle- and Upper-Class Women in the Antebellum South

Sally McMillen

Southern mothers had strong reasons for suckling their newborn, the most common of which was their acceptance of traditional patterns of childrearing. Widespread, almost silent, acceptance of tradition causes a lack of comment by writers of letters and journals, and with few exceptions, which included women who had difficulty lactating, most southern mothers wrote little on the subject. The only comment one might find after reading dozens of letters on infant rearing might be a cryptic reference or the brief comment, "weaned baby from breast." Mothers were far more eager to discuss their babies' uncertain state of health and their changing behavior, and they often wrote pages about infant antics.

Many southern mothers may have been influenced by medical and maternal advice books and by their own observations about infant health. Physicians and advisers, eager to define women's commitment to child care and family improvement, were unanimous in proclaiming a mother's duty to breast-feed her baby. A major theme in maternal advice books and medical guides written during the antebellum period was that mothers should assume the central role in childrearing. Lydia H. Sigourney and Lydia Maria Child, popular authors who promoted female domesticity, heralded the joys of infant care. As if she alone had discovered a new occupation for women, Mrs. Sigourney declared that through motherhood, women had now "taken a higher place in the scale of being." She urged mothers to create a "season of quietness" during lactation, forgoing their presumably gay social lives for the tranquil rewards of infant care. . . .

One of the most troublesome and fatal illnesses experienced by antebellum southern infants and children was cholera infantum. The 1860 federal census reported the incidence of the disease to be 5½ times greater in the South than in the North. This bacterial disease, now commonly referred to as summer diarrhea, is a severe intestinal disorder, particularly common from late spring through early autumn. Symptoms include severe diarrhea, vomiting, headache, dehydration, and debilitation. Southern mothers observed that youngsters between the ages of six months and two years were most susceptible to cholera infantum, and they commented on its being endemic to the South. Jean Syme noted of the Virginia county in which she lived, "this place is already getting sickly for infants, as many as six died in the course of this week, with bowel complaints." Jane Woodruff of Charleston wrote that she lost four of her young children to "the bowel complaint." Phoebe Elliott of Beaufort, South Carolina, remarked that the young children of three of their local doctors had all been sick with dysentery. Although doctors often linked the disease to urban areas, comments like these indicate that it was prevalent throughout the South.

If the number of journal articles on a subject provides an indication of general concern, cholera infantum apparently caused antebellum physicians much anxiety. It was endemic and virulent, and doctors tried, without success, to pinpoint its causes and discover effective remedies. So poorly understood was this illness that parents and physicians often blamed the disease on teething, since it usually occurred when a child was cutting its first teeth. From our present understanding of bacterial diseases, we know that the causes of cholera infantum were many, though the most common one, undoubtedly, was spoiled food and milk, particularly during the time when a child was being weaned. Mothers who breast-fed their infants had the greatest success in delaying, and occasionally preventing, the disease.

Mothers valued their maternal role and the enjoyment they derived from breast feeding. Motherhood and its attendant duties were highly prized during the antebellum years and touted as women's "sacred" occupation. Feminine pride was tied up with breast feeding, and when a woman could not perform this maternal task, she often felt guilty or inadequate. Just as it was assumed that most women could bear children, so was it assumed that most mothers could suckle their babies. Kate de Rosset Meares in 1854 had to supplement feedings because her milk supply was inadequate. She wrote her mother that she had accepted a slave's offer to help breast-feed her infant son but noted, "if I was certain that it was right, I would be delighted to have him well filled twice a day." Laura Norwood of Hillsboro, North Carolina, regretted her inability to breast-feed and wished that she could be a "good" mother—something she and her husband equated with an adequate supply of breast milk. Many men encouraged their wives to be competent nurturers and praised their ability to feed the newborn. In 1801 Daniel Anderson remarked to his brother-in-law that his infant son "has not had one hour's sickness" because his wife Mary "has aplenty for him." Breast feeding was a task that most people assumed mothers were well able to perform. . . .

Southern mothers may have favored breast feeding because they understood that lactation delayed conception. How widely this idea was known and used as a means of contraception is uncertain. In the absence of other effective forms of birth control—except coitus interruptus, abstinence, and abortion—lactation may have been considered. Current studies indicate that suckling an infant can limit birth to every two years, depending on the frequency of breast feeding and the degree of the infant's dependency on maternal milk. Lactation usually prolongs the cessation of the menses following pregnancy, which would prevent conception. In addition, nursing often implied that an infant slept with its mother, perhaps curtailing coitus as well. Though most southern women found motherhood a satisfying role, many must have agreed with Ella Gertrude Clanton Thomas, who remarked during her third pregnancy in as many years of marriage, "I would dislike to think I would never have other children but then I would willingly have a considerable lapse of time between them." The *Charleston Medical Journal and Review* carried an article by Robert Barnes, a nineteenth-century physician, analyzing the effectiveness of lactation as a method of contraception. Based on his survey of one hundred English women, Barnes determined that "mammary activity" retarded uterine action. He concluded that mothers who breast-fed their infants had a lower rate of conception. Despite the appearance of this article in a well-respected southern journal, the topic of birth control was rarely discussed in medical advice books. Physicians must have been aware of the idea, though whether they privately encouraged the method is unknown. Southern men did not usually wish to limit family size, and many seemed to take pride in their large families. Southern women, however, may secretly have shared the knowledge that breast feeding delayed conception, but they seldom, if ever, discussed it in the privacy of their letters and journals. In the personal correspondence consulted for this study, no woman mentioned using breast feeding as a method of contraception. . . .

Imbued with the crucial importance of their maternal duties, southern women accepted breast feeding as an initial rite of motherhood. Perhaps the fact that slaves existed in the South and could have been used as wet nurses makes a southern woman's commitment to infant nurturing even stronger. Southern mothers believed that early contact with the newborn could influence a child's character. By observation, they recognized that maternal milk was conducive to an infant's health during its early months of life. Most exhibited great pride in their offspring and enjoyed the happy moments surrounding breast feeding. Some women even sacrificed their own health and well-being to insure their baby's future. Lactation as a method of contraception may also have encouraged maternal feeding. Slaves and white women sometimes served as wet nurses, and bottle feeding was used on occasion, but usually only when an emergency demanded an alternative method of feeding. Healthy middle- and upper-class women chose to breast-feed their young.

5

Ironically, despite the application of advanced medical technology to conception and childbirth, many parents currently favor "natural" forms of childbirth and prefer breast-feeding over bottle-feeding. The historian Lynn Y. Weiner discusses the formation of the La Leche League in 1956 and the league's promotion of "natural" mothering, free from interference by medical experts (1994).

Reconstructing Motherhood
The La Leche League in Postwar America

Lynn Y. Weiner

For almost four decades, the La Leche League—a voluntary association of women—has championed its cause of "good mothering through breastfeeding" in the United States and around the world. Although the league has been largely overlooked in scholarly discussions of women in the postwar era, it represents an important piece in the puzzle of twentieth-century social history. The league's publication, *The Womanly Art of Breastfeeding*, has sold some two million copies since 1958, and millions of women have attended league support groups, read league literature, or otherwise encountered league ideology. By the mid-1980s, the league claimed over four thousand support groups in forty-eight countries, and in the United States it had a reputation among many women as the primary source of expertise on motherhood—a position earlier held by the United States Children's Bureau.

The La Leche League was organized during a turbulent period when the social roles of American women as mothers and as workers were contested in both ideology and practice. Nineteenth-century middle-class cultural definitions had promoted "the intense, essentially private nature of the mother-child bond and the primary responsibility of mothers for the well-being of their children." In the mid-twentieth century, those definitions were challenged by developments in fertility patterns, new scientific childbirth and infant-feeding techniques, feminism, and the rapid growth of the female labor force. Science had entered the nursery, which growing numbers of women would soon leave behind.

The La Leche League arose to defend traditional domesticity against the assaults of modern industrial life and to dignify the physical, biological side of motherhood in ways that proved to have surprising appeal to many Americans.

Whereas the nineteenth-century version of middle-class "true womanhood" emphasized moral purity and piety in a secular and industrializing age, the league, in the scientific twentieth century, emphasized naturalism. Mother and baby were not so much icons of purity as symbols of nature and simplicity. But they were not just symbols. The founders of the league had a social outlook that can be called maternalist; that is, they implied that an empowered motherhood defined by "female" qualities would improve society. Their faith in this maternalist prescription enabled La Leche League women to focus their efforts. From the mid-1950s to the present, the La Leche League has pursued a steadfast mission: to "bring mother and baby together again" through the "womanly art of breastfeeding."

That mission attracted a variety of supporters. To those suspicious of the intrusion of experts into family life, the league presented a social role for mothers that restored a sense of autonomy to the private domestic realm. Health benefits to mother and child from breastfeeding, childbirth as a natural process, trust in one's own instincts—these notions found favor among women who questioned "scientific motherhood," an ideology initially developed during the late nineteenth and early twentieth centuries that promoted the authority of experts in the realm of child rearing. By the 1950s, "scientific motherhood" dominated mainstream approaches to family life. In addition, the social movements of the 1960s and 1970s welcomed the "natural" methods of the league and its challenge to the patriarchy of the medical establishment.

The league grew rapidly, especially in the 1960s and 1970s. From one meeting of twelve friends in the fall of 1956, the number of league groups multiplied to 43 in 1961, 430 in 1966, 1,260 in 1971, and to about 3,000 in 1976. By 1981, some 17,000 women had been trained as league leaders. While it is difficult to ascribe credit for the rise in breastfeeding in the United States from the mid-1950s through the mid-1980s, the incidence of breastfeeding by new mothers grew from about 20 to about 60 percent.

If some women saw the league's vision of motherhood as empowering and progressive, there was a catch. To meet league standards of on-demand breastfeeding, mother and infant must remain together. This was not too difficult in the 1950s, when fewer than one in five married mothers of young children under the age of six worked outside the home, but by 1980, that number had risen to almost one in two. As maternal employment norms changed, a posture critical of working mothers made the La Leche League seem increasingly conservative. Like maternalist ideologies of past centuries, La Leche League motherhood gave public purpose to the private activities of domestic life; like advocates of those past ideologies, too, the league urged that women subsume their individualism for the greater good of the family and society. This essay will introduce the history of the league and explore the paradox embedded in the league's maternalist ideology—the way in which it simultaneously promoted women's autonomy and restricted women's roles.

*

At a picnic in the Chicago suburb of Elmhurst, Illinois, during the summer of 1956, two mothers—Mary White and Marian Tompson—sat under a tree nursing their babies. As other women approached them and admired what seemed a difficult and unusual task in an era when bottle-feeding was the norm, these mothers determined to help others learn the "womanly art" of breastfeeding. With five friends they formed the La Leche League, to give "mother to mother" help to women who wanted to nurse their infants. The "founding mothers" at first struggled to find a suitable name, for in those days, according to founder Edwina Froehlich, "you didn't mention 'breast' in print unless you were talking about Jean Harlow." The solution of "La Leche League" was offered by Mary White's husband, obstetrician Gregory White, who often gave his pregnant patients medals from a shrine in St. Augustine, Florida, dedicated to a Spanish madonna, Nuestra Señora de La Leche y Buen Parto, or, loosely translated, "Our Lady of Happy Delivery and Plentiful Milk." . . .

The creation of small all-female groups of peers seems to have been an important source of the league's strength. The groups may have helped to break down the isolation of mothering in nuclear families—a growing problem during the era of rapid suburbanization and geographic mobility. In moving to the new postwar suburbs, many women moved farther away from relatives who in earlier times might have provided information and support for the task of mothering. One grandmother wrote the league, for example, that her daughter had moved away to a new city and felt lonely "until she discovered the existence of La Leche League there." . . . The breastfeeding groups enabled women to practice collectively what might have been difficult for them to achieve on their own. And like the later consciousness-raising groups of the women's liberation movement, the breastfeeding support groups made common the problems of individual women and nurtured their sense of belonging to a special subculture. One league member, Mary Jane Brizzolara, recalled attending a meeting in 1957 and finding "instant rapport" with every woman in the room. "In those days, any woman who wanted to have her baby naturally and breastfeed it thought she was the only person in the world who wanted those things," she said, "but to go to that first meeting and discover a whole room full of women who had the same feelings and the same values—it was great."

The woman-to-woman approach of the groups was also evident in the league's hot-line telephone service and its publications. The league from the start received letters and telephone calls from women seeking advice about specific breastfeeding problems. The founders answered these queries "at home surrounded by . . . babies and children," and it was in response to the "never-ending stream of mail and the frantic phone calls" that the first version of *The Womanly Art of Breastfeeding* was put together, in loose-leaf folders sold as a "Course By Mail." The league newsletter first appeared in May of 1958 and was meant "to keep mothers in touch and give them somebody else to relate to or identify with . . . because at that time few mothers had anyone in their circle of friends who was breastfeeding," recalled founder Marian Tompson. The newsletter featured communications, poetry, photographs, and articles by league members. By 1960, four years after the founding of the organization, its headquarters averaged three hundred telephone calls and four hundred letters monthly. One member explained the reason she turned to the league for information. "My doctor has never had a baby. My doctor has never nursed a baby . . . Sally Jones . . . has nursed three babies. Darlene Smith has nursed four. . . . So this is why I called them instead of my doctor." According to the league, breastfeeding was not a medical issue but rather a "womanly art," and "it's up to women who have learned it to pass it on." Emphasizing the experience and wisdom of mothers rather than the expertise of doctors, the league by the mid-1950s anticipated later feminist calls for a women's health movement by questioning the medicalization of birth and infant care and challenging the influence of "experts" on changing definitions of motherhood. . . .

The popularity of the league also reflected unease with approaches to motherhood and family life common among physicians and other experts in the 1950s. The kind of motherhood experts advocated was anything but "natural"—instead it was "scientific." Professional advice was to replace maternal instinct, and so child-rearing manuals, mothers' clubs, and physicians' counsel brought "modern" ideas about motherhood into the home. Earlier maternalist women's groups, such as the National Congress of Mothers, had argued that motherhood was so important to society that women must be trained to "be the best mothers possible for the good of the race." A School of Mothercraft, for example, was established in New York in 1911 to train mothers in the "intelligent and efficient" art of child care. By the 1930s, the authority of professionals on the subject of motherhood was institutionalized in the disciplines of social work, child guidance, preschool education, and, above all, medicine. Scientific motherhood came to favor the bottle over breastfeeding, medicated hospital birth over natural home birth, and rigidly scheduled days and nights over a more fluid approach to time. Motherhood, in short, was to be controlled by experts rather than directed by instinct. Rationality and order, then important in such other arenas of industrial American culture as business, home economics, and education, informed proper mothering as well. Standards of efficiency, time, and measurement were to control a baby's day as well as a factory's routine.

Bottle-feeding was the preferred way to nourish a baby in 1956. The incidence of breastfeeding at one week of age had fallen to about 18 percent, a decline from about 38 percent in 1948 and from over 80 percent before 1920. Bottle-feeding first became popular in the United States in the late nineteenth century in part because of concerns about high infant mortality rates among the urban poor. Middle-class women soon adopted the new infant feeding method because of a desire to be fashionable and scientific. . . .

In the mid-twentieth century, bottle-feeding was a complicated and time-consuming affair. Mothers followed elaborate methods for preparing formula using evaporated, powdered, or whole milk, carefully calculated total milk volume spread over a certain number of bottles per day, and conscientiously sterilized bottles, rubber nipples, and bottle caps. Babies were often weighed before and after feedings. Advice books insisted that mothers consult their doctors about techniques and schedules; doctors were to "prescribe" breastfeeding or bottle-feeding and to mandate all aspects of mothering. Dr. Benjamin Spock, for example, in the 1946 edition of *The Pocket Book of Baby and Child Care*, offered advice on schedules "only for those parents who are unable to consult a doctor regularly" and suggested that ideally "your doctor will prescribe the baby's schedule on the basis of his needs, and you should consult him about any changes." A 1953 publication circulated by the Beech Nut Company, *Happy Mealtimes for Babies*, stated:

> Before we go any further, let's emphasize one important point: your doctor knows your baby—and he knows you. How your particular baby should be cared for, *whether he's sick or well*, is a matter that should be decided by your doctor—not by the neighbors, relatives or books.

The Federal Children's Bureau, in the 1940 edition of its popular booklet *Infant Care*, offered a detailed daily schedule for infants, which could "be varied according to the directions of the physician."

Childbirth, like infant feeding, was defined as "scientific" in the 1950s. Advocates of scientific motherhood had by the 1920s and 1930s labeled childbirth a medical problem rather than a natural function, in part as a response to high infant and maternal mortality rates. As childbirth became medicalized, control of the birthing process fell away from women and their midwives and into the hands of physicians. . . .

Scientific motherhood was not uncontested. There was a "motherhood reform" community made up of people—health care providers as well as mothers and fathers—interested in returning mothering from the artificial or scientific to the "natural" sphere. By the mid-1950s there were throughout North America and Europe critics representing a variety of social perspectives who challenged invasive childbirth methods, artificial infant-feeding techniques, and rigid child-rearing practices. Some, for example, the British natural childbirth educator Grantly Dick Read, believed that motherhood embodied "essential femininity" and that childbirth was "woman's supreme triumph." Others presented arguments for woman-centered childbirth or more general critiques of modern industrial life. La Leche League founders communicated with many of these varied reformers, including the advocates of family-centered maternity care who in 1960 formed the International Childbirth Education Association. League founders read about natural childbirth, nutrition, and child-rearing techniques in *Child-Family Digest*, published in the United States, and in the *Natural Childbirth Trust Newsletter* from Great Britain. They corresponded with Read about his manual *Childbirth without Fear*, and in 1957 they sponsored him as their first guest speaker. In short, they began to communicate, founder Froehlich recalled, with a growing network of "people who had this healthy thinking about the body." . . .

La Leche League leaders built strong ties with others in the international motherhood reform community of the postwar years, but they were especially influenced by two Chicago-area physicians critical of scientific motherhood:

Gregory White, the husband of league founder Mary White, and White's former teacher, Herbert Ratner, a Chicago-area health commissioner. During the early 1950s, these doctors encouraged their patients to attempt home birth, natural childbirth, and breastfeeding, and they urged their patients to talk with each other about natural mothering techniques. Founder Mary Ann Cahill recalled how White recognized the importance "of mother-to-mother help in breastfeeding" and "recognized that one woman needed another" for advice and support. Several of the league's founders were patients of White and Ratner, who, with a medical advisory board, provided La Leche League with "credibility and acceptability in the scientific community." This was especially important during the early years of the organization, when some considered mothers talking about infant feeding to be, according to founder Froehlich, "interfering with medicine."

Doctors Ratner and White urged league founders to broaden their interests from breastfeeding to the more general issue of mothering. Like many in the motherhood reform community, these men held an essentialist view of women that presupposed a natural and biologically based social role. To Ratner, breastfeeding symbolized woman's place in the social order. At the first league convention in 1964, his keynote address focused on the "art of mothering." He believed Americans had abandoned a family ideology that nurtured women and children. "Motherhood," he stated, "is an opportunity for growth. Three children nurture motherhood more than one. Each mothering experience enriches." He also suggested that women who bottle-fed their babies could too easily separate from them and "become vulnerable to other persuasions," and that a decision to bottlefeed "may be a sign of emotional difficulties in the mother." White also saw breastfeeding as a key to good motherhood. The mother who bottle-feeds, he stated, does not have high levels of prolactin, the hormone that contributes to milk production, and therefore she does not have the same physical feelings toward her baby. "She's handicapped," he said, "she may turn out to be a pretty good mother. But she could have been a lot better mother if she had breastfed." By 1958, league founders had begun to shape a maternalist philosophy centered on "good mothering through breastfeeding" that reflected this essentialist model of womanhood.

At the heart of the La Leche League's philosophy was the notion that the needs of the infant—as interpreted by the mother rather than a doctor—should determine the practice and pace of mothering. League founder Cahill said that "one of our mottos was 'give the baby back to the mother, that's who it belongs to.' " The basic need of the infant was for mother's milk and for mother herself. Therefore breastfeeding and bottle-feeding were not two equally acceptable options for mothers, as the Children's Bureau and Dr. Spock had advised. In the words of a league publication, breastfeeding was a moral imperative, no less than "God's plan for mothers and babies."

6

This 1981 newspaper account of a high-risk pregnancy and labor illustrates the lengths to which some women will go to give birth, and the advances in medical technology that make such births possible.

Amazing Births
Medical History in "Miracle" Births

Charles Petit

It took almost miraculous luck, ferocious determination, and nearly every trick in the book of medical technology.

After seven miscarriages and a stillbirth, 42-year-old watercolor artist Po-Ying Chern of Moraga rested yesterday in Alta Bates Hospital in Berkeley, mother of twin girls.

Even her obstetrician, Dr. Robert Neff, can scarcely believe the odyssey of medicine, surgery and sheer willpower it took to get her through her "one last try" for another child beyond the one beautiful, healthy daughter she bore six years ago. Having twins was a bonus miracle.

He thinks the affair has made minor medical history just from the number of techniques employed to bring tiny Stella and Regina Chern into the world, and the number of things that could have, but didn't, go wrong.

The mother underwent delicate tests to determine if genetic abnormalities she carries had been passed to the developing embryos. She spent months nearly motionless in bed with her feet elevated. She took drugs that could easily kill her if taken in quantities just slightly too large. She underwent emergency surgery never before tried by her doctors to sew her cervix shut to retard premature delivery.

So delicate was her condition for the past two months that Neff forbade the plucky woman from walking to the bathroom for fear that gravity would start her into premature labor.

"I had to crawl," she said yesterday. "It was worth it," added the Formosa-born woman, smiling at her husband, Bechtel Corp. engineer Chii Chern at her side. "But it was so nice to finally be able to stand up."

She married Chii Chern, a Ph.D. graduate from UC Berkeley, 14 years ago. After a number of miscarriages and a stillborn child, in 1974 everything went right, leading to the birth of Eugenia, who is now in kindergarten. But, for Mrs. Chern, it was the last pregnancy to go right for the next six years. She suffered four consecutive miscarriages, all of them difficult and complicated.

"Most miscarriages result from a congenital defect in the fetus," Neff said. Suspecting this was the case with his patient, he sent a sample of aborted tissue in 1979 to Dr. Sanford Sherman, a medical geneticist at Children's Hospital Medical Center in Oakland.

Normal human cells carry 46 chromosomes, the structures within the nucleus whose coils of DNA molecules carry the genetic information to make a full human being. They normally come in 23 pairs. The cells of the doomed fetus contained 47 chromosomes.

Analysis of Mrs. Chern's own tissues found she carried a rare genetic disorder called mosaicism. She is literally a mosaic of two kinds of cells. Most of them were normal, but about 10 percent carried an extra chromosome.

Neff consulted with Sherman and other genetics experts, and concluded that, despite the dismal record, his patient stood a good statistical chance that most of the eggs her ovaries produced would have a normal number of chromosomes.

He and his patient drew up a plan to give her every possible chance of successful delivery, on one last try. "I knew I would soon be too old for children," she said yesterday from her hospital bed. "But I wanted another baby so much."

In October last year, she was pregnant again.

On January 12, she visited Alta Bates for the critical test. Doctors first scanned her swollen abdomen with sound waves, in a technique called ultrasound imaging, to locate the developing baby.

Instead of one, there were two. Both babies appeared normal, a finding confirmed by amniocentesis, a clinical test in which a sampling of fetal cells were extracted for a chromosome check.

Things went quickly from good to bad, however. The years of miscarriages had left the hopeful mother with a severely weakened cervix (the mouth to the uterus). On January 23, 18 weeks into the 40 weeks of a full-term pregnancy, Neff ordered partial bedrest for his patient, up only to eat or go to the bathroom. By February 27, it was total bedrest.

On March 17, 26 weeks into the pregnancy, she phoned Neff and reported heavy bleeding and fluid loss. "I was sick," he recalled. "I thought we'd lost it." No baby has ever survived birth after only 26 weeks of gestation. "I was just praying for at least two weeks more."

At the office, one look at his patient and Neff's heart sank. Her cervix was dilated 6 centimeters. Birth usually occurs at 10. Neff and Po-Ying's husband picked her up by hand, ran to the Cherns' car, and raced to Alta Bates. She was injected with a powerful drug, Terbutalene, to stop the contractions.

The drug is dangerous. It can easily cause congestive heart failure and fatal accumulation of fluid in the lungs. Furthermore, it made Mrs. Chern severely nauseous and upset her blood-sugar level.

By lucky coincidence, Neff had one week earlier read an account by two

Canadian medical researchers, Olefemi A. Olatunbosun and Dr. Frank Dyck, of a new method called cervical cerclage for reversing a dilated cervix with protruding membranes. It involves lacing surgical sutures around the cervical opening, then gently pulling them out and around the extremely delicate membranes. Additional sutures are used to pull the cervix shut, like closing a drawstring purse.

Neff hadn't done that before. He stood his patient almost on her head, on a bed inclined at 30 degrees, to get gravity on his side. All she remembers is that her neck hurt. The procedure, however, worked.

For four days, Mrs. Chern's body tried to go into labor again. For four days, delicately dripping Terbutalene into her veins through a tube, an around-the-clock nursing staff kept the contractions to a minimum.

Two weeks later she went home from the hospital. For four more weeks, she was back in bed, but this time with her feet elevated several degrees. She learned to ration the potentially deadly Terbutalene herself, swallowing pills whenever the contractions began.

Finally, last Sunday, she went into labor again. The pregnancy was in its 32nd week, still early, but far from hopeless. "We went through all the same tricks," Neff said while trying to delay birth at least 48 hours. This was to give yet another drug, a steroid called Betamethazone, time to act on the infants' lungs and speed their maturation.

Finally, on Tuesday, "there was no holding her back," and the girls were delivered by Caesarean section. Stella was delivered first, weighing 4 pounds 5 ounces. Regina arrived next, weighing 4 pounds 6 ounces.

"They looked great," Neff said, "but I didn't dare let myself feel good about it until a pediatrician had looked at them and told me they were OK."

In another week or so, he said, mother and children should be going home.

7

Advances in medical technology have transformed not just pregnancy and labor but conception as well. This 1978 article announces the birth of the first test-tube baby.

Woman Gives Birth to Baby Conceived outside the Body

New York Times

The first authenticated birth of a baby conceived in laboratory glassware and then placed in the uterus of an otherwise infertile mother occurred last night, apparently without complications.

Reports from Oldham General and District Hospital in Lancashire said the baby, a girl, was delivered by Caesarian section, appeared normal and weighed 5 pounds 12 ounces.

The birth culminated more than a dozen years of research and experimentation by Dr. Patrick C. Steptoe, a gynecologist, and Dr. Robert G. Edwards, a Cambridge University specialist in reproductive physiology.

The parents are Mrs. Lesley Brown, 31 years old, and her husband, John, 38, a railway truck driver from Bristol.

Mrs. Brown in more than 10 years of marriage had been unable to conceive a child because of a defect in the oviducts, or Fallopian tubes, which each month carry egg cells from the ovaries to the uterus. It is during this passage that the egg cells are fertilized.

In the procedure that culminated in last night's birth, an egg cell was removed surgically from Mrs. Brown's ovaries last Nov. 10 and fertilized with sperm from her husband in a petri dish. After two or more days in a laboratory culture, the fertilized embryo was injected into Mrs. Brown's uterus.

More conventional methods had been attempted in an effort to get Mrs. Brown to conceive, including surgical reconstruction of her oviducts. But the efforts failed, and about two years ago she turned to Dr. Steptoe and Dr. Edwards for treatment.

There have been previous reports of so-called "test-tube babies" but none have been authenticated. The Steptoe-Edwards efforts, which failed a number of times, have been followed closely by the medical profession.

While the experimenters have often been frowned upon, they also are highly regarded by many in the field of obstetrics.

Working with a succession of patients, Dr. Edwards has gradually improved his ability to manipulate the hormones that control the reproductive cycle.

Dr. Steptoe has used a surgical procedure known as laparoscopy to enter a woman's abdomen at the appropriate moment in her monthly cycle to retrieve one or more egg cells. The device, placed through a small incision near the navel, illuminates the target area and allows the surgeon to identify and withdraw by suction nearly mature egg cells.

Once the egg cells have been exposed to sperm, and once microscopic examination after a few days has shown that an embryo is developing normally, the embryo is placed in the uterus with a tube inserted through the cervix.

It is estimated that one-fifth to one-half of women who are sterile are unable to bear children because of absent, defective or blocked oviducts. Because of that, it can be assumed that there will be considerable pressure on physicians to repeat the performance of Drs. Steptoe and Edwards, even though their work is still at a very experimental stage.

The chief problem encountered by the two doctors has been obtaining a satisfactory implant of the embryo in the wall of the uterus.

In normal reproduction, the embryo lingers a day or more in the oviducts after fertilization and does not implant itself until, through cellular division, it has reached a multicelled stage.

This process is controlled by hormones issued from various organs, including the ovaries, and from the embryo itself. The early efforts of Drs. Steptoe and Edwards were frustrated because their performing part of this process outside the body upset the hormonal signalling system.

Furthermore, the woman in many of the attempts was given added hormones to induce multiple egg production. The doctors hoped that this would give them more egg cells, improving their chances of success, but the added hormones seemed to throw the normal reproductive system off-balance.

Another fear was that culturing the embryo in glassware for four and a half days, as had been done, might place too severe a strain on it.

Shortly before their removal of one or more egg cells from Mrs. Brown last Nov. 10, it was learned from experiments at the University of Birmingham Medical School that rhesus monkey-embryos inserted into the uterus after only one or two cell divisions could survive.

This suggested that the embryos of primates, including man, might differ from other mammals in being able to withstand implantation into the uterus at so early a stage.

Some specialists therefore suspect that Drs. Steptoe and Edwards may have decided to implant Mrs. Brown's embryo after only two days, allowing it to enter the uterus well before its normal implantation stage.

Reports from the hospital this morning said that the baby was born just before midnight and that its condition was "excellent." Mrs. Brown and her husband were reported to be jubilant.

Once the fetus began developing, its own hormonal signals generated all the effects of a normal pregnancy. Mrs. Brown is reported to have experienced the sort of cravings often reported by pregnant women—in this case, a yearning for mints.

8

In vitro fertilization and other advanced medical technologies have raised new ethical and personal issues for parents and for society. A mother describes her dilemma in deciding what to do with the frozen embryos she has stored now that she has the three children she wants (1997).

The Eggs, Embryos, and I

Melissa Moore Bodin

I have six potential children on ice in a hospital in southern California, and I don't know what to do with them. For seven years my husband and I suffered with the '90s affliction—infertility. Our problem started in 1986 when we threw out the diaphragm; the next month I was pregnant. Unfortunately, the embryo didn't make the whole journey. It started to develop in one of my tubes, and emergency surgery was necessary to remove it. "Don't worry, this happens, try again," the experts told us.

Eight months later, pregnant—again in the fallopian tube. More surgery. After an evaluation, we were told that my tubes weren't clear (what a surprise) but that an operation could help. By now I knew I was never wearing a bikini again, so what's another scar? After the procedure, we kept on trying, with no results. Then it was time for a little chemical help. I tried Clomid, a drug that increases the production of eggs from the normal one per month to four or more. The rationale is that the more eggs out there, the better the odds of hitting the jackpot. Finally, after a year and a half of monthly ovaries the size of softballs, another tubal pregnancy that needed surgery. You hit yourself in the head with a phone book enough times and something tells you to stop.

The last stop on the Infertility Highway is in vitro fertilization. IVF is expensive and not covered by insurance, but we scraped together every penny and went for it. To begin, I had to shut down my regular reproductive hormones by giving myself a shot in the thigh every morning for 10 days. It wasn't too bad, since I used a tiny diabetic needle. Then I moved on to the big guns, Metrodin and Pergonal, to chemically regulate my cycle. These drugs are suspended in sesame oil, so they have to be injected into the big gluteus muscles with a *large* needle. Now the husband comes into play, reluctantly. Although it was my body on the receiving end of the needle, David had a very hard time making the plunge. We had to do these injections twice a day for 10 days. One side effect: a lot of bruising and a huge lump at the site of each injection. Not a pretty picture, but since actual sex was not part of the process, looks weren't that important.

The big day came, and the infertility clinic harvested 15 eggs, an operation more unpleasant than it sounds. The eggs were then mixed with my husband's sperm in a petri dish. For 36 hours we waited to hear that we'd made 11 embryos. The doctor decided that six was the magic number for us and froze the other five. The only really happy part of the whole ordeal was that before the six embryos were placed in my womb, my husband was allowed to look through a microscope and see the tiny cells waiting to go home. Afterward I had to lie in an uncomfortable position: on my stomach, feet much higher than my head, for four hours in a dark room by myself. The nurse said to think positive thoughts— all I could think about was the enormous dent the end of the gurney was putting in the top of my head. The trip home was a sight to behold; suffice it to say I kept my feet higher than my head in the car, too. I stayed in bed for a week and watched afternoon talk shows about multiple births. Another week went by before the blood test.

Ever heard that you can't be "a little bit pregnant"? Wrong. The pregnancy test was positive, but the "numbers" weren't high enough. The test measures the level of a hormone in the mother's blood, and the doctors want to see a number around 100. Mine was 54. We spent a horrible week before the next blood test, half pregnant. In the end, the one tenacious embryo out of six slipped away. We had our frozen embryos left over, but only three survived the thaw, and that attempt was unsuccessful.

It took two years to recover from the failure, but after promising my husband that it would be the last attempt, we tried IVF again. The day of the pregnancy test I felt premenstrual and crampy, certain I wasn't pregnant. I made my husband call for results. "Does positive mean positive?" he said into the phone. Nine months later Jesse was born. When Jesse had his first birthday, I began thinking about the 18 frozen embryos left over from this IVF cycle. I never thought I had a shot of succeeding (my odds were about 11 percent), but we went ahead and had six of the thawed embryos "put back." (Six others did not survive.) Two weeks later, when I had the pregnancy test, I'd already grown out of my bra, so I knew something was up. Not only was I pregnant, but the hormone level was 412. Our twins, Paul and Samuel, were born nine months later.

I am 42 and my husband is 50. We have three children in diapers—exactly three more than we ever thought we'd have. In Jesse's preschool class we're always 15 to 20 years older than the other parents. My silver-haired husband shows his buddies baby pictures and their response is "Are these your grand-kids?" Parents in the play group are worried about buying their first house; I'm worried about menopause. Most parents are concerned about saving for college; we're concerned about being able to feed ourselves when the kids are college age. We've already spent their college money to get them. Our bank account is empty, and we're both going to have to work full time until we're in our 90s. Of course, we have three of the most wonderful, intelligent, beautiful children on earth, so none of this really matters.

But we still have six frozen embryos. We have only two choices—donate or destroy. As painful as the infertility was, we never considered adoption an alternative. Giving our embryos to another infertile couple would be like giving our children up for adoption. We know this is a very selfish attitude and have struggled mightily with the issue. After all we've gone through, the concept of destroying the embryos is hard to imagine.

So we pay our $50 a month storage fee, raise our boys and wonder what we are going to do.

9

Originally in vitro fertilization changed only the site of conception, not the process. The essayist Margaret Talbot explores the ethical oddities involved in egg donation and the purchase of "stranger eggs" by infertile couples (1998).

The Egg Women

Margaret Talbot

The bold advertisement in a local magazine made me stop, fold back the page, and look again. "Become an egg donor or surrogate mother," it urged. "Help an infertile couple become a family!" And then, in smaller print: "There is a special need for Jewish and Asian women." It was that concluding observation that kept me from turning the page. I have known people who expressed a special need for Jewish and Asian women, but this wasn't exactly what they meant. And this ovular entreaty soon gave rise to more unusual speculation. If an egg donor were Jewish, would that ensure, under the Jewish law of matrilineal descent, that the resulting child was Jewish? Does an egg have an ethnic identity? A religious one? Is an egg donor the same thing as a mother? The anxiety about authenticity was suddenly raised to a new height.

In the field of "assisted reproductive technology," mined as it is with ethical dilemmas, egg donation still presents a special case. It's not that it's a new technique or even an experimental one. Over the last decade, about 6,000 women in the United States have conceived with the help of an egg provided by another, usually younger, woman. Yet egg donation challenges some of our most cherished notions of maternity in a way that neither sperm donation nor even surrogate mothering does. For a start, egg donation is harder to excise from the story of a child's conception than sperm donation, if only because the harvesting of women's eggs is a bigger deal. It entails months of hormone treatments followed by a surgical procedure. The donor is around, on the periphery of your life, for a longer time.

On the other hand, an egg donor is clearly less involved in the process than a surrogate mother, who carries a developing baby for nine months on behalf of another woman. While surrogacy at least resembles the cultural ideal of motherhood as nurturing and self-sacrificing (even if it is often a for-cash transaction), egg donation is more like sperm donation: a drop-your-genes-and-run proposition. When it comes to telling curious children how they came to be, it's easier to write an egg donor out of the picture than a surrogate mother, but easier still, it seems, to write out a sperm donor. Of 35 sperm donor families interviewed by psychologist Susan Klock, 86 percent had no plans to tell the children that they were the product of somebody other than daddy's seed. Families with children conceived through egg donation, on the other hand, tend to be more confused about whether and how to tell them, according to a recent front-page story in *The New York Times*.

But that's not the only ethical oddity of egg donation. In the marketing of eggs to infertile couples, a sort of commercially driven genetic determinism has become the language of choice. Egg brokerages guarantee you "Jewish" eggs. (Warning: they don't write, they don't call.) They promise to provide couples with the SAT and I.Q. scores of prospective egg donors, along with their hair and eye color, their hobbies, their favorite books. In catalog-style entries on their websites, they offer chatty and always glowing profiles. (The same goes for sperm donors: a current listing on the Cryogenic Laboratories, Inc., website, for example, introduces you to Donor 255, who, at "5' 11" and 160 lbs. . . . has a slim athletic build," "thick, straight dark blond hair," and "an oval face." When he isn't busy with his Ph.D. work in psychology, Donor 255 "plays golf as often as possible." Introverted Donor 182, on the other hand, "likes nature tours, gardening, and maintaining his properties.") These companies are not in the business of surprises. For them, the old adage that you cannot choose your parents or your children is only half true. Filial love needs guarantees, or warranties. Indeed, these companies boast that they can improve on the kind of control you exert when you produce offspring with a spouse picked out, in part, perhaps, for his or her admirable heritable traits. As one sperm-bank director put it, "You will know more about the donor than you do about your husband." The sympathetic reading is that these firms want to take the gamble out of babymaking for couples who are already gambling on getting a baby at all. The less sympathetic reading is that they are a sort of Home Shopping Network for the marketing of chromosomes. QVC DNA.

I decided to call the company whose ad I'd seen: the Center for Surrogate Parenting & Egg Donation, Inc., of Beverly Hills, California. The woman I spoke with identified herself as the egg-donor administrator, and she offered a cheery, consumer-oriented philosophy of genetic selection. The center, she said, does not accept egg donations from women who are on welfare or AFDC. "We want to make sure," she explained, "that we are offering our clients quality women, women with goals and aspirations of their own."

The motivations of these quality women might surprise an evolutionary psychologist. On the one hand, they are women with children of their own who "simply" want to help someone else become pregnant. They are "compensated for their time and inconvenience" at a rate of about $2,500 (some centers pay more like $5,000), but few seem to do it primarily for the money. "A lot of them have seen a friend or family member struggle with infertility," says the egg-donor administrator. But then she adds something a little jarring: "I also have girls who say, 'I'm bright. I'm beautiful. I have my own children. I can't see why

I shouldn't pass on more of my genetic material.' And I say, 'Oh, and you're modest, too, huh?' Some of these donors are extremely proud women." So, like many men who give to sperm banks, like the doctor who kept using his own sperm in artificial inseminations until somebody noticed that all the babies at his fertility clinic looked an awful lot like him, some women want to spread their genetic goods far and wide. Alpha females! And this is an urge that is apparently unlinked to what we generally call maternal instinct. Counselors at other egg brokerages have found that prospective donors are less discouraged by the idea that they might have children living nearby but unknown to them than by the prospect of big needles bearing hormone injections.

Maybe once you decide to buy an egg—at a considerable cost once you add in medical bills—you figure you might as well shop for what you really, really want. But all this, I think, is a little nuts. The catalog-style browsing for top-drawer genes and specific attributes (I want a child who can understand Ashberry, damn it!) subtly corrupts the single most significant attribute of parental love, which is that it is love for what one has been *given*. Its unconditionality is owed not least to the fact that the children have not been designed by the parents. But here are these egg dealers, proposing to cancel the surprises and the contingencies that test and toughen the bonds between parents and children. I'm not sure quality is worth it.

10

Despite the eagerness of many to have children, throughout the last twenty years some couples have sought to remain childless. This 1986 article, which explores the phenomenon through interviews with voluntarily childless couples, suggests how modern work patterns as well as the new leisure have influenced this decision. Of course, these couples assume that they can predictably limit their fertility, something the seventeenth- and eighteenth-century women that Scholten describes could not do.

Choosing Childlessness

Newsweek

He works long and often unpredictable hours at the office. So does she. No time to cook at the end of the day: they usually meet for dinner at a trendy restaurant or one of them stops to pick up gourmet takeout on the way home. Their car is an expensive, sporty two-seater—just right for weekend getaways. Their white livingroom rug has never known the muddy footprints of little feet. These are not traditional scenes from a marriage; there are no kids around. But more and more couples are painting a new kind of American family portrait—one with just two faces, the husband's and the wife's.

The percentage of couples without children has doubled in the last few decades. In 1960 only about 13 percent of married women between 25 and 29 were childless; last year 29 percent were. In the past, motherhood was virtually the only option for married women. That is no longer the case. Today 1 out of 4 ever-married women between the ages of 25 and 34 has never had a child—a total of nearly 3.3 million women—compared to 1 out of 10 women in 1960. It is still possible that some will go on to have children; many childless women say they intend to have babies, although they often have no timetable for translating those expectations into reality. Medical advances have made it easier for women to have healthy babies well into their late 30s or even early 40s, and many do; the rate of first pregnancy for women over 35 has risen dramatically in the last decade. Still, there are not enough women over 35 having children to make up for all the younger women who are deciding not to have children. And while the number of childless couples climbs, the percentage of women who are unable to have babies has been falling—again thanks to medical progress—from 11.2

percent in 1965 to 8.4 percent in 1982. Thus it is clear that more couples are actively deciding to remain childless.

The result is a generation of contrasts. Because most of the women currently in their prime childbearing years are baby boomers, the 76 million people born between 1946 and 1964, there are more potential mothers and fathers than ever before. Although many are having children, they are having far fewer than their parents did. This continues a trend that started in the early 19th century, says Andrew J. Cherlin, a sociologist at Johns Hopkins University who has written several books on the family. "The only exception to this rule was during the 1950s," Cherlin says. "Each generation has had fewer children for the last 150 years, probably because we have moved from a rural, agricultural society to an urban, industrial one and children aren't needed as much."

The current overall rates of childlessness are the highest since the end of the Depression but for very different reasons. In the 1930s it was the lack of a reliable income that kept people from starting families. In the 1980s a good salary may be the main reason to delay or forgo parenthood. Childlessness has increased as women have moved into well-paying careers in record numbers. Faced with new options, many wives decide that motherhood is not an essential or even desirable role. They see their friends juggling the incessant and often conflicting demands of work and family. And, in the absence of widespread governmental or corporate support for working parents, many feel compelled to choose between children and jobs. "Women who are very career-oriented suddenly find themselves impaled by the demands of child rearing," says UCLA population expert Judith Blake. "When a woman sees this happening to other people, it makes her fairly leery." Younger women—now in their early 20s—may not feel quite so torn. Some demographers predict that changes in attitudes toward working parents—and changes in the roles that men and women play in the home—may reduce the rate of childlessness in the future. . . .

Some people are so sure of their decision that they leave no room for a change of heart. Voluntary sterilization is rising; 39 percent of all married couples were surgically sterile in 1982, compared with 16 percent in 1965. Leslie Pam, a 42-year-old family therapist in Los Angeles, decided when he was a teenager that he didn't want children; he had a vasectomy at the age of 24. "I had to lie, cheat and steal to do it," he says, "because the physician thought I was too young to make such a decision. He was certain I'd change my mind." Two years ago Pam married Ann Christie, also a family therapist. She had been married before; her first husband had also had a vasectomy. "I seem to be drawn to safe men," she says. "The problem is taken out of my hands so I don't have to deal with it."

More often, however, the decision to remain childless is less clear cut. Most couples begin their lives together planning a family that includes Mom, Dad *and* kids. And, at least until the mid-'60s, the road from the altar did seem to point in only one direction—toward the nursery. But with the availability of birth control and abortion, parenthood is no longer inevitable. Men and women are marrying later and putting children on hold—often until after their careers are in full gear and there's money in the bank. Some of those couples eventually do have children. But others find that by waiting, they have made a de facto decision to limit their family to two. "In your mind, you always think there's some more time," says Christine Irvin Ranhosky, a systems-development manager at a Wall Street firm. But Ranhosky, who is in her mid-30s, knows that she and her husband, Alan, a doctor, will probably never have children. "You reach an economic point where you don't need to use a calculator in the supermarket," she says. Now, she says, the decision would be financial as well as emotional and the bottom line just doesn't add up to children. "I enjoy what I'm doing," Ranhosky says. "Having children isn't necessarily going to buy me more contentment."

The Puritans did not have child-rearing manuals, but they thought deeply about how children should be reared. The poet Anne Bradstreet left reflections on parenting that included a compelling understanding of the different ways children of varying dispositions should be treated, and a commentary on God's inscrutability and its consequences for parental responsibility (1662).

Thoughts on Child Rearing

Anne Bradstreet

Diuerse children, haue their different natures, some are like flesh wch nothing but salt will keep from putrefaction, some again like tender fruits that are best preserued wth sugar, those parents are wise that can fit their nurture according to their Nature.

All the works and doings of god are wonderfull, but none more awfull then his great worke of election and Reprobation, when we consider how many good parents haue had bad children, and againe how many bad parents haue had pious children, it should make vs adore the Souerainty of god, who will not be tyed to time nor place, nor yet to persons, but takes and chuses, when and where and whom he pleases, it should alsoe teach the children of godly parents to walk wth feare and trembling, lest they through vnbeleif fall short of a promise, it may also be a support to such as haue or had wicked parents, that if they abide not in vnbeleif, god is able to grafte them in, the vpshot of all should make vs wth the Apostle to admire the iustice and mercy of god and say how vnsearchable are his wayes and his footsteps past finding out.

Modern child-rearing advice begins with John Locke, whose philosophical essays on education and the formation of the self were fundamental to the modern devotion to childhood as the basis of individual character. Locke views children as ready to be molded, and is committed to using reason and example in the raising of children. He opposes frequent physical correction both because it is "a passionate tyranny" and because it will not teach the child voluntarily to do what is right. Crying, however, according to Locke, must not be tolerated (1690).

The Use of Reason in Child Rearing

John Locke

§81. It will perhaps be wondered that I mention *reasoning* with children: and yet I cannot but think that the true way of dealing with them. They understand it as early as they do language; and, if I misobserve not, they love to be treated as rational creatures sooner than is imagined. 'Tis a pride should be cherished in them and, as much as can be, made the great instrument to turn them by.

But when I talk of *reasoning* I do not intend any other but such as is suited to the child's capacity and apprehension. Nobody can think a boy of three or seven years old should be argued with as a grown man. Long discourses and philosophical reasonings at best amaze and confound, but do not instruct children. When I say therefore that they must be *treated as rational creatures* I mean that you should make them sensible by the mildness of your carriage and the composure even in your correction of them that what you do is reasonable in you and useful and necessary for them and that it is not out of *caprichio*, passion, or fancy that you command or forbid them anything. This they are capable of understanding; and there is no virtue they should be excited to nor fault they should be kept from which I do not think they may be convinced of, but it must be by such *reasons* as their age and understanding are capable of and those proposed always in very *few and plain words*. The foundations on which several duties are built and the fountains of right and wrong from which they spring are not perhaps easily to be let into the minds of grown men not used to abstract their thoughts from common received opinions. Much less are children capable of *reasonings* from remote principles. They cannot conceive the force of long deductions: the *reasons* that move them must be *obvious* and level to their thoughts, and such as may (if I may so say) be felt and touched. But yet, if their age, temper, and inclinations be considered, there will never want such motives as may be sufficient to convince them. If there be no other more particular, yet these will always be intelligible and of force to deter them from any fault fit to be taken notice of in them, viz. that it will be a discredit and disgrace to them, and displease you.

§82. But of all the ways whereby children are to be instructed and their manners formed, the plainest, easiest, and most efficacious is to set before their eyes the *examples* of those things you would have them do or avoid. Which, when they are pointed out to them in the practice of persons within their knowledge with some reflection on their beauty or unbecomingness, are of more force to draw or deter their imitation than any discourses which can be made to them. Virtues and vices can by no words be so plainly set before their understandings as the actions of other men will show them, when you direct their observation and bid them view this or that good or bad quality in their practice. And the beauty or uncomeliness of many things in good and ill breeding will be better learned and make deeper impressions on them in the *examples* of others than from any rules or instructions can be given about them.

This is a method to be used not only whilst they are young, but to be continued even as long as they shall be under another's tuition or conduct. Nay, I know not whether it be not the best way to be used by a father as long as he shall think fit, on any occasion, to reform anything he wishes mended in his son: nothing sinking so gently and so deep into men's minds as *example*. And what ill they either overlook or indulge in them themselves, they cannot but dislike and be ashamed of when it is set before them in another.

§83. It may be doubted concerning *whipping*, when as the last remedy it comes to be necessary, at what time and by whom it should be done: whether presently upon the committing the fault, whilst it is yet fresh and hot; and whether parents themselves should beat their children. As to the first, I think it should *not* be done *presently* lest passion mingle with it and so, though it exceed the just proportion, yet it lose of its due weight: for even children discern when we do things in passion. But, as I said before, that has most weight with them that appears sedately to come from their parents' reason, and they are not without this distinction. Next, if you have any discreet servant capable of it and [who] has the place of governing your child (for if you have a tutor, there is no doubt), I think it is best the *smart* should come more immediately *from another's hand*, though by the parent's order who should see it done; whereby the parent's authority will be preserved and the child's aversion for the pain it suffers rather be turned on the person that immediately inflicts it. For I would have a *father seldom strike his child* but upon very urgent necessity and as the last remedy: and then perhaps it will be fit to do it so that the child should not quickly forget it. . . .

§111. *Crying* is a fault that should not be tolerated in children not only for the unpleasant and unbecoming noise it fills the house with, but for more considerable reasons in reference to the children themselves, which is to be our aim in education.

Their *crying* is of two sorts: either *stubborn* and *domineering* or *querulous* and *whining*.

1. Their *crying* is very often a striving for mastery and an open declaration of their insolence or obstinacy: when they have not the power to obtain their desire, they will by their *clamor* and *sobbing* maintain their title and right to it. This is an avowed continuing of their claim and a sort of remonstrance against the oppression and injustice of those who deny them what they have a mind to.

§112. 2. Sometimes their *crying* is the effect of pain or true sorrow and a *bemoaning* themselves under it.

These two, if carefully observed, may by the mien, looks, and actions, and particularly by the tone of their crying be easily distinguished; but neither of them must be suffered, much less encouraged.

1. The obstinate or *stomachful crying* should by no means be permitted because it is but another way of flattering their desires and encouraging those passions which it is our main business to subdue; and if it be, as often it is, upon the receiving any correction, it quite defeats all the good effects of it. For any chastisement which leaves them in this declared opposition only serves to make them worse. The restraints and punishments laid on children are all misapplied and lost as far as they do not prevail over their wills, teach them to submit their passions, and make their minds supple and pliant to what their parents' reason advises them now, and so prepare them to obey what their own reason shall advise hereafter. But if in anything wherein they are crossed they may be suffered to go away *crying*, they confirm themselves in their desires and cherish the ill humor with a declaration of their right and a resolution to satisfy their inclination the first opportunity. This therefore is another argument against the frequent use of blows: for whenever you come to that extremity, it is not enough to whip or beat them, you must do it till you find you have subdued their minds, till with submission and patience they yield to the correction, which you shall best discover by their *crying* and their ceasing from it upon your bidding. Without this, the beating of children is but a passionate tyranny over them; and it is mere cruelty and not correction to put their bodies in pain without doing their minds any good. As this gives us a reason why children should seldom be corrected, so it also prevents their being so. For if, whenever they are chastised, it were done thus without passion, soberly and yet effectually too, laying on the blows and smart not furiously and all at once, but slowly with reasoning between and with observation how it wrought, stopping when it had made them pliant, penitent, and yielding, they would seldom need the like punishment again, being made careful to avoid the fault that deserved it. Besides, by this means, as the punishment would not be lost for being too little and not effectual, so it would be kept from being too much if we gave off as soon as we perceived that it reached the mind and that was bettered. For since the chiding or beating of children should be always the least that possibly may be, that which is laid on in the heat of anger seldom observes that measure, but is commonly more than it should be, though it prove less than enough.

§113. 2. Many children are apt to *cry* upon any little pain they suffer, and the least harm that befalls them puts them into *complaints* and *bawling*. This few children avoid: for it being the first and natural way to declare their sufferings or wants before they can speak, the compassion that is thought due to that tender age foolishly encourages and continues it in them long after they can speak. It is the duty, I confess, of those about children to compassionate them whenever they suffer any hurt; but not to show it in pitying them. Help and ease them the best you can, but by no means bemoan them. This softens their minds and makes them yield to the little harms that happen to them, whereby they sink deeper into that part which alone feels and make larger wounds there than otherwise they would. They should be hardened against all sufferings, especially of the body, and have no tenderness but what rises from an ingenuous shame and a quick sense of reputation. The many inconveniences this life is exposed to require [that] we should not be too sensible of every little hurt. What our minds yield not to makes but a slight impression and does us but very little harm: it is the suffering of our spirits that gives and continues the pain. This brawniness and insensibility of mind is the best armor we can have against the common evils and accidents of life; and being a temper that is to be got by exercise and custom more than any other way, the practice of it should be begun betimes, and happy is he that is taught it early. That effeminacy of spirit which is to be prevented or cured, as nothing that I know so much increases in children as *crying*, so nothing, on the other side, so much checks and restrains [it] as their being hindered from that sort of *complaining*. In the little harms they suffer from knocks and falls, they should not be pitied for falling, but bid do so again; which, besides that it stops their *crying*, is a better way to cure their heedlessness and prevent their tumbling another time than either chiding or bemoaning them. But let the hurts they receive be what they will, stop their *crying*, and that will give them more quiet and ease at present and harden them for the future.

13

The most influential writer on children in the first half of the nineteenth century was the prolific English author Maria Edgeworth, whose didactic tone should not distract us from her often sage advice. Here she advises parents on the toys that are most conducive to learning. She shares other nineteenth-century experts' new tolerance for children's natural playfulness, but also makes clear that it should be directed to useful ends (1825).

Toys

Maria Edgeworth

Toys which afford trials of dexterity and activity, such as tops, kites, hoops, balls, battledores and shuttlecocks, ninepins, and cup-and-ball are excellent; and we see that they are consequently great and lasting favourites with children; their senses, their understanding, and their passions, are all agreeably interested and exercised by these amusements. They emulate each other; but, as some will probably excel at one game, and some at another, this emulation will not degenerate into envy. There is more danger that this hateful passion should be created in the minds of young competitors at those games, where it is supposed that some *knack* or *mystery* is to be learned before they can be played with success. Whenever children play at such games, we should point out to them how and why it is that they succeed or fail; we may show them, that in reality, there is no *knack* or *mystery* in any thing, but that from certain causes certain effects will follow; that, after trying a number of experiments, the circumstances essential to success may be discovered; and that all the ease and dexterity, which we often attribute to the power of natural genius, is simply the consequence of practice and industry. This sober lesson may be taught to children without putting it into grave words or formal precepts. A gentleman once astonished a family of children by his dexterity in playing at bilboquet: he caught the ball nine or ten times successively with great rapidity upon the spike: this success appeared miraculous; and the father, who observed that it had made a great impression upon the little spectators, took that opportunity to shew the use of spinning the ball, to make the hole at the bottom ascend in a proper direction. The nature of centrifugal motion, and its effect in preserving the *parallelism of motion*, if we may be allowed the expression, was explained, not at once, but at different intervals, to the young audience. Only as much was explained at a time as the children could understand, without fatiguing their attention, and the abstruse subject was made familiar by the mode of illustration that was adopted.

It is surprising how much children may learn from their playthings, when they are judiciously chosen, and when the habit of reflection and observation is associated with the ideas of amusement and happiness. A little boy of nine years old, who had had a hoop to play with, asked "why a hoop, or a plate, if rolled upon its edge, keeps up as long as it rolls, but falls as soon as it stops, and will not stand if you try to make it stand still upon its edge?" Was not the boy's understanding as well employed whilst he was thinking of this phenomenon, which he observed whilst he was beating his hoop, as it could possibly have been by the most learned preceptor?

When a pedantic schoolmaster sees a boy eagerly watching a paper kite, he observes, "What a pity it is that children cannot be made to mind their grammar as well as their kites!" And he adds, perhaps some peevish ejaculation on the natural idleness of boys, and that pernicious love of play against which he is doomed to wage perpetual war. A man of sense will see the same thing with a different eye; in this pernicious love of play he will discern the symptoms of a love of science, and, instead of deploring the natural idleness of children, he will admire the activity which they display in the pursuit of knowledge. He will feel that it [is] his business to direct this activity, to furnish his pupil with materials for fresh combinations, to put him or to let him put himself, in situations where he can make useful observations, and acquire that experience which cannot be bought, and which no masters can communicate. . . .

Card, pasteboard, substantial but not sharp-pointed scissors, wire, gum and wax, may, in some degree, supply the want of carpenter's tools at that early age when we have observed that the saw and plane are useless. Models of common furniture should be made as toys, which should take to pieces, so that all their parts, and the manner in which they are put together, might be seen distinctly; the name of the different parts should be written or stamped upon them: by these means the names will be associated with realities; children will retain them in their memory, and they will neither learn by rote technical terms, nor will they be retarded in their progress in mechanical invention by the want of language. Before young people can use tools, these models will amuse and exercise their attention. From models of furniture we may go on to models of architecture; pillars of different orders, the roofs of houses, the manner of slating and tiling, &c. Then we may proceed to models of machines, choosing at first such as can be immediately useful to children in their own amusements, such as wheelbarrows, carts, cranes, scales, steelyards, jacks, and pumps, which children ever view with eager eyes.

From simple, it will be easy to proceed gradually to models of more complicated, machinery: it would be tiresome to give a list of these; models of instruments used by manufacturers and artists should be seen; many of these are extremely ingenious; spinning-wheels, looms, paper-mills, wind-mills, water-mills, might with great advantage be shown in miniature to children. . . .

When the powers of reason have been cultivated, and the inventive faculty exercised; when general habits of voluntary exertion and patient perseverance, have been acquired, it will be easy, either for the pupil himself, or for his friends, to direct his abilities to whatever is necessary for his happiness.

14

One of the most widely read child-raising manuals of the late nineteenth and early twentieth centuries was The Care and Feeding of Children *(1923) by L. Emmett Holt. His view of crying is similar to Locke's, but allows greater flexibility. Like most of its successors, Holt's manual is easy to read, avoids philosophizing, and is meant to instruct mothers about all the essential issues they would no longer learn about from family or neighbors.*

The Cry

L. Emmett Holt

When is crying useful?

In the newly-born infant the cry expands the lungs, and it is necessary that it should be repeated for a few minutes every day in order to keep them well expanded.

How much crying is normal for a very young baby?

From fifteen to thirty minutes a day is not too much.

What is the nature of this cry?

It is loud and strong. Infants get red in the face with it; in fact, it is a scream. This is necessary for health. It is the baby's exercise.

When is a cry abnormal?

When it is too long or too frequent. The abnormal cry is rarely strong, often it is a moaning or a worrying cry, sometimes only a feeble whine.

What are the main causes of such crying?

Pain, temper, hunger, illness, and habit.

What is the cry of pain?

It is usually strong and sharp, but not generally continuous. It is accompanied by contraction of the features, drawing up of the legs, and other symptoms of distress.

What is the cry of hunger?

It is usually a continuous, fretful cry, rarely strong and lusty.

What is the cry of temper?

It is loud and strong and accompanied by kicking or stiffening of the body, and is usually violent.

What is the cry of illness?

There is usually more of fretfulness and moaning than real crying, although crying is excited by very slight causes.

What is the cry of indulgence or from habit?

This is often heard even in very young infants, who cry to be rocked, to be carried about, sometimes for a light in the room, for a pacifier to suck, or for the continuance of any other bad habit which has been acquired.

What is the most certain way of causing a child to develop the crying habit?

By giving him everything he cries for. This will soon do it even in one with a most amiable disposition.

How is such a habit to be broken?

By never giving a child what he cries for.

How can we be sure that a child is crying to be indulged?

If he stops immediately when he gets what he wants, and cries when this is withdrawn or withheld.

What should be done if a baby cries at night?

One should see that the child is comfortable—the clothing smooth under the body, the hands and feet warm, and the napkin not wet or soiled. If all these matters are properly adjusted and the child [is] simply crying to be taken up, he should not be further interfered with. If the night cry is habitual some other cause should be sought.

How is a baby to be managed that cries from temper, from habit, or to be indulged?

He should simply be allowed to "cry it out." This may require an hour, and, in extreme cases, two or three hours. A second struggle will seldom last more than ten or fifteen minutes, and a third will rarely be necessary. Such discipline is not to be carried out unless one is sure as to the cause of the habitual crying.

Is it likely that rupture will be caused from crying?

Not in healthy young infants if the abdominal band is properly applied, and very seldom after infancy even when [there is] no abdominal support.

15

The behaviorist John B. Watson was the most influential psychologist in America before World War II. In Psychological Care of Infant and Child *(1928) he chastises mothers for spoiling their children with affection; he also offers mothers rigorous advice on how to systematically and scientifically "create" their children.*

Too Much Mother Love

John B. Watson

Now over-conditioning in love is the rule. Prove it yourself by counting the number of times your child whines and wails "Mother." All over the house, all day long, the two-year-old, the three-year-old and the four-year-old whine "Mamma, Mamma," "Mother." Now these love responses which the mother or father is building in by over conditioning, in spite of what the poet and the novelist may have to say, are not constructive. They do not fight many battles for the child. They do not help it to conquer the difficulties it must meet in its environment. Hence just to the extent to which you devote time to petting and coddling—and I have seen almost all of the child's waking hours devoted to it— just to that extent do you rob the child of the time which he should be devoting to the manipulation of his universe, acquiring a technique with fingers, hands and arms. He must have time to pull his universe apart and put it together again. Even from this standpoint alone—that of robbing the child of its opportunity for conquering the world, coddling is a dangerous experiment.

The mother coddles the child for two reasons. One, she admits; the other, she doesn't admit because she doesn't know that it is true. The one she admits is that she wants the child to be happy, she wants it to be surrounded by love in order that it may grow up to be a kindly, goodnatured child. The other is that her own whole being cries out for the expression of love. Her mother before her has trained her to give and receive love. She is starved for love—affection, as she prefers to call it. It is at bottom a sex-seeking response in her, else she would never kiss the child on the lips. Certainly, to satisfy her professed reason for coddling, kissing the youngster on the forehead, on the back of the hand, patting it on the head once in a while, would be all the petting needed for a baby to learn that it is growing up in a kindly home.

But even granting that the mother thinks she kisses the child for the perfectly logical reason of implanting the proper amount of affection and kindliness in it, does she succeed? The fact I brought out before, that we rarely see a happy child, is proof to the contrary. The fact that our children are always crying and always whining shows the unhappy, unwholesome state they are in. Their digestion is interfered with and probably their whole glandular system is deranged.

Should the mother never kiss the baby?

There is a sensible way of treating children. Treat them as though they were young adults. Dress them, bathe them with care and circumspection. Let your behavior always be objective and kindly firm. Never hug and kiss them, never let them sit in your lap. If you must, kiss them once on the forehead when they say good night. Shake hands with them in the morning. Give them a pat on the head if they have made an extraordinarily good job of a difficult task. Try it out. In a week's time you will find how easy it is to be perfectly objective with your child and at the same time kindly. You will be utterly ashamed of the mawkish, sentimental way you have been handling it.

If you expected a dog to grow up and be useful as a watch dog, a bird dog, a fox hound, useful for anything except a lap dog, you wouldn't dare treat it the way you treat your child. When I hear a mother say "Bless its little heart" when it falls down, or stubs its toe, or suffers some other ill, I usually have to walk a block or two to let off steam. Can't the mother train herself when something happens to the child to look at its hurt without saying anything, and if there is a wound to dress it in a matter of fact way?

16

Watson's influence was eclipsed after World War II by a newer, more permissive attitude that advocated emotional sustenance rather than conditioning. The historian Nancy Pottishman Weiss analyzes the shift in the child-rearing advice offered by the U.S. Children's Bureau, which began to emphasize the well-being of the child at the expense of the mother (1998).

The Mother-Child Dyad Revisited
Perceptions of Mothers and Children in Twentieth-Century Child-Rearing Manuals

Nancy Pottishman Weiss

Thousands of letters from rural women, from immigrant mothers written in the hand of their young children, from women of urban slums as well as comfortable suburbs share a common quest for help and advice on raising children. Child-rearing guides can tell us what prevailing professional opinion offered on the subject. Documents such as mail to the United States Children's Bureau in response to the child care pamphlet, *Infant Care*, women's journals concerning children, and archives of groups like the Baby Hygiene Committee of the American Association of University Women corroborate the evidence we have from the large sales of these books: Women craved informed opinion and advice on rearing their young, a need once filled by informal female networks of family and friends and the prevalence of a folk tradition in child rearing. . . .

Admonitions for rearing children involve a tacit list of rules for mothers to follow. As a genre, then, child-rearing manuals can also be referred to as mother-rearing tracts. One example of the dual nature of manual objectives is the discussion of toilet training. Toilet training recommendations have changed markedly over fifty years. Babies of three months were held over a chamber in the mother's lap early in the century; manual writers expected the training to be fully completed by the age of one. By the 1940s the program changed considerably, and the time to initiate controls moved to between 18 and 24 months. But it is not only the time span that has changed, but the very meaning of the process itself. "Being in a hurry to get a baby trained could cause a lot more trouble than having dirty diapers," *Infant Care* of 1951 read. "What you're after is not having fewer diapers to wash, but having a baby who feels like working with you

instead of against you." The changed pattern of toilet training is generally credited to the acceptance of Freudian caveats about disturbances that can abound in
the adult personality when the oral, anal, and genital phases of infancy are
inadequately met. But toilet training involved two principals, not the child alone.
One can view this change in toileting procedures differently by asking a set of
questions addressed to the mother. What is a mother's day like when she trains
a child at three months or, conversely, waits until two years?

Early impositions of sphincter controls, characteristic of childcare advice until
the 1940s, probably had a closer relationship to technology than psychology.
Toilet training at two assumes something like 5000 diapers to wash per child
(using a low average estimate of 7 diapers a day). Without electric washing
machines, diaper services, disposable diapers, laundry workers available for hire,
or alternatively a cultural acceptance of inverse diapering where the child is not
clothed *until* he or she is continent, it seems hard to imagine a permissive mode
of toilet training taking hold. Toilet training before the age of one had utilitarian
implications for women early in the century, for such a procedure actually served
to reduce the work load of the mother. One is reminded that in 1914 women
ordinarily not only had to wash diapers by hand, they also had to sew them at
the outset.

The new pediatrics at the turn of the century advocated early sphincter controls, strict scheduling, early suppers and bedtimes for their salutary nature and
for their utility in character and habit training. However, these same childcare
techniques were also touted by people like Mary West—author of the 1914 and
1921 editions of *Infant Care* and, as she put it, "an experienced mother of five"—
for their usefulness in a busy woman's workday. To a harried mother of three
children under the age of three, Mrs. West wrote:

> If you have not tried putting away your children at six o'clock, you have no
> idea what a relief it will be to you. It can be done . . . and no mother who knows
> the satisfaction of having the care of her children cease before her own evening
> meal, and the quiet comfort of a still household in the evening, would fail to
> immediately begin the training necessary to make it possible.

And to the thousands of readers of *Infant Care* of 1914, Mary West noted:

> The care of a baby is readily reduced to a system unless he is sick. Such a
> system is not only one of the greatest factors in keeping the baby well and in
> training him in a way which will be of value to him all through life, but reduces
> the work of the mother to the minimum and provides for her certain assured
> periods of rest and recreation.

The first two editions of *Infant Care* emphasized the practical nature of child-
rearing advice women demanded—how to raise healthy offspring, reduce sickness, nurture children successfully through the precarious period of infancy. . . .

Psychohistorians, psychologists, and researchers in the field of child development see changes from rigid child-rearing prescriptions to permissive approaches

as linear in nature, claiming that social practices are improving. These favorable assessments of permissive child-rearing practices fail to ask how the changing set of guidelines shaped the lives of women expected to follow them. While experts pay increasing attention to the emotional and psychological facets of child rearing, they still conceive of these dimensions within the narrow structure of the dyad—what anthropologist Laura Nader calls the "intimate environment"—as opposed to a larger set of social forces affecting the rearing process. They also neglect to assess the impact on the caregiver. The result of this omission in the post-forties manuals is a considerable enlargement of the tasks connected with child rearing. While the rudiments of physical nurture emphasized early in the century, are limited, those of psychology and the emotions are spiraling. For example, Spock not only advises mothers to offer children vitamin rich food, he also cautions them to "enjoy him," "don't be afraid of him," and to remember "feeding is learning."

The newer manuals charged the mother with responsibility for the child's cognitive growth, emotional adjustment, and chances for future happiness, in effect, reassigning all the time spared from her earlier tasks of washing diapers by hand, preparing baby food from scratch, sewing or knitting infant garments. The task of the mother in permissive literature is freighted with new significance, replacing the earlier concerns over physical survival of the child. Now a misstep could spell both psychological mischief and cognitive harm, just as earlier mistaken care could result in severe physical illness. . . .

Just as the dyadic ideal often informed public policy decisions, child rearing materials themselves were instrumental in making policy in the home. Popular childcare literature, past and present, has something to tell us about changing views of the rights and responsibilities of children in home settings—and about the mirror image, rights and responsibilities of mothers. With certain exceptions already discussed, the child-rearing advice emanating from the Children's Bureau early in the century depicted a sympathetic dyad with a synchrony of interests. Early toilet training relieved women of laundry burdens and also built good habits for the child. Early supper and bedtime were healthy for a child and also gave a frayed mother time to recoup her energies and regroup her forces for an assault on other home chores. Strict scheduling spared the mother from being on call all day and developed habits of regularity in the baby. This, on the whole, sympathetic orchestration of the rights and responsibilities of mother and child changed character over the years.

Researchers and new professionals in the field of child development—people as disparate as John Watson and Arnold Gesell—have revamped childcare standards. Manual authors began to incorporate scientific information from the field of psychology. The dissonant note in the literature is a reinterpretation and expansion of maternal obligations and a winnowing of the mutuality of interest between mother and child. In the first editions of *Infant Care*, what was good for the mother was good for the child. By World War II, what benefited the child was not necessarily in the mother's best interests.

In the shift to more permissive childcare standards, two changes occur. By the 1940s mothers lose certain rights in the home, and children, in turn, are marked by a moral neutrality, a kind of moral tabula rasa. Difficult as child rearing might have been in the past, what was not allowed the mother was not permitted the child either. By the late 1940s in both the Children's Bureau's *Infant Care* and Spock's *Baby and Child Care* a reversal occurs. Leeway is allowed the child, with the mother expected to pick up the slack. By the period of World War II, babies are no longer described in judgmental terms as "fussy" or "spoiled," as they were in the earlier literature. Now they are morally neutral, and also, as a consequence, depicted as more passive in their ability to influence their own lives. Though the mother's environmental influence on the baby increases considerably in this configuration, she also becomes a more blameworthy person if things go awry. This is true even in very small ways. For example, instead of the exhausting chase of the toddler or the recommendation of Mrs. West to keep the baby in a playpen out of harm's way, now it is solely the mother's fault if the child happens to upset and break a treasured vase: "The mother should not have left it where the baby could get hold of it." Even in a recent poem in a popular women's journal, the mother's responsibility is emphasized:

> When our baby learned to crawl,
> I hung my wedgwood on the wall,
> I didn't take it down in time . . .
> Today the rascal learned to climb.

Another small example of the changed perception of women's rights in the home occurs in feeding the child. Women are not only expected to serve children nourishing food like oatmeal and mashed meats, they are expected to eat them along with the baby. Mothers in this instance are increasingly identified with the baby and lose to some degree the status of adult:

> Babies turn away from certain foods sometimes because they see an older person refuse them. *Parents often have to learn to eat what they want their baby to like.*

. . . Although permissiveness has often been viewed as detrimental to children's character and Spock himself has frequently been attacked on this score for the unruly behavior of youngsters of the 1960s, the negative dimension of permissiveness for mother's lives is little commented on.

The job description for both mother and child changes considerably in permissive literature. From a rough equality, at least in psychological terms, in the shared work of child rearing, now the mother is required to bear a disproportionate amount of the emotional labor attending the process. This psychic work is often explained by pointing to the decline in physical energy needed to keep a house. Although the rapid technological advances of the 1940s, like electric washing machines, are associated with improvement in women's home work lives, the advantages are more mythic than real. The development of the washing machine, for example, brought with it not more time for women to choose to use as they wanted, but escalated standards of cleanliness for home and family. In proportion to the extent that technology freed women's roles, the same blocs of time and even extra time borrowed from other activities were taken over by demands for child-rearing practices that fostered emotional health, cognitive growth, and psychological balance, to be solely mother administered.

Moreover, despite the imprint of psychology in the child-rearing materials of the post-forties period, there is a striking absence of attention to real life problems. Although the early child-rearing advice of the Children's Bureau paid only negative attention to atypical family settings, such as culturally distinct homes, poverty, divorce, presumed unwholesome standards of the foreign nursemaid, it did acknowledge the existence of these factors, just as the pamphlets would speak of the dangers threatening children from illness, careless handling of food, and contaminated milk, and allude as well to the difficult and exhausting jobs that befell the mother. These pamphlets unflinchingly recognized what one might appropriately call the underbelly of child rearing, and mentioned there might be dark days as well as sunny ones. What emerges in the permissive literature is in fact a repression of realistic difficulties and the takeover of what Martha Wolfenstein refers to as the "fun morality." But as Wolfenstein indicates, having fun all the time is hard, even exhausting work. . . .

The nether side of life is unacknowledged, if not banished entirely. But such erasures of cultural differences, the problems of poverty or emotional stress women may experience in child rearing serve to erode women's rights in the home as well. Even the simple right of a mother's variation from the mean average is removed from this literature.

17

The prevalence of child-rearing advice depended on a new science of the child. The historian Joseph M. Hawes analyzes the development of this new child science in the 1920s, its support by foundations and universities, and the dissemination of its findings to the general public (1997).

Child Science and the Rise of the Experts

Joseph M. Hawes

The key figure in the development of child science was Lawrence K. Frank, who, when he began his work in the early 1920s, was a young recent graduate in economics from Columbia. He used the money of large foundations to carry out a design that at first emphasized the development of a science of the normal child and then sought to disseminate the findings of this new science throughout the nation as a way of improving children's lives and thereby ensuring the future health of the nation.

The program of child science Lawrence K. Frank developed while he was working with the Laura Spelman Rockefeller Memorial included not only the development of science but also its popular dissemination. In 1963 Frank recalled:

> The Rockefeller Memorial decided to establish a number of Centers for the study of child growth and development as a way of contributing to the welfare of children by providing more dependable understanding and knowledge of their growth and development, and hopefully, by influencing parents through a program of parent education. . . .

Thus these factors came together for Frank and the child scientists of the twenties. At first, the study of children was linked explicitly to child welfare (and Frank probably preferred to maintain that link), but if the study of children was going to gain academic respectability, it had to be more closely associated with science than with child welfare. Thus much of the money in the 1920s went to the development of child science itself, rather than to child-helping projects. . . .

Although the development of a new science was paramount in the minds of the academics associated with the early days of the child development movement, there was an applied child welfare dimension—parent education, the process whereby scientific findings would be communicated to the general public. Implicit in Lawrence K. Frank's original design was the view that some parents (notably immigrants, urban working classes, and all African-Americans) needed expert advice about how to raise their children in a modern urban and industrial society. Ironically, the parents who responded most enthusiastically were well-off and middle class—the very ones who needed it least, according to Frank and other advocates. As the design evolved, most scientists concentrated on research and academic publication and left the public distribution of their findings to other professionals and popularizers.

As child science expanded and became more professionalized, a certain disdain for ordinary parents emerged. For example, one educational psychologist wrote the following about the parents of nursery school children:

> Many parents, willing as they may be to assume the entire responsibility, are unfitted for the task of presenting the proper kind of stimulation and example for the child. Since the behavior of parents is frequently inadequate, and their personalities may be anything but balanced, the example they set for their children is an unfortunate one. All of this leads to the assertion that the needs of the child of today are adequately met by parents so seldom that it is necessary for the larger social group to become interested in the welfare of children before their personalities have become too definitely set in the wrong direction.

... One proponent of using nursery schools to reach parents was Arnold Gesell. . . . [who argued that] "The nursery school at present is simply on the skirmishing line, and it must be used as a method of developing and defining techniques of parental guidance, and pre-parental education." The beauty of this device, he concluded, was that "if we use it in that way we shall not in any sense weaken the home, but we shall strengthen the home." Parent education was necessary because of myriad threats to American civilization: crime, divorce, insanity, and a lower birthrate. Thus, he concluded, "We must find means of strengthening the psychological stamina of the next generation. And if we must find means we shall get back to the very beginning of things, to the cradle and that is the reason that science is taking and that scientific studies are taking new shape." ...

Another way in which parent education took place was over the radio and in syndicated newspaper columns by well-known personalities such as Angelo Patri. He wrote newspaper columns from 1923 to 1962 and spoke on radio programs from 1928 to 1943. He claimed he received thousands of letters each month from troubled parents, thus documenting strong parental interest in the new expertise. An immigrant from Italy, Patri himself had taken courses at Columbia from John Dewey and had been a school administrator in New York City. For the most part, Patri offered nonjudgmental, commonsense advice, but he dealt mostly with older children and was very sympathetic to children's needs, at times taking the child's viewpoint instead of the parents'. The following is an example from a radio program broadcast in December 1931 in which Patri reads a letter from a 15-year-old girl whose father became angry when a boy walked her home:

the girl whose father roars at the sight of a boy in the house knows that father is wrong. She knows that there is nothing to fear where she and that boy are concerned. She knows that father's attitude is unreasoning and absurd. But father does not know that he will be the last one to whom she will go in time of need. He does not know that she will evade him and he will become a stranger to his own child.

Patri was not unsympathetic to parents, however. "No child can bring himself up," he said in November 1931, "and make a success of it."

Patri's long run as a columnist and radio broadcaster illustrates an important point—much of the information about children that parents sought and used was popular, rather than academic.

18

In the twentieth century experts have scrutinized all aspects of child development—physical health, emotional expression, and intellectual processes. The most prominent and often invoked authority on children's cognitive development is Jean Piaget. Here he discusses the earliest processes of learning, by which the child comes to know him/herself in relation to the environment (1954).

The Construction of Reality in the Child

Jean Piaget

Until the age of three to six months, that is, until the prehension of visual objectives, the child's main activities, from the point of view of space, merely lead him to analyze the content of sensory images: analysis of forms as a whole, or of figures, positions, and displacements. Each behavior pattern or each class of behavior patterns thus results in the formation of a particular category of perceptual clusters which are more or less stable but are not yet realized in objects and are of a type corresponding to spaces: the gustatory or "buccal" space of Stern, visual space, auditory space, tactile space and many others (postural and kinesthetic spaces, etc.). These spaces can be more or less interconnected according to the degree of coordination of the sensorimotor schemata which engender them, but they remain primarily heterogeneous, that is, they are far from constituting together a single space in which each one would be situated. Consequently they do not yet suffice at all for the evaluation of sizes, of distances, of related positions, or above all for the elaboration of objective displacement groups. By virtue of the very fact that there is no single space there could be no question of the subject locating his own activities in space and thus understanding them as related to the displacements of objects. Quite to the contrary, far from knowing himself to be in space, the subject confers on his perceptions only those spatial qualities whose reality is created, as needed, by the immediate action, and he conceives of displacements of things only as extensions of his activity. If there are groups they are therefore only practical, unaware of themselves, and do not include the subject as such; in short, action creates space but is not yet situated in it. . . .

There is no doubt that changes of position are gradually differentiated from changes of state during the earliest months of life. From the chaos of sensory impressions the child comes sooner or later to find certain stable elements in the changes perceived and thus to dissociate irreversible changes from those which can be compensated by body movements. For example, when Jacqueline at 1;7 (sixth stage of the evolution of object concept) finds a hidden object by noting its successive and partly invisible displacements, it is clear that she is distinguishing changes of position from changes of state—that is, she considers the vanished object not as being altered in structure or as having returned to nothingness, but as having been subjected to displacements constituting a coherent "group." . . .

In our first study of the beginnings of mental life we analyzed the origins of intelligence in children and tried to show how the forms of intellectual activity are constructed on the sensorimotor level. In the current work we have tried, on the other hand, to understand how the real categories of sensorimotor intelligence are organized, that is, how the world is constructed by means of this instrument. . . . The time has come to show the unity of these various processes and their relations with those of the child's thought, envisaged in their most general aspect.

The successive study of concepts of object, space, causality, and time has led us to the same conclusions: the elaboration of the universe by sensorimotor intelligence constitutes the transition from a state in which objects are centered about a self which believes it directs them, although completely unaware of itself as subject, to a state in which the self is placed, at least practically, in a stable world conceived as independent of personal activity. How is this evolution possible?

It can be explained only by the development of intelligence. Intelligence progresses from a state in which accommodation to the environment is undifferentiated from the assimilation of things to the subject's schemata to a state in which the accommodation of multiple schemata is distinguished from their respective and reciprocal assimilation. To understand this process, which sums up the whole evolution of sensorimotor intelligence, let us recall its steps, starting with the development of assimilation itself.

In its beginnings, assimilation is essentially the utilization of the external environment by the subject to nourish his hereditary or acquired schemata. It goes without saying that schemata such as those of sucking, sight, prehension, etc., constantly need to be accommodated to things, and that the necessities of this accommodation often thwart the assimilatory effort. But this accommodation remains so undifferentiated from the assimilatory processes that it does not give rise to any special active behavior pattern but merely consists in an adjustment of the pattern to the details of the things assimilated. Hence it is natural that at this developmental level the external world does not seem formed by permanent objects, that neither space nor time is yet organized in groups and objective series, and that causality is not spatialized or located in things. In other words, at first the universe consists in mobile and plastic perceptual images centered about personal activity. But it is self-evident that to the extent that this activity is undifferentiated from the things it constantly assimilates to itself it remains unaware of its own subjectivity; the external world therefore begins by being confused with the sensations of a self unaware of itself, before the two factors become detached from one another and are organized correlatively.

On the other hand, in proportion as the schemata are multiplied and differentiated by their reciprocal assimilations as well as their progressive accommodation to the diversities of reality, the accommodation is dissociated from assimilation little by little and at the same time insures a gradual delimitation of the external environment and of the subject. Hence assimilation ceases merely to incorporate things in personal activity and establishes, through the progress of that activity, an increasingly tight web of coordinations among the schemata which define it and consequently among the objects to which these schemata are applied. In terms of reflective intelligence this would mean that deduction is organized and applied to an experience conceived as external. From this time on, the universe is built up into an aggregate of permanent objects connected by causal relations that are independent of the subject and are placed in objective space and time. Such a universe, instead of depending on personal activity, is on the contrary imposed upon the self to the extent that it comprises the organism as a part in a whole. The self thus becomes aware of itself, at least in its practical action, and discovers itself as a cause among other causes and as an object subject to the same laws as other objects.

In exact proportion to the progress of intelligence in the direction of differentiation of schemata and their reciprocal assimilation, the universe proceeds from the integral and unconscious egocentrism of the beginnings to an increasing solidification and objectification. During the earliest stages the child perceives things like a solipsist who is unaware of himself as subject and is familiar only with his own actions. But step by step with the coordination of his intellectual instruments he discovers himself in placing himself as an active object among the other active objects in a universe external to himself.

19

Jerome Kagan has been prominent among contemporary theorists of child develop-
ment for supporting the idea that the infant develops according to an inner com-
pass. By acknowledging that infants have inborn characteristics and distinct per-
sonal qualities, Kagan provides a new space for biology, and moves away from the
assumption, dominant since Locke, that parenting practices determine a child's
character. His emphasis on the interaction between preexisting tendencies and
environmental factors represents the newest turn in child development theory
(1984).

Understanding the Infant

Jerome Kagan

When most Europeans lived their entire lives in the same villages in which they were born, and 40 percent of all children died by their fifth birthday, a deep understanding of the infant was of neither interest nor value, for the adult profile of any child who survived the first few years was determined in large measure by the parents' economic security and class position. But by the middle of the seventeenth century, both ascent and descent in social status had become a real possibility for a significant proportion of youth whose families had acquired some measure of freedom and the expectation that their children's lives might be different from their own. Historical events had made each child's future less knowable and, therefore, a source of parental apprehension. Now, the community needed an explanation of the variations in life histories that implied some simple practices that parents could implement in order to reduce the uncertainty that invaded consciousness when they wondered about the position their child might occupy two decades later.

Of all the causes thoughtful observers might have invented to explain the dramatic differences in adult talent, wealth, happiness, status, and morality, most Western theorists assumed that the experiences of infancy (either quality of physical care or specific encounters with objects and people) were the most relevant. The moods, values, skills, and habits created during the first few years were supposed to persist indefinitely and to form the adult's character, competence, and capacity for joy. Contemporary American parents are ready to believe that the adult's happiness, which has become the most popular criterion for a successful life, is influenced by the events of infancy.

There is also a political motivation that ensures a preoccupation with the first period of childhood, at least among American families. The disturbing differences in economic resources and technical competence between adolescents from disadvantaged ethnic minorities and youngsters from middle-class families are inconsistent with the American ideal of an egalitarian society. Most Americans believe that if the conditions of early rearing were improved and the proper environments engineered, our social problems would be eased. Hence, discovery of the principles of growth would reveal the correct pattern of encounters for all children. This chapter considers some of the important information we have gained about the infant, even though the most profound insights continue to evade us.

The properties of the infant are so distinct from those of the older child that it is not surprising that all societies regard the first two years of life as a special period of development. Infants are often defined not by what they can do but by absence of the qualities adults possess, especially language, intention, appreciation of right and wrong, symbolism, planfulness, guilt, empathy, and self-consciousness. William James's description of the baby's world as a ''blooming, buzzing confusion'' was rendered credible by the popular notion of the infant as an inherently helpless creature with little power to resist environmental intrusion.

The behavior of the infant is so ambiguous it is easy for the culture's beliefs about human nature to influence observers' interpretations of what they think they see. These influences are nicely illustrated in the different descriptions of the infant by Sigmund Freud, Erik Erikson, and Jean Piaget. Each of these influential theorists highlighted a special aspect of the child's first year because of suppositions originating in the larger cultural context in which each scholar lived.

At the turn of the century, when Freud was forming his theoretical ideas, Darwinian evolutionary theory was a source of metaphors for human behavior. Darwinian theory held that the human infant was the link between animals and human adults. Ernst Haeckel's famous declaration that ontogeny recapitulates phylogeny suggested one form that link might take: the human infant should be governed by the same forces that control primitive animal forms for whom a single orifice served both ingestion of food and sexuality. This imaginative idea—combined with the new doctrine that nerves have specific energies that are linked to different qualities of experience, and the older principle of the conservation of physical energy—probably led Freud to suggest that each child was born with a fixed amount of libidinal energy, with the mouth, tongue, lips, and their usual functions serving as the initial reservoir for this force. Although the bold hypothesis of the oral stage sounds strange today, it was more credible during the early decades of the century—in part, because it bore a close resemblance to major principles in the respected disciplines of zoology, physiology, and physics and satisfied the desire held by many scholars to bring humans and animals conceptually closer.

But half a century later, when Erik Erikson was developing the eight stages of man, politically liberal scholars wanted to increase the psychological distance between animals and humans and to make social experience, rather than inherited instincts, the source of the obvious variation in human talent and character. One reason for this theoretical preference was a desire to quiet a small but vocal group of eminent biologists and psychologists who claimed that the economic and social failure of European immigrant groups was partially biological in origin. Because a growing audience of intellectuals was receptive to the view that social experience, not biology, was formative, it was reasonable for a theorist, during the years between the two world wars, to see the actively nursing infant as a passively fed child and to transform a solitary, instinctive behavior into a social event. Two important qualities in this dyadic relation are the caregiver's affective involvement and her reliability. If she does not feed the crying baby within a reasonable period of time, the infant becomes extremely distressed. Erikson's labeling the first era of development as a time of trust had the same ring of truth in the 1950s that Freud's oral stage had had half a century earlier.

Piaget's conception of infancy, like Freud's, was influenced by debates on the mechanisms of evolutionary change. Piaget sided with those who wanted to award most of the power for change to the organism's commerce with the environment rather than to genetic mutation. Piaget likened the development of cognitive functions to the evolution of organs and bodily processes because, in his conception, the infant's cognitive abilities derive from active interaction with objects in the world and from successive accommodations to new challenges. When Piaget looked at the infant, he saw a baby playing with the mother's face and fingers. Nursing, being nurtured, and exploring the caregiver's fingers are all characteristic of infancy. It is not obvious that one of these functions is most central; theory awards one of them greater status than the others.

The ease with which scholars attribute special meaning to an aspect of infancy reflects a general tendency to ascribe to the young child properties that are opposite to or undeveloped beginnings of the characteristics adults prize. Americans, who value independence and individuality, see the baby as dependent, undifferentiated, and not yet aware of being separate from others—undesirable contrasts to the qualities the Western adult is supposed to attain.

But dependence on others and an undifferentiated self are not ascribed universally to young children. The Japanese, who prize close interdependence between child and adult, regard the infant as having a small component of autonomy that is part of the baby's unique nature. Japanese mothers, who believe they must tempt the infant into a dependent role, rush to soothe a crying infant, respond quietly to the baby's excited babbling, and sleep with the young child at night in order to encourage the mutual bonding necessary for adult life.

Historical shifts in the traits theorists ascribe to infants can reveal secular changes in the qualities that are admired. During the 1930s, when control of childhood aggression was regarded as both highly desirable and attainable, the British psychoanalyst Melanie Klein awarded to the infant unrestrained aggressive impulses and explained the nursing infant's biting of the mother's nipple as an expression of that primitive instinct. Since the Second World War, childhood aggression has become more acceptable and, accordingly, Klein's description has become obsolete.

When strict conformity to parents and benevolent authority was the ideal, nineteenth-century American children were described as willful. The goal of socialization was to teach them the mature posture of obedience to elders. As historical events began to taint the moral imperatives laid down by authority, theorists felt it necessary to promote a private conscience. Hence, children who regularly conformed to the commands of adults out of fear of punishment were reclassified as immature, because anxiety over the disapproval of others is not as desirable a foundation for morality as is an inhibition that rests on an internal commitment to be good.

Attitudes toward the restraint of strong desire have also changed profoundly during the last two centuries. The inhibition of behavior motivated by anger, the promise of sensory delight, or enhanced power—called *self-control*—was the central criterion for morality in the early nineteenth century. But by the first decade of this century, adjustment to social demands began to replace self-control as the ideal each child was supposed to attain. Successful adjustment required yielding to desires for pleasure, friends, status, and wealth; hence, excessive self-control was undesirable, and the profile valued in 1800 had been reclassified as potentially detrimental to happiness.

Contemporary psychologists have chosen to celebrate two other characteristics of the infant. One group, partly derivative of the Eriksonian view, regards affectionate and playful interaction between mother and infant as critical for the attachment of baby to caregiver—a distinguishing feature of this era. A second group has selected for study qualities that comprise the central interests of modern cognitive science: perception, memory, and categorical functioning. If the renewed concern with morality continues to grow, it is possible that, by the end of this century, many observers, like those who wrote at the end of the last century, will award centrality to the behavioral previews of will, intention, and choice because they are the essential elements of conscience.

This chapter attempts to summarize a conception of infancy that is informed by three ideas. The first awards primacy to maturing cognitive talents: in part, because these qualities were ignored in past descriptions; and, in part, because I believe developmental changes in emotions and social behavior are best understood by relating them to the growth of cognitive processes. I shall argue that the most essential catalyst for change is the relation between the events that enter the child's perceptual field and his knowledge at that moment, and that the child's corpus of knowledge is monitored by inherent biases in the way experience is segmented and by a growing ability to remember the past and to compare it with the present.

The infant's attachment to those who provide care is a second initial process in the first year. The actualization of this process also involves a relation between the child and the world outside, but the attachment relation unites the infant's inborn repertoire of actions with the responsiveness of those persons who care for and play with the infant.

Acquiring knowledge and forming attachments are universal, but there is extraordinary variation among children in the rate and form of these acquisitions. Although differences in rearing environments make a substantial contribution to this variation, an infant begins life with a particular temperamental style, which profoundly influences the way others treat the child and how he or she reacts to the unexpected. . . .

Three ideas have dominated this discussion of the human infant. The first provides substance to the earlier suggestion that maturation of the central nervous system makes possible a sequence of intellectual abilities that include recognition and retrieval of the past, the ability to compare past and present, and inhibition of the primitive and automatic reflexes that humans inherit from their primate ancestors. As each of these new competences matures, like new organs in the growth of the embryo, reorganizations occur in the bases of behavior, thought, and emotion. The fears of a stranger and of loss of a mother cannot occur until the infant is able to compare the known with the unknown, but is still unable to put the recognition aside when comprehension fails. Although nineteenth-century observers appreciated the importance of maturation, they shared the twentieth-century commitment to the catalytic power of social experience. What modern science is discovering, however, is that some of these competences are so deeply engrained in the human genome that they require less interaction with others than we have wanted to believe. . . .

The attachment of infant to caregiver is also an inherent capacity that is difficult to suppress. Even though we cannot measure with sensitivity the variations in the emotional quality of an infant's attachment, there is good reason for believing in the theoretical utility of this idea, for most infants living in neglecting environments are more fearful, more labile, and less gleeful than those who have the benefit of predictable and loving care.

The second idea represents the return of an old and popular conviction. Most cultures acknowledge the distinctive temperamental styles of infants, and most parents accommodate to these inborn biases. It is probably not an accident that modern research finds differences in fearfulness to be a persistent quality, for the essence of this characteristic is present in most of the homespun personality theories that can be traced to Plato and Aristotle.

20

The pediatrician T. Berry Brazelton has become probably the most highly regarded contemporary adviser on child development. Here he reassures mothers that they can work and rear children at the same time, and encourages fathers to become more active and responsible parents (1995).

Mothers and Fathers Working and Rearing Children

T. Berry Brazelton

Can a woman decide to take on and competently carry out two roles at once? I certainly think so, and it seems time for us to face this fact as a national trend. It is important to figure out how it can be done so that our next generation of babies and their parents do not suffer.

We learn about ourselves as mature people in the process of being responsible for and nurturing a baby. Mothers who work must learn two very different approaches to life. Abraham Zaleznik in a speech given at the Harvard Business School said that these two approaches, which can never really be reconciled, will be different for each woman. In the workplace, a woman needs to be pragmatic, somewhat isolated emotionally, and forceful and direct in managing her job and those around her. She must be efficient. But an efficient woman could be the worst kind of mother for her children. For at home, a woman must be flexible, warm, and concerned; willing to experience and to learn from her failures, and open to change. She must always be ready for things to go wrong and be able to compensate. To be able to shift gears quickly and without too much anguish, from one approach to the other, may be the key to success in these two, very different roles.

In planning this book, I first saw the problem as one of "mothers who work." The working mothers of my small patients disabused me of that quickly. They said, "If you blame women for the problems that arise, you are ignoring a large part of the issue. It is not just a problem for women but for men, too. Men expect to work but most don't expect to help at home. And yet they must. The problem in a working family is that no one is there all the time to care for the children. Why not see it as a problem for 'working parents,' so that fathers too can see their roles as changing? Men must be more active in nurturing as well as at breadwinning. At least half the problem today is that men haven't been prepared well for their new roles. Women need to learn to do two jobs well, but so do men."

There is an increasing number of studies about the effect of father involvement on children's development in early infancy. Some of the most provocative ones demonstrate that children whose fathers were actively involved with them in their infancy enter school with higher IQs and a better chance for success in the future. But what is even more exciting, these children have better relationships with their peers, a better sense of humor, and appear to have a stronger self-image. In a father's involvement there are many opportunities to strengthen the child as well as the whole family. That shouldn't surprise any of us.

Research in our laboratory at Children's Hospital in Boston (with co-workers Suzanne Dixon, Michael Yogman, Edward Tronick, and Heidi Als) has demonstrated that the father of a small baby shows a very different yet predictable kind of behavior while playing with his infant. A father touches and pokes more. He is likely to speak and react in playful, stimulating ways that produce a heightened reaction in his baby. Whereas a mother will hold, soothe, and play gently with her baby, a father seems to respond differently. Very quickly (as early as the first month) babies demonstrate an expectancy for these playful responses. At one month, an infant's shoulders and eyebrows rise in an expression of expectant joy when father's voice is heard in the distance. The importance to the baby of this different, more playful response is already reflected in this behavior of joyful expectancy, which contrasts clearly with the more urgent and "hungry" expectancy for the mother. At one month, a baby with an actively involved father is already learning about two different kinds of people in the world. . . .

Why has it taken so long as a society to begin actively to include fathers in the family's adjustment to a new baby? The new emphasis on father participation at delivery and in childbirth classes helps recruit fathers for a more involved role with their babies and wives at home. My hope is that these more involved and more motivated fathers will feel a kind of responsibility for baby and spouse that will serve to cement the endangered family structure in our society today. . . .

Men need more and more support and preparation to become successful nurturers. Boys need to be around babies and to be made to feel responsible for them. Adolescent males need to be incorporated into child-care settings and to be educated on early child development. We all need to see, as a cultural goal, the successful accomplishment of the two roles by all mature adults—men and women alike—both in the marketplace and, more important, at home, as nurturers for spouses and children. I hope fathers will feel supported by this book as they take on their new role in working families.

Role strain, especially around emergencies such as a new baby or an illness in the family, can be a sign that it's time to reevaluate the balances within the family. Job dissatisfaction can be compounded by crises at home. Family stress can in turn create job stress. Studies of working mothers show that women who are happy in their work are more likely to perceive the need for and to create higher values at home, and their children profit by it. I try to offer working parents some insights into the normal developmental periods in a child's life that inevitably place extra stress on parents. This stress can be more intense when both parents work. I hope that, by knowing ahead when these periods occur, working families can turn a normal stress into a learning experience.

John Wollaston, *Mann Page and His Sister Elizabeth*, c. 1757. Courtesy of the Virginia Historical Society.

Part Two

Boys and Girls

Social gender identity is established and promoted from the moment of birth. Children learn about their individual gender from their parents and relatives, from their schools, and from their peers. Each generation of adults has a somewhat different attitude about gender, and defines it in new ways more congruent with its needs. In that sense, adults reinvent gender identity, although as the following segments indicate, the maintenance of gender roles has been tenacious over the past four hundred years of history. Only in the very recent past has the elimination of gender distinctions become a conspicuous part of the social agenda.

21

In Anne Bradstreet's lovely ode to her children, she draws an important distinction between her daughters and her sons. When her daughters leave the nest they take flight with their "mates," while the sons go it alone. Note also the poem's affectionate and tender tone, which some may consider unusual for seventeenth-century Puritans. Bradstreet may have been an exception, or perhaps we have overlooked the Puritans' devotion to their children as we focus on their sense of community responsibility and religious piety.

In Reference to Her Children, 23 June, 1659

Anne Bradstreet

I had eight birds hatcht in one nest,
Four Cocks there were, and Hens the rest,
I nurst them up with pain and care,
Nor cost, nor labour did I spare,
Till at the last they felt their wing.
Mounted the Trees, and learn'd to sing;
Chief of the Brood then took his flight,
To Regions far, and left me quite:
My mournful chirps I after send,
Till he return, or I do end,
Leave not thy nest, thy Dam and Sire,
Fly back and sing amidst this Quire.
My second bird did take her flight,
And with her mate flew out of sight;
Southward they both their course did bend,
And Seasons twain they there did spend:
Till after blown by *Southern* gales,
They *Norward* steer'd with filled sayles.
A prettier bird was no where seen,
Along the Beach among the treen.
I have a third of colour white,
On whom I plac'd no small delight;
Coupled with mate loving and true,
Hath also bid her Dam adieu:
And where *Aurora* first appears,
She now hath percht, to spend her years;

One to the Academy flew
To chat among that learned crew:
Ambition moves still in his breast
That he might chant above the rest,
Striving for more then to do well,
That nightingales he might excell.
My fifth, whose down is yet scarce gone
Is 'mongst the shrubs and bushes flown,
And as his wings increase in strength,
On higher boughs he'l perch at length.
My other three, still with me nest,
Untill they'r grown, then as the rest,
Or here or there, they'l take their flight,
As is ordain'd, so shall they light.
If birds could weep, then would my tears
Let others know what are my fears
Lest this my brood some harm should catch,
And be surpriz'd for want of watch,
Whilst pecking corn, and void of care
They fall un'wares in Fowlers snare:
Or whilst on trees they sit and sing,
Some untoward boy at them do fling.
Or whilst allur'd with bell and glass,
The net be spread, and caught, alas.
Or least by Lime-twigs they be foyl'd,
Or by some greedy hawks be spoyl'd.
O would my young, ye saw my breast,
And knew what thoughts there sadly rest,
Great was my pain when I you bred,
Great was my care, when I you fed,
Long did I keep you soft and warm,
And with my wings kept off all harm,
My cares are more, and fears then ever,
My throbs such now, as 'fore were never:
Alas my birds, you wisdome want,
Of perils you are ignorant,
Oft times in grass, on trees, in flight,
Sore accidents on you may light.
O to your safety have an eye,
So happy may you live and die:
Mean while my dayes in tunes Ile spend,
Till my weak layes with me shall end,
In shady woods I'le sit and sing,
And things that past, to mind I'le bring.
Once young and pleasant, as are you,
But former toyes (no joyes) adieu.
My age I will not once lament,
But sing, my time so near is spent.

And from the top bough take my flight,
Into a country beyond sight,
Where old ones, instantly grow young,
And there with Seraphims set song:
No seasons cold, nor storms they see;
But spring lasts to eternity,
When each of you shall in your nest
Among your young ones take your rest,
In chirping languages, oft them tell,
You had a Dam that lov'd you well,
That did what could be done for young,
And nurst you up till you were strong,
And 'fore she once would let you fly,
She shew'd you joy and misery;
Taught what was good, and what was ill,
What would save life, and what would kill.
Thus gone, amongst you I may live,
And dead, yet speak, and counsel give:
Farewel my birds, farewel adieu,
I happy am, if well with you.

The most prominent boyhood ritual in the seventeenth and eighteenth centuries was "breeching," that point at which boys, around the age of seven, were for the first time allowed to wear pants rather than the gowns worn by all young children. After they were breeched, boys assumed their superior place alongside their fathers. In this letter, written in 1679, a woman describes the breeching of her grandson and the excitement that accompanied the event.

Girls had fewer specific rituals or marks of progression through childhood. A wedding was the transformative event that marked a woman's transition from dependency on her father to a new dependency on her husband.

Breeching Little Ffrank

A. North

Dear Son:

You cannot beleeve the great concerne that was in the whole family here last Wednesday, it being the day that the taylor was to helpe to dress little ffrank in his breeches in order to the making an everyday suit by it. Never had any bride that was to be drest upon her weding night more handes about her, some the legs, some the armes, the taylor butt'ning, and others putting on the sword, and so many lookers on that had I not a ffinger amongst I could not have seen him. When he was quite drest he acted his part as well as any of them for he desired he might goe downe to inquire for the little gentleman that was there the day before in a black coat, and speak to the man to tell the gentleman when he came from school that there was a gallant with very fine clothes and a sword to have waited upon him and would come again upon Sunday next. But this was not all, there was great contrivings while he was dressing who should have the first salute; but he sayd if old Joan had been here, she should, but he gave it to me to quiett them all. They were very fitt, everything, and he looks taller and prettyer than in his coats. Little Charles rejoyced as much as he did for he jumpt all the while about him and took notice of everything. I went to Bury, and bo^t everything for another suitt which will be finisht on Saturday so the coats are to be quite left off on Sunday. I consider it is not yett terme time and since you could not have the pleasure of the first sight, I resolved you should have a full relation from

Yo^r most aff^{nate} Mother
A North.

When he was drest he asked Buckle whether muffs were out of fashion because they had not sent him one.

Children's dress and play usually reflect gender attitudes. Here the historian Karin Calvert discusses the new children's dress of the eighteenth and nineteenth centuries and the distinctions made between the play of girls and boys. She also notes some of the other important changes affecting children generally beginning in the late eighteenth century as the views of John Locke increasingly influenced social practices toward children in the American colonies (1992).

Suits and Frocks

Karin Calvert

In 1757, Mann Page and his sister Elizabeth posed for the artist John Wollaston at their home in Virginia. As one would expect of a boy of ten, Mann wore a fashionable frock coat, waist coat, and knee breeches; his younger sister wore a stylish silk gown over a pair of stays. Unlike David Mason of an earlier generation, however, Mann did not look exactly like a small version of an adult male in every regard. A grown man of fashion in 1757 powdered his hair, or wore a powdered wig, and swaddled his neck in a long white linen cravat. Mann wore his hair simply and without powder; instead of a cravat, only the loosely gathered neck of his shirt, fastened with a black ribbon, showed beneath his coat. These simple modifications of standard male attire were less restrictive and more comfortable than the formal cravat and the hot, itchy, and cumbersome wig expected of mature gentlemen.

From about 1750, boys old enough to wear breeches were spared some of the more uncomfortable aspects of adult dress. The relaxation of the accepted dress code for boys between about the ages of seven and ten accompanied the development of more positive attitudes toward childhood in general. Mann Page would one day be a mature member of his society, but that society no longer felt the need to push the issue. Between the skirts of infancy and the breeches and wig of maturity, Americans accepted a slight modification of dress as a gentler entry into the business of growing up. In Wollaston's painting the image of young Page incorporates the developing man (in breeches) and the playful child (holding a pet bird). Americans had created a separate and special stage of life for their growing sons. They no longer sought to maintain the fiction of maturity that had made eight-year-old David Mason seem pleasing in the eyes of his contemporaries of 1670. Childishness and playfulness were no longer shortcomings, but accepted characteristics of childhood—accepted enough, in fact, to be included in an expensive, formal portrait that would be displayed by generations of the Page family.

The young Mann Page dressed in the distinctive costume of youth for his portrait, but the development of his sister, Elizabeth, still held too little significance to their society to be marked by a special costume. Like Joanna and Abigail Mason, Elizabeth Page dressed in a fashion suitable for females at any age. However, instead of giving her the typical feminine attributes of a fan or a flower, Wollaston portrayed Elizabeth cradling a doll on her lap. She still dressed as a little woman, but Wollaston portrayed her as a child at play. Young girls were accepted as children, but society still viewed their development as limited, not worthy of particular attention. Women and girls were perceived as still much the same. Put simply, males changed; females didn't.

Between 1750 and 1770, only a small percentage of portraits of children suggest the newly accepted playfulness of childhood by including toys or a playful pose in the composition. Nonetheless, these portraits mark the beginning of a new acceptance of play as a natural and acceptable part of childhood. Particularly after 1770, children's portraits frequently included toys: with girls, dolls, doll furniture and dishes, grace hoops, and dominoes; with boys, balls, rolling hoops, toy wagons and sleds, toy horses, and tin soldiers. All of these toys definitely signalled a new attitude toward play. In the first place, they clearly suggested that it was acceptable for children. Locke had pronounced play a learning process necessary for young people's development, believing that playthings were the natural tools of childhood and arguing that "recreation is as necessary as labour or food." A century later, American families tended to agree with him. After reading Locke, Eliza Pinckney of South Carolina went out and bought her son a set of alphabet blocks so that he might "play himself into learning," noting that she began early "for he is not yet four months old."

When play became not only acceptable but even encouraged for children, it also became closely associated with them. Instead of youngsters joining in with the games of adults as they had in earlier generations, they now were engaged in games considered suitable for their age. Society had created and defined childhood as a separate stage of development, with its own needs and virtues, and provided it with its own activities. Play and toys became the province of childhood. Young people now engaged in socially defined and approved children's games, while adults pursued other forms of recreation. Children no longer gambled at cards, and adults stopped playing hunt-the-bean. The generations increasingly inhabited different worlds.

Play was also strictly segregated by gender in the eighteenth and early nineteenth centuries. Girls played with girls; "we were seldom permitted to play with any boys except our brothers," noted Lucy Larcom. And girls played with dolls. John Mason's shop in Philadelphia, like many others, advertised "drest dolls, naked ditto and Lilliputian dolls" for sale. Whatever the size of the doll, it was carved of wood to represent a lady of fashion. As such, it gave the child the opportunity to practice the graces and skills she would need as a woman. "She can dress and undress her doll; and carry it through all those ceremonies of giving and receiving visits," and she can make "those things" for the doll "for which women are usually dependent upon milliners." The doll also served as a baby that the little girl "nurses, instructs, and corrects." Even without formal toys, girls' imaginary games centered on imitating the activities of adult women. Philip Fithian described the young daughters of Robert Carter "tying strings to a chair" and then walking back and forth pretending to spin yarn, "getting rags and washing them without water," scrubbing the floor, and "knitting with straws." Little Fanny and Harriet Carter also played at the "womanish Fribble" of "stuffing rags . . . under their Gowns just below their Apron-strings" and were "prodigiously charmed at their resemblance to Pregnant Women." Girls' play was pointedly preparatory to their future roles in society.

Boys' playthings were meant for more active games. They rode in wheelbarrows and sleds, walked on stilts, jumped rope (strictly a boys' game until about 1830), rolled a hoop, and played cricket, marbles, ball, and battledore. The games for boys were far more diverse than those for girls; no one activity summed up the socializing and training process for boys the way the doll did for their sisters. Whatever the game, play had merit as a way of refreshing the mind and exercising the body, so that children could return to their studies invigorated and able to absorb the more serious lessons of growing up. Play was not an end in itself so much as a tool to facilitate the child's development.

Children could not indulge in much active play in the costumes fashionable before 1770; to inhibit childish exuberance was, in fact, their function. With changing attitudes, radical modifications in the clothing of toddlers began to appear during the 1770s. Those old enough to walk gave up their long baby dresses for ankle-length frocks. Unlike earlier generations, they did not wear stiff corsets, tight bodices, high-heeled shoes, or tight sleeves. Instead, little children like Henry Tallmadge wore relatively loose muslin frocks and soft flat slippers. As one might expect, Locke had been among the first to rail against the restrictive clothing children had habitually worn. "Narrow breasts, short and stinking breath, ill lungs, and crookedness" were the natural results of "hard bodices and clothes that pinch," he argued late in the seventeenth century. The actual application of dress reform for young children only began about one hundred years later. The new style of frock was only lightly belted with a ribbon sash and was usually short-sleeved to permit considerably more freedom of movement than had been possible with earlier fashions. The very thin fabric and short sleeves were also in accordance with Locke's recommendations against dressing children too warmly. Following Locke's advice, Mrs. Bloomsgrove, in Hitchcock's 1790 novel, made certain that her children were "temperately clad both summer and winter, varying their dress but little" according to the seasons. "The idea," Hitchcock explained, "she probably received from Mr. Locke, who tells of persons in England who wear the same clothes summer and winter, without any inconvenience, or more sense of cold than others." Like the cold bath and the lightly covered bed, the cotton gown was in keeping with the new conception of the naturalness of children. Adults had grown soft and weak from pampering themselves with luxuries, but they could protect their children from a similar fate by trusting to the strength of the natural constitution of the child. Parents were convinced that exposure to the cold would make their offspring less mindful of it and less likely to take sick. The new cotton frock offered little children greater freedom for active play, and greater need for such increased activity in chilly weather.

The white muslin frock that young children wore after 1770 represented a dramatic break with previous conventions of dress in America because it was strikingly different from the costume worn by adult women. Simpler, lighter, and looser than a mature woman's gown, it offered children greater freedom and (at least in warm weather) comfort. The frock visually distinguished children from women, while still setting them apart from men and boys in knee breeches. Both women and children still held subordinate positions within the family, but by visually dividing them into two separate groups the frock broke the long-accepted link between femininity and childishness. It had become possible to be one without being the other.

The changes in clothing styles after 1770 were particularly important in the lives of little girls. The new childish frock signified a greater emphasis on the development of a young girl, for she now wore a costume quite different from the one she would assume as an adult. From the time she began walking until her early teens, a girl wore her simple muslin frock; she then graduated to the far more complex gowns of silk or muslin, stays, and heels of a grown woman. The transition from one style of dress to the other served to mark her passage from childhood to maturity. For the first time, society visually recognized significant differences between girls and women. And also for the first time, the process of growing older for a little girl was also the process of growing up.

The distinctions between women and children were further accentuated by the popularity of a new hairstyle, worn by boys and girls but not by men or women. Until this time, children had adopted the adult hairstyle appropriate to their sex as soon as their hair grew long enough to dress. The most vivid image of the custom occurs in the sixteenth-century portrait Hans Holbein painted of his own family. In the painting, the artist's two-year-old daughter Katherina sits on her mother's lap, her wispy baby-fine hair plaited into thin little braids that are not long enough to encircle her head in the style typical of women of that time. Instead, a piece of string tied to the end of each braid bridges the gap to complete the coronet in the prescribed fashion. When nature fell short, parents resorted to artifice to bring their children in line with social expectation. In America, boys had worn their hair in long curls, cascading over their shoulders, in the seventeenth and early eighteenth centuries, then tied back in a queue around midcentury. Girls had piled their hair on top of their heads and covered it with a cap that became progressively smaller as the eighteenth century advanced.

By contrast, during the last quarter of the century children of both sexes no longer adopted adult hairstyles as soon as physically possible. Instead, they wore their hair straight and loose to the shoulder and cut in bangs across the forehead.

24

After studying the autobiographical writings of girls in the nineteenth century, the historian Anne Scott MacLeod concludes that girls were not as constrained as we might imagine, and that their activities were not always strictly differentiated from boys' activities. The texture of real children's lives can be very different from the scenarios of novelists or the reconstructions of historians (1994).

American Girlhood in the Nineteenth Century

Anne Scott MacLeod

Any image of prim and proper little girls who imbibed with their mother's milk a deep concern for the state of their clothing dissolves before the autobiographical accounts. These American girls climbed trees, fell into rain barrels, fished in the horse troughs. "We played I Spy, mumblety-peg, stalked about on forked-stick stilts, skinned up the trees, bent limbs for a teeter, climbed on and jumped off the stable roof," recalled Sarah Bonebright. With the clarity of hindsight, they recorded years later how they had abused their clothes: "I often climbed trees and tore my clothes," wrote one, and Anna Clary told of climbing a tree with her skirt filled with grapes. After a while she slid down the tree trunk, to the considerable detriment of both grapes and dress.

City children—a minority in nineteenth-century accounts, as they were in the population—obviously had less of the natural world available to them, but they were not necessarily housebound or sedentary for that reason. Una Hunt grew up in Cincinnati in the 1870s and 1880s, climbing "every tree and shed in the neighborhood." There is no reason to assume that the trees and sheds were low, easy ones, either, since she also recorded that "I was often badly hurt, but after each fall, when vinegar and brown papers had been applied, [my mother's] only comment was 'You must learn to climb better,' and I did." She topped her career by climbing to the tip of the church belfry, where she panicked and had to be helped down. Her mother drew the line then, but only at belfries; and Una went back to slightly less exalted heights.

This girl, like some others, also invented some vigorous indoor sports, not always with family approval. She and the other children in her family liked best what they called "indoor coasting." They used tea trays to slide down the stairs, but only, she confessed, when the family was all out. Elizabeth Allan stayed home from church one Sunday during a visit with some city cousins. Long afterward, she remembered the "wild hilarity" of the afternoon in the 1850s. "I initiated my city cousins in the fun of playing 'Wild Indian.' . . . I amazed them by leaping from tops of high bureaus and tables, and boasting how many more spots in the carpet I could jump over than their prim little legs could encompass." Later her "Presbyterian conscience pricked [her] sharply," not for the wildness of the games, however, but because they had been played on a Sunday.

Nineteenth-century American families did differentiate in their treatment of girls and boys; most twentieth-century families do also. But the distinctions insisted upon in nineteenth-century America may have been fewer and less strict than we commonly suppose while children were preadolescent. Even the strictures against boys and girls playing together, familiar from novels and memoirs, seem to have been unevenly applied. Some girls were indeed forbidden to play with boys, unless perhaps with their brothers, but others chose boys as companions and met no objection from their parents.

Most nineteenth-century children knew work at least as well as play. In a woman's memoirs of childhood, we expect to read that domestic chores dominated her share of the work, and it is true that nearly every autobiography written by a woman records some housekeeping skills acquired young. Girls learned how to knit, sew, and cook, to wash clothes, clean house, and preserve food. They gathered eggs and picked berries, washed dishes, and carried wood for the kitchen stove. They were expected to help care for younger children in the family, sometimes to the point where a woman referred to a younger brother or sister as "my child." Under normal circumstances, the tasks, though constant, were not overly arduous. When the mother of the family was ill or dead, however, the weight of domestic responsibility on a young girl might be considerably heavier. Several accounts tell of virtually full responsibility for housekeeping passed to girls at an early age.

The point about housework, however, was not whether girls were expected to do some of it, or even a good deal of it, as children; of course they were. Children's help was indispensable in most American homes where servants were few and chores were endless. The question is whether work was divided along strict sex lines, with some activities reserved strictly for one sex or another. And here the answer is less absolute. In some rural families, at least, autobiographies indicated that boys helped with domestic work before they were old enough to work beside their fathers in the fields. And while most girls learned housekeeping in the expectation that they would eventually have houses to keep, their autobiographies show that they also learned other, less domestic skills during their childhood years. Virginia-born Ellen Mordecai was brought up by her aunts after her mother's death. They were capable women, who could "do anything," according to Mordecai, and they taught her to fish and trap. Ellen was deft with wild things. She caught a woodpecker in her hand once, just to admire his feathers. Once, she climbed a tree to investigate a hole. She put her hand in, felt something soft, and ran back home for a large silver spoon. Up in the tree again, she put the spoon gently into the hole, to scoop up several baby flying squirrels.

These, too, she admired without harming and put back into the tree. And Ellen, taught by her aunts, fished enthusiastically, as they did.

The parents of Frances Willard (who ultimately became president of the Women's Christian Temperance Union) enforced no connection at all between sex and kinds of work. "Mother did not talk to us as girls, but simply as human beings, and it never occurred to me that I ought to 'know house-work' and do it. Mary took to it kindly by nature; I did not, and each one had her way. Mother never said 'you must cook, you must sweep, you must sew' but she studied what we liked to do and kept us at it with no trying at all. I knew all the carpenter's tools and handled them: made carts and sleds, cross-guns and whip handles. . . . But a needle and a dishcloth I could not abide—chiefly, perhaps, because I was bound to live out-of-doors." Sunday dinner preparation in the Willard household rotated among mother, father, and Oliver, the latter two being, in Frances's words, "famous cooks." The Willards represented a thoroughly open-minded attitude toward child nurture which cannot be considered typical of American households in general. Yet their approach, and that of others more conventional, suggests that American parents were often flexible and common-sensical, rather than rigidly doctrinaire in teaching skills or allocating tasks to children. Many parents seem to have been willing to consider convenience and children's tastes rather than some arbitrary view of what was "suitable" work for girls or boys.

This kind of pragmatic latitude is a key note in many American women's childhood memories. The early years of childhood offered a certain psychic as well as a physical freedom to most American children. "We were a neighborhood of large families," wrote Lucy Larcom in *A New England Girlhood*, "and most of us enjoyed the privilege of 'a little wholesome neglect.' Our tether was a long one, and when, grown a little older, we occasionally asked to have it lengthened, a maternal 'I don't care' amounted to almost unlimited liberty." Larcom, who read mostly English books as a child, contrasted the picture of an English childhood she found there with her own American experience: "We did not think those English children had so good a time as we did; they had to be so prim and methodical. It seemed to us that the little folks across the water [were] never allowed to romp and run wild. . . . [We had] a vague idea that this freedom of ours was the natural inheritance of republican children only."

Though the children of pioneering families faced greater hazards than did those of long-settled places, their parents were no more inclined to hover over them, according to Sarah Bonebright, who grew up on a pioneer farm in Iowa. "We had received instructions and the warning admonition from our parents and were expected to circumvent the [wild] creatures or avoid the danger." Girls as well as boys were expected to cope. Bonebright told of being sent on an errand three-quarters of a mile away, across the river and deep in the woods. She lost her way, making three false starts before finding it again, and was home late. "I do not recall that I was questioned about the delay, or that anxiety was expressed at my unusually long absence. I had accomplished the mission. To be able to 'make a shift' for any contingency was expected of both young and old."

25

Boys' literature in the nineteenth century often enforced an ideal of hard work and enterprise, but by midcentury many boys' stories were full of fantasy and had turned against the explicit moralism of an earlier day. The historian Daniel T. Rodgers discusses some of the newer romantic literature for boys and puts Horatio Alger's stories in a new light (1978).

Nineteenth-Century Boys' Literature

Daniel T. Rodgers

What place children's tales occupied in the welter of socializing influences that bore on children growing up in industrial America, how they compared in influence with the official homilies of schools and churches or the far more powerful pressures of peers and families, it is impossible to say. Like so many other aspects of nineteenth-and early twentieth-century culture, children's reading divided along lines of class and respectability. That which was admitted to library shelves in an age when children's librarians took their censoring responsibilities with immense seriousness was the work of writers whose values belonged to Protestant, middle-class, moralistic America. Louisa May Alcott, Jacob Abbott, and *St. Nicholas Magazine* occupied a social world clearly distinct from that of *Elsie Dinsmore*, the dime and nickel novelists, and *The Boys of New York*. Children's tales divided along lines of sex as well, though there was some half-ashamed crossing over on the part of boys and more adventurous forays on the part of girls into each other's libraries. Finally, children form a relationship with their fiction that is unfathomed and still quite mysterious. Certainly they do not read in any humdrum, literal way, but as persons engaged—extraordinarily impressionable and extraordinarily obtuse. Specific incidents gouge indelible tracks in the memory, as any adult who has gone back to his childhood books discovers, while page upon page rolls off into oblivion. The English historian of children's literature, F. J. H. Darton, reread the *Swiss Family Robinson* of his youth and came away from the reencounter amazed at his "wholly erroneous recollections" of one of his favorite boyhood stories. "I never knew . . . that it was full of the most extravagantly laboured piety," he remarked. "All I remembered was that a very large snake swallowed the donkey and was killed when comatose from repletion; that the family had a house in a tree; that they tamed and rode ostriches, made lassoes, built a boat, tapped the india-rubber tree, . . . and found a salt mine." For generations before that, American children reared on *Pilgrim's Progress* had likewise managed to skirt its theology, overleap its moral, and fasten upon what one of them recalled as the "gorgeous and bloody romance" of Christian's duels with Apollyon and the Giant Despair. All children's stories in this sense are twice-told tales—the teller's words revised, elaborated, and severely edited in the intermediary of the child's imagination. The children's tale and the adult's tale are not the same story. . . .

A generation after 1850, the openly didactic, work-tied tale seemed a relic of the past. . . . One of the signs of the "new era" in children's literature, as its partisans hailed it, was the ascendancy of the fairy tale. Early nineteenth-century moralists had distrusted stories "calculated to entertain the imagination, rather than to improve the heart or cultivate the understanding." William S. Cardell, author of the immensely popular *Jack Halyard*, dismissed the Mother Goose rhymes and fables as "trash" not written by "sensible" people. But in the wake of Hans Christian Andersen's stories, which came to America in the late 1840s, the publication of imaginative tales, both old and new, grew rapidly. The *Youth's Companion* held out against the trend, but in the children's magazines of the second half of the century its resistance was lonely and eccentric.

Joined with the triumph of the fairies was the retreat of the intrusive moralist. Twain announced baldly at the outset of *Huckleberry Finn* that anyone trying to find a moral in it would be banished; but far more conservative writers than he turned against what one reviewer called "the old-fashioned stories, with a moral or pious reflection impending at the close of every sentence." Increasingly, children began to speak up in children's tales, to tease their fanciful and indulgent storytelling papas, and to demand, and sometimes to get, stories without any moral to them. Yet another sign was the appearance of a new kind of boys' tale— a nostalgia-filled story of boys still half-savage, the best part of them not yet broken to the prim, restrictive conventions of civilization. Thomas Bailey Aldrich's *The Story of a Bad Boy*, which appeared in *Our Young Folks* in 1869, was the first of the line which led through Twain to Booth Tarkington's *Penrod*. In one of these tales, Charles Dudley Warner told the young readers of *St. Nicholas*: "Of course the perfectly good boy will always prefer to work and to do 'chores' for his father and errands for his mother and sisters, rather than enjoy himself," and he would always rather split kindling than "go a-fishing." But Warner had only heard of one boy like that, and he had died of a morbid case of obedience.

All of this amounted to a heady infusion of romantic ideals into the children's book world. The new children's writers turned deliberately from the understanding to cultivate the imagination; they overran Abbott's world of wise adults and "sensible" things and planted the standard of the innocent, glory-trailing child, fresh from the dews of heaven. By 1865 a reviewer in the *Atlantic Monthly* could contend: "We have ceased to think it the part of wisdom to cross the first instincts of children, and to insist upon making of them little moralists, metaphysicians, and philosophers, when great Nature determines that their first education shall be in the senses and muscles, the affections and fancies."

What accounted for the sudden new turn of children's tales is hard to determine. Part of it, clearly, was due to the same slow diffusion of romantic ideals that seeped into the churches in the second half of the nineteenth century, sent Henry Ward Beecher sprawling and gazing in the midst of nature, and gave sanctity to the term "play." By the turn of the century, opponents of industrial child labor had turned to the same conventions to argue that the real harm of early factory toil was that it crippled the soul of the child at the time when it was just opening itself to love, to poetry, to "the eternal and infinite" truths. But it is also unmistakably true that after 1850 many children's writers turned away from "sensible" things in recoil at the directions of economic change. The fairies were never needed more, they insisted, than in the modern, relentlessly matter-of-fact world where children "grope up and down the tunnels of brick and stone." Retreating to preserves of the imagination or to rural and child-centered oases of boyhood memory, children's writers tried to carve out a place unviolated by either industrial society or sharp-elbowed didacticians. A child's magazine should be a "pleasure-ground," the editor of the model of them all, *St. Nicholas*, proposed in 1873. "Let there be no sermonizing, . . . no wearisome spinning out of facts, no rattling of the dry bones of history." . . .

In casting off the old formulas, the new storytellers assumed an awkward pack of burdens. They wanted both to win a child's freely given imagination and to control it; they wanted both to shelter children and to thrust them out, if only for a trial moment, into adulthood; they needed to find adult roles for boys that would win a boy's imagination and not violate the writers' own nagging doubts about industrial society. It was not surprising that things often fell apart. . . . Boys' story writers announced their aims in conventional ways and professed their faith in the centrality of work and self-discipline. But the announced story and the one actually told were rarely quite the same; the preface and the tale itself were often disconcertingly out of joint. One of the results of an age of dislocating change was that its counsel to the young grew increasingly split and uncertain.

William T. Adams is a case in point. Though he is forgotten now, under his pen name Oliver Optic he was one of the late nineteenth century's most prolific and successful boys' authors. . . .

Optic helped to usher in the full-blown boys' adventure story. And yet he never admitted what he was doing. His prefaces continued to point back to the virtues of diligence and Christian forbearance; no matter that his heroes showed little of either. Adult figures continued to point to morals of self-restraint that the stories undercut. Occasionally a critic caught the troubling doubleness of the Optic tales, and Adams himself knew his dilemma. At the outset of his writing career he had announced that he would try to combine "healthy moral lessons" with enough "exciting interest" to attract the young. He hoped he had "not mingled these elements of a good juvenile book in disproportionate quantities," but that question of balance troubled him throughout his career. "Perhaps" his heroes were too smart, he warned, their circumstances extraordinary, and some of their actions doubtful. In his revival of Samuel Goodrich's merger of travel stories and geography primer, Optic admitted he found it easier to write an exciting tale than to contrive ways to insinuate the useful information he had studiously collected. But he refused to capitulate to his temptations. The Sunday school superintendent wrestled with his tales, the moralist with the writer of stirring and surprising incidents, each going their increasingly separate ways.

If Optic was a particularly striking example of the peculiarly divided counsel offered to boys growing up in post–Civil War America, of the persistence of the rhetorical shell of the work ethic in increasingly incongruous settings, he was by no means unique. A second case in point is that of Optic's younger friend and protégé, Horatio Alger. Optic was instrumental in starting Alger on his postministerial career as a boys' story writer, and Optic's conventions flowed easily from Alger's pen: the autonomous boys, the crippled fathers, the cruel and exploiting guardians, and the overbearing mortgagees. As everyone knows, Alger joined these elements with pecuniary ingredients of his own into a celebration of upward mobility. His stories insisted that even the poorest boy could rise in the world if he had energy, industry, ambition, and character. He defended the dignity of labor fervently and interminably. His very titles told the tale: *Strive and Succeed, Forging Ahead, Struggling Upward, Slow and Sure*. But, as almost everyone also knows by now, Alger was all but incapable of actually showing the steady, sober advance he talked about so much. His heroes could be picked out by their eagerness to take a job and their toil-soiled hands, but, aside from city bootblacks and newsboys, he rarely showed them working. They saved their money, but luck and patronage were the architects of their fortunes. As Russel Crouse noted years ago, after puzzling through the improbable coincidences of the typical Alger tale: "Mr. Alger could have done much better by the work-and-win theory."

There was no single formula to Alger's near-endless stream of stories but at least four of them. The central one, the one he talked about so often, was the story of the poor boy who made his own way in the world by a steady growth in moral habits to reap "the legitimate consequences of industry and frugality." *Ragged Dick* (1868) and *Risen from the Ranks* (1874) came as close to that formula as Alger ever managed, and in them one finds, soberly and carefully laid bare, the bedrock of prudential virtues that underlay Alger's moral cosmos. Lessons in self-education and self-control were at the bottom of both tales. By turning their energies from a boy's extravagances to study and self-discipline, by forswearing oyster-stew banquets for their dog-eared French primers and their carefully husbanded savings books, by diligence, respectability, and thrift, Ragged Dick rises to the brink of a clerkship and Harry Walton to a country editorship. But much as Alger believed this carefully fashioned tale and repeated its cautiously optimistic moral somewhere in virtually all the stories he wrote, most of them were critically different.

Several of Alger's tales, as Michael Zuckerman has pointed out, were not stories of success at all but were stories of nurture and guardianship. Mark the matchboy was the first of Alger's weak and protection-needing orphans, and, though the sheltering theme was never again as strong as in Alger's first street-urchin stories of the late 1860s, it returns in snatches long thereafter. More common was a third kind of tale, as much a success story as Harry Walton's saga, but with only the shell of that story's moral. For in these tales Alger's heroes did not work out their careers but had them thrust upon them. Over and over again an Alger hero performed a crucial act of kindness, honesty, or heroism in reward for which fortunes fell at his feet. Critics have often tried to link this imposition on providence to a lingering Calvinism in Alger, but the real affinity of these stories is to the conventions of the classic, European fairy tales. Boot-blacks and farm boys took the place of Cinderellas, and the magic helpers who turn the fortunes of the hero were disguised as hermits or merchant-patrons, but the formula was the same. In the enchanted Alger cosmos, if a good boy acted at the crucial moment—if he stopped a runaway horse or returned the honest change—the magic gifts were his and the princess and her father's fortune as well.

Finally, in the 1880s, yet another formula pushed all these aside—the tale of lost and recovered fortunes. In these stories fortune was not built through work and self-denial, nor was it the reward of bravery and goodness; it was a stolen legacy, and the hero's mission was not to earn it but to find it. Almost invariably the quest began in a village where the Alger hero endured the persecution of the town's rich man and the snobbery of his prideful son. And almost as invariably it ended there as well, with the revelation that the criminal was none other than the squire himself. In the last, obligatory scene, justice set things right; the squire became the poor man, and the boy assumed his rightful place.

Fortune was the central constant throughout these shifting formulas. Alger wrote for every boy who had been snubbed by his schoolmates, who felt ashamed of his patched trousers, or who chafed at the dull ordinariness of small town life. He took the theme of ambition, so distrusted by the moralists of Jacob Abbott's generation, and made a romance of it. But the boy whom Alger caught up in Aladdin-like daydreams might be pardoned if he failed to follow Alger's moral. Alger insisted on the centrality of industry, but virtually all the crucial, testing incidents he showed came to his heroes at their leisure, and in the tales of recovered fortune it was essential that the hero lose his job at the outset to free him for the quest. By the same token, the rich men whom one rarely saw, the distant strangers of the city, were inspiring examples of men who had worked their way up from poverty. But there was every chance that the rich man a boy knew well, the owner of the nearest mansion, was a thief. Alger talked of life as an endeavor; but he showed it as a magical web of coincidences and, increasingly, as a detective story. The tale of rising in the world by "the legitimate consequences of industry and frugality" eluded him, and like a modern Midas he turned his moral tales into simple pecuniary fantasies.

26

Despite some initial resistance by moralists, the great European fairy tales of the Brothers Grimm, Charles Perrault, and Hans Christian Andersen became popular in nineteenth-century America (see Gillian Avery's chapter in part 11 for further discussion of this point). Like other children's stories, fairy tales provide important insight into a culture's definition of gender. In the tale of Briar Rose, we watch as the passive girl ("beautiful, modest, kind, and clever") is awakened by the prince.

Briar Rose

The Brothers Grimm

A long time ago there lived a king and a queen, who said every day, "If only we had a child!" But for a long time they had none.

It happened once as the Queen was bathing that a frog crept out of the water onto the land and said to her, "Your wish shall be fulfilled. Before a year has passed you shall bring a daughter into the world."

The frog's words came true. The Queen had a little girl who was so beautiful that the King could not contain himself for joy, and he prepared a great feast. He invited his relatives, friends and acquaintances, and also the fairies, in order that they might be favorably and kindly disposed towards the child. There were thirteen of them in the kingdom, but as the King had only twelve golden plates for them to eat from, one of the fairies had to stay at home.

The feast was held with all splendor, and when it came to an end the fairies all presented the child with a magic gift. One gave her virtue, another beauty, a third riches, and so on, with everything in the world that she could wish for.

When eleven of the fairies had said their say, the thirteenth suddenly appeared. She wanted to revenge herself for not having been invited.

Without greeting anyone or even glancing at the company, she called out in a loud voice, "The Princess shall prick herself with a distaff in her fifteenth year and shall fall down dead." And without another word she turned and left the hall.

Everyone was terror-stricken, but the twelfth fairy, whose wish was still unspoken, stepped forward. She could not cancel the curse but could only soften it, so she said, "It shall not be death, but a deep sleep lasting a hundred years, into which your daughter shall fall."

The King was so anxious to guard his dear child from the misfortune that he sent out a command that all the distaffs in the whole kingdom should be burned.

As time went on, all the promises of the fairies came true. The Princess grew up so beautiful, modest, kind, and clever that everyone who saw her could not but love her. Now it happened that on the very day when she was fifteen years old, the King and Queen were away from home and the Princess was left quite alone in the castle. She wandered about over the whole place, looking at rooms and halls as she pleased, and at last she came to an old tower. She ascended a narrow winding staircase and reached a little door. A rusty key was sticking in the lock, and when she turned it the door flew open. In a little room sat an old woman with a spindle, spinning her flax busily.

"Good day, Granny," said the Princess. "What are you doing?"

"I am spinning," said the old woman, and nodded her head.

"What is the thing that whirls around so merrily?" asked the Princess. And she took the spindle and tried to spin too. But she had scarcely touched it before the curse was fulfilled, and she pricked her finger with the spindle. The instant she felt the prick she fell upon the bed which was standing near, and lay still in a deep sleep which spread over the whole castle.

The King and Queen, who had just come home and had stepped into the hall, went to sleep, and all their courtiers with them. The horses went to sleep in the stable, the dogs in the yard, the doves on the roof, the flies on the wall. Yes, even the fire flickering on the hearth grew still and went to sleep, and the roast meat stopped crackling. The cook, who was pulling the scullion's hair because he had made some mistake, let him go and went to sleep. The wind dropped, and on the trees in front of the castle not a leaf stirred.

But round the castle a hedge of briar roses began to grow up. Every year it grew higher, till at last it surrounded the whole castle so that nothing could be seen of it, not even the flags on the roof.

But there was a legend in the land about the lovely sleeping Briar Rose, as the King's daughter was called. And from time to time princes came and tried to force a way through the hedge into the castle. They found it impossible; for the thorns, as though they had hands, held them fast, and the princes remained caught in them without being able to free themselves. And so they died a miserable death.

After many, many years a prince came again to the country and heard an old man tell of the castle which stood behind the briar hedge, in which a most beautiful maiden called Briar Rose had been asleep for the last hundred years, and with her the King, the Queen, and all their courtiers. He knew also from his grandfather that many princes had already come and sought to pierce the briar hedge, and had remained caught in it and died a sad death.

Then the young Prince said, "I am not afraid. I am determined to go and look upon the lovely Briar Rose."

The good old man did all in his power to dissuade him, but the Prince would not listen to his words.

Now, however, the hundred years were just ended, and the day had come when Briar Rose was to wake up again. When the Prince approached the briar hedge it was in blossom, and was covered with beautiful large flowers which made way for him of their own accord and let him pass unharmed, and then closed up again into a hedge behind him.

In the courtyard he saw the horses and brindled hounds lying asleep. On the roof sat the doves with their heads under their wings. And when he went into the house, the flies were asleep on the walls. And near the throne lay the King and Queen. In the kitchen was the cook, with his hand raised as though about to strike the scullion, and the maid sat with the black fowl in her lap, which she had been about to pluck.

He went on farther, and all was so still that he could hear his own breathing. At last he reached the tower and opened the door into the little room where Briar Rose was asleep. There she lay, looking so beautiful that he could not take his eyes off her. He bent down and gave her a kiss.

As he touched her, Briar Rose opened her eyes and looked lovingly at him. Then they went down together, and the King woke up, and the Queen, and all the courtiers, and looked at each other with astonished eyes. The horses in the stable stood up and shook themselves, the hounds leaped about and wagged their tails, the doves on the roof lifted their heads from under their wings, looked around, and flew into the fields. The flies on the walls began to crawl again; the fire in the kitchen roused itself and blazed up and cooked the food. The meat began to crackle, and the cook boxed the scullion's ears so soundly that he screamed aloud, while the maid finished plucking the fowl.

Then the wedding of the Prince and Briar Rose was celebrated with all splendor, and they lived happily till they died.

27

Nineteenth-century Americans adopted what are commonly identified as Victorian gender ideals, which drew sharp distinctions between girls and boys in terms of their virtues and personal characteristics. These distinctions are evident in children's and young adult literature—for example, in the description of the four sisters in Louisa May Alcott's Little Women *(1868). The girls' mother has advanced views for her time: she makes clear that her daughters' happiness is more important than marriage. However, her ideal for each is still a happy married life.*

Little Women

Louisa May Alcott

Margaret, the eldest of the four, was sixteen, and very pretty, being plump and fair, with large eyes, plenty of soft, brown hair, a sweet mouth, and white hands, of which she was rather vain. Fifteen-year-old Jo was very tall, thin, and brown, and reminded one of a colt; for she never seemed to know what to do with her long limbs, which were very much in her way. She had a decided mouth, a comical nose, and sharp, grey eyes, which appeared to see everything, and were by turns fierce, funny, or thoughtful. Her long, thick hair was her one beauty; but it was usually bundled into a net to be out of her way. Round shoulders had Jo, big hands and feet, a fly-away look to her clothes, and the uncomfortable appearance of a girl who was rapidly shooting up into a woman, and didn't like it. Elizabeth—or Beth, as every one called her—was a rosy, smooth-haired, bright-eyed girl of thirteen, with a shy manner, a timid voice, and a peaceful expression, which was seldom disturbed. Her father called her "Little Tranquillity," and the name suited her excellently; for she seemed to live in a happy world of her own, only venturing out to meet the few whom she trusted and loved. Amy, though the youngest, was a most important person—in her own opinion at least. A regular snow maiden, with blue eyes, and yellow hair curling on her shoulders; pale and slender, and always carrying herself like a young lady mindful of her manners. . . .

Holding a hand of each, and watching the two young faces wistfully, Mrs. March said, in her serious yet cheery way,—

"I want my daughters to be beautiful, accomplished, and good; to be admired, loved, and respected, to have a happy youth, to be well and wisely married, and to lead useful, pleasant lives, with as little care and sorrow to try them as God sees fit to send. To be loved and chosen by a good man is the best and sweetest thing which can happen to a woman; and I sincerely hope my girls may know this beautiful experience. It is natural to think of it, Meg; right to hope and wait for it, and wise to prepare for it; so that, when the happy time comes, you may feel ready for the duties and worthy of the joy. My dear girls, I *am* ambitious for you, but not to have you make a dash in the world—marry rich men merely because they are rich, or have splendid houses, which are not homes because love is wanting. Money is a needful and precious thing—and, when well used, a noble thing—but I never want you to think it is the first or only prize to strive for. I'd rather see you poor men's wives, if you were happy, beloved, contented, than queens on thrones, without self-respect and peace."

"Poor girls don't stand any chance, Belle says, unless they put themselves forward," sighed Meg.

"Then we'll be old maids," said Jo stoutly.

"Right, Jo; better be happy old maids than unhappy wives, or unmaidenly girls, running about to find husbands," said Mrs. March decidedly. "Don't be troubled, Meg; poverty seldom daunts a sincere lover. Some of the best and most honoured women I know were poor girls, but so love—worthy that they were not allowed to be old maids. Leave these things to time; make this home happy, so that you may be fit for homes of your own, if they are offered you, and contented here if they are not. One thing remember, my girls: mother is always ready to be your confidante, father to be your friend; and both of us trust and hope that our daughters, whether married or single, will be the pride and comfort of our lives."

28

Children's and young adult literature of the first half of the twentieth century illustrated the changing gender roles of boys and girls. The popular Nancy Drew series featured an eighteen-year-old girl who shows initiative and independence in solving mysteries, yet is still very feminine (1930).

Nancy Drew and the Secret of the Old Clock

Carolyn Keene

With the instinct of a detective who dared not miss a clue, Nancy deliberately moved closer to the bench on which the Topham girls were seated.

"If there *should* be another will, I'm afraid we'd be out of luck." The words, in Ada's nasal voice, came clearly to Nancy.

Isabel's reply was in so low a tone that the young sleuth could just manage to catch the words, "Well, I, for one, don't believe Josiah Crowley ever made a later will." She gave a low laugh. "Mother watched him like a hawk."

"Or thought she did," Isabel retorted. "The old man got out of her clutches several times, don't forget."

"Yes, and what's worse, I'm sure Nancy Drew thinks he made a later will. That's why she's taking such an interest in those Hoover girls. I actually saw them go into Mr. Drew's office yesterday and it wasn't to deliver eggs! If Nancy gets her father interested, he might dig up another will. Oh, how I hate that interfering girl!"

At this Nancy could barely refrain from laughing. So the Tophams *were* concerned about the existence of a second will. With bated breath she listened further.

"You're such a worry wart, Ada. You can trust Dad and Mother to take care of things, no matter what happens," Isabel commented dryly. "They won't let that pile of money get away from us. It's ours by right, anyhow."

"You've got something there," Ada conceded. "We should have old Josiah's money after supporting and putting up with him for three years. That was pretty clever of Mother, never accepting any board money from Josiah Crowley!"

The conversation ended as Isabel and Ada arose from the bench and walked away. Nancy waited until they were out of sight, then emerged from her hiding place. Seating herself on the bench vacated by the Topham sisters, Nancy mulled over the remarks she had just overheard.

"There's no doubt in my mind now that if there is a later will, the Tophams haven't destroyed it. How thrilling! But where can it be?"

Nancy realized that to find it was a real challenge. "And I'd better hurry up before the Tophams stumble on it!"

For another ten minutes Nancy sat lost in thought, sifting all the facts she had gleaned so far.

"There must be some clue I've overlooked," she told herself. Suddenly, with a cry of delight, she sprang to her feet. "Why didn't I think of that before! The Hoover girls and the Turners aren't the only ones who should have figured in this will. There are other relatives of Mr. Crowley who have filed a claim. I wonder who they are. If I could only talk with them, I might pick up a clue!"

Immediately Nancy set off for her father's office. He was engaged in an important conference when she arrived, and she had to wait ten minutes before being admitted to the inner office.

"Now what?" Mr. Drew asked, smiling, as she burst in upon him. "Have you solved the mystery or is your purse in need of a little change?"

Nancy's cheeks were flushed and her eyes danced with excitement. "Don't tease me," she protested. "I need some information!"

"At your service, Nancy."

The young sleuth poured out the story of the Topham sisters' conversation in the park, and told him of her own conclusions. Mr. Drew listened with interest until she had finished.

"Excellent deducting," he praised his daughter. "I'm afraid, though, I can't help you obtain the relatives' names. I don't know any of them."

Nancy looked disappointed. "Oh dear!" she sighed. "And I'm so anxious to find out right away. If I delay even a single day the Tophams may locate that other will—and destroy it."

The next instant her face brightened. "I know! I'll drive out and see the Turner sisters. They might be able to tell me who the other relatives are." Nancy arose and headed for the door.

"Just a minute," said the lawyer. "I wonder if you realize just what you are getting into, Nancy?"

"What do you mean?"

"Only this. Detective work isn't always the safest occupation in which to engage. I happen to know that Richard Topham is an unpleasant man when crossed. If you do find out anything which may frustrate him, the entire Topham family could make things extremely difficult for you."

"I'm not afraid of them, Dad."

"Good!" Mr. Drew exclaimed. "I was hoping you would say that. I'm glad you have the courage of your convictions, but I didn't want you to march off into battle without a knowledge of what you might be up against."

29

Early-twentieth-century psychologists began to examine gender in childhood from a psychosexual perspective. Here Sigmund Freud discusses the undifferentiated sexuality in the pregenital period of infancy and then the different psychosexual identifications and libidinal drives of girls and boys, making reference specifically to the male Oedipal complex and noting its inverse pattern in girls (1920).

The Sexual Life of the Child

Sigmund Freud

Thus we can now define the forms taken by the sexual life of the child before the primacy of the genital zone is reached; this primacy is prepared for in the early infantile period, before the latent period, and is permanently organized from puberty onwards. In this early period a loose sort of organization exists which we shall call *pre-genital*; for during this phase it is not the genital component-instincts, but the *sadistic* and *anal*, which are most prominent. The contrast between *masculine* and *feminine* plays no part as yet; instead of it there is the contrast between *active* and *passive*, which may be described as the forerunner of the sexual polarity with which it also links up later. That which in this period seems masculine to us, regarded from the stand-point of the genital phase, proves to be the expression of an impulse to mastery, which easily passes over into cruelty. Impulses with a passive aim are connected with the erotogenic zone of the rectal orifice, at this period very important; the impulses of skoptophilia (gazing) and curiosity are powerfully active; the function of excreting urine is the only part actually taken by the genital organ in the sexual life. . . .

Now you will be impatiently waiting to hear what this terrible Oedipus complex comprises. The name tells you: you all know the Greek myth of King Oedipus, whose destiny it was to slay his father and to wed his mother, who did all in his power to avoid the fate prophesied by the oracle, and who in self-punishment blinded himself when he discovered that in ignorance he had committed both these crimes. I trust that many of you have yourselves experienced the profound effect of the tragic drama fashioned by Sophocles from this story. The Attic poet's work portrays the gradual discovery of the deed of Oedipus, long since accomplished, and brings it slowly to light by skilfully prolonged enquiry, constantly fed by new evidence; it has thus a certain resemblance to the course of a psycho-analysis. In the dialogue the deluded mother-wife, Jocasta, resists the continuation of the enquiry; she points out that many people in their dreams have mated with their mothers, but that dreams are of no account. To us dreams are of much account, especially typical dreams which occur in many people; we have no doubt that the dream Jocasta speaks of is intimately related to the shocking and terrible story of the myth. . . .

Now what does direct observation of children, at the period of object-choice before the latency period, show us in regard to the Oedipus complex? Well, it is easy to see that the little man wants his mother all to himself, finds his father in the way, becomes restive when the latter takes upon himself to caress her, and shows his satisfaction when the father goes away or is absent. He often expresses his feelings directly in words and promises his mother to marry her; this may not seem much in comparison with the deeds of Oedipus, but it is enough in fact; the kernel of each is the same. Observation is often rendered puzzling by the circumstance that the same child on other occasions at this period will display great affection for the father; but such contrasting—or, better, *ambivalent*—states of feeling, which in adults would lead to conflicts, can be tolerated alongside one another in the child for a long time, just as later on they dwell together permanently in the unconscious. One might try to object that the little boy's behaviour is due to egoistic motives and does not justify the conception of an erotic complex; the mother looks after all the child's needs and consequently it is to the child's interest that she should trouble herself about no one else. This too is quite correct; but it is soon clear that in this, as in similar dependent situations, egoistic interests only provide the occasion on which the erotic impulses seize. When the little boy shows the most open sexual curiosity about his mother, wants to sleep with her at night, insists on being in the room while she is dressing, or even attempts physical acts of seduction, as the mother so often observes and laughingly relates, the erotic nature of this attachment to her is established without a doubt. Moreover, it should not be forgotten that a mother looks after a little daughter's needs in the same way without producing this effect; and that often enough a father eagerly vies with her in trouble for the boy without succeeding in winning the same importance in his eyes as the mother. In short, the factor of sex preference is not to be eliminated from the situation by any criticisms. From the point of view of the boy's egoistic interests it would merely be foolish if he did not tolerate two people in his service rather than only one of them.

As you see, I have only described the relationship of a boy to his father and mother; things proceed in just the same way, with the necessary reversal, in little girls. The loving devotion to the father, the need to do away with the superfluous mother and to take her place, the early display of coquetry and the arts of later womanhood, make up a particularly charming picture in a little girl, and may cause us to forget its seriousness and the grave consequences which may later result from this situation. Let us not fail to add that frequently the parents themselves exert a decisive influence upon the awakening of the Oedipus complex in a child, by themselves following the sex attraction where there is more than one child; the father in an unmistakable manner prefers his little daughter with marks of tenderness, and the mother, the son.

30

In the mid-twentieth century, the psychologist Karen Horney challenged Freud's male-centered theories, specifically the theory of penis envy and the assumption that girls are merely wounded boys.

Feminine Psychology

Karen Horney

The question then is how far analytical psychology also, when its researches have women for their object, is under the spell of this way of thinking, insofar as it has not yet wholly left behind the stage in which frankly and as a matter of course masculine development only was considered. In other words, how far has the evolution of women, as depicted to us today by analysis, been measured by masculine standards and how far therefore does this picture fail to present quite accurately the real nature of women.

If we look at the matter from this point of view our first impression is a surprising one. The present analytical picture of feminine development (whether that picture be correct or not) differs in no case by a hair's breadth from the typical ideas that the boy has of the girl.

We are familiar with the ideas that the boy entertains. I will therefore only sketch them in a few succinct phrases, and for the sake of comparison will place in a parallel column our ideas of the development of women.

THE BOY'S IDEAS	OUR IDEAS OF FEMININE DEVELOPMENT
Naïve assumption that girls as well as boys possess a penis	*For both sexes it is only the male genital which plays any part*
Realization of the absence of the penis	*Sad discovery of the absence of the penis*
Idea that the girl is a castrated, mutilated boy	*Belief of the girl that she once possessed a penis and lost it by castration*
Belief that the girl has suffered punishment that also threatens him	*Castration is conceived of as the infliction of punishment*
The girl is regarded as inferior	*The girl regards herself as inferior. Penis envy*

| The boy is unable to imagine how the girl can ever get over this loss or envy | *The girl never gets over the sense of deficiency and inferiority and has constantly to master afresh her desire to be a man* |
| The boy dreads her envy | *The girl desires throughout life to avenge herself on the man for possessing something which she lacks* |

. . . The fundamental conclusions to which Freud's investigations of the specific character of feminine development have led him are as follows: first, that in little girls the early development of instinct takes the same course as in boys, both in respect of the erotogenic zones (in the two sexes only one genital organ, the penis, plays a part, the vagina remaining undiscovered) and also in respect of the first choice of object (for both the mother is the first love object). Secondly, that the great differences that nevertheless exist between the two sexes arise from the fact that this similarity of libidinal trend does not go with similar anatomical and biological foundations. From this premise it follows logically and inevitably that girls feel themselves inadequately equipped for this phallic orientation of their libido and cannot but envy boys their superior endowment in that respect. Over and above the conflicts with the mother, which the girl shares with the boy, she adds a crucial one of her own; she lays at her mother's door the blame for her lack of a penis. This conflict is crucial because it is just this reproach which is essential for her detachment from her mother and her turning to her father.

Hence Freud has chosen a happy phrase to designate the period of blossoming of childish sexuality, the period of infantile genital primacy in girls as well as boys, which he calls the *phallic phase*.

I can imagine that a man of science who was not familiar with analysis would in reading this account pass over it as merely one of the many strange and peculiar notions that analysis expects the world to believe. Only those who accept the point of view of Freud's theories can gauge the importance of this particular thesis for the understanding of feminine psychology as a whole. Its full bearings emerge in the light of one of Freud's most momentous discoveries, one of those achievements which, we may suppose, will prove lasting. I refer to the realization of the crucial importance for the whole subsequent life of the individual of the impressions, experiences, and conflicts of early childhood. If we accept this proposition in its entirety, i.e., if we recognize the formative influence of early experience on the subject's capacity for dealing with his later experience and the way in which he does so, there ensue, at least potentially, the following consequences as regards the specific psychic life of women:

(1) With the onset of each fresh phase in the functioning of the female organs—menstruation, coitus, pregnancy, parturition, suckling, and the menopause—even a normal woman (as Helene Deutsch has in fact assumed) would have to overcome impulses of a masculine trend before she could adopt an attitude of wholehearted affirmation toward the processes taking place within her body.

(2) Again, even in normal women, irrespective of race and of social and individual conditions, it would happen altogether more readily than in men that the libido adhered, or came to be turned, to persons of her own sex. In a word, *homosexuality* would be incomparably and unmistakably more common among women than among men. Confronted with difficulties in relation to the opposite sex, a woman would plainly fall back more readily than a man into a homosexual attitude. For according to Freud, not only are the most important years of her childhood dominated by such an attachment to one of her own sex, but when she first turns to a man (the father), it is in the main only by way of the narrow bridge of resentment. "Since I cannot have a penis I want a child instead and 'for this purpose' I turn to my father." . . .

(4) If we accept a second axiom of psychoanalysis, namely, that the individual's attitude in sexual matters is the prototype of his attitude toward the rest of life, it would follow, that woman's whole reaction to life would be based on a strong subterranean resentment. For according to Freud, the little girl's penis envy corresponds to a sense of being at a radical disadvantage in respect to the most vital and elementary instinctual desires. Here we have the typical basis upon which a general resentment is liable to be built up. It is true that such an attitude would not follow inevitably; Freud says expressly that *where development proceeds favorably*, the girl finds her own way to the man and to motherhood. But here again, it would contradict all our analytical theory and experience if an attitude of resentment so early and so deeply rooted did not manifest itself extremely easily—by comparison much more easily than in men under similar conditions—or at any rate were not readily set going as an undercurrent detrimental to the vital feeling-tone of women.

These are the very weighty conclusions with regard to the whole psychology of women, which follow from Freud's account of early feminine sexuality. When we consider them, we may well feel that it behooves us to apply again and again the tests of observation and theoretical reflection to the facts on which they are based and to their proper appraisal.

It seems to me that analytic experience alone does not sufficiently enable us to judge the soundness of some of the fundamental ideas that Freud has made the basis of his theory. I think that a final verdict about them must be postponed until we have at our disposal systematic observations of *normal* children, carried out on a large scale by persons trained in analysis. Among the views in question I include Freud's statement that "it is well-known that a clearly defined differentiation between the male and the female character is first established after puberty." The few observations that I have made myself do not confirm this statement. On the contrary I have always been struck by the marked way in which little girls between their second and fifth years exhibit specifically feminine traits. For instance, they often behave with a certain spontaneous feminine coquetry toward men, or display characteristic traits of maternal solicitude. From the beginning I have found it difficult to reconcile these impressions with Freud's view of the initial masculine trend of the little girl's sexuality. . . .

I speak of an "instinctive" knowledge of the sexual processes because we meet typically with ideas of this sort—e.g., in the anxieties and dreams of early childhood—at a period when as yet there is no intellectual knowledge derived from observation or from explanations by others. It may be asked whether such instinctive knowledge of the processes of penetration into the female body necessarily presupposes an instinctive knowledge of the existence of the vagina as the organ of reception. I think that the answer is in the affirmative if we accept Freud's view that "the child's sexual theories are modelled on the child's own sexual constitution." For this can only mean that the path traversed by the sexual theories of children is marked out and determined by spontaneously experienced impulses and organ sensations. If we accept this origin for the sexual theories, which already embody an attempt at rational elaboration, we must all the more admit it in the case of that instinctive knowledge which finds symbolic expression in play, dreams, and various forms of anxiety, and which obviously has not reached the sphere of reasoning and the elaboration which takes place there. In other words, we must assume that both the dread of rape, characteristic of puberty, and the infantile anxieties of little girls are based on vaginal organ sensations (or the instinctual impulses issuing from these), which imply that something ought to penetrate into that part of the body. . . .

It remains to consider the question of what importance the existence of early vaginal sensations or the "discovery" of the vagina has for our whole conception of early feminine sexuality. Though Freud does not expressly state it, it is nonetheless clear that if the vagina remains originally "undiscovered," this is one of the strongest arguments in favor of the assumption of a biologically determined, primary penis envy in little girls or of their original phallic organization. For if no vaginal sensations or cravings existed, but the whole libido were concentrated on the clitoris, phallically conceived of, then and then only could we understand how little girls, for want of any specific source of pleasure of their own or of any specific feminine wishes, must be driven to concentrate their whole attention on the clitoris, to compare it with the boy's penis, and then, since they are in fact at a disadvantage in this comparison, to feel themselves definitely slighted. If on the other hand, as I conjecture, a little girl experiences from the very beginning vaginal sensations and corresponding impulses, she must from the outset have a lively sense of this specific character of her own sexual role, and a primary penis envy of the strength postulated by Freud would be hard to account for.

31

Although the anthropologist Margaret Mead was deeply influenced by Freudian psychology, she urged that women and men not accept sex stereotypes that deny to each the full range of human potential. Mead was an important expert on childhood and gender issues throughout the mid-twentieth century (1949).

Male and Female
Sex and Temperament

Margaret Mead

The growing child in any society is confronted then by individuals—adults and adolescents and children—who are classified by his society into two groups, males and females, in terms of their most conspicuous primary sex characters, but who actually show great range and variety both in physique and in behaviour. Because primary sex differences are of such enormous importance, shaping so determinatively the child's experience of the world through its own body and the responses of others to its sex membership, most children take maleness or femaleness as their first identification of themselves. But once this identification is made, the growing child then begins to compare itself not only in physique, but even more importantly in impulse and interest, with those about it. Are all of its interests those of its own sex? "I am a boy," but "I love colour, and colour is something that interests only women." "I am a girl," but "I am fleet of foot and love to run and leap. Running and leaping, and shooting arrows, are for boys, not girls." "I am a boy," but "I love to run soft materials through my fingers; an interest in touch is feminine, and will unsex me." "I am a girl," but "My fingers are clumsy, better at handling an axe-handle than at stringing beads; axe-handles are for men." So the child, experiencing itself, is forced to reject such parts of its particular biological inheritance as conflict sharply with the sex stereotype of its culture.

Moreover, a sex stereotype that decrees the interests and occupations of each sex is usually not completely without a basis. The idea of the male in a given society may conform very closely to the temperament of some one type of male. The idea of the female *may* conform to the female who belongs to the same type, or instead to the female of some other type. For the children who do not belong to these preferred types, only the primary sex characters will be definitive in helping them to classify themselves. Their impulses, their preferences, and later much of their physique will be aberrant. They will be doomed throughout life to sit among the other members of their sex feeling less a man, or less a woman, simply because the cultural ideal is based on a different set of clues, a set of clues no less valid, but different. And the small rabbit man sits sadly, comparing himself with a lionlike male beside whom he is surely not male, and perhaps for that reason alone yearning forever after the lioness woman. Meanwhile the lioness woman, convicted in her inmost soul of lack of femininity when she compares herself with the rabbity little women about her, may in reverse despair decide that she might as well go the whole way and take a rabbity husband. Or the little rabbity man who would have been so gently fierce and definitely masculine if he had been bred in a culture that recognized him as fully male, and quite able to take a mate and fight for her and keep her, may give up altogether and dub himself a female and become a true invert, attaching himself to some male who possesses the magnificent qualities that have been denied him. . . .

A recognition of these possibilities would change a great deal of our present-day practices of rearing children. We would cease to describe the behaviour of the boy who showed an interest in occupations regarded as female, or a greater sensitivity than his fellows, as "on the female" side, and could ask instead what kind of male he was going to be. We would take instead the primary fact of sex membership as a cross-constitutional classification, just as on a wider scale the fact of sex can be used to classify together male rabbits and male lions and male deer, but would never be permitted to obscure for us their essential rabbit, lion, and deer characteristics. Then the little girl who shows a greater need to take things apart than most of the other little girls need not be classified as a female of a certain kind. In such a world, no child would be forced to deny its sex membership because it was shorter or taller, or thinner or plumper, less hairy or more hairy, than another, nor would any child have to pay with a loss of its sense of its sex membership for the special gifts that made it, though a boy, have a delicate sense of touch, or, though a girl, ride a horse with fierce sureness.

If we are to provide the impetus for surmounting the trials and obstacles of this most difficult period in history, man must be sustained by a vision of a future so rewarding that no sacrifice is too great to continue on the journey towards it. In that picture of the future, the degree to which men and women can feel at home with their own bodies, and at home in their relationships with their own sex and with the opposite sex, is extremely important.

32

In his argument that girls and boys replicate their sexual roles in their play activity, the psychologist Erik H. Erikson set forth a vision that for many years defined the psychological perspective on gender (1963). According to Erikson, the differences between girls' and boys' constructions are guided as if by some "inner design."

Infantile Sexuality

Erik H. Erikson

I will [describe] observations made on a large number of children who were not patients, but the subjects of a developmental study made at the University of California. Neither were they children of play age. Ten, eleven, and twelve years old, they had already been interviewed and observed regularly for a decade, and all discernible aspects of the growth and development of their bodies, their minds, and their personalities had been carefully recorded. When I joined the staff of the study to review their records, we thought it might be interesting to test on this large sample the clinical proposition . . . that play observation can add significant pointers to available data from other sources. Would an appropriate procedure provide me with specimens of play which could serve as live clues to the data accumulated in the files of the study? Here, maybe, what I had learned from case histories, could be applied to ongoing life histories.

I set up a play table and a random selection of toys and invited the boys and girls of the study, one at a time, to come in and to imagine that the table was a movie studio and the toys, actors and sets. I then asked them to "construct on the table an exciting scene out of an imaginary moving picture." This instruction was given to spare these children, the majority of whom were eleven years old, the indignity of having to play at "kids' stuff"; at the same time it was thought to be a sufficiently impersonal "stimulus" for an unself-conscious use of the imagination. But here was the first surprise: although, for over a year and a half, about 150 children constructed about 450 scenes, not more than a half dozen of these were movie scenes, and only a few dolls were named after a particular actor. Instead, after a moment of thoughtfulness, the children arranged their scenes as if guided by an inner design, told me a brief story with more or less exciting content, and left me with the task of finding out what (if anything) these constructions "meant." I remembered, however, that years before, when I had tried out an analogous method on a smaller group of Harvard and Radcliffe students, all English majors, who were asked to construct a "dramatic" scene, not one scene was reminiscent of a Shakespearean or any other drama. It appears, then, that such vague instructions do accomplish what the encouragement to "associate freely" (i.e., to let thoughts wander and words flow without self-censorship) effects in a psychoanalytic interview, as does, indeed, the suggestion to play in interviews with children: seemingly arbitrary themes tend to appear which on closer study prove to be intimately related to the dynamics of the person's life history. In the present study, what I came to call "unique elements" often provided the key to such significance. For example, one of the few colored boys in the study, and the smallest of these, is the only child to build his scene *under* the table. He thus offers stark and chilling evidence of the meaning of his smiling meekness: he "knows his place." Or consider the only scene in which the piano chair is pushed under the piano so that it is quite clear that nobody is playing. Since the girl who constructed the scene is the only subject whose mother is a musician, it becomes probable that the dynamic meaning of musical noise in her childhood (if suggested in other data as well) deserves our attention. Finally, to mention one of the main instances where a child reveals in her play an awareness of something she was not supposed to know: a girl, since deceased, who suffered from a malignant blood disease was said to be ignorant of the fact that she was kept alive only by a new medical invention then in its experimental stages. She constructed the only ruin built by a girl and put in the center of her scene "a girl who miraculously returned to life after having been sacrificed to the gods." These examples do not touch on the difficult problem of interpreting unconscious content, but they indicate that the scenes often enough proved to be close to life. However, this is not what is to be discussed at this point. Here, I intend only to consider the manifestations of the power of organ modes in spatial modalities.

In order to convey a measure of my surprise in finding organ modes among what (in contrast to *unique* elements) I came to call the *common* elements in these children's constructions, it is necessary to claim what is probably hard to believe, namely, that I tried not to expect anything in particular, and was, in fact, determined to enjoy the freshness of the experience of working with so many children, and healthy ones. To be ready to be surprised belongs to the discipline of a clinician; for without it clinical "findings" would soon lose the instructive quality of new (or truly confirming) finds.

As one child after another concentrated with a craftsman's conscientiousness on configurations which had to be "just right" before he would announce that his task was done, I gradually became aware of the fact that I was learning to expect different configurations from boys than from girls. To give an example which brings us immediately to the mode of female inclusion, girls much more often than boys would arrange a room in the form of a circle of furniture, without walls. Sometimes a circular configuration of furniture was presented as being intruded upon by something threatening, even if funny, such as a pig or "father coming home riding on a lion." . . .

So I set out to define these configurations in the simplest terms, such as towers, buildings, streets, lanes, elaborate enclosures, simple enclosures, interiors with walls, and interiors without walls. I then gave photographs of the play scenes to two objective observers to see whether they could agree on the presence or the absence of such configurations (and of combinations of them). They did agree "significantly," whereupon it could be determined how often these configurations were said by these observers (who did not know of my expectations) to have occurred in the constructions of boys and of girls. I will abstract their conclusions here in general terms. The reader may assume that each item mentioned occurs more (and often considerably more) than two thirds of the time in the constructions of the sex specified and that in the remaining one third special conditions prevail which often can be shown to "prove the rule."

The most significant sex difference was the tendency of boys to erect structures, buildings, towers, or streets (see fig. 1); the girls tended to use the play table as the interior of a house, with simple, little, or no use of blocks.

High structures, then, were prevalent in the configurations of the boys. But the opposite of elevation, i.e., *downfall*, was equally typical for them: ruins or fallen-down structures were exclusively found among boys. . . . In connection with the very highest towers, something in the nature of a downward trend appears regularly, but in such diverse forms that only "unique" elements can illustrate it: one boy, after much indecision, took his extraordinarily high and well-built tower down in order to build a final configuration of a simple and low

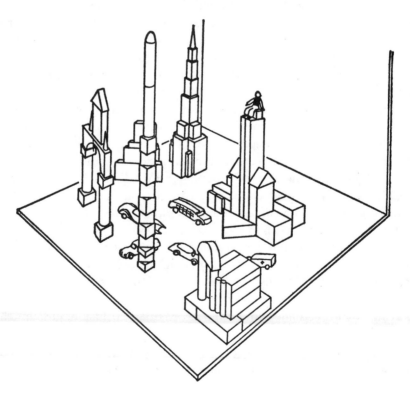

FIGURE 1

structure without any "exciting" content; another balanced his tower very precariously and pointed out that the immediate danger of collapse was the "exciting" element in his story, in fact, *was* his story. One boy who built an especially
high tower laid a boy doll at the foot of it and explained that this boy had fallen
from the top of the tower; another boy left the boy doll sitting high on one of
several elaborate towers but said that the boy had had a mental breakdown (fig.
1). The very highest tower was built by the very smallest boy; and, as pointed
out, a colored boy built his *under* the table. All these variations make it apparent
that *the variable high-low* is a *masculine variable*. Having studied a number of the
histories of these children I would add the clinical judgment that extreme height
(in its combination with an element of breakdown or fall) reflects a need to
overcompensate a doubt in, or a fear for, one's masculinity.

The boys' structures enclosed fewer people and animals inside a house.
Rather, they channeled the traffic of motorcars, animals, and Indians. And they
blocked traffic: the single policeman was the doll used most often by boys!

Girls rarely built towers. When they did, they made them lean against, or stay
close to, the background. The highest tower built by any girl was not on the table
at all but on a shelf in a niche behind the table.

If "high" and "low" are masculine variables, "open" and "closed" are feminine modalities. Interiors of houses without walls were built by a majority of
girls. In many cases the interiors were expressly peaceful. Where it was a home
rather than a school, a little girl often played the piano: a remarkably tame
"exciting movie scene" for girls of that age. In a number of cases, however, a
disturbance occurred. An intruding pig throws the family in an uproar and forces
the girl to hide behind the piano; a teacher has jumped on a desk because a tiger
has entered the room. While the persons thus frightened are mostly women, the
intruding element is always a man, a boy, or an animal. If it is a dog, it is
expressly a boy's dog. Strangely enough, however, this idea of an intruding
creature does not lead to the defensive erection of walls or to the closing of
doors. Rather, the majority of these intrusions have an element of humor and of
pleasurable excitement.

Simple enclosures with low walls and without ornaments were the largest
item among the configurations built by girls. However, these enclosures often
had an elaborate gate (fig. 2): the only configuration which girls cared to construct and to ornament richly. A blocking of the entrance or a thickening of the
walls could on further study be shown to reflect acute anxiety over the feminine
role.

The most significant sex differences in the use of the play space, then, added
up to the following modalities: in the boys, the outstanding variables were height
and downfall and strong motion (Indians, animals, motorcars) and its channelization or arrest (policemen); in girls, static interiors, which are open, simply
enclosed, and peaceful or intruded upon. Boys adorned high structures; girls,
gates.

It is clear by now that the spatial tendencies governing these constructions are
reminiscent of . . . *genital modes*, . . . and that they, in fact, closely parallel the

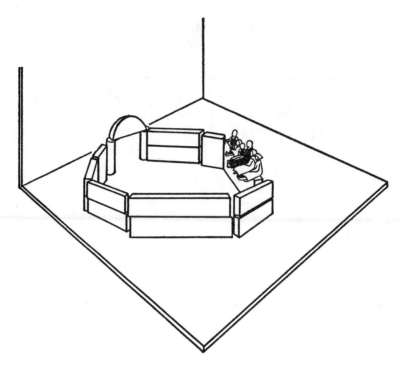

FIGURE 2

morphology of the sex organs: in the male, *external* organs, *erectable* and *intrusive* in character, *conducting* highly *mobile* sperm cells; *internal* organs in the female, with a vestibular *access* leading to *statically expectant* ova. Does this reflect an acute and temporary emphasis on the modalities of the sexual organs owing to the experience of oncoming sexual maturation? My clinical judgment (and the brief study of the "dramatic productions" of college students) incline me to think that the dominance of genital modes over the modalities of spatial organization reflects a profound difference in the sense of space in the two sexes, even as sexual differentiation obviously provides the most decisive difference in the ground plan of the human body which, in turn, co-determines biological experience and social roles. . . .

We may accept, then, the evidence of organ-modes in these constructions as a reminder of the fact that experience is anchored in the ground plan of the body. Beyond the organ-modes and their anatomical models, we see a suggestion of a male and a female experience of space. Its outlines become clearer if, instead of mere configurations, we note the specific functions emphasized in the various ways of using (or not using) blocks. Some constructions (lanes, tunnels, crossings) serve the *channelization* of traffic. Other structures are an expression of an *erecting, constructing,* and *elaborating* tendency. Simple walls, on the other hand, *include* and *enclose*, while open interiors *hold safely* without the necessity of an exclusion of the outside.

Together, then, the space structured and the themes depicted suggest [an] interpenetration of the biological, cultural, and psychological. . . . If psychoanalysis as yet differentiates the psychosexual from the psychosocial, I have endeavored . . . to build a bridge between the two.

Cultures . . . elaborate upon the biologically given and strive for a division of function between the sexes, which is, simultaneously, workable within the body's scheme, meaningful to the particular society, and manageable for the individual ego.

33

Most models and measures of child development have used boys as their standard. The psychologist Carol Gilligan argues that girls develop differently and should not be evaluated on the same terms as boys. In the following, Gilligan challenges the dominant psychological models by taking specific aim at the arguments of Jean Piaget and Lawrence Kohlberg that girls fail to reach the same levels of abstract moral reasoning as boys. On the basis of interviews with individual boys and girls, Gilligan concludes that girls reason differently in coming to their moral and ethical conclusions, but no less well (1982).

Moral Reasoning in Girls and Boys

Carol Gilligan

Asking different questions that arise from different conceptions of the moral domain, the children arrive at answers that fundamentally diverge, and the arrangement of these answers as successive stages on a scale of increasing moral maturity calibrated by the logic of the boy's response misses the different truth revealed in the judgment of the girl. To the question, "What does he see that she does not?" Kohlberg's theory provides a ready response, manifest in the scoring of Jake's judgments a full stage higher than Amy's in moral maturity; to the question, "What does she see that he does not?" Kohlberg's theory has nothing to say. Since most of her responses fall through the sieve of Kohlberg's scoring system, her responses appear from his perspective to lie outside the moral domain.

Yet just as Jake reveals a sophisticated understanding of the logic of justification, so Amy is equally sophisticated in her understanding of the nature of choice. Recognizing that "if both the roads went in totally separate ways, if you pick one, you'll never know what would happen if you went the other way," she explains that "that's the chance you have to take, and like I said, it's just really a guess." To illustrate her point "in a simple way," she describes her choice to spend the summer at camp:

> I will never know what would have happened if I had stayed here, and if something goes wrong at camp, I'll never know if I stayed here if it would have been better. There's really no way around it because there's no way you can do both at once, so you've got to decide, but you'll never know.

In this way, these two eleven-year-old children, both highly intelligent and perceptive about life, though in different ways, display different modes of moral understanding, different ways of thinking about conflict and choice. . . . Jake relies on theft to avoid confrontation and turns to the law to mediate the dispute. Transposing a hierarchy of power into a hierarchy of values, he defuses a potentially explosive conflict between people by casting it as an impersonal conflict of claims. In this way, he abstracts the moral problem from the interpersonal situation, finding in the logic of fairness an objective way to decide who will win the dispute. But this hierarchical ordering, with its imagery of winning and losing and the potential for violence which it contains, gives way in Amy's construction of the dilemma to a network of connection, a web of relationships that is sustained by a process of communication. With this shift, the moral problem changes from one of unfair domination, the imposition of property over life, to one of unnecessary exclusion, the failure of the druggist to respond to the wife.

This shift in the formulation of the moral problem and the concomitant change in the imagery of relationships appear in the responses of two eight-year-old children, Jeffrey and Karen, asked to describe a situation in which they were not sure what was the right thing to do:

JEFFREY

When I really want to go to my friends and my mother is cleaning the cellar, I think about my friends, and then I think about my mother, and then I think about the right thing to do. (*But how do you know it's the right thing to do?*) Because some things go before other things.

KAREN

I have a lot of friends, and I can't always play with all of them, so everybody's going to have to take a turn, because they're all my friends. But like if someone's all alone, I'll play with them. (*What kinds of things do you think about when you are trying to make that decision?*) Um, someone all alone, loneliness.

While Jeffrey sets up a hierarchical ordering to resolve a conflict between desire and duty, Karen describes a network of relationships that includes all of her friends. Both children deal with the issues of exclusion and priority created by choice, but while Jeffrey thinks about what goes first, Karen focuses on who is left out.

The contrasting images of hierarchy and network in children's thinking about moral conflict and choice illuminate two views of morality which are complementary rather than sequential or opposed. But this construction of differences goes against the bias of developmental theory toward ordering differences in a hierarchical mode. The correspondence between the order of developmental theory and the structure of the boys' thought contrasts with the disparity between existing theory and the structure manifest in the thought of the girls. Yet in neither comparison does one child's judgment appear as a precursor of the other's position. Thus, questions arise concerning the relation between these perspectives: what is the significance of this difference, and how do these two modes of thinking connect? . . .

The contrast between a self defined through separation and a self delineated through connection, between a self measured against an abstract ideal of perfection and a self assessed through particular activities of care, becomes clearer and the implications of this contrast extend by considering the different ways these children resolve a conflict between responsibility to others and responsibility to self. The question about responsibility followed a dilemma posed by a woman's conflict between her commitments to work and to family relationships. While the details of this conflict color the text of Amy's response, Jake abstracts the problem of responsibility from the context in which it appears, replacing the themes of intimate relationship with his own imagery of explosive connection:

JAKE   AMY

(*When responsibility to oneself and responsibility to others conflict, how should one choose?*)

You go about one-fourth to the others and three-fourths to yourself.	Well, it really depends on the situation. If you have a responsibility with somebody else, then you should keep it to a certain extent, but to the extent that it is really going to hurt you or stop you from doing something that you really, really want, then I think maybe you should put yourself first.

34

A 1995 report by the American Association of University Women analyzes the differential treatment of girls and boys in classroom instruction. Although girls often do as well as or better than boys in school, the report argues that girls receive less attention and encouragement from teachers and are subject to harassment from male students, to the detriment of their learning and development.

How Schools Shortchange Girls

American Association of University Women Report

Despite a narrowing of the "gender gaps" in verbal and mathematical performance, girls are not doing as well as boys in our nation's schools. The physical sciences is one critical area in which girls continue to trail behind boys. More discouraging still, even girls who take the same mathematics and science courses as boys and perform equally well on tests are much less apt to pursue scientific or technological careers than are their male classmates. This is a "gender gap" our nation can no longer afford to ignore.

Research on sex, race, ethnicity, and socioeconomic status suggests that girls of low socioeconomic status have better test scores than boys of like background in the lower grades, but that by high school this advantage has disappeared. Furthermore, among students of high socioeconomic status, boys from all racial and ethnic groups have better test scores than girls. Nevertheless, girls generally receive better grades than boys, regardless of race or socioeconomic status. . . .

Teacher-Student Interactions

Whether one looks at preschool classrooms or university lecture halls, at female teachers or male teachers, research spanning the past twenty years consistently reveals that males receive more teacher attention than do females. In preschool classrooms boys receive more instructional time, more hugs, and more teacher attention. The pattern persists through elementary school and high school. One reason is that boys demand more attention. Researchers David and Myra Sadker have studied these patterns for many years. They report that boys in one study of elementary and middle school students called out answers significantly more often than girls did. When boys called out, the typical teacher reaction was to listen to the comment. When girls called out, they were usually corrected with comments such as, "Please raise your hand if you want to speak."

The issue is broader than the inequitable distribution of teacher *contacts* with male and female students; it also includes the inequitable *content* of teacher comments. Teacher remarks can be vague and superficial or precise and pene-trating. Helpful teacher comments provide students with insights into the strengths and weaknesses of their answers. Careful and comprehensive teacher reactions not only affect student learning, they can also influence student self-esteem.

The Sadkers conducted a three-year study of more than 100 fourth-, sixth- and eighth-grade classrooms. They identified four types of teacher comments: praise, acceptance, remediation, and criticism.

They found that while males received more of all four types of teacher com-ments, the difference favoring boys was greatest in the more useful teacher reactions of praise, criticism, and remediation. When teachers took the time and made the effort to specifically evaluate a student's performance, the student receiving the comment was more likely to be male. These findings are echoed in other investigations, indicating that boys receive more precise teacher comments than females in terms of both scholarship and conduct.

The differences in teacher evaluations of male and female students have been cited by some researchers as a cause of "learned helplessness," or lack of aca-demic perseverance, in females. Initially investigated in animal experiments, "learned helplessness" refers to a lack of perseverance, a debilitating loss of self-confidence. This concept has been used to explain why girls sometimes abandon while boys persistently pursue academic challenges for which both groups are equally qualified.

One school of thought links learned helplessness with attribution theory. While girls are more likely to attribute their success to luck, boys are more likely to attribute their success to ability. As a result of these different causal attribu-tions, boys are more likely to feel mastery and control over academic challenges, while girls are more likely to feel powerless in academic situations.

Studies also reveal that competent females have higher expectations of failure and lower self-confidence when encountering new academic situations than do males with similar abilities. The result is that female students are more likely to abandon academic tasks.

However, research also indicates that the concepts of learned helplessness and other motivation constructs are complex. Psychologist Jacquelynne Eccles and her colleagues have found that there is a high degree of variation within each individual in terms of motivational constructs as one goes across subject areas. New evidence indicates that it is too soon to state a definitive connection between a specific teacher behavior and a particular student outcome. Further research on the effects of teacher behavior and student performance and motivation is needed.

The majority of studies on teacher-student interaction do not differentiate among subject areas. However, there is some indication that the teaching of certain subjects may encourage gender-biased teacher behavior while others may foster more equitable interactions. Sex differences in attributing success to luck versus effort are more likely in subject areas where teacher responses are less frequent and where single precise student responses are less common.

Two recent studies find teacher-student interactions in science classes particularly biased in favor of boys. Some mathematics classes have less biased patterns of interaction overall when compared to science classes, but there is evidence that despite the more equitable overall pattern, a few male students in each mathematics class receive particular attention to the exclusion of all other students, male and female. . . .

Problems in Student Interactions

The ways students treat each other during school hours is an aspect of the informal learning process, with significant negative implications for girls. There is mounting evidence that boys do not treat girls well. Reports of student sexual harassment—the unwelcome verbal or physical conduct of a sexual nature imposed by one individual on another—among junior high school and high school peers are increasing. In the majority of cases a boy is harassing a girl.

Incidents of sexual harassment reveal as much about power and authority as they do about sexuality; the person being harassed usually is less powerful than the person doing the harassing. Sexual harassment is prohibited under Title IX, yet sex-biased peer interactions appear to be permitted in schools, if not always approved. Rather than viewing sexual harassment as serious misconduct, school authorities too often treat it is as a joke.

When boys line up to "rate" girls as they enter a room, when boys treat girls so badly that they are reluctant to enroll in courses where they may be the only female, when boys feel it is good fun to embarrass girls to the point of tears, it is no joke. Yet these types of behaviors are often viewed by school personnel as harmless instances of "boys being boys."

The clear message to both girls and boys is that girls are not worthy of respect and that appropriate behavior for boys includes exerting power over girls—or over other, weaker boys. Being accused of being in any way like a woman is one of the worst insults a boy can receive.

Rock n' roll goes worldwide. Courtesy of the Library of Congress, Prints and Photographs Division, subject file [LCUSZ 6254400].

Part Three

Adolescence and Youth

As a psychosocial concept, adolescence was invented in the late nineteenth and early twentieth centuries, although youth as a stage of anticipation to adulthood has a much longer history. In nineteenth-century Europe and the United States, adolescence increasingly came to be seen as a period of emotional dissonance and romantic agonizing. Part 3 examines the experience of young people in love and war in the nineteenth century, the origin of the concept of adolescence, and various aspects of the experience of twentieth-century adolescents from the writings of social scientists and in literary works. The part concludes with an article that raises questions about the end point of adolescence in the modern world.

35

In her history of courting behavior, Hands and Hearts *(1984), Ellen K. Rothman discusses the difficulties young men and women faced in the mid-nineteenth century as they set about choosing a partner and embarking on marriage. Then as now, mating was the fundamental issue at the intersection between childhood and youth. But in the nineteenth century this was an especially difficult matter since girls and boys were assumed to be so fundamentally different in their dispositions, interests, goals, and values.*

Courtship and Gender Differences

Ellen K. Rothman

When Mary Ballard married William Ross, she had behind her two years at a school dedicated, in the words of its founders, to "drawing forth the mental energies," rather than "ornamenting the surface," of its students. The Western Female Seminary was one of dozens of institutions founded in the second quarter of the nineteenth century to give girls some of the same intellectual discipline available to boys in their academies and colleges. And yet even as the female seminaries moved closer to the curriculum of their male models, with physiology and astronomy supplanting embroidery and painting, a fundamental difference persisted. Young men pursued higher education as preparation for the ministry, law, medicine. Even as they studied moral philosophy and Latin, young women were in training for the one career open to them—as wives to men and as mothers (or, at least, teachers) to children.

This state of affairs had profound implications for—and roots in—the world beyond the classroom. The eighteenth century had recognized differences between men and women, but the nineteenth century made distinctions based on gender in every aspect of life, from the most mundane to the most metaphysical. On his visit to America in 1831, Alexis de Tocqueville was struck by the "constant care" taken to "trace two clearly distinct lines of action for the two sexes ... in two pathways that are always different." In the 1830s, these lines were relatively new features of American social geography; but in the next fifty years, they would dominate the landscape, demarcating clear roles for—and boundaries between—people in the family, in the community, and in the world of work. The definition of gender differences provided the context for courtship and had important consequences for how young men and women experienced the transition to marriage. It created separate spheres and the need to bridge them; it impelled young people to balance idealization against the fear of disappointment; and it made romance and self-revelation essential accomplishments for any couple en route to marriage.

By the time they reached courting age, young men and women looked at the world—and each other—through a lens that magnified the "natural," as well as the circumstantial, differences between men and women. A Harvard divinity student reported approvingly on Ralph Waldo Emerson's "remarks upon marriage, in which he gave the characteristic differences of the sexes." The father of New England Transcendentalism was hardly breaking new ground here: "Man's sphere is out of doors and among men—woman's is in the house—Man seeks for power and influence—woman for order and beauty—Man is just—Woman is kind." Emerson's view was echoed in every corner of the land; ministers, reformers, pedagogues portrayed male and female in sharp contrast to each other. An 1854 volume on *The Sphere and Duties of Woman* declared, "Woman despises in man everything like herself except a tender heart"; and man presumably felt the same disgust for any sign of masculine qualities in a woman.

Ordinary men and women shared this view. Like John Patch, a struggling editor and poet, they believed that "the spheres of action are different" for men and women. "Where courage, activity and endurance are required, there is the place for man—where cleanliness, order, affection and all the finer sensibilities of the heart and soul are needed for comfort and consolation in the difficulties and trials of life, there should bloom the never fading rose of woman's constancy and affection," he wrote in 1848. Woman did more than comfort and console man; she improved him as well. As a young midwesterner told his fiancée, "The true female character was perfectly adapted and designed by its influence often exerted to soften and beautify the wild rough and turbulent spirit of man." William Lloyd Garrison II put it more simply: "Men would be much better if they acted always as if [woman] were looking at them."

This expectation shaped individual relationships as much as it did general views of "female character." Every woman was empowered by reason of her sex. Twenty-three-year-old Ulysses S. Grant was a junior officer with the Fourth Infantry in Louisiana when he wrote to Julia Dent at home in St. Louis:

> You can have but little idea of the influance you have over me, even while so far away. If I feel tempted to do anything that I now think is not right I am shure to think, "Well now if Julia saw me would I do so" and thus it is, absent or present, I am more or less governed by what I think is your will.

A woman could, by her very existence, help a man keep to the path of virtue. A Wisconsin lawyer told his intended, "I expect you to infuse strength into all my intellectual and moral powers."

It was the latter that women were especially well equipped to enhance. Harry Pierce credited his fiancée with reconciling him to the church and improving him "in the moral sphere." The Indianapolis attorney told Libbie Vinton: "Your presence drew me to church after I had neglected every thought not worldly for years," and he believed that her love was "a greater mainspring to excellence and the magnet to draw [him] nearer the better locality" of her views. Women, it was believed, had an innate sense of direction that enabled them to find "the better locality," while men wandered in darkness. The Protestant clergy looked out from their pulpits at a flock in which women outnumbered men, and conceded that woman was naturally more religious than man. Medical authorities agreed. As one physician explained in 1847, woman's was "a pious mind. Her confiding nature leads her more readily than man to accept the proffered graces of the Gospel."

While women may have shared the culture's obeisance to the moral superiority of the female sex, they were uncomfortable with its implications for their own behavior. In the face of regular pleas from the pulpit, the popular press, and the men they knew to uphold and embody the peculiar virtues of True Womanhood, some women asserted their common humanity instead. *"I am not an angel,"* Mollie Clark declared in a letter to her suitor, a man who was only looking "to find . . . a Woman noble & true." Another New Yorker objected to her fiancé, "As to my being your superior in every respect and my mind's being of a more lofty order than yours—*I don't believe one word of it. . . .* Our minds may be different but that don't go to show that either is of a higher order than the other." Some women simply declined to accept responsibility for the moral uplift of the men who loved them. Winan Allen, a student at the University of Michigan in the 1860s, wrote Annie Cox, "I constitute you, if you'll accept so burdensome a charge, my spiritual doctor exclusively and unreservedly." But Annie insisted that she herself was "but an abcedarian in the spiritual school. . . . We may council together," she concluded.

If a man and woman were to "council together"—if a woman was to exercise the influence that was hers by birth—she had to have access to the men in her life, but the prevailing definition of the male role made such access problematical. The assumption that men were preoccupied and absorbed by worldly matters was as pervasive at midcentury as the expectation that women were naturally inclined toward moral virtue. In the course of the nineteenth century, middle-class men became increasingly defined by their involvement in the world. In this era of the "self-made" man, ideals of manhood all emphasized man's pursuit of worldly—if not purely material—success. "Man is made for action, and the bustling scenes of moving life," wrote one youth just starting out on his own.

Those "bustling scenes" had no room for women—as girls, even in adolescence, understood. "A young man can occupy himself with his business and look forward to his life and prospects, but all we [young women] have to do is to pass our time agreeably to ourselves," one Boston girl observed in 1838. Thirty years later, Mollie Clarke reflected to a suitor, "I often think it is so different from men from what it is with us women. Love is our life our reality, business yours. We stake our all and if it is lost our all is gone." A young Ohio woman had a similar sense of the risks involved; she believed that "a lady could not shape the future . . . she went down or up as her husband did . . . he led the way, made the reputation, the fortune of both." Men perceived this situation too, of course. In 1820, George Cutler had observed that a wife was more dependent on marriage than was her husband, whose "business leads him out of doors." By midcentury, more men were working away from home, and the distance between married men and women had widened.

36

During the Civil War many boys in their mid-teens signed up for military service in the Union and Confederate armies. Emmy E. Werner describes their experiences (1998).

Children's Voices from the Civil War

Emmy E. Werner

When word of Fort Sumter's fall reached President Abraham Lincoln in Washington, D.C., he issued a call to the governors of the states and territories to furnish seventy-five thousand volunteers to put down the insurrection. From Maine to Minnesota, from Illinois to New York, men rushed to arms. The Union held that a recruit had to be at least eighteen years old, but thousands of boys in their early and middle teens managed to slip into the army as drummers, fifers, or buglers and enlisted for duty in the infantry and cavalry. Their enthusiasm was contagious.

In Michigan the *Detroit Press* noted on April 18: "The Star Spangled Banner rages most furiously. The national anthem is . . . whistled by juveniles . . . hammered on tin pans by small boys, and we had almost said barked by the dogs." At Shenango, Pennsylvania, young boys organized a "company," elected a thirteen-year-old captain and held weekly drills in the school yard, accompanied by a dinner-bucket drum corps.

Jane Stuart Woolsey wrote from Boston to a friend in Paris on May 10, 1861:

We all have views now [on the war], men, women, and little boys—"children with drums betwixt their thumbs"—from the modestly patriotic citizen who wears a postage stamp on his hat to the woman who walks on Broadway in a "Union bonnet," composed of alternate layers of red, white and blue. . . . So much intense emotion has been crowded into the last two or three weeks that the "time before Sumter" seems to belong to some dim antiquity. It seems as if we never were alive . . . never had a country till now.

There were some twenty-one million people in the North, and just nine million in the Southern Confederacy, among them three and a half million slaves. Between ten and twenty percent of all new recruits who enlisted in both armies were underage and eager to go to war. At the beginning, each side thought the other would collapse within a few months.

Most boys from the North signed up to take part in an exciting adventure that promised reprieve from the boring routines of farm life or school. Others joined the Union Army because they wanted to teach the defiant South a lesson and set the rebels straight. A few, mostly from the Midwest and New England, felt a strong desire to stamp out slavery. When sixteen-year-old Chauncy Cooke left home with the Twenty-fifth Wisconsin Regiment, he was told by his father: "Be true to your country, my boy, and be true to the flag, but before your country or the flag, be true to the slave."

Southern boys sought adventure and glory in the Confederate Army. They joined "to fight the Yankees—all fun and frolic." But they also wanted to defend their homes against an invading army. North or South, the process of enlistment was relatively simple, especially if parents supported the boy's decision to volunteer.

William Bircher was fifteen years old when he ran away from home to the recruiting depot in St. Paul, Minnesota. He was looking for adventure, and he was in a hurry. When informed that he was too young to serve, he returned home and convinced his Swiss-born father that they should join up together. Ulrich Bircher was a farmer and knew how to handle animals. He became a wagoner, and young William became a drummer boy. Father and son were both assigned to the Second Minnesota Volunteer Regiment and served together throughout the entire war. William remembered: "The happiest day of my life was when I put on my blue uniform for the first time and received my drum."

In Texas, sixteen-year-old Albert Blocker signed up as a musician as well, becoming a "boy bugler" in the Third Texas Cavalry. Drummers, fifers, and buglers were considered nonfighting positions, so a recruiter usually allowed a youngster to sign on without worrying about his age. Some twenty thousand boys, like Blocker, served as musicians in the Confederate Army, and over forty thousand drummer boys, like Bircher, served in the Union Army during the Civil War.

Private Harvey Reid in a letter to his brother gave a glimpse of the life of twelve-year-old Johnnie Walker, a drummer boy in the Twenty-second Wisconsin Regiment:

> Johnnie is a drummer in the band and when they play at dress parades . . . the ladies see the little soldier-boy [and] always give him apples, cakes or something. . . . When we are marching Johnnie always keeps up with the big men, and is always singing and laughing. . . . Everybody in the regiment likes Johnnie because he is a good little boy, is always pleasant and polite and not saucy. . . . His mother sent him a suit of clothes made exactly like officer's clothes, and Lieutenant Bauman says he will get him a pair of shoulder straps with silver drum sticks upon them.

The most famous of the Union drummers was Johnny Clem, who ran away from home to join the army in May 1861 when he was barely ten years old. When he offered his services as a drummer to a company commander of the Third Ohio Volunteer Regiment, the captain laughed and said "he wasn't enlisting infants." Johnny then went to the Twenty-second Michigan Regiment. "I went along with the regiment just the same as a drummer boy," he later wrote, "and though not on the muster roll, drew a soldier's pay of thirteen dollars a month." The officers of the regiment adopted him as a mascot. Each chipped in to pay his salary and made sure he had a uniform cut to his size.

A drummer boy's job was to render the calls of reveille, breakfast, assembly, and "tattoo," which later in the war became "taps." When in camp, the boys might have to play twelve to fifteen times a day, starting at about five o'clock in the morning. During the day the drummers were busy providing the beat for marching drills. Other duties included such tasks as carrying water, rubbing down horses, digging trenches, gathering wood, cooking, and acting as guards, barbers, or chaplain's assistants.

On the battlefield, the boys communicated orders to the troops, such as "Charge!" or "Retreat!" Often drummer boys were required to help remove the wounded from the battlefield and to assist the doctors, honing the surgeon's instruments, removing amputated legs and arms, and burying the dead. In spite of the heavy responsibilities put on these young boys, few deserted their posts. Most stuck out their first and even second terms of enlistment. As the war dragged on, many became old enough to sign on as regular soldiers.

Many boys, especially tall, strong fifteen- or sixteen-year-olds, found it surprisingly easy to join regular infantry and cavalry units—an enlistment that would eventually take them into the thick of fighting. On the evening of April 15, 1861, three days after the fall of Fort Sumter, Thomas Galwey went to the armory of the Hiberian Guards in Cleveland, Ohio. "They seemed to like me," he wrote in his diary, "and I liked them. . . . My name was the first on the company's roll to enlist. I didn't tell them that I was only fifteen. So I became a soldier." . . .

Down south in Mississippi, sixteen-year-old George Gibbs, beardless and still shy with the girls, enlisted in the Eighteenth Mississippi Infantry Regiment only days after he heard the news of the firing on Fort Sumter. His parents were opposed to secession, and they pleaded with him, saying that he was too young and delicate to go to war. "Nothing would do me but to enlist," he wrote later. "Nothing could shake my resolution to be a soldier." But when the time came to part from his parents, he hid from the other soldiers and had a big cry. "This seemed to help me," he remembered, "and I felt better about leaving home."

Not all Southern youths who enlisted in their mid-teens were dirt-poor farm boys. William H. S. Burgwyn joined the Thirty-Fifth North Carolina Infantry Regiment at age fifteen, after a stint as a cadet at the Hillsboro Military Academy. He was first appointed drillmaster and then promoted to second lieutenant before he turned sixteen. The educated son of a wealthy Southern planter whose mother came from a prominent Boston family, he was accompanied throughout most of the war by a slave who was his servant.

37

John Demos and Virginia Demos were the first scholars to examine the concept of adolescence as a historical invention. In this seminal 1969 article they show how the "new" late-nineteenth-century concept of adolescence was related to earlier ideas about childhood.

Adolescence in Historical Perspective

John Demos and Virginia Demos

The idea of adolescence is today one of our most widely held and deeply imbedded assumptions about the process of human development. Indeed most of us treat it not as an idea but as a *fact*. Its impact is clear in countless areas of everyday life—in newspapers, magazines, and books; in various forms of popular entertainment; in styles of dress and of language. Its causes and meaning have been repeatedly analyzed in the work of psychologists and sociologists. Its effects are endlessly discussed by teachers, social workers, officers of the law, and parents everywhere.

Yet all of this has a relatively short history. The concept of adolescence, as generally understood and applied, did not exist before the last two decades of the nineteenth century. One could almost call it an invention of that period; though it did incorporate, in quite a central way, certain older attitudes and modes of thinking. It will be our purpose in this paper to describe the roots and the growth of the concept, to the point in the early twentieth century when it had become well established in the public consciousness. We shall limit our attention to developments in the United States, since adolescence was on the whole an American discovery. . . .

The literature of child-rearing advice is one of the most revealing, and least exploited, sources for the history of the American family. Its beginnings can be located in the early part of the nineteenth century; and it has been growing steadily, and changing in character, ever since. Before about 1825 relatively few books on child-rearing could be found in this country, and those that were available came chiefly from England. In general, they were mild in tone and full of simple moral homilies strung endlessly together. They do not, in short, seem to have been directed to any very pressing needs or problems in the lives of their readers.

After 1825 the situation, for this country at least, changed rapidly. Child-rearing books by American authors began to appear, some of which went through numerous editions and sold many thousands of copies. This development was owing to several different factors. In the first place it was related to a deepening interest in the fact of childhood itself as a distinct period of life and one which was little comparable to the years of maturity. Secondly, it expressed the broad impulse of nationalism that engulfed the country at this time. English books on child-rearing could no longer be regarded as suitable to American conditions. Finally, the new and authentically "native" literature on this subject reflected deep anxieties about the quality of American family life.

Most of the concern which was evident in these books related to problems of authority. In one form or another they all imparted the same message: the authority of parents must be established early in a child's life and firmly maintained throughout the years of growth. Even the smallest infant reveals a "willfulness" that "springs from a depraved nature and is intensely selfish." This must be suppressed by strict training in obedience, or it will rapidly develop beyond the possibility of control with dire implications for the later (adult) personality.

These injunctions seemed all the more necessary because—so many people thought—parental authority was steadily on the wane. In describing the average home, the writers of the child-rearing books repeatedly used words like "disorder," "disobedience," "licentiousness," and above all "indulgence" (i.e., of the children). Statements such as the following were typical:

> It must be confessed that an irreverent, unruly spirit has come to be a prevalent, an outrageous evil among the young people of our land. . . . Some of the good old people make facetious complaint on this. . . . "There is as much family government now as there used to be in our young days," they say, "only it has changed hands."

This seeming change in the traditional family pattern had other dimensions as well. Thus many authors noted the growth of a kind of "child-centered" attitude and condemned it out of hand. More and more parents, for example, appeared to feel compelled to show off their children before any and all guests. Similarly, there was in many households far too much concern with efforts to amuse and entertain the young. Children who were often made the center of attention in this manner would inevitably become conceited and selfish. Another alarming development was the increasing tendency of children to seek social satisfactions outside of the family, among groups of their own peers. Mrs. Lydia Child, whose *Mother's Book* went through many editions, returned again and again to the theme that "youth and age are too much separated." She and many of her contemporaries decried the "new custom" of holding parties exclusively for young people and urged that parents should always be the closest friends and confidants of their children.

Lest it be imagined that Americans of the nineteenth century had no special concern whatsoever for the period which we now call adolescence (and which in their day was simply termed "youth"), we must turn to another category of books that were written specifically *for* the "youth" of the time and about their particular problems. The general nature of these writings is implicit in their titles: *A Voice to Youth; How to be a Man; Papers for Thoughtful Girls; The Young Lady's Companion; On the Threshold; Lectures to Young Men.*

From all of these works there emerges quite clearly a sense of "youth" as a critical transition period in the life of nearly everyone. It is a time, first of all, when people are extremely impressionable, extremely open to a wide range of outside influences. It is—to quote from Joel Hawes's *Lectures to Young Men* (1832)—

> pre-eminently . . . the forming, fixing period. . . . It is during this season, more than any other, that the character assumes its permanent shape and color.

Words such as "pliant," "plastic," and "formative" appear again and again in the discussions of youth.

Because of this characteristic openness, young people are vulnerable to many kinds of "danger." To begin with, boys and girls entering their teens experience a sudden and sharp upsurge of the "passions." They become highly emotional; their mood fluctuates unpredictably from exuberance to melancholy. Henry Ward Beecher, whose *Lectures to Young Men* were among the best known examples of the genre, declared:

> A young man knows little of life; less of himself. He feels in his bosom the various impulses, wild desires, restless cravings he can hardly tell for what, a sombre melancholy when all is gay, a violent exhilaration when others are sober.

In keeping with their Victorian conventions, these writers never directly mentioned the physiological changes that occur at puberty, in particular the strong new charge of sexual energy and tension. Occasionally one finds an allusion to "internal revolutions" and "occult causes, probably of a physical kind"; but for the most part people were content to define youth in the above terms, that is, as a vast outpouring of the emotions.

As if to complement these disruptive changes within the personality, the world at large was full of "seductive temptations," of inducements to all manner of wicked and ruinous behavior. As Beecher said,

> These wild gushes of feeling, peculiar to youth, the sagacious tempter has felt, has studied, has practiced upon, until he can sit before that most capacious organ, the human mind, knowing every step and all the combinations.

Here, then, was the wider, social dimension of the problems which confront the young person. The world lies in wait for him, and "ardent, volatile, inexperienced, and thirsting for happiness," he is

> exceedingly liable to be seduced into the wrong paths—into those fascinating but fatal ways, which lead to degradation and wretchedness.

There are, at this stage of life, dangers both within and without.

Most of the material considered so far has been drawn from the period 1825–1850. As the years passed and the century neared its end, the picture of youth that we have been describing was embellished somewhat in certain important respects. Thus, for example, the sexual factor began to receive some attention. And some writers were struck by a kind of aimlessness and indecision that seemed increasingly common among American young people. Theodore T. Munger, whose book *On the Threshold* was published in 1881, declared that

> Young men of the present years . . . are not facing life with that resolute and definite purpose that is essential both to manhood and to external success. . . . [They] hear no voice summoning them to the appointed field, but drift into this or that, as happens.

Moreover, towards the end of the century, many writers identified the "dangers" and "temptations" which threatened youth directly with urban life. Something of this had been implicit from the beginning, but now it came clearly into the open. The city loomed as the prime source of corrupting influences for the young. Its chaotic social and economic life, its varied population, its frenzied commercial spirit, and its dazzling entertainments were all sharply antagonistic to proper growth towards adulthood.

At roughly the same time, meanwhile, the formal concept of adolescence was receiving its first public expression. The immediate context of this development was a new movement for systematic "child study," inspired and guided by G. Stanley Hall. Hall was, of course, one of the major figures in the early history of American psychology. After a lengthy period of study in Germany, he became in 1881 a professor at Johns Hopkins, and six years later he accepted the presidency of Clark University. There he remained for the rest of his life, presiding over a wide range of research and teaching activities.

The aim of the child-study movement was to enlist large numbers of ordinary citizens in a broad effort to deepen both public and scientific understanding of human development. The mothers who belonged to the various local organizations were encouraged to keep detailed records of the behavior of their children and to participate in regular discussions about such records. They were also exposed to, and themselves reflected back, the major themes in Stanley Hall's own work—not least, his theory of adolescence.

The essentials of Hall's view of adolescence appeared in one of his earliest papers on psychology: "The Moral and Religious Training of Children," published in 1882 in the *Princeton Review*. The great point of departure, then as later, was the idea of "storm and stress," of severe crisis characterized by

> lack of emotional steadiness, violent impulses, unreasonable conduct, lack of enthusiasm and sympathy. . . . The previous selfhood is broken up . . . and a new individual is in process of being born. All is solvent, plastic, peculiarly susceptible to external influences.

The suggestions contained in this article were subsequently elaborated in much greater detail by some of Hall's students at Clark. Efforts were made to link the adolescent "crisis" with a wide range of personal and social phenomena—with religious conversion, for example, and with the rising rate of juvenile delinquency. Hall himself provided the capstone to this whole sequence of activity, with the publication in 1904 of his encyclopedic work *Adolescence: Its Psychology, and Its Relations to Physiology, Anthropology, Sociology, Sex, Crime, Religion, and Education*. It is impossible to summarize here the many ideas and vast assortment of data embraced therein, but certain underlying themes can at least be singled out. From the very start Hall's thinking had been profoundly influenced by Darwinism, and the psychology he proposed was explicitly bound to an evolutionary, or "genetic," model. He urged a kind of "archaeology of the mind," in which all the various stages in the development of human consciousness would be rediscovered and understood in their proper order. A key link here was the theory known as "recapitulation," which affirmed that every individual "lives through" each of the major steps in the evolution of the race as a whole. Adolescence assumed a special importance in this scheme, for it represented (and "recapitulated") the most recent of man's great developmental leaps. The adolescent, Hall believed, reveals truly enormous possibilities of growth and "is carried for a time beyond the point of the present stage of civilization." This is not, however, an easy situation, for it encompasses a variety of contradictions and "antithetic impulses." Among the impulses which Hall paired in this context were hyperactivity and lassitude, happiness and depression, egotism and self-abasement, selfishness and altruism, gregariousness and shyness, sensitivity and cruelty, radicalism and conservatism. Caught in the midst of so much change and conflict, the adolescent was bound to experience "storm and stress" more or less continuously.

Hall's work on adolescence quickly exerted a considerable influence in many different directions. Its impact was clear in general texts on psychology, studies of education, the new literature on child-rearing, and a variety of books on child labor, religious training, vocational guidance, and the like. Even critical comments showed the extent to which the idea of adolescence had captured the public imagination: there were those who complained that "we are today under the tyranny of the special cult of adolescence." . . .

It would be easy to overstate the element of innovation in Hall's thinking. If we compare the kind of adolescence that he was describing with some of the ideas that were current just before his time, we find a considerable degree of continuity. His achievement lay in reshaping certain aspects of popular belief about youth, combining them with some of the most exciting new ideas in science (i.e., evolution), gathering data on a large scale, and presenting the whole in a persuasive and meaningful fashion.

Yet certain questions about the rise of the concept of adolescence remain. What larger developments in American society did it reflect? To what popular attitudes, or needs, or anxieties, did it minister? We offer, in conclusion, the following very tentative suggestions—some of which we have simply lifted from contemporary thinking about adolescence in the fields of psychology and sociology.

We propose, as a starting point, the long-term transformation of the United States from an agricultural into an urban and industrial society; for this change—which has, of course, been basic to so much of our history during the last 150 years—has exerted a profound influence on the structure of American families. Consider that most farm families are characterized by a high degree of internal unity. Children and adults share the same tasks, the same entertainments, the same friends, the same expectations. There is a continuum between the generations. The child appears not so much as a child per se but as himself a potential farmer; he is, then, a miniature model of his father. Such, we would argue, was the prevalent situation in nearly *all* the families of this country before the nineteenth century.

But when Americans began to move to the city, all this changed. City children, for example, do not often have a significant economic function within the family as a whole. (Or alternatively—as in the case of poor children employed as factory hands—their work is likely to be quite different from that of their parents.) Moreover, they are thrust into close proximity with other families and have the opportunity to form numerous contacts among their own peers. Thus there develops in the urban setting an important "discontinuity of age-groups." Children and adults are much more obviously separated from each other than is ever the case in a rural environment.

This second configuration was starting to show itself in some American families during the early part of the nineteenth century, and perhaps it helps to explain the material presented in our opening section. Now—i.e., with the new, typically urban family structure—childhood as such is "discovered"; it is no longer feasible to regard children simply as miniature adults. Now, too, "child-centered" families become possible. The behavior of the young is increasingly seen as bizarre and also as appropriate to their particular time of life. A new tolerance for such behavior develops, and parental authority appears to weaken. Finally, there is an obvious place for a literature on child-rearing.

Most cultures with sharp discontinuities of this kind possess a system of "age-grading," which defines the various steps in the transition from childhood to adulthood. In many cases there are elaborate initiation rites to dramatize this change. But our society lacks such rites; ceremonies like confirmation and graduation exercises are losing whatever significance in this regard they once had. It is in such situations, as Kenneth Keniston has suggested, that a "youth culture" is likely to develop. "Youth culture" may be defined, somewhat carelessly, as institutionalized adolescence. It refers, of course, to the special way of life characteristic of large groups of young people of approximately the same age. It is more than a simple substitute for formal age-grading and initiation rites. It is not, Keniston writes,

so obviously transitional . . . [but is] . . . more like a waiting period . . . a temporary stopover in which one can muster strength for the next harrowing stage of
the trip.

Its pattern is "not always or explicitly anti-adult, but it is belligerently *non-
adult.*" In many respects adulthood looks rather forbidding when compared with
the life of a child, and youth culture reflects some reluctance to bridge this gap.

It is pertinent to recall at this point the deep concern of many nineteenth-
century Americans about the growth of peer-group contacts. We suggest that
these people were witnessing the rudimentary beginnings of a youth culture. Of
course, there were none of the artifacts so prominent in our own modern-day
youth culture (e.g., "rock 'n roll," "teen magazines," special kinds of dress, and
so forth). But the very fact of "wanting to be with and for [their own] kind" was
significant. By about 1900 the situation had become more clear. The many and
varied writings on "gangs," on juvenile delinquency, and on vocational guidance
all show some feeling for the special characteristics of a youth culture.

Keniston argues that a second kind of discontinuity—that between specific
generations—is also important in the formation of youth culture. By this he
means a clear separation between the parents and the children within an individual family. In such cases the situation of the parents offers no viable goal at
which their children may aim. Intra-family conflict is likely to become chronic,
and the adolescent is on his own in the formation of an identity. This pattern is
characteristic of societies with a high rate of social change and a plurality of
alternatives in regard to careers, moral codes, and life styles. The young person
shrinks from such a bewildering array of choices and becomes part of the youth
culture, where a clear-cut, if temporary, identity comes ready-made.

All of this seems to describe nineteenth-century America fairly well, especially
the new life of the cities. Social and economic change was everywhere apparent;
ambitions were high; there was an astonishing diversity of people, ideologies,
occupations. The disparity between generations was assumed; it became, indeed,
a part of the national mythology. Immigrant families presented an especially
dramatic case in point; likewise those families in which the children of unedu-
cated parents had the chance to go to school. Thus, once again, there was the
youth culture.

The growth of the concept of adolescence was the final step in this long and
somewhat devious process. It was the response to an observable *fact*—the fact of
a youth culture, of many young people seemingly in distress (or at least behaving
in ways that distressed their elders). Americans needed some means of understanding the problems of, and the problems created by, these young people. We
have tried to show them groping toward such an understanding through much
of the nineteenth century. And we have located, chiefly in the work of G. Stanley
Hall, a kind of culmination of these efforts: the first comprehensive theory of
adolescence in modern history.

38

The psychologist G. Stanley Hall was the single most important theorist of adolescence. His immense and comprehensive study, Adolescence *(1904), helped define the field. The biological roots of Hall's views are evident, but his scope is enormous; he views adolescence as a complex problem of physical growth, mental development, and emotional expression.*

The Physiology and Psychology of Adolescence

G. Stanley Hall

As we know more of adolescence, it will probably be apparent that many, if not indeed most of its minor disorders are due to disproportionate development. If increase in height is too rapid and excessive, not only growing pains in the limbs due to failure of the muscles to develop *pari passu* with the bones, but venous disturbances, particularly varicosities in the legs, now so common, and even aortic disorders may be caused, to say nothing of curvatures and torsions, because young people become self-conscious and perhaps ashamed of their sudden height, and the fully upright posture is hard to maintain. Acromegalia, or excessive development of the limbs or bones of the face, probably illustrates this same disturbed equilibrium. Some headaches and eye troubles have here their cause. Closely related too, no doubt, are some forms of heterotopy and still more heterochrony or anomalous changes in the direction or order of the various growth stresses. We must probably here too invoke the principle laid down by Roux that different organs and tissues or determinants compete for the available nutritive material in the blood, and some for a time get ahead of others in this internal struggle for survival among the different parts or independently variable growth units. If functions or tissues that ought to develop at the age of twenty appear at fifteen, or earlier, we have here on a small scale what, if excessive, constitutes, from an evolutionary standpoint, the very interesting body of facts treated in teratology. We shall later see how this principle must be appealed to in genius, in some aspects of insanity and crime as well as in sexual and mental precocity. Its more restricted range is a matter of common observation as seen in children, who are precocious and belated in one or many respects. . . . We must regard the adolescent stage as especially characterized by either a loosening of the bonds between the manifold factors of our ego, somatic and psychic, or else by a sudden and independent growth of single elements which leaves their former associative bonds relatively weakened, or perhaps by both together. The fact that the growth factors are increased, some more and some less, and thus brought into new relations with each other, makes this the most favorable field for the genetic study of character and temperament, whether mental, as seen in the now recognized difference of eye, ear, motor-minded, etc., or emotional and active, as seen in the dominance of different classes of temperaments, so apparent in the observation of individual and particularly of peculiar and exceptional children or adults. . . .

Boys are more likely than girls to grow unsymmetrically, and there are many cases where even bilateral symmetry, especially of limbs and shoulders, is lost for a time and then regained, as if boys grew first, and most on one side and then on the other. Indeed all the facts that support the doctrine of nascent periods show that for a time growth tends to focalize upon one group of qualities and then upon another, and the newer developments even in brain anatomy suggest, as we saw, a difference between the period of development for the projection system, which reacts through the senses and muscles to the outer world, and the associative functions which combine these capsular and sensory centers with each other into new and higher unities. . . .

We now pass to consider the special morbidities of adolescence. Very prominent among the physiological disturbances of this age are those of indigestion and disorders of the alimentary canal, and especially of the stomach. The rapid bone growth requires more lime, the blood needs iron, the increased metabolism more oxygen and more fats for heat, perhaps the brain more phosphorus, the muscles require more protein and muscle work more inogen and myosin to break down, and normally the food supply is increased with height and weight, and the chemical bookkeeping of income and expenditure readjusted. . . .

These general considerations, which I conceive to be the basis of the new genetic psychology of the future, may serve to give us due appreciation of the special importance for adolescence of the general law that there is a trophic or nutritive background to everything and to suggest that the profound metamorphoses of puberty involve adjustments far more radical than are usually imagined. . . .

I am convinced that the dawn of adolescence is marked by much emotional intensification of dream life, and that at no age is its influence so important upon the moods and dispositions of waking consciousness. Somnambulism often first appears at this age and trancoidal states of inner absorption midway between sleeping and waking are now most frequent. The new emotional life seems if not to create and project, at least to take command of mental imagery and association, and indeed this may be a part of nature's method of making the intellectual sphere better fit that of instincts. In some of our cases, dreams are so intense as to be one cause of the chronic fatigue and even morning tire common in the teens. Sometimes young people wake with the soul suffused with a sense of nameless and unaccountable rapture from nearly or quite forgotten dreams, or perhaps with a new and strong predisposition toward some person of the other sex unattractive before, which lingers hours and perhaps days before it fades.

These presentiments and previsions of love, which often first arise spontaneously and naturally in sleep, seem to illustrate the old trope that the stars of other and larger systems come out best when the sun of our own personal consciousness has set. Indeed in the reverie and day dreaming common at this stage, when the soul transcends its individual limitations and expatiates over the whole field of humanity, past, present, or future, it is perhaps quite as near the world of our habitual, but generally unremembered dreams, as it is to the waking world of memory. In the new horizon now opening to the mind, unconscious cerebration generally has a larger rôle and for a time is more uncontrolled by the consciousness, over into which it shades by imperceptible gradations. Many psychic processes are so absorbing as to be almost a narcosis akin to the dreamy states that Crichton-Browne characterizes, so that if at first the soul falls to sleep with a great drop from waking life, the two states are later brought into manifold *rapport* and perhaps linked into unity. . . .

Our returns show great reason for believing that near the dawn of sexual life there is not only a new balance struck between the processes of repair and anabolism and those of katabolic expenditure of energy, but that there is a marked tendency to irregularities in sleep. Sometimes a sense of fatigue, lassitude, and sleepiness, rarely narcoleptic, may supervene, and the time of actual sleep for days, weeks, or greater periods be prolonged, but wakeful tendencies and special aversions to retire and to sleep follow and alternate. Some rebel at this period against the necessity of losing so much time from the life of active consciousness, dread night, and rejoice every morning on waking up that they have a long day before sleep is again imperative. There are almost always spells of sitting up late and sometimes, though far more rarely, of preposterously early rising to utilize the maximum of time. Normal adolescent boys especially wish to explore night out-of-doors, to rove about perhaps with adventurous or romantic thoughts, and on moonlight nights particularly there is a pathos about the necessity of rest. A part of this suggests an atavistic recrudescence of what may have been in primitive man the need of watchfulness, the custom of predatory adventures or amatory excursions of ancient courtships by night, still reverberating in the attenuated form of periods of nocturnal restlessness. The child's fever of early candle-light is metamorphosed by puberty into the youth's impulse to use darkness as a motive of abandon and license, as if the responsibilities of the day could be dispensed with by night in roving nocturns of riotous freedom analogous to the start on falling to sleep, due to the sudden removal of the habitual cerebral repression upon the lower spinal and midbrain centers. This passion to occasionally be out or to work late nights shades down the psychophysical scale into increased dream activity and power to work evenings. The wonted irregularity of the diurnal rhythm, no matter how well established before, is now like every other function for a time disturbed.

39

Just as adolescence was being defined physiologically and psychologically, it was given an enormous boost socially by the extension of schooling. By the early twentieth century, schooling beyond the elementary level was becoming a compulsory part of growing up, and this meant that older children — adolescents — were increasingly at school. Not everyone believed that childhood should be extended in this way. The historian Stephen A. Lassonde explains why some Italian immigrant parents in the early twentieth century objected to the education being offered to their children (1998).

Compulsory Schooling and Parent-Adolescent Relations

Stephen A. Lassonde

One of the quiet cultural transformations of the twentieth century in the United States has been the widespread consensus over the meaningfulness of age gradations among children and youths. . . .

Who could have predicted at the dawn of the twentieth century the swift success of the "adolescent idea" and the subdivision of stages in growing up that has occurred since? Certainly the rise of the expert and the medicalization of "deviance" have contributed significantly to the broad acceptance of age gradations and the developmental perspective. But schooling, the most pervasive of all modern institutions has had the greatest influence on the willingness of Americans to think through novel categories of cognitive, emotional, and physiological growth and well-being in young people. While the passage and enforcement of compulsory schooling and a concomitant need to make distinctions among children's school performance (which led to age-grading) established the framework for thinking about pupils developmentally, it was the voluntary extension of schooling that proved the true measure of parents' willing adoption of the developmental view. The critical period of growth in schooling beyond the minimum required by law occurred between 1910 and 1940, when high school attendance grew dramatically. . . .

From the perspective of Italian immigrant parents, the consignment of sons and daughters to school and thus, effectively, to a state of suspended childhood threatened not only to create family hardship, but also to teach their children the *wrong* lessons about their obligations to others. In this respect Italian immigrant parents at the turn of the century differed little from their working-class predecessors in the United States, many of whom had resisted the introduction and enforcement of compulsory schooling from the 1870s to the end of the century. However, because compulsory education and the legal apparatus that supported had been phased in gradually over the latter half of the nineteenth century in Connecticut, immigrant families arriving after 1900 encountered a highly-integrated system of enforcement. . . . Given the *contadini's* [peasants] limited exposure to schooling in Italy, they could only have experienced the demands of the local schools as yet another manifestation of their cultural separateness—as the consequence of ethnic differences that marked off the host culture in which they dwelt as alien and hostile.

Indeed, here was a challenge to the *contadino's* most basic understanding of human relations, involving heretofore unquestioned elements of power and sentiment in family life: the respect of children for the authority of parents, the prerogatives of age, male privilege, and most generally, a sense of devotion to parental welfare as the center of a child's concerns. Thus, expressions of astonishment at the reversal of the order of things—so characteristic of Italian immigrant parents' reactions to the length of schooling in the United States—encapsulated two basic reactions: first, to the disturbing priority given to children in American society (and its implicit dangers); and then alarm at the role of the state in imposing and maintaining what Italian parents regarded as an insidious "dependence" of children upon their parents. In addition to upsetting a sociocultural tradition in the provinces of southern Italy that viewed education in the most narrowly pragmatic terms, schooling in America implied a conception of children's roles that clashed with Italian immigrants' ideas about age and familial responsibility. The variety of distinctions between age groups in the United States and the role of the schools in upholding these threatened mores about the process of socializing young people.

Leonard Covello's published writings, as well as the mounds of unpublished notes, observations, and interviews compiled during his tenure as a high school principal in Italian Harlem during the 1930s and 1940s incisively mirror the attitudes of Italian parents and children toward schooling throughout the industrial northeast. Covello's penetrating appraisal of adolescence as seen through the eyes of Italian immigrants displays a remarkable acuity about the constructedness of childhood, adolescence, and youth in the United States. . . . "The status of American youth," observed Covello, "amazed" the *contadino*,

> but also filled him with apprehension. . . . Boys and even girls, were compelled to go to school up to a certain age regardless of parental feelings, the child's aptitudes and desires. Below a certain age, work by children was prohibited. And when the child neither goes to school nor attends to useful work, the enforced leisure and idleness detach the child from the orbit of family life and remove him from the wholesome influence of familial tradition.

More familiar to Italian immigrant families was a process of incremental, seam-less emergence into adult society, "as gradual and uneventful as . . . [the] physi-cal transformation of the infant into an adult. . . . There were no sharp age divi-sions, each shaded with the older and the younger." There were, fundamentally "two groups," he says, "children and adults: helpless infants and very old feeble folks (and playful tots, young men and young women) but never what we call [adolescents]." Where the father was sufficiently comfortable financially and the sole earner in the family, "the parent could indulge a sentimental attitude toward the adolescent and make a concession to the social pattern of America. But most were not in this position." Of greater significance, in any case, he concludes, "[T]he American school system . . . created a group of idle [youths]. . . . The old Italian equilibrium in which adolescents [fit] well and in a useful way into the family struct[ure] and its economy, had entirely broken; youth was hardly [any] longer an integral part of the Italian family institution. From the ages of seven to fourteen years of age, it was said, the Italian boy in American society did nothing but play in the streets." This perception, of course, expressed the general frustra-tion experienced by many Italian immigrant parents who felt that the indiscrim-inate compulsion of schooling, *apart* from depriving families of needed income, failed to recognize the variability of children's inclination toward formal learning and forced the same lengthy course of schooling on all.

Play among *contadini* children had always been directed toward some useful activity, such as participating in the harvesting of grapes or making a game out of clearing stones from a field. By the same token, the extent to which boys "played in the streets" in America—and the fact that they had so much spare time—grated against the familiar rhythms of children's diurnal obligations in southern Italy: " 'I don't remember [that] we ever played ball, or cops and robbers, or hide-and-seek games,' " a Sicilian immigrant told Covello. " 'We were supposed to play only such games as would be of use when we grew up.' " At an early age, between six and eight, children were supposed to be occupied with chores and activities that would establish a lifelong sense of responsibility. This "responsible work" meant that "the child (even considering his age) was also a real worker who used real tools, like those of adults except for their size." The variety of skills that had been required of a peasant, fisherman, or even a crafts-man in southern Italy could be learned at an early age in the parental household or by apprenticeship. Therefore, Covello points out, formal education was re-garded as superfluous, since the skills and techniques of a peasant economy required only the most straightforward transmission from father to son, or from mother to daughter. And finally, the role of schooling in laying a foundation for a "moral" upbringing—one of the fundamental purposes of all rudimentary systems of mass schooling—was viewed as redundant at best but potentially insidious as well. For the moral code in a relatively homogeneous society, he says, was a "reasonably uniform body of rules learned in daily contact and social relations. The moral customs, unshaken for centuries, were effectively transmit-ted, without any stimulation of a person's logical faculties. . . . [B]eyond a few proverbs, some legends and other bits of generalized wisdom, [formalized] knowledge was at some distance from popular comprehension and consumption." . . .

That American schools did a good job of teaching their children it was widely admitted, but a typical lament was expressed by a man who asked, " 'What good is it if a boy is bright and intelligent, and then does not know enough to respect his family. Such a boy would be worth nothing! That's the trouble with American kids; they're smart, but the schools don't teach them to respect their families.' " Worry about a relative lack of discipline in the schools translated into a further sense that American schools were insufficiently "serious." Again, while many parents were satisfied with the scholastic emphasis of the American schools, others felt that whatever academic discipline might be instilled in their children was simultaneously undercut by a distracting focus on frivolous, non-pedagogical activities. One mother complained that " 'when you pass by a school all you hear is singing or the steps of dancing, or the noise of playing, playing, playing.' " Another instance of the comparative frivolousness of American schools (in the opinion of this same mother) was the way her daughter's teacher one year had instructed every girl in the classroom to bring a present for a boy classmate at Christmas time. This request seemed to her to epitomize the shortcomings of schooling in America and provoked the woman to remark: " 'As if there were not [already] enough love-making in the American schools!' " Thus the significant contributions made by children to household and agricultural tasks in Italy—herding sheep, weeding, harvesting, and stone-clearing for peasant boys; making and repairing lines and nets in fishing families, and for all girls, cleaning, cooking, sewing, spinning, mending, and finishing garments—served as fundamental training for children. Taken together, these tasks were closer to the sense of "education" held by Italian immigrants than was the formal, routinized education offered by schooling in the United States.

40

Among other adolescent characteristics, youthful clannishness has been one of the primary concerns of twentieth-century commentators. In The Gang *(1927), the sociologist Frederic M. Thrasher frames the classic statement about the tendency of urban adolescents to separate out by youthful allegiances. At Thrasher's time, as now, the concern was that this behavior led to deviant social acts, but Thrasher defines the youths' bonding activities as a normal part of adolescent life. The gang, he argues, develops only if it meets with social opposition and in a context that fails to provide young people with various services and opportunities.*

The Natural History of the Gang

Frederic M. Thrasher

The beginnings of the gang can best be studied in the slums of the city where an inordinately large number of children are crowded into a limited area. On a warm summer evening children fairly swarm over areaways and sidewalks, vacant lots and rubbish dumps, streets and alleys. The buzzing chatter and constant motion remind one of insects which hover in a swarm, yet ceaselessly dart hither and thither within the animated mass. This endless activity has a tremendous fascination, even for the casual visitor to the district, and it would be a marvel indeed if any healthy boy could hold himself aloof from it.

In this ubiquitous crowd of children, spontaneous play-groups are forming everywhere—gangs in embryo. Such a crowded environment is full of opportunities for conflict with some antagonistic person or group within or without the gang's own social milieu. The conflict arises on the one hand with groups of its own class in disputes over the valued prerogatives of gangland—territory, loot, play spaces, patronage in illicit business, privileges to exploit, and so on; it comes about on the other, through opposition on the part of the conventional social order to the gang's unsupervised activities. Thus, the gang is faced with a real struggle for existence with other gangs and with the antagonistic forces in its wider social environment.

Play-groups easily meet these hostile forces, which give their members a "we" feeling and start the process of ganging so characteristic of the life of these unorganized areas. . . .

On this basis of interests and aptitudes, a play-group emerges whose activities vary from "hide-and-go-seek" to crap-shooting.

> This was a group of about nine boys, whose ages varied from sixteen to twenty years. There were both Protestants and Catholics, some of whom attended school, while others worked. Their hang-out was in the front room of the home of one of the members, whose mother, known as "Aunt Sarah," allowed the boys the freedom of her house. Two of the number were piano-players. The boys sang, jigged, played cards, or just talked. There was no formal organization, no one was considered as leader, but the word of one or two had more weight than that of others. There was a group-consciousness and most of the wishes of the members were met in the bunch; yet there was no antagonism to outsiders; they never intruded. During the years the bunch lasted no new members were taken in. It disintegrated as members grew up and moved away or married.

Such a play-group may acquire a real organization. Natural leaders emerge, a relative standing is assigned to various members and traditions develop. *It does not become a gang, however, until it begins to excite disapproval and opposition, and thus acquires a more definite group-consciousness.* It discovers a rival or an enemy in the gang in the next block; its baseball or football team is pitted against some other team; parents or neighbors look upon it with suspicion or hostility; "the old man around the corner," the storekeepers, or the "cops" begin to give it "shags" (chase it); or some representative of the community steps in and tries to break it up. This is the real beginning of the gang, for now it starts to draw itself more closely together. It becomes a conflict group.

It would be erroneous, however, to suppose that a gang springs immediately from an ordinary street crowd like Minerva, full-grown from Jove's forehead. The gang has its beginning in acquaintanceship and intimate relations which have already developed on the basis of some common interest. These preliminary bonds may serve to unite pairs or trios among the boys rather than the group as a whole. The so-called "two-boy gang" is often a center to which other boys are attracted and about which they form like a constellation. Thus, the gang may grow by additions of twos and threes as well as of single individuals. The notorious Gloriannas were originally a two-boy gang. . . .

Gangs represent the spontaneous effort of boys to create a society for themselves where none adequate to their needs exists. What boys get out of such association that they do not get otherwise under the conditions that adult society imposes is the thrill and zest of participation in common interests, more especially in corporate action, in hunting, capture, conflict, flight, and escape. Conflict with other gangs and the world about them furnishes the occasion for many of their exciting group activities.

The failure of the normally directing and controlling customs and institutions to function efficiently in the boy's experience is indicated by disintegration of family life, inefficiency of schools, formalism and externality of religion, corruption and indifference in local politics, low wages and monotony in occupational activities, unemployment, and lack of opportunity for wholesome recreation. All these factors enter into the picture of the moral and economic frontier, and, coupled with deterioration in housing, sanitation, and other conditions of life in the slum, give the impression of general disorganization and decay.

The gang functions with reference to these conditions in two ways: It offers a substitute for what society fails to give; and it provides a relief from suppression and distasteful behavior. It fills a gap and affords an escape. Here again we may conceive of it as an interstitial group providing interstitial activities for its members. Thus the gang, itself a natural and spontaneous type of organization arising through conflict, is a symptom of disorganization in the larger social framework.

41

The pioneer anthropologist Margaret Mead turned against Hall's biogenetic determinism (and away from his concentration on boys) when she used her experiences in Samoa to propose that modern Western adolescence, although based on a physical transformation, is a social and cultural construct, and its peculiarities lay in the stresses of modern life. This excerpt from her famous study Coming of Age in Samoa *(1928) illustrates the degree to which her research in the South Seas was driven by her interest in modern America and her special concern with the experiences of adolescent girls in modern society.*

Adolescent Girls in Samoa and America

Margaret Mead

For many chapters we have followed the lives of Samoan girls, watched them change from babies to baby-tenders, learn to make the oven and weave fine mats, forsake the life of the gang to become more active members of the household, defer marriage through as many years of casual love-making as possible, finally marry and settle down to rearing children who will repeat the same cycle. As far as our material permitted, an experiment has been conducted to discover what the process of development was like in a society very different from our own. Because the length of human life and the complexity of our society did not permit us to make our experiment here, to choose a group of baby girls and bring them to maturity under conditions created for the experiment, it was necessary to go instead to another country where history had set the stage for us. There we found girl children passing through the same process of physical development through which our girls go, cutting their first teeth and losing them, cutting their second teeth, growing tall and ungainly, reaching puberty with their first menstruation, gradually reaching physical maturity, and becoming ready to produce the next generation. It was possible to say: Here are the proper conditions for an experiment; the developing girl is a constant factor in America and in Samoa; the civilisation of America and the civilisation of Samoa are different. In the course of development, the process of growth by which the girl baby becomes a grown woman, are the sudden and conspicuous bodily changes which take place at puberty accompanied by a development which is spasmodic, emotionally charged, and accompanied by an awakened religious sense, a flowering of idealism, a great desire for assertion of self against authority—or not? Is adolescence a period of mental and emotional distress for the growing girl as inevitably as teething is a period of misery for the small baby? Can we think of adolescence as a time in the life history of every girl child which carries with it symptoms of conflict and stress as surely as it implies a change in the girl's body?

Following the Samoan girls through every aspect of their lives we have tried to answer this question, and we found throughout that we had to answer it in the negative. The adolescent girl in Samoa differed from her sister who had not reached puberty in one chief respect, that in the older girl certain bodily changes were present which were absent in the younger girl. There were no other great differences to set off the group passing through adolescence from the group which would become adolescent in two years or the group which had become adolescent two years before. . . .

But when we have answered the question we set out to answer we have not finished with the problem. A further question presents itself. If it is proved that adolescence is not necessarily a specially difficult period in a girl's life—and proved it is if we can find any society in which that is so—then what accounts for the presence of storm and stress in American adolescents? First, we may say quite simply, that there must be something in the two civilisations to account for the difference. If the same process takes a different form in two different environments, we cannot make any explanations in terms of the process, for that is the same in both cases. But the social environment is very different and it is to it that we must look for an explanation. What is there in Samoa which is absent in America, what is there in America which is absent in Samoa, which will account for this difference?

Such a question has enormous implications and any attempt to answer it will be subject to many possibilities of error. But if we narrow our question to the way in which aspects of Samoan life which irremediably affect the life of the adolescent girl differ from the forces which influence our growing girls, it is possible to try to answer it.

The background of these differences is a broad one, with two important components; one is due to characteristics which are Samoan, the other to characteristics which are primitive.

The Samoan background which makes growing up so easy, so simple a matter, is the general casualness of the whole society. For Samoa is a place where no one plays for very high stakes, no one pays very heavy prices, no one suffers for his convictions or fights to the death for special ends. Disagreements between parent and child are settled by the child's moving across the street, between a man and his village by the man's removal to the next village, between a husband and his wife's seducer by a few fine mats. Neither poverty nor great disasters threaten the people to make them hold their lives dearly and tremble for continued existence. No implacable gods, swift to anger and strong to punish, disturb the even tenor of their days. . . .

And next there is the most striking way in which all isolated primitive civilisation and many modern ones differ from our own, in the number of choices which are permitted to each individual. Our children grow up to find a world of choices dazzling their unaccustomed eyes. In religion they may be Catholics, Protestants, Christian Scientists, Spiritualists, Agnostics, Atheists, or even pay no attention at all to religion. This is an unthinkable situation in any primitive society not exposed to foreign influence. There is one set of gods, one accepted religious practice, and if a man does not believe, his only recourse is to believe less than his fellows; he may scoff but there is no new faith to which he may turn. Present-day Manu'a approximates this condition; all are Christians of the same sect. There is no conflict in matters of belief although there is a difference in practice between Church-members and non-Church-members. And it was remarked that in the case of several of the growing girls the need for choice between these two practices may some day produce a conflict. But at present the Church makes too slight a bid for young unmarried members to force the adolescent to make any decision.

Similarly, our children are faced with half a dozen standards of morality: a double sex standard for men and women, a single standard for men and women, and groups which advocate that the single standard should be freedom while others argue that the single standard should be absolute monogamy. Trial marriage, companionate marriage, contract marriage—all these possible solutions of a social impasse are paraded before the growing children while the actual conditions in their own communities and the moving pictures and magazines inform them of mass violations of every code, violations which march under no banners of social reform.

The Samoan child faces no such dilemma. Sex is a natural, pleasurable thing; the freedom with which it may be indulged in is limited by just one consideration, social status. Chiefs' daughters and chiefs' wives should indulge in no extra-marital experiments. Responsible adults, heads of households and mothers of families should have too many important matters on hand to leave them much time for casual amorous adventures. Every one in the community agrees about the matter, the only dissenters are the missionaries who dissent so vainly that their protests are unimportant. But as soon as a sufficient sentiment gathers about the missionary attitude with its European standard of sex behaviour, the need for choice, the forerunner of conflict, will enter into Samoan society. . . .

The Samoan picture shows that it is not necessary to channel so deeply the affection of a child for its parents and suggests that while we would reject that part of the Samoan scheme which holds no rewards for us, the segregation of the sexes before puberty, we may learn from a picture in which the home does not dominate and distort the life of the child.

The presence of many strongly held and contradictory points of view and the enormous influence of individuals in the lives of their children in our country play into each other's hands in producing situations fraught with emotion and pain. In Samoa the fact that one girl's father is a domineering, dogmatic person, her cousin's father a gentle, reasonable person, and another cousin's father a vivid, brilliant, eccentric person, will influence the three girls in only one respect, choice of residence if any one of the three fathers is the head of a household. But the attitudes of the three girls towards sex, and towards religion, will not be affected by the different temperaments of their three fathers, for the fathers play too slight a rôle in their lives. They are schooled not by an individual but by an army of relatives into a general conformity upon which the personality of their parents has a very slight effect. And through an endless chain of cause and effect, individual differences of standard are not perpetuated through the children's adherence to the parents' position, nor are children thrown into bizarre, untypical attitudes which might form the basis for departure and change. It is possible that where our own culture is so charged with choice, it would be desirable to mitigate, at least in some slight measure, the strong rôle which parents play in children's lives, and so eliminate one of the most powerful accidental factors in the choices of any individual life.

The Samoan parent would reject as unseemly and odious an ethical plea made to a child in terms of personal affection. "Be good to please mother." "Go to church for father's sake." "Don't be so disagreeable to your sister, it makes father so unhappy." Where there is one standard of conduct and only one, such undignified confusion of ethics and affection is blessedly eliminated. But where there are many standards and all adults are striving desperately to bind their own children to the particular courses which they themselves have chosen, recourse is had to devious and non-reputable means. Beliefs, practices, courses of action, are pressed upon the child in the name of filial loyalty. In our ideal picture of the freedom of the individual and the dignity of human relations it is not pleasant to realise that we have developed a form of family organisation which often cripples the emotional life, and warps and confuses the growth of many individuals' power to consciously live their own lives.

42

After World War II teenagers and their commercial culture became a national obsession and a common feature of popular culture (e.g., the film Rebel without a Cause*). In response, psychologists like Erik H. Erikson and Kenneth Keniston became famous interpreters of the psychology of adolescence. Erikson's definition of adolescence as a "life stage" marked by conflicts in allegiance and the quest for a stable identity (which derived from Hall and Freud) and his coinage "identity crisis" became widely disseminated (1968).*

Identity, Youth, and Crisis

Erik H. Erikson

Among the indispensable co-ordinates of identity is that of the life cycle, for we assume that not until adolescence does the individual develop the prerequisites in physiological growth, mental maturation, and social responsibility to experience and pass through the crisis of identity. We may, in fact, speak of the identity crisis as the psychosocial aspect of adolescing. Nor could this stage be passed without identity having found a form which will decisively determine later life.

Let us, once more, start out from Freud's far-reaching discovery that neurotic conflict is not very different in content from the "normative" conflicts which every child must live through in his childhood, and the residues of which every adult carries with him in the recesses of his personality. For man, in order to remain psychologically alive, constantly re-resolves these conflicts just as his body unceasingly combats the encroachment of physical deterioration. However, since I cannot accept the conclusion that just to be alive, or not to be sick, means to be healthy, or, as I would prefer to say in matters of personality, *vital*, I must have recourse to a few concepts which are not part of the official terminology of my field.

I shall present human growth from the point of view of the conflicts, inner and outer, which the vital personality weathers, re-emerging from each crisis with an increased sense of inner unity, with an increase of good judgment, and an increase in the capacity "to do well" according to his own standards and to the standards of those who are significant to him. The use of the words "to do well" of course points up the whole question of cultural relativity. Those who are significant to a man may think he is doing well when he "does some good" or when he "does well" in the sense of acquiring possessions; when he is doing well in the sense of learning new skills and new knowledge or when he is not much more than just getting along; when he learns to conform all around or to rebel significantly; when he is merely free from neurotic symptoms or manages to contain within his vitality all manner of profound conflict.

There are many formulations of what constitutes a "healthy" personality in an adult. But if we take up only one—in this case, Marie Jahoda's definition, according to which a healthy personality *actively masters* his environment, shows a certain *unity of personality*, and is able to *perceive* the world and himself *correctly*—it is clear that all of these criteria are relative to the child's cognitive and social development. In fact, we may say that childhood is defined by their initial absence and by their gradual development in complex steps of increasing differentiation. How, then, does a vital personality grow or, as it were, accrue from the successive stages of the increasing capacity to adapt to life's necessities—with some vital enthusiasm to spare?

Whenever we try to understand growth, it is well to remember the *epigenetic principle* which is derived from the growth of organisms *in utero*. Somewhat generalized, this principle states that anything that grows has a ground plan, and that out of this ground plan the parts arise, each part having its time of special ascendancy, until all parts have arisen to form a functioning whole. This, obviously, is true for fetal development where each part of the organism has its critical time of ascendance or danger of defect. At birth the baby leaves the chemical exchange of the womb for the social exchange system of his society, where his gradually increasing capacities meet the opportunities and limitations of his culture. How the maturing organism continues to unfold, not by developing new organs but by means of a prescribed sequence of locomotor, sensory, and social capacities, is described in the child-development literature. As pointed out, psychoanalysis has given us an understanding of the more idiosyncratic experiences, and especially the inner conflicts, which constitute the manner in which an individual becomes a distinct personality. But here, too, it is important to realize that in the sequence of his most personal experiences the healthy child, given a reasonable amount of proper guidance, can be trusted to obey inner laws of development, laws which create a succession of potentialities for significant interaction with those persons who tend and respond to him and those institutions which are ready for him. While such interaction varies from culture to culture, it must remain within "the proper rate and the proper sequence" which governs all epigenesis. Personality, therefore, can be said to develop according to steps predetermined in the human organism's readiness to be driven toward, to be aware of, and to interact with a widening radius of significant individuals and institutions.

It is for this reason that, in the presentation of stages in the development of the personality, we employ an epigenetic diagram . . . for an analysis of Freud's psychosexual stages. It is, in fact, an implicit purpose of this presentation to bridge the theory of infantile sexuality (without repeating it here in detail) and our knowledge of the child's physical and social growth. . . .

[In] the diagram, . . . the double-lined squares signify both a sequence of

	1	2	3	4	5	6	7	8
VIII								INTEGRITY vs. DESPAIR
VII							GENERATIVITY vs. STAGNATION	
VI						INTIMACY vs. ISOLATION		
V	Temporal Perspective vs. Time Confusion	Self-Certainty vs. Self-Consciousness	Role Experimentation vs. Role Fixation	Apprenticeship vs. Work Paralysis	IDENTITY vs. IDENTITY CONFUSION	Sexual Polarization vs. Bisexual Confusion	Leader- and Followership vs. Authority Confusion	Ideological Commitment vs. Confusion of Values
IV				INDUSTRY vs. INFERIORITY	Task Identification vs. Sense of Futility			
III			INITIATIVE vs. GUILT		Anticipation of Roles vs. Role Inhibition			
II		AUTONOMY vs. SHAME, DOUBT			Will to Be Oneself vs. Self-Doubt			
I	TRUST vs. MISTRUST				Mutual Recognition vs. Autistic Isolation			

stages and a gradual development of component parts; in other words, the diagram formalizes a progression through time of a differentiation of parts. This indicates (1) that each item of the vital personality to be discussed is systematically related to all others, and that they all depend on the proper development in the proper sequence of each item; and (2) that each item exists in some form before "its" decisive and critical time normally arrives. . . .

Each comes to its ascendance, meets its crisis, and finds its lasting solution in ways to be described here, toward the end of the stages mentioned. All of them exist in the beginning in some form, although we do not make a point of this fact, and we shall not confuse things by calling these components different names at earlier or later stages. A baby may show something like "autonomy" from the beginning, for example, in the particular way in which he angrily tries to wriggle his hand free when tightly held. However, under normal conditions, it is not until the second year that he begins to experience the whole critical alternative between being an autonomous creature and being a dependent one, and it is not until then that he is ready for a specifically new encounter with his environment. The environment, in turn, now feels called upon to convey to him its particular ideas and concepts of autonomy in ways decisively contributing to his personal character, his relative efficiency, and the strength of his vitality.

It is this encounter, together with the resulting crisis, which is to be described for each stage. Each stage becomes a crisis because incipient growth and awareness in a new part function go together with a shift in instinctual energy and yet also cause a specific vulnerability in that part. . . .

Each successive step, then, is a potential crisis because of a radical change in perspective. Crisis is used here in a developmental sense to connote not a threat of catastrophe, but a turning point, a crucial period of increased vulnerability and heightened potential, and therefore, the ontogenetic source of generational strength and maladjustment. The most radical change of all, from intrauterine to extrauterine life, comes at the very beginning of life. But in postnatal existence, too, such radical adjustments of perspective as lying relaxed, sitting firmly, and running fast must all be accomplished in their own good time. With them, the interpersonal perspective also changes rapidly and often radically, as is testified by the proximity in time of such opposites as "not letting mother out of sight" and "wanting to be independent." Thus, different capacities use different opportunities to become full-grown components of the ever-new configuration that is the growing personality. . . .

Adolescence

As technological advances put more and more time between early school life and the young person's final access to specialized work, the stage of adolescing becomes an even more marked and conscious period and, as it has always been in some cultures in some periods, almost a way of life between childhood and adulthood. Thus in the later school years young people, beset with the physiological revolution of their genital maturation and the uncertainty of the adult roles ahead, seem much concerned with faddish attempts at establishing an adolescent subculture with what looks like a final rather than a transitory or, in fact, initial identity formation. They are sometimes morbidly, often curiously, preoccupied with what they appear to be in the eyes of others as compared with what they feel they are, and with the question of how to connect the roles and skills cultivated earlier with the ideal prototypes of the day. In their search for a new sense of continuity and sameness, which must now include sexual maturity, some adolescents have to come to grips again with crises of earlier years before they can install lasting idols and ideals as guardians of a final identity. They need, above all, a moratorium for the integration of the identity elements ascribed . . . to the childhood stages: only that now a larger unit, vague in its outline and yet immediate in its demands, replaces the childhood milieu—"society." A review of these elements is also a list of adolescent problems.

If the earliest stage bequeathed to the identity crisis an important need for trust in oneself and in others, then clearly the adolescent looks most fervently for men and ideas to have *faith* in, which also means men and ideas in whose service it would seem worth while to prove oneself trustworthy. . . . At the same time, however, the adolescent fears a foolish, all too trusting commitment, and will, paradoxically, express his need for faith in loud and cynical mistrust.

If the second stage established the necessity of being defined by what one can *will* freely, then the adolescent now looks for an opportunity to decide with free assent on one of the available or unavoidable avenues of duty and service, and at the same time is mortally afraid of being forced into activities in which he would feel exposed to ridicule or self-doubt. This, too, can lead to a paradox, namely, that he would rather act shamelessly in the eyes of his elders, out of free choice, than be forced into activities which would be shameful in his own eyes or in those of his peers.

If an unlimited *imagination* as to what one *might* become is the heritage of the play age, then the adolescent's willingness to put his trust in those peers and leading, or misleading, elders who will give imaginative, if not illusory, scope to his aspirations is only too obvious. By the same token, he objects violently to all "pedantic" limitations on his self-images and will be ready to settle by loud accusation all his guiltiness over the excessiveness of his ambition.

Finally, if the desire to make something work, and to make it work well, is the gain of the school age, then the choice of an occupation assumes a significance beyond the question of remuneration and status. It is for this reason that some adolescents prefer not to work at all for a while rather than be forced into an otherwise promising career which would offer success without the satisfaction of functioning with unique excellence.

In any given period in history, then, that part of youth will have the most affirmatively exciting time of it which finds itself in the wave of a technological, economic, or ideological trend seemingly promising all that youthful vitality could ask for.

Adolescence, therefore, is least "stormy" in that segment of youth which is gifted and well trained in the pursuit of expanding technological trends, and thus able to identify with new roles of competency and invention and to accept a more implicit ideological outlook. Where this is not given, the adolescent mind becomes a more explicitly ideological one, by which we mean one searching for some inspiring unification of tradition or anticipated techniques, ideas, and ideals. And, indeed, it is the ideological potential of a society which speaks most clearly to the adolescent who is so eager to be affirmed by peers, to be confirmed by teachers, and to be inspired by worth-while "ways of life." On the other hand, should a young person feel that the environment tries to deprive him too radically of all the forms of expression which permit him to develop and integrate the next step, he may resist with the wild strength encountered in animals who are suddenly forced to defend their lives. For, indeed, in the social jungle of human existence there is no feeling of being alive without a sense of identity.

Having come this far, I would like to give one example (and I consider it representative in structure) of the individual way in which a young person, given some leeway, may utilize a traditional way of life for dealing with a remnant of negative identity. I had known Jill before her puberty, when she was rather obese and showed many "oral" traits of voracity and dependency while she also was a tomboy and bitterly envious of her brothers and in rivalry with them. But she was intelligent and always had an air about her (as did her mother) which seemed to promise that things would turn out all right. And, indeed, she straightened out and up, became very attractive, an easy leader in any group, and, to many, a model of young girlhood. As a clinician, I watched and wondered what she would do with that voraciousness and with the rivalry which she had displayed earlier. Could it be that such things are simply absorbed in fortuitous growth?

Then one autumn in her late teens, Jill did not return to college from the ranch out West where she had spent the summer. She had asked her parents to let her stay. Simply out of liberality and confidence, they granted her this moratorium and returned East.

That winter Jill specialized in taking care of newborn colts, and would get up at any time during a winter night to bottle feed the most needy animals. Having apparently acquired a certain satisfaction within herself, as well as astonished recognition from the cowboys, she returned home and reassumed her place. I felt that she had found and hung on to an opportunity to do actively and for others what she had always yearned to have done for her, as she had once demonstrated by overeating: she had learned to feed needy young mouths. But she did so in a context which, in turning passive into active, also turned a former symptom into a social act.

One might say that she turned "maternal" but it was a maternalism such as cowboys must and do display; and, of course, she did it all in jeans. This brought recognition "from man to man" as well as from man to woman, and beyond that the confirmation of her optimism, that is, her feeling that something could be done that felt like her, was useful and worth while, and was in line with an ideological trend where it still made immediate practical sense.

Such self-chosen "therapies" depend, of course, on the leeway given in the right spirit at the right time, and this depends on a great variety of circumstances. I intend to publish similar fragments from the lives of children in greater detail at some future date; let this example stand for the countless observations in everyday life, where the resourcefulness of young people proves itself when the conditions are right.

The estrangement of this stage is *identity confusion*, [expressed in] . . . Biff's formulation in Arthur Miller's *Death of a Salesman*: "I just can't take hold, Mom, I can't take hold of some kind of a life." Where such a dilemma is based on a strong previous doubt of one's ethnic and sexual identity, or where role confusion joins a hopelessness of long standing, delinquent and "borderline" psychotic episodes are not uncommon. Youth after youth, bewildered by the incapacity to assume a role forced on him by the inexorable standardization of American adolescence, runs away in one form or another, dropping out of school, leaving jobs, staying out all night, or withdrawing into bizarre and inaccessible moods. Once "delinquent," his greatest need and often his only salvation is the refusal on the part of older friends, advisers, and judiciary personnel to type him further by pat diagnoses and social judgments which ignore the special dynamic conditions of adolescence. It is here, as we shall see in greater detail, that the concept of identity confusion is of practical clinical value, for if they are diagnosed and treated correctly, seemingly psychotic and criminal incidents do not have the same fatal significance which they may have at other ages.

In general it is the inability to settle on an occupational identity which most disturbs young people. To keep themselves together they temporarily over-identify with the heroes of cliques and crowds to the point of an apparently complete loss of individuality. Yet in this stage not even "falling in love" is entirely, or even primarily, a sexual matter. To a considerable extent adolescent love is an attempt to arrive at a definition of one's identity by projecting one's diffused self-image on another and by seeing it thus reflected and gradually clarified. This is why so much of young love is conversation. On the other hand, clarification can also be sought by destructive means. Young people can become remarkably clannish, intolerant, and cruel in their exclusion of others who are "different," in skin color or cultural background, in tastes and gifts, and often in entirely petty aspects of dress and gesture arbitrarily selected as the signs of an in-grouper or out-grouper. It is important to understand in principle (which does not mean to condone in all of its manifestations) that such intolerance may be, for a while, a necessary defense against a sense of identity loss. This is unavoid-able at a time of life when the body changes its proportions radically, when genital puberty floods body and imagination with all manner of impulses, when intimacy with the other sex approaches and is, on occasion, forced on the young person, and when the immediate future confronts one with too many conflicting possibilities and choices. Adolescents not only help one another temporarily through such discomfort by forming cliques and stereotyping themselves, their ideals, and their enemies; they also insistently test each other's capacity for sustaining loyalties in the midst of inevitable conflicts of values.

The readiness for such testing helps to explain . . . the appeal of simple and cruel totalitarian doctrines among the youth of such countries and classes as have lost or are losing their group identities—feudal, agrarian, tribal, or national. The democracies are faced with the job of winning these grim youths by convincingly demonstrating to them—by living it—that a democratic identity can be strong and yet tolerant, judicious and still determined. But industrial democracy poses special problems in that it insists on self-made identities ready to grasp many chances and ready to adjust to the changing necessities of booms and busts, of peace and war, of migration and determined sedentary life. Democracy, therefore, must present its adolescents with ideals which can be shared by young people of many backgrounds, and which emphasize autonomy in the form of independence and initiative in the form of constructive work. These promises, however, are not easy to fulfill in increasingly complex and centralized systems of industrial, economic, and political organization, systems which increasingly neglect the "self-made" ideology still flaunted in oratory. This is hard on many young Americans because their whole upbringing has made the development of a self-reliant personality dependent on a certain degree of choice, a sustained hope for an individual chance, and a firm commitment to the freedom of self-realization.

We are speaking here not merely of high privileges and lofty ideals but of psychological necessities. For the social institution which is the guardian of identity *is* what we have called *ideology*. One may see in ideology also the imagery of an aristocracy in its widest possible sense, which connotes that within a defined world image and a given course of history the best people will come to rule and rule will develop the best in people. In order not to become cynically or apathetically lost, young people must somehow be able to convince themselves that those who succeed in their anticipated adult world thereby shoulder the obligation of being best. For it is through their ideology that social systems enter into the fiber of the next generation and attempt to absorb into their lifeblood the rejuvenative power of youth. Adolescence is thus a vital regenerator in the process of social evolution, for youth can offer its loyalties and energies both to the conservation of that which continues to feel true and to the revolutionary correction of that which has lost its regenerative significance. . . .

Beyond Identity

. . . . It is only when identity formation is well on its way that true intimacy— which is really a counterpointing as well as a fusing of identities—is possible. Sexual intimacy is only part of what I have in mind, for it is obvious that sexual intimacies often precede the capacity to develop a true and mutual psychosocial intimacy with another person, be it in friendship, in erotic encounters, or in joint inspiration. The youth who is not sure of his identity shies away from interpersonal intimacy or throws himself into acts of intimacy which are "promiscuous" without true fusion or real self-abandon.

43

In the past thirty years eating disorders have become a common feature of the adolescence of American girls. The medical historian Joan Jacobs Brumberg discusses the most common of these, anorexia nervosa, *and its possible causes (1989).*

Anorexia Nervosa in the 1980s

Joan Jacobs Brumberg

While boys are developing muscles as a consequence of biological development, girls experience an increase in adiposity, particularly in the breasts and hips. This increased fat is a necessity for the menstrual cycle. In our fat-phobic society, where female self-worth is so intimately tied to a slim figure, these biological differences have critical and distinctive emotional consequences.

For adolescent boys, growing larger is frequently a source of pleasure and power; for girls, an increase in size is often confusing, awkward, and stressful. In her influential treatise *The Second Sex* (1949), Simone de Beauvoir noted the normal adolescent girl's fear of "becom[ing] flesh . . . and show[ing] her flesh. . . ." This "distaste is expressed by many young girls through the wish to be thin; they no longer want to eat, . . . they constantly watch their weight. Others become pathologically timid. . . . From such beginnings psychoses may now and then develop." In this sense, normal maturation in our society "sets up" young women for anorexia nervosa. . . .

Psychological models of anorexia nervosa fall into three basic groups born of psychoanalysis, family systems theory, and social psychology. In the first two in particular, anorexia nervosa is seen as a pathological response to the developmental crisis of adolescence. Refusal of food is understood as an expression of the adolescent's struggle over autonomy, individuation, and sexual development. "Anorexia [nervosa] is a pathology of the ordinary issues of adolescent passage," writes a contemporary clinician. Much of current psychotherapeutic thinking about anorexia nervosa takes its direction from Sigmund Freud and, more recently, from Hilde Bruch. Freud regarded the anorectic as a girl who feared adult womanhood and heterosexuality. In 1895 he wrote: "The famous anorexia nervosa of young girls seems to me (on careful observation) to be a melancholia *where sexuality is undeveloped*" (italics added). In Freudian terms, eating, like all appetites, is an expression of libido or sexual drive. Clinicians confirm the direction of the Freudian interpretation: anorectics generally are not sexually active adolescents.

Hilde Bruch, in the spirit of Freud and his early followers, considered the contemporary anorectic unprepared to cope with the psychological and social consequences of adulthood as well as sexuality. Because of the anorectic's paralyzing sense of ineffectiveness and anxiety about her identity, she opts, furiously, for control of her body. Bruch argued that the anorectic makes her body a stand-in for the life that she cannot control. She experiences a disturbance of "delusional proportions" with respect to her body image, and she eats in a peculiar and disorganized fashion. By refusing food, the anorectic slows the processes of sexual maturation: her menses stop and her body remains childlike. The preoccupation with controlling her appetite directs the young woman inward so that she becomes increasingly estranged from the outside world. She lives a bizarre life, obsessed with thoughts of food, while struggling with her parents over her right not to eat.

We have seen that there have been numerous efforts to place anorexia nervosa within other established psychiatric categories such as schizophrenia, depression, and obsessional neurosis. Recent psychoanalytic literature suggests that anorexia nervosa is a popular form of classic obsessive-compulsive disorder. Unlike depression, where there is a true reduction of appetite, in anorexia nervosa the patient is constantly aware of her hunger. Simultaneously, she ruminates about calories and exercises frantically, all the while dwelling on images of the very food that she fears. These preoccupations can become excessive and involuntary. Patients usually are stubborn, rigid, and strongly defensive about their behavior, and they espouse elaborate and highly intellectual theories about food and exercise. Many display other behavior patterns associated with obsessive-compulsive disorders: perfectionism, excessive orderliness and cleanliness, meticulous attention to detail, and self-righteousness. The anorectic is, then, a "good girl" who alternates between compliance and rebellion. In the beginning, at least, her refusal to eat is a form of overcontrol that is subtly hostile and rebellious in its nature.

In the 1980s a great deal of attention is being paid also to values and patterns of interaction within anorexic families. Indeed, family systems therapy provides one of today's most important theoretical perspectives on anorexia nervosa. According to family systems theorist Salvador Minuchin, certain kinds of family environments encourage passive methods of defiance (for example, not eating) and make it difficult for members to assert their individuality. Minuchin describes this "psychosomatic family" as controlling, perfectionistic, and nonconfrontational, adjectives that apply equally well to their anorexic daughter. On the basis of clinical work with these families, mental health professionals have come to describe the anorectic as "enmeshed," meaning that the normal process of individuation is blocked by the complex psychological needs of the girl, her parents, even her siblings. In family systems theory not just the patient has anorexia nervosa: the family too has the disease.

When a parent *is* implicated in anorexia nervosa, it is almost always the mother. Kim Chernin, a psychoanalytically inspired feminist writer, argues that eating disorders are rooted in the problems of mother-daughter separation and identity. Mothers and daughters, she writes, express emotions around issues of food and eating rather than sexuality. The "hunger knot" experienced by so many modern daughters represents issues of failed female development, fear, and the daughter's guilt over her desire to surpass her mother. Chernin asserts that women who have disordered relationships to food are unconsciously guilty of symbolic matricide and their obsessive dieting is an expression of their desire to reunite or bond with the mother.

Other recent discussions of anorexia nervosa by psychiatrists suggest that anorectics may have mothers of a certain kind. It has been suggested that the mother of the anorectic is all of the following: frustrated, depressed, perfectionistic, passive and dependent, and unable to "mirror" her child. (The inability to mirror means that the mother is unable to see and reflect her daughter as an independent being. Consequently, a specific conflict emerges within the child, between her invisible sense of self and her visible body. Refusing to eat and losing weight is a desperate appeal to her mother to make emotional contact with the unseen person.)

Research in social psychology and in the field of personality also proposes interesting approaches to anorexia nervosa. At least two different predictive tests for eating disorders have been developed since the late 1970s: the Eating Attitudes Test (EAT) and the Eating Disorders Inventory (EDI). The EDI evaluates an individual on a number of different subscales including drive for thinness, body dissatisfaction, sense of ineffectiveness, perfectionism, interpersonal distrust, and maturity fears. A 1984 study by University of Toronto psychiatrist David Garner used the EDI to compare eating habits, weight-related symptoms, and psychological characteristics of anorectics with two other groups: women who were highly weight preoccupied and those who were not. The study concluded that while weight-preoccupied women and anorectics were indistinguishable on many of the test subscales, the anorexia nervosa group had significantly higher scores on measures of ineffectiveness. Some theorists propose an actual cognitive problem with body imaging. Others, following Carol Gilligan's theory of female moral development, regard the anorectic as a young woman in conflict with the dominant male values of her society, while yet another group posits that anorectics are overly socialized to the feminine role, as indicated by their scores on the Bem Sex Role Inventory.

Another fascinating and potentially promising line of research utilizes models drawn from the study of addiction and substance abuse. Anorexia nervosa does involve a habitual behavior (starvation) which, like intoxication or drug addiction, alters the individual's psychological and physical state. Although each of the behaviors may be unpleasant initially, they can, with prolonged indulgence, come to feel "right." Even when the behavior is patently self-destructive, the anorectic and the alcoholic will characteristically deny the problem—a response that stands in marked contrast to neurotic disorders, in which patients apparently exaggerate the abnormality of their symptoms. According to George I.

Szmukler and Digby Tantam, British psychiatrists, anorexia nervosa is most usefully conceived as a dependence disorder, specifically as "an addiction to starvation." In effect, individuals with anorexia nervosa may be dependent on both the psychological and the physiological effects of starvation.

In the end, no single psychological model provides a full explanation of anorexia nervosa. The psychological paradigm is incomplete, just as the biomedical model is, in that it fails to provide an adequate answer to the same thorny problems of social address, changing incidence, and gender. After reading the psychological literature, one still asks: Why is the anorexia nervosa "epidemic" restricted by class and confined to societies like our own? Why are we experiencing more anorexia nervosa today than we did fifty or one hundred years ago? Why is it that adolescent girls and not adolescent boys engage in this form of developmental struggle? These particular questions suggest that we look closely at what the cultural model has to offer.

The cultural explanation of anorexia nervosa is popular and widely promoted. It postulates that anorexia nervosa is generated by a powerful cultural imperative that makes slimness the chief attribute of female beauty. In casual conversation we hear this idea expressed all the time: anorexia is caused by the incessant drumbeat of modern dieting, by the erotic veneration of sylphlike women such as Twiggy, and by the demands of a fashion ethic that stresses youth and androgyny rather than the contours of an adult female body. The common wisdom reflects the realities of women's lives in the twentieth century. In this respect the cultural model, more than any other, acknowledges and begins to explain why eating disorders are essentially a female problem.

Important psychological studies by Susan and Orlando Wooley, Judith Rodin, and others confirm that weight is woman's "normative obsession." In response to the question, "How old were you when you first weighed more than you wanted?" American women report a preoccupation with overweight that begins before puberty and intensifies in adolescence and young adulthood. Eighty percent of girls in the fourth grade in San Francisco are dieting, according to researchers at the University of California. At three private girls' schools in Washington, D.C., 53 percent of the students said they were unhappy with their bodies by age thirteen; among those eighteen or older, 78 percent were dissatisfied. In the same vein, a 1984 *Glamour* magazine survey of thirty-three thousand women between the ages of eighteen and thirty-five demonstrated that 75 percent believed they were fat, although only 25 percent were actually overweight. Of those judged underweight by standardized measures, 45 percent still thought they were too fat. Clinicians often refer to people with weight preoccupations of this sort as "obesophobic."

The women in the *Glamour* survey confirm that female self-esteem and happiness are tied to weight, particularly in the adolescent and young adult years. When asked to choose among potential sources of happiness, the *Glamour* respondents chose weight loss over success at work or in interpersonal relations. The extent to which "feeling fat" negatively influences female psychological adjustment and behavior is only beginning to be explored. A 1984 study, for example, demonstrates that many college-age women make weight a central feature of their cognitive schema. These women consistently evaluate other women, themselves, and their own achievements in terms of weight. A 1986 study revealed that "feeling fat" was significantly related to emotional stress and other external stimuli. Obviously, being and feeling thin is an extremely desirable condition in this culture, whereas feeling fat is not: "I became afraid of getting fat, of gaining weight. [There is] something dangerous about becoming a fat American."

All indications are that being thin is particularly important to women in the upper classes. (This social fact is reflected in the widely quoted dictum, attributed to the Duchess of Windsor, "A woman can never be too rich or too thin.") A study by Stanford University psychologist Sanford M. Dornbusch revealed a positive correlation between gender, social class, and desire to be thin. Controlling for the actual level of fatness, Dornbusch's data, based on a nationwide sample of more than seventy-five hundred male and female high school students, showed that adolescent females in higher social classes wanted to be thinner more often than those in the lower classes. (Not surprisingly, most obese women come from the working class and the poor.) By contrast, the relationship between social class and the desire to be thin was minimal in males. Because body preference differs among girls according to social class, those from middle-class and upper-class families are the most likely to be dissatisfied and troubled by the normal development associated with sexual maturation.

According to the cultural model, these class-specific ideas about body preference pervade the larger society and do enormous harm. The modern visual media (television, films, video, magazines, and particularly advertising) fuel the preoccupation with female thinness and serve as the primary stimulus for anorexia nervosa. Female socialization, in the hands of the modern media, emphasizes external qualities ("good looks") above all else. As a consequence, we see few women of real girth on television or in the movies who also have vigor, intelligence, or sex appeal. Young girls, fed on this ideological pablum, learn to be decorative, passive, powerless, and ambivalent about being female. Herein lies the cause of anorexia nervosa, according to the cultural model.

44

Girls today are confronted by a culture in which sexuality is up-front and often impersonal. In her best-selling book Reviving Ophelia *(1994), the psychologist Mary Pipher discusses some of the social pressures and hazards facing girls today.*

Reviving Ophelia
Saving the Selves of Adolescent Girls

Mary Pipher

There are more magazines for girls now, but they are relatively unchanged in the thirty years since I bought my copies of *Teen*. The content for girls is makeup, acne products, fashion, thinness and attracting boys. Some of the headlines could be the same: TRUE COLORS QUIZ, GET THE LOOK THAT GETS BOYS, TEN COMMAND-MENTS OF HAIR, THE BEST PLACES TO MEET AVAILABLE MEN and TEN WAYS TO TRIM DOWN. Some headlines are updated to pay lip service to the themes of the 1990s: TWO MODELS CHILL OUT AT OXFORD UNIVERSITY IN SEASON'S GREATEST GRAY CLOTHES or ECO-INSPIRED LOOKS FOR FALL. A few reflect the greater stress that the 1990s offer the young: REV UP YOUR LOOKS WHEN STRESS HAS YOU DOWN, THE STD OF THE MONTH, GENITAL WARTS and SHOULD I GET TESTED FOR AIDS? Some would never have appeared in the 1950s: WHEN YOU'RE HIGHLY SEXED, IS ONE PARTNER ENOUGH? and ADVICE ON ORGASMS.

Cassie listens to music by The Dead Milkmen, 10,000 Maniacs, Nirvana and They Might Be Giants. She dances to Madonna's song "Erotica," with its sado-masochistic lyrics. The rock-and-roll lyrics by 2 Live Crew that make Tipper Gore cringe don't upset her. Sexist lyrics and the marketing of products with young women's naked bodies are part of the wallpaper of her life.

Cassie's favorite movies are *The Crying Game, Harold and Maude,* and *My Own Private Idaho.* None of these movies would have made it past the theater owner of my hometown.

Our culture has changed from one in which it was hard to get information about sexuality to one in which it's impossible to escape information about sexuality. Inhibition has quit the scene. In the 1950s a married couple on TV had to be shown sleeping in twin beds because a double bed was too suggestive. Now anything—incest, menstruation, crotch itch or vaginal odors—can be dis-cussed on TV. Television shows invite couples to sell their most private moments for a dishwasher.

The plot for romance movies is different. In the fifties people met, argued, fell in love, then kissed. By the seventies, people met, argued, fell in love and then had sex. In the nineties people meet, have sex, argue and then, maybe, fall in love. Hollywood lovers don't discuss birth control, past sexual encounters or how a sexual experience will affect the involved parties; they just do it. The Hollywood model of sexual behavior couldn't be more harmful and misleading if it were trying to be.

Cassie has seen *Playboys* and *Penthouses* on the racks at local drugstores and Quick Stops. Our city has adult XXX-rated movie theaters and adult bookstores. She's watched the adult channels in hotel rooms while bouncing on "magic fingers" beds. Advertisements that disturb me with their sexual content don't bother her. When I told her that I first heard the word "orgasm" when I was twenty, she looked at me with disbelief.

Cassie's world is more tolerant and open about sex. Her friends produced a campy play entitled *Vampire Lesbians of Sodom*. For a joke she displays Kiss of Mint condoms in her room. She's a member of her school's branch of Flag— Friends of Lesbians and Gays—which she joined after one of her male friends "came out" to her. She's nonjudgmental about sexual orientation and outspoken in her defense of gay rights. Her world is a kinder, gentler place for girls who have babies. One-fifth of all babies today are born to single mothers. Some of her schoolmates bring their babies to school.

In some ways Cassie is more informed about sex than I was. She's read books on puberty and sexuality and watched films at school. She's seen explicit movies and listened to hours of explicit music. But Cassie still hasn't heard answers to the questions she's most interested in. She hasn't had much help sorting out when to have sex, how to say no or what a good sexual experience would entail.

Cassie is as tongue-tied with boys she likes as I was, and she is even more confused about proper behavior. The values she learned at home and at church are at odds with the values broadcast by the media. She's been raised to love and value herself in a society where an enormous pornography industry reduces women to body parts. She's been taught by movies and television that sophisticated people are sexually free and spontaneous, and at the same time she's been warned that casual sex can kill. And she's been raped.

Cassie knows girls who had sex with boys they hardly knew. She knows a girl whose reason for having sex was "to get it over with." Another classmate had sex because her two best girlfriends had had sex and she didn't want to feel left out. More touching and sexual harassment happens in the halls of her school than did in the halls of mine. Girls are referred to as bitches, whores and sluts.

Cassie has been desensitized to violence. She's watched television specials on incest and sexual assaults and seen thousands of murders on the screen. She's seen *Fatal Attraction* and *Halloween II*. Since Jeffrey Dahmer, she knows what necrophilia is. She wasn't traumatized by *The Diary of Anne Frank*.

Cassie can't walk alone after dark. Her family locks doors and bicycles. She carries Mace in her purse and a whistle on her car keys. She doesn't speak to men she doesn't know. When she is late, her parents are immediately alarmed.

Of course there were girls who were traumatized in the fifties, and there are girls who lead protected lives in the 1990s, but the proportions have changed significantly. We feel it in our bones. . . .

Things that shocked us in the 1950s make us yawn now. The world has changed from one in which people blushed at the term "chicken breast" to one in which a movie such as *Pretty Woman* is not embarrassing. We've gone from a world with no locks on the doors to one of bolt locks and handguns. The issues that I struggled with as a college student—when I should have sex, should I drink, smoke or hang out with bad company—now must be considered in early adolescence.

45

Although the rate of teenage pregnancies has remained relatively stable, the propor-tion of babies born to unmarried teenagers has risen. The demographer Jane Maul-don analyzes the reasons for this "crisis" and its implications (1998).

Families Started by Teenagers

Jane Mauldon

Families in the United States are more diverse than they have ever been, and almost every type of family has its proponents—with the exception of families started by teenagers. In late-twentieth-century America, teenagers are not sup-posed to have children. "Adolescent parenthood"—the phrase only entered the lexicon of social problems in the early 1970s—is a problem almost by definition. Adolescents do not have the rights and responsibilities of adults; parenthood is quintessentially an adult role; ergo, adolescents should not be parents.

But many are. Nearly one million teenagers become pregnant each year in the United States and about a half million give birth. About 7 percent of women are parents before they turn eighteen, and 20 percent are before age twenty; about 13 percent of all births are to women under age twenty. The proportion of teens giving birth has fluctuated modestly over the past twenty-five years, hovering around fifty or sixty births each year per one thousand teens aged fifteen to nineteen. Despite the long-term stability of the teen birth rate, teenage parent-hood has been elevated to the status of a "crisis" in the list of problems facing America today. In his 1995 State of the Union Address, President Clinton called it "our most serious social problem." Whether and in what ways the facts war-rant such extreme concern is the subject of this chapter.

Teen parenting appears problematic for many reasons, but chiefly because it is, from a middle-class perspective, premature. Adolescents should be acquiring education and experience to prepare themselves to work at the highest level they are capable of. Young men have long been expected to use their youth in this way, but women have not. Teenage childbearing occasioned no public concern in the 1950s and early 1960s, even though it was considerably more common than now, partly because most of the young mothers at that time were married but also because women were not expected to have jobs. Now, motherhood is not an acceptable alternative to employment, and a woman's earnings depend largely on the skills she brings to the workplace. Because early parenthood interferes with a young woman's acquisition of education and job-related skills, it seems to guarantee a lifetime of poverty and hardship for a teenage mother and her baby. Indeed, precisely because it seems incompatible with developing a middle-class career trajectory, adolescent childbearing is perceived by many as reflecting, and perpetuating across generations, the values of an "underclass" whose behavior is shaped by a "culture of poverty."

Central to the perceived link between teenage motherhood and "underclass" behaviors is concern about *unwed* teenage births. Unlike the 1950s, the majority of young mothers today are unmarried. Only about one in four—28 percent—of teenage births are in wedlock, and only 35 percent of all teenagers with children are married (a few teenagers do marry after they give birth). The younger the teenage mother, the less likely she is to be married: only 19 percent of births to mothers under eighteen are marital births. The large fraction of teenage births that are outside marriage troubles many people. For one-third of adults, any sex outside marriage is immoral, and for a larger number, unmarried teenage sex is inappropriate. Hillary Rodham Clinton probably spoke for many when she re-marked, "My theory is, don't do it till you're twenty-one and then don't tell me about it." As well as violating norms against premarital teenage sex, unmarried teenage parenthood seems to exclude the babies' fathers from the obligations of parenthood. Only 15 percent of never-married teenage mothers ever have a child support order against the father of their child, and even those who have orders typically receive only one-third of the amount originally awarded to them. In short, very few of these fathers, on paper at least, are required to provide financial support for their children over the long term, and many of their children grow up in persistent, unremitting poverty.

The frustration of middle-class adults at the seeming folly of teenage mother-hood, and at its persistence, is palpable: "If these girls would only wait to have children, everyone would be so much better off! They would be able to get the education they need to support themselves, their children would be better off, and the family would not be a burden on the taxpaying public." On the face of it, the facts confirm these views. Throughout her first twelve years of parenthood, the income of the typical adolescent mother averages barely 40 percent of the median income of all families with children—just $15,300 annually in 1993 dol-lars. About 20 percent of that income comes from AFDC. More than 60 percent of African-American teenage mothers, half of Latinas, and just over one-quarter of whites are still in poverty when they are in their late twenties. And these young mothers must support, on average, at least half a child more than do women who start childbearing later, including a larger number of children who were not wanted when they were conceived. By age thirty, women who gave birth before turning age eighteen have on average 2.5 children. Among women who start childbearing before age twenty and who have more than two children, 51 percent have at least one child who when conceived was not wanted.

Given the low educational attainment of so many teen mothers, their poverty is not surprising. Only 30 percent of women who give birth before age eighteen earn a regular high school diploma and a further 27 percent earn a GED (the high school equivalency certificate, which is less valued in the labor market than a regular diploma), compared to a high school completion rate of 87 percent among all young adults. The children of teen mothers have numerous problems, which is no surprise given that most are born to low-income, poorly educated mothers and grow up in persistent poverty. Compared to children born to older mothers, they are more likely to be born at low birth weight, less likely to be rated in "excellent" health by their parents, more likely to be abused or neglected, more likely to repeat a grade in school, and more likely to run away from home. As adolescents, they more often drop out of high school; daughters are more likely to become adolescent mothers themselves and sons are more likely to be in trouble with the juvenile justice system and go to prison.

Clearly, teenage mothers and their children need help, and their problems are costing the nation dearly. To many people, teenage motherhood, especially unmarried teenage motherhood, seems grossly irresponsible, the result of carelessness at best and outright selfishness at worst. Young mothers want the rewards of parenthood, so critics argue, before they are financially or emotionally able to handle its responsibilities. Most teenagers seem too immature to be good parents: not yet adult, they are too self-centered or irresponsible to properly care for a child. And certainly, a young woman who allows her education to be interrupted by motherhood may never get back on track to support herself and her children above the poverty line. And all too often, critics say, the price of their self-indulgence is paid by their children, and by the taxpayer.

The view of teenage motherhood as a life gone badly awry seems indisputable—until we take a close look at the young mothers themselves, study their lives, and listen to their experiences. Then the picture becomes more complicated. To many of the young women who become mothers, early parenthood does not seem such a disaster. Most middle-class girls see that motherhood would dash their hopes for college, travel, jobs, boyfriends, and fun; they do not become parents, and if they become pregnant they are much more likely to abort. But what is true for middle-class teenagers is not so for the poor—and more than 80 percent of teenage mothers are poor or low-income before they ever give birth.

A Portrait of a Teenage Mother-to-Be

Jackie, sixteen, the second of four children, has just learned she is pregnant. She is bright and strong-willed—for several years she was placed in the "gifted and talented" classes in her school, until she had to leave because of her disruptive behavior. Jackie fights often with her mother, who is worried by her daughter's willfulness and tries to impose strict rules about where she goes and with whom. Jackie's mother has struggled against the odds to raise her children. Having dropped out of high school when she was pregnant, she later took her GED and some community college classes. The family was on welfare until Jackie was three, but since then her mother has worked continuously, mainly in retail jobs.

Over the last two years Jackie's behavior in school has become quite erratic. While she can be passionately enthusiastic and involved when leading the cheerleading squad and in her music and PE classes, she is more often disaffected and "difficult," sometimes cutting school and often talking and playing jokes in her classes. She wants attention and affection from her peers, a job, and independence. Now she is startled to find herself pregnant by her new twenty-year-old boyfriend.

Jackie does not long ponder what to do. She decides to say nothing about her pregnancy until she is far enough along that nobody will nag her to have an abortion, for she has always been adamantly opposed to abortion on principle. She figures that even if she has to drop out of high school, she will eventually get her GED. She has already given up on her earlier ambition of going to college, because her grades are not good enough for a scholarship and her mother could not afford to help her with fees and living expenses. And while she is anxious about telling her family she is pregnant and wonders how she will cope, she is also excited to imagine herself a mother.

Jackie is a real person (with a different name) who is typical of teenage mothers in several ways, chief among them that she did not deliberately intend to become pregnant. More than 80 percent of all teen pregnancies, and more than 90 percent of pregnancies to unmarried teens, are inadvertent. While many of these unplanned pregnancies are aborted, many others are carried to term, sometimes because a young mother decides she wants the baby, sometimes because she is opposed to or frightened by abortion, and often because she does not acknowledge her pregnancy early enough for an abortion or does not have ready access to abortion services. Indeed, 73 percent of all births to teenagers (and about 86 percent of births to unmarried teenagers) are not planned babies: the mothers say they would have preferred to be pregnant later, or not at all. These teenagers failed to take steps to prevent pregnancy. If teenagers needed to plan ahead in order to become pregnant—if, for example, they had to take a pill to do so, instead of taking a pill to avoid pregnancy—there might be only about one-fifth as many unmarried teen births as there are now.

Unplanned Pregnancy among Teenagers

Teenagers are relative novices in sexual matters and are still acquiring the intellectual and emotional skills to act "responsibly" in sexual matters—that is, in accord with what they see as their own long-term goals. Many become pregnant precisely because sex is still relatively unfamiliar to them and because it evokes powerful and conflicting desires. Most adolescents—like, indeed, many adults—find it difficult to integrate sexuality into their lives in a way that keeps them emotionally and physically healthy and avoids unplanned pregnancies or births. Even higher-income, educationally promising teens can get pregnant. In a recent letter to the editor in the *San Francisco Chronicle*, one woman writes, "I grew up . . . in a white middle-class family. Although . . . always a good student, . . . I became pregnant during my last year of high school. As far as I can determine there were no deep psychological reasons I became pregnant—simply that old adolescent bugaboo, denial—the "it-can't-happen-to-me" syndrome." . . .

Jackie herself is midway in age between the oldest and the youngest teenage mothers. In all, there were about 710,000 teenage women with children in 1993, comprising about 9 percent of teenage women aged fifteen to nineteen. About three-fourths of these mothers were actually young adults, aged eighteen or nineteen, one-fourth were aged fifteen to seventeen, while fewer than 2 percent of teen mothers were under fifteen. Of the 402,000 teens who gave birth *for the first time* in 1994, just over half (55 percent) were eighteen or nineteen; 42 percent were fifteen to seventeen, while only 3 percent were aged under fifteen.

Even though girls under age fifteen are a very small fraction of teenage mothers—only two or three junior-high girls (aged twelve to fourteen) in a thousand give birth each year (although the numbers are rising)—this group rightfully attracts considerable media and policy attention. Being so young, they are very vulnerable to abuse. Many of them have been victims of rape and molestation. Among teenagers who started to have sex before age fifteen, 60 percent report having had sex involuntarily, and 43 percent report that they have had *only* involuntary sex. Even among those who have not been abused, such early motherhood is associated with very serious problems for teenage parents and their infants. Still children themselves, these girls have difficulty functioning effectively as parents. Most are not yet capable of the logical and objective thinking needed to make good decisions for themselves and their children. Poor health at birth is common among the infants of very young mothers, who frequently receive no prenatal care or delay it until the third trimester of pregnancy. School failure is almost guaranteed for these mothers, who have not yet made the difficult transitions between middle school or junior high school and high school. And the chances that their first teenage birth will be followed by another is very great. Nearly one-fourth (22 percent) of teen births are second or higher-order births, usually to teenagers who had their first child in their adolescence. These families face exceptionally bleak prospects.

Teenage parenthood is a community phenomenon as well as an individual one, and efforts to understand or change it need to keep that perspective in mind. Research suggests that young people respond to the cues provided by their neighborhoods as well as to their family environments. Some neighborhoods and communities (defined for statistical purposes as a shared zip code) have persistently high teenage childbearing rates, exceeding 150 births each year per thousand teenagers, while others have persistently low rates, fewer than ten births per year. Thus, some children grow up seeing adolescents all around them having babies, while others do not know a single teenage mother.

Jackie herself knows many teenage mothers. Her family lived in a public housing project until Jackie was twelve, when her mother finally earned enough to move the family out. Jackie still has many friends there and visits often. To the casual observer, it looks as though all the teenage girls living there are either pregnant or have children; in fact, about half do, while the other half are babysitting their friends' or their sisters' children. From Jackie's perspective, being a mother is something that every woman will come to sooner or later, and being young has its advantages. The teen mothers that she knows have a lot of energy for their babies and seem to enjoy them. Jackie knows that she will be at least as good a mother as most of them are. After all, her own mother was a teenage parent too.

We can imagine two broad types of explanations for the highly localized variations in birth rates evident in the statistical data. One explanation is cultural. In the United States, with its history and present practices of racial, ethnic, and linguistic segregation, culturally similar people often live close to each other. Women who live nearby might share a set of cultural norms about families, women's roles, marriage, and sex, that would tend to lead to early childbearing. If culture did distinguish neighborhoods in this way, we would expect to find exactly the kinds of local patterns of childbearing that occur in the zip code data. The other explanation focuses on how the local economic and institutional context could influence birth rates. Adolescents living in a particular community may make similar choices about sex and childbearing in response to the generally similar educational and economic opportunities they encounter. The cultural and structural explanations can coexist—indeed, cultural practices and norms can be shaped by the economic and educational context.

Research does suggest that the structural constraints and opportunities of the local environment, especially educational and economic opportunities, partially account for the marked differences in teen birth rates between ethnic and racial groups. For example, African Americans have teen birth rates nearly three times as high as whites do. Data from the 1990 Census show that three of every ten poor blacks live in a "concentrated poverty neighborhood," meaning a census tract where at least 40 percent of their neighbors are also poor. Poor whites are much more likely to live in economically diverse areas—only one in ten poor whites lives in a concentrated poverty neighborhood. A concentrated poverty neighborhood probably has appalling schools and few jobs for teenagers. Adults can offer young people little practical assistance in finding work or furthering their education. In such a neighborhood, young, low-income women, whether black or white, may be less vigilant in avoiding pregnancy, and they will be less likely to find employed or educated young men to marry. . . .

Who Are the Fathers?

A word is in order at this point about the fathers of babies born to teenagers. Fewer teen boys become fathers than teen girls become mothers. One-third of the California birth certificates for teenage mothers reported a teenage father. Nationally, in 1988, twenty-two teenage males per one thousand fathered a child. Most of the fathers of babies born to teenage women are adults between the ages of eighteen and twenty-four (75 percent, according to California birth certificate data from 1990). On average, they are two and a half years older than the young women, so typical young couples would be a mother of seventeen and her boyfriend of twenty, or a mother of nineteen and her boyfriend of twenty-one. Some people may find these age differences troubling, for an age gap of two or three years is more significant in teenage than in adult relationships. And a significant minority of fathers are much older than the teen mothers. About 17 percent of fathers in 1990 were reported as aged twenty-five or older, and about one-fifth (19 percent) of teen mothers report that their partner is at least six years older than they are.

Older fathers pose different challenges for policy than do the younger men and boys who have children with teenage girls. They are no longer engaged in the transitions of adolescence, and many of them dropped out of school long ago, so school-completion programs are unlikely to help them. Their relationships with their children's mothers may be more exploitative than those of younger men. Certainly policymakers and the general public appear to think this is so. As for young men, there is evidence that early fatherhood imposes developmental and economic burdens on them which can disrupt their maturing or their educational attainment. Many find it hard to maintain relationships with their children even when they want to, if they are no longer intimate with the mother. And whatever their age, most fathers of children born to teen mothers live apart from their children (although a substantial number of them have regular contact at least while the children are young), so policymakers are now searching for ways to compel them to pay child support. However, any difficulties fathers may encounter in finding work that pays enough to support a child are rarely addressed. Jackie's boyfriend, like many of the fathers just discussed, is not a teenager but is still very young, and he has neither a high school diploma nor a job.

Partly as a way to strengthen fathers' ties to their children, some policymakers and researchers have proposed trying to increase marriages among teenagers. However, given the notorious instability of teenage marriages, the realistic fear that a young mother might be less likely to complete high school if she marries, and the low levels of education and work experience of many of the fathers, marriage may not be a solution to the problems of teenage mothers (even if public policy were able to encourage it). As one study concluded, "For a majority of young women, early marriage has proven to be a temporary and unsatisfactory solution to adolescent motherhood. The immediate benefit is far outweighed by the foreclosure of life options by lack of education and underemployability [arising from early marriage]."

For a young woman like Jackie who does not expect to go to college, there may be no compelling incentives to avoid pregnancy or to abort a pregnancy once conceived, just as there are no compelling reasons to marry the father of her child. While becoming a teenage single parent was not what Jackie had planned for herself, neither is she particularly worried by the prospect—in fact, she is happy about it. Teenagers, even more than older parents-to-be, underestimate the demands of babies and the long-term challenges of parenthood. They simply do not anticipate the efforts they will have to make in the future to get an education, a job, or even a steady boyfriend, nor how much more difficult those tasks will be with a baby than without one. Nor do they think that their children would suffer by having a young mother. Rather, they look around them and see families started when the mother was a teenager and others started by older women and, for the most part, do not see any noticeable differences between those two types of families. In low-income neighborhoods, raising children is difficult for all families.

46

In April 1999 in Littleton, Colorado, two young men, aged seventeen and eighteen, killed twelve schoolmates, a teacher, and then themselves. The massacre was the latest in a series of school shootings by teenagers that shocked Americans and led to widespread speculation about the biological, cultural, and social reasons for adolescent violence. As this Newsweek *article makes clear, commentators blamed everything from lax family life to widespread availability of guns to the influence of the media.*

Why the Young Kill

Sharon Begley

The temptation, of course, is to seize on one cause, one single explanation for Littleton, and West Paducah, and Jonesboro and all the other towns that have acquired iconic status the way "Dallas" or "Munich" did for earlier generations. Surely the cause is having access to guns. Or being a victim of abuse at the hands of parents or peers. Or being immersed in a culture that glorifies violence and revenge. But there isn't one cause. And while that makes stemming the tide of youth violence a lot harder, it also makes it less of an unfathomable mystery. Science has a new understanding of the roots of violence that promises to explain why not *every* child with access to guns becomes an Eric Harris or a Dylan Klebold, and why not *every* child who feels ostracized, or who embraces the Goth esthetic, goes on a murderous rampage. The bottom line: you need a particular environment imposed on a particular biology to turn a child into a killer.

It should be said right off that attempts to trace violence to biology have long been tainted by racism, eugenics and plain old poor science. The turbulence of the 1960s led some physicians to advocate psychosurgery to "treat those people with low violence thresholds," as one 1967 letter to a medical journal put it. In other words, lobotomize the civil-rights and antiwar protesters. And if crimes are disproportionately committed by some ethnic groups, then finding genes or other traits common to that group risks tarring millions of innocent people. At the other end of the political spectrum, many conservatives view biological theories of violence as the mother of all insanity defenses, with biology not merely an explanation but an excuse. The conclusions emerging from interdisciplinary research in neuroscience and psychology, however, are not so simple-minded as to argue that violence is in the genes, or murder in the folds of the brain's frontal lobes. Instead, the picture is more nuanced, based as it is on the discovery that experience rewires the brain. The dawning realization of the constant back-and-forth between nature and nurture has resurrected the search for the biological roots of violence.

Early experiences seem to be especially powerful: a child's brain is more malleable than that of an adult. The dark side of the zero-to-3 movement, which emphasizes the huge potential for learning during this period, is that the young brain also is extra vulnerable to hurt in the first years of life. A child who suffers repeated "hits" of stress—abuse, neglect, terror—experiences physical changes in his brain, finds Dr. Bruce Perry of Baylor College of Medicine. The incessant flood of stress chemicals tends to reset the brain's system of fight-or-flight hormones, putting them on hair-trigger alert. The result is the kid who shows impulsive aggression, the kid who pops the classmate who disses him. For the outcast, hostile confrontations—not necessarily an elbow to the stomach at recess, but merely kids vacating en masse when he sits down in the cafeteria—can increase the level of stress hormones in his brain. And that can have dangerous consequences. "The early environment programs the nervous system to make an individual more or less reactive to stress," says biologist Michael Meaney of McGill University. "If parental care is inadequate or unsupportive, the [brain] may decide that the world stinks—and it better be ready to meet the challenge." This, then, is how having an abusive parent raises the risk of youth violence: it can change a child's brain. Forever after, influences like the mean-spiritedness that schools condone or the humiliation that's standard fare in adolescence pummel the mind of the child whose brain has been made excruciatingly vulnerable to them.

In other children, constant exposure to pain and violence can make their brain's system of stress hormones unresponsive, like a keypad that has been pushed so often it just stops working. These are the kids with antisocial personalities. They typically have low heart rates and impaired emotional sensitivity. Their signature is a lack of empathy, and their sensitivity to the world around them is practically nonexistent. Often they abuse animals: Kip Kinkel, the 15-year-old who killed his parents and shot 24 schoolmates last May, had a history of this; Luke Woodham, who killed three schoolmates and wounded seven at his high school in Pearl, Miss., in 1997, had previously beaten his dog with a club, wrapped it in a bag and set it on fire. These are also the adolescents who do not respond to punishment: nothing hurts. Their ability to feel, to react, has died, and so has their conscience. Hostile, impulsive aggressors usually feel sorry afterward. Antisocial aggressors don't feel at all. Paradoxically, though, they often have a keen sense of injustices aimed at themselves.

Inept parenting encompasses more than outright abuse, however. Parents who are withdrawn and remote, neglectful and passive, are at risk of shaping a child who (absent a compensating source of love and attention) shuts down emotionally. It's important to be clear about this: inadequate parenting short of Dickensian neglect generally has little ill effect on most children. But to a vulnerable baby, the result of neglect can be tragic. Perry finds that neglect impairs the development of the brain's cortex, which controls feelings of belonging and attachment. "When there are experiences in early life that result in an underdeveloped capacity [to form relationships]," says Perry, "kids have a hard time empathizing with people. They tend to be relatively passive and perceive themselves to be stomped on by the outside world."

These neglected kids are the ones who desperately seek a script, an ideology that fits their sense of being humiliated and ostracized. Today's pop culture offers all too many dangerous ones, from the music of Rammstein to the game of Doom. Historically, most of those scripts have featured males. That may explain, at least in part, why the murderers are Andrews and Dylans rather than Ashleys and Kaitlins, suggests Deborah Prothrow-Smith of the Harvard School of Public Health. "But girls are now 25 percent of the adolescents arrested for violent crime," she notes. "This follows the media portrayal of girl superheroes beating people up," from Power Rangers to Xena. Another reason that the schoolyard murderers are boys is that girls tend to internalize ostracism and shame rather than turning it into anger. And just as girls could be the next wave of killers, so could even younger children. "Increasingly, we're seeing the high-risk population for lethal violence as being the 10- to 14-year-olds," says Richard Lieberman, a school psychologist in Los Angeles. "Developmentally, their concept of death is still magical. They still think it's temporary, like little Kenny in 'South Park'." Of course, there are loads of empty, emotionally unattached girls and boys. The large majority won't become violent. "But if they're in a violent environment," says Perry, "they're more likely to."

There seems to be a genetic component to the vulnerability that can turn into antisocial-personality disorder. It is only a tiny bend in the twig, but depending on how the child grows up, the bend will be exaggerated or straightened out. Such aspects of temperament as "irritability, impulsivity, hyperactivity and a low sensitivity to emotions in others are all biologically based," says psychologist James Garbarino of Cornell University, author of the upcoming book *Lost Boys: Why Our Sons Turn Violent and How We Can Save Them*. A baby who is unreactive to hugs and smiles can be left to go her natural, antisocial way if frustrated parents become exasperated, withdrawn, neglectful or enraged. Or that child can be pushed back toward the land of the feeling by parents who never give up trying to engage and stimulate and form a loving bond with her. The different responses of parents produce different brains, and thus behaviors. "Behavior is the result of a dialogue between your brain and your experiences," concludes Debra Niehoff, author of the recent book *The Biology of Violence*. "Although people are born with some biological givens, the brain has many blank pages. From the first moments of childhood the brain acts as a historian, recording our experiences in the language of neurochemistry."

There are some out-and-out brain pathologies that lead to violence. Lesions of the frontal lobe can induce apathy and distort both judgment and emotion. In the brain scans he has done in his Fairfield, Calif., clinic of 50 murderers, psychiatrist Daniel Amen finds several shared patterns. The structure called the cingulate gyrus, curving through the center of the brain, is hyperactive in murderers.

The CG acts like the brain's transmission, shifting from one thought to another. When it is impaired, people get stuck on one thought. Also, the prefrontal cortex, which seems to act as the brain's supervisor, is sluggish in the 50 murderers. "If you have violent thoughts that you're stuck on and no supervisor, that's a prescription for trouble," says Amen, author of *Change Your Brain/Change Your Life*. The sort of damage he finds can result from head trauma as well as exposure to toxic substances like alcohol during gestation.

Children who kill are not, with very few exceptions, amoral. But their morality is aberrant. "I killed because people like me are mistreated every day," said pudgy, bespectacled Luke Woodham, who murdered three students. "My whole life I felt outcasted, alone." So do a lot of adolescents. The difference is that at least some of the recent school killers felt emotionally or physically abandoned by those who should love them. Andrew Golden, who was 11 when he and Mitchell Johnson, 13, went on their killing spree in Jonesboro, Ark., was raised mainly by his grandparents while his parents worked. Mitchell mourned the loss of his father to divorce.

Unless they have another source of unconditional love, such boys fail to develop, or lose, the neural circuits that control the capacity to feel and to form healthy relationships. That makes them hypersensitive to perceived injustice. A sense of injustice is often accompanied by a feeling of abject powerlessness. An adult can often see his way to restoring a sense of self-worth, says psychiatrist James Gilligan of Harvard Medical School, through success in work or love. A child usually lacks the emotional skills to do that. As one killer told Garbarino's colleague, "I'd rather be wanted for murder than not wanted at all."

That the Littleton massacre ended in suicide may not be a coincidence. As Michael Carneal was wrestled to the ground after killing three fellow students in Paducah in 1997, he cried out, "Kill me now!" Kip Kinkel pleaded with the schoolmates who stopped him, "Shoot me!" With suicide "you get immortality," says Michael Flynn of John Jay College of Criminal Justice. "That is a great feeling of power for an adolescent who has no sense that he matters."

The good news is that understanding the roots of violence offers clues on how to prevent it. The bad news is that ever more children are exposed to the influences that, in the already vulnerable, can produce a bent toward murder. Juvenile homicide is twice as common today as it was in the mid-1980s. It isn't the brains kids are born with that has changed in half a generation; what has changed is the ubiquity of violence, the easy access to guns and the glorification of revenge in real life and in entertainment. To deny the role of these influences is like denying that air pollution triggers childhood asthma. Yes, to develop asthma a child needs a specific, biological vulnerability. But as long as some children have this respiratory vulnerability—and some always will—then allowing pollution to fill our air will make some children wheeze, and cough, and die. And as long as some children have a neurological vulnerability—and some always will—then turning a blind eye to bad parenting, bullying and the gun culture will make other children seethe, and withdraw, and kill.

47

Several twentieth-century American novelists have helped define what it means to be an adolescent by assuming the personae of the youth of their time. In This Side of Paradise *(1920) F. Scott Fitzgerald helped make adolescence a national obsession for the first time. J. D. Salinger would do something similar for the 1950s with his novel* The Catcher in the Rye *(1951).*

Petting

F. Scott Fitzgerald

On the Triangle trip Amory had come into constant contact with that great current American phenomenon, the "petting party."

None of the Victorian mothers—and most of the mothers were Victorian—had any idea how casually their daughters were accustomed to be kissed. "*Servant*-girls are that way," says Mrs. Huston-Carmelite to her popular daughter. "They are kissed first and proposed to afterward."

But the Popular Daughter becomes engaged every six months between sixteen and twenty-two, when she arranges a match with young Hambell, of Cambell & Hambell, who fatuously considers himself her first love, and between engagements the P. D. (she is selected by the cut-in system at dances, which favors the survival of the fittest) has other sentimental last kisses in the moonlight, or the firelight, or the outer darkness.

Amory saw girls doing things that even in his memory would have been impossible: eating three-o'clock, after-dance suppers in impossible cafés, talking of every side of life with an air half of earnestness, half of mockery, yet with a furtive excitement that Amory considered stood for a real moral let-down. But he never realized how wide-spread it was until he saw the cities between New York and Chicago as one vast juvenile intrigue.

Afternoon at the Plaza, with winter twilight hovering outside and faint drums down-stairs . . . they strut and fret in the lobby, taking another cocktail, scrupulously attired and waiting. Then the swinging doors revolve and three bundles of fur mince in. The theatre comes afterward; then a table at the Midnight Frolic—of course, mother will be along there, but she will serve only to make things more secretive and brilliant as she sits in solitary state at the deserted table and thinks such entertainments as this are not half so bad as they are painted, only rather wearying. But the P. D. is in love again . . . it was odd, wasn't it?—that though there was so much room left in the taxi the P. D. and the boy from Williams were somehow crowded out and had to go in a separate car. Odd! Didn't you notice how flushed the P. D. was when she arrived just seven minutes late? But the P. D. "gets away with it."

The "belle" had become the "flirt," the "flirt" had become the "baby vamp." The "belle" had five or six callers every afternoon. If the P. D., by some strange accident, has two, it is made pretty uncomfortable for the one who hasn't a date with her. The "belle" was surrounded by a dozen men in the intermissions between dances. Try to find the P. D. between dances, just *try* to find her.

The same girl . . . deep in an atmosphere of jungle music and the questioning of moral codes. Amory found it rather fascinating to feel that any popular girl he met before eight he might quite possibly kiss before twelve.

"Why on earth are we here?" he asked the girl with the green combs one night as they sat in some one's limousine, outside the Country Club in Louisville.

"I don't know. I'm just full of the devil."

"Let's be frank—we'll never see each other again. I wanted to come out here with you because I thought you were the best-looking girl in sight. You really don't care whether you ever see me again, do you?"

"No—but is this your line for every girl? What have I done to deserve it?"

"And you didn't feel tired dancing or want a cigarette or any of the things you said? You just wanted to be—"

"Oh, let's go in," she interrupted, "if you want to *analyze*. Let's not *talk* about it."

When the hand-knit, sleeveless jerseys were stylish, Amory, in a burst of inspiration, named them "petting shirts." The name travelled from coast to coast on the lips of parlor-snakes and P. D.'s.

48

Even in the second half of the twentieth century, discussions of young adolescents and literary portraits often emphasize male experiences. In her powerful coming-of-age novella The Member of the Wedding *(1947), Carson McCullers re-creates the fear, self-doubt, and emotionality of an adolescent girl.*

The Member of the Wedding

Carson McCullers

She stood before the mirror and she was afraid. It was the summer of fear, for Frankie, and there was one fear that could be figured in arithmetic with paper and a pencil at the table. This August she was twelve and five-sixths years old. She was five feet five and three quarter inches tall, and she wore a number seven shoe. In the past year she had grown four inches, or at least that was what she judged. Already the hateful little summer children hollered to her: ''Is it cold up there?'' And the comments of grown people made Frankie shrivel on her heels. If she reached her height on her eighteenth birthday, she had five and one-sixth growing years ahead of her. Therefore, according to mathematics and unless she could somehow stop herself, she would grow to be over nine feet tall. And what would be a lady who is over nine feet high? She would be a Freak.

In the early autumn of every year the Chattahoochee Exposition came to town. For a whole October week the fair went on down at the fair grounds. There was the Ferris Wheel, the Flying Jinney, the Palace of Mirrors—and there, too, was the House of the Freaks. The House of the Freaks was a long pavilion which was lined on the inside with a row of booths. It cost a quarter to go into the general tent, and you could look at each Freak in his booth. Then there were special private exhibitions farther back in the tent which cost a dime apiece. Frankie had seen all of the members of the Freak House last October:

The Giant

The Fat Lady

The Midget

The Wild Nigger

The Pin Head

The Alligator Boy

The Half-Man Half-Woman

The Giant was more than eight feet high, with huge loose hands and a hang-jaw face. The Fat Lady sat in a chair, and the fat on her was like loose-powdered dough which she kept slapping and working with her hands—next was the squeezed Midget who minced around in little trick evening clothes. The Wild Nigger came from a savage island. He squatted in his booth among the dusty bones and palm leaves and he ate raw living rats. The fair gave a free admission to his show to all who brought rats of the right size, and so children carried them down in strong sacks and shoe boxes. The Wild Nigger knocked the rat's head over his squatted knee and ripped off the fur and crunched and gobbled and flashed his greedy Wild Nigger eyes. Some said that he was not a genuine Wild Nigger, but a crazy colored man from Selma. Anyway, Frankie did not like to watch him very long. She pushed through the crowd to the Pin Head booth, where John Henry had stood all afternoon. The little Pin Head skipped and giggled and sassed around, with a shrunken head no larger than an orange, which was shaved except for one lock tied with a pink bow at the top. The last booth was always very crowded, for it was the booth of the Half-Man Half-Woman, a morphidite and a miracle of science. This Freak was divided completely in half—the left side was a man and the right side a woman. The costume on the left was a leopard skin and on the right side a brassiere and a spangled skirt. Half the face was dark-bearded and the other half bright glazed with paint. Both eyes were strange. Frankie had wandered around the tent and looked at every booth. She was afraid of all the Freaks, for it seemed to her that they had looked at her in a secret way and tried to connect their eyes with hers, as though to say: we know you. She was afraid of their long Freak eyes. And all the year she had remembered them, until this day.

"I doubt if they ever get married or go to a wedding," she said. "Those Freaks."

"What freaks you talking about?" asked Berenice.

"At the fair," said Frankie. "The ones we saw there last October."

"Oh, those folks."

"I wonder if they make a big salary," she said.

And Berenice answered: "How would I know?"

John Henry held out an imaginary skirt and, touching his finger to the top of his big head, he skipped and danced like the Pin Head around the kitchen table.

Then he said: "She was the cutest little girl I ever saw. I never saw anything so cute in my whole life. Did you, Frankie?"

"No," she said. "I didn't think she was cute."

"Me and you both," said Berenice.

"Shoo!" John Henry argued. "She was, too."

"If you want my candy opinion," said Berenice, "that whole crowd of folks down yonder at the fair just give me the creeps. Ever last one of them."

Frankie watched Berenice through the mirror, and finally she asked in a slow voice. "Do *I* give you the creeps?"

"You?" asked Berenice.

"Do you think I will grow into a Freak?" Frankie whispered.

"You?" said Berenice again. "Why, certainy not, I trust Jesus."

Frankie felt better. She looked sidewise at herself in the mirror. The clock ticked six slow times, and then she said: "Well, do you think I will be pretty?"

"Maybe. If you file down them horns a inch or two."

Frankie stood with her weight resting on her left leg, and she slowly shuffled the ball of her right foot on the floor. She felt a splinter go beneath the skin. "Seriously," she said.

"I think when you fill out you will do very well. If you behave."

"But by Sunday," Frankie said. "I want to do something to improve myself before the wedding."

"Get clean for a change. Scrub your elbows and fix yourself nice. You will do very well."

Frankie looked for a last time at herself in the mirror, and then she turned away. She thought about her brother and the bride, and there was a tightness in her that would not break.

"I don't know what to do. I just wish I would die."

"Well, die then!" said Berenice.

And: "Die," John Henry echoed in a whisper.

The world stopped.

"Go home," said Frankie to John Henry.

He stood with his big knees locked, his dirty little hand on the edge of the white table, and he did not move.

"You heard me," Frankie said. She made a terrible face at him and grabbed the frying pan that hung above the stove. She chased him three times around the table, then up through the front hall and out of the door. She locked the front door and called again: "Go home."

"Now what makes you act like that?" asked Berenice. "You are too mean to live."

Frankie opened the door to the stairway that led to her room, and sat down on one of the lower steps. The kitchen was silent and crazy and sad.

"I know it," she said. "I intend to sit still by myself and think over everything for a while."

This was the summer when Frankie was sick and tired of being Frankie. She hated herself, and had become a loafer and a big no-good who hung around the summer kitchen: dirty and greedy and mean and sad. Besides being too mean to live, she was a criminal. If the Law knew about her, she could be tried in the courthouse and locked up in the jail. Yet Frankie had not always been a criminal and a big no-good. Until the April of that year, and all the years of her life before, she had been like other people. She belonged to a club and was in the seventh grade at school. She worked for her father on Saturday morning and went to the show every Saturday afternoon. She was not the kind of person ever to think of being afraid. At night she slept in the bed with her father, but not because she was scared of the dark. . . .

She knew she ought to leave the town and go to some place far away. For the late spring, that year, was lazy and too sweet. The long afternoons flowered and lasted and the green sweetness sickened her. The town began to hurt Frankie. Sad and terrible happenings had never made Frankie cry, but this season many things made Frankie suddenly wish to cry. Very early in the morning she would sometimes go out into the yard and stand for a long time looking at the sunrise sky. And it was as though a question came into her heart, and the sky did not answer. Things she had never noticed much before began to hurt her: home lights watched from the evening sidewalks, an unknown voice from an alley. She would stare at the lights and listen to the voice, and something inside her stiffened and waited. But the lights would darken, the voice fall silent, and though she waited, that was all. She was afraid of these things that made her suddenly wonder who she was, and what she was going to be in the world, and why she was standing at that minute, seeing a light, or listening, or staring up into the sky: alone. She was afraid, and there was a queer tightness in her chest.

One night in April, when she and her father were going to bed, he looked at her and said, all of a sudden: "Who is this great big long-legged twelve-year-old blunderbuss who still wants to sleep with her old Papa." And she was too big to sleep with her father any more. She had to sleep in her upstairs room alone. She began to have a grudge against her father and they looked at each other in a slant-eyed way. She did not like to stay at home.

She went around town, and the things she saw and heard seemed to be left somehow unfinished, and there was the tightness in her that would not break. She would hurry to do something, but what she did was always wrong. She would call her best friend, Evelyn Owen, who owned a football suit and a Spanish shawl, and one would dress in the football suit and the other in the Spanish shawl and they would go down to the ten-cent store together. But that was a wrong thing and not what Frankie wanted. Or after the pale spring twilights, with the smell of dust and flowers sweet and bitter in the air, evenings of lighted windows and the long drawn calls at supper time, when the chimney swifts had gathered and whirled above the town and flown off somewhere to their home together, leaving the sky empty and wide; after the long twilights of this season, when Frankie had walked around the sidewalks of the town, a jazz sadness quivered her nerves and her heart stiffened and almost stopped.

Because she could not break this tightness gathering within her, she would hurry to do something. She would go home and put the coal scuttle on her head, like a crazy person's hat, and walk around the kitchen table. She would do anything that suddenly occurred to her—but whatever she did was always wrong, and not at all what she had wanted. Then, having done these wrong and silly things, she would stand, sickened and empty, in the kitchen door and say:

"I just wish I could tear down this whole town."

49

Manchild in the Promised Land *(1965), Claude Brown's depiction of growing up African American in New York in the 1950s, has become a classic. Brown describes the early sexuality, the drug scene, the fights, and the scams to stay alive. In this excerpt, Brown discusses his concerns about his younger brother, Pimp, and how the particular issues relating to migration from the South and the problems on the Harlem streets were affecting Pimp's adolescence.*

Manchild in the Promised Land

Claude Brown

When I went uptown now, I always had a definite purpose. I was going up to see Pimp to try and get him interested in something. I would take him out to the Flatbush section of Brooklyn and to Brighton, and we'd just walk. We'd walk around in Washington Heights. Sometimes on Sundays I liked to take him bike riding with me and show him other parts of New York City, hoping he could really get to see something outside of Harlem.

I was kind of worried about him now, because he was at that age, fifteen, where it was time to start doing something to be older and get into street life and do the things that the other cats out there were doing. . . .

I knew he had problems now. He had that problem of staying home and taking all that stuff from Dad. Mama had told me that he had had a fight with Dad. He was fighting back now. He was declaring his independence. I couldn't say anything. I didn't know what to do when he started complaining about how Dad and Mama and Papa, my grandfather, were still in the woods and he was growing up. He was getting away from all that old down-home stuff, and he didn't go for hearing it all the time around the house. I knew he was right, because I'd had the same feeling. You feel as though they're trying to make something out of you that you couldn't be and didn't want to be if you could, as though they're trying to raise you as a farm boy in New York, in Harlem.

I knew he was right, but I couldn't agree with him. I couldn't say, "Yeah, man. You got to get outta there." I wasn't sure that he was ready to leave, and I didn't have anyplace for him to go.

He would come down to my place after he'd had a fight with Dad and stay for a night. I knew Mama was all upset, because she'd get on the phone and start calling until he got there. She'd be real upset every time he stayed out after twelve o'clock. She was afraid that he was going to run away. She'd had her troubles with me, and I guess she figured history was repeating itself. Mama had really been through something with me, and I knew this. She had not had any trouble out of Carole and Margie. She'd always said she hoped she wouldn't have any grandsons, because if she had it all to do over again, she'd never have any boys.

I knew she had one reason for saying that, but I didn't want her to have another. I was trying to cool Pimp. I didn't feel that this cat was really ready to make it out on his own. He'd been a good boy all his life, and good boys weren't supposed to be pulling up and leaving home at fifteen.

I had to stop him from coming down to my place, because he was liking it too much. He'd come down, I'd give him money to go to school, money to blow. It was better than being home, because he didn't have anybody to answer to. I never asked him where he'd been or where he was going. He could stay out as late as he wanted to. Cats were always jamming at my place, all the young jazz musicians, the cats playing at the joints around where I lived. They'd be coming up all times of the night, getting high smoking pot and having jam sessions.

There'd be all kinds of bitches up there. We'd be partying way into the wee hours. This was a hip life, the way he saw it, and he wanted to get in. But I knew he wasn't ready for anything like this. It might have had a bad effect on him. The last thing I had to worry about was having my morals corrupted. But Pimp was younger, and he wasn't ready for this thing, the way I saw it. I was afraid for him, so I had to pull a mean trick on him to stop him from coming.

One night he came down, and he said he was tired of Mama and Dad and wanted me to look for a place for him. This was about twelve-thirty.

I said, "Okay, man," and pretended that I was serious about finding him a place. It was a cold night. I said, "Look, I only have one blanket." I put him in the little room across from me, and he almost froze. The next morning, he was in a hurry to get out of there and get back uptown to his warm bed.

I still didn't think he was ready, and more than that, I just didn't want him to hurt Mama as much as I had. I decided to go up there and talk to him, find out just what was going on. I could ask Mama about it, but she'd say, "That boy just thinks he's grown; he's gon fight his daddy, and he gon go outta here and stay as late as he wants." Mama couldn't understand Pimp any more than he could understand her.

I tried to talk to her. I said, "Look, Mama, Pimp grew up here in New York City. He's kind of different. He didn't grow up on all that salt pork, collard greens, and old-time religion. You can't make a chitterlin' eater out of him now."

Mama said, "Now, look here, nigger, you ate a whole lot of chitterlin's yourself, and chitterlin's wasn't too good for you back there in the early forties when your daddy wasn't doing too good on his job."

"Look, Mama, why don't you listen sometime, just for a little while. I'm telling you your son's got problems, Mama. It's not problems down on the farm. He's got problems here in New York City. And the only way he's going to solve these problems is that you try and help him."

"Oh, boy, sometimes I don't know what's wrong with you. You gon get involved in all that psychology you're always talkin' about and go stone crazy."

"Yeah, Mama, forget it." I just couldn't talk to her. . . .

Pimp was still in this thing, and I was afraid for him. I knew it was a hard thing for him to fight. I suppose when I was younger, I fought it by stealing, by not being at home, by getting into trouble. But I felt that Pimp was at a loss as to what to do about it. It might have been a greater problem for him.

It seemed as though the folks, Mama and Dad, had never heard anything about Lincoln or the Emancipation Proclamation. They were going to bring the South up to Harlem with them. I knew they had had it with them all the time. Mama would be telling Carole and Margie about the root workers down there, about somebody who had made a woman leave her husband, all kinds of nonsense like that.

I wanted to say, "Mama, why don't you stop tellin' those girls all that crazy shit?" But I couldn't say anything, because they wouldn't believe me, and Mama figured she was right. It seemed as though Mama and Dad were never going to get out of the woods until we made them get out.

Many times when I was there, Mama would be talking all that nonsense about the woods and about some dead person who had come back. Her favorite story was the time her mother came back to her and told her everything was going to be all right and that she was going to get married in about three or four months. I wanted to say, "Look, Mama, we're in New York. Stop all that foolishness."

She and Dad had been in New York since 1935. They were in New York, but it seemed like their minds were still down there in the South Carolina cotton fields. Pimp, Carole, and Margie had to suffer for it. I had to suffer for it too, but because I wasn't at home as much as the others, I had suffered less than anybody else.

I could understand Pimp's anxieties about having to listen to Grandpapa, who was now living with Mama and Dad, talk that old nonsense about how good it was on the chain gang. He'd tell us about the time he ran away from the chain gang. He stayed on some farm in Georgia for about two or three weeks, but he got lonesome for his family. He knew if he went home, they would be waiting for him, so he went back to the chain gang. The white man who was in charge of the chain gang gave him his old job back and said something like, "Hello there, Brock. Glad to see you back." He said they'd treated him nice. I couldn't imagine them treating him nice, because I didn't know anybody in the South who was treated nice, let alone on a chain gang. Still, Papa said the chain gang was good. I wanted to smack him. If he weren't my grandfather, I would have.

I felt sorry for Pimp, and I wished I were making a whole lot of money and could say, "Come on, man. Live with me and get away from that Harlem scene, and perhaps you can do something." But before he made the move from Harlem, he'd have to know where he was going, every step of the way, all by himself.

He was lost in that house. Nobody there even really knew he was alive. Mama and Dad were only concerned about the numbers coming out. Papa, since he was so old, would just sit around and look for the number in Ching Chow's ear in the newspaper comic section. When the number came out, he'd say, "I knew that number was comin'. I could've told you before."

I used to watch Pimp sometimes when I'd go up there. Papa would be talking this stuff about the number, and it seemed to be just paining Pimp. It hadn't bothered me that much. But I suppose it couldn't have. I used to be kind of glad that they were involved in this stuff. I guess I had an arrogant attitude toward the family. I saw them all as farmers. It made me feel good that they were involved in this stuff, because then they couldn't be aware of what I was doing and what was going down. The more they got involved in that old voodoo, the farther they got away from me and what I was doing out in the street.

Papa used to make me mad with, "Who was that old boy you was with today, that old tar-black boy?" Mama used to say things like that about people too, but I never felt that she was really color struck. Sometimes I used to get mad when she'd say things about people and their complexion, but she always treated all the people we brought up to the house real nice, regardless of whether they were dark- or light-skinned.

I knew that Pimp was at an age when he'd be bringing his friends around, and Papa would be talking that same stuff about, "Who's that black so-and-so?" If you brought somebody to the house who was real light-skinned, Papa would say, "They're nice," or "They're nice lookin'." All he meant was that the people were light-skinned. . . .

With Dad, I suppose it was just as bad at home. He would never read anything but the *Daily News*, and he always read about somebody cutting up somebody or killing somebody. He liked to read about the people in the neighborhood, and he'd point the finger at them. He'd say, "There goes another one." Just let it be one of my friends and, oh, man, he'd ride Pimp about it.

He'd say, "You remember that old no-good boy Sonny use to hang out with? He went to the chair last night," or "He got killed in a stickup someplace." He'd tell him, "You remember that old boy Sonny Boy use to bring up here years ago?" Pimp would never answer. "Well, they found him around there in the backyard on 146th Street dead, with a needle in his arm, last night. All of 'em just killin' theirselves. They ain't no damn good, and they ain't never had no sense. They didn't have enough sense to go out there and get a job, like somebody who knows something, and act halfway decent. They just gon hang out around here and rob the decent people, and break into people's houses. Somebody had to kill them, if they didn't kill theirselves. So I suppose they just might as well go ahead and use too much of that stuff and kill theirselves, no-good damn bums, old triflin', roguish dope addicts. They all ought to kill theirselves."

He'd be preaching this at Pimp as though he were one of them. It bothered Pimp. It would bother anybody. Dad never messed with me with this sort of thing. I was on my own, I was clean, and I was certain that I had as much money in my pocket as he had, if not more. I was his equal, and he couldn't run down all that nonsense to me.

50

Because sexuality plays such a large part in adolescent identity formation, homosexual desire can be particularly problematic in a culture where heterosexual norms predominate. Paul Monette remembers how he dissembled about his sexual interests in order to seem like one of the guys. As a result, instead of defining himself, he argues, he sought to bury "every trace of Paul Monette" (1992).

Becoming a Man
Half a Life Story

Paul Monette

Our two California roommates arrived in tandem: Sean and Jake, respectively a rock climber from Marin and a tennis jock from Santa Barbara. Outsize figures from the moment they walked through the door. They'd been buddies at the Trimble School—best of the West, old California gold, where every boy was required to keep a horse because it built character. Jake was third generation Trimble himself, grandson of the founding gentleman cowboy. He and Sean were smart as anybody from Andover, but not so polished, and proud of that. As to the mores and climate of Yale, everything struck them as being so *Eastern*, which only fortified their free-range superiority.

I was smitten by them both inside of twenty minutes. Not sexually, exactly—sexually was the least of it. Though they were strapping good athletes and frontier rugged, they never occupied a slot in the Olympian frieze of my fantasies. I needed them both to be more real than that, or else how would they ever transform my doggy life? For I quickly came to see them as my salvation, the pals I never had among the Apollo and Dionysus ranks of Andover. I'd never been on the inside before, shooting the breeze in a bull session. Never been anyone's confidant about women.

I took to the role with near-demented enthusiasm. To curry the favor of Sean and Jake I underwent a personality change—voluble where I'd been tongue-tied before, flattering them at every turn, adopting their sneering distaste for the East, I who'd never been west of the Hudson. I dressed like they did, took every meal I could with them. *Courtier* is far too pretty a term for my servile hero worship; *sycophant* is closer. Yet it wasn't at all unconscious: I saw my new friends as a last chance to leave behind the nothing I was in high school.

Thus I stopped answering Francis's letters from Georgetown, sealing the tomb on our old playful style, because it felt tainted with faggotry. Till the first snow-fall I'd get up with Sean on Sunday mornings and pile in a van with the Mountaineering Club, to spend hair-raising afternoons climbing the sheer faces of northern Connecticut's bony hills. Graceless and panting, biting the tongue of my acrophobia, I clambered up the gorse till my knuckles bled, all for a macho nod from Sean at the summit. Back at the dorm, I laughed myself hoarse at Jake's razor wit, becoming his personal buffoon and comic foil. He wanted to be a writer, and therefore so did I. Prose was his meat and potatoes, and therefore I took poetry.

It amazes me now, that I made life choices for no other reason than to get in Sean and Jake's good graces. Today I haven't a clue where they live or what they've done since Yale. I realize college provides a classic ground for reinvention of self, but self had nothing to do with this. The very opposite: all I wanted to be was the two of them, burying every trace of Paul Monette.

Bury especially the hungry voyeur with the secrets. Jake had what amounted to a knee-jerk loathing of queers, every third remark a withering bash of anybody who seemed the least bit eccentric. He'd pout his lips and affect a nancy lisp and a wobbly wrist, dismissing whatever felt effete or even intellectual. Since there were so many closeted teachers about, Yale was fertile territory for his HUAC-style snipery, every bachelor guilty till proven innocent. And I was the first to go along, frantic to hide my own fellow-traveling. Eagerly I learned how to mock my brothers behind their backs—anything to make Jake laugh.

But more was required to prove one's manhood than just the putting down of queers. In those pre-coed days, Yale men hardly talked of anything except getting laid, unless it was getting drunk. The best of all worlds therefore was scoring in both at once: a dream Saturday night where you'd be shitfaced from the rotgut punch at a mixer and mauling some poor townie girl. Jake and Sean were more than eager to get in on the action, pestering me to set them up with dates since I was the one with the East Coast connections. I could no more admit I'd never dated than I could my heterosexual virginity. So I invented my own modest tales of carnal prowess, cobbling details here and there from other men's boasting.

For Dartmouth weekend I invited a girl I knew from Rosemary Hall, who arrived with a blushing pair of her classmates. I hated attending the football game, having no idea what was going down on the field, but the worst was the mixer that night. Guys throwing up in the bushes outside and a general air of male entitlement, showing off their women and making their moves in the shadows to the tawdry strains of *Louie Louie*. I was engaged in the upstream battle of *not* scoring, avoiding sex at all costs. Here my four-year schizophrenic pattern laid itself out: the requisite girl on my arm, the looking good, the frenzied round of sports and museums and parties, anything to avoid too much time *à deux*, the compulsory makeout.

I wasn't unaware even at the time what a grim sham I was putting the girls through. Oh, I made up for my carnal detachment with frantic charm and witticisms, and for a while at least found dates who seemed relieved not to be mauled. But I would almost never see a girl twice, for fear of the expectations. The girl from Rosemary Hall kept writing till Christmas, and I was too frozen to answer. Every minute of a date felt like a lie, but if you didn't date, you couldn't be one of the guys. My guys anyway, whose opinion I cared about more than my own.

For Harvard weekend I invited Missy Cabot to come down from Middlebury, spending my self-imposed month's allowance just on tickets for The Game. As Missy wasn't due in till six on Friday, I spent the afternoon out at the soccer field, timing the freshman match between Harvard and Yale. I hadn't suddenly developed a fondness for the sport that gave me chilblains all through four rotten autumns at Andover. It was because Sean and Jake were playing for Yale, and I their constant companion could get no closer than sitting on the bench with a stopwatch. . . .

With ever renewed vigor I went on mimicking Sean and Jake, as spellbound and singleminded as Eve Harrington studying Margo Channing. It's a wonder I got any work done at all. Indeed I barely remember those freshman courses— Physics at 8 A.M. with Dr. Dandruff, or the English 25 seminar with sherry in a book-lined study, taught by a loser who used the occasion to get sloshed like a priest on Communion wine. My only intellectual coup was to land in a pair of upper division courses in art history, *Painting and Sculpture in the Twentieth Century* and *Modern Architecture*. I had to work my butt off to keep up with the seniors, flailing through Kandinsky's theory of the spirit in art, memorizing all the blank walls of the Bauhaus.

But I learned the collection in the Yale Art Gallery cold, forging myself a new sanctuary. What seems in memory a daily pilgrimage to the Van Gogh *Night Café*, the boiling light above the billiards table, the delirium of genius rendering, in Vincent's words, "the passions of humanity in red and green." And to reinforce the spell of art, I had two vivid mentors. Paoletti from Andover, who was finishing up his dissertation at Yale, steered me past the freshman survey and onto the upper floors of the Bauhaus. His comrade in the doctoral trenches, Peter Bunnell, was breaking ground in elevating the discourse on photography as art. I cared about being smart enough to talk to these men in their own argot, despite Jake's dismissal of them both as "fag intellectuals."

They certainly gave me more sensitive counsel than the live-in freshman adviser of Bingham Hall, Entry A, whose roaring binges usually ended with the rolling of empty beer kegs down the stairs. This singular thug, who suited up as an ROTC admiral two days a week, was otherwise distinguished by a bulletin board displaying several pairs of pinned-up panties, trophies of his many conquests. He was also a fourth generation Yalie and pledge chairman of the animal-house fraternity. Not notable for his opinions on Kandinsky. . . .

By junior year the pressure to date had taken a further turn of the screw. Men on every side of me were connecting up with steady girls. The girls came down every weekend from Smith and Vassar, with Breck hair and circle pins and Loden coats. They still nominally stayed in the Taft Hotel or the Whitney Motor Inn, for parietal hours were in strict force: no women in the rooms after midnight on weekends. Even so, a lot of them stayed over secretly, smuggled in and out of the bathrooms.

I was the sort who would check if the coast was clear for them, puckish as Juliet's nurse, always glad to assist in the joys of Eros. I charmed the regular girls in the dining hall, everyone's favorite fifth wheel, and they were always trying to fix me up with the shy girl in their dorm. Mostly I managed to sidle away from these good offices, cultivating the role of the solitary poet, too burning with private fires and mysteries to have anything left over for worldly passion. In fact I was the college fool, straining for hilarity and a knockabout enthusiasm, thinking by ingratiation to keep them all so entertained they wouldn't probe too much my bachelor status.

There was one steady girl who resisted my charms completely, barely a thin polite smile for all my manic patter and volley of one-liners. Natalie was from Mount Holyoke, pre-law, with a steel-trap mind and a low tolerance for fools. She was also Cody's girlfriend. They'd dated through four years of high school and two at Yale. A starry-eyed shot of them at the prom, peeking through a rose trellis, perched on Cody's desk. Yet for all her independent spirit and braininess— as if every conversation were a moot court proceeding—Natalie's take on Cody was hero worship, same as mine. And three was very definitely a crowd. . . .

Everyone at Yale seemed to drink too much, almost as a badge of honor. Holding your liquor was the mark of a man, but *not* holding it wasn't such a crime either; it proved a man was still a boy at heart, prone to mischief. I don't know how much I drank myself, a great deal more than I needed, but a small Puritan caution kept me from trying to keep up with Cody, in that at least. Otherwise I was like a mirror of his every word and gesture, increasingly trying to encourage him as his doubts about being an artist made him ever more savagely cynical.

Seething with that bitterness, he would tear canvases in half, then on a sudden impulse invite Natalie down for a midwinter weekend. I froze when I heard him make the phone call, and pretended to be very busy all the week before, so I wouldn't show how devastated I was. When he stayed overnight with her at the Taft, I sat in the dark staring out at the rainy courtyard, feeling as if I would die from the double paralysis of jealousy and envy. So lost was I in the realms of psych, all those lies on all those questionnaires, I couldn't have even said which of them I ached to be: Natalie, so Cody would love me, or Cody, so I could love a woman. I only knew I would never be happy and no one would ever hold me.

I can't recall how many more weekends like that there were—maybe once a month, maybe oftener. But I could see, even with my suffering, how at odds the two of them were—Cody drunk and surly, Natalie red-eyed with crying. But the pain between them made me as envious as their laughter, because it was real and expressible, blood-red with passion, and not the invisible pain of a ghost like me. Sometimes my head filled with a scream that went on for hours but was silenced by the dungeon walls of the closet. My face still wearing its social smile fixed in place as if by a stroke.

Let's go sit with Paul, they all said to their dates in the dinner line. *He's so funny.*

51

At the end of the twentieth century many Americans are coming to believe that adolescence has become so prolonged and socially diffuse that it is hardly a stage of development any longer, but a way of life. This is effectively captured in the following article from the Los Angeles Times *(1997).*

Adulthood?
Later, Dude!

D. James Romero

Adulthood has become a dirty word in America. No one, it seems, wants to live the Cleaver life. Some would just as soon be in prison as be beholden to family, job and community. They see it as the antithesis of freedom. Others dream of suburbia and strollers, but simply don't have the means.

That much is clear on a gleaming day along the bustling row of bars, restaurants and boutiques that line Pasadena's Colorado Boulevard.

"I'm basically still in the process of growing up," says waiter Domenico Fragomeno, 24, as he stands in the doorway of La Dolce Vita. "I'm working day to day to get my own home, my own business, my own family. I hope it will happen . . . in the next five to eight years."

Down the block, Joseph Ferris pooh-poohs such idealized visions of adulthood.

"Adults are boring," the 54-year-old bachelor says as he sits in a darkened saloon, pitcher of beer at his side, book at the fore. "They have to be too responsible and worry about things that should not be worried about—possessions."

What's happening here?

America, some say, has become a nation of adolescents. The nation has been transformed so that self-indulgence takes precedence over family values, some experts argue. As some people in their 30s, 40s, and 50s see no need to take charge of the world in the way their parents once did, the very young—adolescents and teens—are sometimes forced to act old prematurely for lack of guiding hands.

As the clock ticks toward 2000, it becomes clear that adulthood is what you make of it. No longer is 18 a ticket to ride into a world of responsibility, family and ethics. These have been reduced to lifestyle choices in a lifetime of endless choices. Being grown up is but a dull subculture with its own fashion (wood-paneled sportutes), clubs (Price Club) and music (can you say "anthology?").

"Adulthood," contends the cynical cyber zine Suck, "sucks."

The grown-up state of mind is coming at later and later ages, if at all. Many culture watchers and sociologists argue that true adulthood in America is post-poned until at least after 30. It comes, they say, when people master responsibilities—ethics, finances, psychological stability—worthy of parent-hood, regardless of whether they have children. Dictionaries list the word, a mix of Latin and French, as meaning the end of childhood, or the state of full physical and mental development.

Statistically, fewer people fit these definitions. Those ages 35 and older account for 43% of reported cocaine-related hospital emergencies, according to the National Household Survey on Drug Abuse—more than double the percentage for that age group in 1980. At the same time, there was a 76% rise in violent crime arrests for the 30–49 age group from 1980 to 1995, according to Michael A. Males, author of *The Scapegoat Generation: America's War on Adolescents* (Common Courage Press, 1996).

Meanwhile, people stay in school longer (nearly half of those ages 35–54 attend adult and college courses), marry later (age 25 for the average woman, versus 21 in 1970; 27 for the average man, versus 23 in 1970), buy homes later (one-fifth of 25-year-olds live with parents) and get divorced faster (nearly half of all marriages end in divorce).

Diane Crispell, executive editor of *American Demographics* magazine, says there's one very good reason people are growing up at older ages: money.

Higher paying jobs go to those who have better educations, so people stay in school and reach for higher degrees. Housing prices are through the roof (the Census Bureau reports that two-thirds of those ages 25 to 34 can't afford a median-priced home in their area), so twentysomethings rent. The cost of living is at an all-time high, so young people take on college-style living arrangements with roommates or stay at home with Mom or Dad.

"Becoming a fully fledged adult is taking longer," Crispell says, "partly because you have lots more people going to college for at least four years. There's a sense in college at any age that you are still a dependent and you are not required to fully grow up.

"Then there is the delay in marriage and home buying, which is an extension of the idea of spending more time to think about their lives and trying to do it right."

Author Gail Sheehy blames expanding life spans for prolonged adolescence. Average life expectancy is 75 and rising, with some experts predicting that people will live well into the triple digits in the next few decades. That pushes all phases of life into older years. Adolescence reaches into the 20s, midlife into the 50s.

Yet author Neil Howe, one of the country's foremost experts on generational sociology, takes a bit different view. He says each generation has its own tempo for turning adult, and that it's not necessarily young adults who are acting like kids. In fact, people in their 20s and 30s actually grew up fast, he maintains.

"They grew up at a time of massive child under-protection," Howe says, "so they raised themselves."

With nearly half of them products of broken homes, young people are fiercely mobile and nomadic—"quick to jump ship" in work life, living arrangements and love life.

"Their lifestyle is one of great autonomy," Howe says. "They're redefining adulthood."

Indeed.

"I have grown-up responsibilities, like paying for my rent and school," says Heather Garner, 22, a marine biology major at USC, whose parents divorced. She has supported herself since she was 18, working at such places as Banana Republic, an upscale chain store where she sells clothes. "Adulthood means being true to yourself—no longer depending on others."

Baby boomers are said to have pioneered prolonged adolescence by tripping in the '60s, dancing in the '70s, snorting in the '80s—all the while challenging traditional sex, race and class roles. More than anything, Howe says, the questioning of values defined their relationship with adulthood. If that meant long hair and bong tokes, civil disobedience, even conservative reactivity, it was all in the name of weighing values. . . .

The term "coming of age" was coined more than a century ago by French sociologists to describe dying as a child and being reborn as an adult. Sometime during the 20th century, traditional agrarian rites welcoming the young into cultural, religious and matrimonial adulthood—American "sweet 16s," Jewish bar mitzvahs, Mexican *quinceañeras*—lost any ties to coming of age and were transformed into teenage house parties.

"Today," Howe says, "coming out doesn't have that kind of clarity. It's no longer clear who in society is supposed to contribute and who is supposed to be dependent."

That is the main assertion of Robert Bly, author of *The Sibling Society* (Addison Wesley, 1996).

"People don't bother to grow up," he writes, "and we are all fish swimming in a tank of half adults."

Elders are unwilling to lead, even when implored, Bly has argued, and thus new generations are left to wallow in a childlike state without grown-ups to help "pull the adolescents over that mysterious line drawn on the ground into adulthood."

At the same time, kids are forced to act like adults because many adults abandon parental responsibility. Teenagers, Bly writes, "seem to have a kind of emotional knowledge that is far older than they are."

Argues author Males: "Kids today are being raised by the most violent, drug-abusing parents in history."

This leads to what Bly refers to as "the leveling process"—kids grow up fast while adults act young, and we are left with a nation of siblings.

But R. U. Sirius, Bay Area cyber-culture expert and author, says people can be responsible without acting under traditional—and perhaps outdated—notions of adulthood.

"Adulthood is an authoritarian concept," says Sirius, 45, and never married. "To have to adhere to some handed-down set of behaviors and values is intrusive.

"I think it's clear that just like everything else in our culture, the definitions of adulthood are up for grabs."

A Father Uses the Shingle on His Son, c. 1897. Courtesy American Antiquarian Society.

Part Four

Discipline

Beliefs and practices concerning the disciplining of children evolved dramatically in the the first three centuries of American history. In the colonial period child discipline was both harsh and consistent, but over time new religious views, changing attitudes toward childhood, and new democratic social patterns radically altered beliefs and introduced enormous variety in the practices of an increasingly complex population.

Two conflicting approaches to discipline have emerged in the late twentieth century. On the one hand, child-rearing manuals oppose the use of corporal punishment in any form. On the other hand, in response to growing violence in some schools and the disturbing increase of very young murderers, the law has begun to treat children harshly, especially those who commit violent crimes. Today the death penalty can be imposed on sixteen-year-olds.

52

*In seventeenth-century New England discipline was a critical part of the hierarchi-
cal structure of the household. The community expected parents to discipline their
children and use severe corporal punishment when necessary, but there were limits
on this discipline as historian John Demos makes clear in the following (1970).*

Family Life in Plymouth Colony

John Demos

Egalitarianism formed no part of seventeenth-century assumptions about the
proper relationship of parents and children. But at Plymouth this relationship
involved a set of *reciprocal* obligations.

From the standpoint of the child, the Biblical commandment to "Honor thy
father and mother" was fundamental—and the force of law stood behind it. The
relevant statute directed that "If any Childe or Children above sixteen years old,
and of competent Understanding, shall Curse or Smite their Natural Father or
Mother; he or they shall be put to Death, unless it can be sufficiently testified
that the Parents have been very Unchristianly negligent in the Education of such
Children, or so provoked them by extreme and cruel Correction, that they have
been forced thereunto, to preserve themselves from Death or Maiming." A corollary order prescribed similar punishment for behavior that was simply "Stubborn or Rebellious"—or indeed, for any sort of habitual disobedience.

The rightful authority of the parents is clear enough here, but it should also
be noted that this authority was limited in several ways. In the first place, a child
less than sixteen years old was excluded from these prescriptions; he was not
mature enough to be held finally responsible for his actions. Disobedience and
disrespect on the part of younger children were surely punished, but on an
informal basis and within the family itself. In such cases, presumably, the purpose of punishment was to form right habits; it was part of a whole pattern of
learning. But for children of more than sixteen different assumptions applied.
Ultimate responsibility could now be imputed, and an offense against one's
parents was also an offense against the basic values of the community. Hence the
full retributive process of the laws might properly be invoked.

The clause relating to "extreme and cruel correction" implied a second limitation on parental power. The child did have the right to protect his own person
from any action that threatened "Death or Maiming." Finally, it seems significant

that the arbiter of *all* such questions was not the parental couple directly involved but rather the constituted authorities of the Colony as a whole. The correct response to gross disobedience in a child was as follows: "his Father and Mother, . . . [shall] lay hold on him, and bring him before the Magistrates assembled in Court, and testifie unto them, that their Son is Stubborn and Rebellious, and will not obey their voice and chastisement." This may sound rather menacing, but it did imply an important kind of negative. The parents shall *not* take matters completely into their own hands. The child shall also have *his* say in Court; and presumably he may try, if he wishes, to show that his behavior was provoked by some cruelty on the part of his parents.

It must be said that only a few cases of youthful disobedience to parents actually reached the Courts, and that these few are not very revealing. Certainly the death penalty was never invoked on such grounds; only once, in fact, was it even mentioned as a possibility. In 1679 "Edward Bumpus for stricking and abusing his parents, was whipt att the post; his punishment was alleviated in regard hee was crasey brained, otherwise hee had bine put to death or otherwise sharply punished." In other instances the Court's function was to mediate between the affected parties or to ratify an agreement which had already been worked out on an informal basis. In 1669, for instance, it heard various testimonies about the "crewell, unnaturall, and extreame passionate carriages" of one Mary Morey toward her son Benjamin, and his own "unbeseeming" response. The situation was described as being so "turbulent . . . that severall of the naighbours feared murder would be in the issue of it." Yet in the end the Court took no action beyond admonishing both principals and making them "promise reformation." Some years earlier Thomas Lumbert of Barnstable complained formally that "Jedediah, his sone, hath carryed stuburnly against his said father," and proposed that the boy be "freed, provided hee doe dispose himselfe in some honest family with his fathers consent." The Court merely recorded this arrangement and decided not to interfere directly unless Jedediah neglected to find himself a good foster home. In sum, then, the role of the Court with regard to specific cases of this type, was quite limited. The laws on the matter should be viewed as expressing broad and basic values rather than an actual pattern of intervention in the day-to-day affairs of Old Colony households. In fact, most parents must have tried to define and enforce their authority very much on an individual basis. Quite likely an appeal to the Courts was a last resort, to be undertaken only with a keen sense of failure and personal humiliation. . . .

But if the child owed his parents an unceasing kind of obedience and respect, there were other obligations which applied in the reverse direction. The parent for his part must accept responsibility for certain basic needs of his children— for their physical health and welfare, for their education (understood in the broadest sense), and for the property they would require in order one day to "be for themselves." There were, moreover, legal provisions permitting the community to intervene in the case of parents who defaulted on these obligations. One statute affirmed that when "psons in this Gourment are not able to provide Competent and convenient food and raiment for theire Children," the latter might be taken in hand by local officials and placed in foster families where they would be more "comfortably provided for." Another, more extended set of enactments dealt with the whole educational side of the parental role. Children should be taught to read, "at least to be able duely to read the Scriptures." They should be made to understand "the Capital Laws" and "the main Grounds and Principles of Christian Religion." And they should be trained "in some honest lawful calling, labour or employment, that may be profitable for themselves, or the Country." Parents who neglected any of this were subject to fines; and once again the ultimate recourse of transferring children into new families might be applied if the neglect were habitual. Unfortunately we cannot discover how often these procedures were actually set in motion. The responsibility for specific cases was assigned to local authorities in the various towns, and records of their actions have not survived. But the basic intent behind the laws which covered such matters is clear—and in itself significant.

53

Most orphans and other children were "put to service" (indentured) under a master. While the community allowed severe discipline, the law also protected the child servant from extreme abuse, as revealed in these seventeenth-century Massachusetts court records. In the first case, the master was found guilty of manslaughter in the death of his twelve-year-old servant; in the second the master was fined and warned.

Protecting Children from Abusing Masters

Colonial Documents

Massachusetts Court Order, 1655

We, whose names are underwritten, being appointed a jury by Master John Alden to view the dead body of John Walker, servant to Robert Latham, of this town, and to find the cause how he came to his untimely end:

We, upon due search and examination, do find that the body of John Walker was blackish and blue, and the skin broken in divers places from the middle to the hair of his head, viz., all his back with stripes given him by his master, Robert Latham, as Robert himself did testify; and also we found a bruise of his left arm, and one of his left hip, and one great bruise of his breast; and there was the knuckles of one hand and one of his fingers frozen, and also both his heels frozen, and one of the heels the flesh was much broken, and also one of his little toes frozen and very much perished, and one of his great toes frozen, and also the side of his foot frozen; and also, upon the reviewing the body, we found three gaules like holes in the hams, which we formerly, the body being frozen, thought they had been holes; and also we find that the said John was forced to carry a log which was beyond his strength, which he endeavoring to do, the log fell upon him, and he, being down, had a stripe or two, as Joseph Beedle doth testify; and we find that it was some few days before his death . . . and also we find the flesh much broken of the knees of John Walker, and that he did want sufficient food and clothing and lodging, and that the said John did constantly wet his bed and his clothes, lying in them, and so suffered by it, his clothes being frozen about him; and that the said John was put forth in the extremity of cold, though thus unabled by lameness and soreness to perform what was required;

and therefore in respect of cruelty and hard usage he died; and also, upon the second review, the dead corpse did bleed at the nose.

[Signatures of twelve men]

Massachusetts Court Record, c. 1680–85

Phillip Fowler was presented for abusing his servant, Richard Parker, and although court justified any person in giving meet correction to his servant, which the boy deserved, yet they did not approve of the manner of punishment given in hanging him up by the heels as butchers do beasts for the slaughter, and cautioned said Fowler against such kind of punishment. He was ordered to pay costs.

54

John Locke's ideas on disciplining children were influential with American parents in the eighteenth century. Locke urged parents not to use the rod; rather, they should inculcate self-discipline in their children, and not give in to children's whims and cravings (1690).

Inculcating Self-Discipline

John Locke

§103. I told you before that children love *liberty* and therefore they should be brought to do the things [that] are fit for them without feeling any restraint laid upon them. I now tell you they love something more: and that is *dominion*; and this is the first origin of most vicious habits that are ordinary and natural. This love of *power* and dominion shows itself very early, and that in these two things:

§104. 1. We see children (as soon almost as they are born, I am sure long before they can speak) cry, grow peevish, sullen, and out of humor, for nothing but to have their *wills*. They would have their desires submitted to by others; they contend for a ready compliance from all about them, especially from those that stand near or beneath them in age or degree, as soon as they come to consider others with those distinctions. . . .

§106. 1. That a child should never be suffered to have what he *craves*, much less what he *cries for*, I would have said *or so much as speaks for*. But that being apt to be misunderstood and interpreted as if I meant a child should never speak to his parents for anything, which will perhaps be thought to lay too great a curb on the minds of children to the prejudice of that love and affection which should be between them and their parents, I shall explain myself a little more particularly. It is fit that they should have liberty to declare their wants to their parents and that with all tenderness they should be hearkened to and supplied at least whilst they are very little. But it is one thing to say, I am hungry; another to say, I would have roast meat. Having declared their wants, their natural wants, the pain they feel from hunger, thirst, cold, or any other necessity of nature, it is the duty of their parents and those about them to relieve them; but children must leave it to the choice and ordering of their parents what they think properest for them and how much, and must not be permitted to choose for themselves and say, I would have wine or white bread; the very naming of it should make them lose it.

§107. That which parents should take care of here is to distinguish between the wants of fancy and those of nature, which Horace has well taught them to do in this verse: *Queis humana sibi doleat natura negatis.*

Those are truly natural wants which reason alone, without some other help, is not able to fence against nor keep from disturbing us. The pains of sickness and hurts, hunger, thirst, and cold, want of sleep and rest or relaxation of the part wearied with labor are what all men feel; and the best disposed minds cannot but be sensible of their uneasiness and therefore ought by fit applications to seek their removal, though not with impatience or overgreat haste upon the first approaches of them where delay does not threaten some irreparable harm. The pains that come from the necessities of nature are monitors to us to beware of greater mischiefs, which they are the forerunners of, and therefore they must not be wholly neglected nor strained too far. But yet the more children can be inured to hardships of this kind by a wise care to make them stronger in body and mind, the better it will be for them. I need not here give any caution to keep within the bounds of doing them good and to take care that what children are made to suffer should neither break their spirits nor injure their health, parents being but too apt of themselves to incline, more than they should, to the softer side.

But whatever compliance the necessities of nature may require, the wants of fancy children should never be gratified in nor suffered to *mention.* The very *speaking* for any such thing should make them lose it. Clothes, when they need, they must have; but if they *speak* for this stuff or that color, they should be sure to go without it. Not that I would have parents purposely cross the desires of their children in matters of indifferency: on the contrary, where their carriage deserves it, and one is sure it will not corrupt or effeminate their minds and make them fond of trifles, I think all things should be contrived, as much as could be, to their satisfaction that they might find the ease and pleasure of doing well. The best for children is that they should not place any pleasure in such things at all nor regulate their delight by their fancies, but be indifferent to all that nature has made so. This is what their parents and teachers should chiefly aim at; but till this be obtained, all that I oppose here is the liberty of *asking,* which in these things of conceit ought to be restrained by a constant forfeiture annexed to it.

This may perhaps be thought a little too severe by the natural indulgence of tender parents: but yet it is no more than necessary. For since the method I propose is to banish the rod, this restraint of their tongues will be of great use to settle that awe we have elsewhere spoken of and to keep up in them the respect and reverence due to their parents. Next, it will teach them to keep in and so master their inclinations. By this means they will be brought to learn the art of stifling their desires as soon as they rise up in them, when they are easiest to be subdued. For giving vent gives life and strength to our appetites, and he that has the confidence to turn his wishes into demands will be but a little way from thinking he ought to obtain them. This, I am sure, everyone can more easily bear a denial from himself than from anybody else. They should therefore be accus-

tomed betimes to consult and make use of their reason before they give allowance to their inclinations. 'Tis a great step towards the mastery of our desires to
give this stop to them and shut them up in silence. This habit, got by children, of
staying the forwardness of their fancies and deliberating whether it be fit or no
before they *speak*, will be of no small advantage to them in matters of greater
consequence in the future course of their lives. For that which I cannot too often
inculcate is that, whatever the matter be about which it is conversant, whether
great or small, the main (I had almost said only) thing to be considered in every
action of a child is what influence it will have upon his mind; what habit it tends
to and is likely to settle in him; how it will become him when he is bigger; and
if it be encouraged, whither it will lead him when he is grown up.

For nineteenth-century parents, control of the child was an important goal, but affection was considered important too, according to the historian Carl N. Degler (1980).

Introducing Children into the Social Order

Carl N. Degler

A time-honored way of raising children has been to coerce them physically, thereby inculcating not only proper behavior but perhaps proper thoughts as well. And just because the ends were so important, physical disciplining occurred early in the life of the child, not only prior to the 19th century but in the years after 1800 as well. The immediate purpose of this early discipline was to subdue the child's self-assertiveness. Until that was done, it was then believed, little true education or spiritual growth could be expected. Historian Lawrence Stone tells us that in early 17th-century England, schools and parents alike undertook, as contemporaries put it, "to break the child's will." One 17th-century New England minister, for example, ruefully observed that "there is in all children . . . a stubbornness and stoutness of mind, arising from natural pride, which must in the first place be broken and beaten down." He further advised parents that "children should not know, if it could be kept from them, that they have a will of their own."

In 17th-century England whipping was one of the favorite ways of breaking the child's will. The practice was so common that when one theologian sought to be graphic in describing the torments of Hell he said that they were "worse a thousand times than whippings," and that "God's anger is worse than your father's anger." The common use of the whip or cane in disciplining children in the early modern period is suggested by a comment made by King Henry IV of France to the governess of his son, the future King Louis XII. "I have a complaint to make," Henry began, "you do not send word that you have whipped my son. I wish to command you to whip him every time that he is obstinate or mischievous, knowing well for myself that there is nothing in the world which will be better for him than that. I know it from experience, having myself profited, for when I was his age I was often whipped. That is why," the King concluded, "I want you to whip him and to make him understand why." Whipping of children and other dependents persisted well into the 18th century. In the diary of William Byrd children seem to be whipped for little or nothing. And sometimes even more violent methods were used; Byrd claimed to have forced a child to drink "a pint of piss" for wetting the bed.

The idea that it was imperative to "break the will" of the child continued into the 19th century. The new child-rearing literature that began to appear in large quantities in the 1830s and 1840s stressed the need to subdue the child early and at almost any cost. "No child," wrote Theodore Dwight in a book of advice to fathers in 1834, "has ever been known since the earliest period of the world, to be destitute of an evil disposition—however sweet it appears." Dwight's implication, however, that children were innately depraved was not typical of child-rearing thinking at that time. He expressed a line of thought that was by then outmoded. More typical was Lydia Maria Child, writer and abolitionist, who specifically denied any belief in infant depravity, however much she believed in control over the child. It was necessary, she insisted, to provide a good environment if the child's "bad propensities" were to be kept under control until he was able to resist evil on his own. "Evil," she wrote in 1831, "is within and without." By the early 19th century, the breaking of the child's will was as much for the future benefit of the child as for any other consideration. That, too, marked a change from earlier centuries.

The concern expressed in the child-rearing literature for early control over the child appears again and again in the letters of parents as well. In 1860, for example, Mary Mallard described her two-year-old daughter to a close female friend: "She is a child of wonderful life and great activity of mind, so that I have constantly to be on my guard; and she often gets into trouble." She then went on to say it was "no easy matter rightly to control a child," but that she had no doubt that control was essential for proper upbringing. By way of illustration she recounted an incident of a few evenings earlier. After the father had reproved his young daughter for some act of misconduct, the child turned and looked at her father "in the most quizzical way and said; 'Oh, darling, don't talk so; you will scare this child into fits!'" Mary Mallard's pointed conclusion from the incident was that "native depravity shows itself pretty often, but I hope in a few months more she will be quite an obedient little girl." The incident is doubly revealing; it shows not only a clear parental concern for controlling the child, but also a mildness of reaction that is typically 19th-century. No 18th-century parent would have ignored such a challenge. Mary Mallard's mother also testified to a concern about controlling children. In writing to her widower son Charles about his daughter, who was being reared by her, she noted the progress of the two-year-old and concluded with the observation, "I do not think she will ever be a difficult child to govern."

How to "govern" a child was Mary Waterman Rice's concern, too, in 1875 when she wrote to her father about her baby, then only twelve weeks old. After pointing out how attractive he was and how pleased she was to have him, she noted that "the other side of the story is . . . that even at this early age he shows that he possesses a furious temper and a most determined will, and I anticipate trouble in the future, if we [are] not very judicious in his government." The problem of control, of course, could become more serious as the children matured. Thus some mothers, like Juliet Janin, took measures to anticipate problems of discipline and control. When she was in New York in 1847 with her three young sons, she allowed only two of them to take the ferry to Staten Island. "I kept Louis with me because I feared he would be too wild and dispute with his brothers," she wrote her husband. "There is not a milder, better behaved boy than he is when by himself and with those who will give up to him, but with older boys and his brothers who will not, he appears in a different light. He is very self-willed and passionate and unstable to a degree—that is alarming. Those are the worst traits of his character."

Control over her sons was just as important to Charlena Anderson as it was to Juliet Janin, but her confidence was less. In 1881 she wrote her husband that her two sons, neither of whom was yet six years old, were "a great care, the little rascals. Balfour does not mind a whipping in the least," she reported, suggesting that she had tried her hand at that in her husband's absence; "and Playfair is growing bold and it keeps me busy to study out different ways of keeping them in check." Then she offered a succinct statement of her view of the responsibility for discipline and its justification. "I shall be glad when you get with them again to *help* in the responsibility of controlling them, and I know how much their character will depend upon how they are governed."

If concern with subduing the will of the child and "governing" it properly did not alter substantially from the 17th to the 19th century, the way in which that governance was accomplished certainly did. The idea that whipping was good for the child—as Henry IV had said and which many 17th- and 18th-century parents believed—was generally frowned upon by 19th-century middle-class parents and the advice books they read. "Affectionate persuasion addressed to the understanding, the conscience, and the heart," advised Herman Humphrey in *Domestic Education* in 1840, "is the grand instrument to be employed in family government." Whipping, the advice books told them, should be only a last resort. In 1847 Augusta Larned, in her book *Talks with Girls*, put physical punishment at the end of a list of six devices for controlling children. The first, significantly, was "love," the second "reason," and the third "authority." The shift, of course, reflected the new appreciation of children and the sentimentality toward them that had been growing ever since the dawning of Romanticism. Nor was it accidental that the decline of physical punishment coincided with the rise in the importance of women within the family and their increasing concentration upon child-rearing and home. As the gentler sex, traditionally, it was only to be expected that under their aegis a more gentle approach would be taken toward children.

As the listing in *Talks with Girls* makes clear, however, physical punishment was not prohibited even in the late 19th century. Instead there was a shift in priorities rather than an abandonment of physical coercion. In fact, as we saw in the last chapter, as late as the 1860s William Pender was justifying whipping in almost the same terms that Henry IV had used. And one mother in 1834 wrote in *Mother's Magazine* of her efforts to subdue her sixteen-month-old daughter's will, offering us, thereby, a good illustration of how whipping was no longer the first step to control, though it was not dropped entirely. Because the child would not say "dear mama" on her father's orders, the mother banished the child to a room alone. Although she screamed wildly for ten minutes, she still would not comply with the mother's command. It was at that point that the mother spanked the child before putting her back into the room. After four hours of isolation, the child complied with her parent's demand.

A missionary couple, living on the Oregon frontier in the 1840s, also resorted to physical violence to induce proper behavior in their children. When two-year-old Cyrus Walker was told by his father to say please in asking for milk, the child refused, even though denied the milk. "He has gone to sleep with a smile of exultation depicted on his countenance," his mother recorded in her diary. "I hope if he is ever called to suffer at the stake he will be as unrelenting." The parents' reaction to a stubborn child, however, took a different turn with another son in 1846. Again the child was only two years of age; he requested some sugar. The mother told him to say please, but the child would only repeat, "I want some sugar." At that juncture the mother decided "to try the rod which I continued to do with increasing severity till his father came when I delivered him to him, and he followed the same course till noon when the child became so much exhausted that we concluded to let him sleep, but he did not seem to yield at all." After he had awakened, apparently refreshed, they resolved not to give him any food or drink until he said "please." The response was "I don't want to say please." He was then put to bed without food. The next morning he was beaten again until "we feared to longer." No temptations of food or drink moved the child, even though he had been without either for more than twenty-four hours. And apparently he never did yield, though that is not clear since the diary is damaged. But once food and drink had been given him he did say "please" many times. The experience shook the mother's confidence in the use of physical punishment. "I regret the course we pursued," she conceded once he began freely to say "please," even though she did "not perceive that he is much injured by it except for the time but less severity would I think have been just as well." Her reasoning was revealing since it seemed to stem from her equating the child's personality with her own. "I often fear being guilty of the very thing for which I punish my child."

Other more sophisticated 19th-century parents found it necessary to use physical coercion when less violent means failed. But there, too, the use was reluctant. Mary Waterman Rice, who had predicted trouble in governing her newborn child, reported to her father ten years later in 1885 that she had broken his favorite hairbrush while giving her son a spanking. She wrote that since the boy had disobeyed her on two recent occasions, "I saw that a spanking was an immediate and positive necessity, and I do not generally do things by halves, therefore the spanking was a good and complete one, but I did make *halves* out of your brush."

Although physical punishment continued to be used, less violent means were usually relied upon for the control and discipline of children. The internalizing of proper standards of behavior, which John Locke had advocated at the end of the 17th century, had become the practice as well as the ideal by the early 19th century. Rather than continual correction of the child, the Victorian aim was to develop in the child early in its life a proper sense of self that made further correction unnecessary. To achieve this Lockean ideal, 19th-century parents resorted to a variety of devices, not all of them novel, among which physical punishment was the last to be taken up. (Locke himself advised against any physical chastisement.) Much more common were shaming, playing upon the child's guilt, and depriving the child of company, food, or self-respect. Again, the cause for the change probably should be sought in the new prominence of women within the family. It is not surprising that 19th-century women would resort to verbal means of control like shaming, arousing guilt, or denying love.

In Catharine Sedgwick's widely read novel *Home* (1835), the method whereby the rod is spared and the child is saved was graphically depicted. When young Wallace Barclay impetuously threw his sister's kitten into a pot of boiling water because the animal had torn his kite, he was neither whipped nor even deprived of food. Instead he was removed from the company of the family by being sent to his room for all the hours he was not at school. The intention was to cause him to think about the enormity of his deed. After considerable rumination Wallace told his father that he believed he could now resist temptation and control his temper. Twice, he reported to his father, he had been provoked by comrades at school, but in both instances he had successfully resisted. The father gave his blessing to the boy, convinced that the lesson had been well learned.

56

A new solicitude for children became notable in the mid-nineteen century. This new tenderness and concern were apparent in the gentler discipline promoted by the influential minister and religious educator Horace Bushnell in Christian Nurture *(1849).*

A Milder and Warmer Family Government

Horace Bushnell

There is, then, to be such a thing as penalty, or punishment, in the government of the house. And here again is a place where large consideration is requisite. First of all, it should be threatened as seldom as possible, and next as seldom executed as possible. It is a most wretched and coarse barbarity that turns the house into a penitentiary, or house of correction. Where the management is right in other respects, punishment will be very seldom needed. And those parents who make it a point of fidelity, that they keep the flail of chastisement always a going, have a better title to the bastinado themselves than to any Christian congratulations. The punishments dispensed should never be such as have a character of ignominy; and therefore, except in cases of really ignominious wickedness, it would be better to avoid, as far as may be, the infliction of pain upon the person. For the same reason the discipline should, if possible, be entirely private; a matter between the parent and child. Thus it is well said by Dr. Tiersch, "If ever a severe punishment is necessary, it must be carried out so as to spare the child's self-respect; not in the presence of his brothers and sisters, nor of the servants. For a wholesome terror to the others, it is enough if they perceive, at a distance, something of that which happens. And if only the smallest triumph over his misfortune, the least degree of mockery arise, bitterness and a loss of self-respect are the consequences to the child."

Punishments should be severe enough to serve their purpose; and gentle enough to show, if possible, a tenderness that is averse from the infliction. There is no abuse more shocking, than when they are administered by sheer impatience, or in a fit of passion. Nor is the case at all softened, when they are administered without feeling, in a manner of uncaring hardness. Whenever the sad necessity arrives, there should be time enough taken, after the wrong or detection, to produce a calm and thoughtful revision; and a just concern for the wrong, as evinced by the parent, should be wakened, if possible, in the child. I would not be understood, however, in advising this more tardy and delicate way of proceeding, to justify no exceptions. There are cases, now and then, in the outrageous and shocking misconduct of some boy, where an explosion is wanted; where the father represents God best, by some terrible outburst of indignant violated feeling, and becomes an instant avenger, without any counsel or preparation whatever. Nothing else expresses fitly what is due to such kind of conduct. And there is many a grown up man, who will remember such an hour of discipline, as the time when the ploughshare of God's truth went into his soul like redemption itself. That was the shock that woke him up to the staunch realities of principle; and he will recollect that father, as God's minister, typified to all dearest, holiest, reverence, by the pungent indignations of that time.

There is great importance in the closing of a penal discipline. Thus it should be a law never to cease from the discipline begun, whatever it be, till the child is seen to be in a feeling that justifies the discipline. He is never to be let go, or sent away, sulking, in a look of willfulness unsubdued. Indeed, he should even be required always to put on a pleasant, tender look, such as clears all clouds and shows a beginning of fair weather. No reproof, or discipline, is rightly administered till this point is reached. Nothing short of this changed look gives any hope of a changed will. On the other hand, when the face of disobedience brightens out into this loving and dutiful expression, it not only shows that the malice of wrong is gone by, but, possibly, that there is entered into the heart some real beginning of right, some spirit of really Christian obedience. Many a child is bowed to holy principle itself, at the happy and successful close of what, to human eyes, is only a chapter of discipline.

57

Louisa May Alcott's novel Little Women *(1868) reflects a more liberal view of discipline. She portrays the mother, Marmee, as the embodiment of new, feminine values that emphasize kindness and gentleness in child rearing. The emphasis is also on hard-won self-control.*

Learning Self-Control

Louisa May Alcott

"Laurie did it all; I only let her go. Mother, if she *should* die, it would be my fault;" and Jo dropped down beside the bed, in a passion of penitent tears, telling all that had happened, bitterly condemning her hardness of heart, and sobbing out her gratitude for being spared the heavy punishment which might have come upon her.

"It's my dreadful temper! I try to cure it; I think I have, and then it breaks out worse than ever. O mother, what shall I do? what shall I do?" cried poor Jo, in despair.

"Watch and pray, dear; never get tired of trying, and never think it is impossible to conquer your fault," said Mrs. March, drawing the blowzy head to her shoulder, and kissing the wet cheek so tenderly that Jo cried harder than ever.

"You don't know; you can't guess how bad it is! It seems as if I could do anything when I'm in a passion; I get so savage, I could hurt any one, and enjoy it. I'm afraid I *shall* do something dreadful some day, and spoil my life, and make everybody hate me. O mother, help me, do help me!"

"I will, my child, I will. Don't cry so bitterly, but remember this day, and resolve, with all your soul, that you will never know another like it. Jo, dear, we all have our temptations, some far greater than yours, and it often takes us all our lives to conquer them. You think your temper is the worst in the world; but mine used to be just like it."

"Yours, mother? Why, you are never angry!" and, for the moment, Jo forgot remorse in surprise.

"I've been trying to cure it for forty years, and have only succeeded in controlling it. I am angry nearly every day of my life, Jo; but I have learned not to show it; and I still hope to learn not to feel it, though it may take me another forty years to do so."

The patience and the humility of the face she loved so well was a better lesson to Jo than the wisest lecture, the sharpest reproof. She felt comforted at once by the sympathy and confidence given her; the knowledge that her mother had a fault like hers, and tried to mend it, made her own easier to bear and strengthened her resolution to cure it; though forty years seemed rather a long time to watch and pray, to a girl of fifteen.

"Mother, are you angry when you fold your lips tight together, and go out of the room sometimes, when Aunt March scolds, or people worry you?" asked Jo, feeling nearer and dearer to her mother than ever before.

"Yes, I've learned to check the hasty words that rise to my lips; and when I feel that they mean to break out against my will, I just go away a minute, and give myself a little shake, for being so weak and wicked," answered Mrs. March, with a sigh and a smile, as she smoothed and fastened up Jo's dishevelled hair.

"How did you learn to keep still? That is what troubles me—for the sharp words fly out before I know what I'm about; and the more I say the worse I get, till it's a pleasure to hurt people's feelings, and say dreadful things. Tell me how you do it, Marmee dear."

"My good mother used to help me—"

"As you do us—" interrupted Jo, with a grateful kiss.

"But I lost her when I was a little older than you are, and for years had to struggle on alone, for I was too proud to confess my weakness to any one else. I had a hard time, Jo, and shed a good many bitter tears over my failures; for, in spite of my efforts, I never seemed to get on. Then your father came, and I was so happy that I found it easy to be good. But by-and-by, when I had four little daughters round me, and we were poor, then the old trouble began again; for I am not patient by nature, and it tried me very much to see my children wanting anything."

"Poor mother! what helped you then?"

"Your father, Jo. He never loses patience—never doubts or complains—but always hopes, and works, and waits so cheerfully that one is ashamed to do otherwise before him. He helped and comforted me, and showed me that I must try to practise all the virtues I would have my little girls possess, for I was their example. It was easier to try for your sakes than for my own; a startled or surprised look from one of you, when I spoke sharply, rebuked me more than any words could have done; and the love, respect, and confidence of my children was the sweetest reward I could receive for my efforts to be the woman I would have them copy."

"O mother, if I'm ever half as good as you, I shall be satisfied," cried Jo, much touched.

"I hope you will be a great deal better, dear; but you must keep watch over your 'bosom enemy,' as father calls it, or it may sadden, if not spoil your life. You have had a warning; remember it, and try with heart and soul to master this quick temper, before it brings you greater sorrow and regret than you have known to-day."

"I will try, mother; I truly will. But you must help me, remind me, and keep me from flying out. I used to see father sometimes put his finger on his lips, and look at you with a very kind but sober face, and you always folded your lips tight or went away; was he reminding you then?" asked Jo softly.

"Yes; I asked him to help me so, and he never forgot it, but saved me from many a sharp word by that little gesture and kind look."

Jo saw that her mother's eyes filled and her lips trembled as she spoke; and, fearing that she had said too much, she whispered anxiously "Was it wrong to watch you, and to speak of it? I didn't mean to be rude, but it's so comfortable to say all I think to you, and feel so safe and happy here."

"My Jo, you may say anything to your mother, for it is my greatest happiness and pride to feel that my girls confide in me, and know how much I love them."

58

The nineteenth-century slave child experienced discipline in its most extreme form from his master, not his parents. James W. C. Pennington, a Presbyterian minister and an escaped slave, describes his whippings and dread of the overseer (1849).

The Life of a Slave Child

James W. C. Pennington

My feelings are always outraged when I hear [ministers] speak of "kind masters,"—"Christian masters,"—"the mildest form of slavery,"—"well fed and clothed slaves," as extenuations of slavery; I am satisfied they either mean to pervert the truth, or they do not know what they say. The being of slavery, its soul and body, lives and moves in the chattel principle, the property principle, the bill of sale principle; the cart-whip, starvation, and nakedness, are its inevitable consequences to a greater or less extent, warring with the dispositions of men. . . .

Another evil of slavery [is] . . . the want of parental care and attention. My parents were not able to give any attention to their children during the day. I often suffered much from hunger and other similar causes. To estimate the sad state of a slave child, you must look at it as a helpless human being thrown upon the world without the benefit of its natural guardians. It is thrown into the world without a social circle to flee to for hope, shelter, comfort, or instruction. The social circle, with all its heaven-ordained blessings, is of the utmost importance to the tender child; but of this, the slave child, however tender and delicate, is robbed.

There is another source of evil to slave children, which I cannot forbear to mention here, as one which early embittered my life,—I mean the tyranny of the master's children. My master had two sons, about the ages and sizes of my older brother and myself. We were not only required to recognize these young sirs as our young masters, but they felt themselves to be such; and, in consequence of this feeling, they sought to treat us with the same air of authority that their father did the older slaves.

Another evil of slavery that I felt severely about this time, was the tyranny and abuse of the overseers. These men seem to look with an evil eye upon children. I was once visiting a menagerie, and being struck with the fact, that the lion was comparatively indifferent to every one around his cage, while he eyed with peculiar keenness a little boy I had; the keeper informed me that such was always the case. Such is true of those human beings in the slave states, called overseers. They seem to take pleasure in torturing the children of slaves, long before they are large enough to be put at the hoe, and consequently under the whip.

We had an overseer, named Blackstone; he was an extremely cruel man to the working hands. He always carried a long hickory whip, a kind of pole. He kept three or four of these in order, that he might not at any time be without one.

I once found one of these hickories lying in the yard, and supposing that he had thrown it away, I picked it up, and boy-like, was using it for a horse; he came from the field, and seeing me with it, fell upon me with the one he then had in his hand, and flogged me most cruelly. From that, I lived in constant dread of that man; and he would show how much he delighted in cruelty by chasing me from my play with threats and imprecations. I have lain for hours in a wood, or behind a fence, to hide from his eye.

59

After World War II, Dr. Benjamin Spock's manual Baby and Child Care *(first published in 1945) quickly eclipsed all others in popularity and influence. Spock discarded much of John B. Watson's insistence on conditioning, shifted the emphasis to affection and emotional sustenance, and discouraged the use of physical punishment. His mode of child rearing is often described as permissive since it moves away from discipline toward loving acceptance.*

Managing Young Children

Benjamin Spock

Is Punishment Necessary?

The only sensible answer is that many good parents feel that they have to punish once in a while. But other parents find that they can successfully manage their children without ever having to punish. A lot depends on how the parents were brought up. If they were punished occasionally for good cause, they naturally expect to have to punish in similar situations. And if they were kept in line by positive guidance alone, they are apt to find that they can do the same with their children.

On the other hand, there are also a fair number of poorly behaved children. The parents of some of them punish a lot and the parents of others never do. So we can't say either that punishment always works or that lack of it always works. It all depends on the nature of the parents' discipline in general.

Before we go further with the subject of punishment, we ought to realize that it is *never* the main element in discipline—it's only a vigorous additional reminder that the parents feel strongly about what they say. We have all seen children who were slapped and spanked and deprived plenty, and yet remained ill-behaved. Many chronic criminals have spent half their adult years in jail, and yet each time they get out they promptly become involved in another crime.

The main source of good discipline is growing up in a loving family—being loved and learning to love in return. We want to be kind and cooperative (most of the time) because we like people and want them to like us. (Habitual criminals are people who in childhood were never loved enough to make much difference to them, and many of them were abused, besides.) Children gradually lessen their grabbing and begin to share, somewhere around the age of 3 years, not primarily because they are reminded by their parents (though that may help some) but because their feelings toward other children—of enjoyment and affection—have developed sufficiently.

Another vital element is children's intense desire to be as much like their parents as possible. They work particularly hard at being polite and civilized and responsible in the 3-to-6-year-old period. They pretend very seriously to take care of their doll children, keep house, go out to work, as they see their parents do. A boy tries to be grown up just like his father in interests and manners, a girl like her mother.

Though children do the major share in civilizing themselves, through love and imitation, it still leaves plenty for parents to do, as all of you know. In automobile terms, the child supplies the power but the parents have to do the steering. Children's motives are good (most of the time), but they don't have the experience or the stability to stay on the road. The parents have to be saying, "No, crossing the street is too dangerous," "You can't play with that, you'll hurt someone," "Say thank you to Mrs. Griffin," "You have to come in now because lunch is ready," "You can't take the wagon home because it belongs to Harry," "You have to go to bed to grow big," etc., etc. How well the guidance works depends on such factors as whether the parents are reasonably consistent (nobody can be completely consistent, whether they mean what they say (are not just sounding off), and whether they are directing or prohibiting the child for a good reason (not just because they're feeling mean or bossy).

The everyday job of the parent, then, is to keep the child on the right track by means of firmness. (You don't sit by and watch a small child destroy something and then punish him afterward.) You come to punishment (if you use it at all) once in a while when your system of firmness breaks down. Maybe your son, sorely tempted, wonders whether you still mean the prohibition that you laid down a couple of months ago. Or maybe he is angry and misbehaves on purpose. Perhaps he breaks something that's very precious to you, by foolish carelessness. Or he's slightly rude to you at a moment when you are tense about another matter. Maybe he narrowly escapes being run over because he didn't look. Indignation or righteous anger wells up in you. At such a moment you punish, or at least you feel like punishing.

The best test of a punishment is whether it accomplishes what you are after, without having other serious effects. If it makes a child furious, defiant, and worse behaved than before, then it certainly is missing fire. If it seems to break the child's heart, then it's probably too strong for him. Every child reacts somewhat differently.

There are times when a child breaks a plate or rips his clothes because of accident or carelessness. If he gets along well with his parents, he feels just as unhappy as they do, and no punishment is needed. (In fact, you sometimes have to comfort him.) Jumping on a child who feels sorry already sometimes banishes his remorse and makes him argue.

If you're dealing with an older child who is always fooling with the dishes and breaking them, it may be fair to make him buy replacements from his allowance. A child beyond the age of 6 is developing a sense of justice and sees the fairness of reasonable penalties. However, I'd go light on the legalistic, "take-the-consequences" kind of punishment before 6, and I wouldn't try to use it at all before 3. You don't want a small child to develop a heavy sense of guilt. The job of a parent is to keep the child from getting into trouble rather than act as a severe judge after it's happened.

In the olden days children were spanked plenty, and nobody thought much about it. Then a reaction set in, and many parents decided that it was shameful. But that didn't settle everything. If parents keep themselves from spanking, they may show their irritation in other ways: for instance, by nagging the child for half the day, or trying to make him feel deeply guilty. I'm not particularly advocating spanking, but I think it is less poisonous than lengthy disapproval, because it clears the air, for parents and child. You sometimes hear it recommended that you never spank a child in anger but wait until you have cooled off. That seems unnatural. It takes a pretty grim parent to whip a child when the anger is gone.

Some parents find that putting a child in his room works well. One theoretical disadvantage is that it may make his room seem like a prison. Having the young child sit in a special chair for a few minutes is an effective reminder in some families.

Avoid threats as much as possible. They tend to weaken discipline. It may sound reasonable to say, "If you don't keep out of the street with your bicycle, I'll take it away." But in a sense a threat is a dare—it admits that the child may disobey. It should impress him more to be firmly told he must keep out of the street, if he knows from experience that his parents mean what they say. On the other hand, if you see that you may have to impose a drastic penalty like taking away a beloved bike for a few days, it's better to give fair warning. It certainly is silly, and quickly destroys all a parent's authority, to make threats that aren't ever carried out or that can't be carried out. Scary threats, such as of bogeymen and cops, are 100% wrong in all cases.

Parents Who Can't Control Their Children or Who Have to Punish Frequently Need Help

A few parents have extreme difficulty controlling their children. They say their child "won't obey" or that he's "just bad." The first thing you see when you watch such a parent (let's say it's a mother) is that she doesn't appear to be really trying, even though she wants to and thinks she is. She threatens or scolds or punishes frequently. But one such mother almost never carries out a threat. Another, though she punishes, never in the end makes the child do what she said he had to do. And another makes him obey once, but 5 minutes later and 10 minutes later she lets him get away with it. Another laughs in the middle of a scolding or punishment. Another just keeps shouting at the child that he's bad or asks a neighbor, right in front of the child, whether she ever saw a worse one.

Parents like these unconsciously expect the child's bad behavior to go right on and can do nothing effective to stop it. They are inviting it, without realizing it. Their scolding and punishing are only an expression of frustration. In their complaints to neighbors they are only hoping to get some comforting agreement that the child is truly impossible. Frustrated parents like these have often had an unsatisfactory childhood during which they never received sufficient assurance that they were basically good and well behaved. As a result they don't have enough confidence in themselves or in their children. They need a lot of help from a child guidance clinic or from a family social agency.

60

While corporal punishment was discouraged by Dr. Spock and others, the U.S. Supreme Court in 1975 affirmed the right of teachers to use corporal punishment even over the objections of parents.

Corporal Punishment

Middle District, North Carolina Court

Baker v. Owen

395 F. Supp. 294 (M.D.N.C.), *aff'd without opinion*, 423 U.S. 907 (1975)

Craven, Circuit Judge.

This three-judge court was convened to consider the claims of Russell Carl Baker and his mother that their constitutional rights were violated when Russell Carl was corporally punished by his teacher over his mother's objections and without procedural due process. Russell Carl, a sixth-grader, was paddled on December 6, 1973, for allegedly violating his teacher's announced rule against throwing kickballs except during designated play periods. Mrs. Baker had previously requested of Russell Carl's principal and certain teachers, that Russell Carl not be corporally punished, because she opposed it on principle. Nevertheless, shortly after his alleged misconduct her son received two licks in the presence of a second teacher and in view of other students.

Mrs. Baker alleges that the administration of corporal punishment after her objections violated her parental right to determine disciplinary methods for her child. Russell Carl charges that the circumstances in which the punishment was administered violated his right to procedural due process, and that the punishment itself in this instance amounted to cruel and unusual punishment. This special court was convened because both Mrs. Baker in her claim and Russell Carl in his procedural due process claim have challenged the constitutionality of North Carolina General Statutes §115-146. They claim that this statute, which empowers school officials to "use reasonable force in the exercise of lawful authority to restrain or correct pupils and to maintain order," is unconstitutional insofar as it allows corporal punishment over parental objection and absent adequate procedural safeguards.

We hold that fourteenth amendment liberty embraces the right of parents generally to control means of discipline of their children, but that the state has a countervailing interest in the maintenance of order in the schools, in this case sufficient to sustain the right of teachers and school officials to administer reasonable corporal punishment for disciplinary purposes. We also hold that teachers and school officials must accord to students minimal procedural due process in the course of inflicting such punishment. We further hold that the spanking of Russell Carl in this case did not amount to cruel and unusual punishment.

61

Youthful crime and the appropriate punishment for violent children became regular news issues in the late twentieth century. After a series of shootings of classmates by high school students in the 1990s, the public called for stricter punishments for youthful offenders (1998).

Cracking Down on Kids

Annette Fuentes

When Kipland Kinkel, Mitchell Johnson and Andrew Golden reportedly unloaded mini arsenals of guns at their classmates, they fulfilled the worst fears about young people that now dominate the nation's adult consciousness. Kinkel, 15, of Springfield, Oregon, allegedly is responsible for the deaths of two students as a result of an incident on May 21, as well as for the deaths of his parents. Johnson, 13, and Golden, 11, were charged in connection with the March 24 deaths of four students and a teacher in Jonesboro, Arkansas. All were instantly transformed from average American boys, perhaps a bit on the wild side, into evil incarnate. Forget that Mitchell sobbed next to his mother in court, or that Drew learned to sling a shotgun from Dad and Grandpa the way many boys learn to swing a bat. "Let 'em have it" was the sentiment, with catchy phrases like "adult crime, adult time."

After the Arkansas incident, Attorney General Janet Reno scoured federal laws for some way to prosecute Johnson and Golden so they could be locked up till age 21 if convicted, a stiffer sentence than the state could mete out. One *Washington Post* Op-Ed called for states to adopt a national uniform minimum age for juveniles to be tried as adults for violent crimes.

The three boys are believed to have committed terrible deeds, no question. But twenty years ago, a Greek chorus would have been clamoring to understand why they went bad. The events themselves would have been seen as aberrations. Redemption might have been mentioned, especially since these were not career delinquents. Instead, we have proposals like the one from Texas legislator Jim Pitts, who wants his state to use the death penalty on children as young as 11. And he's got plenty of support, because this is the era of crime and punishment and accountability for all constituencies without wealth or power to shield them. And the young are such a class of people.

In the past two decades, our collective attitude toward children and youth has undergone a profound change that's reflected in the educational and criminal justice systems as well as in our daily discourse. "Zero tolerance" is the mantra in public schools and juvenile courts, and what it really means is that to be young is to be suspect. Latino and black youth have borne the brunt of this growing criminalization of youth. But the trend has spilled over racial and ethnic boundaries—even class boundaries, to a degree. Youth, with all its innocence and vulnerability, is losing ground in a society that exploits both.

In fact, youth crime has not changed as dramatically as our perceptions of it. Data from the National Center for Juvenile Justice show that between 1987 and 1996, the number of juvenile arrests increased 35 percent. Juvenile violent-crime arrests were up 60 percent, but they represent a sliver of all juvenile arrests— about 5 percent of the 1996 total of 135,100. A 1997 study by the center found that "today's violent youth commits the same number of violent acts as his/her predecessor of 15 years ago." As to whether criminals are getting younger, a 1997 report from the Justice Department answers clearly: Today's serious and violent juvenile offenders are not significantly younger than those of 10 or 15 years ago."

What's more, from 1994 to 1995 there was a 3 percent decline in juvenile arrests for violent crime, and from 1995 to 1996 there was a 6 percent decline. "I have people call me up and ask, 'Why is juvenile crime down?'" says Robert Shepherd Jr., a law professor at the University of Richmond in Virginia. "I say, 'Why was it up?' It could be just one of history's cycles. Over the thirty years I've been involved in juvenile justice issues, I've seen very little change in the incidence of violent crime by kids."

One thing that has changed is the prominence of guns and their role in violence. A 1997 Justice Department report looked at homicides by youths aged 13 and 14 with and without guns. In 1980 there were 74 murders committed with guns and 68 without by that age group. In 1995 gun-related murders totaled 178; there were 67 nongun murders.

Exaggerated claims about juvenile crime would be a hard sell if people weren't ready to believe the worst about young people. A 1997 report from Public Agenda, a nonprofit policy group, called "Kids These Days: What Americans Really Think About the Next Generation," found that 58 percent of those surveyed think children and teens will make the world a worse place or no different when they grow up. Even kids aged 5 to 12 weren't spared, with 53 percent of respondents characterizing them in negative terms. Only 23 percent had positive things to say about children. What America really thinks about its kids, in short, is: not much.

The generation gap is old news, but this sour, almost hateful view of young people is different. Adults aren't merely puzzled by young people; they're terrified of them. It can't be a coincidence that the shift in adult attitudes began roughly a generation after the height of political and social movements created by young people of all colors. Policy-makers now propelling anti-youth agendas remember how effective young people can be as a force for change. Demographics and the shifting nature of U.S. families also foster the anti-youth bias. According to census statistics, the number of people under age 65 has tripled since 1900, while the population aged 65 or over has increased elevenfold. One-quarter of all households are people living alone. And children are no longer integral to family structure: In 51 percent of all families there are no children under 18 living at home. Young people are easily demonized when their worlds don't coincide with ours. The sense of collective responsibility in raising children disappears as the building blocks of community change.

To an older America in a postindustrial world, children have become more of a liability than an asset. Middle-class parents calculate the cost of raising kids, including an overpriced college education, as they would a home mortgage. Low-income parents are bludgeoned by policies designed to discourage having children, from welfare reform to cuts in higher-education assistance. Young people's place in the economic order is uncertain, and a threat to those elders who are scrambling for the same jobs at McDonald's or in Silicon Valley. Says Barry Feld, professor at the University of Minnesota Law School and author of the upcoming *Bad Kids: Race and the Transformation of Juvenile Court*, "Parents raised kids so they could take care of them when they're old. As caring for the old has shifted to the public sector, the elderly no longer have that fiscal investment in their kids. They know Social Security will be there for them."

Another reason adults are willing to condemn children is that it saves them from taking responsibility when kids go wrong. Take this statistical nugget: From 1986 to 1993, roughly the same period of the youth crime "explosion," the number of abused and neglected children doubled to 2.8 million, according to the Justice Department. And just three years later, the total of all juvenile arrests was 2.8 million. What goes around comes around.

Historically, U.S. criminal law followed the definitions of adulthood and childhood laid down by William Blackstone in his *Commentaries on the Laws of England* (1765–69). Children up to 7 were considered incapable of criminal responsibility by dint of their immaturity. At 14, they could be held as responsible as adults for their crimes; the years in between were a gray area of subjective judgment on culpability. But by 1900, reformers had created a separate system of juvenile courts and reform schools based on the principles that delinquency had social causes and that youth should not be held to adult standards. Eighteen was generally held as the entryway to adulthood. . . .

We are marching backward to a one-size-fits-all system for youth and adults in which punishment, not reform, is the goal. From 1992 to 1995, forty-one states passed laws making it easier to prosecute juveniles in adult criminal court, and today all fifty states have such laws. In more than half the states, children under 14 can be tried in adult court for certain crimes. In thirteen states, there is no minimum age at which a child can be tried in adult court for felonies. New York permits prosecution of a 7-year-old as an adult for certain felonies. The Hatch-Sessions bill now in the U.S. Senate continues the assault on youthful offenders. It would use block grants to encourage states to toughen further their juvenile justice procedures. One provision eliminates the longstanding mandate to separate incarcerated juveniles and adults. "You're going to see more suicides and assaults if that happens' " says Robert Shepherd.

Violent crimes like those in Oregon and Arkansas are a rarity, but they've become the rationale for a widespread crackdown on youth at school and on the streets. If Dennis the Menace were around, he'd be shackled hand and foot, with Mr. Wilson chortling as the cops hauled his mischievous butt off to juvenile hall. In Miami recently, a 10-year-old boy was handcuffed, arrested and jailed overnight because he kicked his mother at a Pizza Hut. His mother protested the police action—it was a waitress who turned him in. The boy now faces domestic battery charges in juvenile court.

Last October at the Merton Intermediate School in Merton, Wisconsin, four boys aged 12 and 13 were suspended for three days and slapped with disorderly conduct citations and fines (later dropped) by the local sheriff after they yanked up another boy's underwear "wedgie style." "The boys were playing, wrestling around in the schoolyard, and there was a pile-on," says Kevin Keane, an attorney who represented one of the boys. "One kid was on the ground and the others gave him a wedgie. He wasn't hurt or upset, and they all went back to class." But the principal learned about the incident and termed it a sexual assault.

Anti-youth analysts prefer to think more juvenile arrests means more kids are behaving recklessly. But it's just as plausible to argue that the universe of permissible behavior has shrunk. Look at curfews, which were virtually unknown twenty years ago. Curfews generated 185,000 youth arrests in 1996—a 113 percent increase since 1987. Disorderly conduct arrests of youth soared 93 percent between 1987 and 1996, with 215,000 arrests in 1996 alone.

Public schools are at ground zero in the youth crackdown. A report released in March by the National Center for Education Statistics surveyed 1,234 public schools on crime and security measures. Three-fourths have "zero tolerance" policies on drugs, alcohol and weapons, which means ironclad punishment for any transgression. Six percent of the schools surveyed use police or other law enforcement on campus at least thirty hours a week, while 19 percent of high schools have stationed cops full time. Public schools are even using dogs to search for illegal drugs. The Northern California A.C.L.U., filed suit in March 1997 against the Galt, California, school district on behalf of two students and a teacher who were subjected to dog searches during a course on criminal justice. "It's a real state police-prison element introduced into the schools," says A.C.L.U. lawyer Ann Bick. "It tells kids, 'We don't trust you.' And they'll live down to those expectations."

Lewis Hine, Three boys holding newspapers, 1910. Courtesy of the Library of Congress, Prints and Photographs Division, Lot 7480, vol. 2, #1616.

Part Five

Working Children

Until the twentieth century (and up to the present for some families), parents depended on the labor of their children for the survival of the family unit. Children worked in the fields, at home, and in factories; some worked on the streets as peddlers or entertainers. Children could begin work as early as five and become full-time workers with adult responsibilities by age ten. Schooling, when offered, was fitted around the work schedule.

The kind of work children performed was determined by the race, class, and ethnic background of their parents. It was also influenced by geography. Black slave children worked in the fields, as did many children of white farmers or sharecroppers. In New England and the South children were often hired as factory workers in the growing textile industry. Children of immigrants from southern and eastern Europe worked in stores or clothing sweatshops or sometimes on the street. Children who had no parents or whose parents could not care for them were apprenticed or placed out to masters, who used their labor in many different work situations.

It was not until the beginning of the twentieth century that the state passed child labor laws that seriously restricted the work of children. At around the same time, new mandatory education laws required children to spend time in school. This pattern of school rather than work has persisted for most of the century until the recent sharp rise of part-time teen workers, fueled by the needs of the new service industries of fast-food and video entertainment.

62

In the colonial era nearly all children worked. Those who did not work under their fathers' supervision usually served as apprentices. Mary Ann Mason discusses these child labor arrangements (1994).

Fathers/Masters: Children/Servants

Mary Ann Mason

Masters and Servants

A very large proportion of children in the colonial era did not spend their whole childhood under the custody and control of their own parents or stepparents. These children were put under the custody and control of masters (and sometimes mistresses), to whom they were indentured. "Binding out," "putting out," or "apprenticing" were all variations on the well-established English custom of placing children in the home of a master who was obliged to provide ordinary sustenance and some training in return for services. This training could be as specific as teaching a skilled craft or it could be as general as instruction in basic reading and the catechism. Laws under common law differed pertaining to articles of indenture for servants and for apprentices. In the New World the distinction between indentures for servants and apprentices was less clear. Binding out or apprenticing became a catch-all concept that both provided a controllable and skilled labor force to the new country and parent figures to thousands of children who had no parents. Whatever the terms of the indenture contract, it was ratified and supervised by the local court.

The master-servant relationship established by the indenture contract closely reflected the parent-child relationship. Master and servant shared mutual obligations, as did parent and child, and for the most part these obligations were the same; courts often described the master as serving in loco parentis. While the affectional bonds between a father and his child may have been of an entirely different nature, the legal responsibilities of father and master were not. Many laws . . . assigned identical duties to fathers and masters regarding the care and training of the children in their charge. In return masters could expect labor from their charges, just as fathers could. Blackstone clearly supported this analogy. "The father has the benefit of his children's labor while they live with him and are maintained by him; and this is no more than he is entitled to from his apprentices or servants."

In a society where production relied on the economic services of children, the law strongly supported this master-servant relationship. In the absence of social workers and children's protective services, the courts cooperated with poor officials in creating and supervising the indentures of orphaned or impoverished children. They also settled the disputes between parents and masters over the treatment of apprentices and ordered runaway apprentices back to their masters if they could not prove gross abuse. While courts rarely, if ever, heard custody disputes following divorce, colonial courts every day struggled with problems relating to the "placing out" of children.

Courts supervised a broad variety of indentures, roughly divided into two categories: 1. voluntary apprenticeships, where a parent voluntarily arranged with a third party, usually to train the child in a specific trade in exchange for the child's services; and 2. involuntary apprenticeships, where the parents were dead or unable to properly raise their children and the town poor law officials placed them with a master, primarily in order to relieve the town of the financial burden. In the absence of the legal form of adoption involuntary apprenticeships were also used to ratify the legal position of close relatives who took in a child upon the death of the child's parents. Both types of indenture contracts were under the jurisdiction of the county court and were usually not enforced by other courts if the master moved.

Involuntary Apprenticeships

Children who came to America as indentured servants without parents provided critical labor for the settlement of the colonies. More than half of all persons who came to the colonies south of New England were indentured servants, and most servants were under nineteen years old. Whether these children who came alone to the colonies came as voluntary or involuntary servants is unknown. Certainly, some of the older children voluntarily signed their own indentures, as did adults, in hopes of a fresh start in an uncrowded country. However, many children were orphans, or children of the poor, and their indentures, like those of all impoverished children, were not voluntary.

In 1617 the Virginia Company actively solicited the lord mayor of London to send poor children to settle the colony. The lord mayor complied by authorizing a charitable collection to grant five pounds apiece for equipment and passage money, while the children were to be apprenticed until the age of twenty-one and afterward to have fifty acres of land in the plantation to be held in fee simple at a rent of one shilling a year. This arrangement apparently worked well, and was initiated again in 1619 for "one hundred children out of the multitude that swarm in that place to be sent to Virginia."

The children, like all settlers, did not survive long in deadly Virginia, and the London City Council once again complied with a request in 1622 for the transportation of another hundred children, "being sensible of the great loss which [the plantation] lately susteyned by the barbarous cruelty of the savage people there."

A similar process occurred in New Netherland (later named New York), where the directors of the West India Company asked for and received several shiploads of poor and/or orphaned children from Amsterdam. An official of Fort New Amsterdam asked for more children in 1658 but specified their age: "Please to continue sending others from time to time: but, if possible, none ought to come less than fifteen years of age and somewhat strong, as little profit is to be expected here without labor."

Other children, many of whom were not orphans or under the control of the poor law officials, were tricked into indentured servitude by "spiriters" who gained a healthy profit for each suitable child (or adult) they could deliver to the colonies, where they sold their indentures. The custom grew out of hand by the middle of the seventeenth century; victims often were blatantly kidnapped and held prisoner for a month or so until sent off to sea. One father obtained a warrant to search the ship for his eleven-year-old son whom he claimed had been spirited away. The search uncovered nineteen servants, eleven of whom had been taken by "spirits," most against their will. The spirit trade provoked public outrage and fear. Petitioned by merchants, planters, and masters of ships, the attorney general of Charles II established in 1664 a central registry recording the contracts of all servants leaving for the colonies. This remedy was supplemented by fierce prosecution of those caught spiriting.

Given the circumstances of immigration, many children arrived with irregular indentures or none at all. The law required the would-be master to bring the child before the court to determine the terms of the indenture. Most common was the term set by the Virginia legislature: "Such persons as shall be imported, having no indenture or covenant, either men or women, if they be above sixteen years old shall serve four years, if under fifteen to serve till he or she shall be one and twenty years of age, and the courts to be judges of their ages." Other colonies fixed eighteen years of age or marriage as the termination date of indentures for girls.

The law did not require that masters teach these child immigrants a specific trade but rather allowed them to put the children to whatever service they wished. At the termination of the indenture, however, the law required masters to provide the servant with a suitable wardrobe and some provisions. A North Carolina law specified: "Every Christian servant shall be allowed by their master or mistress at the expiration of his or her time of service three barrels of Indian corn and two new suits of apparel of the value of five pounds at least or, in lieu of one suit of apparel, a good well-fixed gun, if he be a man servant."

In the New England colonies and in colonies south of New England, following the first decades of intense immigration, children were most often involuntarily apprenticed when their parents were unable or unwilling to care for them properly. Adoption was not then a legal option, and orphanages and asylums for children were rare until the end of the eighteenth century. The town of the child's "settlement" was responsible for the child's welfare. Elaborate laws determined how "settlement" would be carried out, since no town was eager to take on an unnecessary burden. Generally, the child's place of birth was its settlement if neither his mother nor father had one. However, if the father or the mother had a town of settlement, that was the child's, in that order of preference. Bastards, however, as *filius nullius*, had only the town in which they were born.

The officials of the child's town of settlement charged with administering the poor laws took charge of these children and, with appropriate approval of the court, "bound them" to an appropriate master who gained full custody and control of the child, but under continued court supervision. Once the child was bound out the parents, if alive, lost any legal claim to its custody. In the case of orphans the child was often bound out to a close relative, providing the legal custodial authority to the relatives that was not available by adoption. If the child was an infant, poor law officials might pay a family to nurse the child until it was old enough to bind out. In this instance poor law officials maintained legal control of the child. These infants were often bastards. The records for one parish in Virginia between 1748 and 1753 indicate that fully half of the poor relief paid out went to families for the purposes of keeping a bastard child for a year.

63

The southern colonies were particularly needy of labor. Virginia attempted to persuade the mayor of London to ship street children to the New World to serve as apprentices. Slave children were also put to work alongside their parents at an early age, and were treated as harshly as their parents were.

Children's Involuntary Labor

Colonial Documents

Request by Virginia Company to Mayor of London, 1619

The Treasurer, Council, and Company of Virginia assembled in their great and general Court the 17th of November 1619 have taken into consideration the continual great forwardness of his honorable City [London] in advancing the plantation of Virginia and particularly in furnishing out one hundred children this last year, which by the goodness of God there safely arrived (save such as died in the way), and are well pleased we doubt not for their benefit, for which your bountiful assistance, we in the name of the whole plantation do yield unto you due and deserved thanks.

And forasmuch as we have now resolved to send this next spring very large supplies for the strength and increasing of the Colony . . . and find that the sending of those children to be apprentices hath been very grateful to the people: we pray your Lordship and the rest in pursuit of your former so pious actions to renew your like favors and furnish us again with one hundred more for the next spring. Our desire is that we may have them of twelve years old and upward with allowance of three pounds apiece for their transportation and forty shillings apiece for their apparel as was formerly granted. They shall be apprentices the boys till they come to twenty-one years of age the girls till the like age or till they be married, and afterwards they shall be placed as tenants upon the public land with best conditions where they shall have houses with stock of corn and cattle to begin with, and afterward the moiety of all increase and profit whatsoever. And so we leave this motion to your honorable and grave consideration.

Request by Virginia Company to Principal Secretary of James I, 1620

Right Honorable:

Being unable to give my personal attendance upon the Lords, I have presumed to address my suit in these few lines unto your Honor. The City of London have by act of their Common Council, appointed one hundred children out of their superfluous multitude to be transported to Virginia; there to be bound apprentices for certain years, and afterward with very beneficial conditions for the children. And have granted moreover a levy of five hundred pounds among themselves for the appareling of those children, and toward their charges of transportation. Now it falleth out that among those children, sundry being ill disposed, and fitter for any remote place than for this City, declare their unwillingness to go to Virginia, of whom the City is especially desirious to be disburdened, and in Virginia under severe masters they may be brought to goodness. But this City wanting authority to deliver, and the Virginia Company to transport, these persons against their wills, the burden is laid upon me, by humble suit unto the Lords to procure higher authority for the warranting thereof. May it please your Honor therefore, to vouchsafe unto us of the Company here, and to the whole plantation in Virginia, that noble favor, as to be a means unto their Lordships out of their accustomed goodness, and by their higher authority, to discharge both the City and our Company of this difficulty, as their Lordships and your Honors in your wisdom shall find most expedient. For whose health and prosperity our Company will always pray.

Declaration by Privy Council of England, 1620

January 31, 1620.

Whereas we are informed that the City of London hath, by an act of the Common Council, appointed one hundred children, out of the multitudes that swarm in that place, to be sent to Virginia, there to be bound apprentices for certain years with very beneficial conditions for them afterwards, and have moreover yielded to a levy of five hundred pounds for the appareling of those children and towards the charge of their transportation; wherein, as the City deserveth thanks and commendations for redeeming so many poor souls from misery and ruin and putting them in a condition of use and service to the State; so forasmuch as information is likewise made that among that number there are divers unwilling to be carried thither and that it is conceived that both the City wanteth authority to deliver and the Virginia Company to receive and carry out these persons against their wills, we have thought meet, for the better furtherance of so good a work, hereby to authorize and require as well such of the City as take charge of that service as the Virginia Company, or any of them, to deliver, receive, and transport into Virginia all and every the foresaid children as shall be most expedient. And if any of them shall be found obstinate to resist or otherwise to disobey such directions as shall be given in this behalf, we do likewise hereby authorize such as shall have the charge of this service to imprison, punish, and dispose any of those children, upon any disorder by them or any of them committed, as cause shall require, and so to ship them out for Virginia with as much expedition as may stand with conveniency. For which this shall be unto all persons whom the same may any way concern a sufficient warrant.

64

The terms of an indenture contract typically provided certain limited rights to apprentices: they were to be provided adequate food, clothing, and shelter; they were also protected from mistreatment. At the completion of the contract, usually at age twenty-one, the apprentice normally received clothing, some money, and, in the southern colonies, a piece of land from his or her master. In most colonies, the apprentice system was regulated by law as well as contract.

Apprentices, Servants, and Child Labor

Colonial Documents

Standard Form of Indenture for an Apprentice, Virginia, 1659

This indenture made the 6th day of June in the year of our Lord Christ 1659, witnesseth, that Bartholomew Clarke the son of John Clarke of the City of Canterbury, sadler, of his own liking and with the consent of Francis Plumer of the City of Canterbury, brewer, hath put himself apprentice unto Edward Rowzie of Virginia, planter, as an apprentice with him to dwell from the day of the date above mentioned unto the full term of four years from thence next ensuing fully to be complete and ended, all which said term the said Bartholomew Clarke well and faithfully the said Edward Rowzie as his master shall serve, his secrets keep, his commands most just and lawful he shall observe, and fornication he shall not commit, nor contract matrimony with any woman during the said term; he shall not do hurt unto his master, nor consent to the doing of any, but to his power shall hinder and prevent the doing of any; at cards, dice or any unlawful games he shall not play; he shall not waste the goods of his said master nor lend them to anybody without his master's consent; he shall not absent himself from his said master's service day or night, but as a true and faithful servant, shall demean himself. [A]nd the said Edward Rowzie in the mystery, art, and occupation of a planter . . . the said Bartholomew shall teach or cause to be taught, and also during said term shall find and allow his apprentice competent meat, drink, apparel, washing, lodging with all other things fitting for his degree, and in the end thereof, fifty acres of land to be laid out for him, and all other things which according to the custom of the country is or ought to be done.

New York City Statute, 1731

No merchant, shopkeeper or handy craft tradesman shall take any apprentice to teach or instruct them in their trade or calling within this City, without being bound by indenture before the Mayor, Recorder or one of the Aldermen of the said City, and enroling the same in the Town Clerk's Office. And that at the expiration of the said indentures the said apprentice shall be made free of this City by the master, if he hath well and truly served him. And the Clerk shall have for enroling each indenture of apprenticeship the sum of three shillings to be paid by the master of such apprentice bound as aforesaid. . . .

And whereas the emigration of poor persons from Europe hath conduced greatly to the settlement of this State, while a colony; and whereas doubts have arisen tending to the discouragement of further importation of such poor persons; therefore be it further enacted by the authority aforesaid, That every contract already made or hereafter to be made by any infant or other person, coming from beyond sea . . . the party entering into the same, for such term and for such services as shall be therein specified. . . . But that no contract shall bind any infant longer than until his or her arrival to the full age of twenty one years; excepting such as are or shall be bound in order to raise money for the payment of their passages, who may be bound until the age of twenty four years, provided the term of such service shall not exceed four years in the whole. . . .

And whereas, many persons are taken as apprentices or servants, when they are very young, and for several years of their apprenticeships or service, are rather a burthen, than otherwise, to their masters or mistresses: And whereas it frequently happens that such apprentices or servants, when they might be expected to be useful to their masters or mistresses, absent themselves from their service: And whereas the laws in being are not sufficient to prevent these inconveniences: For remedy whereof: Be it further enacted by the authority aforesaid, That from and after the passing of this act, if any apprentice or servant shall absent him or herself, from his or her master's or mistress's service, before the term of his or her apprenticeship or service shall be expired, every such apprentice or servant shall, at any time or times thereafter, whenever he or she shall be found, be compelled to serve his or her said master or mistress, for double the time he or she shall have so absented him or herself from such service, unless he or she shall make satisfaction to his or her master or mistress for the loss he or she shall have sustained by such absence from his or her service; and so from time to time, as often as any such apprentice or servant, shall, without leave of his or her master or mistress, absent himself or herself from his or her service, before the term of his or her contract shall be fulfilled.

Provided always. . . . That nothing in this clause of this act shall extend to any apprentice, whose master or mistress shall have received with such apprentice any sum or sums of money to learn such art, craft, mystery, profession, trade or employment. And also that no apprentice or servant shall be compelled to serve for any time or term or to make any satisfaction to any master or mistress, after the expiration of three years, next after the end of the term for which such apprentice or servant, shall have contracted to serve; any thing herein contained to the contrary notwithstanding.

South Carolina Statute, 1740

All and every person and persons whatsoever, that now are or at any time or times after the passing of this Act shall be bound by indentures to serve as an apprentice within this Province, in any lawful employment, calling, art, mystery or trade, although such apprentice or any of them have been or shall be within the age of twenty-one years at the time of making their several indentures, shall be bound to serve for the years in their several indentures contained, as fully and effectually, to every intent, as if the said apprentice had been of full age at the time of making such indentures, and shall be bound, accepted and taken as an apprentice, accordingly ... and provided also, that nothing in this Act contained shall extend to oblige any male apprentice to serve after he shall have attained the age of one-and-twenty years, or a female after she shall have attained the age of eighteen years.

... Every person or persons under the age of one-and-twenty years, and hereafter intending to be bound by indenture as an apprentice, in this Province, shall execute such indenture in the presence and with the approbation of his or her father, mother or guardian; and if such intended apprentice hath neither father, mother or guardian, in the presence and with the approbation of the church-wardens of the parish where such person is indented ... which indenture or indentures, so executed ... shall be good and effectual, to all intents and purposes, as if such apprentice had been of full age and by indenture of covenant had bound him or herself, or otherwise shall be void and of none effect. ...

... It shall and may be lawful to and for the master or mistress of any apprentice, indented to serve within this Province as aforesaid, upon sufficient cause, to be approved of by the parent or guardian, or where there is no parent or guardian, by the church-wardens of the parish where such master or mistress resides, to assign and transfer the indenture of such apprentice to any other master or mistress, exercising within this Province the same employment, calling, trade, art or mystery; which said indenture, so assigned, shall be valid and effectual to the assignee as to the time remaining unexpired, as if the said apprentice had been originally indented to such assignee; and the said assignee, on accepting such assignment, shall be equally bound to the said apprentice, according to the tenor or the said indenture, as the original master or mistress was. ...

And it be further enacted by the authority aforesaid, That if any master or mistress within this Province shall misuse or evilly intreat his or her apprentice, or if the said apprentice shall have any just cause to complain, or do not his or her duty to the said master or mistress, then and in such case the said master, mistress or apprentice being grieved, and having just cause to complain, shall repair and make such complaint to any two justices of the peace within the county where such master or mistress resides, who shall and are hereby authorized and required by their wisdom and discretion to make such order and give such direction between the said master, mistress and apprentice, as the equity and justice of the case shall require.

*Alexander Hamilton, the first U.S. secretary of the treasury, believed that child labor was central to the country's future economic prosperity. He was particularly enthusiastic about putting children to work in the new textile industries (*Report on Manufactures, *1795).*

Children and Manufactures

Alexander Hamilton

As to the additional employment of classes of the community not originally engaged in the particular business, this is not among the least valuable of the means by which manufacturing institutions contribute to augment the general stock of industry and production. In places where those institutions prevail, besides the persons regularly engaged in them, they afford occasional and extra employment to industrious individuals and families who are willing to devote the leisure resulting from the intermissions of their ordinary pursuits to collateral labors, as a resource for multiplying their acquisitions or their enjoyments. The husbandman himself experiences a new source of profit and support from the increased industry of his wife and daughters, invited and stimulated by the demands of the neighboring manufactories. . . .

It is worthy of particular remark that, in general, women and children are rendered more useful, and the latter more early useful, by manufacturing establishments, than they would otherwise be. Of the number of persons employed in the cotton manufactories of Great Britain, it is computed that four-sevenths, nearly, are women and children; of whom the greatest proportion are children, and many of them of a tender age.

And thus it appears to be one of the attributes of manufactures, and one of no small consequence, to give occasion to the exertion of a greater quantity of industry, even by the same number of persons, where they happen to prevail, than would exist if there were no such establishments.

Benjamin Franklin had no interest in apprenticing to his father as a chandler. In his autobiography (1791) he describes his choice, at age twelve, to apprentice in the printing trade.

Choosing a Trade

Benjamin Franklin

I continu'd thus employ'd in my Father's Business for two Years, that is till I was 12 Years old; and my Brother John, who was bred to that Business, having left my Father, married and set up for himself at Rhode Island. There was all Appearance that I was destin'd to supply his Place and be a Tallow Chandler. But my Dislike to the Trade continuing, my Father was under Apprehensions that if he did not find one for me more agreeable, I should break away and get to Sea, as his Son Josiah had done to his great Vexation. He therefore sometimes took me to walk with him, and see Joiners, Bricklayers, Turners, Braziers, &c. at their Work, that he might observe my Inclination, & endeavor to fix it on some Trade or other on Land. It has ever since been a Pleasure to me to see good Workmen handle their Tools; and it has been useful to me, having learned so much by it, as to be able to do little Jobs myself in my House, when a Workman could not readily be got; & to construct little Machines for my Experiments while the Intention of making the Experiment was fresh & warm in my Mind. My Father at last fix'd upon the Cutler's Trade, and my Uncle Benjamin's Son Samuel, who was bred to that Business in London, being about that time establish'd in Boston, I was sent to be with him some time on liking. But his Expectations of a Fee with me displeasing my Father, I was taken home again.

From a Child I was fond of Reading, and all the little Money that came into my Hands was ever laid out in Books. Pleas'd with the Pilgrim's Progress, my first Collection was of John Bunyan's Works, in separate little Volumes. I afterwards sold them to enable me to buy R. Burton's Historical Collections; they were small Chapmen's Books and cheap, 40 or 50 in all. My Father's little Library consisted chiefly of Books in polemic Divinity, most of which I read, and have since often regretted, that at a time when I had such a Thirst for Knowledge, more proper Books had not fallen in my Way, since it was now resolv'd I should not be a Clergyman. Plutarch's Lives there was, in which I read abundantly, and I still think that time spent to great Advantage. There was also a Book of Defoe's, called an Essay on Projects, and another of Dr. Mather's, call'd Essays to do Good which perhaps gave me a Turn of Thinking that had an Influence on some of the principal future Events of my Life.

This Bookish Inclination at length determin'd my Father to make me a Printer, tho' he had already one Son, (James) of that Profession. In 1717 my Brother James return'd from England with a Press & Letters to set up his Business in Boston. I lik'd it much better than that of my Father, but still had a Hankering for the Sea. To prevent the apprehended Effect of such an Inclination, my Father was impatient to have me bound to my Brother. I stood out some time, but at last was persuaded and signed the Indentures, when I was yet but 12 Years old. I was to serve as an Apprentice till I was 21 Years of Age, only I was to be allow'd Journeyman's Wages during the last Year. In a little time I made great Proficiency in the Business, and became a useful Hand to my Brother.

67

Many children worked in factories in the nineteenth century and well into the twentieth. In response to anti–child labor fervor, August Kohn, a journalist, defends the practice of hiring children to work in cotton mills in the South in the early twentieth century (1907).

Children in the Mills

August Kohn

There has been very much more interest shown by the outside world in the matter of the employment of children in the cotton mills—more indeed than any other phase of cotton mill life. The employment of children has always been a matter of concern to the public at large. It is probably very well that there is so much interest in this phase of mill life. Most of those who have undertaken to present the matter of child labor have done so from the sensational or sentimental view point, and very many of those who have undertaken to arouse a sentiment against the employment of children have added an appeal for subscriptions to a fund with which to prosecute this work against the employment of children, but suggest no other means of the children making a livelihood. My purpose shall be to present the matter as fairly as I can, with due regard to the sentimental side; the injury that is done by the employment of children; the reason that these children are employed, and the law in South Carolina and how it is enforced; and what, if anything, can be done, or ought to be done, to minimize the employment of children . . .

The best way to get at the actual facts is to visit the cotton mills. I went through at least twenty-five cotton mills; one of the chief purposes of my visits being to see with my own eyes and to hear with my own ears the facts relative to the employment of children. In a recent magazine paragraph it is stated: "Sixty thousand little children are to-day toiling in Southern cotton mills; little girls, eight years old, work through a twelve-hour night." In *The Outlook* this advertisement was printed: "The national child labor committee wants your help to rescue two million children from premature labor. The sweat-shop, the coal mine, the glass factory, the silk mill, the cotton mill, the cigar shop, and the whiskey bottling works invade the school and the home to capture the American child. Our work is a campaign against race deterioration. Child labor is a menace to industry, education and good citizenship."

This may be a very good scheme by which to gather money for the committee which is undertaking the work of minimizing child labor, but when one considers that, according to the census, out of the 1,750,178 children employed in "gainful occupations" there are 1,061,971 of this number engaged in agricultural pursuits, the force of the advertisement is very considerably weakened. It should be remembered, too, that of the total number of children reported who are engaged in "gainful occupations" 688,207 are children between 10 and 15, and 501,844 are 14 and 15 years of age, and this number will have to be eliminated from the claims made in the advertisement. In other words, almost 90 per cent of the number given as engaged in "gainful occupations" are eliminated, first, by being in agricultural pursuits, and then on account of being 14 years of age or over. And, if the whole thing were dissected in the same way as to the remaining number, it would be found that very few of the 2,000,000 are left—certainly in the Southern cotton mills—for the GOOD offices of the committee that is raising general subscriptions for the work. The fact of the matter is that the census report does not show more than 95,000 employed in the various occupations itemized in the advertisement, and yet it is claimed that 2,000,000 children are to be saved, and this 95,000 includes children of 14 and 15 years of age engaged in "gainful occupations. . . ."

As stated before, the trouble with so many of these sensationalists is that they do not begin at the right place. If they could only compare the conditions of these families to-day with what they were twenty years ago they would probably write in a more conservative strain. In a recent article by Mr. D. A. Tompkins published in the *Textile Manufacturers' Journal*, he refers to the conditions in the South immediately after the war and reconstruction. And then he goes on to say: ". . . Here was a possible opportunity to escape the smouldering ashes of reconstruction and the pinching poverty of five-cent cotton. The problem was not one of seeking wealth, but of human welfare. It would have been peculiarly unnatural if the welfare of children should not have been left behind in this life-saving movement. They were not left behind, but, on the contrary, their welfare has been as assiduously pressed as any other phase of development in the South. It was regarded that the first prerequisites in the interest of children were Christian training in church and mental training in school. From the very beginning both these essentials have been provided, and are still provided. Any exception is so rare that it may be omitted. The age limit has been constantly increased, and the purpose has been, and is still, to replace the better training as the mill training is displaced. . . . The great benefactors are those who have formulated plans for the industrial development of the South, and accomplished the maintenance of regular work and a cash pay roll at regular intervals. Whoever finds the way to keep people employed at profitable wages may depend upon it that they, in turn, will, in time, be more instrumental than anybody else in their own betterment. Working together, the mills and the operatives, there have been found ways in all the mills for building churches, establishing and maintaining schools, shortening the work day, increasing the pay per day, stopping night work, and bringing about other reforms by natural means."

68

The historian David Nasaw describes the lives of children—usually immigrants— who worked as peddlers and street performers in the early twentieth century (1985).

Children at Work in the City

David Nasaw

The children who earned their money as street traders peddled whatever they could buy cheaply, fit into their pockets or the canvas bag slung over their shoulders, and sell for a profit. Bessie Turner Kriesberg, a Russian émigré whose oral history translated from the Yiddish is found in the YIVO archives, was astounded on her arrival in Chicago by the number of boys on the streets—and the variety of items they sold. "She enjoyed watching the young boys acting as businessmen. They were shouting out the merchandise they had for sale. One was selling newspapers, one chewing gum, one peanuts, one theater tickets, and the youngest carried on his shoulder a small wooden box with tools to clean shoes for people."

Many children sold more than one item at a time. The newsies in particular were always adopting "side lines" to hawk with their papers. Hy Kraft, the future Broadway playwright, who claimed to have held more jobs as a child "than there are categories in the Yellow Pages of the phone book," sold newspapers with his brother Willie "at the corner of 116th Street and Lenox Avenue, in front of the pool parlor next to the subway kiosk, defying the onrush of bicycles and streetcars. We almost got ourselves killed, but we never got rich. So we took on a side line—Spearmint gum. We had the same deal as we had on the newspapers—two for a penny and sold them for a penny a slice, when we sold them. Packages were two for a nickel; we sold them at a nickel a pack. A 100 percent profit."

George Burns claims in his autobiography that he sold so many different items he "became sort of a one-man conglomerate. And that was before I became a man, or before I knew what conglomerate meant. . . . One of my many big business ventures lasted exactly two hours and twenty minutes. I thought there was money to be made by selling vanilla crackers. I'd go into a grocery store and buy a bunch of vanilla crackers at ten for a penny. Then on the street I'd sell them eight for a penny. . . . The problem here was by the time I sold eight crackers I'd eaten two crackers. It didn't take me long to realize that this was the wrong business for a kid who was hooked on vanilla crackers."

Al Jolson and his brother Harry sold newspapers in Washington, D.C. In the summer, they went into the watermelon business. "We could buy watermelons at the wharves at a wholesale price, three for a nickel. Sometimes we could get four for a nickel. We had a patched and battered wagon, for which we had traded. We would load it with melons, and haul them to a promising section of town for resale. Here our voices . . . became part of our stock-in-trade. We made up a little song which Al and I [Harry] would sing in tones that carried far:

> Wa————a-termelons
> Red to da rind
> Five cents a piece
> And you eat 'em all da time."

As the Jolsons and the other young hustlers quickly discovered, their youth was their greatest selling point. There was something irresistible about innocent-looking children trying so hard to earn money. The incongruity between their size and their salesmanship attracted customers. In their own neighborhoods, the children were helped out by working-class and immigrant adults who had children of their own. Downtown, they were patronized by prosperous Americans who found the little hustlers too cute to pass by.

All the street traders had to perform for their customers. One needed a bit of bravado and an immunity from embarrassment to survive on the streets. Children with a surfeit of each—and a bit of talent—went a step further. The streets of the city were filled with young hustlers who clowned, pantomimed, sang, and danced, some for the sheer sport of it, others for the change they hoped to collect from bystanders. The Jewish neighborhoods in particular were, as Irving Howe has written, the training grounds for future generations of comics, dancers, and singers. "There are the famous or once-famous names: Al Jolson, George Jessel, Eddie Cantor, Sophie Tucker, Fanny Brice, Ben Blue, Jack Benny, George Burns, George Sidney, Milton Berle, Ted Lewis, Bennie Fields, and others. And there are the hundreds who played the small towns, the ratty theaters, the Orpheum circuit, the Catskills, the smelly houses in Brooklyn and the Bronx."

The children of the streets observed from the outside the great panorama of urban life, taking it all in, and then, if they had the talent, representing it in comic or melodramatic form from the stage (and later on the screen, over the radio, on television). They learned to mimic the dialects, the dialogues, the patter of peddlers, policemen, and "the hoity-toity Irish teacher who recited Browning in high school." They began by entertaining each other. Only later would they begin charging for it.

At the age of six, Eddie Cantor began keeping "late hours . . . with a band of boys two and three times [his] age who spent their nights in a revelry of song. For the East Side at night is not only menaced by the caterwauling of cats, but by gangs of youngsters who sit on the stoops and the corner stands, singing all the popular songs with all their might at an age when their voices are changing."

The Jolson brothers, George Burns, and Fanny Brice began their careers in similar fashion, singing or clowning on street corners and in backyards and alleyways with their friends. When they discovered that adults were willing to throw pennies their way, they quickly abandoned their amateur status. Fanny Brice roamed with her gang through backyards until they found "a likely-looking tenement" to perform for. The children sang all the popular songs of the day and, when they were lucky, were rewarded with a "brief, scattered shower of pennies." When the Jolson brothers and their gang in Washington, D.C., "found that grown people would stop to listen" and even throw coins at them, they moved away from the street corners they had been gathering on to well-situated sidewalks where they were sure to meet adults with change in their pockets. "Our favorite stage was the sidewalk in front of the Hotel Raleigh. In those days, congressmen, high government officials, and even Supreme Court Justices would sit on chairs on the sidewalks during spring and summer evenings, just as people did in small towns. They not only appreciated our singing, but they became an unusual source of income for us. We sang all the popular songs, such as: Sweet Marie, The Sidewalks of New York, Who Threw the Overalls in Mrs. Murphy's Chowder, Daisy Bell, and Say Au Revoir But Not Goodbye. We soon learned that statesmen and jurists preferred the songs that carried them into the romantic past, the songs of Stephen Foster, and Listen to the Mocking Bird, Come Where My Love Lies Dreaming, and When You and I Were Young, Maggie. Songs such as these brought a shower of nickels, dimes, and even quarters."

For children whose songs or clowning met with applause, laughter, and pennies, there was no turning back. George Burns and the three friends who mixed syrup with him in Rosenzweig's basement began work as the Peewee Quartet after school one afternoon "at the corner of Columbia and Houston." "We stood there and sang from three-thirty to six, and made exactly four cents." The boys did not give up. They continued to sing—in saloons until they were thrown out, on the Staten Island ferry until "Mortzy" got seasick, and in backyards where they were greeted by rotten fruit and occasional pennies.

Though future show business characters tell the best stories about performing on the streets, they were by no means the only children who tried to make some money this way. Of the four friends who made up the Peewee Quartet, only George Burns went into show business. Two others went into the taxi business; the third became an insurance broker. Similarly, the dozens of children who sang in groups with Eddie Cantor on the Lower East Side, Fanny Brice in Brooklyn, and the Jolson brothers in Washington, D.C., had neither the talent nor the inclination to go into show business.

69

Many children worked with their parents in small businesses or stores. In her autobiography (1918) Rose Cohen, a Jewish immigrant, describes her experience in New York City's garment industry, where she worked with her tailor father in the late nineteenth century.

A Child Worker in the Garment Industry

Rose Cohen

On the following day father came home at noon and took me along to the shop where he worked. We climbed the dark, narrow stairs of a tenement house on Monroe Street and came into a bright room filled with noise. I saw about five or six men and a girl. The men turned and looked at us when we passed. I felt scared and stumbled. One man asked in surprise:

"Avrom, is this your daughter? Why, she is only a little girl!"

My father smiled. "Yes," he said, "but wait till you see her sew."

He placed me on a high stool opposite the girl, laid a pile of pocket flaps on the little narrow table between us, and showed me how to baste.

All afternoon I sat on my high stool, a little away from the table, my knees crossed tailor fashion, basting flaps. As I worked I watched the things which I could see by just raising my eyes a little. I saw that the girl, who was called Atta, was very pretty.

A big man stood at a big table, examining, brushing and folding coats. There was a window over his table through which the sun came streaming in, showing millions of specks of dust dancing over the table and circling over his head. He often puffed out his cheeks and blew the dust from him with a great gust so that I could feel his breath at our table.

The machines going at full speed drowned everything in their noise. But when they stopped for a moment I caught the clink of a scissors laid hastily on a table, a short question and answer exchanged, and the pounding of a heavy iron from the back of the room. Sometimes the machines stopped for a whole minute. Then the men looked about and talked. I was always glad when the machines started off again. I felt safer in their noise.

Late in the afternoon a woman came into the shop. She sat down next to Atta and began to sew on buttons. Father, who sat next to me, whispered, "This is Mrs. Nelson, the wife of the big man, our boss. She is a real American."

She, too, was pretty. Her complexion was fair and delicate like a child's. Her upper lip was always covered with shining drops of perspiration. I could not help looking at it all the time.

When she had worked a few minutes she asked father in very imperfect Yiddish: "Well, Mr.——, have you given your daughter an American name?"

"Not yet," father answered. "What would you call her? Her Yiddish name is Rahel."

"Rahel, Rahel," Mrs. Nelson repeated to herself, thoughtfully, winding the thread around a button; "let me see." The machines were going slowly and the men looked interested.

The presser called out from the back of the room: "What is there to think about? Rahel is Rachel."

I was surprised at the interest every one showed. Later I understood the reason. The slightest cause for interruption was welcome, it broke the monotony of the long day.

Mrs. Nelson turned to me: "Don't let them call you Rachel. Every loafer who sees a Jewish girl shouts 'Rachel' after her. And on Cherry Street where you live there are many saloons and many loafers. How would you like Ruth for a name?"

I said I should like to be called Ruth.

Father made the life for me as easy as he could. But there were many hardships he could not prevent.

We began the day at six in the morning. I would stand dressing with my eyes closed and feel about for my buttons. But once I was out on the street and felt the moist early morning air I was wide awake at once.

When we had been in the shop about an hour a grey-bearded little old man used to come in lugging a big basket of food covered with black oil cloth. He was the shop pedlar. He always stopped near the door, rested his basket against it and groaned: "Oh, the stairs, the stairs in America!" The men looked at him with pity and Atta at the sight of him would sometimes begin to sing "The Song of the Pedlar." If the boss was not in the shop or the men were not very busy, one of them would take the basket from the pedlar and place it on a chair in the middle of the room. Then each shop hand picked out a roll and the little old man poured him out a tiny glass of brandy for two cents. Father used to buy me an apple and a sweetened roll. We ate while we worked. I used to think two cents a good deal to spend for my breakfast. But often I was almost sick with hunger. At noon we had our big meal. Then father would send me out for half a pound of steak or a slice of beef liver and a pint of beer which he sometimes bought in partnership with two or three other men. He used to broil the steak in the open coal fireplace where the presser heated his irons, and cut it into tiny squares. He always picked out the juiciest bits and pushed them to my side of the plate, and while there was still quite some meat he would lay down his fork and push his chair away from the table with an air as if he had had more than enough. He also got me to drink beer. Before long I could drink a full glass. But I did not like it. One day it made me quite sick. After that I refused to drink it.

I liked my work and learned it easily, and father was pleased with me. As soon as I knew how to baste pocket-flaps he began to teach me how to baste the coat edges. This was hard work. The double ply of overcoat cloth stitched in with canvas and tape made a very stiff edge. My fingers often stiffened with pain as I rolled and basted the edges. Sometimes a needle or two would break before I could do one coat. Then father would offer to finish the edge for me. But if he gave me my choice I never let him. At these moments I wanted so to master the thing myself that I felt my whole body trembling with the desire. And with my habit of personifying things, I used to bend over the coat on my lap, force the obstinate and squeaking needle, wet with perspiration, in and out of the cloth and whisper with determination: "No, you shall not get the best of me!" When I succeeded I was so happy that father, who often watched me with a smile, would say, "Rahel, your face is shining. Now rest a while." He always told me to rest after I did well. I loved these moments. I would push my stool closer to the wall near which I sat, lean my back against it, and look about the shop. . . .

I liked the life in the shop yet there were times when I felt unhappy. The men often told vulgar jokes. The first time this happened father looked at me and groaned.

"Don't listen," he said, "or pretend you don't hear."

But I could never keep my face from turning red.

One day when Atta and I were alone at our table she said:

"It is too bad that you have a 'tell tale face.' You better learn to hide your feelings. What you hear in this shop is nothing compared with what you will hear in other shops. Look at me." But when I would look over at Atta it seemed to me that her needle actually flew in and out of her sleeve lining and her pretty little mouth looked more pursed than usual.

When I learned to find my way home alone my hours were not so long. For father was a piece worker and as I was only helping him he could do as he pleased with my time. And so now I came into the shop at seven o'clock in the morning and found my roll and apple already waiting for me. And when I went home at seven o'clock in the evening it was still broad daylight.

Our room was a dingy place where the sun never came in. I always felt lonely and a little homesick on coming into it. But I would soon shake off the feeling. I would cook and eat some soup and then go and stand on the stoop and watch the children playing.

One night as I came out of our room into the hall I caught a few strains of music coming from the roof. I went up and found under the sky, blue and bright with the stars and the city lights twinkling all around, a group of Irish-American girls and boys waltzing to the music of a harmonica. I sat down in the shadow near one of the chimneys and watched the stars and the dancing and listened to the song of "My Beautiful Irish Maid."

After this I went up every evening. At first the girls and boys showed that I was not welcome by making ugly grimaces at me. But as I persisted, for I wanted to know the Americans, they became used to seeing me. And soon they paid no more attention to me than to the chimney near which I sat.

On Friday I worked only the first half of the day, then I would go home to do the washing and cleaning in our room. All morning I would count the hours and half hours and my heart beat with joy at the thought that I would soon leave the shop. When at last I heard the noon whistle from the big paper factory on Water Street I used to bend my head low to hide this joy. I felt ashamed at my eagerness to leave off work. When I came out into the street I had to stand still for a while and look about. I felt dazed by the light and the air and the joy of knowing that I was free. For at these moments I did not remember the work at home. I would start to walk along slowly, linger under the trees, of which there was one here and there on Cherry Street, and watch the children on the way home from school to lunch. In their white summery dresses and with books under their arms, they appeared to me like wonderful little beings of a world entirely different from mine. I watched and envied them. But I often consoled myself with the thought, "When our children come they too will go to school."

On the stoop I lingered too. I watched the children playing jacks and from minute to minute I put off going in. At last with a feeling of guilt I would realise that the afternoon was almost gone and my work not even begun. But it was at such moments that I did my best and quickest work. I would rush upstairs, catch up the bundle of soiled clothes under my arm and run down into the cellar to the wash tubs. Once the washing was done I did not feel so guilty, and by the time I was at the floor, which I scrubbed with great swishes of water, I sang cheerfully, "After the Ball is Over."

70

The sociologist Viviana A. Zelizer describes how child labor laws changed our conception of the worth of children (1985).

The Changing Social Value of Children

Viviana A. Zelizer

The 1900 U.S. Census reported that one child out of every six between the ages of ten and fifteen was gainfully employed. It was an undercount: The total figure of 1,750,178 excluded many child laborers under ten as well as the children "helping out" their parents in sweatshops and on farms, before or after school hours. Ten years later, the official estimate of working children reached 1,990,225. But by 1930, the economic participation of children had dwindled dramatically. Census figures registered 667,118 laborers under fifteen years of age. The decline was particularly marked among younger children. Between 1900 and 1930, the number of children ten to thirteen years old in nonagricultural occupations alone decreased more than six fold, from 186,358 to under 30,000.

The exclusion of children from the marketplace involved a difficult and prolonged battle lasting almost fifty years from the 1870s to the 1930s. It was partly an economic confrontation and partly a legal dispute, but it was also a profound "moral revolution." Two groups with sharply conflicting views of childhood struggled to impose their definition of children's proper place in society. For child labor reformers, children's early labor was a violation of children's sentimental value. As one official of the National Child Labor Committee explained in 1914, a laboring child "is simply a producer, worth so much in dollars and cents, with no standard of value as a human being. . . . How do you calculate your standard of a child's value? . . . as something precious beyond all money standard." On the other hand, opponents of child labor reform were just as vehement in their support of the productive child, "I say it is a tragic thing to contemplate if the Federal Government closes the doors of the factories and you send that little child back, empty-handed; that brave little boy that was looking forward to get money for his mother for something to eat."

The child labor conflict is a key to understanding the profound transformation in the economic and sentimental value of children in the early twentieth century. The price of a useful wage-earning child was directly counterposed to the moral value of an economically useless but emotionally priceless child. In the process, a complex reassessment of children's economic roles took place. It was not just a matter of whether children should work or not. Even the most activist of child labor reformers were unwilling to condemn all types of child work, while their opponents were similarly reluctant to condone all child labor. Instead, their argument centered over conflicting and often ambiguous cultural definitions of what constituted acceptable work for children. New boundaries emerged, differentiating legitimate from illegitimate forms of economic participation by children.

It was not a simple process. As one perplexed contemporary observer noted: "To work or not to work—that is the question. But nobody agrees upon the answer. . . . Who among the controversialists is wrong? And just what is work anyway? When and where does it step across the dead line and become exploitation?" Child work and child money were gradually redefined for the "sacred" twentieth-century child into primarily moral and instructional tools. While child labor laws regulated exclusively working-class children, the new rules for educational child work cut across classes, equally applicable to all "useless" children.

In recent studies, economists and historians have documented the vital significance of child labor for working-class families in the late nineteenth century. Using extensive national data from the 1880s and 1890s, Michael Haines concludes that child labor "appears to have been the main source of additional support for the late nineteenth-century urban family under economic stress." In her analysis of U.S. Federal Population Census manuscripts for Philadelphia in 1880, Claudia Goldin found that Irish children contributed between 38 and 46 percent of the total family labor income in two-parent families; German children 33 to 35 percent, and the native-born 28 to 32 percent. Unlike the mid-twentieth century when married women entered the labor force, in the late nineteenth century a child, not a wife, was likely to become the family's secondary wage earner.

To use children as active participants in the household economy of the working class was not only economically indispensable but also a legitimate social practice. The middle class, with its own children in school, still wistfully admired the moral principle of early labor. As late as 1915, one observer recognized: "There is among us a reaction to be noted from the . . . overindulgence of our children and a realization that perhaps more work and responsibility would do them good. . . ." Even children's books and magazines, aimed at an educated middle-class audience, "hymned the joys of usefulness," praising the virtues of work, duty, and discipline to their young readers. The standard villain in these stories was an idle child.

Child labor as a morally righteous institution was not a nineteenth-century invention. American children had always worked. In his classic study of family life in Plymouth Colony, John Demos suggests that by the time children turned six or eight, they were expected to assume the role of "little adults," engaged in useful tasks in their own homes, or apprenticed elsewhere. Laws governing the poor in the seventeenth and eighteenth centuries similarly reflected prevalent

Puritan views on the virtue of work by providing employment for dependent children.

Industrial work created different job opportunities for young children in the late eighteenth century. Employers welcomed their nimble "little fingers" for the "gigantic automatons of labor saving machinery." Indeed, the first workers in the American spinning mill set up in Rhode Island by Samuel Slater in 1790, were nine children between the ages of seven and twelve. By 1820, young boys and girls constituted 55 percent of the operatives employed in Rhode Island's textile mills. An enthusiastic writer for *Nile's Register* eagerly anticipated the pecuniary payoffs of child labor for local economies: "If we suppose that before the establishment of these manufactories, there were two hundred children between seven and sixteen years of age, that contributed nothing towards their maintenance and that they are now employed, it makes an immediate difference of $13,500 a year to the value produced in the town!"

71

During the Depression many children had to work to help their needy families. The black civil rights leader Anne Moody describes her efforts as a child in her 1976 memoir.

Coming of Age in Mississippi

Anne Moody

Times really got hard at home. Mama was trying to buy clothes for the three of us, feed us, and keep us in school. She just couldn't do it on five dollars a week. Food began to get even scarcer. Mama discovered that the old white lady living in the big white two-story house on the hill sold clabber milk to Negroes for twenty-five cents a gallon. Mama started buying two or three gallons a week from her. Now we ate milk-and-bread all the time (milk with crumbled corn-bread in it). Then Mrs. Johnson started giving her the dinner leftovers and we ate those. Things got so bad that Mama started crying again. And she cried until school was out.

One Saturday I went to get some clabber milk and the old white lady asked me to sweep her porch and sidewalks. After I had finished she gave me a quarter and didn't take the quarter Mama had given me for the milk. When I got home and told Mama, she laughed until she cried. Then she sent me up there every day to see if the old lady wanted her porch swept. I was nine years old and I had my first job. I earned seventy-five cents and two gallons of milk a week.

Soon after I started working for that old lady, I stopped drinking her milk. One evening, I was cleaning the back porch where she kept it, when a little Negro boy came to buy two gallons. She came in to get them while he waited out in the backyard. She kept the milk in three old safes with screen doors. I saw her open one of them and pour some milk out of a big dishpan. Then she went out to the yard, leaving the safe door open. Now this old lady had eight cats that also lived on the back porch. About five of them scrambled into the open safe and began lapping up the milk in the dishpan. She was fussy about her cats so I didn't yell at them or shoo them away. I just let them eat. "She'll run them out and pour that milk out when she come back in," I thought.

But when she came back, she just let those cats help themselves. When they had had enough, she pushed them away from the milk and closed the safe door. I stood there looking at all of this and I thought of how many times I had drunk that milk. "I'll starve before I eat any more of it," I thought.

I could hardly wait to tell Mama, but when I did she didn't believe me. "She probably is gonna give the rest of that milk to them cats too. I don't think that woman would sell us milk she let cats eat out of," Mama said. I didn't argue with her. "I will still bring the milk home," I thought. "Y'all can eat it but not me."

I didn't keep that job long. That big old white house had the biggest porches I had ever seen. It had a porch on the bottom and top floors circling the entire house, which gave the house a rounded look. Pretty soon the old lady even had me sweeping the inside of the house downstairs where she lived and dusting the furniture. She started keeping me up there all day. Mama didn't like that. One day she kept me up there until after dark. Mama came up there and got me.

"What she got you doing she have you up there all day?" Mama asked me when we got home.

"I sweep the porches and dust the furniture and sweep the bottom house. I was washing out some stockings for her today," I told her.

"You go up there tomorrow and you tell her you ain't gonna come back no more, you heah. She been trying to kill you for seventy-five cent and that little shittin' milk she gives you. Tell her you gotta stay at home with Adline and Junior."

The next morning I went and swept the porches and cleaned the house and stayed up there all day. When I had finished, I told her what Mama told me to tell her. I didn't really want to quit working for her. I got a good feeling out of earning three quarters and two gallons of milk a week. It made me feel good to be able to give Adline and Junior each a quarter and then have one for myself.

72

The New Deal often created educational opportunities under the cover of work programs for young Americans. Thus, it encouraged millions of young people to help their families by working in the Civilian Conservation Corps, while others were enabled to finish their education through part-time work in the National Youth Administration according to historian Paula Fass (1989).

Children and the New Deal

Paula S. Fass

The New Deal entered the educational arena through the back door, as it were, not as an agent of education, but as a dispenser of relief. Throughout the thirties, the Roosevelt administration never overtly questioned the local basis of educational policy or the autonomy of the states in decisions about schooling and did not set out to establish a federal responsibility for education. Instead, in the course of its relief efforts, the New Deal developed educational programs and facilities that paralleled those of traditional educational institutions. Those programs were federally administered and controlled but did not technically interfere with or challenge local and state control over education. In devising and administering relief programs, the federal government not only became an active participant in all phases of social life, including education, but also uncovered basic inequities, inefficiencies, and "perplexing problems" that had been dormant or taboo subjects. In the end, the Roosevelt administration injected the federal government into the educational arena in such a way that it both exposed educational failures and defined their redress as a federal responsibility.

Roosevelt and the relief administrators most immediately involved—Harry Hopkins and Harold Ickes—responded to the school emergency of the depression not by assisting the schools as organizations but by assisting school people and school plants. They did this through a mixed bag of work relief programs, work-study schemes, supplementary social work enterprises, and public works construction and repair projects, organized and administered through FDR's alphabet-soup agencies—the Public Works Administration (PWA), Works Progress Administration (WPA), Federal Emergency Relief Administration (FERA), Civilian Conservation Corps (CCC), and the National Youth Administration (NYA). These separately run agencies, relying heavily on discretionary administrative policies whose purpose was to provide maximum individual relief, were coordinated with a variety of federal departments but almost never responsible to the Office of Education. Thus, to speak of the New Deal's educational activities is both to describe a massive program of improvements—school construction and repair, teacher employment, courses in literacy and naturalization, vocational training and rehabilitation, nursery schools, correspondence courses, educational radio programs, and subventions to high-school and college students—and to describe no educational policy at all. In most cases (the NYA was in part an exception to this), education was a by-product of work relief, and the educational content and purpose were defined in the course of the agencies' activities by the need to find appropriate employment for teachers, carpenters, masons, students, nurses, and unskilled laborers.

Since many of its educational endeavors were unfocused, the New Deal often discovered its educational commitments in the process of program administration. When the CCC, the most popular of the New Deal work projects, got under way, the aim was to provide out-of-work youth from relief families with immediate employment in conservation work. The expectation was that CCC recruits would pick up what they needed to learn in the process. Despite resistance from CCC director Robert Fechner, it soon became clear that explicit instruction, not only in the technical aspects of conservation but also in basic literacy, was often urgently needed. Additionally, as the officials of the CCC sought to occupy and stimulate camp enrollees in their nonworking hours, they turned to education in subjects such as Latin, mathematics, and history, as well as in vocational skills and literacy. At first these activities were entirely voluntary, but the moral pressure on enrollees to occupy their time usefully made the educational supplements almost as basic to CCC activities as the work regime.

By 1938–39, more than 90 percent of the members of the corps were enrolled in some instruction, averaging four hours per week. Two-thirds of these enrollees were in job-related classes. . . . An educational adviser had early been attached to each CCC camp, and it is clear that the camps, by utilizing various local resources, helped to educate thousands of young men, providing many with basic literacy and remedial instruction and some with welcome advanced education. When it extended the life of the CCC in 1937, Congress formalized the educational activities of the CCC by providing each camp with a school building and by increasing specifically educational appropriations. By 1941, credit for educational work completed in CCC camps was provided by forty-seven states and the District of Columbia. The CCC had certainly become the center of a federally administered educational enterprise, but the camps were run by the War Department, with personnel and responsibilities shared with the Departments of Agriculture, Labor, and Interior and, to only a limited degree, the United States Office of Education.

The National Youth Administration, while more focused in its goals, was even more administratively fragmented. Established in 1935 as an autonomous division of the WPA, the NYA had a clear objective: to permit students in secondary schools and colleges to continue their education by providing them with part-time, often on-campus, jobs as clerks, janitors, and research assistants or jobs on construction projects, on playgrounds, and in nursery schools. The NYA also provided work relief with a prevocational objective to unemployed, out-of-school youths of school age. In 1938, the NYA channeled its grants through 26,751 colleges and secondary schools and reached 368,921 students. At the height of its activities, in 1935–36, NYA provided almost half a million students with various kinds of work-based financial assistance. . . . Despite administrative complexity and professional hostility, the NYA was sufficiently able to enlist the cooperation of local school officials to become one of the New Deal's most successful programs, popular with students and the public and effective in terms of New Deal policies whose principal objective was to keep young people out of the labor market.

In addition to the CCC and NYA, the only exclusively youth-oriented programs, the New Deal also provided various educational programs through the WPA. These included worker education, nursery schools, vocational retraining, and parent education. In all these programs, the federal government's stated objective was simply to provide relief funds. It chose personnel on the basis of relief needs but left program content to various professional groups and state departments of education. . . .

The New Deal programs encouraged an awareness of how poverty often underlay inequalities in educational attainment. Before the 1930s, equal educational opportunity was more often a catch phrase for providing people with only as much education as they could use than it was a platform for eliminating inequalities in access to education. But New Deal programs and especially the NYA subsidies provided a challenge to this perspective. As Harry Hopkins made clear in an informal address to NYA state administrators:

> Well, I think we have started something. It seems to me that what we are starting is this: that anyone who has capacities should be in college and should get a higher education, and that he is going to get it irrespective of his economic status. That is the crux of the thing, to decide once and for all that this business of getting an education and going to law school and medical school and dental school and going to college is not to be confined to the people who have an economic status at home that permits them to do it. . . . All this about anyone being able to go to school who wants to go to school is sheer nonsense and always has been, in my opinion. I grant you there are a few exceptional students who can do it, but the great majority of people cannot; and anyone who knows anything about this game at all knows that in the good old days of '28 and '29 tens of thousands of young people were leaving school to go to work for no other reason than that they were poor. They were quite capable of going to college, far more so than some of us in this room.

Hopkins was not alone in this challenge to the educational status quo, nor in his slap at college-bred egos. Fresh from his experiences as chief of the NYA, Aubrey Williams came to the very center of elite education, Harvard University, to give the coveted Inglis Lecture in 1940. His address was on vocational education, but he made clear that "I am not talking now of vocational training. In fact, I think there has been an overemphasis in the past on a strict division between vocational and academic education." He proceeded to condemn the idea that education was the preserve of the gentleman and training that of the laborer. "I do not believe that our democracy can afford to provide less educational opportunity for any of our people. On the contrary, I think it should provide more adequately so that children in all parts of the country, from all races, and all economic groups, may have the best we know to give them." To do this, Williams insisted, required that "we find a way to extend to them the opportunity to work during the period of their schooling."

73

The historian Robert William Kirk describes how children in the 1940s were encouraged to participate in scrap collection drives to aid the war effort (1994).

American Children in the Second World War

Robert William Kirk

After Pearl Harbor, material and psychological necessities impelled government authorities, industrialists, educators, parents, adult leaders of children's groups, and others to add their voices to that of President Roosevelt to ask youngsters to participate in scrap drives. Psychological factors include improving character through practicing diligence, enhancing patriotism, developing a sense of purpose in children in order to reach a common goal, preventing their delinquency, and lessening children's fears and insecurity. Material needs refer, of course, to war industries' critical shortage of scrap rubber, metal, paper, and other items.

Concerned adults believed that children's participation in scrap drives would nurture patriotism within them. The 1940 White House Conference on Children in a Democracy, the Wartime Commission of the National Education Association, the US Office of Education, educators on the state and local level, and the mass media all called attention to increased patriotism as a benefit to children as well as a motive for their participation. Proponents of progressive education concluded that community service would help break down the walls between the classroom and community life, leading children to an appreciation of democratic values. The Wartime Policies Commission asked schools to "emphasize the ideals of freedom and equality for which we are fighting," and at the same time "to provide many opportunities for community service...." *Parents' Magazine* echoed the NEA Commission's policy statement when it exhorted: "It isn't enough to drive ... youngsters to do their part in the war effort to collect scrap, to take the grease to the butcher, to save pennies for war stamps, to draw the curtains for the dimout...." Rather, children too young to join the armed forces "must learn to understand and live by the principles for which this country fights." ...

If collecting scrap had merely assuaged children's fears and stemmed delinquency, salvage could have been well justified as a beneficial developmental activity like creative play. However, federal authorities desperately needed materials necessary to augment scarce commodities. At various times between 1941 and 1945, rubber, metals, and paper were in short supply. Shortages resulted because war plants tried to replace vintage weapons and to supply America's allies, while at the same time other manufacturers sought to furnish the needs of increasingly affluent civilians. It was not until the spring of 1942 that the War Production Board emphasized national security needs by forbidding consumer industries to use materials essential for defense production. Shortages, however, were to remain no less acute. The United States had either enough natural resources, or the technical capability of making sufficient substitute materials, such as rubber, to win the war. But the nation had insufficient workers to extract, process, and fabricate these resources. War production had created millions of new jobs at the same time that men went away to war. From 1941 to 1945, the work force increased from 45 to 55 million. Because paid work enrolled increasing numbers of women, Blacks, Chicanos, the unskilled, the handicapped, and the long-term unemployed, opportunities were opened for 14- to 17-year olds. By 1944, 1,350,000 of the nation's 14- to 17-year-olds worked full-time, and 1,400,000 worked part-time while attending school. Employment of 14–18-year-old boys increased 169 percent between 1940 and 1944, and the employment of girls in that age group increased 243 percent during the same four-year period. When older teenagers enrolled in part- or full-time employment, opportunities were created for children under age 14. It was as if children as an age group had moved up a notch.

To many, children's efforts appeared to be a partial solution to the shortage of workers and to be well within legal, moral, and ethical bounds. Although the United States Children's Bureau had reported that 37 percent of children illegally employed during the war were under age 14, and that of those, 12 percent were 11 or younger, those who favored children collecting scrap did not advocate breaking the law. Instead, they favored mobilizing children as volunteers and making their tasks at least appear to be fun, competitive, and patriotic. Because boys and girls were to volunteer during non-school hours, and because they would not, at least ostensibly, become the victims of exploitative private employers, editors of popular journals signified their approval. *Better Homes and Gardens* pointed out, "There are still plenty of odd jobs crying to be done, which boys and girls of 12 or 13, or even younger ones can do. These younger citizens can do wonders with paper- and scrap- collection routes. . . ." Calling children "great little scavengers," *Parents' Magazine* urged readers to organize their sons and daughters to collect salvage items from neighbors. "Don't delay," the editor warned, "start now."

Because reformers had fulfilled the promise of their long crusade to liberate the young from exploitation, officials who wanted children to collect scrap had to make volunteer work appear to children as well as to parents to be desirable rather than coercive. In order to do so they made use of the groups into which children were already organized. Children were divided by gender into two primary groups with ascribed roles. Prepubescent girls might be mobilized along with boys to collect discarded materials; because they were judged by the amount of materials they brought in, collecting scrap provided a better opportunity for young girls to participate with boys on the basis of equality than did playing games. But older girls were mobilized under their own leaders and often performed tasks separate from those assigned to boys. Members of a girls club, for example, performed duties such as caring for small children, rolling bandages, or knitting socks. In addition, neighborhood children organized themselves into informal, *ad hoc* groups under their natural leaders. To motivate these children, adults made use of children's "communal feeling," of what David Riesman called the "brooding omnipresence of the peer group." In addition, many boys and girls belonged to formal groups such as the Future Farmers of America, Boy Scouts, Girl Scouts, Cubs, and Camp Fire Girls, the adult leaders of which pledged their followers to work for the cause of victory. Moreover, almost all of the nation's children were compulsorily divided and supervised in schools and could be reached in the classroom with any message the school authorities agreed to relay.

To motivate boys and girls, educators, government authorities, and the media used the organizations and pervasive culture of children as a fulcrum and the child's desire to be perceived as a valued member of that culture as a lever. They gave salvage campaigns compelling names such as *Salvage for Victory*. They awarded children titles reminiscent of those borne by soldiers; for instance, the WPB bestowed the title *Paper Trooper* on children all over the nation. Paper Troopers wore cloth shoulder insignias that gave them "official status." Authorities set schools in competition for the largest aggregate amount of scrap and the largest average total per pupil in each state. Occasionally, they sought to motivate children, as they did adults, through material rewards such as free movie tickets to be exchanged for donations of scrap. But, usually they relied on nonmonetary rewards such as advancement in rank. With incentives such as these, children showed themselves eager to earn their stripes.

74

In 1944 the U.S. Supreme Court defended the constitutionality of child labor laws against the challenges of religious groups who claimed that the laws interfered with First and Fourteenth Amendment rights.

Child Labor and the Law

U.S. Supreme Court

Prince v. Massachusetts
321 U.S. 158 (1944)

Mr. Justice RUTLEDGE delivered the opinion of the Court.

The case brings for review another episode in the conflict between Jehovah's Witnesses and state authority. This time Sarah Prince appeals from convictions for violating Massachusetts' child labor laws, by acts said to be a rightful exercise of her religious convictions.

When the offenses were committed she was the aunt and custodian of Betty M. Simmons, a girl nine years of age. Originally there were three separate complaints. They were, shortly, for (1) refusal to disclose Betty's identity and age to a public officer whose duty was to enforce the statutes; (2) furnishing her with magazines, knowing she was to sell them unlawfully, that is, on the street; and (3) as Betty's custodian, permitting her to work contrary to law. The complaints were made, respectively, pursuant to §§79, 80 and 81 of Chapter 149, Gen. Laws of Mass. (Ter. Ed.). The Supreme Judicial Court reversed the conviction under the first complaint on state grounds; but sustained the judgments founded on the other two. 313 Mass. 223, 46 N.E.2d 755. They present the only questions for our decision. These are whether §§80 and 81, as applied, contravene the Fourteenth Amendment by denying or abridging appellant's freedom of religion and by denying to her the equal protection of the laws. . . .

. . . Mrs. Prince, living in Brockton, is the mother of two young sons. She also has legal custody of Betty Simmons, who lives with them. The children too are Jehovah's Witnesses and both Mrs. Prince and Betty testified they were ordained ministers. The former was accustomed to go each week on the streets of Brockton to distribute "Watchtower" and "Consolation," according to the usual plan. She had permitted the children to engage in this activity previously, and had been warned against doing so by the school attendance officer, Mr. Perkins. But, until December 18, 1941, she generally did not take them with her at night.

That evening, as Mrs. Prince was preparing to leave her home, the children asked to go. She at first refused. Childlike, they resorted to tears; and, motherlike, she yielded. Arriving downtown, Mrs. Prince permitted the children "to engage in the preaching work with her upon the sidewalks." That is, with specific reference to Betty, she and Mrs. Prince took positions about twenty feet apart near a street intersection. Betty held up in her hand, for passers-by to see, copies of "Watchtower" and "Consolation." From her shoulders hung the usual canvas magazine bag on which was printed: "Watchtower and Consolation 5cts. per copy." No one accepted a copy from Betty that evening and she received no money. Nor did her aunt. But on other occasions, Betty had received funds and given out copies.

Mrs. Prince and Betty remained until 8:45 p.m. A few minutes before this, Mr. Perkins approached Mrs. Prince. A discussion ensued. He inquired and she refused to give Betty's name. However, she stated the child attended the Shaw School. Mr. Perkins referred to his previous warnings and said he would allow five minutes for them to get off the street. Mrs. Prince admitted she supplied Betty with the magazines and said, "[N]either you nor anybody else can stop me. . . . This child is exercising her God-given right and her constitutional right to preach the gospel, and no creature has a right to interfere with God's commands." However, Mrs. Prince and Betty departed. She remarked as she went, "I'm not going through this any more. We've been through it time and time again. I'm going home and put the little girl to bed." It may be added that testimony, by Betty, her aunt and others, was offered at the trials, and was excluded, to show that Betty believed it was her religious duty to perform this work and failure would bring condemnation "to everlasting destruction at Armageddon."

As the case reaches us, the questions are no longer open whether what the child did was a "sale" or an "offer to sell" within §69 or was "work" within §81. The state court's decision has foreclosed them adversely to appellant as a matter of state law. The only question remaining therefore is whether, as construed and applied, the statute is valid. . . .

[Appellant's argument] rests squarely on freedom of religion under the First Amendment, applied by the Fourteenth to the states. She buttresses this foundation, however, with a claim of parental right as secured by the due process clause of the latter Amendment. Cf. Meyer v. Nebraska, 262 U.S. 390. These guaranties, she thinks, guard alike herself and the child in what they have done. Thus, two claimed liberties are at stake. One is the parent's to bring up the child in the way he should go, which for appellant means to teach him the tenets and the practices of their faith. The other freedom is the child's, to observe these; and among them is "to preach the gospel . . . by public distribution" of "Watchtower" and "Consolation," in conformity with the scripture: "A little child shall lead them." . . .

To make accommodation between these freedoms and an exercise of state authority always is delicate. . . . On one side is the obviously earnest claim for freedom of conscience and religious practice. With it is allied the parent's claim to authority in her own household and in the rearing of her children. The parent's conflict with the state over control of the child and his training is serious enough when only secular matters are concerned. It becomes the more so when an element of religious conviction enters. Against these sacred private interests, basic in a democracy, stand the interests of society to protect the welfare of children, and the state's assertion of authority to that end, made here in a manner conceded valid if only secular things were involved. . . . It is the interest of youth itself, and of the whole community, that children be both safeguarded from abuses and given opportunities for growth into free and independent well-developed men and citizens. Between contrary pulls of such weight, the safest and most objective recourse is to the lines already marked out, not precisely but for guides, in narrowing the no man's land where this battle has gone on.

The rights of children to exercise their religion, and of parents to give them religious training and to encourage them in the practice of religious belief, as against preponderant sentiment and assertion of state power voicing it, have had recognition here, most recently in West Virginia State Board of Education v. Barnette, 319 U.S. 624. Previously in Pierce v. Society of Sisters, 268 U.S. 510, this Court had sustained the parent's authority to provide religious with secular schooling, and the child's right to receive it, as against the state's requirement of attendance at public schools. And in Meyer v. Nebraska, 262 U.S. 390, children's rights to receive teaching in languages other than the nation's common tongue were guarded against the state's encroachment. It is cardinal with us that the custody, care and nurture of the child reside first in the parents, whose primary function and freedom include preparation for obligations the state can neither supply nor hinder. Pierce v. Society of Sisters, supra. And it is in recognition of this that these decisions have respected the private realm of family life which the state cannot enter.

But the family itself is not beyond regulation in the public interest, as against a claim of religious liberty. Reynolds v. United States, 98 U.S. 145; Davis v. Beason, 133 U.S. 333. And neither rights of religion nor rights of parenthood are beyond limitation. Acting to guard the general interest in youth's well being, the state as parens patriae may restrict the parent's control by requiring school attendance, regulating or prohibiting the child's labor and in many other ways. Its authority is not nullified merely because the parent grounds his claim to control the child's course of conduct on religion or conscience. Thus, he cannot claim freedom from compulsory vaccination for the child more than for himself on religious grounds. [Jacobson v. Massachusetts, 197 U.S. 11.] The right to practice religion freely does not include liberty to expose the community or the child to communicable disease or the latter to ill health or death. The catalogue . . . is sufficient to show what indeed appellant hardly disputes, that the state has a wide range of power for limiting parental freedom and authority in things affecting the child's welfare; and that this includes, to some extent, matters of conscience and religious conviction.

75

Many contemporary immigrant children, especially Asian children, work for long hours after attending school. The journalist Samuel G. Freedman describes one such child in a New York City high school in the 1980s.

Working Children in Contemporary Chinatown

Samuel G. Freedman

See Wai entered P.S. 130 in September 1980, equipped with his parents' advice to dress drably and say little. He was a *sang sau*, "one without experience," and he would do best to listen and obey. But even wordlessly, See Wai unsettled the school, for he was an eleven-year-old with fewer than two years of formal education. Academically, he belonged in the second grade, socially in the sixth. The school compromised by placing him in a fifth-grade class for English as a Second Language, and there he learned the alphabet and the family members and the different types of transportation. He carried with him a small thick book entitled *A New Essential English — Chinese Dictionary*, and he thumbed it until the shine was gone from the jade green cover. With its definitions from "a" to "zoology," with its charts of tenses and conjugations, the book served as See Wai's Rosetta stone.

As it had in China, however, free education exacted a hidden price. Each day after school, See Wai hurried down Canal Street to work beside his parents in a garment factory owned by a cousin and her husband. It was an oppressive place, a single square room with flaking paint and swirling lint and drifts of cardboard cartons and machines whining like a chorus of dental drills. Bent forward on a metal stool, Sau Ling stitched until her eyes burned and her back throbbed, and then she stitched more. Let Keung pressed the finished garments, sheathed them in cellophane, and arranged them on metal racks. It was common to find children in the factory, some simply collecting there because Chinatown had a dire shortage of day care, and many more laboring because on garment factory wages, making the rent was a family-wide campaign. Sau Ling worked seventy-two hours a week, and even with See Wai assisting her for twenty hours, they brought home a total of $200 on the piecework pay scale. Only when his shift ended at 10 P.M. could See Wai begin the normal task of an eleven-year-old, doing his homework.

Gradually, the Muis hardened their hold on America. Let Keung repaid his brother and then pulled himself, Sau Ling, and See Wai out of the garment factory, infuriated at how his cousins, his blood, had abused them. He worked as a cook and then a noodle maker, and with Sau Ling's income from a new factory job, he saved enough money by 1984 to open a sidewalk vegetable stall, his own tiny version of the Chinese-American dream. Through the sixth and seventh grades, See Wai had his afternoons and evenings free for study. He won a school prize for his sketch of a Taishan landscape and wrote simple poems and essays to improve his English. He taped his drawings and writings over the holes in his bedroom wall. Sometimes See Wai dreamed of China, but the dreams were not sentimental; in one, he stumbled upon snakes while hiking through a forest and in another, he returned to Yong He Li to find the village deserted. He was trying to become an American now, and the more the intricacies of language defied him, the more he relied on the external emblems of belonging. On the small portable television in the kitchen, he watched "The Little Rascals." When he posed for his graduation portrait in junior high school, he affected a Beatlesque moptop. At about the same time, he and his sisters took part in an informal ritual of renaming themselves, a common moment of passage for the children of Chinatown. As an older cousin read a list of American names, each of the three Muis chose one. May Fong took Christine; So Fong selected Cindy; and, finally, See Wai, "Calm Famous," set aside the brand of his birth for the prosaic alias of Andy.

The Chinatown that was home to See Wai and hundreds of other Seward Park students contradicted not only the Chinese vision of *Gum San* [gold mountain] but the American image of an ethnic idyll, peopled by industrious parents and their scholarly children. Industry and scholarship certainly abounded in Chinatown, but so did youth gangs, sweatshops, and tuberculosis. The stereotype of Chinese Americans, or more broadly Asian Americans, as the "model minority" left little room for the realities of life in New York's fastest-growing ghetto. . . .

The most unifying factor in Chinatown was, unfortunately, its subsistence economy. Despite such prominent Chinese-American successes as the architect I. M. Pei and the computer executive An Wang, the new immigrants typically had more in common with Let Keung and Sau Ling. The 1980 census found that 55 percent of New York's Chinese spoke no English and 71 percent had not completed high school. Six of every ten families staked their lives on two industries, food and textiles. A waiter generally earned $200 a month in base pay, predicated on a sixty-hour week without overtime, medical care, or job security, and a seamstress could expect to bring home $500 a month for similar hours and similar conditions, her lot softened only by a union health care plan. Even the youngest girls referred to themselves as *yee chong ah mo*, "garment factory old woman."

Chinatown's poverty coexisted with Chinatown's plenty, for at the same time that peasants were thronging into one small, discrete sector of Manhattan, desperate for any bed and any job, Asian investors fleeing the forthcoming Communist assumption of Hong Kong were sowing their millions in the same soil.

Only two banks served Chinatown in 1940, but there was business enough for twenty-seven in 1986, and they tallied assets above $2 billion. The money made Chinatown, if not the golden mountain, then at least the golden ghetto, a study in staggering contrasts, with high-tech shopping arcades rising beside turn-of-the-century tenements where tuberculosis raged at almost twice the national rate. While the waiters and seamstresses saved toward opening their own small restaurant or factory, the neighborhood's soaring rents, narrow profits, and vicious competition felled such businesses at the rate of two a week. The days of buying a dream for $25,000 were over in Chinatown.

The single uncomplicated success of Chinatown, it appeared, was its youth. In 1985, when Asian-American children made up but 5.5 percent of the city's public school populace, they accounted for about 30 percent of the students in the most selective academic high schools—Bronx Science, Brooklyn Tech, and Stuyvesant. From there, the immigrants marched off to Harvard, the Massachusetts Institute of Technology, and the University of Chicago, brandishing 1,400-point scores on the Scholastic Achievement Test and Westinghouse Talent Search plaques. The very personification of the Asian American superstudent was a boy named Chi Luu, an ethnic Chinese who escaped Vietnam by boat, reached New York in his teens, and graduated from City College in 1984 as the valedictorian. The explanation of such achievements struck many as simple: Chinese culture venerated scholarship, as it had since Confucius, and children of superior character excelled, as they always had in America.

All the accolades were grounded in truth, but there was more than one truth at work in the Chinese-American experience. A poll of Chinese immigrant children conducted by author and academic Betty Lee Sung in 1987 found that while three-quarters believed they could succeed in America if they tried, an almost comparable majority said they were *not* better off in this country. The dichotomy derived, in part, from the shifting nature of Chinese immigrants. Students like See Wai, rural peasants unschooled in English and barely literate in their own tongue, were supplanting the urban, educated elite of Hong Kong and Taiwan in New York's classrooms. Nearly half the pupils in See Wai's elementary school required bilingual courses, and a 1984 study found that only 28 percent of the elementary school pupils in Chinatown were reading at grade level, compared to 55 percent of their peers citywide. One-third of the neighborhood's teenagers worked at least twenty hours a week. The combination of the need to learn a bewildering new language and to contribute to the family coffers drove the failure and dropout rates for Chinese-American children steadily higher. And whenever a student grew disaffected, a youth gang stood ready to recruit him for its protection and extortion rackets and to pay him as much in a week as his father made in a month. The promising candidate who demurred at gang membership often had a change of heart after being beaten by his suitors.

The degree to which many Chinese-American students surmounted the obstacles and mastered their schoolwork reflected cultural factors, but not necessarily those most widely assumed. The process of learning the 1,000 ideograms required for basic literacy in their own language heightened the ability of Chinese immigrants to memorize material. Their particular skill in science and mathematics had much to do with the limited role English plays in quantitative subjects. The Chinese-American affinity for such courses, and at Seward Park for the business curriculum as well, gave lie to the legend of Confucian scholarship. The major reason the ancient Chinese hurled themselves into study for the imperial examinations, the major reason their [descendants] in New York crammed for tests in chemistry and computer science, was that achievement promised employment and employment promised upward mobility. What the Chinese immigrants shared with the Jewish immigrants who had once slept in the same tenements and sat in the same schoolrooms and slaved in the same sweatshops was not a religious belief in Education, the god on the wall of the Seward Park auditorium. What they shared was the pragmatic judgment of a landless people with a diasporic past that one could survive best by one's wits, for they were the single possession no despot could plunder.

Winslow Homer, *The Noon Recess. Harper's Weekly*, June 28, 1873.

Part Six

Learning

Modern conceptions of childhood in the Western world are intimately linked to issues of schooling and learning. In the United States learning has been fundamental to child rearing since the Puritans insisted that children be made literate and trained to a livelihood. Educational reform spread from New England to the rest of the country in the mid-nineteenth century. Learning has been a fundamental part of child life, but schooling, which expanded greatly in the early twentieth century to encompass more and more years of a child's life, has been a much more contested and politicized matter. Today schools are a contentious political battlefield and education an arena in which American failures toward children seem to be most manifest.

76

While Americans today trace their roots to all parts of the earth, the fundamental social definitions of childhood and the political and cultural institutions that sustain them are of European origin. The French historian Philippe Ariès wrote a seminal book on the history of childhood in Europe and, in effect, initiated the field of childhood studies in the United States as well (1962). Here Ariès makes the critical link between the evolution of modern childhood and the separation from adult life that is enforced by schooling.

Education and the Concept of Childhood

Philippe Ariès

In the Middle Ages, at the beginning of modern times, and for a long time after that in the lower classes, children were mixed with adults as soon as they were considered capable of doing without their mothers or nannies, not long after a tardy weaning (in other words, at about the age of seven). They immediately went straight into the great community of men, sharing in the work and play of their companions, old and young alike. The movement of collective life carried along in a single torrent all ages and classes, leaving nobody any time for solitude and privacy. In these crowded, collective existences there was no room for a private sector. The family fulfilled a function; it ensured the transmission of life, property and names; but it did not penetrate very far into human sensibility. Myths such as courtly and precious love denigrated marriage, while realities such as the apprenticeship of children loosened the emotional bond between parents and children. Medieval civilization had forgotten the *paideia* of the ancients and knew nothing as yet of modern education. That is the main point: it had no idea of education. Nowadays our society depends, and knows that it depends, on the success of its educational system. It has a system of education, a concept of education, an awareness of its importance. New sciences such as psycho-analysis, pediatrics and psychology devote themselves to the problems of childhood, and their findings are transmitted to parents by way of a mass of popular literature. Our world is obsessed by the physical, moral and sexual problems of childhood.

This preoccupation was unknown to medieval civilization, because there was no problem for the Middle Ages: as soon as he had been weaned, or soon after, the child became the natural companion of the adult. The age groups of Neolithic times, the Hellenistic *paideia*, presupposed a difference and a transition between the world of children and that of adults, a transition made by means of an initiation or an education. Medieval civilization failed to perceive this difference and therefore lacked this concept of transition.

The great event was therefore the revival, at the beginning of modern times, of an interest in education. This affected a certain number of churchmen, lawyers and scholars, few in number in the fifteenth century, but increasingly numerous and influential in the sixteenth and seventeenth centuries when they merged with the advocates of religious reform. For they were primarily moralists rather than humanists: the humanists remained attached to the idea of a general culture spread over the whole of life and showed scant interest in an education confined to children. These reformers, these moralists . . . fought passionately against the anarchy (or what henceforth struck them as the anarchy) of medieval society, where the Church, despite its repugnance, had long ago resigned itself to it and urged the faithful to seek salvation far from this pagan world, in some monastic retreat. A positive moralization of society was taking place: the moral aspect of religion was gradually triumphing in practice over the sacred or eschatological aspect. This was how these champions of a moral order were led to recognize the importance of education. . . . Their writings extended from Gerson to Port-Royal, becoming increasingly frequent in the sixteenth and seventeenth centuries. The religious orders founded at that time, such as the Jesuits or the Oratorians, became teaching orders, and their teaching was no longer addressed to adults like that of the preachers or mendicants of the Middle Ages, but was essentially meant for children and young people. This literature, this propaganda, taught parents that they were spiritual guardians, that they were responsible before God for the souls, and indeed the bodies too, of their children.

Henceforth it was recognized that the child was not ready for life, and that he had to be subjected to a special treatment, a sort of quarantine, before he was allowed to join the adults.

This new concern about education would gradually install itself in the heart of society and transform it from top to bottom. The family ceased to be simply an institution for the transmission of a name and an estate—it assumed a moral and spiritual function, it moulded bodies and souls. The care expended on children inspired new feelings, a new emotional attitude, to which the iconography of the seventeenth century gave brilliant and insistent expression: the modern concept of the family. Parents were no longer content with setting up only a few of their children and neglecting the others. The ethics of the time ordered them to give all their children, and not just the eldest—and in the late seventeenth century even the girls—a training for life. It was understood that this training would be provided by the school. Traditional apprenticeship was replaced by the school, an utterly transformed school, an instrument of strict discipline, protected by the law-courts and the police-courts. The extraordinary development of the school in the seventeenth century was a consequence of the new interest taken by parents in their children's education. The moralists taught them that it was their duty to send their children to school very early in life:

"Those parents," states a text of 1602, "who take an interest in their children's education [*liberos erudiendos*] are more worthy of respect than those who just bring them into the world. They give them not only life but a good and holy life. That is why those parents are right to send their children at the tenderest age to the market of true wisdom [in other words to college] where they will become the architects of their own fortune, the ornaments of their native land, their family and their friends."

Family and school together removed the child from adult society. The school shut up a childhood which had hitherto been free within an increasingly severe disciplinary system, which culminated in the eighteenth and nineteenth centuries in the total claustration of the boarding-school. The solicitude of family, Church, moralists and administrators deprived the child of the freedom he had hitherto enjoyed among adults. It inflicted on him the birch, the prison cell—in a word, the punishments usually reserved for convicts from the lowest strata of society. But this severity was the expression of a very different feeling from the old indifference: an obsessive love which was to dominate society from the eighteenth century on. It is easy to see why this invasion of the public's sensibility by childhood should have resulted in the now better-known phenomenon of Malthusianism or birth-control. The latter made its appearance in the eighteenth century just when the family had finished organizing itself around the child, and raised the wall of private life between the family and society.

77

In seventeenth-century New England the law required that parents both instruct and discipline their children. Parents were held to account for their children's adequate guidance, as shown in this Massachusetts Statute.

Family Instruction in Early Massachusetts

Colonial Document

Massachusetts Statute, 1648

Forasmuch as the good education of children is of Singular behoof and benefit to any commonwealth, and whereas many parents and masters are too indulgent and negligent of their duty in that kind: It is therefore ordered that the selectmen of every town, in the several precincts and quarters where they dwell, shall have a vigilant eye over their brethren and neighbors to see, first, that none of them shall suffer so much barbarism in any of their families as not to endeavor to teach by themselves, or others, their children and apprentices so much learning as may enable them perfectly to read the English tongue and knowledge of the capital laws, upon penalty of twenty shillings for each neglect therein.

Also that all masters of families do once a week (at the least) catechize their children and servants in the grounds and principles of religion. . . . If any be unable to do so much, that then at least, they procure such children or apprentices to learn some short orthodox catechism without book, that they may be able to answer unto the questions that shall be propounded to them out of such catechism by their parents or masters or any of the selectmen when they shall call them to a trial of what they have learned in this kind.

And further that all parents and masters do breed and bring up their children and apprentices in some honest lawful calling, labor, or employment, either in husbandry, or some other trade profitable for themselves and the commonwealth, if they will not or cannot train them up in learning to fit them for higher employments. And if any of the selectmen, after admonition by them given to such masters of families, shall find them still negligent of their duty in the particulars aforementioned, whereby children and servants become rude, stubborn, and unruly, the said selectmen with the help of two Magistrates or the next County Court for that shire, shall take such children or apprentices from them and place them with some masters for years (boys till they come to twenty-one, and girls eighteen years of age complete) which will more strictly look unto, and force them to submit unto government according to the rules of this order, if by fair means and former instructions they will not be drawn unto it.

78

In the United States the colonial historian Edmund S. Morgan was a pioneer in the historical study of families (1944). Here he discusses the vocational education, literacy training, and catechism that were required by law and were together considered essential parts of the learning experience of children in Puritan New England.

A Puritan Education

Edmund S. Morgan

A parent had to provide for his children, because they were unable to provide for themselves. If he was ever to free himself of the obligation, he must see to it that they knew how to earn a living. "If you're careful to bring them up diligently in proper business," Benjamin Wadsworth advised parents, "you take a good method for their comfortable subsistence in this World (and for their being serviceable in their Generation) you do better for them, then if you should bring them up idly, and yet leave them great Estates." According to law every father had to see that his children were instructed "in some honest lawful calling, labour or imployment, either in husbandry, or some other trade profitable for themselves, and the Common-wealth if they will not or cannot train them up in learning to fit them for higher imployments."

For the first few years of a child's life he was not seriously disturbed by the process of learning a calling. John Cotton did not consider it idleness for young children to "spend much time in pastime and play, for their bodyes are too weak to labour, and their minds to study are too shallow . . . even the first seven years are spent in pastime, and God looks not much at it." Probably most children were set to some kind of useful work before they reached seven. . . .

Samuel Sewall . . . took care that his children should have more to do than play in the streets. In a letter to Daniel Allen, on March 28, 1687, he wrote: "I have two small daughters who begin to goe to schoole: my wife would intreat your good Lady to pleasure her so far as to buy for her, white Fustian drawn, enough for curtins, wallen counterpaine for a bed, and half a duz. chairs, with four threeded green worsted to work it." The young seamstresses whom Sewall expected to ply the green worsted through so much fustian and counterpain were Elizabeth and Hannah Sewall, aged five and seven years respectively. That he intended the materials for them is shown by his request on the same date to his London financial agent, Edward Hull, "to furnish my Cousin Allen with what mony she calls for towards a piece of service my wife Intreat her help in, that so she may set her two Little daughters on work and keep them out of Idlenes."

The daughters of a family could begin the study of a calling at such an early age, because there was little likelihood of their ever following any career but that of a housewife, whether as daughter, wife, or mother. Boys did not ordinarily undertake training in a life's occupation until they had reached a riper age. If the boy was to follow his father's calling, he might begin to pick up the rudiments of it while still very young; but in large families with children of varying talents, not all would be willing or qualified to follow their father's trade. In most cases probably one son inherited the father's business while the others took up some different occupation. They could not begin to learn it until they had decided what it should be, but they were doubtless kept busy about the house with chores of a general nature.

A boy usually chose his calling between the ages of ten and fourteen. Since the training for almost every trade was gained through an apprenticeship of seven years to some master of the trade, if a child wished to be free and able to earn his living by the time he became twenty-one, he had to begin his apprenticeship not later than his fourteenth year. If he began it before then, as many children did, he usually remained an apprentice until he reached twenty-one. Of course if he was so fortunate as to go to college, he might put off the choice of a calling until later; for the mere fact of possessing a college degree narrowed the choice: anyone with a "liberal" education would adopt a "liberal" calling, that is, a calling which required no manual labor and no long period of apprenticeship. About half the graduates of Harvard College in the seventeenth century entered the ministry. Thus for many boys the decision to go to college must have constituted in itself the choice of a calling. In any case most persons had to decide their vocation in life at a comparatively early age, for unless a man underwent the long training necessary either for a liberal education or for a skilled trade, he could look forward to spending his life in a position of servitude as a common laborer. . . .

As far as his children's material welfare was concerned, a Puritan parent could call his duty done when he saw them established in their callings with good husbands and wives. But he was responsible for the well-being of their souls as well as their bodies. If he considered only their material welfare without attention to their spiritual needs, he was, the Puritans thought, like those "who are very careful for the shooe, and take no care for the foot." He lacked common sense. He also lacked religion. Cotton Mather pointed out to the earnest inhabitants of Boston that "If your *main concern* be, to get the *Riches of this World* for your *Children,* and leave a *Belly full* of this *World* unto them, it looks very suspiciously, as if you were yourselves the People of *this World,* whose *Portion* is only in *this Life.*" The point was a telling one, but the Puritans did not rely on mere exhortation to persuade parents of their spiritual duties. In 1642 Massachusetts enacted a law requiring masters of families to teach their children and apprentices to read . . .

[See the amplified law of 1648 in the previous chapter.]

The grounds of the law are clear: the Puritans insisted upon education in order to insure the religious welfare of their children. This motive certainly explains the requirement that children learn a catechism. It also explains in large measure why they should know the capital laws, for the capital laws were simply the most important of the laws of God, an understanding of which was essential to the welfare of the smallest child. In the printed codes of law, the capital laws alone had the distinction of being supported by biblical citation. It might be contended that the reading requirement arose from a pure love of knowledge in itself, but the reasons which the Puritans offered elsewhere in defense of reading make it plain that here again a religious motive was present. In 1647 the General Court of Massachusetts provided for the establishment of reading schools, because it was *"one chief project of that old deluder, Satan, to keep men from the knowledge of the Scriptures."* Children were taught to read in order that they might gain a first-hand knowledge of the Bible. When John Cotton was urging parents to educate their children, he did not say, "Learn them to read," but "Learn them to read the Scriptures." Benjamin Wadsworth exhorted young persons to the same purpose. "If we are not able to *Read*, we should use all regular means, and imploy all opportunities for our learning; but if we can *read*, we should not (unless some extraordinary matter prevents) suffer one day to pass, without reading some portion of the Word of God." Thomas Foxcroft was even more explicit in his explanation of the need for education:

> The Word Written and Preacht is the ordinary Medium of Conversion and Sanctification. Now in order to obtaining these Benefits by the Word, it is requisite, that Persons be diligent in *Reading and Hearing* of it; And in order to these, how expedient and necessary is it, that there be Schools of Learning; those of a Lower Character, for the instructing of Youth in Reading, and those of an Higher, for the more Liberal Education of such, as may be devoted to the Work of the Ministry?

The Puritans sought knowledge, therefore, not simply as a polite accomplishment, nor as a means of advancing material welfare, but because salvation was impossible without it. They retained throughout the seventeenth century a sublime confidence that man's chief enemy was ignorance, especially ignorance of the Scriptures. By keeping the world in ignorance, they thought, the Roman Church had stifled true religion. When the people finally recovered knowledge of the Scriptures, the light of the gospel broke out in the Reformation, and as long as the people had this knowledge, the light would continue to shine. The Puritans rested their whole system upon the belief that "Every *Grace* enters into the Soul through the *Understanding*." Upon this premise it followed naturally that "The *Devotion* of *Ignorance*, is but a *Bastard* sort of *Devotion*," or that "Ignorance is the Mother (not of Devotion but) of HERESY." In order to be saved, men had to understand the doctrines of Christianity, and since children were born without understanding, they had to be taught. Samuel Willard, in a sermon to the members of the Old South Church, explained the dangers to which all children were exposed by their ignorance. John Hull copied down the minister's words as follows:

> 1. they are all born in Ignorance rom. 3.17. without the knowledge and fear of god they must have it by doctrine and institution 2ly this ignorance layeth them open to satan to lead them whither he will. 3ly holdeth them under the Power [and] efficacy of sin a blind mind and dead conscience are companions. hence they sin without shame ignorance stopps the activity of all the faculties. 4ly as long as they remain in their naturall ignorance there is no hope of being freed from everlasting misery. if you have any Compassion for them take Pains that they may know god. 5ly Hardness of heart allienation from god Springs from ignorance and 6ly they hence are inclined to fullfill their owne evill will.

Such doctrines make it apparent that if children were not to remain forever *"Alienated from the Life of God,"* parents must teach them "the *Worth* of a Christ, and their *Want* of Christ, and a way of closing with a *Christ."* *"After* all, (nay, *Before* all, and *Above* all,)" said Cotton Mather,

> Tis the *Knowledge* of the *Christian Religion*, that *Parents* are to *Teach* their *Children*. . . . The *Knowledge* of other things, though it be never so desirable an Accomplishment for them, our *Children* may arrive to Eternal Happiness without it. But the *Knowledge* of the *Godly Doctrine in the words of the Lord Jesus Christ*, is of a Million times more Necessity for them; without that *Knowledge*, our Children are Miserable to all *Eternity*.

In other words, the main business of education was to prepare children for conversion by teaching them the doctrines and moral precepts of Christianity.

79

The great Enlightenment philosopher Jean-Jacques Rousseau drew the important and consequential connection between the rights of man and those of children. His thinking ultimately changed the way Western societies looked at children, particularly in matters of education (1769).

Émile

Jean-Jacques Rousseau

Never tell the child what he cannot understand: no descriptions, no eloquence, no figures of speech, no poetry. The time has not come for feeling or taste. Continue to be clear and cold; the time will come only too soon when you must adopt another tone.

Brought up in the spirit of our maxims, accustomed to make his own tools and not to appeal to others until he has tried and failed, he will examine everything he sees carefully and in silence. He thinks rather than questions. Be content, therefore, to show him things at a fit season; then, when you see that his curiosity is thoroughly aroused, put some brief question which will set him trying to discover the answer.

On the present occasion when you and he have carefully observed the rising sun, when you have called his attention to the mountains and other objects visible from the same spot, after he has chattered freely about them, keep quiet for a few minutes as if lost in thought and then say, "I think the sun set over there last night; it rose here this morning. How can that be?" Say no more; if he asks questions, do not answer them; talk of something else. Let him alone, and be sure he will think about it.

To train a child to be really attentive so that he may be really impressed by any truth of experience, he must spend anxious days before he discovers that truth. If he does not learn enough in this way, there is another way of drawing his attention to the matter. Turn the question about. If he does not know how the sun gets from the place where it sets to where it rises, he knows at least how it travels from sunrise to sunset, his eyes teach him that. Use the second question to throw light on the first; either your pupil is a regular dunce or the analogy is too clear to be missed. This is his first lesson in cosmography.

As we always advance slowly from one sensible idea to another, and as we give time enough to each for him to become really familiar with it before we go on to another, and lastly as we never force our scholar's attention, we are still a long way from a knowledge of the course of the sun or the shape of the earth; but as all the apparent movements of the celestial bodies depend on the same principle, and the first observation leads on to all the rest, less effort is needed, though more time, to proceed from the diurnal revolution to the calculation of eclipses, than to get a thorough understanding of day and night.

Since the sun revolves round the earth it describes a circle, and every circle must have a centre; that we know already. This centre is invisible, it is in the middle of the earth, but we can mark out two opposite points on the earth's surface which correspond to it. A skewer passed through the three points and prolonged to the sky at either end would represent the earth's axis and the sun's daily course. A round teetotum revolving on its point represents the sky turning on its axis, the two points of the teetotum are the two poles; the child will be delighted to find one of them, and I show him the tail of the Little bear. Here is another game for the dark. Little by little we get to know the stars, and from this comes a wish to know the planets and observe the constellations.

We saw the sun rise at midsummer, we shall see it rise at Christmas or some other fine winter's day; for you know we are no lie-a-beds and we enjoy the cold. I take care to make this second observation in the same place as the first, and if skilfully lead up to, one or other will certainly exclaim, "What a funny thing! The sun is not rising in the same place; here are our landmarks, but it is rising over there. So there is the summer east and the winter east, etc." Young teacher, you are on the right track. These examples should show you how to teach the sphere without any difficulty, taking the earth for the earth and the sun for the sun.

As a general rule—never substitute the symbol for the thing signified, unless it is impossible to show the thing itself; for the child's attention is so taken up with the symbol that he will forget what it signifies.

I consider the armillary sphere a clumsy disproportioned bit of apparatus. The confused circles and the strange figures described on it suggest witchcraft and frighten the child. The earth is too small, the circles too large and too numerous, some of them, the colures, for instance, are quite useless, and the thickness of the pasteboard gives them an appearance of solidity so that they are taken for circular masses having a real existence, and when you tell the child that these are imaginary circles, he does not know what he is looking at and is none the wiser.

We are unable to put ourselves in the child's place, we fail to enter into his thoughts, we invest him with our own ideas, and while we are following our own chain of reasoning, we merely fill his head with errors and absurdities.

80

Schooling in the United States became free and common, at least in the Northeast and the more settled parts of the Midwest, in the middle of the nineteenth century. Historian Carl F. Kaestle discusses how morality and citizenship were intertwined in the ideology and programs of these nineteenth-century schools (1983).

Moral Education for Citizenship

Carl F. Kaestle

Morality was the most important goal of common education, and it promised many benefits. Among those most often cited were good work habits, deference to adults, restraint from vicious and debilitating habits, a reduction of crime, and the protection of property. Orville Taylor's popular *District School* emphasized that teachers had a heavy responsibility to parents and to the future of society in shaping the character of "pliable, susceptible" children. "Society expects that teachers will make children and youth social, honorable, and benevolent members." In another widely read teacher's manual, Alonzo Potter urged teachers to "inspire the young with deep reverence for parents and for old age" and give them training "which will lead them, without surrendering their own independence, to have due respect for the recorded wisdom and experience of the past." Schools needed to introduce American boys to a "humanizing culture," said Potter, lest as adults, "in the absence of higher sources of exhilaration, they rush to the gaming table, and, above all, to the intoxicating cup." In Germany, where the fine arts were cultivated, he claimed that "drunkenness is almost unknown." Horace Mann advocated vocal music on the same grounds. Music had a "harmonizing, pacificating tendency" that could be "applied in the management and discipline of children in school." Music promotes "peace, hope, affection, generosity, charity, and devotion." In Prussia, that fount of good educational ideas, vocal music pervaded schools, families, and social occasions. "It saves the people from boisterous and riotous passions."

Throughout discussions of education, of course, there was a strong emphasis on obedience, discipline, and order, for the good of the school, for the good of the parents, and for the good of the children when they grew up. "If there is any place on the surface of the earth where order is the first, and last, and highest law, that place is the schoolroom," said Charles Northend, author of *The Teacher and the Parent* (1853). The "spirit of obedience and subordination" children learned would "also tend to prepare them for higher spheres of usefulness and happiness." Some educators, however, qualified the theme of subordination to authority. Although schools should develop "the highest respect for textbooks and established maxims," said an Illinois report, they should also "fully awaken the idea of bold and independent thinking and manly research." Support for plain old-fashioned obedience was widespread, but many of the leading antebellum reformers urged authority mixed with affection, discipline more internal than imposed, morality more by example than precept, and lessons emphasizing understanding more than rote memorization. These pedagogical aspects of the reform were widely discussed in journals, teachers' institutes, and education reports. Classroom memoirs suggest that some budding young professionals tried hard to implement these concepts, while many other teachers relied on traditional authority and the threat of corporal punishment. Teachers tending in either direction, though, could subscribe to the proposition that the central purpose of common schooling was moral education, and that moral education would reduce vicious behavior and crime.

To maintain law through moral education was part of the republican experiment. Moral education thus overlapped citizenship education. Future citizens— and the women who as mothers and teachers would train them—not only needed to know some United States geography, history, and law but also needed to be impressed with the moral responsibility of protecting American institutions. In conservative hands this doctrine extended to the denigration of labor organizations and the denunciation of foreign culture in America; but in its general form it elicited broad support as an important and almost self-evident purpose of common schooling. Ignoring the fact that the majority of Americans could not vote, Pennsylvania's superintendent stated in 1842 the democratic principle that animated citizenship education: "The foundations of our political institutions rest upon man's capacity for self-government; not the capacity of one, of a hundred, of a thousand, but of *all*. . . . Enlightened public opinion will be a wall of fire around our free institutions, and preserve them inviolate forever." Twenty years later, the superintendent of public instruction in Illinois reiterated the main purpose of public schooling: "The chief end is to make GOOD CITIZENS. Not to make precocious scholars . . . not to impart the secret of acquiring wealth . . . not to qualify directly for professional success . . . but simply to make good citizens." Moral education in common schools would produce virtuous citizens.

81

It is sometimes difficult to know what the young learned at schools in the past, and girls' schooling especially is often shrouded in myth. But historian Harvey J. Graff's reading of Mary Anna Longstreth's memoirs is an important exception. Here we get a sense of a middle-class girl's education that is as fully developed as that of boys; we also learn why some girls themselves went on to teach school (1995).

The Education of Mary Anna Longstreth

Harvey J. Graff

Mary Anna Longstreth's memoir introduces us to middle-class experience as it was forming. Born to Philadelphia Quaker parents, Mary Anna (1811–1884) was "an infant greatly desired and joyfully welcomed." Hers were "modern" parents, and the infant responded to their love. In perfect health, she "was never heard to cry." Concern about precocity being as yet uncommon, Mary Anna began school at the age of two and a half when her sister was born.

At first she went to a dame school. "Actual study" began at age five. Mary Anna attended a school run by the Misses Cox for five years. Although fond of reading and grammar, she had difficulty learning to write. When she was seven, her father died, and her mother's sister joined the family to assist in socializing and educating her nieces and nephews. Since no school in Philadelphia taught Latin or Greek to girls, a private master was employed. A minister awaiting missionary assignment in Burma, he sparked Mary Anna's lifelong interest in and support of missionaries. Greek and French masters followed him.

In 1824 John Brewer opened a girls' school that taught Latin and Greek. Thirteen-year-old Mary Anna was one of the first scholars and one of the best. She also taught Latin to her younger sister. Before she was twelve, Mary Anna had read all of Virgil. Brewer engaged her as an assistant while she continued her own studies over the next three years. The first payment for her services was a great delight: a "little diary" that "bears witness to the deepening earnestness with which she looked upon her vocation as a teacher."

In the diary Mary Anna thanked family and God for their aid and blessings, and vowed to repay them with her life by always improving, always doing good. She was grateful for the peace and tranquillity she felt in her soul. On her eighteenth birthday, confessing a deep sense of responsibility, Mary Anna rededicated her purpose, surrendering herself to her God to do "my 'most reasonable service.' " In the spring of 1829 the sisters began to teach "on their own account." Mary Anna, eighteen, and Susan, sixteen, opened a school for girls "under the protection of their mother's roof." After a week, it "succeeds delightfully" with eight students, and after two weeks with fourteen. On her nineteenth birthday, the school "prospering," Mary Anna repeated her covenant. She made education her career, a proper path for a middle-class woman: working for the young, aiding them along their way.

Always improving themselves, the sisters took lessons in drawing and perspective, attended lectures on chemistry and natural philosophy, read constantly. Mary Anna also "loved an innocent jest as much as any one, and her habitual brightness, even gayety of manner, her quick smile and genial laughter, and above all, the rare sweetness of face, the very 'lineaments of gospel books,' left no room for the reproach that her religion was an austere one." Little disturbed her. Combining in her patience and spirituality the qualities of "true women," fashioning in growing up a life of virtue and a contribution to her class and gender, Mary Anna Longstreth served spiritually and maternally three generations of Philadelphia children.

82

Some may tend to romanticize the old nineteenth-century schoolhouse and the schoolmarm who presided there, but Mark Twain, America's greatest humorist, took his aim at schooling as well as other pieties of the culture. Here Twain pokes fun at the conventional educational products of the period, like sentimental poetry and eloquent patriotic speeches (1876).

Tom Sawyer's Examination Day

Mark Twain

Vacation was approaching. The schoolmaster, always severe, grew severer and more exacting than ever, for he wanted the school to make a good showing on "Examination" day. His rod and his ferule were seldom idle now—at least among the smaller pupils. Only the biggest boys, and young ladies of eighteen and twenty, escaped lashing. Mr. Dobbins's lashings were very vigorous ones, too; for although he carried, under his wig, a perfectly bald and shiny head, he had only reached middle age and there was no sign of feebleness in his muscle. As the great day approached, all the tyranny that was in him came to the surface; he seemed to take a vindictive pleasure in punishing the least shortcomings. The consequence was that the smaller boys spent their days in terror and suffering and their nights in plotting revenge. They threw away no opportunity to do the master a mischief. But he kept ahead all the time. The retribution that followed every vengeful success was so sweeping and majestic that the boys always retired from the field badly worsted. At last they conspired together and hit upon a plan that promised a dazzling victory. They swore-in the sign-painter's boy, told him the scheme, and asked his help. He had his own reasons for being delighted, for the master boarded in his father's family and had given the boy ample cause to hate him. The master's wife would go on a visit to the country in a few days, and there would be nothing to interfere with the plan; the master always prepared himself for great occasions by getting pretty well fuddled, and the sign-painter's boy said that when the dominie had reached the proper condition on Examination Evening he would "manage the thing" while he napped in his chair: then he would have him awakened at the right time and hurried away to school.

In the fullness of time the interesting occasion arrived. At eight in the evening the schoolhouse was brilliantly lighted, and adorned with wreaths and festoons of foliage and flowers. The master sat throned in his great chair upon a raised platform, with his blackboard behind him. He was looking tolerably mellow. Three rows of benches on each side and six rows in front of him were occupied by the dignitaries of the town and by the parents of the pupils. To his left, back of the rows of citizens, was a spacious temporary platform upon which were seated the scholars who were to take part in the exercises of the evening; rows of small boys, washed and dressed to an intolerable state of discomfort; rows of gawky big boys; snowbanks of girls and young ladies clad in lawn and muslin and conspicuously conscious of their bare arms, their grandmothers' ancient trinkets, their bits of pink and blue ribbon and the flowers in their hair. All the rest of the house was filled with non-participating scholars.

The exercises began. A very little boy stood up and sheepishly recited, "You'd scarce expect one of my age to speak in public on the stage, etc."—accompanying himself with the painfully exact and spasmodic gestures which a machine might have used—supposing the machine to be a trifle out of order. But he got through safely, though cruelly scared, and got a fine round of applause when he made his manufactured bow and retired.

A little shamefaced girl lisped "Mary had a little lamb, etc.," performed a compassion-inspiring curtsy, got her meed of applause, and sat down flushed and happy.

Tom Sawyer stepped forward with conceited confidence and soared into the unquenchable and indestructible "Give me liberty or give me death" speech, with fine fury and frantic gesticulation, and broke down in the middle of it. A ghastly stagefright seized him, his legs quaked under him and he was like to choke. True, he had the manifest sympathy of the house—but he had the house's silence, too, which was even worse than its sympathy. The master frowned, and this completed the disaster. Tom struggled a while and then retired, utterly defeated. There was a weak attempt at applause, but it died early.

"The Boy Stood on the Burning Deck" followed; also "The Assyrian Came Down," and other declamatory gems. Then there were reading exercises, and a spelling fight. The meager Latin class recited with honor. The prime feature of the evening was in order now—original "compositions" by the young ladies. Each in her turn stepped forward to the edge of the platform, cleared her throat, held up her manuscript (tied with dainty ribbon), and proceeded to read, with labored attention to "expression" and punctuation. The themes were the same that had been illuminated upon similar occasions by their mothers before them, their grandmothers, and doubtless all their ancestors in the female line clear back to the Crusades. "Friendship" was one; "Memories of Other Days"; "Religion in History"; "Dream Land"; "The Advantages of Culture"; "Forms of Political Government Compared and Contrasted"; "Melancholy"; "Filial Love"; "Heart Longings," etc., etc.

A prevalent feature in these compositions was a nursed and petted melancholy; another was a wasteful and opulent gush of "fine language"; another was a tendency to lug in by the ears particularly prized words and phrases until they were worn entirely out; and a peculiarity that conspicuously marked and marred them was the inveterate and intolerable sermon that wagged its crippled tail at the end of each and every one of them. No matter what the subject might be, a brain-racking effort was made to squirm it into some aspect or other that the moral and religious mind could contemplate with edification. The glaring insincerity of these sermons was not sufficient to compass the banishment of the fashion from the schools, and it is not sufficient today; it never will be sufficient while the world stands, perhaps. There is no school in all our land where the young ladies do not feel obliged to close their compositions with a sermon; and you will find that the sermon of the most frivolous and least religious girl in the school is always the longest and the most relentlessly pious. But enough of this. Homely truth is unpalatable.

Let us return to the "Examination." The first composition that was read was one entitled "Is this, then, Life?" Perhaps the reader can endure an extract from it:

> "In the common walks of life, with what delightful emotions does the youthful mind look forward to some anticipated scene of festivity! Imagination is busy sketching rose-tinted pictures of joy. In fancy, the voluptuous votary of fashion sees herself amid the festive throng, 'the observed of all observers.' Her graceful form, arrayed in snowy robes, is whirling through the mazes of the joyous dance; her eye is brightest, her step is lightest in the gay assembly.

> "In such delicious fancies time quickly glides by, and the welcome hour arrives for her entrance into the elysian world, of which she has had such bright dreams. How fairylike does everything appear to her enchanted vision! each new scene is more charming than the last. But after a while she finds that beneath this goodly exterior, all is vanity: the flattery which once charmed her soul, now grates harshly upon her ear; the ballroom has lost its charms; and with wasted health and embittered heart, she turns away with the conviction that earthly pleasures cannot satisfy the longings of the soul!"

And so forth and so on. There was a buzz of gratification from time to time during the reading, accompanied by whispered ejaculations of "How sweet!" "How eloquent!" "So true!" etc., and after the thing had closed with a peculiarly afflicting sermon the applause was enthusiastic.

Then arose a slim, melancholy girl, whose face had the "interesting" paleness that comes of pills and indigestion, and read a "poem." Two stanzas of it will do:

A MISSOURI MAIDEN'S FAREWELL TO ALABAMA

Alabama, good-bye! I love thee well!
    But yet for awhile do I leave thee now!
Sad, yes, sad thoughts of thee my heart doth swell,
    And burning recollections throng my brow!
For I have wandered through they flowery woods;

    Have roamed and read near Tallapoosa's stream;
Have listened to Tallassee's warring floods,
    And wooed on Coosa's side Aurora's beam.
Yet shame I not to bear an o'er-full heart,

> Nor blush to turn behind my tearful eyes;
> 'Tis from no stranger land I now must part,
>   'Tis to no strangers left I yield these sighs.
> Welcome and home were mine within this State,
>   Whose vales I leave—whose spires fade fast from me;
> And cold must be mine eyes, and heart, and tête,
>   When, dear Alabama! they turn cold on thee!

There were very few there who knew what "*tête*" meant, but the poem was very satisfactory, nevertheless.

Next appeared a dark complexioned, black-eyed, black-haired young lady, who paused an impressive moment, assumed a tragic expression and began to read in a measured, solemn tone.

A Vision

Dark and tempestuous was night. Around the throne on high not a single star quivered; but the deep intonations of the heavy thunder constantly vibrated upon the ear; whilst the terrific lightning reveled in angry mood through the cloudy chambers of heaven, seeming to scorn the power exerted over its terror by the illustrious Franklin! Even the boisterous winds unanimously came forth from their mystic homes, and blustered about as if to enhance by their aid the wilderness of the scene.

At such a time, so dark, so dreary, for human sympathy my very spirit sighed; but instead thereof,

> "My dearest friend, my counsellor, my comforter and guide—
> My joy in grief, my second bliss in joy," came to my side.

She moved like one of those bright beings pictured in the sunny walks of fancy's Eden by the romantic and young, a queen of beauty unadorned save by her own transcendent loveliness. So soft was her step, it failed to make even a sound, and but for the magical thrill imparted by her genial touch, as other unobtrusive beauties, she would have glided away unperceived—unsought. A strange sadness rested upon her features, like icy tears upon the robe of December, as she pointed to the contending elements without, and bade me contemplate the two beings presented.

This nightmare occupied some ten pages of manuscript and wound up with a sermon so destructive of all hope to non-Presbyterians that it took the first prize. This composition was considered to be the very finest effort of the evening. The mayor of the village, in delivering the prize to the author of it, made a warm speech in which he said that it was by far the most "eloquent" thing he had ever listened to, and that Daniel Webster himself might well be proud of it.

It may be remarked, in passing, that the number of compositions in which the word "beauteous" was overfondled, and human experience referred to as "life's page," was up to the usual average.

Now the master, mellow almost to the verge of geniality, put his chair aside, turned his back to the audience, and began to draw a map of America on the blackboard, to exercise the geography class upon. But he made a sad business of it with his unsteady hand, and a smothered titter rippled over the house. He knew what the matter was and set himself to right it. He sponged out lines and re-made them; but he only distorted them more than ever, and the tittering was more pronounced. He threw his entire attention upon his work now, as if determined not to be put down by the mirth. He felt that all eyes were fastened upon him; he imagined he was succeeding, and yet the tittering continued; it even manifestly increased. And well it might. There was a garret above, pierced with a scuttle over his head; and down through this scuttle came a cat, suspended around the haunches by a string; she had a rag tied about her head and jaws to keep her from mewing; as she slowly descended she curved upward and clawed at the string, she swung downward and clawed at the intangible air. The tittering rose higher and higher—the cat was within six inches of the absorbed teacher's head—down, down, a little lower, and she grabbed his wig with her desperate claws, clung to it and was snatched up into the garret in an instant with her trophy still in her possession! And how the light did blaze abroad from the master's bald pate—for the sign-painter's boy had *gilded* it!

That broke up the meeting. The boys were avenged. Vacation had come.

NOTE—The pretended "compositions" quoted in this chapter are taken without alternation from a volume entitled *Prose and Poetry, by a Western Lady*—but they are exactly and precisely after the schoolgirl pattern and hence are much happier than any mere imitations could be.

83

One of America's greatest philosophers, John Dewey, was not coincidentally also its most renowned educational theorist. In the late nineteenth and early twentieth centuries, education became a fundamental issue in the social transformation of America. Dewey was interested in how knowledge about child development could become a means to maintain democracy in the midst of change. He proposed to revolutionize the manner in which children were educated so that the child's growth and human experience would be at the center of instruction. In this way, learning would engage the child's propensities and children would retain initiative and individuality. Dewey's views have remained a serious stimulus to educational reform throughout the twentieth century (1902).

The Child and the Curriculum

John Dewey

What, then, is the problem? It is just to get rid of the prejudicial notion that there is some gap in kind (as distinct from degree) between the child's experience and the various forms of subject-matter that make up the course of study. From the side of the child, it is a question of seeing how his experience already contains within itself elements—facts and truths—of just the same sort as those entering into the formulated study; and, what is of more importance, of how it contains within itself the attitudes, the motives, and the interests which have operated in developing and organizing the subject-matter to the plane which it now occupies. From the side of the studies, it is a question of interpreting them as outgrowths of forces operating in the child's life, and of discovering the steps that intervene between the child's present experience and their richer maturity.

Abandon the notion of subject-matter as something fixed and ready-made in itself, outside the child's experience; cease thinking of the child's experience as also something hard and fast; see it as something fluent, embryonic, vital; and we realize that the child and the curriculum are simply two limits which define a single process. Just as two points define a straight line, so the present stand-point of the child and the facts and truths of studies define instruction. It is continuous reconstruction, moving from the child's present experience out into that represented by the organized bodies of truth that we call studies.

On the face of it, the various studies, arithmetic, geography, language, botany, etc., are themselves experience—they are that of the race. They embody the cumulative outcome of the efforts, the strivings, and the successes of the human race generation after generation. They present this, not as a mere accumulation, not as a miscellaneous heap of separate bits of experience, but in some organized and systematized way—that is, as reflectively formulated.

Hence, the facts and truths that enter into the child's present experience, and those contained in the subject-matter of studies, are the initial and final terms of one reality. To oppose one to the other is to oppose the infancy and maturity of the same growing life; it is to set the moving tendency and the final result of the same process over against each other; it is to hold that the nature and the destiny of the child war with each other.

If such be the case, the problem of the relation of the child and the curriculum presents itself in this guise: Of what use, educationally speaking, is it to be able to see the end in the beginning? How does it assist us in dealing with the early stages of growth to be able to anticipate its later phases? The studies, as we have agreed, represent the possibilities of development inherent in the child's immediate crude experience. But, after all, they are not parts of that present and immediate life. Why, then, or how, make account of them?

Asking such a question suggests its own answer. To see the outcome is to know in what direction the present experience is moving, provided it move normally and soundly. The far-away point, which is of no significance to us simply as far away, becomes of huge importance the moment we take it as defining a present direction of movement. Taken in this way it is no remote and distant result to be achieved, but a guiding method in dealing with the present. The systematized and defined experience of the adult mind, in other words, is of value to us in interpreting the child's life as it immediately shows itself, and in passing on to guidance or direction.

Let us look for a moment at these two ideas: interpretation and guidance. The child's present experience is in no way self-explanatory. It is not final, but transitional. It is nothing complete in itself, but just a sign or index of certain growth-tendencies. As long as we confine our gaze to what the child here and now puts forth, we are confused and misled. We cannot read its meaning. Extreme depreciations of the child morally and intellectually, and sentimental idealizations of him, have their root in a common fallacy. Both spring from taking stages of a growth or movement as something cut off and fixed. The first fails to see the promise contained in feelings and deeds which, taken by themselves, are uncompromising and repellent; the second fails to see that even the most pleasing and beautiful exhibitions are but signs, and that they begin to spoil and rot the moment they are treated as achievements. . . .

Just as, upon the whole, it was the weakness of the "old education" that it made invidious comparisons between the immaturity of the child and the maturity of the adult, regarding the former as something to be got away from as soon as possible and as much as possible; so it is the danger of the "new education" that it regard the child's present powers and interests as something finally significant in themselves. In truth, his learnings and achievements are fluid and moving. They change from day to day and from hour to hour.

It will do harm if child-study leave in the popular mind the impression that a child of a given age has a positive equipment of purposes and interests to be cultivated just as they stand. Interests in reality are but attitudes toward possible experiences; they are not achievements; their worth is in the leverage they afford, not in the accomplishment they represent. To take the phenomena presented at a given age as in any way self-explanatory or self-contained is inevitably to result in indulgence and spoiling. Any power, whether of child or adult, is indulged when it is taken on its given and present level in consciousness. Its genuine meaning is in the propulsion it affords toward a higher level. It is just something to do with. Appealing to the interest upon the present plane means excitation; it means playing with a power so as continually to stir it up without directing it toward definite achievement. Continuous initiation, continuous starting of activities that do not arrive, is, for all practical purposes, as bad as the continual repression of initiative in conformity with supposed interests of some more perfect thought or will. It is as if the child were forever tasting and never eating; always having his palate tickled upon the emotional side, but never getting the organic satisfaction that comes only with digestion of food and transformation of it into working power.

As against such a view, the subject-matter of science and history and art serves to reveal the real child to us. We do not know the meaning either of his tendencies or of his performances excepting as we take them as germinating seed, or opening bud, of some fruit to be borne. The whole world of visual nature is all too small an answer to the problem of the meaning of the child's instinct for light and form. The entire science of physics is none too much to interpret adequately to us what is involved in some simple demand of the child for explanation of some casual change that has attracted his attention. The art of Raphael or of Corot is none too much to enable us to value the impulses stirring in the child when he draws and daubs. . . .

If, once more, the "old education" tended to ignore the dynamic quality, the developing force inherent in the child's present experience, and therefore to assume that direction and control were just matters of arbitrarily putting the child in a given path and compelling him to walk there, the "new education" is in danger of taking the idea of development in altogether too formal and empty a way. The child is expected to "develop" this or that fact or truth out of his own mind. He is told to think things out, or work things out for himself, without being supplied any of the environing conditions which are requisite to start and guide thought. Nothing can be developed from nothing; nothing but the crude can be developed out of the crude—and this is what surely happens when we throw the child back upon his achieved self as a finality, and invite him to spin new truths of nature or of conduct out of that. It is certainly as futile to expect a child to evolve a universe out of his own mere mind as it is for a philosopher to attempt that task. Development does not mean just getting something out of the mind. It is a development of experience and into experience that is really wanted. And this is impossible save as just that educative medium is provided which will enable the powers and interests that have been selected as valuable to function.

They must operate, and how they operate will depend almost entirely upon the stimuli which surround them and the material upon which they exercise themselves. The problem of direction is thus the problem of selecting appropriate stimuli for instincts and impulses which it is desired to employ in the gaining of new experience. What new experiences are desirable, and thus what stimuli are needed, it is impossible to tell except as there is some comprehension of the development which is aimed at; except, in a word, as the adult knowledge is drawn upon as revealing the possible career open to the child. . . .

How, then, stands the case of Child vs. Curriculum? What shall the verdict be? The radical fallacy in the original pleadings with which we set out is the supposition that we have no choice save either to leave the child to his own unguided spontaneity or to inspire direction upon him from without. Action is response; it is adaptation, adjustment. There is no such thing as sheer self-activity possible—because all activity takes place in a medium, in a situation, and with reference to its conditions. But, again, no such thing as imposition of truth from without, as insertion of truth from without, is possible. All depends upon the activity which the mind itself undergoes in responding to what is presented from without. Now, the value of the formulated wealth of knowledge that makes up the course of study is that it may enable the educator *to determine the environment of the child*, and thus by indirection to direct. Its primary value, its primary indication, is for the teacher, not for the child. It says to the teacher: Such and such are the capacities, the fulfilments, in truth and beauty and behavior, open to these children. Now see to it that day by day the conditions are such that *their own activities* move inevitably in this direction, toward such culmination of themselves. Let the child's nature fulfil its own destiny, revealed to you in whatever of science and art and industry the world now holds as its own.

The case is of Child. It is his present powers which are to assert themselves; his present capacities which are to be exercised; his present attitudes which are to be realized. But save as the teacher knows, knows wisely and thoroughly, the race-expression which is embodied in that thing we call the Curriculum, the teacher knows neither what the present power, capacity, or attitude is, nor yet how it is to be asserted, exercised, and realized.

84

In the early twentieth century Dewey's progressive philosophy challenged schools to become more democratic and more child-centered. But as the schools expanded and the student body included more and more children of immigrants, administrators sought pragmatic solutions to their many problems. According to Paula Fass, IQ testing was a convenient tool that justified the creation of a tracking system and allowed educators to shift the blame from inadequate schools to inadequate students (1989).

Testing the IQ of Children

Paula S. Fass

Progressive social reformers hoped to use education to revitalize democracy through the reconstruction of the elements of individual political responsibility. To this faith in democratic renewal through education, progressives added a new faith—in science, technical expertise, and the symbolic power of numbers. Amidst the disorders of the late nineteenth-century and early twentieth-century world, science and numbers seemed to promise just that fundamental knowledge and access to order that would result in control. Science was more than a form of data-collecting; it would also provide a method for solving social problems and making social policy. In the early twentieth century, education and science went hand-in-hand with the euphoria of reform.

The science that had the most profound effect on educational practice was psychology, a hybrid calling which was part biology, part philosophy, and in good part linked with the evolving profession of education. Most significant for education was the fact that American psychology had by the first two decades of the twentieth century become deeply involved in mental measurement, especially in devising tests to measure mental capacity. . . .

In the United States, mental testing first surfaced in a relatively minor way in the 1890s in a report by the pioneer psychologist James Cattell. But the early interest among psychologists and a few educators was nothing compared with what was soon to follow. For it was only as the French concern with personality and abnormality was joined to the English preoccupation with the measurement of individual and group differences in the form of aggregates and norms that mental testing as an American science was born. Despite its European ancestry, testing became a major preoccupation only in American psychology, where, in the words of an early historian of testing, the "movement . . . swept everything else before it" during the second and third decades of the twentieth century. As Harlan Hines observed in his book popularizing intelligence testing, "It is doubtful whether so much public interest has been aroused since Darwin propounded his theories about the descent of man." . . .

The Americanization of mental testing began in 1911 when Lewis Terman, the Stanford psychologist, adopted Alfred Binet's age-mentality scale to test, sort, and classify American schoolchildren. Terman was not the first American to use Binet's tests, but he was the first to use them with normal children. With Terman's adoption of the Binet scale and his subsequent modification and introduction of the concept of intelligence quotient (IQ) in 1916, the history of IQ testing in America properly began. Terman's work with normal children clearly anticipated the use of IQ tests in the schools, and he was a vigorous proponent of their large-scale adoption. His enthusiasm for the method was virtually unbounded, since it was, in his words, "from the practical point of view . . . the most important in all the history of psychology." By 1911, Terman had already claimed that "by its use it is possible for the psychologist to submit, after a forty-minute diagnostication, a more reliable and more enlightened estimate of the child's intelligence than most teachers can after a year of daily contact in the schoolroom." Educators like Elwood Cubberly, probably the most influential educational spokesman of the time, also foresaw the educational implications. In introducing Terman's book in 1916, he observed that "The present volume appeals to the editor [Cubberly] of this series as one of the most significant books, viewed from the standpoint of the future of our educational theory and practice, that has been issued in years."

At the same time, Terman's tests and the IQ scale were not quite fitted to the needs of the American school system. First, they required costly individual administration on a one-to-one basis. Second, Terman and other early testers jealously guarded their own expertise in this scientific procedure and insisted on expert administration. American entrance into the First World War changed that. As Americans prepared to fight a war to save democracy, they also found themselves with the kind of heterogeneous fighting force that resulted from democratic immigration policies. That army needed to be organized for maximum efficiency and effectiveness. For this task, a group of psychologists volunteered their services. This committee of the American Psychological Association at once hoped to assist the war effort and to raise psychology's still shaky status as a scientific profession in the eyes of the public. Mental testing seemed to provide a way to fulfill both the needs of the army and of the profession. As a science, testing could call on the enthusiasm for the exactitude of numbers for practical results. Mental testing seemed like the perfect instrument in a progressive crisis: it was socially useful, numerical, and had reform implications.

Although the army tests were based on and still linked to the individual Binet scale, the army test was a "group test," organized and routinized around pen and paper exercises which required only one administrator to provide general instructions to a large group. Over 1,700,000 men were eventually tested in this way. The army tests demonstrated the feasibility of mass testing, and as one textbook on testing noted, "The possibility of measuring an individual's intelligence by a short and simple test has captured the imagination of school people and of the general public." In the long run, the army tests were a significant administrative breakthrough. . . .

As they proceeded to refine the test results, psychologists went beyond comparing and ranking individuals within a large population. They also correlated differences in scores with social categories like region, education, race, and country of origin of the draftees. While there were marked differences within all categories, the attention of testers and the public was riveted by the markedly lower scores registered by blacks and the recent immigrants, like Italians and Slavs, who did worse than native-white Americans on both tests administered to those literate in English (Alpha) and those not literate or non-English speaking (Beta). The army tests made the crucial link between mental ability and race, not for the first time, but on a mass scale and in the full glare of public attention.

What had begun as a way of eliminating the feebleminded, proceeded to a ranking of individuals according to talent, and finally became a means for ordering a hierarchy of groups. Mental testing as a measuring device was a defining and sorting instrument, a way of distinguishing and differentiating which, given the cultural concerns of the time and in the context of statistical techniques like normal distributions, correlations, and factor analysis, led predictably to racial comparisons. In so doing, of course, intelligence testing sharpened and confirmed the cultural awareness of individual and group differences. Since Americans were, in the first thirty years of the century, inundated by dozens of immigrant groups who were so radically different first from "Americans" and then from each other, the emphasis on differences, now measurable by scientifically validated tests, was translated from the realm of the senses to that of statistics. At a time when democracy seemed threatened by heterogeneity, counting, sifting, and ranking provided a form of order and containment. . . .

The incipient search for a racialist explanation for differences informed American perceptions of the usefulness of testing, and perhaps more significantly helped to determine what the tests would be interpreted to mean. . . .

One of the truly remarkable aspects of the early history of IQ testing is the rapidity of its adoption in American schools nationwide. In the twenties, the tests were taken from the laboratory, where they were still being tested, retested, and modified, and were fast on the way to becoming an entrenched part of educational administration. As early as 1919–20, New York City's *Bulletin of High Points* (a teacher's journal) contained numerous articles on IQ testing, including a symposium on the subject and an account of the successful application of testing at Evander Childs High School. In Mt. Vernon, New York, all students from elementary through the first year of high school had already been tested by 1920. One Detroit educator boldly announced in the *Yearbook of the National Society for the Study of Education* in 1922 that "the adoption of the group method [of testing] by hundreds of school systems is now an old story."

Immediately after the war, the same group of psychologists who had constructed the army Alphas developed the National Intelligence Test. Over 575,000 copies were sold within a year of its issuance—800,000 copies the following year, 1922–23. By 1922, it was competing with numerous other tests of a similar kind. In 1922–23, over 2,500,000 intelligence tests were sold by just one firm which specialized in their development and distribution. Forty different group intelligence tests were by then available on the national market. Many more were rapidly being produced as psychologists suddenly found themselves in a lucrative business, possessing skills very much in demand. Indeed, tests were rushed into press before they were adequately evaluated. Some were a hodgepodge of different forms, completely unintegrated and uncoordinated. Edward Thorndike, éminence grise of psychological measurement and objective testing, was moved to declaim: "In the elementary schools we now have many inadequate tests and even fantastic procedures parading behind the banner of educational science. Alleged measurements are reported and used which measure the fact in question about as well as the noise of the thunder measures the voltage of lightning. To nobody are such more detestable than to the scientific worker with educational measurements."

While the rapidity with which IQ tests were adopted was remarkable, it was not really surprising. From the beginning, Terman and others had targeted the schools as the principal beneficiaries of the tests. And school administrators, eager to adopt scientific tools to cope with problems of curriculum development, a heterogeneous population, and the progressive challenge to tailor school programs to individual needs, responded enthusiastically to an instrument that seemed to slice through their problems efficiently and democratically. Retardation had rung an alarm in schools committed to expansion, and the IQ allowed educators to shift the blame for inadequate schooling to the inadequacy of the pupils. More significantly, IQ could allow the schools to expand and incorporate ever larger and more diverse groups for longer and longer periods, while adjusting to progressive principles.

Education as it was being redefined and reformed in the early twentieth century was turning away from defining learning as the inculcation of information toward issues of socialization that emphasized the acquisition of knowledge in the total process of individual development and growth. John Dewey had most idealistically represented this new direction by passionately rejecting the view that education was the acquisition of the accumulated wisdom of the past and by urging instead that the unfolding of the child's (and society's) potential should be the mission of the schools. By shifting the charge to the schools from the traditional one of instilling an agreed upon body of knowledge to an active development of understanding pegged to individual talent and instrumental in a changing society, Dewey and progressive pedagogy sharpened the challenges facing the schools. Given the schools' design, their dependence on structured grades, central administration, their emphasis on order, and cost efficiency, progressive educational theories propelled the schools to seek ways to define children, not individually, but according to the range of their educability. As Josephine Chase observed in her study of New York schools, "It is to the task of individualizing education, of making the school program elastic enough to fit the needs of each child that the progressive school leaders of New York are bending every effort." To this effort, the IQ was immediately recognized as a powerful ally.

For the schools, the IQ was a concept that seemed ideally suited to their new goals and problems. It seemed to establish a stable educational center by assuming an unvarying constant within each child—his inborn capacity—and was based on a simple testing method designed to discover that potential. On this basis, educators could design programs and curricula that would make education more individually usable and more socially relevant. The IQ thus provided multiple blessings as it was brought to bear on a host of institutional matters. As Elwood Cubberly correctly predicted in his introduction to Terman's *The Measurement of Intelligence*, "The educational significance of the results to be obtained from careful measurements of the intelligence of children can hardly be overestimated. Questions relating to the choice of studies, vocational guidance, schoolroom procedure, the grading of pupils, promotional schemes, the study of retardation of children in schools, juvenile delinquency, and the proper handling of subnormals on the one hand and gifted children on the other—all alike acquire new meaning and significance when viewed in the light of the measurement of intelligence as outlined in this volume."

The IQ categorized students and made it possible for the schools to deal with them in group, class, and hierarchical terms. That the IQ ultimately also predefined children so that students would thenceforth learn only so much as they were at the outset judged able to learn and ironically limited the function of the school by establishing the primacy of innate ability over environmental stimulation was also a blessing. As one judicious authority on tests, Frank Freeman, observed, "The usefulness of measures of intellectual ability depends in part upon their stability and the possibility of predicting the individual's future intelligence from the measure of intelligence made at a given time. If the purpose of the test is, for example, to classify pupils so that the demands made upon them may be adjusted to their abilities, it is necessary that their abilities shall remain more or less constant." In a final irony, the very needs of the schools thus helped to confirm the meaning of IQ.

The growth of American education and specifically the requirements of educational administration, like the American sensitivity to racial differences, meant that whatever instrument was used to place and locate the individual in the increasingly complex school structure had to provide a constant measure of some inherent and unvarying potential. And just as the immigrant presence was crucial to the cultural network that created IQ as a form of organizing perceptions, so the presence of vast numbers of immigrant children in the schools was basic to the educational situation which seemed to make IQ testing an instrumental necessity. The problems facing the schools—the need for better organization, selection, and a curriculum at once more fully tailored to the individual and more socially alert—were not entirely the result of the presence of new immigrants. But the pressures on education to expand beyond the three Rs, the stricter school attendance laws, and the concurrent child-labor legislation which vastly expanded school populations cannot be separated from problems associated with immigration during this period. Immigration made the schools grow exponentially in scope, size, and complexity. At the same time, it made the schools' problems vastly more complicated.

Immigration helped to frame the context for the schools' search for procedures to define children and to order the curriculum, but the tests were not aimed at immigrants alone. They were a convenient necessity to the schools because they made possible a learning process tailored to individual potential, organizable by classes, while still allowing for progression of instruction by age. The best way to describe this network is a "track." Just as age subdivided schools horizontally and permitted instruction to be developed according to progressive levels of advancement, the track subdivided the system vertically and channeled instruction more precisely as determined by individual abilities. The organizational grid that resulted from the intersection of age and ability permitted instruction to be technically more individualized. If IQ is a ratio that compares age and ability, the tracked class system was the map projected from that concept.

85

Many students, often the most original, were inspired by books that they devoured outside school. In the case of African Americans in the segregated South, even after the end of slavery, this education was considered incendiary and had to be carried out surreptitiously. Richard Wright had to use a coworker's library card to fulfill his thirst for reading (1937).

For the Love of Books

Richard Wright

One morning I arrived early at work and went into the bank lobby where the Negro porter was mopping. I stood at a counter and picked up the Memphis *Commercial Appeal* and began my free reading of the press. I came finally to the editorial page and saw an article dealing with one H. L. Mencken. I knew by hearsay that he was the editor of the *American Mercury*, but aside from that I knew nothing about him. The article was a furious denunciation of Mencken, concluding with one, hot, short sentence: Mencken is a fool.

I wondered what on earth this Mencken had done to call down upon him the scorn of the South. The only people I had ever heard denounced in the South were Negroes, and this man was not a Negro. Then what ideas did Mencken hold that made a newspaper like the *Commercial Appeal* castigate him publicly? Undoubtedly he must be advocating ideas that the South did not like. Were there, then, people other than Negroes who criticized the South? I knew that during the Civil War the South had hated northern whites, but I had not encountered such hate during my life. Knowing no more of Mencken than I did at that moment, I felt a vague sympathy for him. Had not the South, which had assigned me the role of a non-man, cast at him its hardest words?

Now, how could I find out about this Mencken? There was a huge library near the riverfront, but I knew that Negroes were not allowed to patronize its shelves any more than they were the parks and playgrounds of the city. I had gone into the library several times to get books for the white men on the job. Which of them would now help me to get books? And how could I read them without causing concern to the white men with whom I worked? I had so far been successful in hiding my thoughts and feelings from them, but I knew that I would create hostility if I went about this business of reading in a clumsy way.

I weighed the personalities of the men on the job. There was Don, a Jew; but I distrusted him. His position was not much better than mine and I knew that he was uneasy and insecure; he had always treated me in an offhand, bantering way that barely concealed his contempt. I was afraid to ask him to help me to get books; his frantic desire to demonstrate a racial solidarity with the whites against Negroes might make him betray me.

Then how about the boss? No, he was a Baptist and I had the suspicion that he would not be quite able to comprehend why a black boy would want to read Mencken. There were other white men on the job whose attitudes showed clearly that they were Kluxers or sympathizers, and they were out of the question.

There remained only one man whose attitude did not fit into an anti-Negro category, for I had heard the white men refer to him as a "Pope lover." He was an Irish Catholic and was hated by the white Southerners. I knew that he read books, because I had got him volumes from the library several times. Since he, too, was an object of hatred, I felt that he might refuse me but would hardly betray me. I hesitated, weighing and balancing the imponderable realities.

One morning I paused before the Catholic fellow's desk.

"I want to ask you a favor," I whispered to him.

"What is it?"

"I want to read. I can't get books from the library. I wonder if you'd let me use your card?"

He looked at me suspiciously.

"My card is full most of the time," he said.

"I see," I said and waited, posing my question silently.

"You're not trying to get me into trouble, are you, boy?" he asked, staring at me.

"Oh, no, sir."

"What book do you want?"

"A book by H. L. Mencken."

"Which one?"

"I don't know. Has he written more than one?"

"He has written several."

"I didn't know that."

"What makes you want to read Mencken?"

"Oh, I just saw his name in the newspaper," I said.

"It's good of you to want to read," he said. "But you ought to read the right things."

I said nothing. Would he want to supervise my reading?

"Let me think," he said. "I'll figure out something."

I turned from him and he called me back. He stared at me quizzically.

"Richard, don't mention this to the other white men," he said.

"I understand," I said. "I won't say a word."

A few days later he called me to him.

"I've got a card in my wife's name," he said. "Here's mine."

"Thank you, sir."

"Do you think you can manage it?"

"I'll manage fine," I said.

"If they suspect you, you'll get in trouble," he said.

"I'll write the same kind of notes to the library that you wrote when you sent me for books," I told him. "I'll sign your name."

He laughed.

"Go ahead. Let me see what you get," he said.

That afternoon I addressed myself to forging a note. Now, what were the names of books written by H. L. Mencken? I did not know any of them. I finally wrote what I thought would be a foolproof note: *Dear Madam: Will you please let this nigger boy*—I used the word "nigger" to make the librarian feel that I could not possibly be the author of the note—*have some books by H. L. Mencken?* I forged the white man's name.

I entered the library as I had always done when on errands for whites, but I felt that I would somehow slip up and betray myself. I doffed my hat, stood a respectful distance from the desk, looked as unbookish as possible, and waited for the white patrons to be taken care of. When the desk was clear of people, I still waited. The white librarian looked at me.

"What do you want, boy?"

As though I did not possess the power of speech, I stepped forward and simply handed her the forged note, not parting my lips.

"What books by Mencken does he want?" she asked.

"I don't know, ma'am," I said, avoiding her eyes.

"Who gave you this card?"

"Mr. Falk," I said.

"Where is he?"

"He's at work, at the M——Optical Company," I said. "I've been in here for him before."

"I remember," the woman said. "But he never wrote notes like this."

Oh, God, she's suspicious. Perhaps she would not let me have the books? If she had turned her back at that moment, I would have ducked out the door and never gone back. Then I thought of a bold idea.

"You can call him up, ma'am," I said, my heart pounding.

"You're not using these books, are you?" she asked pointedly.

"Oh, no, ma'am. I can't read."

"I don't know what he wants by Mencken," she said under her breath.

I knew now that I had won; she was thinking of other things and the race question had gone out of her mind. She went to the shelves. Once or twice she looked over her shoulder at me, as though she was still doubtful. Finally she came forward with two books in her hand.

"I'm sending him two books," she said. "But tell Mr. Falk to come in next time, or send me the names of the books he wants. I don't know what he wants to read."

I said nothing. She stamped the card and handed me the books. Not daring to glance at them, I went out of the library, fearing that the woman would call me back for further questioning. A block away from the library I opened one of the books and read a title: *A Book of Prefaces*. I was nearing my nineteenth birthday and I did not know how to pronounce the word "preface." I thumbed the pages and saw strange words and strange names. I shook my head, disappointed. I looked at the other book; it was called *Prejudices*. I knew what that word meant; I had heard it all my life. And right off I was on guard against Mencken's books. Why would a man want to call a book *Prejudices*? The word was so stained with all my memories of racial hate that I could not conceive of anybody using it for a title. Perhaps I had made a mistake about Mencken? A man who had prejudices must be wrong.

When I showed the books to Mr. Falk, he looked at me and frowned.

"That librarian might telephone you," I warned him.

"That's all right," he said. "But when you're through reading those books, I want you to tell me what you get out of them."

That night in my rented room, while letting the hot water run over my can of pork and beans in the sink, I opened *A Book of Prefaces* and began to read. I was jarred and shocked by the style, the clear, clean, sweeping sentences. Why did he write like that? And how did one write like that? I pictured the man as a raging demon, slashing with his pen, consumed with hate, denouncing everything American, extolling everything European or German, laughing at the weaknesses of people, mocking God, authority. What was this? I stood up, trying to realize what reality lay behind the meaning of the words. . . . Yes, this man was fighting, fighting with words. He was using words as a weapon, using them as one would use a club. Could words be weapons? Well, yes, for here they were. Then, maybe, perhaps, I could use them as a weapon? No. It frightened me. I read on and what amazed me was not what he said, but how on earth anybody had the courage to say it.

Occasionally I glanced up to reassure myself that I was alone in the room. Who were these men about whom Mencken was talking so passionately? Who was Anatole France? Joseph Conrad? Sinclair Lewis, Sherwood Anderson, Dostoevski, George Moore, Gustave Flaubert, Maupassant, Tolstoy, Frank Harris, Mark Twain, Thomas Hardy, Arnold Bennett, Stephen Crane, Zola, Norris, Gorky, Bergson, Ibsen, Balzac, Bernard Shaw, Dumas, Poe, Thomas Mann, O. Henry, Dreiser, H. G. Wells, Gogol, T. S. Eliot, Gide, Baudelaire, Edgar Lee Masters, Stendhal, Turgenev, Huneker, Nietzsche, and scores of others? Were these men real? Did they exist or had they existed? And how did one pronounce their names?

I ran across many words whose meanings I did not know, and I either looked them up in a dictionary or, before I had a chance to do that, encountered the word in a context that made its meaning clear. But what strange world was this? I concluded the book with the conviction that I had somehow overlooked something terribly important in life. I had once tried to write, had once reveled in feeling, had let my crude imagination roam, but the impulse to dream had been slowly beaten out of me by experience. Now it surged up again and I hungered for books, new ways of looking and seeing. It was not a matter of believing or disbelieving what I read, but of feeling something new, of being affected by something that made the look of the world different.

As dawn broke I ate my pork and beans, feeling dopey, sleepy. I went to work, but the mood of the book would not die; it lingered, coloring everything I saw, heard, did. I now felt that I knew what the white men were feeling. Merely because I had read a book that had spoken of how they lived and thought, I identified myself with that book. I felt vaguely guilty. Would I, filled with bookish notions, act in a manner that would make the whites dislike me?

I forged more notes and my trips to the library became frequent. Reading grew into a passion. My first serious novel was Sinclair Lewis's *Main Street*. It made me see my boss, Mr. Gerald, and identify him as an American type. I would smile when I saw him lugging his golf bags into the office. I had always felt a vast distance separating me from the boss, and now I felt closer to him, though still distant. I felt now that I knew him, that I could feel the very limits of his narrow life. And this had happened because I had read a novel about a mythical man called George F. Babbitt.

The plots and stories in the novels did not interest me so much as the point of view revealed. I gave myself over to each novel without reserve, without trying to criticize it; it was enough for me to see and feel something different. And for me, everything was something different. Reading was like a drug, a dope. The novels created moods in which I lived for days. But I could not conquer my sense of guilt, my feeling that the white men around me knew that I was changing, that I had begun to regard them differently.

Whenever I brought a book to the job, I wrapped it in newspaper—a habit that was to persist for years in other cities and under other circumstances. But some of the white men pried into my packages when I was absent and they questioned me.

"Boy, what are you reading those books for?"

"Oh, I don't know, sir."

"That's deep stuff you're reading, boy."

"I'm just killing time, sir."

"You'll addle your brains if you don't watch out."

I read Dreiser's *Jennie Gerhardt* and *Sister Carrie* and they revived in me a vivid sense of my mother's suffering; I was overwhelmed. I grew silent, wondering about the life around me. It would have been impossible for me to have told anyone what I derived from these novels, for it was nothing less than a sense of life itself. All my life had shaped me for the realism, the naturalism of the modern novel, and I could not read enough of them.

86

In its unanimous decision in Brown v. Board of Education of Topeka *(1954), the U.S. Supreme Court ended legal segregation in schools, South and North. According to Chief Justice Earl Warren's written decision, segregation was inherently unequal and therefore separate racial schools could not be retained in an equal society. The following includes the full Warren opinion and excerpts from the influential brief made by social scientists on behalf of the plaintiffs.*

School Desegregation

U.S. Supreme Court

Brown v. Board of Education of Topeka
347 U.S. 483, 74 S.Ct. 686, 98 L.Ed. 873 (1954)

Mr. Chief Justice Warren delivered the opinion of the Court.

We come [t]o the question presented: Does segregation of children in public schools solely on the basis of race, even though the physical facilities and other "tangible" factors may be equal, deprive the children of the minority group of equal educational opportunities? We believe that it does.

[T]o separate them from others of similar age and qualifications solely because of their race generates a feeling of inferiority as to their status in the community that may affect their hearts and minds in a way unlikely ever to be undone. The effect of this separation on their educational opportunities was well stated by a finding in the Kansas case by a court which nevertheless felt compelled to rule against the Negro plaintiffs:

> "Segregation of white and colored children in public schools has a detrimental effect upon the colored children. The impact is greater when it has the sanction of the law; for the policy of separating the races is usually interpreted as denoting the inferiority of the negro group. A sense of inferiority affects the motivation of a child to learn. Segregation with the sanction of law, therefore, has a tendency to [retard] the educational and mental development of negro children and to deprive them of some of the benefits they would receive in a racial[ly] integrated school system."

Whatever may have been the extent of psychological knowledge at the time of Plessy v. Ferguson, this finding is amply supported by modern authority. Any language in Plessy v. Ferguson contrary to this finding is rejected.

We conclude that in the field of public education the doctrine of "separate but equal" has no place. Separate educational facilities are inherently unequal. Therefore, we hold that the plaintiffs and others similarly situated for whom the actions have been brought are, by reason of the segregation complained of, deprived of the equal protection of the laws guaranteed by the Fourteenth Amendment.

The Effects of Segregation and the Consequences of Desegregation: A Social Science Statement

Appendix to Appellants' Briefs

The problem of the segregation of racial and ethnic groups constitutes one of the major problems facing the American people today. It seems desirable, therefore, to summarize the contributions which contemporary social science can make toward its resolutions. . . .

At the recent Mid-century White House Conference on Children and Youth, a fact-finding report on the effects of prejudice, discrimination and segregation on the personality development of children was prepared as a basis for some of the deliberations. This report brought together the available social science and psychological studies which were related to the problem of how racial and religious prejudices influenced the development of a healthy personality. It highlighted the fact that segregation, prejudices and discriminations, and their social concomitants potentially damage the personality of all children—the children of the majority group in a somewhat different way than the more obviously damaged children of the minority group.

The report indicates that as minority group children learn the inferior status to which they are assigned—as they observe the fact that they are almost always segregated and kept apart from others who are treated with more respect by the society as a whole—they often react with feelings of inferiority and a sense of personal humiliation.

[T]he report indicates that minority group children of all social and economic classes often react with a generally defeatist attitude and a lowering of personal ambitions. This, for example, is reflected in a lowering of pupil morale and a depression of the educational aspiration level among minority group children in segregated schools. In producing such effects, segregated schools impair the ability of the child to profit from the educational opportunities provided him. . . .

Segregation is at present a social reality. Questions may be raised, therefore, as to what are the likely consequences of desegregation. . . .

The available scientific evidence indicates that much, perhaps all, of the observable differences among various racial and national groups may be adequately explained in terms of environmental differences. It has been found, for instance, that the differences between the average intelligence test scores of Negro and white children decrease, and the overlap of the distribution increases, proportionately to the number of years that the Negro children have lived in the North. Related studies have shown that this change cannot be explained by the hypothesis of selective migration. It seems clear, therefore, that fears based on the assumption of innate racial differences in intelligence are not well founded.

[A] second problem that comes up in an evaluation of the possible consequences of desegregation involves the question of whether segregation prevents or stimulates interracial tension and conflict and the corollary question of whether desegregation has one or the other effect.

The most direct evidence available on this problem comes from observations and systematic study of instances in which desegregation has occurred. Comprehensive reviews of such instances clearly establish the fact that desegregation has been carried out successfully in a variety of situations although outbreaks of violence had been commonly predicted. Extensive desegregation has taken place without major incidents in the armed services in both Northern and Southern installations and involving officers and enlisted men from all parts of the country, including the South.

[U]nder certain circumstances desegregation not only proceeds without major difficulties, but has been observed to lead [to] the emergence of more favorable attitudes and friendlier relations between races. Relevant studies may be cited with respect to housing, employment, the armed services and merchant marine, recreation agency, and general community life. . . .

The available evidence also suggests the importance of consistent and firm enforcement of the new policy by those in authority. It indicates also the importance of such factors as: the absence of competition for a limited number of facilities or benefits; the possibility of contacts which permit individuals to learn about one another as individuals; and the possibility of equivalence of positions and functions among all of the participants within the unsegregated situation. These conditions can generally be satisfied in a number of situations, as in the armed services, public housing developments, and public schools.

87

The quality of education in the public schools has been a concern throughout much of the twentieth century. When the Soviet Union launched its artificial satellite Sputnik in 1957, U.S. school administrators scrambled to improve curricula and teaching methods. The historian and education policy expert Diane Ravitch describes their efforts and the subsequent redirection of resources in the 1960s to meet the challenges of school desegregation (1983).

Education in the Post-Sputnik Era

Diane Ravitch

Unlike higher education, where the mood was one of confidence and optimism as the 1960s began, America's elementary and secondary schools were struggling to readjust to the new demands of the post-Sputnik era. The Soviet launch of the world's first artificial satellite on October 4, 1957, promptly ended the debate that had raged for several years about the quality of American education. Those who had argued since the late 1940s that American schools were not rigorous enough and that life adjustment education had cheapened intellectual values felt vindicated, and, as one historian later wrote, "a shocked and humbled nation embarked on a bitter orgy of pedagogical soul-searching." National magazines discovered a new crisis in education, and critics like Admiral Hyman Rickover—known as the father of the nuclear submarine—vociferously blamed the schools for endangering the nation's security by falling behind the Russians in science, mathematics, and engineering. Regardless of what was said, there was Sputnik itself, orbiting the earth as a constant reminder that political supremacy was tied to technological prowess. For the first time since the end of World War II, people of all political backgrounds agreed that the national interest depended on improving the quality of America's schools.

Out of the new mood arose a clamor for the federal government to do something, and do it quickly. President Eisenhower had staunchly opposed any general federal aid to schools, on the grounds that federal aid would inevitably lead to federal control. Yet, aware that the baby boom had strained the finances of many school districts, Eisenhower repeatedly tried to gain congressional approval for a federal school construction program. Even so limited a purpose as school construction was stymied by the same political factors—race, religion, and fear of federal control—that had blocked previous federal aid bills. After

Sputnik, however, the broad popular demand for a federal response to meet the Russian challenge prompted Congress to pass the National Defense Education Act in 1958 (NDEA). This act provided fellowships, grants, and loans to encourage the study of science, mathematics, and foreign languages and funded school construction and equipment. The active federal aid lobby, defeated so many times in the past, was happy to latch onto national security as a vehicle to establish the legitimacy of the federal role in supporting education.

Well before Sputnik, there were clear signs of discontent with the quality of American schools. Government officials repeatedly expressed concern about the shortage of graduates in scientific and technological fields. Additionally, the critics of progressivism complained about the neglect of the basic academic disciplines—English, history, science, mathematics, and foreign languages. The historian Arthur Bestor insisted that scholars had a responsibility for the way their disciplines were presented in the public schools. Nor was Bestor alone in his belief that what was taught in the schools was obsolescent, trivial, or insufficiently challenging. Many others, in the academic world and the government, criticized the quality of secondary school teaching, especially in the fields of science and mathematics. In 1952, mathematicians at the University of Illinois organized a project to develop new materials for high school teachers, with the intention of introducing adolescents to the way that mathematicians think. In the spring of 1956, under the leadership of physicist Jerrold Zacharias, a group of scientists at MIT formed the Physical Science Study Committee, which aimed to revise the content and methods of physics teaching in secondary schools, in part to correct what was taught but also to attract more students into careers in science.

Sputnik came to be a symbol of the consequences of indifference to high standards. In popular parlance, Sputnik had happened not because of what the Russians had done but because of what American schools had failed to do. The prototypical response to Sputnik was the Rockefeller Brothers Fund's report *The Pursuit of Excellence*, which appeared in 1958. While the NEA's *Education for All American Youth*, published in 1944, epitomized the progressive educators' expansive vision of the school as a grand social service center meeting the needs of the individual and the community, *The Pursuit of Excellence* presented a contrasting vision of the proper relation between school and society. It advocated the development of human potential as a national goal and insisted that the nation could encourage both excellence and equality without compromising either. It spoke of challenges and greatness, of high performance, of moral and intellectual excellence. Like most reports, it made nothing happen, but it accurately reflected hopes for the renewal of American society through the infusion of higher educational aspirations.

During the late 1950s, the much-discussed "crisis in the schools" attracted the attention of the major foundations, which had previously focused their resources on higher education. In late 1956, almost a year before the orbiting of Sputnik, the Carnegie Corporation agreed to support a series of studies of public education by James B. Conant, former president of Harvard University and ambassador to West Germany. When Conant's first report, *The American High School Today*, was published in 1959, beleaguered school officials seized upon it as a set of practical recommendations to translate the exhortations of *The Pursuit of Excellence* into reality. Conant urged the spread of the comprehensive high school, which he defined (in progressive terminology) as one "whose programs correspond to the educational needs of *all* the youth in the community." To be comprehensive, a high school had to fulfill three tasks: first, to provide "a good general education for *all* the pupils" (which meant that all students were required to take courses in English and American literature and composition, as well as in social studies); second, to offer the noncollege-bound majority good elective nonacademic courses (such as vocational, commercial, and work-study); and third, to provide the academically talented students with advanced courses in fields such as mathematics, science, and foreign languages. He urged the elimination of high schools too small to be "comprehensive," that is, with a senior class smaller than one hundred. Conant opposed tracking of students into separate curricula (for example, "college prep" versus vocational), but he endorsed ability grouping, so that fast and slow students would get the appropriate level of academic challenge. A skillful blend of dedication to both academic excellence and democratic values, Conant's high school study became a surprise best-seller. Though some professional educators complained that Conant's recommendations were too conservative, John Gardner, president of the Carnegie Corporation (and, coincidentally, author of *The Pursuit of Excellence*) noted approvingly that Conant "became overnight the most quoted authority on American education," and his celebrated report "was debated in PTA's, school boards, superintendents' offices, and educational conferences throughout the nation."

During the same period, the Ford Foundation addressed the "crisis in the schools" with two major efforts: a "Comprehensive School Improvement Program" (CSIP), which funded leading communities to serve as model districts for educational reform, and a "Great Cities–Gray Areas Program," to help big-city school systems create compensatory and remedial programs for their increasing numbers of low-income pupils. Unlike the Conant report, which sought to strengthen traditional secondary education, Ford's CSIP encouraged the implementation of innovative practices in curriculum, staffing, technology, and facilities, such as team teaching, nonprofessional personnel, flexible scheduling, programmed instruction, federally sponsored science curricula, teacher-devised curricula, independent study, language laboratories, open-space classrooms, nongraded programs, and school-university cooperation. Both programs were bellwethers of a sort, one by stressing innovation as the key to school improvement, the other by confronting the issues of educating poor children. . . .

At the National Science Foundation (NSF), the furor over Sputnik significantly increased the agency's role in secondary school curriculum reform. Established by Congress in 1950 to promote basic research and education in the sciences, NSF initially had little to do with precollege programs. Soon, however, it began to sponsor science fairs and summer institutes for high school teachers of mathematics and science. In 1956, responding to governmental concern about manpower shortages in scientific and technical fields, NSF funded the MIT Physical Science Study Committee's revision of the secondary school physics curriculum. In the wake of Sputnik, NSF expanded its high school curriculum revision projects to include the fields of mathematics, biology, chemistry, and social science. From these efforts eventually came a number of innovative curricula, including "the new math," "the new social studies," and substantial revisions in the natural sciences. . . .

The curriculum reformers shared a common outlook. They hoped to replace current methods—characterized by teacher-led "telling" and student recitation—with curriculum packages that used "discovery," "inquiry," and inductive reasoning as methods of learning; the rationale was that students would find the field more interesting and would retain longer what they learned if they "figured out," through carefully designed exercises or experiments, the basic principles of the field. They hoped to end the traditional reliance on a single textbook by creating attractive multimedia packages that included films, "hands-on" activities, and readings. They emphasized the importance of understanding a few central concepts in a discipline, rather than trying to "cover" an entire field, the way current courses in science or history did. Where present curricula stressed the informational, descriptive, and applied aspects of a subject (the discipline's "product"), the new curricula would teach the structure of the academic discipline; students would learn how a scientist or mathematician or social scientist thinks (the discipline's "processes"). Put another way, instead of learning "about" science, students would "do" science. The reformers agreed on the importance of cognitive growth, in keeping with the principle enunciated by one of the moving forces of the curriculum reform movement, Harvard psychologist Jerome Bruner, that "any subject can be taught effectively in some intellectually honest form to any child at any stage of development."

As the new curricula were devised and revised in the early years of the 1960s, the climate for educational change was unusually receptive. The political and social context seemed charged by the energy, youth, and dynamism of the Kennedy administration, and the status quo in every area of endeavor was under reexamination. For the first time, the problem of educational change was jointly attacked by federal agencies, university scholars, major philanthropic foundations, big-city school systems, and almost everyone else in the field. On all educational fronts, innovation was the watchword, and some observers confidently spoke of "the revolution in the schools." In 1963, Francis Keppel, U.S. commissioner of education, observed that in the past decade, "more time, talent, and money than ever before in history have been invested in pushing outward the frontiers of educational knowledge, and in the next decade or two we may expect even more significant developments." . . .

The expected pedagogical revolution in the schools was not to be, however. It was swept aside by the onrush of the racial revolution, which presented a forceful challenge to the political, social, and economic basis of American schools. Between 1963 and 1965, the nation's social fabric sustained a series of jolts: violence against blacks and civil rights workers in the South; the assassination of

President Kennedy; the rediscovery of poverty; the beginning of American involvement in Vietnam. Meanwhile, the movement of blacks to northern cities brought the problems of racial segregation and slums to urban schools. Civil rights leaders in North and South brought their demands for integration, equality, and justice to the doors of the public schools; in the context of such transcending demands, the pedagogical revolution was no revolution at all.

Before long, the pursuit of excellence was overshadowed by concern about the needs of the disadvantaged. As the racial crisis and the urban crisis became the nation's most pressing problems, the Cold War competition with the Soviets moved to the back burner and lost its motivating power. Identifying the gifted and stimulating high achievement paled as a national goal in comparison to the urgency of redressing racial injustice. Government agencies and foundations redirected their agendas to search for mechanisms to meet the needs of disadvantaged minority children, and scores of compensatory programs were created throughout the country. Such efforts were multiplied by congressional passage of the Elementary and Secondary Education Act in 1965, with its focus on educating poor children.

The many remedial and compensatory programs initiated by local school systems, state education departments, and federal agencies were born in crisis, and there was neither time enough nor knowledge enough to satisfy the rising expectations of long-denied and angry minorities. Programs were tried, hastily evaluated, declared a failure. In some cities, civil rights groups conducted demonstrations to demand integration and to protest inferior schooling. In others, black community groups demanded control of the public schools by the black community. Critics charged that the curriculum, the professionals, the tests, the bureaucratic organization, and the methods of the conventional school were inherently biased against blacks.

Since none of these demands for change was ever fully satisfied, and, more importantly, since none—even if fully satisfied—had the power to produce in immediate and tangible form the desired goal of full racial equality, the schools bore the brunt of black anger. No matter how well or how badly the schools taught reading or writing or history, poor black children still lived in slums, black unemployment was still double the white rate, and black poverty remained high. Even what the schools could do well, if they were good schools, was not equal to the burden placed on them. And so, because they could not solve the problem of racial inequality and did not have within their power the means to redress demands for justice, the schools became the targets of intense criticism.

88

The psychiatrist Robert Coles interviewed children caught in the crossfires of desegregation in the South. Here he describes a boy who became an unlikely hero as he found himself in the midst of a historic struggle (1967).

Children of Crisis

Robert Coles

Amid the talk we hear these days about "culturally disadvantaged" Negro children, I think we tend to overlook the fact that Negroes—not only those from the skimpy Negro middle class—have had a widespread interest in education, though to be sure it has necessarily been education of a special kind. Negro colleges are scattered all over the South. Negro seminaries seem to be everywhere. Negro boys have aimed for teaching or the ministry as commonly as white boys have hoped to become lawyers, doctors or businessmen. By Northern white standards many of the schools and seminaries are weak indeed. We may, today, scoff at state-supported A. and M. (agricultural and mechanical) colleges as part of the "Uncle Tom" tradition that started with Booker T. Washington and is only now ending. We may be dubious about the endless educational courses and credits taken and achieved by the thousands of Negro teachers in the South's segregated schools—all leading so often and ironically nowhere but to further spiritless, flawed learning. Yet, such efforts have at least enabled the hopes and ambitions of Negro people to find some outlet, however small, during a period in history when nothing else seemed at all possible. . . .

My experience in city after city of the South has taught me to expect no set pattern for the kinds of children who have taken on the leadership in school desegregation, nor any pattern for the criteria imposed by school boards in selecting them. Many Negro parents would not allow their children to face the dangers involved: some because they were poor and afraid that they would lose their jobs; some because they were comfortable and unwilling to risk the loss of that comfort; some because they were (and are) so fearful of whites, or hate them so, that they would not want their children exposed to them even if they were assured it wasn't dangerous.

School boards in Southern states have not always shown a consistent interest in trying to select the students whose abilities would augur well for making desegregation work. In many instances the age of the child and his place of residence were the only considerations observed. Indeed, often the school boards regarded themselves as under legal attack, and accommodated themselves minimally, and only under court order. Frequently they would agree to desegregate, and announce that fact publicly; later on they set a time for those who wished to apply for transfer. In Atlanta a large number applied when they learned that the eleventh and twelfth grades of several white schools would be open to them.

John decided on impulse to request a transfer. Like his friends and classmates, he had been paying particular attention to what he once called "race news." He was eleven when the Little Rock crisis occurred, and remembered it vividly. He later told me that he would "never forget that if I live to be one hundred. I was walking every inch with those kids." In 1960, just a year before Atlanta faced its crisis, New Orleans had been the scene of more riots, in a sense worse than any before them in duration and intensity, let alone the vulnerability of the children involved. John had particularly worried for the young children—he had a sister of seven. "I kept on picturing her going through it, and I figured if she did, I'd walk beside her; and just let anyone try anything."

Walking home one day with his friends, he heard some say yes, they would, some say no, they wouldn't think of going through mobs or sitting through insults at a white school. John recalls the atmosphere and conversation as follows: "We were just kidding around, like any other time; only that day it was about integration and what we would do now that it was coming to Atlanta. We kept on daring one another and teasing each other. My friend Kenny said he was going to do it, regardless; and the girls let out a big cheer and hugged and kissed him. Then Larry called him a fool. He said we would be giving up the best two years of our lives for nothing but trouble. He meant the end of high school, and the dances and football games—everything you hope for when you're beginning high school. Well, we most of us said we would do it—I think more to be the hero before the girls. Then they fell to arguing just like we did. My best girl then was Betty, and she told me she would sign up if I would, but we had to promise we both meant it to one another. I can still remember the bargain. She said, 'No joking' and I said, 'No joking,' and that was it. A week later we went down singing to get the forms and apply. I didn't even tell my folks until it came time to get their signatures, and that was where the trouble started. They said no, sir. I tried to tell them we were all going to do it, but it didn't cut any ice with them. Momma started praying out loud, and quoting the Bible to me about getting into heaven by being poor, and if I tried to go to school with whites and rise up, I'll probably lose my soul. And Daddy told me I'd get myself killed, and they'd get him to lose his job, one way or another. For a while I thought I was out of the running before I even started; and a lot of my friends had the same trouble."

In a sense the week of struggle for his parents' signatures became a real time of intimacy and discussion between the three of them. It was also a confrontation of the generations, the past incredulous at what the present seemed to expect as its due. John heard from his parents stories of experiences which they themselves had long since "forgotten": accounts of terror, humiliation and repudiation which had formerly been handed down from parent to child as an inheritance, to be told and later relived. John was particularly moved by his mother's insistence that his generation was the first to be spared the worst of it—the constant possibility of lynching, the near-total lack of hope, the daily scorn that permitted no reply, no leeway. To be free of that, to be safe from night riders, to have steady work, to be left mostly alone, all that seemed enough. "They wanted me to be glad I could walk on the sidewalk," John summarized their conversations, "because they used to have to move into the gutter in their town when a white man approached them. But I told them that once you walk on the sidewalk, you look in the windows of the stores and restaurants, and you want to go there, too. They said, maybe *my* children, and I said *me*, so that my children will be the first really free Negroes. They always told me that they would try to spare me what they went through; so I told them I wanted to spare my children going through any mobs. If there were mobs for us to face, we should do it right now. And besides, I told them they were contradicting themselves. My mother always brags about how wonderful the farm life was, and my daddy says he thought the city would save him, and it drove him to drink, so it's too bad he ever left South Carolina. Suddenly, though, all the truth was coming out." When I asked him how *he* explained their opposing sentiments he replied briefly—and for me his words are unforgettable—"I guess people can believe different things at different times."

As he persisted they relented. Eventually they gave their reluctant, apprehensive endorsements. They apparently were proud as well as filled with foreboding as they signed their names, itself not an easy task for either of them. John must have sensed their pride. He described an unexpected rise of sentiment in himself as he watched his parents sign their permission: "I think I got more emotional over that than anything else that happened; even more than walking in the building the first day."

Before walking into any school building for white children he would have to meet the standards of school officials worried about how to implement an uncongenial court order in the face of an uncertain and fearful population. John expected to be one of hundreds of new Negro students. He may have been dimly aware that no Southern city had yet taken more than a handful of Negro children to start desegregation, but neither he nor his friends ever gave much thought to the likelihood that only a few of them might be chosen. To some extent they believed—and correctly—that their city was determined to secure their safety. That belief, that faith, helped these children forget or "overlook" some of the possible dangers in the future. John put it to me quite concisely one day several weeks before those dangers actually started coming to his attention: "I try not to think about what's going to happen when school starts. I just go from day to day. We never thought it would be a picnic, but we figured we'd just take what comes, and then we could have stories to tell afterward."

John was interviewed, along with many of his friends, by school officials who were trying to make their choices more rationally and thoughtfully than some of their counterparts had done in other Southern cities. John realized during the interviews that a quiet and sincere presence was wanted, that an inflammatory or argumentative one was feared. He was asked by the school system's deputy superintendent how he would manage insults and even attacks upon himself. He replied that he would ignore them. If anyone threatened to injure him or interfere with his activities, he would call for help from others, namely his teachers. He was pointedly asked whether he would strike back if hit. He said he would not. He was asked why. He said he would only be inviting worse injury by doing so; he would, after all, be outnumbered, literally a thousand to one. I asked him, on hearing him tell of this exchange, how he expected to maintain that degree of almost fearless restraint. My question was: "John, in your own mind—apart from what you told them in the interview—do you think you would act that way if one or two boys pushed or shoved you, and called you names?" He replied: "That's where my daddy is right. He told me a long time ago, 'The only way a colored man can win is to fool the white man into thinking he's won.' I don't think that's always right, but it has to be like that until we get strong enough to make it even steven."

John was chosen, one of ten in a city of a million. He was surprised and quite disappointed rather than honored to learn that he and a girl he casually knew would be the only two of their race to enter the large "white" high school near his "old" one. Again he made light of his worries by speculating that since they were so few, none of them would be allowed to enter at all. In fact, one of the girls selected for another school soon decided to forgo her chance. She took stock of the threats and dangers about to begin and decided they were too much for her. . . .

For three summer months he awaited his role in desegregation. He worked at cutting lawns, emptying trash, helping his father by substituting at the gas station, or selling Cokes at local baseball games. I saw very little evidence of anxiety in him. He did become concerned with his "strength," and accordingly set himself a routine of exercise. His sister asked him whether he was worried about trouble in the fall, and he impatiently denied it. He had noticed he was short-winded on occasion, and that alone was the reason for his exercise. I was on the lookout for "trouble," but his appetite held up; he slept well; he seemed to his family quieter and more relaxed than usual.

The week before school started, the threats on his life, on his family's life, reached their terrible and bizarre peak. The telephone calls came in round the clock, angry voices talking of dynamite, alarmed voices talking of "racial amalgamation," plaintive voices urging John to reconsider his ill-advised decision "before it is too late." His parents—and especially his older sisters—wanted the phone changed. A city detective watching their home advised them to change their number. John would not hear of it: "I'm going to have to get used to that, so we might as well start now." Such a response showed how firmly and stubbornly he was girding himself. As I look back—and only in retrospect can I see it and say it—his willingness to take on the constant irritation and heckling of the telephone calls foreshadowed his future capacity to deal with similar episodes in school. At the time I failed to understand why he wouldn't let his family follow their inclinations and the advice of the police department. Oversensitive as I was to the possibility of incipient neurotic illness under stress, I failed to recognize this youth's desire to have his preliminary struggle with the enemy on "home territory," and win it.

On the first day of school he was escorted and driven to school by city detectives. I watched him walk up to the door of the high school, heavily guarded by police, the students and teachers waiting inside for him, and wondered how he felt, what he was thinking, and whether in fact he had any words to describe those seconds. Everybody else seemed to have words: national and local political leaders, reporters, observers, all noted how important it was for a Southern city to initiate school desegregation without violence. There was none.

Certainly the white children and their teachers felt themselves in the presence of history; and so did John. He told his mother later that he said a prayer she long ago taught him as he left the police car; when that was finished, still walking toward the school, he looked quickly at the building and thought of words he had heard from his grandparents as a boy: "It's going to get better for us, don't you ever forget that." Approaching the front door, he thought of the classroom and pictured the students sitting, waiting for him to enter, and then watching him as he did.

They were doing just that, watching closely, and would continue to do so for two years. They stared at him and looked away from him. At the end of the first class some of them heckled him. A few days later he found insulting words scribbled on his books. Some of the students tried very hard to be friendly, though most of them kept an apprehensive distance from him. He, too, watched apprehensively; but he also worked hard in school, studied earnestly at home, and took things as they came each day.

During his two years in a desegregated high school I kept trying to learn how he managed to cope with the constant strains. I kept careful track of his moods, particularly so because I became puzzled at his altogether remarkable composure in the face of various social provocations or intellectual hurdles. In the first place, he was woefully unprepared for the transfer academically. He had prepared himself for unfriendliness, but not for the long hours of homework required to catch up with, not to say keep abreast of, his fellow students. Meeting these problems daily and a host of others he had never expected, he survived and—I came to see—flourished. I had a hard time understanding why.

89

For many immigrants and their children, the learning process has required the acquisition of English as a second language, a language not normally spoken at home. Few have written about this with greater insight and poignancy than Richard Rodriguez (1982).

Hunger of Memory
The Education of Richard Rodriguez

Richard Rodriguez

At first, it seemed a kind of game. After dinner each night, the family gathered to practice "our" English. (It was still then *inglés*, a language foreign to us, so we felt drawn as strangers to it.) Laughing, we would try to define words we could not pronounce. We played with strange English sounds, often over-anglicizing our pronunciations. And we filled the smiling gaps of our sentences with familiar Spanish sounds. But that was cheating, somebody shouted. Everyone laughed. In school, meanwhile, like my brother and sister, I was required to attend a daily tutoring session. I needed a full year of special attention. I also needed my teachers to keep my attention from straying in class by calling out, *Rich-heard*— their English voices slowly prying loose my ties to my other name, its three notes, *Ri-car-do*. Most of all I needed to hear my mother and father speak to me in a moment of seriousness in broken—suddenly heartbreaking—English. The scene was inevitable: One Saturday morning I entered the kitchen where my parents were talking in Spanish. I did not realize that they were talking in Spanish however until, at the moment they saw me, I heard their voices change to speak English. Those *gringo* sounds they uttered startled me. Pushed me away. In that moment of trivial misunderstanding and profound insight, I felt my throat twisted by unsounded grief. I turned quickly and left the room. But I had no place to escape to with Spanish. (The spell was broken.) My brother and sisters were speaking English in another part of the house.

Again and again in the days following, increasingly angry, I was obliged to hear my mother and father: "Speak to us *en inglés*." (*Speak.*) Only then did I determine to learn classroom English. Weeks after, it happened: One day in school I raised my hand to volunteer an answer. I spoke out in a loud voice. And I did not think it remarkable when the entire class understood. That day, I moved very far from the disadvantaged child I had been only days earlier. The belief, the calming assurance that I belonged in public, had at last taken hold.

Shortly after, I stopped hearing the high and loud sounds of *los gringos*. A more and more confident speaker of English, I didn't trouble to listen to *how* strangers sounded, speaking to me. And there simply were too many English-speaking people in my day for me to hear American accents anymore. Conversations quickened. Listening to persons who sounded eccentrically pitched voices, I usually noted their sounds for an initial few seconds before I concentrated on *what* they were saying. Conversations became content-full. Transparent. Hearing someone's *tone* of voice—angry or questioning or sarcastic or happy or sad—I didn't distinguish it from the words it expressed. Sound and word were thus tightly wedded. At the end of a day, I was often bemused, always relieved, to realize how "silent," though crowded with words, my day in public had been. (This public silence measured and quickened the change in my life.)

At last, seven years old, I came to believe what had been technically true since my birth: I was an American citizen.

90

Jerome S. Bruner has become John Dewey's successor as the most influential educational philosopher of the late twentieth century. Here he reflects on the purpose and meaning of education (1962).

The Quest for Clarity

Jerome S. Bruner

What the school is. The school is an entry into the life of the mind. It is, to be sure, life itself and not merely a preparation for living. But it is a special form of living, one carefully devised for making the most of those plastic years that characterize the development of *homo sapiens* and distinguish our species from all others. School should provide more than a continuity with the broader community or with everyday experience. It is primarily the special community where one experiences discovery by the use of intelligence, where one leaps into new and unimagined realms of experience, experience that is discontinuous with what went before. A child recognizes this when he first understands what a poem is, or what beauty and simplicity inhere in the idea of the conservation theorems, or that measure is universally applicable. If there is one continuity to be singled out, it is the slow converting of the child's artistic sense of the omnipotence of thought into the realistic confidence in the use of thought that characterizes the effective man.

In insisting upon the continuity of the school with the community on the one side and the family on the other, John Dewey overlooked the special function of education as an opener of new perspectives. If the school were merely a transition zone from the intimacy of the family to the life of the community, it would be a way of life easily enough arranged. In the educational systems of primitive societies, there almost always comes a point, usually at puberty, where there is a sharp change in the life of the boy, marked by a *rite de passage* that establishes a boundary between childhood ways and the ways of the adolescent.

It would be romantic nonsense to pattern our practices upon those found in preliterate societies. I would only ask that we attend to one parallel: education must not confuse the child with the adult and must recognize that the transition to adulthood involves an introduction to new realms of experience, the discovery and exploration of new mysteries, the gaining of new powers. . . .

*

The subject matter of education. The issue of subject matter in education can be resolved only by reference to one's view of the nature of knowledge. Knowledge is a model we construct to give meaning and structure to regularities in experience. The organizing ideas of any body of knowledge are inventions for rendering experience economical and connected. We invent concepts such as force in physics, the bond in chemistry, motives in psychology, style in literature as means to the end of comprehension.

The history of culture is the history of the development of great organizing ideas, ideas that inevitably stem from deeper values and points of view about man and nature. The power of great organizing concepts is in large part that they permit us to understand and sometimes to predict or change the world in which we live. But their power lies also in the fact that ideas provide instruments for experience. Having grown up in a culture dominated by the ideas of Newton, and so with a conception of time flowing equably, we experience time moving inexorably and steadily, marked by a one-way arrow. Indeed, we know now, after a quarter of a century of research on perception, that experience is not to be had directly and neatly, but filtered through the programmed readiness of our senses. The program is constructed with our expectations and these are derived from our models or ideas about what exists and what follows what.

From this, two convictions follow. The first is that the structure of knowledge—its connectedness and the derivations that make one idea follow from another—is the proper emphasis in education. For it is structure, the great conceptual inventions that bring order to the congeries of disconnected observations, that gives meaning to what we may learn and makes possible the opening up of new realms of experience. The second conviction is that the unity of knowledge is to be found within knowledge itself, if the knowledge is worth mastering.

To attempt a justification of subject matter, as Dewey did, in terms of its relation to the child's social activities is to misunderstand what knowledge is and how it may be mastered. The significance of the concept of commutativity in mathematics does not derive from the social insight that two houses with fourteen people in each is not the same as fourteen houses with two people in each. Rather, it inheres in the power of the idea to create a way of thinking about number that is lithe and beautiful and immensely generative—an idea at least as powerful as, say, the future conditional tense in formal grammar. Without the idea of commutativity, algebra would be impossible. If set theory—now often the introductory section in newer curriculums in mathematics—had to be justified in terms of its relation to immediate experience and social life, it would not be worth teaching. Yet set theory lays a foundation for the understanding of order and number that could never be achieved with the social arithmetic of interest rates and bales of hay at so much per bale. Mathematics, like any other subject, must begin with experience, but progress toward abstraction and understanding requires precisely that there be a weaning away from the obviousness of superficial experience. . . .

What then of subject matter in the conventional sense? The answer to the question, "What shall be taught?" turns out to be the answer to the question,

"What is nontrivial?" If one can first answer the question, "What is worth knowing about?" then it is not difficult to distinguish between the aspects of it that are worth teaching and learning and those that are not. Surely, knowledge of the natural world, knowledge of the human condition, knowledge of the nature and dynamics of society, knowledge of the past so that it may be used in experiencing the present and aspiring to the future—all of these, it would seem reasonable to suppose, are essential to an educated man. To these must be added another: knowledge of the products of our artistic heritage that mark the history of our aesthetic wonder and delight.

A problem immediately arises concerning the symbolism in terms of which knowledge is understood and talked about. There is language in its natural sense and language in its mathematical sense. I cannot imagine an educated man a century from now who will not be largely bilingual in this special sense—concise and adept in both a natural language and mathematics. For these two are the tools essential to the unlocking of new experience and the gaining of new powers. As such, they must have a central place in any curriculum.

Finally, it is as true today as it was when Dewey wrote that one cannot foresee the world in which the child we educate will live. Informed powers of mind and a sense of potency in action are the only instruments we can give the child that will be invariable across the transformations of time and circumstance. The succession of studies that we give the child in the ideal school need be fixed in only one way: whatever is introduced, let it be pursued continuously enough to give the student a sense of the power of mind that comes from a deepening of understanding. It is this, rather than any form of extensive coverage, that matters most. . . .

Insofar as possible, a method of instruction should have the objective of leading the child to discover for himself. Telling children and then testing them on what they have been told inevitably has the effect of producing bench-bound learners whose motivation for learning is likely to be extrinsic to the task—pleasing the teacher, getting into college, artificially maintaining self-esteem. The virtues of encouraging discovery are of two kinds. In the first place, the child will make what he learns his own, will fit his discovery into the interior world of culture that he creates for himself. Equally important, discovery and the sense of confidence it provides is the proper reward for learning. It is a reward that, moreover, strengthens the very process that is at the heart of education—disciplined inquiry. . . .

Most important of all, the educational process must be free of intellectual dishonesty and those forms of cheating that explain without providing understanding. I have expressed the conviction elsewhere that any subject can be taught to anybody at any age in some form that is honest. It is not honest to present a fifth-grade social-studies class with an image of town government as if it were a den of cub scouts presided over by a parent figure interpreting the charter—even if the image set forth does happen to mesh with the child's immediate social experience. A lie is still a lie—even if it sounds like familiar truth. Nor is it honest to present a sixth-grade science class with a garbled but concrete picture of the atom that is, in its way, as sweeteningly false as the suburban image of town government given them the year before. A dishonest image can only discourage the self-generating intellectual inquiry out of which real understanding grows.

91

Today classrooms include children who had once been set apart because of behavioral or physical difficulties. Albert Shanker, then president of the American Federation of Teachers, addressed this issue in 1994.

Children and the Individuals with Disabilities Education Act

Albert Shanker

Writing laws is not an exact science. No matter how carefully crafted a piece of legislation is, it can have design flaws—gray areas or big loopholes—which lead to disputes, court cases and, often, decisions that obscure or pervert its intent. This is what's happened to the federal Individuals with Disabilities Education Act (IDEA). IDEA defines services for disabled children, a group whose educational needs used to be largely ignored, but there have been serious problems with a number of its important provisions. . . .

IDEA requires that youngsters with disabilities get a "free and appropriate public education in the least restrictive environment." What does that mean? It has generally been accepted that "least restrictive" depends on the nature of a particular child's disability, so a "continuum of placements" should be available. But now, advocates of "full inclusion" insist on a totally different interpretation of "least restrictive." They say it means that every child must be placed in a regular classroom, regardless of the nature and severity of the child's disability. Full inclusion is equated with fairness, but a one-size-fits-all approach is unfair to youngsters with disabilities, who differ greatly in what they need and can do. It is also unfair to the other kids in the class. By writing "continuum of placements" into the law, Congress can make sure that youngsters with disabilities are treated as individuals.

Those who created IDEA wanted to prevent kids with disabilities from being jerked around from one placement to another. But one of their tools, the "stay-put" provision, has turned out to be a nightmare for other students and teachers. According to "stay-put," once a child has been placed in a class, he can't be excluded because of behavior related to his disability for more than ten days a year without the consent of his parents or a formal hearing process that could take months. This means that a kid with a behavioral disorder who constantly disrupts the class—or even assaults the teacher or other kids—cannot be excluded. Congress can fix this problem by amending the law to allow responsible alternative arrangements for disabled students who are violent or disruptive until the issue of where they should be placed is resolved. Their rights can be protected without sacrificing the education of other students in the class—some or all of whom may also be disabled—or endangering their safety and that of their teachers.

The success of any placement depends to a large extent on the classroom teacher. Teachers who are going to work with disabled children must be adequately trained, but many in regular classrooms are ill-prepared or unprepared to work with students who have disabilities. IDEA needs to be amended to require that districts provide adequate training for all teachers who work with disabled students. . . . Except for parents, teachers know better than anybody else what a child needs. The child's teacher is also in the best position to know whether or not the services called for are actually being provided. The revised IDEA should allow teachers to report failure to provide services and offer protection to teachers who might hesitate to blow the whistle for fear of reprisal.

But a rewrite job alone, no matter how good it is, will not fix IDEA because lack of funding is as responsible for the distortion of the law as murky language. The services IDEA requires are very expensive—New York State now spends 30 percent of all new education money on them—but Congress has never come close to appropriating the 40 percent it promised. Many school districts have simply cut back their regular programs to pay for these unfunded mandates. And many districts are trying to control costs, under the pretext of inclusion, by dumping students with disabilities into regular classrooms without necessary supports for the youngsters or help for the teachers. This undermines the education of *all* students. And because regular programs have been cut back to pay for IDEA services, many kids who are identified as having learning problems, but who could normally get the help they need in a regular classroom, are pushed into special ed.

IDEA was intended to serve the best educational interests of students with disabilities without compromising the education of other students. Some serious attention from Congress, when the reauthorization comes up, will make it possible for IDEA to live up to this aim.

92

While the IQ controversy has by no means died, educators today often think of intelligence in plural terms. Howard Gardner has been an influential advocate of this more complex perspective on intelligence. He urges teachers to redirect the discussion away from IQ testing and focus on how best to educate students with varying talents (1993).

The Theory of Multiple Intelligences

Howard Gardner

I believe that we should get away altogether from tests and correlations among tests, and look instead at more naturalistic sources of information about how peoples around the world develop skills important to their way of life. Think, for example, of sailors in the South Seas, who find their way around hundreds, or even thousands, of islands by looking at the constellations of stars in the sky, feeling the way a boat passes over the water, and noticing a few scattered landmarks. A word for intelligence in a society of these sailors would probably refer to that kind of navigational ability. Think of surgeons and engineers, hunters and fishermen, dancers and choreographers, athletes and athletic coaches, tribal chiefs and sorcerers. All of these different roles need to be taken into account if we accept the way I define intelligence—that is, as the ability to solve problems, or to fashion products, that are valued in one or more cultural or community settings. For the moment I am saying nothing about whether there is one dimension, or more than one dimension, of intelligence; nothing about whether intelligence is inborn or developed. Instead I emphasize the ability to solve problems and to fashion products. In my work I seek the building blocks of the intelligences used by the aforementioned sailors and surgeons and sorcerers.

The science in this enterprise, to the extent that it exists, involves trying to discover the *right* description of the intelligences. What is an intelligence? To try to answer this question, I have, with my colleagues, surveyed a wide set of sources which, to my knowledge, have never been considered together before. One source is what we already know concerning the development of different kinds of skills in normal children. Another source, and a very important one, is information on the ways that these abilities break down under conditions of brain damage. When one suffers a stroke or some other kind of brain damage, various abilities can be destroyed, or spared, in isolation from other abilities. This research with brain-damaged patients yields a very powerful kind of evidence, because it seems to reflect the way the nervous system has evolved over the millennia to yield certain discrete kinds of intelligence.

My research group looks at other special populations as well: prodigies, idiot savants, autistic children, children with learning disabilities, all of whom exhibit very jagged cognitive profiles—profiles that are extremely difficult to explain in terms of a unitary view of intelligence. We examine cognition in diverse animal species and in dramatically different cultures. Finally, we consider two kinds of psychological evidence: correlations among psychological tests of the sort yielded by a careful statistical analysis of a test battery; and the results of efforts of skill training. When you train a person in skill A, for example, does that training transfer to skill B? So, for example, does training in mathematics enhance one's musical abilities, or vice versa?

Obviously, through looking at all these sources—information on development, on breakdowns, on special populations, and the like—we end up with a cornucopia of information. Optimally, we would perform a statistical factor analysis, feeding all the data into a computer and noting the kinds of factors or intelligences that are extracted. Alas, the kind of material with which I was working didn't exist in a form that is susceptible to computation, and so we had to perform a more subjective factor analysis. In truth, we simply studied the results as best we could, and tried to organize them in a way that made sense to us, and hopefully, to critical readers as well. My resulting list of seven intelligences is a preliminary attempt to organize this mass of information.

I want now to mention briefly the seven intelligences we have located, and to cite one or two examples of each intelligence. Linguistic intelligence is the kind of ability exhibited in its fullest form, perhaps, by poets. Logical-mathematical intelligence, as the name implies, is logical and mathematical ability, as well as scientific ability. Jean Piaget, the great developmental psychologist, thought he was studying *all* intelligence, but I believe he was studying the development of logical-mathematical intelligence. Although I name the linguistic and logical-mathematical intelligences first, it is not because I think they are the most important—in fact, I am convinced that all seven of the intelligences have equal claim to priority. In our society, however, we have put linguistic and logical-mathematical intelligences, figuratively speaking, on a pedestal. Much of our testing is based on this high valuation of verbal and mathematical skills. If you do well in language and logic, you should do well in IQ tests and SATs, and you may well get into a prestigious college, but whether you do well once you leave is probably going to depend as much on the extent to which you possess and use the other intelligences, and it is to those that I want to give equal attention.

Spatial intelligence is the ability to form a mental model of a spatial world and to be able to maneuver and operate using that model. Sailors, engineers, surgeons, sculptors, and painters, to name just a few examples, all have highly developed spatial intelligence. Musical intelligence is the fourth category of ability we have identified: Leonard Bernstein had lots of it; Mozart, presumably, had even more. Bodily-kinesthetic intelligence is the ability to solve problems or to fashion products using one's whole body, or parts of the body. Dancers, athletes, surgeons, and craftspeople all exhibit highly developed bodily-kinesthetic intelligence.

Finally, I propose two forms of personal intelligence—not well understood, elusive to study, but immensely important. Interpersonal intelligence is the ability to understand other people: what motivates them, how they work, how to work cooperatively with them. Successful salespeople, politicians, teachers, clinicians, and religious leaders are all likely to be individuals with high degrees of interpersonal intelligence. Intrapersonal intelligence, a seventh kind of intelligence, is a correlative ability, turned inward. It is a capacity to form an accurate, veridical model of oneself and to be able to use that model to operate effectively in life.

These, then, are the seven intelligences that we have uncovered and described in our research. This is a preliminary list, as I have said; obviously, each form of intelligence can be subdivided, or the list can be rearranged. The real point here is to make the case for the plurality of intellect. Also, we believe that individuals may differ in the particular intelligence profiles with which they are born, and that certainly they differ in the profiles they end up with. I think of the intelligences as raw, biological potentials, which can be seen in pure form only in individuals who are, in the technical sense, freaks. In almost everybody else the intelligences work together to solve problems, to yield various kinds of cultural endstates—vocations, avocations, and the like.

This is my theory of multiple intelligence in capsule form. In my view, the purpose of school should be to develop intelligences and to help people reach vocational and avocational goals that are appropriate to their particular spectrum of intelligences. People who are helped to do so, I believe, feel more engaged and competent, and therefore more inclined to serve the society in a constructive way.

These thoughts, and the critique of a universalistic view of mind with which I began, lead to the notion of an individual-centered school, one geared to optimal understanding and development of each student's cognitive profile. . . .

The design of my ideal school of the future is based upon two assumptions. The first is that not all people have the same interests and abilities; not all of us learn in the same way. (And we now have the tools to begin to address these individual differences in school.) The second assumption is one that hurts: it is the assumption that nowadays no one person can learn everything there is to learn. We would all like, as Renaissance men and women, to know everything, or at least to believe in the potential of knowing everything, but that ideal clearly is not possible anymore. Choice is therefore inevitable, and one of the things that I want to argue is that the choices that we make for ourselves, and for the people who are under our charge, might as well be informed choices. An individual-centered school would be rich in assessment of individual abilities and proclivities. It would seek to match individuals not only to curricular areas, but also to particular ways of teaching those subjects. And after the first few grades, the school would also seek to match individuals with the various kinds of life and work options that are available in their culture.

I want to propose a new set of roles for educators that might make this vision a reality. First of all, we might have what I will call "assessment specialists." The job of these people would be to try to understand as sensitively and comprehensively as possible the abilities and interests of the students in a school. It would be very important, however, that the assessment specialists use "intelligence-fair" instruments. We want to be able to look specifically and directly at spatial abilities, at personal abilities, and the like, and not through the usual lenses of the linguistic and logical-mathematical intelligences. Up until now nearly all assessment has depended indirectly on measurement of those abilities; if students are not strong in those two areas, their abilities in other areas may be obscured. Once we begin to try to assess other kinds of intelligences directly, I am confident that particular students will reveal strengths in quite different areas, and the notion of general brightness will disappear or become greatly attenuated.

93

Using drugs to calm children is not new. Mothers used laudanum, an opium derivative, in the nineteenth century. In the late twentieth century drugs like Ritalin are widely prescribed to treat attention deficit disorder. Critics oppose the tendency to medicalize problems associated with learning, but many see Ritalin as a means to allow troubled children to be educated alongside their peers. This Newsweek *article (1996) gives a sense of these divergent views.*

Mother's Little Helper
Ritalin and Attention Deficit Disorder

LynNell Hancock, Pat Wingert, Mary Hager, Claudia Kalb, Karen Springen, and Dante Chinni

It is another medication morning at Winnebago Elementary School in the middle-class Chicago suburb of Bloomingdale. Three pings sound precisely over the intercom at 11:45 a.m. Principal Mark Wagener opens a locked file cabinet and withdraws a giant Tupperware container filled with plastic prescription vials. Nearly a dozen students scramble to the office for their Ritalin, a drug that calms the agitated by stimulating the brain. These children—all ages, mostly boys— have been diagnosed with Attention-Deficit/Hyperactivity Disorder, a complex neurological impairment that takes the brakes off brains and derails concentration. The school nurse places the pills, one by one, in the children's mouths, a rite of safe passage before lunch. "Let me see . . . ," says nurse Pat Nazos, as she checks under each child's tongue for a stray, unswallowed capsule.

A decade ago, Wagener remembers, only two Winnebago students lined up for Ritalin. He is uncertain how many more "take their meds," as some students say. Some take time-released pills before school. Others take their doses at off-hours. One boy's jogging watch is timed to beep for Ritalin at 10 a.m. and 2 p.m. Like many administrators, Wagener is not sure what to make of it. Are doctors just catching this disabling affliction more often? Or has our culture gone so high-band haywire that we have lost patience with the demanding quirks of our children? For some students, Wagener observes, Ritalin can make the crucial difference between failing a test or sitting still long enough to pass it. But for others, he laments, "they've just got an excuse to be bad."

The Ritalin riddle, a brain teaser for the '90s, confounds doctors, parents and, sometimes, children. The stimulant can be a godsend for those who truly need it. Pharmaceutically speaking, "Ritalin is one of the raving successes in psychiatry," says Dr. Laurence Greenhill of Columbia University medical school. Now it's a routinely prescribed drug at distinguished institutions from Johns Hopkins to the Mayo Clinic, a pill that allows children and a growing number of adults to focus their minds and rein in their rampaging attention spans.

But for those who don't need it, Ritalin and its generic twins can be useless, or can even backfire. There is no X-ray, no blood test, no CT scan to determine who needs it; diagnosing attention deficit remains as much art as science. There are no definitive long-term studies to reassure parents that this stimulant isn't causing some hidden havoc to their child. Critics dismiss the drug as just a behavioral "quick fix" for children forced to live in an impatient culture that feeds on deadlines, due dates, sound bites and megabytes. "It takes time for parents and teachers to sit down and talk to kids," says Dr. Sharon Collins, a pediatrician in Cedar Rapids, Iowa, where reportedly 8 percent of the children are on Ritalin. "It takes less time to get a child a pill."

What's clear amid the debate is that a remarkable revolution has taken place in the care and treatment of America's children. ADHD has become America's No. 1 childhood psychiatric disorder. Experts believe that more than 2 million children (or 3 to 5 percent) have the disorder. According to an estimate by the National Institute of Mental Health, about one student in every classroom is believed to experience it. Since 1990, Dr. Daniel Safer of Johns Hopkins University School of Medicine calculates, the number of kids taking Ritalin has grown 2½ times. Among today's 38 million children at the ages of 5 to 14, he reports, 1.3 million take it regularly. Sales of the drug last year alone topped $350 million.

This is, beyond question, an American phenomenon. The rate of Ritalin use in the United States is at least five times higher than in the rest of the world, according to federal studies. It's so common in some upscale precincts that a mini black market has emerged in a handful of playgrounds and campuses. "Vitamin R"—one of its recreational names—sells for $3 to $15 per pill, to be crushed and snorted for a cheap and relatively modest buzz.

Ritalin is the brand name of the drug known as methylphenidate. Doctors have discovered that this and other stimulants work like an antenna adjuster for children whose brains crackle with static interference, as if a dozen stations are coming in on one channel. Technically, the stimulant appears to increase the level of dopamine in the frontal lobe of the brain, where it regulates attention and impulsivity. It is a powerful drug, and one that the U.S. Drug Enforcement Administration has classified as a Schedule II controlled substance, in the same category as cocaine, methadone and methamphetamine. Parent groups are now lobbying to ease the restrictions on Ritalin to avoid monthly doctor's visits. The DEA is opposing them, going so far last month as to enlist the help of the International Narcotics Control Board.

For all the success they've had in treating ADHD, many doctors are convinced that Ritalin is overprescribed. "I fear that ADHD is suffering from the 'disease of the month' syndrome," says Dr. Peter S. Jensen, chief of the Child and Adolescent Disorders Research Branch of NIMH. Teachers—even in preschool—are known to pull parents of active kids aside and suggest Ritalin. Overwhelmed with referrals, school psychologists (averaging one for every 2,100 students) say they feel pressed to recommend pills first before they have time to begin an evaluation. Psychiatrists nationwide say that about half the children who show up in their offices as ADHD referrals are actually suffering from a variety of other ailments, such as learning disabilities, depression or anxiety—disorders that look like ADHD, but do not need Ritalin. Some seem to be just regular kids. A St. Petersburg, Fla., pediatrician says parents of normal children have actually asked him for Ritalin just to improve their grades. "When I won't give it to them, they switch doctors," says Dr. Bruce Epstein. "They can find someone who will."

Finding someone who will is distressingly easy. Doctors themselves admit their methods are too often hasty. Almost half the pediatricians surveyed for a recent report in the Archives of Pediatric and Adolescent Medicine said they send ADHD children home in an hour. With such a rapid turnaround, many doctors never talk to teachers, review the child's educational levels, nor do any kind of psychological work-up—all essential diagnostic elements, Most children only get a prescription.

Making matters worse is that, ADHD experts now say, most children need behavior-modification therapy and special help in school. But most of the surveyed pediatricians said they rarely recommend anything more than pills. "A lot of doctors," says Dr. F. Xavier Castellanos, an ADHD researcher at NIMH, "are lulled into complacency. They think that by giving a child Ritalin, the likelihood of helping him is high and the downside is low."

What is ADHD? The disorder is almost as elusive as its name. More than a century ago, these children were known as "fidgety Phils." In the '50s, they were "hyperkinetic." The term Attention Deficit Disorder was coined in 1980. "Hyperactivity" was added in 1987 to describe the vast majority. (Roughly 20 percent suffer ADD without the hyperactivity.) But the label still isn't quite right. "It's not that they are not paying attention," says Sally L. Smith, founder of The Lab School of Washington, a private K-12 institution for children with learning disabilities. "They are paying *too* much attention, to *too* many things."

Children with attention problems are "lost in space and time," says Smith. Boys are afflicted up to three times as often as girls. They tend to be bright, but are poor students. These are the children who can't wait their turn. They blurt out answers before questions are asked. They can't stop wiggling their legs, tapping their pencils. They lose their bookbags, their homework, their tempers . . . not sometimes, but *constantly*. Decades ago "these children were the outcasts, the losers, the zoned-out kids," says Castellanos. Many just left school. "I had an uncle who dropped out in the fourth grade," says Dr. Martha Denckla, director of cognitive neurology at Johns Hopkins. "The explanation was, 'Milton was not a student'." She is convinced he was ADHD. The difference is, today's schools can't afford to give up on them.

Children in an orphanage nursery, c. 1895. Courtesy of the Chapin Hall Center for Children at the University of Chicago.

Part Seven

Children without Parents

A child in colonial America was considered an orphan when its father died. If the mother did not have the means to support the child, poor law officials gave the child to relatives or placed him/her with a family in exchange for maintenance. When children were formally apprenticed, boys were released at twenty-one and girls at eighteen and given a suit of clothes and some money. Later, agencies took over the supervision of orphans, and they were likely to send them by the trainload to be "placed out" with farm families in the developing West or other rural areas of the country.

As society turned away from child labor toward child nurture, a system of orphanages and then foster homes developed. Adoption, not legally available until the second half of the nineteenth century, also became an option, particularly for very young children. Today we still face the problem of children without parents. Foster care, orphanages, and adoption are the focus of current debate, much as they were at the turn of the century.

94

Many immigrants to colonial America, particularly the Chesapeake Bay colonies (Virginia, Maryland, and North Carolina), came as orphaned apprentices. According to the historian Abbot Emerson Smith, some of these children were kidnapped off the streets of London and "spirited away" on vessels bound for America (1947).

Kidnapping and White Servitude

Abbot Emerson Smith

Meanwhile the government made its first move to check the practice [kidnapping]. An ordinance of Parliament, in 1645, charged all officers and ministers of justice "to be very diligent in apprehending all such persons as are faulty in this kind, either in stealing, selling, buying, inveigling, purloyning, conveying, or receiving Children so stolne, and to keep them in safe imprisonment, till they may be brought to severe and exemplary punishment." The marshals of the Admiralty and of the Cinque Ports were ordered to search all vessels in the river and at the Downs for such children. A further precaution was taken by the Admiralty Commissioners, who ordered that Customs Houses should keep a register of all outgoing passengers to plantations or to foreign parts; this order was repeated by Parliament in January, 1646/7, and the governor of each colony was instructed to return a certificate of the arrival of such persons in his province. Apparently all of these injunctions were ignored; certainly no such lists remain, and the spiriting of servants went on with increasing vigor.

Where Parliamentary orders failed, local regulation succeeded better. In 1654 the city of Bristol passed a corporate ordinance requiring the registry in the Tolzey Book of the names of all departing servants, together with their destinations and the terms of their indentures. A penalty of £20 was imposed on any captain who disregarded this order, and for twenty years it was observed. The registrations of more than 10,000 servants may still be seen at Bristol, and the two volumes containing the entries are almost the only systematic records of servant transportation during the seventeenth century which are known to exist.

The only recourse of persons whose children or apprentices had been kidnapped was a special petition to the highest authorities. Thus a warrant was granted in 1653 for the master of a ship to deliver to Robert Broome his son, aged eleven, who had been spirited on board. In 1657 Sir John Barkstead, Colonel Francis White, and Major Miller were directed to inform themselves what passengers were on board the ship *Conquer*, bound for the West Indies. They found nineteen servants, of whom eleven had been "taken by the spirits," and most of these stated that they were unwilling to go. The ship was allowed to proceed after setting these on shore. In the summer of the Restoration the Privy Council received information on the subject, and in writing to the customs officers of London they described the practices of the spirits, calling them "so barbarous and inhumane, that Nature itself, much more Christians, cannot but abhorre." Continuing, they said that they had been informed "That, at this tyme, there is a Shipp, called the Seven Brothers, lately fallen downe towards Graves-End, and two other Shipps in the River of Thames in good forwardnesse to follow after in which there are sundry such Children and Servants of severall Parents and Masters, so deceived and inticed away Cryinge and Mourninge for Redemption from their Slavery." The officers were accordingly ordered to search all ships, and especially to stop the *Seven Brothers*. In 1663 the clerk of the town of Plymouth took it upon himself to stop the ship *Reserve*, bound for Maryland and legally cleared from Gravesend. A number of servants on board informed the clerk that they had been kidnapped, upon which he set them free. For this he was soundly rebuked by the Privy Council, yet very likely he was justified with respect to a part at least of the cargo.

The need for a regular system of recording the names and indentures of all emigrating servants had by this time become obvious. In November, 1660, two men petitioned the king for letters patent to keep a registry office, to which all servants were to be brought to declare their willingness to go, as well as the parents of all children who were to be transported. A series of other petitions and suggestions poured in on the king and Council. The mayor of Bristol in 1662 recited the situation in his city. In 1664 the Lord Mayor and Court of Aldermen of London presented a memorial on spiriting, saying that it often caused great tumults and uproars in the city, to the breach of the peace and the hazard of men's lives. On July 12, 1664, a group of merchants, planters, and masters of ships trading to the plantations petitioned for the appointment of persons under the Great Seal to enter the name, age, quality, place of birth, and last residence of all those desiring to go to the colonies as servants. This time the matter was referred to the attorney-general, who reported that the mischiefs of spiriting were indeed very great and frequent, and that there was scarcely a voyage to the plantations without some persons being illegally carried away. He recommended a registry office, but remarked that such an office would never be effectually executed without an act of Parliament granting a sufficient salary. The Council of Foreign Plantations favored the scheme, the usual formalities were seen through, and on September 14, 1664, the registry office was officially created. Roger Whitley, "at 40s." was given charge, and was expected to derive his principal reward from fees rather than from a salary. Registration of servants was not, of course, compulsory; the point was supposed to be that if thus registered a servant could have no complaint against the merchant, nor could parents distress ship owners about their children if the children had been properly signed on.

No systematic records of the activities of Whitley's office exist, but specimens of the forms it used have been preserved, showing that a system was worked out, even if not much used. There is an affidavit made out by a servant in 1670, stating the terms on which he had agreed to go to Virginia, and that he was willing to go. With this is a long certificate signed by "Jo: Salladine, Deputy Registrar," which recites the substance of the affidavit, specifies the freedom dues which the master is to give the servant at the end of his term, and announces that he has been properly registered. A place is provided for the special seal of the office.

95

In colonial America children were considered orphans when their fathers died, even when their mothers were still living; orphans' courts often determined their fate. The historian Lois Green Carr describes the operation of the orphans' court in Maryland (1997).

Orphans' Court

Lois Green Carr

The orphans' courts of Maryland and Virginia developed during the seventeenth century in response to a critical social need. A man who immigrated to the Chesapeake in the 1600s, regardless of his social class, had a short time to live compared even to Third World inhabitants today. He was unlikely to see any of his children come of age. A child had perhaps one chance in two of spending part of his childhood in the household of a stepfather or other guardian. Legal protections for the persons and property of children were vital matters, especially in a land where settlement was scattered and settlers were predominantly newcomers.

There were two sides to the problem: nurture of the child and protection of his inheritance, if any, from embezzlement or waste. The executor of William Watts's estate, for example, put Watts's sons to hard labor in the fields "equall to any servt or Slave" with "noe manner of cloathes but such Raggs & old Clouts that scarce would cover their nakedness." William Hollis had three stepfathers in four years and only timely intervention by the judge of probate prevented the father's assets from paying the debts of his successors. In a society where men well outnumbered women, young men on their death beds knew their wives would surely remarry. Wills often expressed concern that a stepfather might waste or steal the children's inheritance or treat the children as servants or let them grow up without education to enable them to improve what estate was left them.

Over much of the century, furthermore, there were no networks of kin to whom widows and orphans could turn for assistance. Most adult settlers of the seventeenth-century Chesapeake were immigrants, who had left their families 3,000 miles across an ocean. New family networks could not grow until the children of immigrants reached maturity and began to marry. The process was slow in Maryland. . . . For example, in the 1660s, 84 percent of the testate men and women who died in St. Mary's County, Maryland, and left minor children behind them, mentioned no kin in their wills. For the 1670s the figure was still 62 percent. By the decade 1700 to 1710 the problem was disappearing. Only 24 percent of the testators who left minors mention no kin upon whom their families might rely. But until late in the century the absence of kin made some institutional substitute an urgent matter: hence the orphans' courts. . . .

The laws were primarily concerned with the protection of property, but they also required guardianship appointments for indigent orphan children. Widows requested the court to find homes for children they could not support. Planters petitioned that orphans left in their care be bound to serve until they came of age, promising maintenance in return. Whether indigent orphan children were ever supported without formal court action is impossible to determine with certainty. The laws clearly intended that no child should be without the protection of the court, but proceedings show that justices rarely placed orphans if no one had petitioned on their behalf. On the other hand, it was in the interest of men who expected to benefit from the future labor of a child to obtain a recorded order of court.

A recent study I have made of Prince George's County, Maryland, at the end of the seventeenth century makes it possible to estimate the proportion in that place and time of decedent fathers whose orphans gained the court's attention. Forty-six men whose estates went through probate died in the county over the ten years from 1696 through 1705 and possibly left minor children. Of these forty-six, there are orphan proceedings for the children of twenty-four. The court bound out the children of four, all landless men. The other twenty were landowners. The court took security for the estates of seventeen, in most instances from a mother or a stepfather. In the other three cases, the court investigated trespasses on the orphans' land. The remaining twenty-two of these forty-six men left estates to children, if there were any, who do not appear in the guardianship records. All but one of these men were landowners. Nine may have died childless, and the orphans of two may have been of age. But at least eleven left minors, and four died intestate. The court should have taken security at least for the estates of these. Besides these forty-six men, twenty-three landless men whose estates were not probated left orphans who were bound out to service. Total identified fathers who may have left orphans not of age thus was sixty-nine. From 71 to 84 percent of them left orphans for whom there are guardianship proceedings (see table).

These figures may be close to the proportion of orphan families in the whole population brought to the notice of the court, but there are some possible holes in the data. Orphaned children not found in the guardianship records are most often identified in wills or other probate records, and estates of some men of property who left minor children may not have gone through probate. However, I have yet to identify a Prince George's County landowner or merchant of this period who died without leaving at least an inventory. Second, stepfathers of poor children whose fathers' estates did not go through probate may not have sought official guardianship of their stepchildren or bound them out to others.

Proceedings for Orphans of Men Who Died, 1696–1705, Prince George's County

(A)	Proceedings		No Proceedings		
	Landowners	Tenants	Landowners	Tenants	Total
Estate probated	20	4	15	7	46
Estate not probated	0	23	0	0	23
Totals	20	27	15	7	69

(B)	Estates Minors Certain		Estates Minors Uncertain		
	Landowners	Tenants	Landowners	Tenants	Total
Security taken	17	0	0	0	17
Children bound	0	27	0	0	27
Other proceedings	3	0	0	0	3
No proceedings	10	1	5	6	22
Totals	30	28	5	6	69

But the tally of tenants represented among the sixty-nine possible fathers suggests otherwise. In 1706 about 35 percent of heads of households in the county owned no land, but 49 percent (thirty-four) of these sixty-nine fathers were tenants. That tenants should be more numerous among decedent men with minor children than in the population of heads of households as a whole is not surprising. A study of dead men who left inventories in four Southern Maryland counties, 1658–1705, shows that tenancy was a stage in a man's career; if he had lived long enough to have a child of age he almost always was a landowner. Thus tenants were proportionately somewhat more likely than were landowners to leave minor children behind them. Nevertheless, the high proportion of tenants among identified decedent fathers suggests that no appreciable number of landless orphans went unnoted. The sixty-nine fathers identified should be close to all of the men who died leaving minor children needing care.

By the end of the seventeenth century, then, the Prince George's County Court was appointing guardians or actively supervising the estates of about three-quarters, and possibly four-fifths, of the orphan families.

96

The biographer David Herbert Donald describes Abraham Lincoln's warm relation-ship with his stepmother, to whom he attributed much of his success in life.

Abraham Lincoln and Sarah Bush Lincoln

David Herbert Donald

Within a year of Nancy's death, Thomas Lincoln recognized that he and his family could not go on alone, and he went back to Kentucky to seek a bride. In Elizabethtown he found Sarah Bush Johnston, whom he had perhaps unsuccess-fully courted before he wed Nancy. She was the widow of the Hardin County jailer and mother of three small children. There was no time for a romantic engagement; he needed a wife and she needed a husband. They made a quick, businesslike arrangement for him to pay her debts and for her to pack up her belongings and move with him to Indiana.

The arrival of Sarah Lincoln marked a turning point in Abraham Lincoln's life. She brought with her, first, her collection of domestic possessions—comfort-able bedding, a walnut bureau that had cost her forty-five dollars, a table and chairs, a spinning wheel, knives, forks, and spoons—so that the Lincoln children felt they were joining a world of unbelievable luxury. Her children—Elizabeth, John D., and Matilda, who ranged from nine to five years in age—brought life and excitement to the depressed Lincoln family. But most of all she brought with her the gift of love. Sarah Bush Lincoln must have been touched to see the dirty, ill-clad, hungry Lincoln children, and she set to work at once, as she said, to make them look "more human." "She soaped—rubbed and washed the children clean," Dennis Hanks remembered, "so that they look[ed] pretty neat—well and clean."

At her suggestion, the whole household was reorganized. Thomas Lincoln and Dennis Hanks had to give up hunting for a while to split logs and make a floor for the cabin, and they finished the roof, constructed a proper door, and cut a hole for a window, which they covered with greased paper. The cabin was high enough to install a loft, reached by climbing pegs driven into the wall, and here she installed beds for the three boys—Dennis Hanks, Abraham, and John D. Downstairs she had the whole cabin cleaned, a decent bedstead was built, and Thomas used his skill as a carpenter to make another table and stools. Remarka-bly, these reforms were brought about with a minimum of friction.

What was even more extraordinary, Sarah Bush Lincoln was able to blend the two families harmoniously and without jealousy. She treated her own children and the Lincoln children with absolute impartiality. She grew especially fond of Abraham. "Abe never gave me a cross word or look and never refused in fact, or even in appearance, to do anything I requested him," she remembered. "I never gave him a cross word in all my life. . . . His mind and mine—what little I had[—]seemed to move together—move in the same channel." Many years later, attempting to compare her son and her stepson, she told an interviewer: "Both were good boys, but I must say—both now being dead that Abe was the best boy I ever saw or ever expect to see."

Starved for affection, Abraham returned her love. He called her "Mama," and he never spoke of her except in the most affectionate terms. After he had been elected President, he recalled the sorry condition of Thomas Lincoln's household before Sarah Bush Johnston arrived and told of the encouragement she had given him as a boy. "She had been his best friend in this world," a relative reported him as saying, "and . . . no man could love a mother more than he loved her."

97

Black slave children were frequently orphaned when they or their parents were sold to another owner. In contrast to the situation of white orphans and servants, the care of slave children was not supervised by the courts. In his autobiography (1845) Frederick Douglass describes his dependence on his master.

A Childhood in Slavery

Frederick Douglass

As to my own treatment while I lived on Colonel Lloyd's plantation, it was very similar to that of the other slave children. I was not old enough to work in the field, and there being little else than field work to do, I had a great deal of leisure time. The most I had to do was to drive up the cows at evening, keep the fowls out of the garden, keep the front yard clean, and run of errands for my old master's daughter, Mrs. Lucretia Auld. The most of my leisure time I spent in helping Master Daniel Lloyd in finding his birds, after he had shot them. My connection with Master Daniel was of some advantage to me. He became quite attached to me, and was a sort of protector of me. He would not allow the older boys to impose upon me, and would divide his cakes with me.

I was seldom whipped by my old master, and suffered little from any thing else than hunger and cold. I suffered much from hunger, but much more from cold. In hottest summer and coldest winter, I was kept almost naked—no shoes, no stockings, no jacket, no trousers, nothing on but a coarse tow linen shirt, reaching only to my knees. I had no bed. I must have perished with cold, but that, the coldest nights, I used to steal a bag which was used for carrying corn to the mill. I would crawl into this bag, and there sleep on the cold, damp, clay floor, with my head in and feet out. My feet have been so cracked with the frost, that the pen with which I am writing might be laid in the gashes.

We were not regularly allowanced. Our food was coarse corn meal boiled. This was called *mush*. It was put into a large wooden tray or trough, and set down upon the ground. The children were then called, like so many pigs, and like so many pigs they would come and devour the mush; some with oyster-shells, others with pieces of shingle, some with naked hands, and none with spoons. He that ate fastest got most; he that was strongest secured the best place; and few left the trough satisfied.

I was probably between seven and eight years old when I left Colonel Lloyd's plantation. I left it with joy. I shall never forget the ecstasy with which I received the intelligence that my old master (Anthony) had determined to let me go to Baltimore, to live with Mr. Hugh Auld, brother to my old master's son-in-law, Captain Thomas Auld. I received this information about three days before my departure. They were three of the happiest days I ever enjoyed. I spent the most part of all these three days in the creek, washing off the plantation scurf, and preparing myself for my departure.

The pride of appearance which this would indicate was not my own. I spent the time in washing, not so much because I wished to, but because Mrs. Lucretia had told me I must get all the dead skin off my feet and knees before I could go to Baltimore; for the people in Baltimore were very cleanly, and would laugh at me if I looked dirty. Besides, she was going to give me a pair of trousers, which I should not put on unless I got all the dirt off me. The thought of owning a pair of trousers was great indeed! It was almost a sufficient motive, not only to make me take off what would be called by pig-drovers the mange, but the skin itself. I went at it in good earnest, working for the first time with the hope of reward.

The ties that ordinarily bind children to their homes were all suspended in my case. I found no severe trial in my departure. My home was charmless; it was not home to me; on parting from it, I could not feel that I was leaving any thing which I could have enjoyed by staying. My mother was dead, my grand-mother lived far off, so that I seldom saw her. I had two sisters and one brother, that lived in the same house with me; but the early separation of us from our mother had well nigh blotted the fact of our relationship from our memories. I looked for home elsewhere, and was confident of finding none which I should relish less than the one which I was leaving. If, however, I found in my new home hardship, hunger, whipping, and nakedness, I had the consolation that I should not have escaped any one of them by staying.

98

In the nineteenth century charities often sent children on trains for placement with farm families in western states. Here Children's Aid Society officials and other educators offer their opinions on the advantages and drawbacks of this practice. At issue are children who are orphaned, neglected, or abused, and also delinquent children.

Placing Orphan Children with Farm Families

Charles Loring Brace and His Critics

Charles L. Brace, "What Is the Best Method for the Care of Poor and Vicious Children?" (1880)

In this country, there was the greatest possible inducement for the "placing out" system, for Reformatories on the family plan, and for Farm Schools. The demand here for children's labor is practically unlimited. A child's place at the table of the farmer is always open; his food and cost to the family are of little account. A widespread spirit of benevolence, too, has inspired all classes—perhaps one of the latest fruits of Christianity—such as opens thousands of homes to the children of the unfortunate. The chances, too, of ill treatment in a new country, where children are petted and favored, and every man's affairs are known to all his neighbors, are far less than in an old. The very constitution, too, of an agricultural and democratic community favors the probability of a poor child's succeeding. When placed in a farmer's family, he grows up as one of their number, and shares in all the social influences of the class. The peculiar temptations to which he has been subject—such, for instance, as stealing and vagrancy—are reduced to a minimum; his self-respect is raised, and the chances of success held out to a laborer in this country, with the influences of school and of religion, soon raise him far above the class from which he sprang.

The cost, too, should have been a powerful inducement. A child's expense in an Asylum, Poor House, or Reformatory for a year, cannot be less than one hundred dollars, and may be much more; the placing out costs but a small sum.

Then, experience has taught that large numbers of poor and neglected children, placed in institutions together, deprave and injure one another. Their virtues, too, have an institutional flavor. They incline to be hypocritical; they lack in independence of character, and are weak under temptation, though outwardly respectable. Being supplied by machinery, they do not learn the small household arts—of making a fire, taking care of lamps, drawing water, cutting wood, and the like—which a poor man is compelled to practice. The most profitable branches of labor in this country for the workingman are agricultural; but the boy of the Asylum and Refuge has usually been trained in the poorest and most simple mechanical trades, such as shoe-pegging and similar occupations, and is comparatively unfitted for farm and garden work.

All these inducements should have led early in this country to the employment of the placing out plan for orphan, homeless and pauper children, and even for those sentenced for trivial offences, such as vagrancy and the like; while for the vicious and those who had committed criminal offences, Farm Schools and Family Reformatories should have taken the place of Congregated Reformatories and large Houses of Refuge.

The great principle at the base of modern criminal reform is *individual influence*, and the nearest approach possible to a natural system. The best influence on a poor child must come from a family life, and no asylum, however well managed, can approach in healthful natural influences an average farmer's family.

If we . . . endeavor to answer the question, "What is the best method for the care of poor and vicious children," we should say,

(1.) All pauper children should be removed as soon as possible from Almshouses, and placed, if possible, at once in families, subject to a careful visitation and inspection by officials or local committees. The poor-house is no place for a child. Nor is there need of intermediate institutions, except for those of unsound mind and body. Under a good system, any pauper children who are of sound mind, and not defective in body, can be at once well placed in families.

(2.) The orphan, homeless, and street-wandering children of villages and cities should be temporarily gathered in asylums, homes for the friendless, lodging houses, and industrial schools, and, as soon as practicable, be distributed in homes and upon farms. No orphan asylum or home of the friendless should detain their inmates after they are ten or twelve years of age, unless they are of peculiarly unfortunate condition, physical or mental. For the expense of one child kept during a year, seven can be placed out; while the chances for improvement are far greater in the farmer's home than in the asylum . . .

(3.) Children who are habitually vicious or who have inherited very bad tendencies, or have an abnormal constitution, or have committed serious offences, should be placed in Farm Schools, arranged after the family plan. There should be small groups of children, say twenty or twenty-five in number, gathered in cottages, each group under a teacher or superintendent, who could learn the habits and characters of each and exert an individual influence upon them. These children should do all the work of the house, garden, and farm. Their great employments should be in the soil. Those are the labors most healthful, needed most in this country, and which in the long run repay the best . . .

As to the petty criminals among children—those convicted of vagrancy, petty thieving, disobedience of parents, quarreling and like offences—they should also be placed in Family Reformatories; but they need be kept there only for a short time, and then should be carefully distributed in families. This class of children are frequently no worse than the great body of those outside, and turn out very well under family influence. Asylum life (if long continued) only weakens their character. A certain amount, however, of punishment and discipline is very useful to them.

The principle lying at the bottom of all these suggested improvements, it cannot too often be said, is the necessity of *individual influence* on each child to be reformed, and the superiority of family life to any other influence in the improvement and reform of children.

Lyman P. Alden, "The Shady Side of the 'Placing-out System'" (1885)

It is well known by all who have had charge of the binding out of children that the great majority of those who apply for children over nine years old are looking for cheap help; and while many, even of this class, treat their apprentices with fairness, and furnish them a comfortable home, a much larger number of applicants do not intend to pay a *quid pro quo*, but expect to make a handsome profit on the child's services, and, if allowed one, will evade, as far as possible, every clause in the contract,—furnishing poor food, shoddy clothing, work the child beyond its strength, send it to school but a few months, and that irregularly, and sometimes treat it with personal cruelty, though this, in a thickly settled country, is not likely to occur so frequently. I could fill this paper with instances in proof of this that have come under my personal observation, in an experience of eight years as superintendent of the Michigan State Public School. These people can always get good indorsements. That my experience may not appear singular, I have taken considerable pains, by correspondence and otherwise, to ascertain the views of old and successful workers in this field, in the East and West; and I find remarkable unanimity of opinion on this point, so far as I have investigated.

Miss Susan Fenimore Cooper, of Cooperstown, N.Y., whose labors for poor children are distinguished, and make her an authority, says:—

Our chief difficulty lies with the families who receive the children when they leave us. In many instances, very respectable people, who have brought the best of references, seem to have no judgment in training children. They are careless of the child's best interests, allow it to associate with evil companions, to run wild, and to read pernicious books and papers.

Mrs. Virginia Ohr, for about fifteen years superintendent of the Illinois Soldiers' and Sailors' Orphans' Home, says:—

Our experience in placing children in homes is very unsatisfactory. I find that the greater number of applicants for children have no other aim in view than to secure cheap help.

Says the committee for placing out children, of the Cleveland Protestant Orphan Asylum, "The larger proportion of homes offered we are compelled to decline." Mrs. Mary E. Cobb, superintendent of the Wisconsin Girls' Industrial School, and one of the most experienced and successful workers in this country, says, "Many more must be rejected than accepted, even when the applications come indorsed according to the strictest rule."

Says A. H. Fetterolf, President of Girard College for Orphan Boys: "Our experience with farmers has not been satisfactory. They are not considerate for the child's welfare, caring only to use him for their profit."

S. W. Pierce, for eighteen years superintendent of the Iowa Soldiers' Orphan Home and Home for Indigent Children, says, "The average family with us wants a child for what they can get out of it in the way of work."

Says Rev. E. Wright, of Normal, Ill., agent for the New York Juvenile Asylum, which during the past thirty years has placed out in Illinois, with the greatest possible care, 4,285 children:—

The beneficence of an apprenticing agency is not attested by the number of children which it disposes of. It is not quantity, but quality, that determines the real excellence of its work. It would be an easy matter for us to place a thousand children annually in homes, in the Western States, if nothing more than that were required. But, of all the outrages that have been perpetrated in the name of Christian charity, none is more reprehensible than that of leaving helpless children without recourse in such situations. That this is not an extravagant assertion could be proved from the experience of this agency during almost any single week of its history.

Now, all this does not prove, nor is it intended to prove, that many good homes cannot be found for children, if proper care is taken. I know that thousands of such homes have been found, where the children are treated with affectionate consideration. But it does prove, I think, that the great majority of those who apply for children should never have them, and that great caution and discrimination should be used in selecting homes. It does prove that, if institutional care for children, where specialists are employed, who are constantly under the eye of the public and of official boards and visiting committees, is not so perfect as it should be, it is still more difficult to secure uniformly wise and kind treatment of children where they are placed in so many different families, scattered, perhaps, all over a State, which, with the best system of supervision practicable, cannot be visited, usually, oftener than once in each year. It does prove that a glamour has been thrown over the work of placing out children, which should be dispelled. It takes something more than a farm of a hundred and sixty acres and well-filled granaries to constitute a good home. There may be all of these, and yet the elements of a good home be entirely wanting. The man may be vulgar, profane, intemperate, penurious, or tyrannical. Or the mistress may be slovenly, sickly, peevish, and an eternal scold. Or, if the parents are all right, there may be disagreeable, overbearing, hateful children; and a child placed in such a home would be living in the antipodes of a heaven on earth, while those who bound it out might complacently imagine that its life was a happy one.

Francis H. White, "The Placing-Out System in the Light of Its
Results" (1894)

The conclusions presented in this paper are founded upon an investigation into the afterlife of the children placed in Kansas by the New York Children's Aid Society. The state, as you know, is centrally located, and its people and physical features are fairly typical of the other states in the Mississippi valley where thousands of children have been given homes. My interest in the work dates back to a time when I was superintendent of the Brooklyn Children's Aid Society. Five years ago I accepted a chair in the State Agricultural College of Kansas, a position which has brought me in contact with the class of people among whom most of the children have been placed.

The agencies within the state engaged in placing-out children are a few private institutions, whose work is not extensive, and a state institution, established a few years ago, which receives and trains dependent children, and finds homes for them through the aid and supervision of the county superintendents of public instruction. There is no organized system of boarding-out children such as is practised in some other states.

Two societies having headquarters outside of Kansas are engaged in placing-out children within it. These are the Chicago Children's Home Society and the New York Children's Aid Society. The first has done little in the state, but the second has accomplished a large work, extending over a long period of time. There are other states in which it has operated more extensively than in this, indeed it has placed out over 75,000 children in various parts of the country since 1857. There is good reason to believe that the work done in Kansas is a fair sample of what it has done everywhere.

At my request, an official of the New York Children's Aid Society made a careful examination of their records and vouches for the following general summary:—

The total number of children placed in homes among the residents of Kansas is 960, of whom 13 per cent were girls.

2 per cent are known to be dead.

10 per cent have no records. These were mainly large boys placed early in the history of the society.

3 per cent were returned as not satisfactory because of some mental or physical disability.

10 per cent left their homes within the first few years.

2 per cent have bad records, that is, were guilty of some serious misdemeanor.

7 per cent have poor records.

22 per cent have very fair records.

44 per cent have excellent records.

The average age of the children was 12.3 years.

84 per cent of those under eight years do well.

It will be noticed that only 66 per cent of the whole work is known to be successful. Let us examine somewhat more closely into the history of these children in order to discover the reasons for this rather low percentage. . . .

Party Placed in Kansas, 1867

1. Reported a good boy, but no record after first year, though many letters have been sent.

2. Wrote once. No trace of him since.

3. Stayed nine months, then went west and has never been heard from.

4. Remained about two years, then ran away. Some years later served a term in the penitentiary. Afterwards wrote his foster-parent he was employed and doing fairly well.

5. Left after staying a few months.

6. Stayed about a year and a half, then went to Michigan, where he married and still lives.

7. Soon left.

8. Remained in place for several years, then went elsewhere in the neighborhood to work. Not been in the vicinity for many years.

9. No replies to letters sent.

10. Was a good boy, but died in second year.

11. Left the first year.

12. A good boy, but met with accident and went east for treatment. Nothing known of him since.

13. Did well. Is now married; has children of his own, and is living near a large western city, employed as a railroad conductor.

14. Left the first year.

15, 16. Brothers. Placed with same man. No record or replies to seven letters sent.

17. Stayed six months, then went to live with another man in the vicinity. Now has considerable property and is highly respected.

18. No record or replies to letters.

The chairman of the committee that found homes for these boys is still living and is a man of some prominence in the community. He remembers very well the disappointment of the farmers when they found the boys were over fourteen, for they had requested younger children, knowing well they could not induce the older ones to remain. The chairman seemed quite sure that the farmers had no intention of doing a charitable act nor of satisfying their own longing for children, but that they simply wished to obtain cheap labor, as the boys were only to receive board and clothes for their services. He says that when he expressed doubt as to whether the boys ought to be placed with these men without any written agreement on the part of the latter to take good care of them, the agent laughed and told him not to worry about that; if the homes were not agreeable to them they would soon leave. Not one of this party now resides in the county, and only two are known to live in Kansas. Over half of the persons with whom they were placed are dead or have moved out of the county, and their present address is unknown to former acquaintances.

Party Placed in Kansas, 1884

1. Age 6. Visited one year later and found he was doing well and had excellent home; frequent good reports; now working out and earning $10 per month; goes by his foster-parents' name.

2. Age 17. Wrote same year thanking Society for home. In 1891 joined regular army, was assigned to infantry band, and stationed in New Mexico. Has written and published some poems, and now employs leisure time studying Spanish and translating poetry. Reports he is saving money and has joined the church.

3. Age 6. Stayed until man with whom placed moved away, then went to live in town near by and is now doing well.

4. Age 12. Stayed until man moved away, then went to live with excellent family; still there and doing well.

5. Age 9. Stayed until man broke up housekeeping, then went elsewhere, and when last heard from was doing well.

6. Age 12. Visited and found to be doing well; letters confirmed report; died in 1888 of consumption.

7. Age 10. Remained six years, then went to New Mexico; returned, and later reported doing well.

8. Age 14. No replies to letters sent.

9. Age 9. Visited and found to be doing well; remained seven years and then went to work for himself; now reported to be making a good living.

10. Age 10. Visited and reported as getting along all right and that he had joined the church; stayed three years; is now in neighborhood and said to be succeeding.

11. Age 8. Visited and reported a good boy; remained till 1889, then left and has worked in several places since.

12. Age 12. Remained for several years, was slow and stubborn, but a good worker; went to Colorado and then returned, and is now reported as in the neighborhood, but "doing no good."

13. Age 16. An excellent young woman; married a relative of the man with whom she was placed, and is doing well.

14. Age 6. Visited and found to have a good home, but after three years left it; reported that he lied and stole and could not be managed; brought back, but was dissatisfied, and was transferred to another home, where he did fairly well. Later, taken to New York and placed in the Eye and Ear Infirmary for treatment.

15. Age 5½. Visited and found to be doing well; failing health of his foster-parent made it necessary to give him another home, where he is now living and getting along well; is well liked.

16. Age 6. Visited and found to be doing well; a letter from foster-parent says boy goes by his name; a recent letter, that "he is satisfied with them and they with him."

17. Age 7½. Stayed until foster-parents gave up housekeeping, then went to another home, where she is reported to be contented, giving fair satisfaction, though she is not very intelligent.

18, 19, 20, 21. Ages 15, 13, 12, 11. Brothers and sisters; all doing well at last account; one of them now owns an eighty-acre farm.

Of the party placed in 1867, composed of boys between the ages of fourteen and seventeen, by far the larger part drifted away or turned out badly; while just the reverse is true of the party placed in 1884, composed of children for the most part twelve years old or under. The histories of other children I have traced confirm me in this opinion. It seems clear that the earlier children are placed, the more likely are the results to be satisfactory.

See, too, the picking and choosing that is necessary in making up a party to go west. From the street, the newsboys' homes, the charitable institutions, come the applicants for western homes, bright, dull, hardened, sad, gay—their natures so different, their friendless and homeless condition so similar. Will the net take all? No! only the gold fish,—the "gilt-edged children," as they are popularly called. This astonishes us at first. Nearly every one pictures the work as an effort to relieve the city of the bad, not the good, dependent children.

Why does the Society refuse to send west the hardened, the incorrigible, the vicious? For two reasons: first, the west would not take them, and second, they could not be induced to remain in the homes provided. The experiment was tried repeatedly in the early history of the work, but almost invariably failed.

99

American literature and folk legend are full of the fatherless and homeless child forced to make it on his own. Probably the most famous such child was created by Mark Twain in The Adventures of Huckleberry Finn *(1885). Here Huck's father tries to reclaim him, with disastrous results.*

Huckleberry Finn

Mark Twain

I had shut the door to. Then I turned around, and there he was. I used to be scared of him all the time, he tanned me so much. I reckoned I was scared now, too; but in a minute I see I was mistaken—that is, after the first jolt, as you may say, when my breath sort of hitched, he being so unexpected; but right away after, I see I warn't scared of him worth bothring about.

He was most fifty, and he looked it. His hair was long and tangled and greasy and hung down, and you could see his eyes shining through like he was behind vines. It was all black, no gray; so was his long, mixed-up whiskers. There warn't no color in his face, where his face showed; it was white, not like another man's white but a white to make a body sick, a white to make a body's flesh crawl—a tree-toad white, a fish-belly white. As for his clothes—just rags, that was all. He had one ankle resting on t'other knee; the boot on that foot was busted and two of his toes stuck through, and he worked them now and then. His hat was laying on the floor—an old black slouch with the top caved in, like a lid.

I stood a-looking at him; he set there a-looking at me, with his chair tilted back a little. I set the candle down. I noticed the window was up; so he had clumb in by the shed. He kept a-looking me all over. By and by he says:

"Starchy clothes—very. You think you're a good deal of a big-bug, *don't* you?"

"Maybe I am, maybe I ain't," I says.

"Don't you give me none o'your lip," says he. "You've put on considerable many frills since I been away. I'll take you down a peg before I get done with you. You're educated, too, they say—can read and write. You think you're better'n your father, now, don't you, because he can't? *I'll* take it out of you. Who told you you might meddle with such hifalut'n foolishness, hey?—who told you you could?"

"The widow. She told me."

"The widow, hey?—and who told the widow she could put in her shovel about a thing that ain't none of her business?"

"Nobody never told her."

"Well, I'll learn her how to meddle. And looky here—you drop that school, you hear? I'll learn people to bring up a boy to put on airs over his own father and let on to be better'n what *he* is. You lemme catch you fooling around that school again, you hear? Your mother couldn't read, and she couldn't write, nuther, before she died. None of the family couldn't before *they* died. *I* can't; and here you're a-swelling yourself up like this. I ain't the man to stand it—you hear? Say, lemme hear you read."

I took up a book and begun something about General Washington and the wars. When I'd read about a half a minute, he fetched the book a whack with his hand and knocked it across the house. He says:

"It's so. You can do it. I had my doubts when they told me. Now looky here; you stop that putting on frills. I won't have it. I'll lay for you, my smarty, and if I catch you about that school I'll tan you good. First you know you'll get religion, too. I never see such a son."

He took up a little blue and yaller picture of some cows and a boy, and says: "What's this?"

"It's something they give me for learning my lessons good."

He tore it up, and says:

"I'll give you something better—I'll give you a cowhide." . . .

Well, pretty soon the old man was up and around again, and then he went for Judge Thatcher in the courts to make him give up that money, and he went for me, too, for not stopping school. He catched me a couple of times and thrashed me, but I went to school just the same, and dodged him or outrun him most of the time. I didn't want to go to school much before but I reckoned I'd go now to spite pap. That law trial was a slow business—appeared like they warn't ever going to get started on it; so every now and then I'd borrow two or three dollars off of the judge for him, to keep from getting a cowhiding. Every time he got money he got drunk, and every time he got drunk he raised Cain around town, and every time he raised Cain he got jailed. He was just suited—this kind of thing was right in his line.

He got to hanging around the widow's too much, and so she told him at last that if he didn't quit using around there she would make trouble for him. Well, *wasn't* he mad? He said he would show who was Huck Finn's boss. So he watched out for me one day in the spring and catched me and took me up the river about three mile in a skiff, and crossed over to the Illinois shore where it was woody and there warn't no houses but an old log hut in a place where the timber was so thick you couldn't find it if you didn't know where it was.

He kept me with him all the time and I never got a chance to run off. We lived in that old cabin and he always locked the door and put the key under his head nights. He had a gun which he had stole, I reckon, and we fished and hunted, and that was what we lived on. Every little while he locked me in and went down to the store, three miles, to the ferry, and traded fish and game for whisky and fetched it home and got drunk and had a good time and licked me. The widow she found out where I was by and by and she sent a man over to try to get hold of me, but pap drove him off with the gun and it warn't long after that till I was used to being where I was and liked it—all but the cowhide part. . . .

But by and by pap got too handy with his hick'ry and I couldn't stand it. I was all over welts. He got to going away so much, too, and locking me in. Once he locked me in and was gone three days. It was dreadful lonesome. I judged he had got drownded and I wasn't ever going to get out any more. I was scared. I made up my mind I would fix up some way to leave there. I had tried to get out of that cabin many a time but I couldn't find no way. There warn't a window to it big enough for a dog to get through. I couldn't get up the chimbly; it was too narrow. The door was thick, solid oak slabs. Pap was pretty careful not to leave a knife or anything in the cabin when he was away; I reckon I had hunted the place over as much as a hundred times; well, I was most all the time at it, because it was about the only way to put in the time. But this time I found something at last; I found an old rusty wood-saw without any handle; it was laid in between a rafter and the clapboards of the roof. I greased it up and went to work. There was an old horse-blanket nailed against the logs at the far end of the cabin behind the table, to keep the wind from blowing through the chinks and putting the candle out. I got under the table and raised the blanket, and went to work to saw a section of the big bottom log out—big enough to let me through. Well, it was a good long job but I was getting towards the end of it when I heard pap's gun in the woods. I got rid of the signs of my work and dropped the blanket and hid my saw, and pretty soon pap come in.

Pap warn't in a good humor—so he was his natural self. He said he was down to town and everything was going wrong. His lawyer said he reckoned he would win his lawsuit and get the money if they ever got started on the trial, but then there was ways to put it off a long time and Judge Thatcher knowed how to do it. And he said people allowed there'd be another trial to get me away from him and give me to the widow for my guardian, and they guessed it would win this time. This shook me up considerable because I didn't want to go back to the widow's any more and be so cramped up and sivilized, as they called it. Then the old man got to cussing and cussed everything and everybody he could think of, and then cussed them all over again to make sure he hadn't skipped any, and after that he polished off with a kind of a general cuss all round, including a considerable parcel of people which he didn't know the names of and so called them what's-his-name when he got to them and went right along with his cussing.

He said he would like to see the widow get me. He said he would watch out and if they tried to come any such game on him he knowed of a place six or seven mile off to stow me in, where they might hunt till they dropped and they couldn't find me. That made me pretty uneasy again but only for a minute; I reckoned I wouldn't stay on hand till he got that chance. . . .

Whenever his liquor begun to work he most always went for the govment. This time he says:

"Call this a govment! why, just look at it and see what it's like. Here's the law a-standing ready to take a man's son away from him—a man's own son, which he has had all the trouble and all the anxiety and all the expense of raising. Yes, just as that man has got that son raised at last, and ready to go to work and begin to do suthin' for *him* and give him a rest, the law up and goes for him. And they call *that* govment!

100

Informal adoption by kin, especially grandparents, is common among many fami-
lies, particularly during tough economic times. The sociologist Charles S. Johnson
observes this pattern in his 1934 study of black residents of Macon County,
Alabama.

Shadow of the Plantation
Separation and Adoption

Charles S. Johnson

The frequency of separations of families with children and the large number of children born outside of formal family relations normally throw a considerable burden of responsibility upon grandparents, and this responsibility, in turn, is accepted as a matter of course. Actually there was a marked sense of social obligation to children, expressed more by grandparents than by parents with numbers of children.

Sadie Thompson not only had a family of her own, now practically grown, but had undertaken the rearing of some of the grandchildren and other adopted ones. She had enterprise and initiative and both virtues were required to keep up her household. There was in her solicitude for the children a feeling rarely expressed, whether experienced or not, by families regarding their own immediate offspring. And with this feeling there was mixed some appreciation of the economic value of the children themselves.

> I got these little motherless children here and got nothing to give them to eat. I never had a mouthful to give them yesterday and last night Mr. Walker just give them boys a dollar and I couldn't buy nothing but a little meal and a spoonful of lard. These children got a father but he don't give them nothing. These my dead daughter's children. Sometimes I look at them and tears get in my eyes. We made fourteen bales of cotton last year, and didn't get a penny for it. The little children was barefooted and didn't have a thing. If they hadn't had a little pig and I made some syrup I don't know what the little things woulda done. Every time they go to the white man they say they can't let you have nothing. Something is wrong somewhere but they ain't letting the nigger know where it is. I hate to go so far and not get nothing. "I don't reckon we will die," said one of my sons. But you will die 'cause every one of you all look sick in the eyes and it's cause you ain't had enough food. This is a starving land. . . .

This is the worst place I ever run on in my life. If you could jest get out of it all you put in it you could live happy. This is good rich land, and you could make money if we was treated right. The mules ain't even got nothing to eat, and we have to pull up the little corn and feed it to them. I look at my children sometimes and I'm sorry I ever born a child in the world. I believe in living like people. My children is smart 'cause I taught them to work. Us never do hire no day hands. We all help one 'nother get through with the chopping. They busy all the time. How they hold up I can't see.

. . . Another woman was explaining the presence of a female relative in the home: "This lady who stays here is my husband's cousin. She gonna have a baby soon. She got two more, but she gie'd dem away. She ain't married; the child's father he 'round here somewheres." In this instance the responsibility of children would obviously be a burden to the woman. The family to which she had given her children regarded them freely and easily as their own, but their own children were regarded primarily as potential helpers in the severe struggle for existence. The comments about their children, and almost always about the adult ones, were followed by some such consideration: "She's a good chile. . . . She bring me something to eat when she can." Or: "I can't let dat boy marry. He all I got to help me."

Separations and divorce frequently divide the children or leave all of them with one parent. The natural handicaps, for illiterate people, of communication contribute to a stretching-out of filial ties, often to the vanishing-point. "My girl, Fannie Mae, is with her father in Pittsburgh. She been gone 'bout ten years. I ain't heard 'bout her since Christmas 'fore last. I speck she still dere." . . .

Adoption of children is a fairly common practice. Several factors appear to be responsible. Children after a certain age are, as indicated earlier, an economic asset. Childless couples, for whatever reason, have not the social standing in the community of families with children. The breaking-up of families, through desertion or migration, results in the turning-over of children to relatives or friends, and since little distinction in treatment enters, they soon are indistinguishable from the natural children, and assist them by dividing the load of heavy families. Moreover, adoption is related to illegitimacy, and frequently the children in families which are referred to as adopted are really the illegitimate offspring of one's own daughter or neighbor's daughter. The child of an unmarried daughter becomes another addition to the children of the parents of the girl with all the obligations. Discipline is in the hands of the original parents and the young mother's relationship to her son is in most respects the same as her relationship to her younger brother. These children call her by her first name and refer to their natural grandparents as "mama" and "papa." It has happened that men have adopted into their legitimate families extra-legal children by other women, and with no apparent distinction that would make them unfavorably conspicuous among the other children. Again, children orphaned by any circumstances are spontaneously taken into childless families.

This girl, we find her when us come down here. She be's both orphan by mother and father, and nobody to look atta her. So we jest tuk her as one of the family, and don't sho' no difference. We don't tell no difference. This little boy is my sister's boy. I can't 'dopt him long as she live, 'cause I don't want no dissatisfaction. But he won't stay with her. She carry him home and have to bring him back.

. . . The ease with which the adoptions are made is interesting. There are few families, indeed, however poor, that would not attempt to rear a child left with them. Adoption, in a sense, takes the place of social agencies and orphans' homes.

No, I ain't got no husband; he ain't dead, I don't guess. I ain't seen him in eight years. He left me here wid these chillun, so I try to take keer of them. The girl is my niece. Her mother and father both dead.

Me and my wife been married thirty-two years. We ain't got no chillun of our own. My wife 'dopted this little boy. He eleven years old. His mamma gie'd him ter my wife soon atta he was born. His mamma 'round here in Shorter somewhere. We don't know nothing 'bout his daddy. His mamma ain't never been married as we knows of.

101

In the late twentieth century divorce rather than death has left a large percentage of children living with only one parent. Psychologists and other social scientists disagree about the impact this has on children. Here the psychologists Judith S. Wallerstein and Joan Berlin Kelly describe behavior they have observed in children of divorced parents (1980).

Surviving the Breakup
How Children Respond to Divorce

Judith S. Wallerstein and Joan Berlin Kelly

The age and developmental groupings into which the children's responses fell, with a regularity which we had not fully anticipated, provided a congenial way of categorizing their concerns, feelings, and behaviors at the time of the marital breakup. Some of our cases illustrate the close similarities as well as the striking differences which emerged.

The Preschool and Kindergarten Children (Three-to-Five-Year-Olds)

Linda's Perspective

Linda, age four, appeared in our office, an attractive, blond, well-groomed child. When asked about what was happening at home, she solemnly explained that her father was living in the city because he didn't like Mommy, and that Mommy felt bad because she (Mommy) still liked Daddy. As was characteristic of many of the children, Linda accompanied her sober and dutiful recitation of the events of the household with play which belied her spoken words.

Linda played in an eerie silence. All the usual and familiar sounds with which children accompany their play were absent. She constructed a serene scene in which mother and father lay in bed together. The children played happily in an adjoining room as the baby slept peacefully in the crib. As the narrative developed, the mother arose to make a bountiful breakfast and the little boy generously brought a bowl of cereal to another child.

At the second meeting the child again arranged a happy family scene. The family members all watched television together. The father held the baby on his lap and the baby was comfortable in the father's arms. The children were seated on the floor in front of their parents. After the show, the family had dinner together and the father continued, tenderly, to hold the baby.

In the third hour with us the child went quickly to the now-familiar dollhouse and arranged the furniture to her satisfaction. The togetherness theme took over with new and rising intensity. Methodically and soberly, the child placed father, mother, and the three children in a bathtub together. She then removed the entire family to the roof and the father and mother and the children were all sitting, one on top of the other, on top of the house. Then, suddenly, her play ended, she jumbled the furniture and the dolls and began a wild puppet play in which large animals bit each other viciously. The whale bit the crocodile, and the crocodile bit the giraffe. And then, finally, apparently carried away by her play, the child broke through the play and bit the crocodile savagely and then pummeled it out of shape. All of this, including her final giving way to anger, attack, and loss of control, occurred in the total absence of any sound.

There is a very moving eloquence to Linda's wordless portrayal. First, there is togetherness and tenderness: parents care lovingly for happy children; the food is abundant; and the family never separates, not even in the bathtub. Suddenly, the peaceful scenes are disrupted and the family, which is perched precariously on the roof, but still together, comes crashing down and is overtaken by cascading aggression, attack, destruction. The child herself leaves her role as director and, caught up in the play, regresses and herself bites one of the main players. Her four-year-old capacity to distinguish between her play and reality is wiped out with the rise in aggression and the weakening of controls as her wish for the close and intact family becomes too painful for her.

The extraordinary silence which accompanies the play may express many feelings—perhaps the child's unexpressed and unexpressable grief, perhaps feelings which we can only guess at at this stage and which would require considerable skill to plumb. One needs, however, no special training to read Linda's agenda for restoring her family, or to follow her perspective on the divorce events.

Fear

The youngest children who came to see us were, like Linda, frightened, bewildered, and very sad. Their immature grasp of the events swirling around them, together with their difficulty in sorting out their own fantasy and dream from reality, rendered them especially vulnerable. Having seen the central relationship between their parents come apart, they concluded, not without logic, that other relationships might similarly come undone, and they might well be left alone.

The routine separations of daily life were suddenly filled with dread. Some clung to the remaining parent, whimpering or crying when the parent left on a routine errand or departed for work at the usual time, or went out for the evening. Parents who returned from work or retrieved their children after school were greeted with angry tears, crankiness, and sometimes tantrums by children sufficiently relieved by the parent's return to express the anguish and frustration which they had suffered during the parental absence. Anxieties rose as darkness approached, and peaked at bedtime, which soon became a tense and unhappy battle of wills between an exhausted angry parent and a panic-stricken child. Throughout the night children became fretful, waking frequently, crying, and begging to be taken into the parent's bed.

Children who attended nursery school or kindergarten became anxious about leaving home to go to school. Like Hansel and Gretel in the fairy tale, they were fearful of not finding their way back home again. Or they feared that no one would be there to greet them. They refused to ride in familiar carpools unless mother came along; they objected to returning to kindergartens which they had previously enjoyed. Youngsters who had adjusted well to their mother's employment found their mother's departure very difficult and greeted her return with tears of relief and the accumulated crankiness of the worrisome day.

Regression

Regression was a common response among the youngest children. Overwhelmed by their anxiety, very young children returned to their security blankets, to recently outgrown toys. Lapses in toilet training and increased masturbatory activity were noted. The difficulty in separating from the custodial parent also reflects regression to earlier modes of relationship, characteristic of the toddler who needs to keep the caregiver in full view or readily accessible. The child who regresses tells us by his behavior that it is all too much, that he must hold back in development, mark time or move backward, in order to gain strength for the next step forward. Although in most instances the regressions lasted a short time, a few weeks or a few months at most, the custodial parent found these particularly difficult because they disrupted household routines and increased the child's need for care at a time when the parent lacked both time and patience. . . .

Macabre Fantasy

. . . One fairly common fantasy which children expressed in their play was their fear of being left hungry by their parents. This fear of hunger was associated with their fear of abandonment and with the consequences of aggression. Children constructed toy scenes of powerful animals with big teeth who snatched food away from hungry little animals who were helpless to defend themselves.

Bewilderment

Children were painfully bewildered and trying anxiously to comprehend the present and future vicissitudes of their relationship with both parents. Their concept of the dependability of human relationships and personal ties had been profoundly shaken. Sometimes the fear of being hurt or betrayed in a relationship spread to the relationship with the teacher at school. Larry begged his teacher to hold him on her lap and then hollered, "Don't get too close to me!" and ran away. Recurrent playroom themes were those of aimless, woebegone searching, and trying dispiritedly to fit objects together. Sometimes they essayed to clarify boundaries and master distinctions and linkages by asking uncomprehendingly and repetitiously of familiar objects, "What's this?"

John explored the room, handling everything in sight. At the slightest rustle outside, however, he would look up apprehensively. "Who's that? Where has daddy gone?" He turned abruptly to the toys. "What's this?" he asked, "What's that?" He obviously knew and answered just a few of his own questions. Boxes intrigued him and he shook them open and scattered the objects, then rapidly moved on to the next box. The play that lasted consisted of poking objects into objects; fitting things together, sticks into clay, tinker toys, cars into boxes, puppets into a house. The central theme of the child's play was what belongs to what, and who belongs to whom.

Fred, age five, played endlessly with a magnet, bringing objects into its magnetic field and releasing them, silently playing out the coming together and the separation, and seemingly unable to integrate the experience or to move on from it.

Karen, age three, became preoccupied with staking out claims all over her house. Crossly and imperiously, she asserted about various objects that seemed selected at random, "That is mine, and that is mine." We observe here not only the child's preoccupation with what is indeed hers, but also her sad recognition of the limits of her claims by her bold, if futile, efforts to undo her loss by claiming dominion over everything.

Replaceability

As the children made heroic efforts to encompass the disturbing events of the separation they reached explanations that caused them great anguish. One unhappy conclusion which the four-to-five-year-olds arrived at was that the departed parent had rejected them and left to replace them with another family elsewhere. It was almost impossible for these children to conceptualize the one parent's departure as being directed at the other parent and not at them.

First seen when he was four years old, Frank had been his mother's favorite child, and his self-esteem, although badly shaken by the divorce, was still high. He was, however, at the time that we saw him, very frightened and especially fearful of abandonment by both parents, and he was clinging, tearful, and petulant. He offered, with a conscious gallant effort to save face, "I don't miss my father. I see him all the time. It's just like always." On the way home, however, following his interview with us he began to question his mother for the first time. Poignantly, he asked her, "Is daddy going to get another wife? Another dog? Another little boy?"

Fantasy Denial

Fantasy was employed extensively, especially by the little girls, to help them cope with their painful sense of rejection and loss. Some of the little girls denied their father's absence with a thousand wish-fulfilling fantasies. "When he grows up he'll come back; he promised." "He'll divorce her [his new wife] and marry me," or "I go see my daddy whenever I want to" [not true]. "I like it better this way" [not true]. These fantasies gradually came to occupy increasing amounts of the time and psychic energy of these children.

Wendy, age four, arrived and seated herself comfortably on the therapist's lap, saying, "You look like a mommy." Arranging the members of the flexible toy family, each in its own separate apartment, she said that her daddy lived in his apartment, and she loved to visit him there. Soon she placed the family all together, with the father's arm around the mother. Later, when drawing her family at the interviewer's request, Wendy said that she sees her father all the time; he has an apartment but, she said, "He lives with *me*. He sleeps in *my* bed every night." "You mean," said the interviewer, "You *wish* he slept with you and that he still lived at your house." Laughingly Wendy replied, "Yes, but someday he really will. He promised me that he would." Later Wendy reported that her sister was such a baby because she cried all the time. "*She* wants her daddy to come home," said the child with mild disdain.

Several little girls, referring to their absent fathers, confided, "He loves me the best." Whether reality or fantasy, or a mixture of both, the sense of having been loved "the best" appeared as a guiding fantasy in undoing the rejection and in maintaining the self-esteem and sense of their own lovability that was threatened by the father's departure. The children's loyalty and intense love for the father remained unchanged, despite repeated disappointments in the postseparation relationship. Several of these little girls remained nourished for many years by vivid fantasies about the father and his expected return. These fantasies clearly served to reverse the unbearable sense of rejection, of not having been loved sufficiently, if at all.

Fantasy was employed by little boys, as well, to undo the painful reality of the family rupture, but they appeared less able than the girls to deny the father's departure. Boys and girls were equally committed to fantasies of a restored family. . . .

Inhibition of Aggression

While for some children the family rupture catalyzed a general rise of aggression, for others the response was the reverse. These children evidenced a massive inhibition of their own aggression and sometimes became acutely fearful of attacks. Nan, age three, assured us unsolicited, "I never, never break things." Tim was afraid to go to sleep at night because he might be killed while he was sleeping. Harold brought little clay balls into his play session to protect himself just in case somebody attacked him. And Edna fearfully approached the interviewer with the repeated admonition, "Don't hurt me, don't hurt me." Several children appeared to listen intently for sound outside the consulting room and to watch every motion as if it were potentially dangerous.

Guilt

As we have said, preschool children were often given to self-blame. Kay told us that her father had left because her play was too noisy. Jennifer said her father objected to her messily trained dog and left for that reason. Max savagely beat the "naughty baby doll." These self-accusations, which severely troubled these children, were highly resistant to change by educational measures or by explanations undertaken by parents or teachers. These children clung to their self-accusations with great tenacity. Their feeling of helplessness on the one side, and of total responsibility for the disaster on the other, were both present in their thinking and they suffered from both.

Emotional Need

Some of the behavior which we saw in these young children has no counterpart in clinical practice. Children are usually brought for help because of symptoms which disturb the adults in their life, or because they are not learning appropriately. In the course of time, however, we became concerned with the general emotional neediness in several of these youngsters. This behavior expressed itself in a random reaching out to new adults, climbing into strange laps, and other behavior reflecting a diffuse need for physical contact, nurturance, and protection. Teachers in nursery school and kindergarten reported the same phenomenon. This almost randomly expressed hunger for affection and physical contact appeared to endure long after some of the immediate responses which we have described had subsided.

Mastery

Finally, these young children tried to cope successfully with the stress in a variety of mature ways. A few appeared able to keep their inner balance, their perspective, and their own distance from parental difficulties.

Harold told us, "You have to keep your anger in." He maintained this calmly and sagely at a time when his parents were threatening each other with guns, and violence was escalating all around him. His stance was sober and mature, and he, at age five, told us seriously about his responsibility to be a big brother to his younger sister. The wishes that Harold confided were for a helicopter and wings. These may well reflect his eagerness for escape and seemed prompted by his wish not to become enmeshed in the family struggles. Apparently he was succeeding: His teachers reported he was an excellent student as well as a cheerful youngster whose behavior had not changed.

A few of the little girls also displayed only moderate change at the time of the family rupture. Although saddened by the father's departure, after several days of greater restlessness, increased tension, and tears these children appeared busy with age-appropriate pursuits and were quickly occupied again with playmates, school, hamsters, and various group games.

Immediately following her father's departure, Nancy built an elaborate tree house which excluded all the other members of his family. Frances told us "The divorce is okay, cause mommy asked him to leave."

Viewed at close range, it is remarkable how some of these five-year-old children showed the capacity for perception in regard to their families and an ability to accept the family rupture with a minimum of subterfuge and self-blame. How much of this reflected a conscious, studied scanning of the family landscape is hard to judge. We were often impressed with the acute social sensitivity of these children. . . .

The anxieties that these children showed in the consulting room can be differentiated, in a general way, from the anxiety other children of the same age show when they are brought to psychiatric clinics for evaluation or treatment. These youngsters had a relatively intact ability to relate to adults and, in fact, their search for adults led them to make very quick contact with us. These were children who had neither been rejected by their parents nor had they been given poor care, but rather they were children whose lives had been disrupted and who therefore expected to be received well by adults and to be treated with kindness and consideration. They did not appear as psychologically disturbed children, but as children responding to severe stress whose life experiences with adults had not been poor until the sudden disruption of their families which, for that very reason, left them unprepared and bewildered. Ease in their relations and a hunger for contact appeared in many of the children.

The interviewer reported, "At the end of the hour John heard a voice in the waiting room and wanted to leave. He panicked as I said, 'Just a minute,' and he dashed to the door, yelling, 'I want Daddy! I want Daddy!' I had been leaning against the door while playing with him and he tried to get out, running over me before I could get up. After this first hour and despite this rather unceremonious leave-taking, he came back and was reluctant to say goodbye, and as I knelt down to say we would see each other again next week, he walked slowly up to me with his head bowed. I repeated several times for him the hour and day that we would see each other. Once up to my face, John broke into a wide grin and kissed me."

102

The sociologist Arlene Skolnick discusses recent custody disputes and the assumptions they reveal about the meaning of parenthood and the "best interests" of the child.

Solomon's Children

The New Biologism, Psychological Parenthood, Attachment Theory, and the Best Interests Standard

Arlene Skolnick

On August 2, 1993, the American television public looked on as a screaming toddler was taken from her mother's arms to be sent to another family in another state. The Michigan Supreme Court had ruled that Jan and Roberta DeBoer had no right to keep Baby Jessica, the child they had raised since shortly after birth. Cara Clausen, the birth mother, and the man she had named as the father had signed the adoption papers. Three weeks later, she changed her mind and said she had named the wrong man. She told her ex-boyfriend, Dan Schmidt, that he was the father and the couple married. They pursued their biological daughter and won.

A similar drama played out as Baby Richard was removed from his adoptive parents at the age of four. At around the same time, Gregory K., an eleven-year-old boy, made headlines around the world when he sued to "divorce" the biological mother who had abandoned him and be adopted by his foster family. Other cases recently in the news include a mother who lost custody because she had placed her child in day care while going to college, and a professional woman who lost custody because the judge thought she spent too much time at the office.

Although few cases attract the kind of media attention these did, custody battles have become everyday events in the nation's courtrooms. In the wake of the dramatic transformations in family life since the 1970s, the courts have been called upon to make increasing numbers of Solomon-like judgments about where and with whom children shall live. According to one estimate, about 50 percent of children born in 1990 are likely to come under court jurisdiction in a custody case. Most of these cases arise out of parental divorce, not contested adoptions. But state intervention in children's living arrangements has also grown, owing to rising numbers of child abuse and neglect cases. Finally, new reproductive technologies, too, have led to custody struggles which raise questions about the very definition of biological parenthood.

At a time when the family has become an explosive political issue, custody disputes have aroused passionate public debates as well as complex and troubling questions for the legal system. How should a family be defined? What qualifies one parent—or one set of parents—to be chosen over the other to retain custody? Should the courts focus on the rights of the adults, or the best interests of the child? What in fact are the child's best interests?

To the vast majority of Americans, as poll after poll revealed, the decision in the Baby Jessica case was heartless and baffling. How could judges take a child away from the only parents she had known? The decision revealed to a public not familiar with family law that, while children may be the central characters in the courtroom dramas that determine their fate, their roles are actually very small. As one family court judge put it, "The single biggest failing in our system today is that the voice of the child is not heard. That goes for adoption cases and custody."

Even when courts do try to focus on the child's well-being, the efforts can seem misguided, as in the case where the mother lost custody because she put her child in day care. The aim of this chapter is to examine the child's emotional stake in custody disputes, no matter how they arise. More than two decades ago, the concept of "psychological parenthood" was introduced to the legal community to designate the person to whom the child has the closest emotional ties, whether or not that person is biologically related to the child. The authors of the concept argued that the child's emotional well-being and future development are critically dependent on maintaining the relationship with the psychological parent. Since then, the concept has been enormously influential, part of the everyday vocabulary used in juvenile and family courts around the country. Yet it has also provoked a great deal of debate.

One major criticism deals with the lack of evidence presented by the authors of the psychological parenthood concept in support of their argument. Indeed, "psychological parenthood" is not a psychological term—it is not used by psychologists except in the context of child custody and placement decisions. Since the concept was first advanced, research and theory concerning children's emotional attachments has become a major focus of developmental research. . . .

Disputes over the custody of children arise in many contexts. Cases like those of Baby Jessica and Baby Richard, where a biological mother or father seeks to undo an adoption and get the child back, are not rare, but they are plainly not the most common kind of situation that comes before a family court judge. . . . Custody battles most often arise when the child is living with two parents and they divorce. But the two adults could also be a biological parent and a stepparent, two biological parents who are unmarried, or two partners of the same sex raising a child. As one example, Martha, a woman with two children of her own, married a man with a deaf daughter. She learned sign language to communicate with the child, something the child's father had not done. Martha and her children, who also learned to sign, became emotionally close to the girl. When Martha and her husband divorced, she sued for custody of the deaf child. As another example, Jane and Jill are a lesbian couple who decided to have children together. Jane became pregnant through artificial insemination, and gave birth to a son. The women defined themselves as the child's two mothers, and shared in his care. When the boy was four, however, Jane and Jill separated. Jane, as the biological mother, had legal custody and, on that basis, refused to allow Jill to visit the child.

In another kind of situation, the child is being cared for by someone who is not the biological parent, and another person seeks custody of the child. For example, a child may have been raised by his mother and her second husband. When the mother dies, this leads to a contest between the child's biological father, the stepfather, and the mother's parents.

In recent years, an increasing number of disputes have been between foster parents and state agencies having legal custody of the child who want to remove the child to the biological parent or parents, another foster home, or relatives or others who want to adopt the child. In one case, for example, Mary, a drug addict, abandoned her infant. The child was placed in a foster home. Three years later, Mary cleaned up her act, found a job, and was ready to reclaim the child. The foster parents, however, had come to love the child and wanted to adopt her.

Finally, there are cases where the child has been in the care of what might be called informal foster parents—grandparents, a friend of the family, a boarding school teacher—who seek to prevent the return of the child to the biological parents. As one illustration, Maria and Eduard were political refugees who had to flee their country, leaving their eighteen-month-old baby behind with a neighbor family. Ten years later they returned, and claimed the child. But neither the child nor the family was willing to make the change.

Traditionally, there has been a presumption in favor of biological parents in disputes with other people. The media spotlight on Jessica, Richard, Gregory, and other children revealed to the public that the focus of the courts was clearly on the legal rights and wrongs of the adults involved, rather than the child's perceptions and emotional needs. However, different jurisdictions and judges place different weights on the rights of parents and the interests of the child. Thus custody decisions are marked by a great deal of uncertainty and inconsistency.

In some states today, unless a parent is found to be unfit or to have abandoned the child, the rights of biological parents are all but inviolate. Thus the courts who decided the fate of Baby Jessica acted without consideration of her "best interests" or the circumstances of her life—the only issue the court considered was whether the parental rights of the biological father had been correctly terminated.

It was this aspect of the case that provoked the most public outrage—that a child could be plucked from her family by a man who happened to have impregnated the birth mother, at a time when she was engaged to another man. Some commentators see this biological preference as a legacy from the era when children were considered property. A dissenting justice in Jessica's case complained that his colleagues were treating Jessica like "a carload of hay" and trying to decide who had the better legal title. (Because Jessica's father was unmarried to her mother at the time of Jessica's birth, legal recognition of his biology-based claims is actually a rather recent development.) A judge in the Baby Richard case compared the outcome of the case to the infamous Dred Scott decision—in which the Supreme Court ruled that an escaped slave should be returned to his "rightful" owner.

Many commentators, however, believe that the child's best interests are in fact served by growing up with biological parents, and that parents not only have a right to their children but that "natural bonds of affection" lead parents to care for their children in a way that no "stranger" could.

This biological slant of the legal system also reflects widespread, but usually unarticulated assumptions about ties based on blood and genes in American culture. Because they are so taken for granted, there is a danger that unless they are made explicit, these assumptions may well guide decision making and discussion of the issues in an unreflective way. The belief that family bonds are the natural and essential product of biological ties is deeply rooted in American kinship beliefs. The saying "blood is thicker than water" tells us that ties not based in biological kinship cannot be as strong as those that are. This belief is enshrined in a host of tales in which children discover their real parents and live happily ever after.

Yet such terms as "natural" and "real" have traditionally raised suspicions among philosophers and cultural anthropologists. Philosophers ask how do you get from "is" to "ought"—from the brute facts of biological reproduction to moral claims of a right to rear. Anthropologists point to the enormous variation around the world in kinship systems as well as concepts of what is "real." Thus anthropologist David Schneider argues that American beliefs in blood kinship are no more rooted in the facts of biology than supernatural beliefs in ghosts are based in the real nature of such beings. Both kinship and religion, he argues, are cultural constructs. To be sure, there are biological facts, but kinship systems make use of these facts in various symbolic ways.

One of the most striking features of the way Americans think about the family, Schneider observes, is the emphasis on the family as natural. The nuclear family—mother and father and child—is a cultural icon; the man and woman are united in physical love—"one flesh"—and a child is imagined to be the "flesh and blood" of both parents. The cultural symbolism of family is very different in other cultures. For example, the traditional Chinese family is understood to be a long line of fathers and sons, including remote ancestors and unborn descendants. Women constitute the links in the male chain of descent, but they are not included in anyone's genealogy.

Schneider distinguishes between "the family" as a cultural symbol, the kinship norms of different ethnic and class practices, and everyday life in families and households. For example, even in cultures in which the three-generation household is the ideal norm, most households may in fact be nuclear, because most people do not live long enough to overlap the lives of their grandchildren. Even in the United States, however, Schneider writes, the cultural symbolism of the "natural" family coexists with a wide variety of actual family patterns. In a number of ethnic groups and regions of the country, for example, much of daily life and child socialization are embedded in social networks, often including extended kin like grandparents, aunts, uncles, and cousins. So-called fictional kin-nonrelatives who are considered "part of the family"—are also common in these networks and are found in many cultures around the world. In many Latin cultures, godparents are a well-institutionalized aspect of child rearing. The exchange of children, or a child going to live for a time with a relative living near or far, is a common custom in American subcultures and around the world.

In recent years, the traditional biological concept of family in American culture and law has been joined by what might be called a new biologism, a growing sense that the true essence of a person is rooted in the primordial differences of gender, race, ethnicity, genes. It's true that the recent advances in genetic research have made biological information about one's family background an important part of a person's medical history. But the new biologism is a much broader cultural phenomenon that encompasses identity politics and the emphasis on ethnic roots, the search movement among adoptees, and the antiadoption movement which has emerged in recent years.

The fact that adopted children or those of surrogate parents may seek out their "natural" parents, however, is not in itself evidence that knowledge about one's genetic heritage is essential to one's sense of identity. Instead of some basic truth about human nature, the search for biological roots may reflect the cultural importance of genes, and the stigma and sense of difference a person feels when growing up in a culture that increasingly defines identity and belongingness in biological terms. As one observer notes, in these postmodern times, the parent-child bond has taken on new and urgent meanings; as the relationship between the sexes becomes more fragile, it has become "the source of the last remaining, irrevocable, unexchangable primary relationship."

Beyond the argument from nature, there are some legal scholars who argue that Jessica's case and the others like it were correctly decided. They advance a number of arguments justifying the legal system's emphasis on biological parents. Most fundamental, perhaps biology provides a clear standard, a "bright line" for making legal judgments. However unfortunate the outcome of any particular case, according to this view, the absence of a presumption in favor of biological parents would open up a Pandora's box of troublesome and unjustified claims.

In 1993, for example, the Kansas Supreme Court rejected the claim by a day care provider that the court should recognize the visitation rights of those who had been close to a child. The court granted that "the realities of modern life mean that individuals . . . may end up caring for a child for weeks, months, or even years, and then have the natural parents . . . abruptly end a relationship that is important to the child. It could be the only stable relationship the child has known." However, the court refused to recognize a visitation right on grounds that it would likely lead to more lawsuits, more court intrusion into families, and misuse of the right by anyone who had taken care of or had a relationship with a child for some period—a nanny, a housekeeper, a teacher, even a parent's former lover.

A more fundamental concern, however, is the issue of justice for the parent as well as for the child. In 1982, the U.S. Supreme Court held that the right of a fit biological parent to the custody of a minor child is a fundamental liberty interest. Historically, poor and minority families have been vulnerable to state intervention and the removal of children. The lack of family rights on the part of slaves was one of the most painful and resented features of that infamous system. The Fourteenth Amendment, which insured the rights of former slaves, was "conceived by people who regarded slavery's denial of family rights as a uniquely deplorable usurpation of fundamental human entitlements."

Ironically, the Iowa court that ruled in favor of Jessica's biological father aroused public outrage in a 1966 case for the opposite reason—ignoring the interests of a father. Harold Painter was a San Francisco man whose wife and daughter were killed in a car accident. At one point when he had trouble arranging for child care, he placed his young son Mark temporarily in the care of his wife's parents in Iowa. When Painter later claimed the child, the grandparents sued for custody and won. The Iowa Supreme Court ruled that while Painter was not an unfit father, Mark's churchgoing, midwestern grandparents provided a better home for him than the more artistic, bohemian setting of his father's home in California. In justifying the decision, the court contrasted many aspects of the father's and the grandparents' lifestyles, including the decor of the Painter house, the state of the paint job on its exterior, and the wild oats growing on the hillside behind it.

In an outraged reaction to this decision, legislatures all over the country wrote laws clarifying and reinforcing the rights of biological parents. The new Iowa law declared that the "best interests of the child" standard could only be invoked if the child had been abandoned or the parent declared unfit.

For a variety of reasons, then, the facts of biological parenthood carry more legal weight than in the past. Courts have shown a strong preference for awarding custody to what they call "natural parents" whether or not a parent-child relationship exists. Large numbers of adults who have actually nurtured and raised children—relatives, stepparents, and foster parents—have no legal standing. As [Mary Ann] Mason points out: "An unwed father who has never lived with a child will probably receive custodial preference over a stepfather who raised the child. Surrogate mothers who give birth to a child are deemed incapable of contracting away their biological rights to that child. Foster parents who raise a child have little hope of adopting the child, except under unusual circumstances."

103

Mary Ann Mason describes how the sexual preference and lifestyle of the mother come under scrutiny in child custody disputes (1999).

Fit to Be a Parent?

Mary Ann Mason

What does it mean to be a fit parent? We have learned that violent criminal behavior—even murder—does not necessarily create a presumption that the perpetrator is an unfit parent in the eyes of the court. Sexual behavior, however, between consenting adults considered deviant for the time and place may do so.

John Ward had served an eight-year prison term for the second-degree murder in 1974 of his first wife, Judy. They were arguing over custody of their children. He shot her six times, reloaded his gun, and shot six more times.

Upon his release Ward found stable employment in a lumberyard, married a woman named Mary, and fathered a daughter, Cassey. The Wards divorced in 1992, and Mary Ward was granted primary custody of their eight-year-old daughter. Three years later Judge Joseph Tarbuck of Escambia County Circuit Court ordered the child to move in with her father after Mr. Ward told the court that Cassey made statements of a sexual nature, exhibited bad table manners and personal hygiene habits, and preferred to wear men's cologne. Mary Ward was granted limited supervised visitation. Mary, who at the time was a restaurant chef living with a girlfriend and two older daughters—one of whom was a lesbian with a live-in girlfriend—denied that she had exposed the child to any sexual behavior in her home. She noted that she had filed for increased child support shortly before Mr. Ward petitioned for custody.

In a written statement released by his lawyers Mr. Ward described the court's decision as one that held that "growing up in a household with a husband and wife residing together in marriage was more beneficial to an 11-year-old girl than growing up in a household with four adults engaged in homosexual relationships." He said that his daughter "very much loves her mother," but has made new friends and "is not embarrassed to bring them home for a visit or introduce them to her father and stepmother."

Gay rights lawyers said Ms. Ward's case was most disturbing because there was no evidence of any improper conduct at her home. "When a decision like this comes down, it does strike fear into the hearts of lesbian and gay parents around the country because they recognize that if it could happen to a parent like Mary Ward it could happen to them," said Kathryn D. Kendell, the executive director of the National Center for Lesbian Rights, which helped represent Ms. Ward.

The appeals court in the ward case upheld the trial court's decision. It dismissed as irrelevant a recently passed Florida law creating a presumption that granting custody to a parent who had been convicted of a felony involving domestic violence would be detrimental to the child. The father, the court said, had "reformed."

Domestic violence and lesbianism—two volatile fronts on which women's rights advocates are struggling to advance in the gender wars—are the central issues of this case. On both fronts women believe they are unfairly pitted against a legal system and a society that discredits them. It is true that gay men share the disadvantage of homophobia, which certainly plays a role in thwarting their paternal rights; and some men are victims of violent domestic assaults. Yet women by far fight the majority of these battles in the custody wars.

On its face this case appears to confirm a deeply rooted prejudice against lesbian mothers. It probably does, but an important piece of information is missing: what does eleven-year-old Cassey want? Is she happy to live with her father and stepmother, or is she simply a pawn in this larger politicized battle? No one disputes that her mother has always been her primary parent; but is she, perhaps, genuinely unhappy and embarrassed in her mother's household? If this is the case, while it may not advance the cause of women's rights, her feelings as a developing adolescent should be taken seriously. Yet the court, political supporters, and opponents—and probably even the warring parents—have lost track of the wishes and feelings of this child; the lesbian lifestyle of the mother has blinded all parties to any other consideration.

The sexual lifestyle of mothers is always of great concern to society, and this concern is faithfully reflected in the law. Mothers took a legal leap in the nineteenth century when courts reversed fathers' paramount claims to custody, focusing instead on mothers as the nurturers of small children; but the tender years doctrine offered only a qualified approval of mothers, usually expressed as: "Children of tender years are awarded to the mother unless the mother is unfit." Lack of fitness might include physical neglect or abuse or mental illness, but in most cases for mothers it meant their sexual behavior. The very high moral standards imposed on mothers in the nineteenth century allowed judges to sometimes view them more positively in custody disputes, but it also meant that the system turned harshly against mothers when they strayed from strict, conventional moral standards. Nineteenth-century judges routinely condemned adulterous women, declaring them unfit to have *any* contact with their children, much less sole custody.

Though adultery may have been an inexcusable act for mothers, in the venerable tradition of the double standard it was not so for fathers. Adultery alone was rarely enough to bar a father's custodial rights; an additional factor such as domestic violence was required. In *Lindsay v. Lindsay*, an 1854 case, Mrs. Lindsay claimed that she was not living in an adulterous relationship since she believed her ex-husband had obtained a total divorce. Furthermore, she argued, she left him because he had his adulterous affair while they were still living together. Nevertheless, the court gave their four-year-old daughter to the father, stating,

> [T]here may be no difference in the sin of the man and the woman, who violate the laws of chastity. But we do know, that in the opinion of society, it is otherwise . . . for when she sins after this sort, she sins against society . . . her associations are with the vulgar, the vile and the depraved. If her children are with her, their characters must be, more or less, influenced and formed by the circumstances which surround them.

In the early twentieth century divorce grew more commonplace and courts grew less publicly attached to religious strictures. Judges began to view mothers' extramarital sexual activities more leniently, provided they had clearly mended their ways and their transgressions had occurred in the more or less distant past. The case of *Harmon v. Harmon* provides a glimpse into the Roaring Twenties, but it also reveals that a woman's sexual conduct was no longer a complete bar to custody, and that adultery alone was no longer always valid grounds for divorce. Two married couples in Kansas, Mr. and Mrs. Harmon and an unnamed husband and wife, associated in the same social circles and became good friends, going on late-night rides together and spending much of their free time as a foursome. One day Mr. Harmon found Mrs. Harmon engaged in an act of adultery with the other husband. He insisted that she must go to live with her parents and renounce custody of their five-year-old daughter. Both men made her sign a written agreement admitting her guilt and agreeing to the custody arrangement. Mr. Harmon then sued for divorce on the ground of adultery and sought custody of their daughter. The trial court found that adultery was committed with "the knowledge, connivance and consent of the plaintiff," and denied the divorce. The court was silent on the custody issue.

On appeal a higher court agreed that the adultery was encouraged by the husband. "He must have known the absurd lengths to which extraordinary intimacy, informality, and unconventionality [with the other couple] had grown, [and] was bound to culminate as it did." The court granted temporary custody of the daughter to the mother, reasoning that "except for defendant's temporary infatuation for her paramour, she was a good mother."

Several decades later, in the Swinging Sixties, sexual activity outside the institution of marriage became so commonplace (at least among the young) that the law gradually reflected the more tolerant attitude expressed by large numbers of Americans. The moral indignation of adultery was no longer necessary or important as a ground for ending a marriage as no-fault divorce swept the country in the 1970s. In a separate but related movement the feminist drive for equal rights abolished the distinction between mothers and fathers in custody law as a matter of gender equality. In most states today custody law is drafted in strictly gender-neutral language and excludes specific references to moral fitness as a factor in custody decisions. On paper the old double standard is largely defunct.

Homosexual activity, which in previous eras would have been an automatic and conclusive factor against a parent, is treated with more tolerance, at least superficially. A few states still consider homosexuality evidence of parental unfitness per se, but most states—including Florida, where the Wards fought for custody of Cassey—require proof that homosexual activity or extramarital heterosexual activity has produced an adverse affect on the child. The Ward case, however, demonstrates that official changes in the law do not necessarily mean changes in attitudes. The judicial focus may have shifted from a mother's adultery to a mother's homosexuality, but mothers are still held to a rigid moral standard.

104

One new feature of modern life is the openly expressed desire of gay and lesbian couples to become parents. But the law is ill-equipped to handle any custody disputes that may arise in these situations.

Lesbian Parents in Custody Disputes

California Court of Appeal

Nancy S. v. Michele G.
228 Cal. App. 3D 831, 279 Cal. Rptr. 212 (1991)

Natural mother commenced action for declaration that LESBIAN partner was not parent of children, that natural mother was entitled to sole legal and physical custody, and that LESBIAN partner was entitled to visitation only upon natural mother's consent. The Superior Court, Alameda County, No. 642975-5, Ronald M. Sabraw, J., found for natural mother, and LESBIAN partner appealed. The Court of Appeal, Stein, J., held that: (1) LESBIAN partner who was not natural or adoptive parent was not parent within meaning of Uniform Parentage Act; (2) custody could not be awarded to LESBIAN partner over objections of mother, absent finding that parental custody by natural mother would be detrimental to children: and (3) status of LESBIAN partner as de facto parent, under doctrine of in loco parentis, by equitable estoppel nor from functional definition of parent-hood did not entitle LESBIAN partner to grant of custody.

Judgment affirmed.

Stein, Associate Justice.

Appellant, Michele G., appeals from a judgment under the Uniform Parentage Act (Civ.Code, s 7000 et seq.) determining that respondent, Nancy S., is the only parent of the two minor children that respondent conceived by artificial insemination during her relationship with appellant. The judgment further provided that respondent, as the only legal parent of the two minor children, is entitled to sole legal and physical custody and that any further contact between appellant and the children shall only be by respondent's consent.

The issue presented is whether the court erred in determining, as a matter of law, that appellant has no right to an award of custody or visitation under the Uniform Parentage Act.

Facts

In August of 1969, appellant and respondent began living together, and in November of that year they had a private "marriage" ceremony. Eventually they decided to have children by artificially inseminating respondent. In June of 1980, respondent gave birth to a daughter, K. Appellant was listed on the birth certificate as the father, and K. was given appellant's family name. On June 13, 1984, respondent gave birth to a son, S. Again appellant was listed as the father on the birth certificate, and S. was given appellant's family name. Both children refer to appellant and respondent as "Mom." Although the parties considered arranging for appellant to adopt the children, they never initiated formal ADOPTION proceedings.

In January of 1985 appellant and respondent separated. They agreed that K. would live with appellant and that S. would live with respondent. They arranged visitation so that appellant would have K. five days a week and respondent would have S. five days a week, but the children would be together, either at appellant's or respondent's home for four days a week. After approximately three years, respondent wanted to change the custody arrangement so that each had custody of both children 50 percent of the time. Appellant opposed any change, and attempts to mediate the dispute failed.

Respondent then commenced this Uniform Parentage Act proceeding. Her complaint sought a declaration that appellant is not a parent of either child, that respondent is entitled to sole legal and physical custody and that appellant is entitled to visitation only with respondent's consent. The court issued a temporary restraining order and granted temporary custody to respondent. Appellant answered the complaint and admitted that respondent is the biological mother of the children. She denied, however, the allegations that she was not also a parent of the children. She sought an order for custody and visitation in accordance with their original custody agreement.

A hearing was held on respondent's order to show cause and appellant's cross-motion for custody and visitation. The parties fully briefed and argued the issue whether appellant could qualify as a parent and seek custody and visitation under the Uniform Parentage Act. Appellant admitted that she was not the biological mother and had not adopted the children. Nonetheless, she argued that she had attained the status of a de facto parent, or that respondent should be estopped to deny appellant's status as a parent. The court determined that appellant was not a parent under the Uniform Parentage Act, and that even if she could prove that she had the status of a de facto parent, that it could not award her custody over the objections of respondent, the natural mother, who did qualify as a parent under the act. The court therefore awarded sole physical and legal custody to respondent.

Analysis

. . . The Uniform Parentage Act defines a parent as one who is the natural or adoptive parent of a child. (Civ.Code, s 7001.) The existence of the relationship of parent and child may be proved between a child and its natural mother by proof of her having given birth to the child (Civ. Code, s 7003, subd. (1)), between a child and an adoptive parent by proof of ADOPTION (Civ.Code, s 7003, subd. (3)), and between a natural father and a child as provided in the act (Civ.Code, s 7003, subd. (2)).

It is undisputed that appellant is not the natural mother of K. and S., and that she has not adopted either child. She does not contend that she and respondent had a legally recognized marriage when the children were born. Based on these undisputed facts, the court correctly determined that appellant could not establish the existence of a parent-child relationship under the Uniform Parentage Act.

Appellant nonetheless asserts that the Uniform Parentage Act does not provide the exclusive definition of a parent. She asserts that her allegations of a long-term relationship in which she has become a "psychological parent" of the children would, if proved, entitle her to seek custody and visitation as if the dispute were between two legally recognized parents. She advances several legal theories to support her assertion that she has acquired "parental rights," i.e., the right to seek custody and visitation on an equal footing with the children's natural mother and over their natural mother's objections. First, she argues that she is either a "de facto" parent, or that she stands "in loco parentis."

A de facto parent is "that person who, on a day-to-day basis, assumes the role of parent, seeking to fulfill both the child's physical needs and his psychological need for affection and care." Appellant alleged that she helped facilitate the conception and birth of both children and immediately after their birth assumed all the responsibilities of a parent. K. lived with appellant until the underlying dispute arose. . . .

We agree with appellant that the absence of any legal formalization of her relationship to the children has resulted in a tragic situation. As is always the case, it is the children who will suffer the most as a result of the inability of the adults, who they love and need, to reach an agreement. We do not, however, agree that the only way to avoid such an unfortunate situation is for the courts to adopt appellant's novel theory by which a nonparent can acquire the rights of a parent, and then face years of unraveling the complex practical, social, and constitutional ramifications of this expansion of the definition of parent.

Conclusion

Although the facts in this case are relatively straightforward regarding the intent of the natural mother to create a parental relationship between appellant and her children, expanding the definition of a "parent" in the manner advocated by appellant could expose other natural parents to litigation brought by child-care providers of long standing, relatives, successive sets of stepparents or other close friends of the family. No matter how narrowly we might attempt to draft the definition, the fact remains that the status of individuals claiming to be parents would have to be litigated and resolution of these claims would turn on elusive factual determinations of the intent of the natural mother, the perceptions of the children, and the course of conduct of the party claiming parental status. By deferring to the Legislature in matters involving complex social and policy ramifications far beyond the facts of the particular case, we are not telling the parties that the issues they raise are unworthy of legal recognition. To the contrary, we intend only to illustrate the limitations of the courts in fashioning a comprehensive solution to such a complex and socially significant issue.

The judgment is affirmed.

Newsom, Acting P.J., and Dossee, J., concur.

105

The new reproductive technology has created ever more variations on the theme of parenthood. The court in Johnson v. Calvert *struggles to determine who is the mother of a child born by means of gestational surrogacy.*

Surrogacy and Child Custody

California Supreme Court

Johnson v. Calvert
5 Cal.4th 84, 851 P.2d 776, 19 Cal.Rptr.2d 494 (1993)
Panelli, Justice.

In this case we address several of the legal questions raised by recent advances in reproductive technology. When, pursuant to a surrogacy agreement, a zygote formed of the gametes of a husband and wife is implanted in the uterus of another woman, who carries the resulting fetus to term and gives birth to a child not genetically related to her, who is the child's "natural mother" under California law? Does a determination that the wife is the child's natural mother work a deprivation of the gestating woman's constitutional rights? And is such an agreement barred by any public policy of this state?

We conclude that the husband and wife are the child's natural parents, and that this result does not offend the state or federal Constitution or public policy.

Facts

Mark and Crispina Calvert are a married couple who desired to have a child. Crispina was forced to undergo a hysterectomy in 1984. Her ovaries remained capable of producing eggs, however, and the couple eventually considered surrogacy. In 1989 Anna Johnson heard about Crispina's plight from a coworker and offered to serve as a surrogate for the Calverts.

On January 15, 1990, Mark, Crispina, and Anna signed a contract providing that an embryo created by the sperm of Mark and the egg of Crispina would be implanted in Anna and the child born would be taken into Mark and Crispina's home "as their child." Anna agreed she would relinquish "all parental rights" to the child in favor of Mark and Crispina. In return, Mark and Crispina would pay Anna $10,000 in a series of installments, the last to be paid six weeks after the child's birth. Mark and Crispina were also to pay for a $200,000 life insurance policy on Anna's life.

The zygote was implanted on January 19, 1990. Less than a month later, an ultrasound test confirmed Anna was pregnant.

Unfortunately, relations deteriorated between the two sides. Mark learned that Anna had not disclosed she had suffered several stillbirths and miscarriages. Anna felt Mark and Crispina did not do enough to obtain the required insurance policy. She also felt abandoned during an onset of premature labor in June.

In July 1990, Anna sent Mark and Crispina a letter demanding the balance of the payments due her or else she would refuse to give up the child. The following month, Mark and Crispina responded with a lawsuit, seeking a declaration they were the legal parents of the unborn child. Anna filed her own action to be declared the mother of the child, and the two cases were eventually consolidated. The parties agreed to an independent guardian ad litem for the purposes of the suit.

The child was born on September 19, 1990, and blood samples were obtained from both Anna and the child for analysis. The blood test results excluded Anna as the genetic mother. The parties agreed to a court order providing that the child would remain with Mark and Crispina on a temporary basis with visits by Anna.

At trial in October 1990, the parties stipulated that Mark and Crispina were the child's genetic parents. After hearing evidence and arguments, the trial court ruled that Mark and Crispina were the child's "genetic, biological and natural" father and mother, that Anna had no "parental" rights to the child, and that the surrogacy contract was legal and enforceable against Anna's claims. The court also terminated the order allowing visitation. Anna appealed from the trial court's judgment. The Court of Appeal for the Fourth District, Division Three, affirmed. We granted review. . . .

Discussion

. . . In deciding the issue of maternity under the [Uniform Parentage] Act we have felt free to take into account the parties' intentions, as expressed in the surrogacy contract, because in our view the agreement is not, on its face, inconsistent with public policy. . . .

Anna urges that surrogacy contracts violate several social policies. Relying on her contention that she is the child's legal, natural mother, she cites the public policy embodied in Penal Code section 273, prohibiting the payment for consent to adoption of a child. She argues further that the policies underlying the adoption laws of this state are violated by the surrogacy contract because it in effect constitutes a prebirth waiver of her parental rights.

We disagree. Gestational surrogacy differs in crucial respects from adoption and so is not subject to the adoption statutes. . . .

It has been suggested that gestational surrogacy may run afoul of prohibitions on involuntary servitude. . . . We see no potential for that evil in the contract at issue here, and extrinsic evidence of coercion or duress is utterly lacking. We note that although at one point the contract purports to give Mark and Crispina the sole right to determine whether to abort the pregnancy, at another point it acknowledges: "All parties understand that a pregnant woman has the absolute right to abort or not abort any fetus she is carrying. Any promise to the contrary is unenforceable." We therefore need not determine the validity of a surrogacy contract purporting to deprive the gestator of her freedom to terminate the pregnancy.

Finally, Anna and some commentators have expressed concern that surrogacy contracts tend to exploit or dehumanize women, especially women of lower economic status. Anna's objections center around the psychological harm she asserts may result from the gestator's relinquishing the child to whom she has given birth. Some have also cautioned that the practice of surrogacy may encourage society to view children as commodities, subject to trade at their parents' will. . . .

We are unpersuaded that gestational surrogacy arrangements are so likely to cause the untoward results Anna cites as to demand their invalidation on public policy grounds. Although common sense suggests that women of lesser means serve as surrogate mothers more often than do wealthy women, there has been no proof that surrogacy contracts exploit poor women of any greater degree than economic necessity in general exploits them by inducing them to accept lower-paid or otherwise undesirable employment. We are likewise unpersuaded by the claim that surrogacy will foster the attitude that children are mere commodities; no evidence is offered to support it. The limited data available seem to reflect an absence of significant adverse effects of surrogacy on all participants.

The argument that a woman cannot knowingly and intelligently agree to gestate and deliver a baby for intending parents carries overtones of the reasoning that for centuries prevented women from attaining equal economic rights and professional status under the law. To resurrect this view is both to foreclose a personal and economic choice on the part of the surrogate mother, and to deny intending parents what may be their only means of procreating a child of their own genetic stock. Certainly in the present case it cannot seriously be argued that Anna, a licensed vocational nurse who had done well in school and who had previously borne a child, lacked the intellectual wherewithal or life experience necessary to make an informed decision to enter into the surrogacy contract. . . .

The judgment of the Court of Appeal is affirmed.

Lucas, C. J., and Mosk, Baxter and George, J. J., concur.

Kennard, Justice, dissenting.

When a woman who wants to have a child provides her fertilized ovum to another woman who carries it through pregnancy and gives birth to a child, who is the child's legal mother? Unlike the majority, I do not agree that the determinative consideration should be the intent to have the child that originated with the woman who contributed the ovum. In my view, the woman who provided the fertilized ovum and the woman who gave birth to the child both have substantial claims to legal motherhood. Pregnancy entails a unique commitment, both psychological and emotional, to an unborn child. No less substantial, however, is the contribution of the woman from whose egg the child developed and without whose desire the child would not exist. . . .

The problem with this argument, of course, is that children are not property. Unlike songs or inventions, rights in children cannot be sold for consideration, or made freely available to the general public. Our most fundamental notions of personhood tell us it is inappropriate to treat children as property. Although the law may justly recognize that the originator of a concept has certain property rights in that concept, the originator of the concept of a child can have no such rights, because children cannot be owned as property. Accordingly, I cannot endorse the majority's "originators of the concept" or intellectual property rationale for employing intent to break the "tie" between the genetic mother and the gestational mother of the child.

Next, the majority offers as its third rationale the notion that bargained-for expectations support its conclusion regarding the dispositive significance of the genetic mother's intent. Specifically, the majority states that " 'intentions that are voluntarily chosen, deliberate, express and bargained-for ought presumptively to determine legal parenthood.' " . . .

It is commonplace that, in real or personal property transactions governed by contracts, "intentions that are voluntarily chosen, deliberate, express and bargained-for" ought presumptively to be enforced and, when one party seeks to escape performance, the court may order specific performance. . . . Just as children are not the intellectual property of their parents, neither are they the personal property of anyone, and their delivery cannot be ordered as a contract remedy on the same terms that a court would, for example, order a breaching party to deliver a truckload of nuts and bolts. . . .

Conclusion

Recent advances in medical technology have made it possible for the human female reproductive role to be divided between two women, the genetic mother and the gestational mother. Such gestational surrogacy arrangements call for sensitivity to each of the adult participants. But the paramount concern must be the well-being of the child that gestational surrogacy has made possible. . . .

In this opinion, I do not purport to offer a perfect solution to the difficult questions posed by gestational surrogacy; perhaps there can be no perfect solution. But in the absence of legislation specifically designed to address the complex issues of gestational surrogacy and to protect against potential abuses, I cannot join the majority's uncritical validation of gestational surrogacy.

I would reverse the judgment of the Court of Appeal, and remand the case to the trial court for a determination of disputed parentage on the basis of the best interests of the child.

106

Foster care has become the dominant mode of placement for children in the twenti-
eth century, but children continue to live in group homes. Here two teenaged foster
children reflect on their experiences with foster parents and with group homes
(1996).

Teenage Voices from Foster Care

Autobiographical Documents

Omar Sharif, "How I Lived a Double Life"

For most of my life I felt different from the "normal" kids. They had parents and families but I didn't, because I lived in a group home.

We'd have assignments in elementary school and if we didn't finish them in class, the teacher would say, "When you go home tonight, ask your parents to help you."

No one knew how hurt I was by that simple remark. It was not my parents but a counselor who would help me with my homework that night.

I was embarrassed by my situation and I began to hide my identity. I was almost two people in one. During the day in school I pretended I was like everyone else, but at night I could be myself, just a "regular" kid in the group home.

It was uncomfortable to go to Parent-Teachers Night because the counselors who went with me weren't my parents. Now when I look back this seems funny, but at the time it was as serious as life and death.

I'd run into my fellow students on those nights and they would ask, "Hey, is that your mom?" or "Is that your dad?" And I would say something off the topic to avoid the question, like, "Do you think you're gonna get in trouble tonight?" That would always change the subject.

I used to practice gymnastics after school at the YMCA. One afternoon when my session was over, a counselor came to pick me up in the group home van, and as it pulled up, a friend asked me, "Is that your van you're gettin' in?"

I was caught on the spot and didn't know how to respond. So I told him, "Nah, that's a friend of mine who works with a cab service." I hoped he believed me and wouldn't ask me any more questions as I stared him in the face. I guess he thought it was the truth, because he never mentioned it again.

I almost blew my cover one morning when I was picked up at the group home by the school bus. There were twelve of us living there. I was ten years old at the time and also the youngest in the house. The oldest kid was seventeen. I and two other young kids, Wesley and Robert, used to get picked up by the bus at 7:15 every morning to go to elementary school. The rest of the older guys left the house around 7:30 to walk to high school, which was only a couple of blocks away. But this morning my bus didn't show up on time. I went back inside to tell the counselors what had happened, then waited on the steps. At 7:30 the bus came down the block to pick up Wesley, Robert, and me. At the same time, the older guys came out of the group home to walk to school.

I never worried about the kids on the bus seeing me each morning with Wesley and Robert. I always assumed that the kids on the bus thought the group home was my own private house. Wesley could pass for my brother any day because we had the same complexion (we're black), the same haircut, and sometimes we used to dress alike. And Robert, who was Puerto Rican, seemed like a friend hanging out with us.

But now, as the kids on the bus watched, the older high school kids were coming out of the group home and they were white, black, Spanish, and Chinese. It was obvious they weren't my family. As soon as I got on the bus I knew someone was going to question me about the older kids. I could see the puzzlement on their faces as everyone's head was turned to look. So I blurted out an explanation. I told them the older kids were my brothers. Since some of the older guys were black, I hoped the kids on the bus would assume they were my brothers and the rest of the guys were my brothers' friends. But I was so humiliated by the lie that I buried my face in a book in the back seat.

When I was in junior high I usually took the bus, but when I woke up late or overslept I had to be driven to school in the group home van. I remember how ashamed I would be when I was dropped off that way. The kids in my junior high had parents with lots of money. They were all middle class or above. They had good-looking cars, and there I was getting dropped off in a big blue van.

To cover myself, I'd always ask the counselor to drop me off a block away from school. Then I'd wait until the traffic was moving before I got out so none of the students across the street would see me.

I kept where I lived a secret because I was afraid the students would make fun of me. Only one kid knew. How Joseph found out I'll never know. But he was cool—he never told anyone my business, and as a matter of fact, we became close friends because I started to hang out with him. His family was so understanding they even wanted to adopt me. Joseph's mother used to pick me up in her car on weekends to bring me to their house and then drop me back at the group home at night.

Joseph once told me I could stay with his family if I ever needed a place. He was a true friend because he offered me his home when I was down and out. He was someone I could trust, someone I could confide in, someone who knew me and didn't feel ashamed to be around me because I lived in a group home.

Joseph never singled me out—I was a regular kid whenever I was with him.

And my main point is that I just wanted to be accepted in the same way by my peers.

As I grew older and became more mature, I began to see that I didn't need to be ashamed about my situation. I began to realize that people looked at me for who I was, not for where I lived or who I lived with. If people liked me before they knew I lived in a group home, they probably wouldn't change their attitude once they found out.

I also realized that "normal" and "regular" kids who live at home are often ashamed of *their* parents. (I don't know why, because all they have in this world are their parents.) You don't have to live in a group home to feel ashamed or awkward, or to feel that you don't really have a family.

My friend Joseph helped me open my eyes and realize that it doesn't matter where you live, just as long as you're true to yourself and to others.

If your friends don't accept you because you live in the system, then they're not your friends and that's their loss. If you are proud of who you are, there will be many more true friends for you down the road of life.

Omar Sharif, 20, is the author of two other pieces in this collection [The Heart Knows Something Different], *"My Foster Mother Is My Best Friend" and "Writing Taught Me about Myself."*

Shameek Williamson, *"Kicked Out Because I Was Gay"*

During my first four years in foster care, I was in nine group and foster homes. My ninth home was different from the others because I had just "come out" as a gay person and I was worried about being accepted by my new foster mother, Sharon.

When I first moved in with Sharon and her two biological daughters, I kept to myself. I felt close to Sharon but not close enough to tell her I was gay. Since I had just come out, I wasn't sure if this was who I really was or if it was only a stage I was going through. I didn't want to tell Sharon until I was sure I was gay.

Before I moved in with Sharon, I came out to my social worker. She thought Sharon would be an excellent foster parent because Sharon had once been in the system, was young, and could probably accept my sexual identity.

After I moved in with Sharon, I used to go to gay clubs by myself or with my friend Carla (who was also gay). I wasn't in a relationship yet and this was my way of exploring the gay scene.

One night at the Octagon, a gay club in Manhattan, Carla introduced me to her ex-girlfriend Bridgette. We only said hello, but I thought about Bridgette throughout the rest of that night and continuously through the week.

The next week I went to Pandora's Box, another gay club, by myself and saw Bridgette. We danced, drank, and at the end of the night exchanged numbers.

But because I had just come out, I felt uneasy about having a relationship with another woman.

After about two weeks of talking on the phone, we decided to go out. We first went to a restaurant and, during the next couple of months, Bridgette took me to get my hair done and brought me flowers, basically treating me like no man ever had. By now I knew that being gay was who I really was.

Sharon, who had been worried because I didn't have any friends, became so happy I now had Bridgette that she encouraged us to see more of each other.

But even though I was sure I was gay, I still had to hide it from my foster mother. Even though Sharon had mentioned to me that she had gay friends, I wasn't sure if she would accept me because I was living in her home.

(Some people think it's okay to have friends who are gay because all friends do basically is hang out together, but having them live in their house is different because many people believe that gay people are sex-crazed and jump on everyone who passes by.)

One time Bridgette and I went out and she brought me flowers. When I got home, Sharon saw the flowers and said to me, "You told me that you were going out with Bridgette, but you two went out with guys and he brought you flowers." Nervously, I just agreed with her, wondering how long this charade would last.

Somehow or other Sharon eventually found out that Bridgette was gay and assumed that I was gay also. To this day I really don't know how she found out. (Maybe it was the way I whispered on the phone every time Bridgette called, or the way I went into the bathroom to continue our conversations.)

After Sharon found out, she told my social worker that she didn't want me in her house anymore because she was afraid I would try something with her twelve-year-old biological daughter. When the social worker told me this, I immediately became angry because I would never invade her daughter's privacy in that way.

The moving didn't bother me because I had moved nine times before that and I had learned not to get close to anyone. So I ended up staying with my uncle for a few weeks until my worker found me a new placement. I didn't want to stay in Sharon's house if she didn't trust me.

In the meantime, I noticed Bridgette had slowly started drifting away. I asked her why our relationship was ending. She explained to me that she became frightened because she had destroyed a relationship between a mother and daughter.

(Little did Bridgette know that Sharon wasn't my mother. As with every placement I had, I was ashamed of being in foster care, so I had told Bridgette that Sharon was my real mother. Now I couldn't tell her that Sharon was my foster mother because Bridgette would think I didn't trust her enough to tell her the truth from the start.)

It's been one and a half years since I left Sharon. Bridgette and I still speak every once in a while, but the relationship is over. Sometimes I choose not to admit it, but I do think I loved Bridgette. I have a hard time admitting it because I try to keep my emotions hidden within myself.

But since that incident, I have been honest at the beginning of my relationships. I tell them I'm in foster care, and if the relationship progresses, I tell them things that happened in my past.

I am presently in kinship care with my grandmother. She doesn't know I'm gay because she wouldn't accept it due to her religious beliefs. I can't afford to have her kick me out of the house because I'm nineteen years old and there is no place for me to go. But when I do move out in January I might decide to tell her, because I'll no longer be living under her roof.

As far as Sharon goes, she was wrong for making me leave because of my sexual preference. I would never have tried anything with her daughter. I would never take advantage of anyone like that. Being gay doesn't mean you want to have sex with everyone you pass by.

I think agencies should warn prospective foster parents who are willing to take teenagers that they might have a gay teen in their home, and should give them training on how to deal with those types of situations. Foster care is supposed to accept all youth, no matter what their sexual identity is.

Sharon may have had gay friends, but she couldn't accept a gay person into her family. Sharon may have lived in foster care, but obviously she didn't understand or care how her rejection would affect me. How could Sharon judge me like that if she had once been in foster care herself?

Personally, I'd rather be moved than live a lie, but no one should have to live a lie for fear of being moved.

Shameek Williamson wrote this story when she was 19. She would like to see better training and evaluation for foster parents. "I've noticed that the foster parents I've lived with either do it for the money, or they try to replace your natural parents." The first person in her family to go to college, Shameek is studying social work at Audrey Cohen College in Manhattan.

107

The family law attorney Nanette Schorr argues that we are too quick to take children away from their parents (1992).

Foster Care and the Politics of Compassion

Nanette Schorr

In 1910, a single mother wrote a poignant appeal to the *Bintel Brief* (letters) section of the *Jewish Daily Forward*. The social supports in her community had failed her, and she had nowhere else to turn.

> My husband deserted me and our three small children, leaving us in desperate need. . . . I am young and healthy, I am able and willing to work in order to support my children, but unfortunately I am tied down because my baby is only six months old. I looked for an institution which would take care of my baby but my friends advise against it. The local Jewish Welfare Agencies are allowing me and my children to die of hunger. . . . It breaks my heart but I have come to the conclusion that in order to save my innocent children from hunger and cold I have to give them away. . . .

The dilemma this woman faced is hardly different from that of many working mothers today. But the editor of the *Forward*, in response to the letter, looked beyond the responsibility of the Jewish social welfare agencies to that of the larger social order that forced parents to consider such desperate measures. The *Forward* editor replied: "What kind of society are we living in that there is no other way out than to sell her three children for a piece of bread? Isn't this enough to kindle a hellish fire of hatred in every human heart for such a system?" The *Forward*'s passionate and righteous anger is unequivocal; the enemy is the capitalist system.

At a time when class-based analyses had greater currency, it was easy to arouse the public's indignation at a skewed division of resources. The moral fault lines were clear—hungry children, innocent parents, guilty social order. But in the course of the twentieth century, denunciation of the social order has been diluted by the need of a large middle class to define social relations in ways that assuage its conscience and shore up its economic position. As a result, contemporary social policy rationalizes unfair distribution of resources without implicating society's fundamental decency. Instead of finding fault in the failure of the current economic system to meet *all* its members' needs, modern social theorists assure us that those who have not achieved a measure of material security are inherently flawed. And as social-service providers, journalists, educators, academics, and others lose faith in a more equitable and meaningful social vision, this view becomes more seductive and powerful.

It is therefore not surprising that "blaming the victim" has become a cornerstone of the way the state provides child-protective services. Partly as a result of the growing sensitivity about oppression within families (an awareness fostered by feminist critiques and the growth of the "children's-rights" movement), but partly as a result of society's unwillingness to acknowledge the social forces that put stress on families, the state's child-protective bureaucracy fosters the notion that we are dealing simply with "good children" and "bad parents." By defining the parent as a personal failure and abstracting that failure from the social reality within which parenting occurs, the state manages to perform a necessary function—protecting the child from extreme forms of abuse—and at the same time denies the existence of the social conditions that often account for bad parenting. Once having identified the primary problem as bad parenting, the state is free to intervene without restraint in its clients' daily lives by removing children from their parents with minimal investigation and little respect for legal procedures—before exploring avenues for keeping the family together.

These interventions rarely touch the sexual abuse, physical violence, or simple neglect that occurs in middle- and upper-middle-class families. This abuse typically comes to light much later in life—in therapy, or in consciousness-raising groups—but not because the state has become involved. Often communities that have already been defined as pathological because they haven't made it in the competitive market economy—Third World people, those on welfare, or the working poor—become the targets of an overzealous bureaucracy.

The case of L. H. is striking in its ordinariness. A mother living in the Bronx in 1987, L. H. was in a position not unlike the mother who wrote to the *Bintel Brief*. She had recently separated from a husband who had abused her and was now alone with three young children, without money or job skills, in a house with broken windows. She sought help from child-welfare authorities—money to fix her windows and someone to watch over her children while she looked for work—but they responded by charging her with neglect for leaving her younger children in the care of her older ones and for causing them emotional distress by arguing with her husband in front of them. As a result, the child-protective system removed L. H.'s children from her care and insisted her problems could be solved with psychology. The institutional foster care providers ignored L. H.'s concerns for the safety of her boys, whom they deemed "fragile," and placed them in separate group homes as a way of treating "parentification" syndrome (older siblings protecting younger ones). L. H. found no justice in the family courts, either. Her court-appointed counsel was inaccessible and unresponsive, and the court itself did not have time to hear her case. L. H. was finally reunited with her children, but only after taking extraordinary legal action. The wounds of the utterly unnecessary separation have yet to fully heal.

I work as a lawyer representing parents who are trying to regain or maintain custody of their children and I see cases like L. H.'s all the time. Most of the time parents don't fight back because they have already come to believe that the system is so rigged against them, and are so steeped in the belief that they are unworthy simply because they are poor, that any serious struggle seems futile. Moreover, the degradation they have suffered—which the child-protective system only compounds by its treatment of poor families—makes some parents doubt their own ability to care for their children.

Of course horrendous things do happen to children in some families. But defining the problem this way provides everyone with an excuse to avoid confronting the way the child-protective system works. . . .

The good child–bad parent definition works very well for those social workers, therapists, and others whose job is to keep the system working smoothly and who long ago have given up any hope of changing the larger society. But the system's very effectiveness is often a disaster for the children and parents caught in its vise. Families are torn apart and children suffer in the process. Children may be separated from their brothers and sisters, moved precipitously from foster home to foster home, or—worst of all for children in such a vulnerable position—abused or neglected in foster care. Their parents are not much better off. As overwhelmed and undertrained caseworkers make arbitrary or impossible demands on them, parents lose hope of being reunited with their children. They complete a drug treatment program only to be told they must find a job. They receive a certificate from a parental skills class, only to be told that they can get their children back only when a therapist determines they are ready. They are told they must find an apartment, but there are no apartments to be rented for what they can afford to pay. Frightened and bewildered, they go to family court hoping to find justice, but instead they are shuffled from one court appearance to the next. Months, sometimes years, pass as cases are repeatedly adjourned and professionals who sit behind closed doors determine the fate of their families.

Children in protective care, meanwhile, are forming bonds with their foster parents and foster parents are becoming attached to their foster children. The longer children live in foster care, the more the state recognizes the bond that is built between foster parent and child—a bond that will be sustained by the state against the aspirations of parents who seek to reunite the natural family. The courts are full of custody battles between foster parents and natural parents, battles in which the state throws its substantial power behind foster parents. Ask yourself to whom a child's affections will naturally turn: the foster parent who daily provides that child's needs (as well as many things above and beyond those needs), or the parent who earns a paltry income or lives on public assistance and is permitted to visit for only an hour once every other week. Social engineering, not child protection, is the net result in this system, as children are taken from poor families and placed in middle-class families that can give them a "better" life. Such interference overextends the role of the state. It is not for the state to decide what constitutes an enlightened upbringing, but rather to establish threshold criteria for the care of children above which its intervention is not required. There are many types of harm from which the state is unable to protect children, such as the emotional harm they experience when their parents argue or divorce, the internalized pain and loss of self-esteem they suffer when discipline is imposed in an arbitrary manner, or the damage they live with when they are punished corporally in ways the state does not deem "excessive." Were every kind of harm subject to state intervention, all children would at some time have been removed from their parents' homes.

Over its century of existence, the child-protective movement has tended to reflect the country's broader political and social context—in the 1940s and 1950s, for example, it adopted the then-burgeoning middle class's rigid definitions of healthy families and began to put growing emphasis on psychiatric labeling. Yet in some sense, the field of child protection has evolved independently of the national discourse; continuities in practice have overshadowed the changes in theory. In the 1900s as in the 1990s, the focus of casework has remained the treatment of individual weaknesses. As a result, caseworkers make little practical distinction between "neglect" and "abuse"—despite the dramatic differences between the two. A neglected child is legally defined as a child whose physical, mental, or emotional condition is impaired or is in imminent danger of impairment because his or her parent fails to supply him or her with adequate food, clothing, shelter, education, supervision, or guardianship. The law defines an abused child as a child whose parent inflicts or allows to be inflicted physical injury, by other than accidental means, that causes or creates a substantial risk of death or serious or protracted disfigurement. Yet whether the case be one of "neglect" or "abuse," the child-protective system treats parents in much the same way.

Until the nineteenth century, when the term "child abuse" entered the national discourse, most Americans saw the suffering of children pragmatically, as part of the human condition. The contemporary child-protective movement reflects internationally recognized human-rights protocols that define children as separate beings of inherent value. But while the discourse of human rights has helped to transcend cultural distinctions and placed the field of "children's rights" squarely within its purview, state intervention has gone far beyond safeguarding the right of children to be protected from harm and provided with basic nurturance. Since child protection became a social institution, compulsory separation of children from their parents has remained the primary form of state intervention in family life. In the nineteenth century, "orphan trains" carried the children of immigrants westward to be loaned out as indentured servants. Now, foster parents and foster-care administrators have an economic incentive to perpetuate the institutionalized practice of child removal and placement. None of this is to say that abuse and neglect do not exist, that parents are not responsible for what happens to their children, or that child protection is merely a capitalist conspiracy to make money by stealing the children of the poor. But one cannot ignore the images evoked by the vocabulary that predicates intervention: Reductive characterizations of parents as "crack mothers," for example, justify dehumanizing social policies and underwrite the state's recourse to criminal sanctions instead of remedial therapies. . . .

The question then becomes: When should children be taken from their parents? Quite simply, when their parents are abusing or neglecting them, when there is imminent risk of harm to their lives or health, or when "reasonable efforts" have been made to ameliorate the problem. While abuse cases may require long-term removal, in the majority of neglect cases a family's needs may be met by limited remedial intervention such as that provided by the Homebuilders' program or the "family preservation" models that are being developed around the country. The cost and pain of family separation should be—but aren't—considered before a child is placed in foster care. . . .

We shrink from the difficult decisions we cannot avoid: The fear of drawing the line too narrowly leads us to draw it too broadly. When we focus on the neglectful and abusive behavior of individual parents, we allow ourselves to avoid recognizing how their failure reflects larger social failures for which we are all ultimately accountable, since the state—in whose operation we are all implicated—is the most neglectful parent of all. The degree of intervention into parent-child relationships must be tailored to fit (and not exceed or fall short of) the needs and circumstances of each individual family. When the state uses untempered intervention as a blunt instrument, and describes all parental failures of children as "child abuse"—provoking the uniform response of removing all the children from the home—we needlessly destroy otherwise viable families. . . .

The courts must respect the rights of parents by ensuring that caseworkers are making "reasonable efforts," both before and after they remove children. The courts can neither rectify the unequal scrutiny given to poor families nor change the social conditions that give rise to neglect. But they can make better efforts to keep families together by ordering and supplying necessary services, even if those services cost money. . . .

The complexity and immediacy of the issue requires us to respond quickly and decisively. Many of the clients in the child-protective system do need help. The question is, what kind of help? Rather than focusing on child removal as a remedy, that help could take the form of funding "family preservation" programs that assist families before their children are removed and maintain the parent-child bond during foster care with frequent visits. "Family preservation" should be broadly defined to include support for poor and working parents in the form of publicly funded day care and health insurance. In addition to providing services, government should support community organizations and mutual-assistance societies such as those formed by many ethnic groups that share day care, provide seed money for new endeavors, and run parenting groups and advocacy efforts.

Recognizing the pain of parental struggle does not mean that all parents are good. It does require recognizing that real support for families must be linked with efforts to change the world of work and reorganize the economy. The social significance of child neglect extends beyond its current impact. Its human impli-

cation is also profound because it shapes the lens through which future generations will filter their memories, and, in turn, their hopes and dreams. A compassionate response to children must include an equally compassionate response to
their parents.

108

As this 1997 New York Times *article reveals, orphanages are once again being suggested as a solution to the growing problem of children whose parents are not competent to care for them.*

Orphanage Revival Gains Ground

Katharine Q. Seelye

Boys' Home is an orphanage, although none of the 41 boys living there are technically orphans. Many are like Reggie. "My daddy's a drunk and my mom's a drug addict," he said.

A grown-up 14-year-old in a starched white shirt with a knotted red tie, he noted matter-of-factly that he escaped the family illnesses. As he put it, "They didn't mess up my brain when I was in birth."

Reggie bounced from three foster homes before landing here in 1996.

"This is mainly my family," he said of Boys' Home, a former potato farm spread across a 1,400-acre patch of the Allegheny Mountains in southwest Virginia. "I don't have anywhere else to go."

Most American orphanages were shuttered more than three decades ago. Several studies had documented the long-term harm of institutionalizing children and condemned orphanages as warehouses that led to abuse of all kinds. Moreover, experts began to believe that every effort should be made to preserve families.

But orphanages never really went away. And while the prevailing view among child-welfare experts is still highly skeptical of them—the costs are exorbitant and orphanages are perceived as damaging to young psyches—the concept has inspired an increasingly vocal following among some who see the current foster-care system, clogged with 500,000 children, as a colossal failure.

Advocates of orphanages say that they can provide a sense of permanence, security, structure and camaraderie, and that they may be the best option for some children who cannot live with their own families or be adopted.

"Children's homes have worked well in the past, are working now and can work even better in the future," said Richard McKenzie, who grew up in an orphanage and is now an organizer of the back-to-orphanage movement.

The question, Mr. McKenzie said, is not when orphanages will return but how fast they can return to spare children from the insecurity of foster care.

Orphanages in the United States were originally built to house children left parentless by war, epidemics and poverty. In the 1920's, as many as 140,000 children lived in more than 1,200 orphanages.

Now, advocates say, such institutions are just as necessary for some of the children left homeless by the plagues of modern times: abuse, crack, alcohol and AIDS.

Heidi Goldsmith, executive director of the International Center for Residential Education, a nonprofit group in Washington estimated that about 25 orphanages existed today. Ms. Goldsmith limited the term "orphanage" to small residential schools or cottages for about 50 children who are disadvantaged, not serious troublemakers or children who need intense psychiatric treatment. And they take children in for the long haul, not just in emergencies.

Many homes are affiliated with religious organizations. On the high end is the much-showcased Milton Hershey School near Harrisburg, Pa., which was founded in 1909 and now has a $3 billion endowment.

A handful of new orphanages have been built in the last few years, notably by SOS Villages, U.S.A., a nonprofit international group, in Florida, Illinois and Wisconsin. Others have sprung up in Estes Park, Colo., Boston, and Ewing Township, N.J., near Trenton. Ms. Goldsmith said she received several calls a month—including one recently from Mayor Rudolph W. Giuliani's office in New York City—inquiring about setting up such residential schools for at-risk children.

Her definition does not include the hundreds of small institutions around the country that serve more difficult children. For example, more than 4,000 of the 42,000 children in foster care in New York City live in group homes with 18 children or less.

"The popular wisdom today is that large, congregate-care institutions are less desirable than foster boarding homes," Nicholas Scoppetta, Commissioner of the Administration for Children's Services, said through a spokesman. But, Mr. Scoppetta added, "there is a place for group homes, although the more closely we duplicate the family setting, the more likely we will be able to help children."

Modern orphanages, advocates say, have evolved from the stereotypes of institutional warehouses full of starving waifs. More likely, they are small and homey, strong on discipline and short on free time.

Donnie Wheatley, 50, who grew up here at Boys' Home and is now its director, said such homes were intended to help children "before their troubling situations turn them into troubled children."

Mr. Wheatley acknowledged some problems, including the regular turnover of the staff because of burnout, and the potential for abuse, although he said there was less opportunity for predators in such settings because other people were almost always around. He also said orphanages "can't provide the intimacy a family can give you." But the biggest problem, he said, was the nation's anti-orphanage prejudice.

"The things they've done to replace orphanages haven't worked," Mr. Wheatley said.

Mr. McKenzie, whose alcoholic mother killed herself when he was 10 and who spent eight years in an orphanage in North Carolina, was quick to say that orphanages were not ideal. But Mr. McKenzie, now a professor at the University of California at Irvine, said he never "pined away" to be adopted.

"If you've been in a failed family situation," he said, "you don't think the next family will be any better."

That is not the case for all boys here. David, for example, who has lived at Boys' Home for a year, said he wanted to return to his most recent foster family. His parents divorced when he was 2, his mother died when he was 6, and, he said, he was abused by his grandparents.

"Boys' Home has helped me a lot socially," said David, 13. "I have better manners. I can choose my words better. I have more self-control. But I want to live with my foster family. She's the closest thing I have to a mother. They love me, and I don't have that up here."

Critics say a large-scale return to orphanages would be a social disaster. Permanence, they say, is precisely what they do not want to encourage because it could close off the possibility of a child's ever living with a family. And living with a family, many experts believe, is best.

When Speaker Newt Gingrich raised the possibility of orphanages in 1994, he was quickly quashed. The North American Council on Adoptable Children, a nonprofit group based in Minnesota, published a position paper strongly opposing them.

Joe Kroll, executive director of the council and an author of the paper, said in an interview that any child could be adopted and that establishing orphanages would be to give up.

Critics of orphanages are also concerned that profit may be the motive behind the push for orphanages. They say that changes in the welfare law, which now allow for-profit companies to compete for the huge supply of Federal dollars available for child welfare, could lure private companies into the business of selling institutional care for profit.

"Are we instilling family values," Ronald Feldman, dean of the Columbia University School of Social Work, asked in an interview, "or is this a way to open up opportunities for the business sector that might not have existed before?"

Advocates of orphanages point to Boys' Home, founded by the Episcopal Church in 1906, as a model.

The home's $20-million endowment is surely a primary factor in its success, along with robust private fund-raising that provides the average annual cost of $35,000 for each boy. About $164,000—less than 8 percent of the annual $2 million budget—comes from tax dollars.

The boys, ages 10 to 19, live in eight brick cottages, with partitions between their beds. A team of six "house parents" oversees two cottages.

Officials screen the boys and accept only those who show potential for success in school. Their days are highly regulated with school, chores and meals from 6 A.M. to lights out at 10:30 P.M. They have a dress code (no sagging clothes), but no uniforms. They operate on a strict system that rewards good behavior with privileges and freedom. The campus, which includes a Christmas tree farm and pastures for sheep, pigs and a goat, is open.

The boys are taught to give something back to the community. On a recent evening, they pooled their gifts for the poorest people in town. Robert, 19, whose parents are divorced and who has lived here since 1993, gave $10. His cottage gave pancake mix and canned corn.

Robert said he considered Boys' Home his home. ''Every boy here is treated as a king,'' he said. ''If you behave.''

Lewis Hine, *Child Labor on the Farm*, 1930. Gift of David Vestal, 1963.353. Photograph by Christopher Gallagher. Courtesy of the Art Institute of Chicago.

The Vulnerable Child

Since the eighteenth century, when portraits of children came into fashion, children have almost always been depicted as innocent and vulnerable. Works by nineteenth-century novelists like Charles Dickens and Harriet Beecher Stowe included portrayals of saintly children, in contrast to earlier images of children as beastly and uncivilized. Many of the changes in nurture, dress, institutions, and practices since the late eighteenth century have resulted from this new view of the child.

The special vulnerability of the child has also resulted in the recognition that not all children are equally well cared for and that the responsibility for them may well lie outside the family. The health and emotional well-being of children in general have become potent symbols of a society's ability to provide for its members, and many of the triumphs of science, like vaccinations for diphtheria and polio, are seen in terms of children's health. But the emphasis on vulnerability has also resulted in a kind of cultural obsession with representing children as victims of disease, institutional neglect, and the greed, lust, and mistreatment of adults.

109

In the late nineteenth century the journalist-reformer Jacob A. Riis described how the children of the poor were vulnerable to disease, mistreatment, and neglect. Here he focuses on the lives of foundling children in New York City (1890).

Waifs of the City's Slums

Jacob A. Riis

[The] Foundling Asylum . . . stands at the very outset of the waste of life that goes on in a population of nearly two millions of people; powerless to prevent it, though it gather in the outcasts by night and by day. In a score of years an army of twenty-five thousand of these forlorn little waifs have cried out from the streets of New York in arraignment of a Christian civilization under the blessings of which the instinct of motherhood even was smothered by poverty and want. Only the poor abandon their children. The stories of richly dressed foundlings that are dished up in the newspapers at intervals are pure fiction. Not one instance of even a well-dressed infant having been picked up in the streets is on record. They come in rags, a newspaper often the only wrap, semioccasionally one in a clean slip with some evidence of loving care; a little slip of paper pinned on, perhaps, with some such message as this I once read, in a woman's trembling hand: "Take care of Johnny, for God's sake. I cannot." But even that is the rarest of all happenings.

The city divides with the Sisters of Charity the task of gathering them in. The real foundlings, the children of the gutter that are picked up by the police, are the city's wards. In midwinter, when the poor shiver in their homes, and in the dog days when the fierce heat and foul air of the tenements smother their babies by thousands, they are found, sometimes three and four in a night, in hallways, in areas and on the doorsteps of the rich, with whose comfort in luxurious homes the wretched mother somehow connects her own misery. Perhaps, as the drowning man clutches at a straw, she hopes that these happier hearts may have love to spare even for her little one. In this she is mistaken. Unauthorized babies especially are not popular in the abodes of the wealthy. It never happens outside of the storybooks that a baby so deserted finds home and friends at once. Its career, though rather more official, is less romantic, and generally brief. After a night spent at Police Headquarters it travels up to the Infants' Hospital on Randall's Island in the morning, fitted out with a number and a bottle, that seldom see much wear before they are laid aside for a fresh recruit. Few outcast babies survive their desertion long. Murder is the true name of the mother's crime in eight cases out of ten. Of 508 babies received at the Randall's Hospital last year 333 died, 65.55 percent. But of the 508 only 170 were picked up in the streets, and among these the mortality was much greater, probably nearer ninety percent, if the truth were told. The rest were born in the hospitals. The high mortality among the foundlings is not to be marvelled at. The wonder is, rather, that any survive. The stormier the night, the more certain is the police nursery to echo with the feeble cries of abandoned babes. Often they come half dead from exposure. One live baby came in a little pine coffin which a policeman found an inhuman wretch trying to bury in an uptown lot. But many do not live to be officially registered as a charge upon the county. Seventy-two dead babies were picked up in the streets last year. Some of them were doubtless put out by very poor parents to save funeral expenses. In hard times the number of dead and live foundlings always increases very noticeably. But whether travelling by way of the Morgue or the Infants' Hospital, the little army of waifs meets, reunited soon, in the trench in the Potter's Field where, if no medical student is in need of a subject, they are laid in squads of a dozen.

Most of the foundlings come from the East Side, where they are left by young mothers without wedding rings or other name than their own to bestow upon the baby, returning from the island hospital to face an unpitying world with the evidence of their shame. Not infrequently they wear the bedtick regimentals of the Public Charities, and thus their origin is easily enough traced. Oftener no ray of light penetrates the gloom, and no effort is made to probe the mystery of sin and sorrow. This also is the policy pursued in the great Foundling Asylum of the Sisters of Charity in Sixty-eighth Street, known all over the world as Sister Irene's Asylum. Years ago the crib that now stands just inside the street door, under the great main portal, was placed outside at night; but it filled up too rapidly. The babies took to coming in little squads instead of in single file, and in self-defense the sisters were forced to take the cradle in. Now the mother must bring her child inside and put it in the crib where she is seen by the sister on guard. No effort is made to question her, or discover the child's antecedents, but she is asked to stay and nurse her own and another baby. If she refuses, she is allowed to depart unhindered. If willing, she enters at once into the great family of the good Sister who in twenty-one years has gathered as many thousand homeless babies into her fold. One was brought in when I was last in the asylum, in the middle of July, that received in its crib the number 20715. The death rate is of course lowered a good deal where exposure of the child is prevented. Among the eleven hundred infants in the asylum it was something over nineteen percent last year; but among those actually received in the twelvemonth nearer twice that figure. Even the nineteen percent, remarkably low for a Foundling Asylum, was equal to the startling death rate of Gotham Court in the cholera scourge.

Four hundred and sixty mothers, who could not or would not keep their own babies, did voluntary penance for their sin in the asylum last year by nursing a strange waif besides their own until both should be strong enough to take their chances in life's battle. An even larger number than the eleven hundred were "pay babies," put out to be nursed by "mothers" outside the asylum. The money thus earned pays the rent of hundreds of poor families. It is no trifle, quite half of the quarter of a million dollars contributed annually by the city for the support of the asylum. The procession of these nursemothers, when they come to the asylum on the first Wednesday of each month to receive their pay and have the babies inspected by the sisters, is one of the sights of the city. The nurses, who are under strict supervision, grow to love their little charges and part from them with tears when, at the age of four or five, they are sent to western homes to be adopted. The sisters carefully encourage the home feeling in the child as their strongest ally in seeking its mental and moral elevation, and the toddlers depart happy to join their "papas and mammas" in the faraway, unknown home.

An infinitely more fiendish, if to surface appearances less deliberate, plan of child murder than desertion has flourished in New York for years under the title of baby farming. The name, put into plain English, means starving babies to death. The law has fought this most heinous of crimes by compelling the registry of all baby farms. As well might it require all persons intending murder to register their purpose with time and place of the deed under the penalty of exemplary fines. Murderers do not hang out a shingle. "Baby farms," said once Mr. Elbridge T. Gerry, the President of the Society charged with the execution of the law that was passed through his efforts, "are concerns by means of which persons, usually of disreputable character, eke out a living by taking two, or three, or four babies to board. They are the charges of outcasts, or illegitimate children. They feed them on sour milk, and give them paregoric to keep them quiet, until they die, when they get some young medical man without experience to sign a certificate to the Board of Health that the child died of inanition, and so the matter ends. The baby is dead, and there is no one to complain." A handful of baby farms have been registered and licensed by the Board of Health with the approval of the Society for the Prevention of Cruelty to Children in the last five years, but none of this kind. The devil keeps the only complete register to be found anywhere. Their trace is found oftenest by the coroner or the police; sometimes they may be discovered hiding in the advertising columns of certain newspapers, under the guise of the scarcely less heartless traffic in helpless children that is dignified with the pretence of adoption—for cash. An idea of how this scheme works was obtained through the disclosures in a celebrated divorce case, a year or two ago. The society has among its records a very recent case of a baby a week old (Baby "Blue Eyes") that was offered for sale— adoption, the dealer called it—in a newspaper. The agent bought it after some haggling for a dollar, and arrested the woman slave trader; but the law was powerless to punish her for her crime. Twelve unfortunate women awaiting dishonored motherhood were found in her house.

One gets a glimpse of the frightful depths to which human nature, perverted by avarice bred of ignorance and rasping poverty, can descend, in the mere suggestion of systematic insurance *for profit* of children's lives. A woman was put on trial in this city last year for incredible cruelty in her treatment of a stepchild. The evidence aroused a strong suspicion that a pitifully small amount of insurance on the child's life was one of the motives for the woman's savagery. A little investigation brought out the fact that three companies that were in the business of insuring children's lives, for sums varying from $17 up, had issued not less than a million such policies! The premiums ranged from five to twenty-five cents a week. What untold horrors this business may conceal was suggested by a formal agreement entered into by some of the companies, "for the purpose of preventing speculation in the insurance of children's lives." By the terms of this compact, "no higher premium than ten cents could be accepted on children under six years old." Barbarism forsooth! Did ever heathen cruelty invent a more fiendish plot than the one written down between the lines of this legal paper?

It is with a sense of glad relief that one turns from this misery to the brighter page of the helping hands stretched forth on every side to save the young and the helpless. New York is, I firmly believe, the most charitable city in the world. Nowhere is there so eager a readiness to help, when it is known that help is worthily wanted; nowhere are such armies of devoted workers, nowhere such abundance of means ready to the hand of those who know the need and how rightly to supply it. Its poverty, its slums, and its suffering are the result of unprecedented growth with the consequent disorder and crowding, and the common penalty of metropolitan greatness. If the structure shows signs of being top heavy, evidences are not wanting—they are multiplying day by day—that patient toilers are at work among the underpinnings. The Day Nurseries, the numberless Kindergartens and charitable schools in the poor quarters, the Fresh Air Funds, the thousand and one charities that in one way or another reach the homes and the lives of the poor with sweetening touch, are proof that if much is yet to be done, if the need only grows with the effort, hearts and hands will be found to do it in ever increasing measure. Black as the cloud is it has a silver lining, bright with promise. New York is today a hundredfold cleaner, better, purer, city than it was even ten years ago.

Two powerful agents that were among the pioneers in this work of moral and physical regeneration stand in Paradise Park today as milestones on the rocky, uphill road. The handful of noble women, who braved the foul depravity of the Old Brewery to rescue its child victims, rolled away the first and heaviest boulder, which legislatures and city councils had tackled in vain. The Five Points Mission and the Five Points House of Industry have accomplished what no machinery of government availed to do. Sixty thousand children have been rescued by them from the streets and had their little feet set in the better way. Their work still goes on, increasing and gathering in the waifs, instructing and feeding them, and helping their parents with advice and more substantial aid. Their charity knows not creed or nationality. The House of Industry is an enormous nursery school with an average of more than four hundred day scholars and constant boarders—"outsiders" and "insiders." Its influence is felt for many blocks around in that crowded part of the city. It is one of the most touching sights in the world to see a score of babies, rescued from homes of brutality and desolation, where no other blessing than a drunken curse was ever heard, saying their prayers in the nursery at bedtime. Too often their white nightgowns hide tortured little bodies and limbs cruelly bruised by inhuman hands. In the shelter of this fold they are safe, and a happier little group one may seek long and far in vain.

110

Beginning in 1909 the White House organized a series of conferences that focused on the health and emotional well-being of children. One of the important issues addressed was whether children should be supported in the home if the family was too poor to raise them.

Preserving the Home

Conference Document

Proceedings of the Conference on the Care of Dependent Children, 1909

The secretary read as follows:

Should children of parents of worthy character, but suffering from temporary misfortune, and the children of widows of worthy character and reasonable efficiency, be kept with their parents—aid being given the parents to enable them to maintain suitable homes for the rearing of the children? Should the breaking of a home be permitted for reasons of poverty, or only for reasons of inefficiency or immorality?

The CHAIRMAN. The opening speaker will be Mr. Michael J. Scanlan, who was for some years a member of the state board of charities of New York, and who has long been one of the most active members of the Society of St. Vincent de Paul, in that city, and who is the president of the New York Catholic Home Bureau for Dependent Children.

Address of Mr. Michael J. Scanlan, President Catholic Home Bureau for Dependent Children, New York

Mr. SCANDLAN. Mr. Chairman and ladies and gentlemen, when I first heard this proposition announced, it struck me that there could be no negative to it, and I said as much to the committee; but they assured me that there might be room for a difference of opinion. So I was induced to jot down a few arguments in favor of the maintenance of family relations. . . .

The question now under discussion, as I apprehend it, is substantially this: Should workers in the field of charity make extraordinary efforts to preserve the family; should the children of those in destitute circumstances be kept with their parents or be taken from them and brought up elsewhere? In other words, should the family of those who have the misfortune to be poor be preserved rather than destroyed? . . .

For us Catholics there can be no question where we stand. The teaching of our church has always been in favor of the preservation of family ties, and the wisdom of this teaching has been commended by those separated from her. For us members of the society of St. Vincent de Paul there can likewise be no question as to where we stand. The special object of our society, its fundamental work, is the visiting of the poor at their homes. Our members are exhorted by all means to keep the family together. Funds are distributed liberally for that purpose. Situations are procured if necessary. It is only a very last resort and for very grave reasons and after many trials that a family group is broken up. And if because of the dissipated lives of parents the household is dispersed, our members are keen to discover symptoms of reformation so that they can rehabilitate that household again. By following out these rules we frequently have the happiness and consolation of seeing the children of those who have been on our relief rolls grow up to be respected and useful members of society. The question here discussed could not be the subject of debate at a meeting of the St. Vincent de Paul Society, because the maintenance of the family is so much a part of our creed. . . . It should be the cardinal aim of charity workers to keep intact the family circle of the poor. Children should be reared in the family where God Almighty has placed them, and while we know from sad experience that cases will arise where the removal of children from their homes is necessary, it should be done reluctantly and only where proper supervision at home has become impossible. Aid should be given to preserve the home in case of poverty, not public aid but aid such as is given by the St. Vincent de Paul Society; and even where children have the misfortune to have dissipated parents, some attempts at reformation should be made before the home is broken up.

111

The first state assistance came in the form of mothers' aid, which usually was given to women who had been widowed. The mothers' aid statute passed in Illinois in 1911 was the first of its kind in the United States. Massachusetts followed suit in 1913.

The Mothers' Aid Movement

Documents from the Child Welfare Movement

Illinois Statute, 1911

Be it enacted by the People of the State of Illinois, represented in the General Assembly: That section 7 of the Act entitled "An Act relating to children who are now or may hereafter become dependent, neglected or delinquent . . . approved June 4, 1907, be and the same hereby amended so as to read as follows:

If the court shall find any male child under the age of seventeen years or any female child under the age of eighteen years to be dependent or neglected within the meaning of the Act, the court may allow such child to remain at its own home subject to the friendly visitation of a probation officer, and if the parent, parents, guardian or custodian consent thereto. . . .

If the parent or parents of such dependent or neglected child are poor and unable to properly care for the said child, but are otherwise proper guardians and it is for the welfare of such child to remain at home, the court may enter an order finding such facts and fixing the amount of money necessary to enable the parent or parents to properly care for such child, and thereupon it shall be the duty of the county board, through its country agent or otherwise, to pay to such parent or parents, at such times as said order may designate the amount so specified for the care of such dependent or neglected child until the further order of the court.

Report by Massachusetts Commission on the Support of Dependent Minor Children of Widowed Mothers

It has long been the practice of charitable agencies in Massachusetts, as elsewhere, to separate children from their mothers when circumstances of whatever kind have made it appear that the members of the family would then be better off. In itself separation is not held to be desirable, and there is little doubt that today it is resorted to with much less readiness than was the case in the earlier period, and that very careful discrimination has come to be employed by the well-managed agencies. Separation takes place for a variety of causes, mainly reducible to two: the mother's unfitness or incapacity for her role, and her economic disabilities. The two causes may, of course, be present together.

Your commission has sought especially to discover how frequent were the cases of economic disability. To this end it requested virtually all the important child-helping agencies of the Commonwealth to report the causes of separation for all new instances arising in the six months' period, Jan. 1 to June 30, 1912, and for all the other active cases of that period. . . .

Returns were secured for 754 children not living with widowed mothers in the six months' period. In the cases of 328, or 43.3 per cent, of these children, removal was reported to have taken place because of the bad conduct of the child or—much oftener—the immorality or other unfitness of the mother. In the cases of 426, or 56.7 per cent, of the children, such causes were not reported to be involved. In a clear majority of the 426 cases economic causes determined separation. . . .

The commission believes . . . that the widow without children or with children grown up is in a situation that she can generally manage. It believes that aid should be given only where there are young children in a good family, and then only in respect of them.

The commission rejects the principle of payment by way of indemnity for loss. It proposes the principle of payment by way of subsidy for the rearing of children. The terms "pension," "indemnity" and "compensation" are irrelevant, but the term "subsidy" implies that a condition exists which, aided, will result in positive good for the State. Subsidy makes it feasible that children should stay with their worthy mothers in the most normal relation still possible when the father has been removed by death. It is intended not primarily for those with least adequate incomes under the present system of aid, but for the fit and worthy poor. What a good mother can do for her own children no other woman can do, and no different device can do. . . .

The commission believes that no aid can be given, except under the poor-law and by private societies, to widows unfit to spend money for the improvements of their families. Aid may have to be given them hesitatingly, without assurance, and under abundant supervision. When even then family life is not really maintained, separation of the children may be resorted to as being genuinely in their interests. Whether it is then best that they be boarded out or placed in institutions must depend on a variety of circumstances.

It seems not undesirable to create in the community a distinction between subsidy and relief. The family receiving the former may desire to live up to the special confidence reposed in it. Its income is regular and adequate. Supervision is less frequent than with other families. Detection of real misuse of the subsidy compels its cessation and reduces the family to the position of the incompetent poor. On the other hand, a family declared ineligible for subsidy may often, through the friendly offices of philanthropic societies, be trained to later eligibility.

112

The historian Charles R. King describes the reasons for the decline in infant mortality rates in the twentieth century, including improved nutrition and living conditions for the population in general, more widely available prenatal and maternal health care, and scientific advances in immunology (1993).

Infant Mortality

Charles R. King

The study of infant mortality was, and is, an especially "sensitive indicator" of community health. It "reflects the positive or negative influences exerted by various social factors" upon children's health. It is "particularly sensitive to environmental conditions, such as housing, sanitation, and pure food and water." In other words, infant mortality is an indicator of the very factors that form the basis of and promote public health. Thus, as Josephine Baker, the first director of the New York City Bureau of Child Hygiene, concluded, "everything that affects the health of the child, from the beginning of the prenatal period to the end of adolescence" forms the basis for children's health in general; and infant mortality is an especially sensitive indicator of the good or bad influence of these factors.

According to most observers, too many American babies died. In 1880, 288 of every 1,000 live-born infants in New York City died. During the following decade in Milwaukee, 10 percent of all deaths were infant deaths, and during the first half of this decade the number of infants dying with gastrointestinal illnesses more than doubled. As late as 1912, more than 1 in 10 New York children died during infancy, while the *Newark Evening News* reported a Russell Sage Foundation study that found that in 1910 more than 1,300 infants under one year of age had died in Newark. These profound tragedies affected some segments of the population more than others. Most frequently, immigrant and minority infants died. For example, twice as many black as white infants died. The biggest difference between the death rates for black and white infants was seen in the rural South, where more than twice as many black babies died. Two-thirds of the deaths of black infants occurred in the first three months of life.

Many factors, including poverty, poor housing, limited nutrition, and inadequate medical care, were responsible for these deaths. Infant deaths increased as the number of family members per room increased, as the family income decreased, and when mothers worked outside the home. In addition, the president of the New Orleans Board of Health was of the opinion that southern black families (other officials included other immigrant and minority groups) were "as savage almost in their ideas of hygiene as their ancestors in Africa." While this statement was clearly prejudicial in word and intent, it underscores the importance of education about the scientific ideas of health and hygiene for black and white, native and immigrant Americans for the reduction of infant mortality. The education of mothers about children's health was, according to the 1912 Annual Report of the American Association for the Study and Prevention of Infant Mortality (AASPIM), "the strongest weapon for fighting infant mortality." By calling mothers to a moral campaign to save their children, physicians and health officers hoped that their educational programs would provide mothers with the tools to reduce infant deaths. . . .

Significant reductions in the frequency of infant death required not only good professional practices but also broad social programs. By the early twentieth century, physicians, health officers, advisers, and laywomen promoted programs that reduced infant mortality. New efforts that emphasized prenatal care and provided special attention to women during pregnancy were started. From Elizabeth Lowell Putnam in Boston to Samuel Crumbine in Kansas, these authorities offered evidence that prenatal care reduced infant mortality. Putnam showed that maternal deaths, premature births, stillbirths, and neonatal deaths were less than half as frequent among Boston women who received prenatal care than those who did not. Crumbine agreed and suggested that diet, exercise, rest, sunshine, fresh air, and cleanliness during pregnancy, among other factors, all reduced infant mortality. The Baltimore obstetrician and leading American authority on pregnancy care, J. Whitridge Williams (1866–1931), concluded that "no other prophylactic measure" than prenatal care provided the means "by which the lives of so many children can be saved."

If prenatal care helped reduce infant mortality, not surprisingly, improved obstetrical care did also. American birthing practices dramatically changed during the early twentieth century. Physicians replaced midwives as birth attendants, operative births replaced spontaneous unassisted births, hospital birthing became standard, anesthesia was utilized, and women increasingly accepted the physician's voice in the birthing chamber. In the middle third of the twentieth century, a more consistent application of sterile technique with childbirth, newly available blood transfusions, safer anesthetic methods, and more skilled operative obstetrical interventions made childbirth safer; but in the first decades of the century, little change in infant mortality accompanied the new birthing practices. In fact, during the first three decades of the twentieth century, maternal and infant deaths were more frequent with physician-assisted births than with those attended by midwives. Rather than addressing the implications of this observation most physicians argued that midwives, not physicians, were responsible for these needless deaths and that the solution to the high frequency of infant deaths was the elimination of midwives. Since physicians were unwilling to accept responsibility for maternal deaths, they also did not alter their obstetrical practices and procedures at the patient's bedside. The result was that while physicians criticized midwives for the problem, through their own failure to adequately wash their hands and avoid needless obstetrical intervention, some mothers and infants died when they should not have.

Although the larger issue of who should attend births remained problematic, simpler measures like eye washes for the newborn to prevent eye infections were available for use by both midwives and physicians. One authority estimated that neonatal infections were responsible for the blindness of 7,000 Americans. The bacterial infections that caused ophthalmia neonatorum were easily prevented with routine instillation of a silver nitrate solution into the baby's eyes. The standardization of birthing practices, including routine eye prophylaxis, as exemplified by the inclusion and specification of these procedures in the publications of the federal Children's Bureau, was evidence not only of growing professional, public, and governmental interest in children's health but also of the expanding authority of governmental officials and programs in promoting the health of the nation's children. . . .

While in the early part of the twentieth century infant mortality remained high, by 1930 the rate was declining because general living conditions were enhanced, disease was prevented by vaccination, nutrition was improved, prenatal and maternal health were advanced, and, perhaps most important, a system of pure milk supply and distribution had been established. While twentieth-century physicians and advisers recommended breast feeding, methods of artificial feeding became more readily available and successful; and more American women employed these alternatives. Successful artificial feeding required the application of the principles of the germ theory, like sterilization of bottles and the provision of pure milk, and nutritional knowledge about the composition of infant formulas. Interest in cow's milk as a nutritional source for infants and children was not new, but attention to measures that ensured its safe supply and healthful composition for infant feeding were. Before 1880 only 13 scientific articles were published about milk and infant health, an indication of the lack of interest by physicians about this topic. Over the next four decades more than 1,200 articles appeared, most after 1890. This newfound knowledge enabled the development of methods for safe and successful artificial feeding. Holt concluded not only that this task was "the most important branch of pediatrics" but also that "at no other time in life does prophylaxis give such results as in the conditions of infancy." Infant feeding was not problematic because it was innately unhealthy, but the methods employed by most turn-of-the-century mothers were improper, inadequate, unsanitary, and often nutritionally incomplete. Consequently, as knowledge about artificial feeding became available from the chemical analysis of milk, the development of better feeding techniques, and the supply of bacteria-free milk, infant feeding became more successful.

Because of its widespread availability and similar composition to human milk, cow's milk became the standard replacement for infant feeding. Pediatricians, led by Thomas Morgan Rotch (1849–1914) in Boston and Emmett Holt in New

York, established milk laboratories for the analysis and compounding of infant formulas based on cow's milk. These often complex formulas, as a former student of Rotch recalled, were compounded "with a chemical composition, including fat, sugar, protein and acidity, that chemically equalled human milk." Because each component was included on a precise percentage basis, this method was termed *percentage feeding*. Not all physicians accepted the percentage feeding methodology. Jacobi, for example, opposed it, and others, including a Boston physician, objected "to doing an algebraic or even considerable arithmetic sum at the bedside." Despite problems with the daily use of percentage feeding, the development of this method not only provided an understanding of the nutritional composition of milk but also promoted the acceptance of milk as a basis for infant feeding. In the process pediatricians advanced their professional stature by becoming the recognized authorities on infant feeding. The complexity of this methodology and the initiative by physicians to gain its acceptance sent American mothers the message that infant feeding was "to be used only under the direction of a physician." By recommending complex formulas that were compounded with difficulty and periodically altered for each baby, pediatricians placed themselves in an indispensable position as advisers about infant feeding. . . .

By mid-century pediatricians tackled more complex children's health problems that required more and more specialized scientific and medical knowledge. Most of the advances in pediatric medical practice followed general medical advances, like the development of surgical techniques and the refinement of the technology for performing X-rays. Immunologic methods that immunized children against childhood infectious diseases were especially important and successful. By the 1960s, immunization against measles, mumps, rubella, and polio was routinely completed. Rather than the widespread epidemics of the early years of the century, which caused frequent childhood deaths, most children were protected against these common yet serious infectious problems. During 1958 more than one million doses of the Salk polio vaccine were administered to suburban Chicago residents. The benefit of these scientific efforts was demonstrated across the city, where only 16 cases of poliomyelitis with three deaths occurred. The dramatic results of this seemingly simple procedure stood in sharp contrast to the frequent deaths that polio had caused half a century before.

The practice of routine immunization was an example of the important changes that more complete medical knowledge, generated from the study of the physiology and biochemistry of infants and children, provided. Endocrinologists isolated hormones and treated diabetes and growth failure, while cardiologists recognized an increasingly complex variety of heart defects and offered the means of their surgical correction. Previously unrecognized medical problems, like Cooley's anemia and cystic fibrosis, were described, and the means of maintaining salt and water balance with intravenous fluids understood. Not only was the biochemical basis of many of the major children's health problems identified, but an understanding of the methods of medical treatment was established. Rickets, for example, long recognized as a cause of ill health and deformed bones, was identified as a problem of calcium deficiency in growing bones. Better living conditions that provided children with sunlight and improved sources of calcium and vitamin D readily prevented the disease. In short, science provided pediatricians with the tools to diagnose disease more accurately and treat its ill effects more adequately. Unfortunately, despite such medical successes, measles cases today are increasing, whooping cough is more frequent, and a growing number of children, mostly victims of poverty, are incompletely immunized against preventable childhood diseases, all because of inadequate knowledge or finances and limited availability of medical services. This resurgence of avoidable health problems is symptomatic of the unresolved social problems that cause ill health for many American children.

113

Like tuberculosis in the nineteenth century, polio in the twentieth century was a scourge that seemed to strike children in particular. After various campaigns to protect the children through quarantine, the campaign to wipe out polio in the 1950s became a children's crusade, and Jonas Salk became a folk hero when he invented the polio vaccine. The public's initial fear and skepticism were alleviated by widely published results of scientific studies on the vaccine.

Polio

U.S. News & World Report

If Polio Strikes, What to Do

- Polio cases this year are running about 12 per cent above 1952, which had record high of 57,626 cases.
- That raises questions of what can be done as a protection against the disease . . .
- And what steps are being taken to fight polio in areas where there are bad epidemics.

With the polio season at hand, parents want to know: What can you do if the disease shows up in your neighborhood? Can you get shots for your child? Not as a general rule. Where there is one case of polio in a neighborhood, not all children living nearby can get injections of the serum that is being used as an antipolio measure. There just is not enough of the serum, which is made from human blood and is known as gamma globulin. But, where a child has been in close contact with another who has been stricken with polio, the parents should see their physician. In case of extremely dangerous exposure, the child may be able to get shots.

Suppose there is a case of polio in your home? Then there should be no trouble in getting gamma globulin inoculations for the young members of the family. First priority for the serum goes to such a household where there are people under 30 years of age or where there is a pregnant woman, regardless of age.

What happens in an area where there is an epidemic? Additional supplies of gamma globulin are rushed to that area and all children below a certain age are given a chance for inoculation. So far this year, three places have been declared emergency areas because of outbreaks of polio. They are Montgomery County, Ala.; Caldwell County, N.C., with a number of cases also reported in nearby Catawba County; and Steuben and Chemung counties, N.Y. Thousands of children were given GG shots in these communities.

Who controls rationing of the serum? Top control is in the U.S. Office of Defense Mobilization. It allots so much to each State on the basis of its experience with polio in recent years. Within each State, the health authorities distribute their share of gamma globulin.

Is this serum a certain preventive? No. But some encouraging results have come from using the serum as a protection against polio. Experiments during past epidemics indicated that fewer children developed polio after receiving the shots. Furthermore, some of those inoculated, when getting the disease, had milder cases with less chance of being badly crippled. If a child has already picked up a polio virus, however, gamma globulin will not help. It is not a cure.

Is a permanent immunity ever provided? No. The effectiveness of gamma globulin serum as a preventive begins about one week after injection and lasts for only five or six weeks.

How much do the shots cost? The serum costs nothing. That's because it is provided by the National Foundation for Infantile Paralysis, which is supported by individual donations, and by the American Red Cross, which collects blood and funds from the public. Physicians usually charge for inoculations; families who cannot pay can get free medical service from hospitals and clinics.

How much GG serum is available? Latest estimates are that there will be enough for about 1 million shots this polio season. Some of this will be used, however, to combat measles and hepatitis, a liver ailment.

What's the outlook for a vaccine to give permanent immunity against polio? Some physicians and scientists are encouraged by work on a vaccine that might give immunity lasting from one year to a lifetime. This vaccine, if successful, is expected to be effective against all three known types of polio. It still is in a testing stage and is not yet available for general use.

Gamma globulin thus is seen to be the main weapon being used against polio this summer. In this connection, Red Cross officials say that many blood donors will be needed. For not only is GG expensive to produce, but it takes one pint of human blood to make an average sized dose of the serum.

What the Polio Tests Really Showed

The official report on the polio vaccine developed by Dr. Jonas E. Salk reveals just how good it really is.

The vaccine offers protection against mild types of polio, works with increasing effectiveness as the severity of the disease increases. It is safe, causes a minimum of reactions, may give long immunity.

Here, from a report written by the deputy director of the group set up at the University of Michigan to evaluate the vaccine, are the basic conclusions of the test.

Following are extracts from the medical summary prepared by Dr. Robert F. Korns, deputy director of the vaccine-evaluation program:

During the spring of 1954 an extensive field trial of the . . . effectiveness of for-malin-inactivated poliomyelitis vaccine, as developed by Dr. Jonas Salk and his associates, was initiated by the National Foundation for Infantile Paralysis.

The Poliomyelitis Vaccine Evaluation Center was established at the University of Michigan for the purpose of impartially collating and analyzing data collected through the combined efforts of many thousands of health department workers, practicing physicians, physical therapists and laboratory people scattered through the 211 participating study areas in 44 States.

The tremendous clinic program was accomplished according to plan during April, May and June. In placebo control areas [where "dummy" shots were given to some, vaccine to others] the study population included 749,236 children; 455,474 (or 60.8 per cent) requested participation; 200,745 (26.8 per cent) received three injections of vaccine, and 201,229 (26.9 per cent) three injections of placebo, an identical material which, however, contained no poliomyelitis virus or mon-key kidney protein. In observed control areas the study population totaled 1,080,680 children in the first three grades; 221,998 second grade children (20.5 percent of the total) received three doses of vaccine.

The first problem of evaluation was that of collecting and verifying basic information on each of the 1,829,916 children in the study population. These data, which included the name, address, age, sex, history of polio or other crippling condition, participation status and dates of vaccination, if any, for each child, were transferred to punch cards, and tables describing the population were prepared which would serve as the denominators over which the discovered cases of polio would be placed for the determination of polio attack rates in vaccinated vs. control and in other segments of the population. . . .

The question of safety of the vaccine was assessed through specific studies of the cause and extent of absenteeism from school following inoculation in Pitts-burgh and Schenectady, N.Y. The experience was identical in vaccinated and control subjects and no significant reactions were observed.

From records obtained during the clinic [vaccination] program, the following distribution of minor reactions was observed: Placebo control areas—931 reac-tions or 0.4 per cent in vaccinated and 939 or 0.4 per cent in those receiving placebo.

Of the so-call "major" reactions, none of which could be clearly attributed to inoculation, 9 or 0.004 per cent occurred in vaccinated and 13 or 0.006 per cent in the placebo control. Those findings . . . fail to implicate the vaccine as a significant cause of untoward reactions. . . .

What the Vaccine Did

A further refinement in analysis was to consider the effect of vaccine in patients from whom poliomyelitis virus was isolated. These furnish a higher degree of confidence in diagnosis. In cases classified as spinal paralytic, the effectiveness was the same in placebo and observed control areas, 82 and 83 per cent respectively, and the corresponding lower limits of effect were 65 and 64 respectively. Enforcement of laboratory criteria for diagnosis apparently eliminated a substantial number of cases which were less influenced by vaccination, and undoubtedly among them were many illnesses which actually were not poliomyelitis. The effect in bulbospinal polio, with laboratory confirmation superimposed, was 91 per cent in placebo control and 60 per cent in observed control areas.

The next step was to examine the effect of vaccine with reference to the specific type of poliomyelitis virus isolated. In placebo control areas the effectiveness was 68 per cent against Type I, 100 per cent against Type II (significant at .05 level), and 92 per cent against Type III. This clearly agrees with the previous demonstrations that most lots of vaccine were less antigenic against Type I than against the other two types. In addition, the effectiveness of different lots of vaccine varied considerably as measured by the occurrence of poliomyelitis.

- From these data it is not possible to select a single value giving numerical expression in a complete sense to the effectiveness of vaccine as a total experience. If the results from the observed study areas are employed, the vaccine could be considered to have been 60 to 80 per cent effective against paralytic poliomyelitis, 60 per cent against Type I poliomyelitis and 70 to 80 per cent effective against disease caused by Types II and III. There is, however, greater confidence in the results obtained from the strictly controlled and almost identical test populations of the placebo study areas.
- On this basis it may be suggested that vaccination was 80 to 90 per cent effective against paralytic poliomyelitis; that it was 60 to 70 per cent effective against disease caused by Type I virus and 90 per cent or more effective against Type II and Type III virus. The estimate would be more secure had larger number of cases been available.

114

In the 1960s public attention turned to the plight of children with disabilities. The Jerry Lewis telethons to raise money for muscular dystrophy and the Easter Seals mail campaigns used images of children to appeal to the conscience of potential donors. In the 1970s the television journalist Geraldo Rivera took his viewers on a tour of the notorious Willowbrook facility for severely retarded children. His report demonstrated television's effectiveness in exposing the abuse of vulnerable children.

"Welcome to Willowbrook"

Geraldo Rivera

When Dr. Wilkins slid back the heavy metal door of B Ward, building No. 6, the horrible smell of the place staggered me. It was so wretched that my first thought was that the air was poisonous and would kill me. I looked down to steady myself and I saw a freak: a grotesque caricature of a person, lying under a sink on an incredibly filthy tile floor in an incredibly filthy bathroom. It was wearing trousers, but they were pulled down around the ankles. It was skinny. It was twisted. It was lying in its own feces. And it wasn't alone. Sitting next to this thing was another freak. In a parody of human emotion, they were holding hands. They were making a noise. It was a wailing sound that I still hear and that I will never forget. I said out loud, but to nobody in particular, "My God, they're children."

Wilkins looked at me and said, "Welcome to Willowbrook." . . .

The residents of the ward bore only a passing resemblance to children I have known. Their heads were swollen. Their bodies were bent and twisted. Their eyes were rolled back. Some were lying on the floor or on the benches; others staggered around the room. A few ran from Ronnie's light; most were attracted to it.

The single attendant was struggling to separate a cluster of children near the center of the ward. I stared at that woman with a look of intense hatred, and she looked back with a kind of half-smile that said, "It isn't my fault."

The kids were either naked or wearing fragments of clothing. Some wore just strait jackets.

Several of the toilet bowls had no seats on them, and all of the facilities were caked with filth. I watched one kid lower his head into the bowl and drink like a dog, while his roommates squatted on the others nearby.

The ward was filled with noise, but none of it seemed human. If I had heard that wail in a sound studio, my guess would have been that it was some kind of weird electronic music. It was the moaning made by all those kids left unattended, uncleaned, and unloved.

The only television set was on, but it wasn't focused. Still, a group of kids sat watching the blur and listening to the static.

Compare it to something? I was two years old at the end of World War II, and I've seen only yellowed photographs of the Nazi death camps, but that was the comparison that came to mind.

The kids were disgusting to look at, and their sound made me want to put my hands over my ears, but the smell was what made me physically sick. It smelled of filth. It smelled of disease. And it smelled of death.

After what seemed a long time, I went looking for Alis. We had to leave before the building supervisor found out we were there. While I was in the bathroom, he had been filming in the dayroom. His eyes were tearing, either from irritation or from something else. I never asked.

"Let's go, Bob."

"Just a minute. I've got to get some more shots."

"No. Let's go. We've got enough."

We left by the same side door we had entered. We had been inside for less than five minutes.

115

Kidnappings have been a feature of American life since the late nineteenth century, but the fear of stranger abduction for the purpose of sexual molestation became especially prominent in the 1980s. The 1979 disappearance of six-year-old Etan Patz was one of the first abductions attributed to a sexual predator.

Kidnapping in Contemporary America

Paula S. Fass

Just before 8 A.M. on Friday, May 25, 1979, six-year-old Etan Patz emerged confidently from his parents' co-op apartment in the SoHo district of New York to begin the two-block walk to the school bus stop. Etan had been eager for some time to do this on his own as a sign of a new maturity, and his mother had finally assented. She watched him briefly from her loft's third-floor fire escape as he proceeded from their home on 113 Prince Street to the intersection of Wooster. She then turned back into the apartment, and Etan vanished into the New York crowds.

Julie Patz did not yet know that when her son vanished from her sight, he had disappeared forever from her life. Indeed, Julie assumed that Etan had boarded the bus and was in his first-grade class at the Independence Plaza School (an annex of P.S. 3) on Greenwich Street throughout the day. It was only when he did not return as usual at 3:30 that afternoon that Julie Patz suspected that something might be wrong. She soon learned from a friend who usually collected him from the bus and whose daughter was in his class that Etan had not been at school and that he never made it to the bus that morning. It was clear to Julie at once and it would eventually become clear to the police, the media, and through them, the city, and the nation that Etan Patz had been taken in broad daylight amidst the commercial bustle of normal life from the streets of New York.

What happened to him has, however, never been made clear. Indeed, the case of Etan Patz—who would now be a young man of twenty-five—remains an open police case of a missing child.

When the police arrived at the Patzes' home at 5:30 that evening, they were confronted by a time lapse of nearly ten hours since the child was last seen. They were also confounded by the fact that it was not only a Friday, but the beginning of the long Memorial Day weekend. As a result, it would be very difficult to recreate the early morning scene the next day, a Saturday, when many possible observers would be absent. And it would be very difficult to piece together evidence or witnesses to that morning's events. Because the weather had been drizzly and because of the delay, the police dogs brought in the next morning to follow the child's scent and to reconstruct the route of his disappearance would be less than completely effective.

In the Patz case, however, unlike many others, the police were not long delayed either by the assumption that Etan had simply run away or just wandered off. Runaways were usually older, and Etan was a happy, well-adjusted child who knew where he was going. Neither was he the victim of a potential custody dispute. Julie and Stanley Patz were, to all appearances, a stable couple with two other children, a two-year-old toddler, Ari, and an eight-year-old daughter, Shira. These were always among the first speculations in any case of a missing child. Whatever had happened to Etan, it was unlikely that he had either run off or been taken by one of the parents. Nor did it seem probable that he was the victim of foul play by one of the parents, as sometimes also happened when children were reported missing to the police. The parents seemed devoted and loving, and they were genuinely distraught. While the police would not discount this last possibility until both Julie and Stanley had taken the first of several polygraph tests, they proceeded on the assumption that Etan had been kidnapped. Etan's disappearance, according to Lieutenant Earl J. Campazzi, who commanded the missing persons squad, was simply "unique."

For a long time, Julie Patz believed that, as an extremely handsome child with blond hair, an upturned nose, and glowing blue eyes (often fetchingly rendered by his photographer father), Etan had been taken by someone who desperately wanted a child of her or his own. "Whoever took him might be desperate for a child, but that person can't make Etan happy," Julie pleaded. "We won't press charges—all we ask is please bring Etan back to us." Almost one half year later, on Etan's birthday, October 9, Julie insisted, "We still think some misguided person who wanted to have a beautiful little boy took Etan." And Etan— friendly, bright, and outgoing, as well as smiling and pretty—would have been a desirable child. By 1979, it was becoming increasingly difficult to find attractive, healthy, white children for adoption. And while most children stolen for such purposes were infants taken directly from the hospital, . . . it was not altogether impossible for a child Etan's age to be taken with these ends in view.

It was similarly unlikely that Etan would serve as the basis for a ransom. The Patzes were far from wealthy—their loft was thinly furnished (Julie ran a child-care center there)—and ransom kidnapping had largely faded in the 1970s. A brief rash of cases followed in the wake of the spectacular abduction of Patty Hearst in 1974, but through that very connection to a political cause, ransom kidnappings became less likely as a simple form of criminal extortion. . . .

None of these explanations seemed to dispel the mystery of Etan's disappearance. "All the questions, it seems, lead nowhere," Etan's father Stanley noted. "Everyone is supposed to love a mystery. Well, we don't." Neither did the police, as Etan's case became the "No. 1 priority of the Police Department" in New York City by the end of May and the beginning of June 1979. One week after Etan's disappearance, the police were fielding 500 calls daily, and a force of forty men had completed repeated searches of all buildings in the four-block square area where Etan was last seen. As many as 500 officers were at one point involved in the police investigation, but the police appeared baffled. Lieutenant Ken Bauman speculated: "Is the child in a building where he is trapped? Is he with a male who is attracted to young boys or is he with a mentally disturbed woman who wishes that the child would be her child?"

Absent meaningful leads, the police were reduced to chasing after "sightings" by concerned citizens. These started coming in large numbers after the city was blanketed by flyers (eventually more than 300,000 were broadcast) with a picture and description of the boy, distributed by the forty neighbors and friends of the Patzes who assembled in their home to aid in the search effort. Etan or someone very like him was soon spotted in many local places, from Sheepshead Bay, to the south in Brooklyn, to Yonkers, north of the city. As the media began to retell the story, the police got calls from as far as Michigan and California. Sightings, posters, and the media became the lifeline of the search effort. Very soon, too, in desperation the Patzes turned to leads by hundreds of psychics who offered their services. . . . Julie Patz tried to use every media occasion to draw attention to her still-missing child, and Etan had become, a month after he vanished from the city's streets, the subject of the "widest and longest search for a missing child undertaken by the city's Police Department in decades." . . . Detective James Williams had been in the missing person's squad for twenty years and observed that "there's never been anything like this before. . . . A child so small, so defenseless has never disappeared for so long."

In fact, the search for Etan Patz would go on much, much longer. After the city had tired of the posters and handbills "plastered on every boutique and loft building" and they had become the site for graffiti and obscenities, the search for Etan would remain an obsession for the child's parents and for at least two law officers: Detective William Butler, who was initially in charge of the police investigation and worked on the case for over a year until his retirement, and much later, federal prosecutor Stuart GraBois. These diehards were haunted by the pretty little boy who disappeared inexplicably off the face of the earth. They remained with the case while other support faded. Two weeks after the disappearance, the police had disassembled the telephone command post they had set up in the Patz home, and after the first few months of rapt interest, the press coverage thinned down significantly to be reawakened only by the occasion of a birthday or an anniversary. But Etan Patz, a "Lost Child," was, in the words of his omnipresent posters, "Still Missing." . . .

. . . The Patzes would suffer intensely the agony of not knowing what had happened to their son. "How," Stanley Patz asked, "do you learn to survive as the family of an abducted child?" "This is a psychological wound that will never heal, never close up, without a resolution of one kind or another." At the outset, the Patzes had refused to allow rewards to be posted for Etan, fearful that this would lead others to steal children in hopes of benefiting from the reward. . . .

When they finally relented three years later, it was in order to provide themselves with some ending to their story. An anonymous donor offered $25,000
" 'for credible information' leading to Etan's return or proof that he is dead." . . .
The Patzes finally used reward money to bring some closure, some end to Etan's
unfinished story. "People get raped or murdered, and those crimes, as horrible
as they are, at least are contained in time," Stanley Patz observed. "In this crime
there was a beginning, but there is no end." Finally, Stanley and especially Julie
Patz had to construct a meaning for their loss, to provide themselves a substitute
for its emotional irresolution. . . . They did so by devoting themselves to the effort
to help find other children. Their meaning now came in subsuming Etan's identity to a larger campaign on behalf of missing children. In 1983, when President
Ronald Reagan proclaimed a new National Missing Children Day, he chose May
25, the date of Etan's disappearance. Since then, the event, with a shifting date in
May, has become an institution. It was fitting that when the New York City
Police Foundation began a "new public campaign to find missing children in
1985," on a date almost exactly six years after Etan's disappearance, it was Etan's
picture that was flashed two times an hour from a large electronic screen above
Broadway. Here it competed with the other lights and icons of twentieth-century
culture. The picture was accompanied by the words "Last seen 5-25-79. Still
Missing."

While his parents learned to cope with their loss and Etan became a symbol
for other missing children, the explanation for his disappearance was beginning
to emerge from another set of cultural concerns that allowed his disappearance
to become meaningful. Only after the initial explosion of interest had subsided
and after they had pieced together every possible shred of testimony (there was
no physical evidence) from passersby who had either seen or been present in the
neighborhood that morning—five full months after the event—did the police
release a sketch of a man who was possibly implicated in Etan's disappearance.
This man was "reportedly seen talking with Etan Patz shortly before the boy
disappeared." By then Stanley and Julie, who had initially sought comfort in the
belief that their son had attracted the attention of some desperate, but maternal,
woman, were hanging onto their shredding hopes. Soon they would even draw
"strength . . . in the story of Steven Stayner, the California boy who was returned
to his family seven years after he was kidnapped." Whatever strength the Patzes
were able to draw from Stayner's return could not possibly have come, contrary
to the phrasing of the *New York Times* report, from his having been returned. On
the contrary, Kenneth Parnell, who kidnapped Stayner in 1972, had just stolen
another boy, five-year-old Timmy Lee White, who he also expected to keep
permanently as "his son." It was Stayner's empathy for the new recruit, and
what he anticipated to be the certain fate of the younger child, that crystalized
Stayner's determination to escape from Parnell and take the new child with him.
By this time, Steven was a strapping young man who, when he did escape, could
not remember much more about his early life than his first name. Stayner had
not "been returned," and his escape eventually led to an extremely tricky and

far from successful reintegration into his family. Steven had been deeply wounded by the regular sexual and physical abuse to which he had been subjected by Parnell.

It was, however, Stayner's story that helped to turn a particular corner in the Patz case as it precipitated a more settled picture of what had likely happened to Etan. Stayner's return from captivity together with other aspects of the Patz case began to jell into a new theory that eclipsed most previous speculations. That theory centered on the sexual abuse of young children and their entrapment by adults driven by uncontrollable urges, even to the extent of abducting their victims.

Both the police and his parents had always been aware of this possible fate for pretty little Etan. It was one of the speculations by Lieutenant Bauman as early as May 31, but the press had hardly followed in depth this line of investigation and had not advertised any police dragnet of suspected sex criminals. The search for Etan had been mostly an open-ended search for a missing child. Even a year after his disappearance, a long piece in the *Sunday New York Times Magazine* by Mary Cantwell had not alluded to the sexual possibilities in the kidnapping but dwelled instead on the existential torments of being a mother who must at some point allow a child to take wing, even with the possibility of such a loss literally lurking around the corner.

By the time Beth Gutcheon's best-selling novel, *Still Missing*, was published in 1981, that new theory had become an all but settled fact. The book was universally believed to be based on the Patz case and full of deep emotional and physical parallels, but Gutcheon had attached an ending to the search. Gutcheon, who had been a neighbor of the Patzes, located "Alex Selky" in the clutches of a pedophile. Alex had been obviously (though never explicitly) abused, and the novel is full of the sexual themes of child exploitation.

One year later, in December 1982, a picture of a child very much resembling a somewhat older Etan was discovered in a police raid on a warehouse in Massachusetts used by NAMBLA (the North American Man Boy Love Association), which had also netted two teenaged boys. By then, what had been previously unspoken, but hardly unimagined—that Etan had been stolen in order to be sexually exploited—had become the governing assumption, even after it was firmly established that the boy pictured in the NAMBLA material was not Etan. It was this picture and its surrounding sexual sensation that eventually drew forth the so-called eyewitness report by the New York cabby. It also renewed the investigation of Etan's disappearance, to which eight New York police officers were once again assigned.

Within a week of the finding in Massachusetts, the Patz case was back in the news. The *New York Times* put the issue bluntly on the front page of its "Living" section with the headline, "Etan Patz Case Puts New Focus on a Sexual Disorder, Pedophilia." Although, according to Dr. A. Nicholas Groh, a clinical psychologist, "abduction of a child by a pedophile was very rare," the *Times* nevertheless stated that "There is an epidemic of sexual abuse of children."

While Etan Patz would never return, and eventually even his parents no longer wished for the media attention that a continued campaign would require, his disappearance could now be "explained." Its explanation lay in the deepest, dirtiest secret of contemporary American culture.

116

In the last two decades fears about the sexual abuse of children by caretakers in day care, at schools, in churches, and in the home have become a national obsession. In 1975 Suzanne M. Sgroi wrote the first article in this latest campaign against child sexual abuse.

The Last Frontier in Child Abuse

Suzanne M. Sgroi

The professional who becomes sufficiently concerned and knowledgeable about sexual abuse of children to be consistently alert to the possibility that sexual molestation *may* have occurred will often face a spectrum of reactions from his colleagues that range from incredulity to frank hostility. For although the pioneering efforts of many distinguished professionals and dedicated lay people over the past decade have made child abuse a national issue, the problem of sexual molestation of children remains a taboo topic in many areas.

This is not to argue that the problem of child abuse has been "solved" anywhere in the United States. It is, however, fair to assert that sexual abuse of children is the last remaining component of the maltreatment syndrome in children that has yet to be faced head-on. In medical parlance, child molestation is the least popular diagnosis. In the vernacular, it is not nearly so "in" a topic as child battering or neglect. Combating these forms of maltreatment is publicly applauded and encouraged. But somehow, protecting children against sex crimes has received far less community sanction. It seems to be "too dirty," "too Freudian" or perhaps "too close to home." Thus one who becomes concerned with this particular aspect of child protection must be prepared to cope with a very high degree of resistance, innuendo and even harassment from some, as well as indifference from others. The pressure from one's peer group as well as the community to ignore, minimize or cover up the situation may be extreme.

Incidence of Molestation

No one knows the true incidence of child molestation in the United States today. Vincent DeFrancis, director of the Children's Division of the American Humane Association, conducted a comprehensive 3-year study of child molestation in

New York City that was reported in 1969. His estimate of approximately 3,000 cases each year in New York City alone is probably conservative. Considering the widespread reluctance to recognize and report this condition, it must be assumed that the reported incidents represent a small fraction of the cases.

Nevertheless, the reporting of suspected sexual abuse of children is encompassed in the child abuse reporting statutes of many states. Recent strengthening of these statutes and the establishment of child abuse hotlines has markedly increased the reporting of all forms of child maltreatment. In Connecticut, for example, passage of an expanded child abuse reporting law (P.A. 73-205, effective October 1, 1973), which involves a $500 fine for mandated reporters who fail to report suspected child abuse, resulted in 1,957 reported cases in fiscal year 1974—an increase of nearly 200 percent over the preceding fiscal year. . . .

The opening of the Care-Line, a 24-hour statewide toll-free child abuse prevention and information line, probably had a significant impact since it facilitated the reporting process for many professionals and private citizens who called to express concern about children. The Connecticut Child Welfare Association (CCWA), a private statewide citizens' organization which operates the Care-Line, has also conducted a continuing education effort aimed at both the general public and the professional groups who have been required to report cases of suspected child abuse since 1971. Connecticut's Municipal Police Training Council has cooperated by incorporating lectures on child abuse detection and reporting into their mandatory training program for all newly-hired police officers in 166 of the state's 169 towns. These child abuse training sessions were initiated in 1972 as part of the CCWA Child Advocacy Project and have been conducted by Association staff at 6-week intervals ever since. In October 1973 the two groups jointly sponsored and taught three one-day seminars on child abuse which were attended by higher ranking police officers from all over the state. It is therefore not surprising that the percentage of reports of suspected child abuse by police officers increased markedly in F.Y. 1974, while reports by hospitals decreased proportionately and those by private physicians remained at the same low level— five percent.

It is noteworthy that during this same reporting period, the total number of reports of suspected sexual abuse of children in Connecticut increased, while the proportion of such reports to total child abuse reporting statistics declined slightly. . . .

In fiscal years 1973 and 1974 in Connecticut, the relationship of the perpetrator to the child in all cases of suspected abuse was that of a parent or a parent-substitute in 80 percent of the cases. This complements DeFrancis' finding that parents were involved in the sexual molestation of children in 72 percent of the cases studied—either by perpetration of the offense (25 percent) or else by acts of omission or commission. The most frequently named perpetrator in cases of sexual abuse is the father or a male relative or boyfriend—virtually always someone who has ready access to the child in his or her home. Ages of victims may range from early infancy (one to two months) all the way to 17 or 18 years.

Recognizing Sexual Abuse

Why is sexual molestation of children the last frontier in child abuse? And what are the major obstacles to identifying the sexually abused child?

In practical terms, the answers are lack of recognition of the phenomenon, failure to obtain adequate medical corroboration of the event, and reluctance to report. If one accepts the premise that it is impossible to protect the child victim of sexual molestation unless we know that he exists, these obstacles take on major importance. Each is rooted in ignorance and taboo and must be considered accordingly.

Recognition of sexual molestation in a child is entirely dependent on the individual's inherent willingness to entertain the possibility that the condition may exist. Unfortunately, willingness to consider the diagnosis of suspected child sexual molestation frequently seems to vary in inverse proportion to the individual's level of training. That is, the more advanced the training of some, the less willing they are to suspect molestation.

The lack of preparation and willingness of many physicians to assist patients with sexual problems in general has often been noted. When the patient is a child, these deficiencies are extremely serious.

If the victim of alleged sexual assault is a child, a complete physical examination with careful attention to any other signs of physical abuse or neglect must accompany the routinized perineal examination and laboratory tests. The examination is not complete unless the child is carefully scrutinized for evidence of oral and/or anal penetration as well as genital sexual contact. This includes inspection for trauma as well as laboratory tests for the presence of semen and venereal disease.

Unfortunately, all too few health professionals are trained to look for or to recognize the signs of rectal and urogenital gonorrhea infections in young children. This not only requires a high index of suspicion but again an inherent willingness to entertain the diagnosis of acquired venereal disease in a child. With the exception of congenital syphilis and gonococcal eye infection in newborns, the presence of a gonorrhea or syphilis infection in a child makes it imperative that sexual molestation be suspected unless or until it is ruled out by a careful joint medical and protective services investigation. The U.S. Public Health Service, which operates the National Communicable Disease Center in Atlanta, Georgia, has recently cautioned that "with gonococcal infection in children, the possibility of child abuse must be considered!"

Medical Corroboration of Abuse

The next major obstacle to identifying and helping the child victim of sexual abuse is failure to obtain immediate medical corroboration of the assault. This occurs most frequently on the grounds that physical examination of the child will aggravate and intensify the psychological trauma that may already have been experienced. However, this attitude has little basis in fact and may be detrimental in the extreme to the future protection of the child. A gentle and thorough examination, as outlined above, conducted by a knowledgeable examiner, will be well tolerated by most children. The experience not only can be non-threatening but it may also be reassuring and welcomed by a child victim who is old enough to worry that he or she may have been harmed by the assault. . . .

Reporting Sexual Abuse

Failure to report to the statutory authority is the last major obstacle to identifying the sexually abused child. Sexual abuse of a minor is a reportable condition in every state in the United States. Such a report is the triggering mechanism for a Protective Services investigation of the child and his family—thereby providing a conduit for professional help and community resources to strengthen and improve the home situation or, occasionally, to remove a child from an untenably dangerous environment. Nevertheless, sexual abuse of children is grossly under-reported.

It is unconscionable that any member of the "helping professions" would violate the law as well as withhold potential help from the child victim by failure to report suspected sexual abuse. In most areas it is particularly inappropriate to withhold reports to the statutory authority on the grounds that more effective therapy for delicate internal family matters can be provided surreptitiously by a private agency or private practitioner. Since the success of the private agency's efforts to monitor the home situation for indications of recurrent abuse is directly dependent upon the family's voluntary compliance (which may cease at any time), such reasoning is fallacious. A far more appropriate course for the private help source who discovers the abuse is to report immediately and request to "service" the case in cooperation with the statutory authority. In most cases, cooperation with the frequently superior resources of the private source of help will be eagerly welcomed by the public agency. The result: a higher level of service available to the family as well as increased protection for the child.

For too long health professionals have skirted the issue of reporting suspected sexual molestation when an unmistakable diagnosis of acquired venereal disease has been made in a child. We have been content to do contact investigation within the family circle and to treat other family members—parents, aunts and uncles, older siblings, etc.—for venereal disease without asking why or how a 6-year-old boy acquired a gonorrheal urethritis or a 3-year-old girl contracted pelvic infection with gonococci. Because of reluctance to entertain the possibility of sexual molestation of a child by an adult, we have often postulated modes of transmission of venereal disease to children within the family circle that were long ago discarded in relation to adults, such as the possibility of transmission via clothing, towels and bedsheets. In view of what we know about the epidemiology of gonorrhea and syphilis in adults, it is absurd to cling to an erroneous double standard when we deal with acquired venereal disease in children. We must assume that these children have had some type of sexual contact, most probably with an adult, and investigate accordingly. . . .

Identifying Abused Children

Since we cannot help the sexually abused child and his family unless we know they exist, how then can the major obstacles to identification detailed in this article be overcome? The key role of the physician in obtaining adequate medical corroboration of sexual abuse has not been minimized. Nevertheless, any concerned individual, especially when professionally involved with some aspect of child care, can do much to enhance recognition and reporting of this phenomenon.

First, since this is a phenomenon that thrives and proliferates in darkness, we need to open windows and doors and promote open public discussion of the topic. Increased public awareness is best stimulated by people who care enough to snatch every opportunity to arouse society's consciousness of the child victim of sexual abuse. Only then will the public sanction so vital to identifying and assisting these children be forthcoming. . . .

Lastly, it behooves every professional who deals with children to be aware that sexual molestation exists, to recognize danger signals—especially in high-risk children—and to be knowledgeable about his or her state's reporting laws and sources of help. Sexual abuse of children is certainly not the problem of any single profession or segment of society. A strong united effort is required to push back the last frontier in child abuse and assist the sexually molested child.

117

In the 1980s public concern over the sexual abuse of children, including ritual (sometimes satanic) abuse, became epidemic and led to suspicions of entire towns. In a small town in Minnesota an investigation of child abuse eventually led to the arrest of two dozen people.

By Silence Betrayed
The Sexual Abuse of Children in America

John Crewdson

It was sometime on the afternoon of September 26, 1983, that Judy Kath and Christine Brown, their ten-year-old daughters in tow, marched into the Jordan, Minnesota, police department. The two girls, their mothers said, wanted to talk to someone about James John Rud, a twenty-seven-year-old trash collector who lived by himself in a shabby mobile home at the Valley Green Trailer Park. Jordan's five-man department had no one on its staff who could qualify as an expert in child sexual abuse, certainly not patrolman Larry Norring. But when the girls announced that Rud had been abusing them sexually, Norring did not take their allegations lightly. Later that evening, while Rud was riding his motorcycle on one of the narrow county roads outside of town, Norring pulled him over and placed him under arrest. Had the matter ended there, with a suspect behind bars, it might have been worth a single headline in the Minneapolis papers. But the matter did not end there, and before it was finally over, it would occasion many headlines.

Norring's superiors took the girls' allegations as seriously as he had, and in the days and weeks that followed, the police interviewed a number of other children. Some of them were playmates of the two girls, others the sons and daughters of Rud's neighbors at the trailer park or of women he had befriended at meetings of Alcoholics Anonymous. To the surprise of no one more than the police, many of the children told essentially the same story. As residents of small American towns will attest, very little happens in such places that does not quickly become common knowledge, and no sooner had the investigation begun than dozens of worried parents, particularly those whose children had known Jim Rud or any of his victims, were asking their own sons and daughters whether anything had happened to them. Those who said it had were taken to talk with the police, who by now were struggling to cope with what would have been a major child-abuse case in a city many times the size of Jordan.

When the children were asked whether they knew of any others who had been abused, nearly every child supplied at least one new name. When they were asked who had abused them, many named several adults, often including their own parents. As it unfolded, the tale being told by the children of Jordan was a most improbable one—nobody in Minnesota law enforcement could remember anything remotely like it—and it was being told in a most improbable setting, a Minneapolis suburb distinguished only by the consummate ordinariness of small-town America. With its spired churches, main-street cafés, and simple, sturdy houses, it was possible from a distance to mistake the village of Jordan for a painting on a calendar, or perhaps for Garrison Keillor's mythical hamlet, Lake Wobegon. Seen from up close, Jordan was less picturesque, a little threadbare in places and beginning to sag, but most of those who lived there were the kind of phlegmatic, reliable folk that Keillor has in mind when he says no true Minnesotan accepts an offer of anything until it has been made at least three times.

At the beginning the investigation focused on the Valley Green trailer park, the first stop for those arriving in town and the last for those on their way to somewhere else, but before long it had expanded to include some of the middle-class families who lived in the large, pleasant houses that were, both literally and figuratively, on the other side of the tracks. By then it wasn't only the children who were talking. One morning a woman walked into the police department to report that Rud had been photographing her five-year-old twin daughters in the nude, and that he had probably abused them sexually as well. When she and her children visited Rud's trailer, the woman said, he often took one girl or the other into a back bedroom for a few minutes at a time. As she was leaving, the woman named three other children Rud had molested, not at his trailer but at the house of Judy Kath, one of the two original complainants in the case, who also happened to be Jim Rud's former fiancée.

Less than a month after Judy Kath and Chris Brown had taken their daughters to see Officer Norring, both women were under arrest themselves, Brown charged with abusing Judy Kath's daughter and one of her own, Kath with promoting a minor, her own daughter, to "engage in obscene works." Brown's current boyfriend, her ex-husband, her sister, and her brother-in-law would eventually be charged with the sexual abuse of several other children. So would a deputy sheriff, a truck driver, a printing-equipment operator, an auto-body painter, a waitress at the local truck stop, an employee of the county assessor's office, an eight-year veteran of the Jordan police department, and both of Jim Rud's parents. A few of the defendants in the case were strangers, a few others related by birth or marriage. Most had become acquainted in the ways that people get to know one another in any small town, as neighbors, parishioners, customers, and friends of friends. On the surface the defendants didn't seem much different from anybody else, but the tales their children were telling were growing more horrifying by the day.

One boy, seeking to pinpoint one of the many occasions on which, he said, he had been abused by his parents, remembered that "we had pizza that night, because Mom and Dad went shopping." A girl recalled being abused by a neighbor lady who had just finished fixing her hair into a ponytail. Another boy said he had been abused by his parents in his own living room while watching "Wonder Woman" on TV. A girl said her grandmother had abused her with a pair of scissors before giving her macaroni and cheese for lunch. But not all of the abuse had been so matter-of-fact. There had also been "parties" that sometimes included ten or fifteen adults and as many children, parties where everyone played hide-and-seek or baseball or some other game, the sort of get-togethers one might expect to find on a summer evening in a small Midwestern town— except that, the children said, the outcome of the games had been their parents' way of determining which adults would have sex with which children.

When they talked about the sex, the children described nearly every permutation imaginable—mothers and fathers with sons and daughters, aunts and uncles with nieces and nephews, grandparents with grandchildren, children with one another and even with their pets. At one party, they said, the abusive games were followed by a hot dog supper. At another, everyone had strawberry ice cream afterward. Though they were copied down in the stilted dialect that is the universal trademark of police reports, the children's stories managed to retain some of their innocent language. One boy said his parents had put their mouths on his "freddie." Another talked of being forced to put his penis in his mother's "chinese." A young girl spoke of having been penetrated in both her "front butt" and her "back butt." Some of the children said they were given drugs and liquor, mostly beer and wine but sometimes peppermint schnapps, to encourage their compliance. Others said they had been threatened with being hurt or "sent to jail" or even killed if they did not submit. Some of the children talked freely to the police. Others talked only to the half-dozen child therapists who had been brought in from Minneapolis to help them deal with the aftereffects of the abuse. A few, mostly very young children, were reluctant to talk at all, and a few older ones could not seem to stop talking. As winter gave way to spring, the pages of police reports numbered in the thousands, and still the questioning went on: Who else hurt you? Do you know any other children who were hurt? Is there anything else you haven't told us?

From the day it surfaced, the Jordan case enjoyed the full attention of Kathleen Morris, then thirty-nine, the local prosecuting attorney who had become known for an aggressiveness that bordered on flamboyance and a penchant for working seven-day weeks. Morris, whose waist-length hair and lack of makeup contrasted sharply with her tailored business suits, had already won a reputation beyond the borders of Scott County, the state's second smallest. As a young assistant prosecutor, Morris had made her first headlines when, while prosecuting a narcotics case, she told a reporter that she favored legalizing marijuana. The offhand remark caused a furor, but within a year Morris had been elected chief prosecutor. When she won six convictions in the first child sexual abuse case in Scott County history, she emerged a self-styled champion of children's rights, crisscrossing the state to make speeches about child abuse and to criticize her fellow prosecutors for steering clear of such difficult cases. It wasn't uncommon to hear people say that someday Kathleen Morris was going to be Minnesota's first female attorney general, or maybe its first female governor, but not everybody felt that way. "People either love me or hate me," Morris was fond of saying. "I guess I'd rather they love me, but I'm not going to worry about it if they don't."

By the spring of 1984 the "Jordan sex case" was beginning to attract some national attention, and most of the news reports reflected one of two points of view. According to the prosecutors and the police, what had happened in Jordan was beyond imagination—two dozen men and women, most of them married, most of them parents, many of them solid citizens, had forged a twisted conspiracy of sex and torture with their own children as its victims. According to the defendants and their lawyers, what had actually happened was just as incomprehensible—two dozen men and women, friends, neighbors, and church-goers, were faced with the loss of their savings, their homes, their jobs, and their reputations because their children had lied. For a black fantasy such as the children described to have taken place, the defendants' lawyers said, was plainly impossible. The only thing more inconceivable, the authorities replied, was that the children had made it all up. Privately, not all the lawyers were quick to insist that all the other defendants were equally innocent, or that the whole case was nothing but a children's conspiracy of lies. Some children, most of them agreed, had clearly been abused, but by whom was another question. Ultimately the case was dropped by the prosecutor because of too much inconsistent and conflicting evidence from the children.

118

The sociologist Neil Gilbert provides an important reminder that the public can be incited to excessive fears about the extent of child sexual abuse. While Gilbert may lean too far in the direction of skepticism, his is an important counterweight to recent fears about the pervasiveness of child sexual exploitation (1994).

Miscounting Social Ills

Neil Gilbert

Social policy deliberations have become muddled in recent years by an increasing tendency among advocates for different groups to generate vast and often questionable estimates of social ills afflicting their clients. Advocacy research has not always been that way. The development of social welfare policy in the United States has benefitted from a long and honorable tradition of advocacy research—studies that seek to measure social problems, heighten public awareness of them, and recommend possible solutions. . . .

The expanding volume and declining quality of advocacy research has spawned the use of emotive statistics—startling figures that purport to document "hidden crises" and "silent epidemics." Frequent reports in the media lend authority to these figures as they are brought to national attention.

Consider the story in *The Los Angeles Times* (July 2, 1990), for example, reporting on a study of 32,000 California children in which 25 percent of those surveyed said that "they had gotten away from someone trying to kidnap them." Is it conceivable that one in four children or almost one child in every other family was a victim of attempted kidnapping? On a little reflection, most people would find it difficult to take these figures seriously, but not the professor of social work who conducted the study. In his view, the survey results indicate that California's extensive statewide program to provide children with training to prevent sexual abuse "is effective in teaching youngsters how to deal with the threat of physical and sexual abuse."

In the mid-1980s, fear of kidnappings was intensified by the widely publicized estimate that 50,000 children were being abducted by strangers annually. According to Child Find, an organization devoted to the plight of missing children, only 10 percent of these children were recovered by their parents, another 10 percent were found dead, and the remaining 40,000 cases per year remained unsolved. Prominently reported by the media, these figures first provided sensational headlines that proclaimed a national crisis. Later they became the grist for a Pulitzer Prize winning analysis of the problem in the *Denver Post*, which criticized the risk of child abduction as recklessly inflated. The *Post* revealed an astonishing discrepancy between the 50,000 estimate put forth by crusaders for missing children and the official number of FBI investigations of children abducted by strangers, which totalled sixty-seven cases in 1984.

A closer analysis of these figures by Joel Best in *The Public Interest* shows that if the advocates' estimates of 50,000 are too high, the FBI count of 67 is too low. The FBI's jurisdiction in kidnapping cases is limited to offenses that violate a federal statute, such as transporting a victim across state lines. Only a fraction of the cases reported to local law enforcement authorities come under the Federal Kidnapping Statute. Best demonstrated, on the basis of data from a study by the National Center for Missing and Exploited Children, which included police records on every reported crime in 1984 that involved kidnapping or attempted kidnapping of children in Jacksonville, Florida and Houston, Texas, that a reasonable extrapolation of serious incidents would yield a nationwide estimate of 550 cases annually—about eight times higher than the FBI count, but still ninety times lower than the incidence rate claimed by advocates. . . .

Unlike cases of missing children who are almost always reported to the authorities, child sexual abuse is a difficult problem to document. In 1992, an estimated 499,120 cases of child sexual abuse were reported to child protective services, approximately 40 percent were substantiated. Although an annual incidence rate of 199,648 substantiated cases (about 3 in 1000 children) represents an immense amount of suffering, it does not begin to yield a 25 to 33 percent prevalence rate over the course of childhood. However, many, if not most, incidents of child sexual abuse are never reported to the authorities. The highly publicized prevalence rates of 25 to 33 percent come from surveys of adult women, who are asked to recall if they had experienced any sexual abuse during childhood. The estimates broadcast by child sexual abuse prevention advocates reveal more about the ambiguities of this problem than its magnitude.

At least fifteen surveys conducted since 1976 have attempted to gauge the prevalence of child sexual abuse through self-reports recalled by victims. These studies estimate that the proportion of women sexually abused during their childhood ranges from 6 percent to 62 percent of the population. This is a rather wide spread with half of the studies showing a prevalence rate of 6 to 15 percent. Some of this variance can be accounted for by different research sampling procedures and data gathering techniques. But the most telling factor is the investigators' assorted working definitions of child sexual abuse.

At the high end of these estimates, one of the most extensive and most widely cited studies was conducted by Diana Russell, who reports in *Sexual Exploitation* that 54 percent of her respondents were victims of incestuous or extrafamilial sexual abuse before the age of eighteen. This prevalence rate was based on a broad definition of child sexual abuse under which children who merely receive unwanted hugs and kisses are classed as victims, as are others who have not been touched at all (for example, children who encounter exhibitionists). A lower rate of 38 percent was registered with a narrower definition that involved "unwanted sexual experiences ranging from attempted petting to rape" by persons outside the family and "any kind of exploitive sexual contact or attempted contact" by relatives. The information, used to determine an episode of sexual abuse, was based on responses to fourteen screening questions such as these:

—Did anyone ever try or succeed in touching your breasts or genitals against your wishes before you turned fourteen?

—Did anyone ever feel you, grab you, or kiss you in a way you felt was threatening?

—At any time in your life has an uncle, brother, father, grandfather, or female relative ever had any kind of sexual contact with you?

What this study characterizes as a "narrower" definition of child sexual abuse actually stretches from attempted petting to any exploitive contact such as touching on the leg or other body parts to forced sexual intercourse, fellatio, and other forms of penetration. When one thinks of child sexual abuse, an incident of attempted petting, a touch on the leg, and an unwanted pat on the buttock hardly come to mind. By lumping together relatively harmless behavior such as attempted petting with the terribly damaging ordeal of child rape, advocates have inflated the estimates of child sexual abuse to critical proportions.

More recently, in an effort to assess the effectiveness of sexual abuse prevention training programs, David Finkelhor and colleagues report in "The Effectiveness of Victimization Prevention Instruction: An Evaluation of Children's Responses to Actual Threats and Assaults" a 42-percent prevalence rate of "victimization" among 2,000 children surveyed. These "victimizations" included fights and attempted assaults by peers, gangs, or family members, kidnapping, and sexual abuse.

Measures of sexual abuse included positive responses to broadly worded questions such as: "Has there ever been a time when an older person tried to feel you, grab you, or kiss you in a sexual way that made you feel bad or afraid?"

By equating as "victimizations," school yard scraps, attempted fights, unwanted squeezes, and kisses that "feel bad" with kidnapping and rape of children, the researchers construct a 42-percent "victimization" rate, which presumably reveals the pressing need for sexual-abuse-prevention training. When sexual victimization is separated out from other forms of victimization, the prevalence rate drops to 6 percent. Since half of these involve attempted cases, the findings show an actual sexual abuse prevalence rate of 3 percent, which includes kisses and touches that felt bad.

119

Sylvia Ann Hewlett's book When the Bough Breaks *is a wide-ranging analysis of the dangers our children face and the unwillingness of parents and society to pay attention to their needs. Here she focuses on the use of psychiatric hospitals by middle-class parents to temporarily rid themselves of troubled kids (1991).*

Psychiatric Hospitals for Juveniles?

Sylvia Ann Hewlett

It's time for a commercial break on a local TV station in Louisiana, and the face of a distraught, weeping father fills the screen. He is talking about how he never listened to his son, how he never paid enough attention to him, and now it is too late. The man pauses, swallows hard, and then tells us that his son has just committed suicide. A violin starts to play, a heart-tugging backdrop to the pathetic sounds of a father crying over his son's suicide. At this point the sales pitch comes on: viewers are urged to consider seeking professional help if they are having difficulty with their children. The not-so-subtle message is: Let your friendly, neighborhood, for-profit, psychiatric hospital fix your kid—before anything really bad happens.

The images conjure up every parent's nightmare. They certainly make for a powerful brand of advertising that's attracting thousands of new patients to psychiatric hospitals around the nation. In 1971, 6,500 children and teenagers were hospitalized in private psychiatric facilities in the United States. By 1989 this figure had reached approximately 200,000. At least some of these youngsters are in dire need of inpatient hospital treatment, but it seems that anxious, preoccupied parents are increasingly using psychiatric admission as a method of "parking" troublesome but otherwise normal teenagers. Psychiatrist Marvin Schwarz, who runs three juvenile psychiatric programs in the Chicago area, blames the swelling tide of hospital admissions on parents "who are too wrapped up in seeking self-satisfaction through careers to set limits for their children." But it's not just a question of absorbing careers. Divorce and single parenthood seem to trigger a large proportion of these psychiatric admissions. A startling percentage of children in residential treatment—over 80 percent—are from families in which the biological parents no longer live together.

Whatever the factors that precipitate psychiatric admission, most of these teens do not suffer from serious mental disorders. A recent study at the University of Michigan found that 70 percent of adolescent psychiatric admissions are "inappropriate and potentially harmful" to the children concerned. A 1988 review by Blue Cross of Minnesota came up with the following examples of teenagers who had been hospitalized unnecessarily:

- A fifteen-year-old boy was hospitalized for 102 days after discharge from a chemical-dependency unit. His mother dropped him off at the psychiatric hospital before going on vacation. He had a history of drug use, fighting with his parents, and running away. When hospitalized he complained of hallucinating and a fear of death, but later admitted that this was a ploy to stay in treatment because he did not want to go home.
- A fourteen-year-old girl was admitted for evaluation because her mother said she had trouble setting limits for her daughter. The girl apparently had left home twice without permission to stay with her father and stepmother. It was determined that the girl did not suffer from depression, but nevertheless she was kept in the hospital for eighty-five days.

As one might expect, the experience of being locked up in a psychiatric hospital for two or three months has "substantial negative effects" on most normal adolescents. These run the gamut from feelings of powerlessness, helplessness, and rage to the trauma of exposure to children who are seriously emotionally disturbed.

And then there is the question of expense. Adolescent psychiatric patients stay in the hospital for 30 to 100 days, at a cost of $500 to $1,000 a day. These costs can quickly mount. In 1988 it cost the Defense Department a whopping $270 million to provide inpatient psychiatric care for the troubled children of military personnel. For many U.S. corporations juvenile psychiatric care is now the fastest-growing medical expense.

For middle-class parents these huge costs are often hidden because most up-front expenses associated with psychiatric hospital care are picked up by an insurance carrier. In the end, of course, we all pay the bill. Medical insurance costs go through the roof and are passed on to employers and workers in the form of higher insurance rates, diminished medical coverage, and lower profits and earnings. . . .

The explosive growth of juvenile psychiatric care in the 1970s and 1980s is a distressing story. The chaos of family life and the pain of neglected adolescents have been cleverly exploited by private entrepreneurs who seduce and entrap desperate parents and their luckless children. "We entice parents, and I can't stand that," says Karen Brugler, director of adolescent programs at the Lutheran General Hospital in Chicago. "We're on television all the time, giving parents the idea that if they take their kids into a hospital, they'll come out scrubbed and fresh and beautiful again. That's not how it works." But if the system is not working for kids it's certainly working for the private sector. Hospital chains like

National Medical Enterprises and Community Psychiatric Corp. are growing at
20 percent a year and raking in large profits. The emotional problems of young
people are now big business.

These extraordinary developments in hospital psychiatric care are powerful
examples of how the integrity of children can be violated by the market. They
also illustrate the potentially disastrous consequences of government inaction. In
an age where neglect, chaos, and rage litter the adolescent landscape, we need
something more substantial than a permissive, minimalist state if we are to save
our children. "Parental discretion," no matter how unbridled, fails to cut the
mustard.

120

In 1987 the issue of extreme child endangerment exploded into the news with the case of Lisa Steinberg, beaten to death by her adoptive parents, white middle-class professionals who were addicted to cocaine. Her death made it clear that all children, regardless of class or color, could face threats from within their own households.

Couple Held in Beating of Daughter

Todd S. Purdum

A Manhattan lawyer and a former children's book editor were charged yesterday with the attempted murder of their 6-year-old daughter after the police answered a call for medical help at the couple's Greenwich Village apartment and found that the girl had been severely beaten.

The lawyer, Joel Barnet Steinberg, 46, and the former editor, Hedda Nussbaum, 45, of 14 West 10th Street, were charged after they refused to make any statements about the girl's injuries. The police said the couple were not married, but had lived together for 17 years.

The girl, Elizabeth, was listed in extremely critical condition at St. Vincent's Hospital, with bleeding in the brain and bruises to her head and spine, the authorities said.

Miss Nussbaum had cuts and bruises around her eyes and a bandage on her nose, and had apparently also been beaten, the police said. She declined to cooperate in the investigation, the police said.

After the couple were arrested, the police said neighbors in their building told them that they had heard "screams and thumping" coming from the family's apartment for some time, but they never reported it.

A spokeswoman for the city's Human Resources Administration, Suzanne Trazoff, said she did not immediately know whether reports of abuse of the children had ever been brought to the city's child welfare agency. If such reports had been made, she said, they would be confidential.

The authorities learned of the case yesterday when Miss Nussbaum called the 911 emergency telephone number at 6:33 A.M. to report that Elizabeth was choking on food and was having trouble breathing.

Officers arrived at the apartment, in a building where Mark Twain once lived.

Officer Vincent Daluise, one of the responding officers, said the girl "was filthy and she wasn't breathing." He said the apartment looked like "it wasn't cleaned in about a year," and although the electricity was on in the apartment, none of the lights were working.

Inside the apartment, the couple's 18-month-old son, Mitchell, had been tied to a playpen with a 3½ foot piece of twine around his waist, and was covered with his urine, according to the commander of Manhattan detectives, Assistant Chief Aaron H. Rosenthal.

"The girl's feet were so black, they had to scrape the dirt off them, and she was suffering from a lack of oxygen," Chief Rosenthal said. She was in a coma yesterday at St. Vincent's, the police said. Mitchell was examined at St. Vincent's and was placed in the custody of the city's Office of Special Services for Children.

A senior police official who spoke on the condition that he not be identified said the children had apparently been adopted with the help of a gynecologist who was a friend of the couple. But the official said the police had questions about the legality of the adoption of the younger child because they were unable to find copies of the boy's adoption papers.

The police said Mr. Steinberg apparently had his own law practice and was not part of any firm, but they said they did not know the details of his business. Court records list him as having been admitted to the bar on July 7, 1970.

Several names and the words Greenwich Petroleum Ltd. appeared under Mr. Steinberg's name on his mailbox at the five-story, red brick house, but the police said they did not know whether he worked at home or elsewhere.

Miss Nussbaum worked for several years as an editor in the juvenile publishing division of Randon House until she was dismissed about six years ago for absenteeism and other reasons, according to an editor of the New York publishing house.

A man who lives on the first floor of the building but would not give his name said he knew Mr. Steinberg. "I had very little contact with him," the man said. "We said hello in the halls."

The man said he had not heard screams or noises coming from the couple's apartment, 3W. He said the couple's daughter "was a really beautiful child when she was younger," but recently the girl "really looked unhappy a lot."

Deputy Inspector Robert R. Frankel told reporters at a news conference at the Sixth Precinct station house yesterday that the police had responded to the couple's apartment on Oct. 6 presumably because Miss Nussbaum had been beaten. He said the police "noticed a slight injury and both were referred to the court" but there was no indication that the children had been abused.

Chief Rosenthal said that when the police and Emergency Medical Service workers went to the apartment yesterday, they found bruises on Elizabeth's right forehead that "were a couple of days old," and other bruises over the rest of her body. When the girl was taken to the hospital, he said, doctors determined the injuries were "obviously not from a fall."

The police said the girl's teacher at Public School 41 on West 11th Street told them yesterday afternoon that she had recently noticed what appeared to be bruises on the girl, but had not reported it. Investigators said the school principal also noticed that the girl had exhibited a diminished interest and alertness at school since last winter. The police did not know when the girl was last seen in school.

Chief Rosenthal said the couple had requested lawyers and had refused to cooperate in the investigation. "They're both very aware of their rights," he said.

They were charged with second-degree attempted murder, first-degree assault and endangering the welfare of a child. They were held pending arraignment.

121

The mistreatment of infants recently caught the attention of child advocates and the American public when British researchers used videotapes to record parental mistreatment (1997).

A Glimpse into a Hell for Helpless Infants

New York Times

Child abuse typically occurs behind a veil of family privacy and deceit. In the current issue of the journal *Pediatrics*, British researchers part that veil a bit. And the picture they present is harrowing.

The researchers got the permission of the British child-welfare authorities to clandestinely videotape parents visiting their children hospitalized after suspected incidents of abuse. From 1986 to 1994, hidden cameras at two hospitals filmed 39 children, aged 2 months to 4 years, alone with their parents. In all but 6 of the cases, the cameras caught either mother or father kicking, slapping, trying to suffocate or otherwise physically abusing his or her child in the hospital. One mother broke her baby's left arm. Many of the abusers adopted affectionate behavior toward their children as soon as nurses walked into the room. Most had serious personality disorders.

The videotaping was set up to gather enough evidence to prosecute abusers but permit nearby hospital staff to intervene when a child's life was in danger. Citing privacy and legal issues, the authorities have declined to make the tapes or names public. But transcripts of written logs kept by those who monitored the videotaping were published in Pediatrics along with the researchers' findings. The logs are excerpted here.

The case: a 6-week-old boy taken to the hospital after three unexplained episodes of near-suffocation. The infant is visited by his father, who three years earlier had been present at the death of his infant stepson, which was classified at the time as sudden infant death syndrome. The videotaping begins:

Day 1, 10:51 P.M.: The father said to the infant, "I will bounce you off the canteen roof."

10:52 P.M.: The father said to the infant that when the infant became older he "will beat, whip, remove fingernails, and amputate his limbs."

Day 2, 2:04 P.M.: The father deliberately wakes[the baby] up.

2:11 P.M.: The father wakes him by tweaking his ear.

2:13 P.M.: Repeated.

2:15 P.M.: Repeated.

2:17 P.M.: Repeated.

2:19 P.M.: The father flicks [the baby's] eyelids while asleep.

2:22 P.M.: The father obstructs his nasal orifices for 20 seconds before a nurse enters.

9:41 P.M.: The father places his hand over the mouth; the infant struggles for 25 seconds. The father hears a noise outside and stops.

Day 3, 9:51 P.M.: The father puts his finger into the infant's throat.

9:53 P.M.: As above; the infant gags and cries, and the mother appears.

10:29 P.M.: The father pinches his hands. Infant wakes from sleep, cries, and then sobs. The father tells the mother who comes in that the infant had "just woke up crying."

Day 6, 9:16 P.M.: The father digs his nail into the infant's palm repeatedly. The infant cries.

9:20 P.M.: The father pinches his left hand.

9:38 P.M.: The infant is asleep. The father shouts, "Wakey, wakey," and the infant wakes up.

9:41 P.M.: The father suffocates the infant by placing his right hand over the nose and mouth and forcing the back of the infant's head into his left hand. The infant struggles for 25 seconds before a noise outside the room causes the father to remove his hand.

Aftermath: Informed of the videotaping, the father admitted to the abuse of his son and to the manslaughter of his stepson earlier. He was committed to a mental institution.

The case: a 3-month-old girl who suffered several episodes of near-suffocation. At the hospital before videotaping begins, nurses find the baby choking and gray after being left alone briefly with her mother, a 19-year-old with a history of behavioral disorders. The videotaping begins:

Day 1, 2:02 P.M.: The mother slaps the infant's head.

2:03 P.M.: Repeated.

2:09 P.M.: Repeated.

2:58 P.M.: The mother swears at the infant, accusing her of being responsible for them having to remain in hospital. There is growing anger, with the mother repeatedly ordering the infant to kiss her. The interaction is as follows:

- "Give me a kiss, you little sod, give me a kiss. Kiss! Kiss! Kiss! Kiss!" . . .
- "I'm sick of it. Bloody sick of it. All the bloody time, mummy, mummy, mummy."
- "Stinking mummy, mummy, mummy." (Bounces roughly on knee.)
- "Rock a bye, rock, rock a bye." (Holds child up by her arms.)
- "Dance, dance, dance." (Shakes, lifts by arms, sings.)

3:01 P.M.: The mother roughly patted the child's face 14 times and then pressed her hand forcibly against the child's face. . . . She then started to shake the infant like a doll.

3:02 P.M.: The mother deliberately and forcefully bent back the infant's left arm at the elbow. The force used led to the elbow going way beyond 180 degrees. The infant started screaming. The mother pressed the nurse alarm call button. When the nurse came in, the mother stated that the child had caught her arm in one of the toys attached to the cot as she was trying to lift her. The child was examined by a doctor, who was unsure as to whether there was a fracture.

Unfortunately, the mother was then left alone for about 30 seconds, and again she forcibly bent back the child's left arm at the elbow, causing her to scream.

3:06 P.M.: The surveillance ends, mother separated from child.

Aftermath: Confronted with the findings of the video surveillance, the mother became enraged and tried to remove the infant from the ward. She was restrained and arrested. The infant, whose arm was broken, was eventually adopted, as was her abused 17-month-old sister.

The case: an 18-month-old girl who had been in and out of the hospital since birth with episodes of near-suffocation, cardiac arrest and other crises. Her mother had a history of behavioral disorders and drug abuse. The log entries:

Day 2, 12:20 P.M.: The mother tells the child that if she doesn't stop making a noise, she will smack her hard and "I don't want to do that in the hospital."

3:18 P.M.: The mother smacks the child with a toy hammer.

3:26 P.M.: The child calls "mummy." The mother smacks her.

4:08 P.M.: The mother deliberately pinches the child, who begins to cry and develops breath-holding. She reaches for comfort from her mother but is ignored. After 20 seconds, the mother presses an alarm to call the nurses. They don't appear. . . . The mother hears the nurse coming but the breath-holding has stopped; she slaps the child hard on the leg. The child cries and the nurse enters the room. The mother appears to be comforting the child.

7:51 P.M.: The mother says "lie down and sleep," then hits her hard on the back. She then immediately strokes the child's back.

7:53 P.M.: The mother smacks her hard on the bottom, then on the top of the leg and says "go to sleep."

8:03 P.M.: The child sits up. The mother smacks her and then pushes tissues up her nose. The child cries.

8:15 P.M.: The mother says, "I'm going out. I don't love you anymore, babe."

Day 4, 11:59 A.M.: The mother slaps the child hard.

1:28 P.M.: The mother slaps the child, the child cries.

1:30 P.M.: The mother is softly rubbing the child's forehead. Suddenly she turns and hits her on the forehead.

2:52 P.M.: The mother is throwing toy bricks into a box past the child's head. Gradually she increases the force of throwing and then a brick hits the child on the head. The child cries out in pain and begins to hold her breath.

3:54 P.M.: The mother picks up the child roughly. She places her hand over the child's mouth for 1 to 2 seconds. She wipes her face hard with tissues. The child is trying to move away but is held tight. The mother then slaps the child hard on the face. The child cries. After 1 minute of crying, the mother cuddles and cuddles her.

4:14 P.M.: The child walks past the mother who deliberately trips her up with her leg and kicks her in the abdomen and back on three occasions. The child cries and reaches for her mother, who initially ignores her and then, suddenly, picks her up and cuddles her.

4:41P.M.: The mother changes the child's nappy. The child is passive and lies on the bed quietly for 2 minutes. She then attempts to get up. The mother takes a pillow and forces it over the child's head. The child struggles to breathe. After 8 seconds the mother removes the pillow but then replaces it for 3 seconds. . . . A nurse enters the room after being alerted by CVS [covert video surveillance] observers.

Aftermath: The mother was convicted of child abuse and her child placed with a foster family.

The videotaping was done at North Staffordshire Hospital in Stoke-on-Trent and Royal Brompton Hospital in London. The researchers, led by Dr. David P. Southall, a pediatrics professor at Keele University in Staffordshire, say such videotaping might help save lives.

122

In a notorious case in Delaware in 1996 two teenagers, both college freshmen, were prosecuted for killing their newborn. They subsequently pleaded guilty.

An Infant's Death, an Ancient "Why?"

Jan Hoffman

Discordant images from a Wilmington, Del., courthouse last week:

Two chipmunk-cheeked college freshmen, blushing, tearful, whispering as they sit at the defense table. After the hearing, their fingertips brush in farewell.

Then both are returned to prison, having just pled not guilty to the intentional or reckless murder of their newborn son, found abandoned last month in a motel Dumpster.

Their lawyers say the baby was brain-damaged and did not survive delivery. But if, as prosecutors say, the infant was born healthy and died from a fractured skull and from being shaken, the couple committed a stark act of incomprehensible immorality. Yet it would be only the latest example of neonaticide, or the killing of an infant within the first 24 hours of life.

Many early civilizations, including the Greeks, left ailing babies on hillsides to die. Eskimos would kill one of most sets of twins; the Chinese would sacrifice an infant daughter to save the cost of a dowry.

As ancient and as much-debated as neonaticide itself is the question of how society should view it. Throughout history, many cultures have uneasily sanctioned the act as a response to severe social, emotional or economic stress.

The English grappled with the not-uncommon killings of newborns by poor mothers and unmarried servant girls. In the early 19th century, according to one scholar, juries were reluctant to send such women to the gallows:"Those juries knew that at or about the time of birth, dogs, cats and sows sometimes kill their own young. They were not prepared to extend less compassion and concern to a mentally sick woman than they would to an excitable bitch."

Since 1922, England has had an infanticide law providing that mothers who kill babies up to a year old should face charges of manslaughter, not murder. Such women are given psychiatric treatment and rarely serve prison terms.

American law is not so forgiving. It does not carve out lenient exceptions in its homicide statutes for certain victims, "regardless of whether they are one second or 50 years old," said Joshua Dressler, a professor at the McGeorge School of Law in Sacramento.

While the facts of neonaticides are often similar, a prosecutor has great discretion over how to charge each case. If Brian C. Peterson, Jr. or Amy S. Grossberg, whose son was found in a trash container outside the Comfort Inn in Newark, Del., are convicted of first-degree murder—lesser charges were not included in the indictment—they could face life in prison or the death penalty. But in the case of a New York college student whose conviction for killing her newborn was upheld last month, prosecutors charged her with manslaughter, a jury found her guilty of the lesser charge of criminally negligent homicide and she was sentenced to one-and-a-third to four years.

Tracking this crime is difficult, because many corpses are never discovered. Using Justice Department statistics, one estimate puts the number at about 250 a year. Dr. Phillip J. Resnick, a professor of psychiatry at Case Western Reserve medical school, who coined the term "neonaticide" in 1970, said that the number is on the decline because of the availability of birth control and abortion.

Typically, neonaticides are committed by young, isolated women in severe denial of their pregnancy. If they have irregular menstrual periods, they may not realize that they are pregnant soon enough to have an abortion. Doctors say that small, fit women may not develop a belly; one mother said she had seen her teen-age daughter naked the night before she gave birth and had not noticed anything remarkable about the girl's figure.

Profoundly unprepared, the women find themselves giving birth in department store bathrooms and college dorms. The trauma of delivery, followed by the crying of a newborn, crashes through the thickest walls of denial. Women try to stifle the wails by strangling the baby, stuffing tissues down its throat, drowning it in the toilet. Then they throw the tiny corpses in trash compactors, leave them in dresser drawers, even toss them out windows.

Such acts are shocking to a society that cherishes the concept of bonding that begins in utero and prompt many to see neonaticide as the most inhuman of murders. But Dr. Resnick said a woman who desperately does not want to be pregnant can mentally foreclose attachment. "This is a foreign body going through her, not a baby, and the bonding never occurs," he said. "She doesn't think of it as her child but as an object to get rid of."

Some psychiatrists believe many of these women are legally sane and should be charged with some offense, since a mother's attempt to hide the body shows that she knew what she did was wrong. Powerful postpartum depression brought on by riotous hormones can be the basis of an insanity defense but it does not set in until days later, some doctors say.

But Dr. Margaret Spinelli, the director of a maternal mental health program at Columbia-Presbyterian Hospital in New York City, said that women she has treated describe a corrosive breakdown. "They're dissociated from pregnancy, intercourse and reproduction," she said. "Then they deliver and they panic because they're not sure what's happening. It's like driving down a highway but not remembering how they got there: they're charged with killing their child and they don't even have their memories as their own defense."

The case of Ms. Grossberg and Mr. Peterson has confounded many experts not because of their privileged background but because the act is almost always done by a woman alone.

Rarer still is an indictment for capital murder for such a crime. Dr. Resnick questioned whether this is appropriate for two people without prior records. Though he takes a stern view of neonaticide, he added, "they're being charged as if they did something worse than robbing a 7-Eleven store and shooting the clerk."

123

By the 1990s the threat to children seemed everywhere. In 1994 Hillary Rodham Clinton spoke out against television news media's obsessive coverage of violent crimes and its possible effects on young viewers.

Media Violence and Children

Hillary Rodham Clinton

American children are immersed in a culture of violence. They see violence on television. They see violence in movie theaters. They see it on the streets where they live. They see it in their schools. They see it in their homes.

In too many neighborhoods, gunfire has become a daily ritual of life. An Uzi has become a badge of honor. A bullet wound has become an emblem of adulthood. Just this last week, on Monday, I was across the country, in New York, where I visited a very large hospital in Brooklyn, a hospital that treats gunshot wounds and knife wounds every hour.

And the doctors there told me that the most discouraging part of their work is that the age of the victims gets younger and younger, and that after they finish patching up a 13 or 14-year old from a gang shooting or a drive-by shooting, or a knife fight, they anticipate they will see that same young person in just a few months or years again.

In Washington, our nation's capital, a young four-year-old girl was shot in the head when young men opened fire on an elementary school playground as a crowd watched a pickup football game.

Last summer, again in Washington, gunshots rang out at a pool as children sought relief from 90-degree heat. A young mother is dragged by the side of her car during a car jacking that had the child in the car and the mother being killed trying to hang on to the car.

I could tell you many, many stories like that, but I think you know what happens every day in every neighborhood. This horrible chronicle of malicious violence goes on and on, every day and every week, every month, across the nation.

The reason we know about these tragic incidents—the murders, the car jackings, the kidnappings, the beatings, the rapes—is because the news media reports about them. And I'm sure that everyone in this audience today would agree that reporting about these sorts of incidents is part of the news media's job.

I think we all agree that the public needs to know about crime and violence. I'm sure that, to some degree, news coverage of crime has heightened public support for deterrents such as gun control. And it might also help this Administration and this President get a crime bill with real possible hope for change this year.

At the same time, we have to stop and ask ourselves some very important questions:

First, has the exhaustive—and perhaps excessive—coverage of violence contributed to increasing alienation and dysfunctional behavior on the part of our children and youth?

And second, does the news coverage engender so much cynicism and distrust among young people that they grow up with no faith in any of our institutions and little motivation to make something of their own lives?

These are questions I hope you will explore and that I think we must answer.

Over the past few years, a lot of attention has been paid to violence in movies and in television programming, and in the records that young people listen to. And on that score, things are beginning to improve. As the President said earlier this week, the entertainment industry has—as a result of public concerns—become much more involved in efforts to reduce violence in network programming. Their willingness to set up a voluntary monitoring system is a step in the right direction.

In the meantime, we're only now beginning to focus on the issue of violence and the news media, and it's a very tricky issue, given that information today comes from so many different sources—newspapers, radio, local television, network television, television tabloids. This is an issue that must be addressed, even as we recognize that these different news media sometimes go about their jobs in different ways.

Just yesterday I read about the results of a new survey put out by the Center for Media and Public Affairs. It showed that network news coverage of murder and violence had doubled last year—even though the nation's overall crime rate had remained the same.

Some of the coverage was a result of unusual cases, like the Branch Davidians, the World Trade Center bombing, the Menendez brothers' trial, the Polly Klass case, and the murders of tourists in Florida.

But what about the rest? Were the stories really newsworthy? Or were they part of a troubling pattern of sensationalism that threatens to desensitize viewers—particularly children—to the point where violence is considered a normal, accepted part of life?

Children Now's recent survey reports that young people are deeply affected by news stories they read or see on television. More than half the children surveyed said they felt angry or depressed after watching or reading the news.

And about 60 percent of kids between the ages of 11 and 16 said the news too often conveyed negative images of young people.

The fact is that we all want to stop violence. We all want our children to experience their childhoods without being afraid, without being vulnerable, and without being insecure.

We want them to be able to be children—to feel safe in school, to enjoy sports and recreation, to develop extracurricular interests, and to build healthy relationships.

But those kinds of positive childhood experiences seem less and less real to children who are routinely bombarded with words and pictures that seldom portray young people living that way. Saturating children with increasingly graphic and sensational stories of violence prevents them from developing the emotional and psychological tools they need to deal with violence.

One of the biggest dangers of excessive coverage of violence is that, in a child's eye, the stories validate, sometimes even glamorize, dysfunctional behavior. Violence becomes normal—and, in an odd way, even painless. It becomes harder for a child to distinguish between fact and fiction. The latest drive-by shooting on the evening news looks a lot like the Terminator blowing his fictional enemy to bits on the movie screen.

The second danger of excessive coverage is that children become numbed—or, as social scientists say, "desensitized"—to violence. Children become so habituated to seeing and hearing about violence that shootings, beatings—even death—come to seem normal to them.

They develop an ironic detachment from life, a fatalism that prevents them from trusting anyone or anything. Recently I read a story about young children planning their own funerals. These children were so sure they were going to die violently that they had told their families what clothes they wanted to wear at their funerals, what music they wanted played, all with a casual detachment about what living and dying really means.

The third danger of excessive coverage of violence is that it exacerbates stereotypes. If African-American and Latino youth are usually portrayed on the news committing crimes, that stereotype is etched into the public consciousness. The same is true for women, who are often portrayed as victims.

Whether coverage of violence actually incites violent acts is one question we have to answer, and I know that researchers have debated it for years. Another equally important question is whether such coverage leaves us—and particularly children—with the impression that no one in our society ever does anything good or anything right.

For example, if children hear story after story about priests or clergy who molest children—but never hear about those priests and clergy members who help children—they are not likely to grow up trusting their churches. And yet, there are far more priests and ministers, and rabbis, in this country helping children than hurting them.

We need to ask ourselves whether some of our news coverage contributes to this lack of trust and whether it perpetuates a cynical detachment which, in turn, leads to abnormal behavior, including violence. Of course, I'm not suggesting that all news coverage of violence is bad or wrong, or that the media's treatment of violence alone accounts for our social ills. As I said earlier, the public has to be kept informed, including children.

124

A teenager living in a foster home tells of the abuse she experienced at the hands of her mother and how she herself often resorted to violence (1996).

A Teenage Voice from Foster Care

Autobiographical Document

Saretta Andrea Burkett, "I Won't Abuse My Kids"

It's a weekday evening. I'm sitting on top of my bed, sobbing profusely. Just received a beating from my mother. What did I do to deserve it? I can't really remember.

Sometimes I'd get beat if I talked back to grandma. Other times, for touching something in the house that didn't belong to me. Or for forgetting to clean out the tub after I'd used it.

Really didn't matter what I'd get beat for. At the end of some whippings, I'd sit on my bed and say to myself, *When I have kids, I'm never gonna beat them.*

Mother demanded that I take my punishment in dignity and silence. "Like a woman," she would sneer. Any yelping or whimpering from me would cause her to strike again. Beatings were endless, until I choked, literally, to hold down the screams.

You will read this, I'm sure, and conclude that I was a victim of abuse. But at the time, it wasn't obvious to either mother or me.

You see, mother thought children were victims of abuse only if they'd been molested sexually, beaten into unconsciousness, or abandoned in the streets. No, to mother I wasn't being abused. She was simply raising me the best way she knew how.

During my first year in the system, after tearful nights and weekly sessions with the resident therapist, I was able to acknowledge to myself that I had been abused. However, I wasn't aware that mother's abusive patterns were very much alive and growing within me.

In the group home I was known for my hot temper and quick, violent ways of ending disputes. Little mistakes made by the girls would send me flying into a hot rage. I'd cool off only after several doors had been kicked and a few glasses broken. Concerned counselors would pull me aside, but I waved away my actions as just "blowing off steam."

One Thanksgiving Day I visited my grandmother's house. (Also residing there are my mother, my aunt Lunette, and her ten-year-old son, my cousin Clyde.)

On this particular weekend, both Auntie Lunette and mother were at work. Grandmother and Clyde were home. After about an hour of chatting and watching television, grandma stepped away to take a shower, leaving me to tend to young Clyde.

Before leaving, she gave me specific instructions to call for her if Clyde misbehaved. "Don't give Saretta trouble, Clyde," she said, and went off.

Well, as soon as Clyde heard water running in the shower, he decided to turn the television from the Thanksgiving parade to the cartoon channel, which grandma had advised him not to do.

"Yo, Clyde," I said sternly, "chill with the TV."

In minutes, a matter as trivial as what television station to watch evolved into a major dispute, which Clyde ended with the words, "You're not my mother. I'm not listening to you."

I felt humiliated. Here I was, eighteen years old, being dictated to by someone eight years my junior. I wanted Clyde to listen. I wanted him to obey me. So I did to him what mother had done to me so many times before: I hit him across the face with the back of my hand.

In doing so, I was careful not to cause him too much pain, but enough to make him realize I was serious. He shouted in agony and rushed my legs with punches as hard as his little hands could throw.

"What?" I said, both shocked and angry that this ten-year-old had actually hit me back. In a moment, faster than it takes for a person to think, I grabbed the remote control and swung it at Clyde's head.

Everything happened so quickly. The remote dropped from my hand and my body trembled as I noticed blood streaming from a gash in Clyde's head.

"Oh my God oh my God oh my God oh my God oh my God oh my God oh my God, Jesus, I didn't mean to hit you, Clyde!"

He was screaming at the top of his lungs. Never had he seen so much blood. I tried to subdue his screams and put my hands over his mouth, but Clyde shoved me away and yelled all the louder.

At this point, I was more worried about stopping the blood than keeping him quiet. Wads of red Kleenex tissue were strewn on the floor. In looking at the amount of blood this kid was shedding, I panicked: Clyde might need medical attention.

Grandma heard the screams and came running out of the shower, wet and dripping, clad only in a towel.

"Oh my gosh! I leave you with Clyde for one minute and this is what happens? Oh my gosh!"

She pulled him into the bathroom and was able to stop the bleeding. I walked back into grandma's room, stared out the window, blankly reflecting on what [had] taken place in a matter of seconds. *My temper*, I said to myself, *I need help*.

Minutes later grandma came back, freshly clothed, along with Clyde. His face and neck were wiped clean of blood. There was nothing but a small Band-aid, smack dab across the center of his forehead.

I could only stand there and look at him. I had wanted him to be afraid of me just so he would obey. And now I had left a scar on him. Grandma split the blame between us: Clyde for not listening and me for hitting him.

But there was nothing she could say to rid me of my guilt. At first I was going to hang around until mother got home from work, but now I decided it wouldn't be such a good idea.

The subway ride from Brooklyn to my group home in lower Manhattan was a most agonizing one. I put on my Walkman in an attempt to forget what happened, but there was no distracting me. Echoes of Clyde's frightful screams filled my brain. I opened my hands and stared at them for a while, not quite believing that I had hurt a child, my own cousin, no less.

A couple of minutes prior to entering Marian Hall, my group home, I looked at my reflection in a car window and checked for any traces of tears. "I'm fine," I assured myself, choked up though I was. I walked into my floor and the area was bustling with activity, as is normal on a Saturday afternoon.

Before I could even duck and hide myself in my room, one of the girls called out, "Hey, Saretta, you got blood on your shirt."

That did it. The protective wall I'd built for myself was crumbling fast and I needed to talk. Barbara, the staff on duty at the time, pulled me to the patio where it was more private. Five cigarettes later, I spilled the beans. I told her everything: how I felt, what I did, and how sincerely sorry I was.

Barbara sympathized with me but did agree that I was in need of help, professional or otherwise. She also pointed out that my violent tendencies may have stemmed from the abuse I experienced as a child.

As mentioned at the start of this article, I did accept having been abused by my mother. But until now I hadn't accepted or even dealt with being a potential abuser of others.

It was somewhat disturbing to think that I was becoming exactly what I hated in my mother. Part of me wanted to remain in the comfort of denial, but I knew that minimizing the seriousness of the situation would lead to more expressions of violence. . . .

No matter what form of help you seek in dealing with anger, none will guarantee you an overnight solution. It's like writing with your left hand your whole life and suddenly deciding to switch to your right.

I still get angry. But there is relief in knowing that I'm doing something about it.

It's also good to know that in the near future, when it's my turn to raise children, I will have had some time to practice being human and more sensitive to the feelings of others.

Saretta Andrea Burkett, 19, entered the system in 1992. She believes foster care should be a last resort, only after the family has received all the help it needs: "If the parents are the ones perpetrating the violence, they should receive care and therapy. The same also for the children . . . We need to redefine abuse and communication issues." A skilled poet and photographer, Saretta was awarded a scholarship to attend Manhattanville College in the fall of 1994.

Photograph by James L. Bixby. Courtesy of the Northwestern University Archives, Bixby Collection.

Part Nine

Sexuality

The sexuality and sexualization of children are some of the most strained and complex issues associated with contemporary childhood. The Lockean notion of children as blank slates presumed childhood sexual innocence, as did nineteenth-century romantic-sentimental images of children's natural goodness. But belief in the asexuality of children was challenged by Darwinian concepts of a direct connection between the human and animal worlds. Freud sexualized even the infant, and thus naturalized sexuality as innately human—a repellent idea for some, while others found it potentially liberating.

125

A haunting, though largely implicit, sexualization of childhood can be found in Henry James's novel The Turn of the Screw *(1898). Note that the narrator is at first convinced that the children's beauty is a sign of their purity, despite a letter from the school that would indicate otherwise.*

The Turn of the Screw

Henry James

I was a little late on the scene of his arrival, and I felt, as he stood wistfully looking out for me before the door of the inn at which the coach had put him down, that I had seen him on the instant, without and within, in the great glow of freshness, the same positive fragrance of purity, in which I had from the first moment seen his little sister. He was incredibly beautiful, and Mrs. Grose had put her finger on it: everything but a sort of passion of tenderness for him was swept away by his presence. What I then and there took him to my heart for was something divine that I have never found to the same degree in any child—his indescribable little air of knowing nothing in the world but love. It would have been impossible to carry a bad name with a greater sweetness of innocence, and by the time I had got back to Bly with him I remained merely bewildered—so far, that is, as I was not outraged—by the sense of the horrible letter locked up in one of the drawers of my room. . . .

Both the children had a gentleness—it was their only fault, and it never made Miles a muff—that kept them (how shall I express it?) almost impersonal and certainly quite unpunishable. They were like those cherubs of the anecdote who had—morally at any rate—nothing to whack! I remember feeling with Miles in especial as if he had had, as it were, nothing to call even an infinitesimal history. We expect of a small child scant enough "antecedents," but there was in this beautiful little boy something extraordinarily sensitive, yet extraordinarily happy, that, more than in any creature of his age I have seen, struck me as beginning anew each day. He had never for a second suffered. I took this as a direct disproof of his having really been chastised. If he had been wicked he would have "caught" it, and I should have caught it by the rebound—I should have found the trace, should have felt the wound and the dishonour. I could reconstitute nothing at all, and he was therefore an angel. He never spoke of his school, never mentioned a comrade or a master; and I, for my part, was quite too much disgusted to allude to them. Of course I was under the spell, and the wonderful part is that, even at the time, I perfectly knew I was. But I gave myself up to it; it was an antidote to any pain, and I had more pains than one. I was in receipt in these days of disturbing letters from home, where things were not going well. But with this joy of my children what things in the world mattered? That was the question I used to put to my scrappy retirements. I was dazzled by their loveliness. . . .

How can I retrace to-day the strange steps of my obsession? There were times of our being together when I would have been ready to swear that, literally, in my presence, but with my direct sense of it closed, they had visitors who were known and were welcome. Then it was that, had I not been deterred by the very chance that such an injury might prove greater than the injury to be averted, my exaltation would have broken out. "They're here, they're here, you little wretches," I would have cried, "and you can't deny it now!" The little wretches denied it with all the added volume of their sociability and their tenderness, just in the crystal depths of which—like the flash of a fish in a stream—the mockery of their advantage peeped up. . . .

What it was least possible to get rid of was the cruel idea that, whatever I had seen, Miles and Flora saw *more*—things terrible and unguessable and that sprang from dreadful passages of intercourse in the past. Such things naturally left on the surface, for the time, a chill that we vociferously denied we felt; and we had all three, with repetition, got into such splendid training that we went, each time, to mark the close of the incident, almost automatically through the very same movements. It was striking of the children at all events to kiss me inveterately with a wild irrelevance and never to fail—one or the other—of the precious question that had helped us through many a peril. "When do you think he *will* come? Don't you think we *ought* to write?"—there was nothing like that enquiry, we found by experience, for carrying off an awkwardness. "He" of course was their uncle in Harley Street; and we lived in much profusion of theory that he might at any moment arrive to mingle in our circle. . . .

"That's it. Out, straight out. What you have on your mind, you know."

"Ah then is *that* what you've stayed over for?"

He spoke with a gaiety through which I could still catch the finest little quiver of resentful passion; but I can't begin to express the effect upon me of an implication of surrender even so faint. It was as if what I had yearned for had come at last only to astonish me. "Well, yes—I may as well make a clean breast of it. It was precisely for that."

He waited so long that I supposed it for the purpose of repudiating the assumption on which my action had been founded; but what he finally said was: "Do you mean now—here?"

"There couldn't be a better place or time." He looked round him uneasily, and I had the rare—oh the queer!—impression of the very first symptom I had seen in him of the approach of immediate fear. It was as if he were suddenly afraid of me—which struck me indeed as perhaps the best thing to make him.

Yet in the very pang of the effort I felt it vain to try sternness, and I heard myself the next instant so gentle as to be almost grotesque. "You want so to go out again?"

"Awfully!" He smiled at me heroically, and the touching little bravery of it was enhanced by his actually flushing with pain. He had picked up his hat, which he had brought in, and stood twirling it in a way that gave me, even as I was just nearly reaching port, a perverse horror of what I was doing. To do it in any way was an act of violence, for what did it consist of but the obtrusion of the idea of grossness and guilt on a small helpless creature who had been for me a revelation of the possibilities of beautiful intercourse? Was n't it base to create for a being so exquisite a mere alien awkwardness? I suppose I now read into our situation a clearness it could n't have had at the time, for I seem to see our poor eyes already lighted with some spark of a prevision of the anguish that was to come. So we circled about with terrors and scruples, fighters not daring to close. But it was for each other we feared! That kept us a little longer suspended and unbruised. "I'll tell you everything," Miles said—"I mean I'll tell you anything you like. You'll stay on with me, and we shall both be all right, and I *will* tell you—I *will*. But not now."

"Why not now?"

My insistence turned him from me and kept him once more at his window in a silence during which, between us, you might have heard a pin drop. Then he was before me again with the air of a person for whom, outside, some one who had frankly to be reckoned with was waiting. "I have to see Luke."

I had not yet reduced him to quite so vulgar a lie, and I felt proportionately ashamed. But, horrible as it was, his lies made up my truth. I achieved thoughtfully a few loops of my knitting. "Well then go to Luke, and I'll wait for what you promise. Only in return for that satisfy, before you leave me, one very much smaller request."

He looked as if he felt he had succeeded enough to be able still a little to bargain. "Very much smaller—?"

"Yes, a mere fraction of the whole. Tell me"—oh my work preoccupied me, and I was off-hand!—"if, yesterday afternoon, from the table in the hall, you took, you know, my letter."

My grasp of how he received this suffered for a minute from something that I can describe only as a fierce split of my attention—a stroke that at first, as I sprang straight up, reduced me to the mere blind movement of getting hold of him, drawing him close and, while I just fell for support against the nearest piece of furniture, instinctively keeping him with his back to the window. The appearance was full upon us that I had already had to deal with here: Peter Quint had come into view like a sentinel before a prison. The next thing I saw was that, from outside, he had reached the window, and then I knew that, close to the glass and glaring in through it, he offered once more to the room his white face of damnation. It represents but grossly what took place within me at the sight to say that on the second my decision was made; yet I believe that no woman so overwhelmed ever in so short a time recovered her command of the *act*. It came to me in the very horror of the immediate presence that the act would be, seeing and facing what I saw and faced, to keep the boy himself unaware. The inspiration—I can call it by no other name—was that I felt how voluntarily, how transcendently, I *might*. It was like fighting with a demon for a human soul, and when I had fairly so appraised it I saw how the human soul—held out, in the tremor of my hands, at arms' length—had a perfect dew of sweat on a lovely childish forehead. The face that was close to mine was as white as the face against the glass, and out of it presently came a sound, not low nor weak, but as if from much further away, that I drank like a waft of fragrance.

"Yes—I took it."

At this, with a moan of joy, I enfolded, I drew him close; and while I held him to my breast, where I could feel in the sudden fever of his little body the tremendous pulse of his little heart, I kept my eyes on the thing at the window and saw it move and shift its posture. I have likened it to a sentinel, but its slow wheel, for a moment, was rather the prowl of a baffled beast. My present quickened courage, however, was such that, not too much to let it through, I had to shade, as it were, my flame. Meanwhile the glare of the face was again at the window, the scoundrel fixed as if to watch and wait. It was the very confidence that I might now defy him, as well as the positive certitude, by this time, of the child's unconsciousness, that made me go on. "What did you take it for?"

"To see what you said about me."

"You opened the letter?"

"I opened it."

My eyes were now, as I held him off a little again, on Miles's own face, in which the collapse of mockery showed me how complete was the ravage of uneasiness. What was prodigious was that at last, by my success, his sense was sealed and his communication stopped: he knew that he was in presence, but knew not of what, and knew still less that I also was and that I did know. And what did this strain of trouble matter when my eyes went back to the window only to see that the air was clear again and—by my personal triumph—the influence quenched? There was nothing there. I felt that the cause was mine and that I should surely get *all*. "And you found nothing!"—I let my elation out.

He gave the most mournful, thoughtful little headshake. "Nothing."

"Nothing, nothing!" I almost shouted in my joy.

"Nothing, nothing," he sadly repeated.

I kissed his forehead; it was drenched. "So what have you done with it?"

"I've burnt it."

"Burnt it?" It was now or never. "Is that what you did at school?"

Oh what this brought up! "At school?"

"Did you take letters?—or other things?"

"Other things?" He appeared now to be thinking of something far off and that reached him only through the pressure of his anxiety. Yet it did reach him. "Did I *steal*?"

I felt myself redden to the roots of my hair as well as wonder if it were more strange to put to a gentleman such a question or to see him take it with allowances that gave the very distance of his fall in the world. "Was it for that you might n't go back?"

The only thing he felt was rather a dreary little surprise. "Did you know I might n't go back?"

"I know everything."

He gave me at this the longest and strangest look. "Everything?"

"Everything. Therefore *did* you—?" But I could n't say it again.

Miles could, very simply. "No. I did n't steal."

My face must have shown him I believed him utterly; yet my hands—but it was for pure tenderness—shook him as if to ask him why, if it was all for nothing, he had condemned me to months of torment. "What then did you do?"

He looked in vague pain all round the top of the room and drew his breath, two or three times over, as if with difficulty. He might have been standing at the bottom of the sea and raising his eyes to some faint green twilight. "Well—I said things."

"Only that?"

"They thought it was enough!"

"To turn you out for?"

Never, truly, had a person "turned out" shown so little to explain it as this little person! He appeared to weigh my question, but in a manner quite detached and almost helpless. "Well, I suppose I ought n't."

"But to whom did you say them?"

He evidently tried to remember, but it dropped—he had lost it. "I don't know!"

He almost smiled at me in the desolation of his surrender, which was indeed practically, by this time, so complete that I ought to have left it there. But I was infatuated—I was blind with victory, though even then the very effect that was to have brought him so much nearer was already that of added separation. "Was it to every one?" I asked.

"No; it was only to—" But he gave a sick little headshake. "I don't remember their names."

"Were they then so many?"

"No—only a few. Those I liked."

Those he liked? I seemed to float not into clearness, but into a darker obscure, and within a minute there had come to me out of my very pity the appalling alarm of his being perhaps innocent. It was for the instant confounding and bottomless, for if he *were* innocent what then on earth was I? Paralysed, while it lasted, by the mere brush of the question, I let him go a little, so that, with a deep-drawn sigh, he turned away from me again; which, as he faced toward the clear window, I suffered, feeling that I had nothing now there to keep him from. "And did they repeat what you said?" I went on after a moment.

He was soon at some distance from me, still breathing hard and again with the air, though now without anger for it, of being confined against his will. Once more, as he had done before, he looked up at the dim day as if, of what had hitherto sustained him, nothing was left but an unspeakable anxiety. "Oh yes," he nevertheless replied—"they must have repeated them. To those *they* liked," he added.

There was somehow less of it than I had expected; but I turned it over. "And these things came round—?"

"To the masters? Oh yes!" he answered very simply. "But I did n't know they'd tell."

"The masters? They did n't—they've never told. That's why I ask you."

He turned to me again his little beautiful fevered face. "Yes, it was too bad."

"Too bad?"

"What I suppose I sometimes said. To write home."

I can't name the exquisite pathos of the contradiction given to such a speech by such a speaker; I only know that the next instant I heard myself throw off with homely force:"Stuff and nonsense!" But the next after that I must have sounded stern enough. "What *were* these things?"

My sternness was all for his judge, his executioner; yet it made him avert himself again, and that movement made *me*, with a single bound and an irrepressible cry, spring straight upon him. For there again, against the glass, as if to blight his confession and stay his answer, was the hideous author of our woe—the white face of damnation. I felt a sick swim at the drop of my victory and all the return of my battle, so that the wildness of my veritable leap only served as a great betrayal. I saw him, from the midst of my act, meet it with a divination, and on the perception that even now he only guessed, and that the window was still to his own eyes free, I let the impulse flame up to convert the climax of his dismay into the very proof of his liberation. "No more, no more, no more!" I shrieked to my visitant as I tried to press him against me.

"Is she *here*?" Miles panted as he caught with his sealed eyes the direction of my words. Then as his strange "she" staggered me and, with a gasp, I echoed it, "Miss Jessel, Miss Jessel!" he with sudden fury gave me back.

I seized, stupefied, his supposition—some sequel to what we had done to Flora, but this made me only want to show him that it was better still than that. "It's not Miss Jessel! But it's at the window—straight before us. It's *there*—the coward horror, there for the last time!"

At this, after a second in which his head made the movement of a baffled dog's on a scent and then gave a frantic little shake for air and light, he was at me in a white rage, bewildered, glaring vainly over the place and missing wholly, though it now, to my sense, filled the room like the taste of poison, the wide overwhelming presence. "It's *he*?"

I was so determined to have all my proof that I flashed into ice to challenge him. "Whom do you mean by 'he'?"

"Peter Quint—you devil!" His face gave again, round the room, its convulsed supplication. "*Where*?"

They are in my ears still, his supreme surrender of the name and his tribute to my devotion. "What does he matter now, my own?—what will he *ever* matter? I have you," I launched at the beast, "but he has lost you for ever!" Then for the demonstration of my work, "There, *there*!" I said to Miles.

But he had already jerked straight round, stared, glared again, and seen but the quiet day. With the stroke of the loss I was so proud of he uttered the cry of a creature hurled over an abyss, and the grasp with which I recovered him might have been that of catching him in his fall. I caught him, yes, I held him—it may be imagined with what a passion; but at the end of a minute I began to feel what it truly was that I held. We were alone with the quiet day, and his little heart, dispossessed, had stopped.

126

The literary scholar James R. Kincaid discusses the perspective of Victorian litera-
ture toward the erotic child, and suggests that the obsession with child sex is of
more recent vintage (1992).

Child-Loving
The Erotic Child and Victorian Culture

James R. Kincaid

To a large extent what we know about the history of pedophilia begins with the nineteenth century.

That is not the same thing as saying that pedophilia itself begins with the nineteenth century. However, it can be argued that the special historical construction of "the child" during this period and slightly before made it available to desire in a way not previously possible, made it available by, among other things, making it different, a strange and alien species that was once, and in some way is still, continuous with the adult. This highlighted, special, and different child was also made radiant, by way of the Romantic exaltation of the child, an exaltation furthered by the revival of fundamentalist Christianity in Victorian England. The contributions of Christianity to pedophilia are hard to measure but probably heavy, considering what force was placed by that religion on purity, how closely purity was associated with children (and, of course, women), and how vital, if partly submerged, was the connection between this purity and the sexually prohibited, desirable, sanctioned, and necessary: violating purity was perhaps the major crime; but the enjoyment of purity was also the reward held out to the faithful, both in marriage and in heaven. Purity was, in any case, defined by and thus riddled through with sexual desire in Victorian England. The alliance of purity and sexuality rules its religion, its poetry, its commerce; it reached its zenith in the home, and in the center of the domestic sphere, the child.

All of which is high-sounding but dubious. So negative a game as purity could never attract so many players, and even sexuality's imperialist claims deserve to be questioned. *I* want to claim that the way in which we have constructed the child, the way in which it has been constructed historically, makes its desirability inevitable. But I do not say that the erotic appeal of the child is the center of the culture or a key with which to unlock its secret. That we have so incessantly disclaimed responsibility for eroticizing the child makes the subject particularly seductive, but it does not guarantee any sort of centering. . . .

We can . . . note some forms of Victorian pedophilia that seem especially marked, perhaps specific to the period. The particular attractions of the sick or dying child seem to have figured importantly for the culture generally, and certainly for pedophiles. The surviving pedophile poetry and what we know of public activity suggests that, next to dying and the even-more-popular flogging, bathing may have provided the most important subject: "Breasting the wavelets, and diving there,/ White boys, ruddy, and tanned and bare." Francis William Bouidillon's "The Legend of the Water Lilies" (1878) is one of several poems of this sort that combine naked bathing with death: when one of the group swims out too far, the others, all of them, try to save their comrade and drown in the attempt. Some water lilies (the ones referred to in the title of the poem) grow there to mark the grave and preserve the erotic image of the bonanza of naked, dying bodies. This memorializing raises another common feature of pedophilia, the action taken against transience on behalf of the desire to possess and hold the child in time. The incessant nineteenth-century (and modern) child-photographing seems to be a form of this erotic urge, and the photographing can, in turn, be related to the close connections between pedophilia and voyeurism. . . . Finally, we can locate in Victorian pedophilic discourse what look like various displaced or substitute fetishes or practices: spanking, most notably, but also enema cults and underwear cults. In *When a Child Loves*, for instance, the chief adult figure, General Hill, was "one of those persons for whom the little lady's underclothing had a great and especial fascination."

This last example leads me, not very artfully, to an acknowledgment of the existence of some erotic or pornographic material directly involving children. . . . I believe we have greatly exaggerated the quantity of this material, probably because we get pleasure in imagining it to have been there, much as we now relish the idea of some "billion-dollar kiddie porn industry." There was at least a little Victorian child erotica. The bulk of what survives focuses on flagellation; . . . there is not a great deal of "straight" material—depictions of seduction, sex play, intercourse between adults and children—that I know of. There is, however, a lot of windy propaganda about the importance of sex starting very young:

> At the age of twelve I had practiced every form of sexual desire that my vigorous imagination could conceive. I had "had" several beautiful boys of my own sge [sic] with whom I indulged in sll [sic] sorts of sexual acts. I had also played with and "had" several young girls from the age of six to twenty, which, together with my carnal knowledge of all of father's farm. . . .

Even this, however, seldom takes narrative form. What we generally find, in place of detailed depictions of adult-child sex, is one form or another of general discussion, extended arguments on the subject. . . . [For example,]

Is it any wonder that men of refinement and feeling, seek above all things the mutual indulgence of sensuel [sic] passion between themselves and pretty child-girls? Surely not. Fors [sic] is not the naked form of a healthy well grown girl of twelwe [sic] or thirteen years . . . a picture for any man's desire?

. . . More intriguing, I think, is the possibility that the Victorians, busy sexualizing the child, still did not invest in the process the degree of anxiety common in this century. It is possible that they did not regard the erotic child as a problem in the way we suppose they must have. What is a commanding problem for us did not always seem a problem at all to those making it so. Even Freud did not bother enough with the issue of sexual attraction to children to make it into a separate category or discuss its etiology and treatment. He usually suggested, in an offhand way, that children become sex objects only with those among the cowardly and the impotent who haven't the occasion for sex with adults. The "uncanny frequency," he says, with which "school teachers and child attendants" turn up as sexual abusers of children can be attributed to the fact that they "have the best opportunity for it," just as, one supposes, those who live near water tend often to go swimming. The nonchalance of this has offended even devout Freudians, who like to point out that the sex doesn't follow the vocation but vice versa, that such people don't have sex with children because they are around them but seek out ways to be around them so as to have sex with them. But that is modern orthodoxy, quite at odds, it appears, with the Victorians who sexualized and made desirable this child, all the while not much noticing the process or, perhaps, noticing but not caring, or caring but not turning the issue into the particular sort of problem that would demand discursive treatment.

127

The late nineteenth century saw a rising awareness of the sexuality of children in various guises. Freud's name is inexorably linked to the explicit investment of the young child with a sexual drive. Here Freud discusses three important components of his psychology—the polymorphous perverse sexuality of infants and children, the incestuous desires of children, and the interpretation of dreams (1920).

Polymorphous Perversity

Sigmund Freud

What we have already ascertained has guided us to the study of the child's mental life, and we may now hope to find in a similar way an explanation of the source of the other kind of prohibited wishes in dreams, i.e. the excessive sexual desires. We are impelled therefore to study the development of the sexual life of the child, and here from various sources we learn the following facts. In the first place, it is an untenable fallacy to suppose that the child has no sexual life and to assume that sexuality first makes its appearance at puberty, when the genital organs come to maturity. On the contrary he has from the very beginning a sexual life rich in content, though it differs in many points from that which later is regarded as normal. What in adult life are termed "perversions" depart from the normal in the following respects: (1) in a disregard for the barriers of species (the gulf between man and beast), (2) in the insensibility to barriers imposed by disgust, (3) in the transgression of the incest-barrier (the prohibition against seeking sexual gratification with close blood-relations), (4) in homosexuality and, (5) in the transferring of the part played by the genital organs to other organs and different areas of the body. All these barriers are not in existence from the outset, but are only gradually built up in the course of development and education. The little child is free from them: he does not perceive any immense gulf between man and beast, the arrogance with which man separates himself from the other animals only dawns in him at a later period. He shows at the beginning of life no disgust for excrement, but only learns this feeling slowly under the influence of education; he attaches no particular importance to the difference between the sexes, in fact he thinks that both have the same formation of the genital organs; he directs his earliest sexual desires and his curiosity to those nearest to him or to those who for other reasons are specially beloved—his parents, brothers and sisters or nurses; and finally we see in him a characteristic which manifests itself again later at the height of some love-relationship—namely, he does not look for gratification in the sexual organs only, but discovers that many other parts of the body possess the same sort of sensibility and can yield analogous pleasurable sensations, playing thereby the part of genital organs. The child may be said then to be *polymorphously perverse*, and even if mere traces of all these impulses are found in him, this is due on the one hand to their lesser intensity as compared with that which they assume in later life and, on the other hand, to the fact that education immediately and energetically suppresses all sexual manifestations in the child. This suppression may be said to be embodied in a theory; for grown-up people endeavour to overlook some of these manifestations, and, by misinterpretation, to rob others of their sexual nature, until in the end the whole thing can be altogether denied. It is often the same people who first inveigh against the sexual "naughtiness" of children in the nursery and then sit down to their writing-tables to defend the sexual purity of the same children. When they are left to themselves or when they are seduced children often display perverse sexual activity to a really remarkable extent. Of course grown-up people are right in not taking this too seriously and in regarding it, as they say, as "childish tricks" and "play," for the child cannot be judged either by a moral or legal code as if he were mature and fully responsible; nevertheless these things do exist, and they have their significance both as evidence of innate constitutional tendencies and inasmuch as they cause and foster later developments: they give us an insight into the child's sexual life and so into that of humanity as a whole. If then we find all these perverse wishes behind the distortions of our dreams, it only means that dreams in *this respect also* have regressed completely to the infantile condition.

Amongst these forbidden wishes special prominence must still be given to the incestuous desires, i.e. those directed towards sexual intercourse with parents or brothers and sisters. You know in what abhorrence human society holds, or at least professes to hold, such intercourse, and what emphasis is laid upon the prohibitions of it. The most preposterous attempts have been made to account for this horror of incest: some people have assumed that it is a provision of nature for the preservation of the species, manifesting itself in the mind by these prohibitions because in-breeding would result in racial degeneration; others have asserted that propinquity from early childhood has deflected sexual desire from the persons concerned. In both these cases, however, the avoidance of incest would have been automatically secured and we should be at a loss to understand the necessity for stern prohibitions, which would seem rather to point to a strong desire. Psycho-analytic investigations have shown beyond the possibility of doubt that *an incestuous love-choice* is in fact the first and the regular one, and that it is only later that any opposition is manifested towards it, the causes of which are not to be sought in the psychology of the individual.

Let us sum up the results which our excursion into child-psychology has brought to the understanding of dreams. We have learnt not only that the material of the forgotten childish experiences is accessible to the dream, but also that the child's mental life, with all its peculiarities, its egoism, its incestuous object-choice, persists in it and therefore in the unconscious, and that our dreams take us back every night to this infantile stage. This corroborates the belief that *the Unconscious is the infantile mental life*, and, with this, the objectionable impression that so much evil lurks in human nature grows somewhat less. For this terrible evil is simply what is original, primitive and infantile in mental life, what we find in operation in the child, but in part overlook in him because it is on so small a scale, and in part do not take greatly to heart because we do not demand a high ethical standard in a child. By regressing to this infantile stage our dreams appear to have brought the evil in us to light, but the appearance is deceptive, though we have let ourselves be dismayed by it; we are not so evil as the interpretation of our dreams would lead us to suppose.

128

In the early twentieth century, the concern with sexually exploited children fueled the age-of-constant campaign. Here the historian Mary E. Odem discusses the cultural context for raising the age-of-consent laws, as well as some of the sexual problems faced by adolescent girls in the early twentieth century (1995).

Delinquent Daughters
The Age-of-Consent Campaign

Mary E. Odem

The age of consent in American law was based on previously established standards developed over the centuries in England. Under English common law, the age of female discretion was held to be twelve years. A parliamentary statute in 1576 lowered the age of consent in sexual relations to ten years and explicitly designated such relations with an underage female, without benefit of clergy, as a felony. According to William Blackstone, the foremost British legal scholar in the eighteenth century, this statute superseded the older common-law standard of female consent in rape cases. Hence, any male over the age of fourteen who had intercourse with a female under twelve, with or without her consent, was guilty of the crime of rape. But whereas, in England, purity reformers had succeeded in pressuring Parliament to raise the age of consent to thirteen in 1875 and to sixteen in 1885, in the United States the ages remained at ten and twelve.

The revelation of these low ages of consent galvanized the American reform community into action. Members of the New York Committee for the Prevention of State Regulation of Vice immediately embarked on a campaign to raise the age of consent in New York. Leaders of the committee circulated a petition demanding that the age be legally raised from ten to eighteen. Aaron Macy Powell and Emily Blackwell met with the chief justice of the New York Supreme Court to draft a model law to be introduced in the state legislature. The organization also used the pages of the *Philanthropist* to incite public concern about the issue. One editorial that appeared in January 1886 stated: "It will doubtless astonish many of our readers, who have hitherto avoided the subject as indelicate, or painful, to be told that the young girl of the Empire State is held by its criminal laws to be legally capable of giving 'consent' to her own corruption at the tender age of TEN YEARS!"

The low age of consent in the United States also stirred the Woman's Christian Temperance Union into action, and the political skills and tactics honed in the temperance movement allowed its members quickly to assume leading roles in the campaign. The WCTU drafted a petition demanding that "the age at which a girl can legally consent to her own ruin be raised to at least eighteen years." This petition circulated among many local WCTU branches throughout the country, provoking a flood of letters to state legislatures in support of more stringent consent laws. The WCTU also organized a national petition drive to institute a higher age of consent in the nation's capital and the territories. Because of its extensive political network, the WCTU was better able than any single organization to build a formidable national campaign that touched every state in the country.

Purity reformers received strong support from white suffragists. The two competing national suffrage organizations—the American Woman Suffrage Association, headed by Lucy Stone and her husband Henry Blackwell, and the National Woman Suffrage Association, led by Elizabeth Cady Stanton and Susan B. Anthony—both considered the age-of-consent campaign an important battle in the larger struggle to overcome the subordination of women in home and society. Stanton denounced the low age of consent as an "invasion of the personal rights of woman, and the wholesale desecration of childhood." The major national suffrage publication of the period, the *Woman's Journal*, edited by Stone and Blackwell, kept its readers abreast of progress of the campaign and urged them to support age-of-consent efforts in their local communities. The many state suffrage organizations joined purity groups in circulating petitions and lobbying legislators. They added the age of consent to their list of legislative priorities for the improvement of women's status, which included the right to vote, liberal divorce laws, married women's property rights, and equal guardianship rights over children.

Age-of-consent reformers found another important source of support among white workingmen's groups. When the WCTU organized its national petition drive, Frances Willard sought the assistance of the Knights of Labor, the largest labor organization in the country at the time. After meeting with Willard, Knights president Terrence Powderly had copies of the petition sent to all local assemblies of the organization. When the petitions were presented to Congress in January 1888, the Knights of Labor had supplied half of the nearly 15,000 signatures.

The great appeal that the age-of-consent campaign had for white workingmen, suffragists, and middle-class women stemmed in large part from purity reformers' particular conception of sexual danger. Influenced by the Victorian belief in inherent female purity and passionlessness, reformers charged that male vice and exploitation were responsible for the moral ruin of young women and girls. In their publications and speeches, reformers recounted numerous tales of seduction that followed a common pattern in which men of status and wealth took advantage of poor, innocent young women, using various forms of trickery and deception, and force if necessary. The fate of female victims was always disas-

Legal Ages of Consent in the United States, 1885 and 1920

State	1885	1920
Alabama	10	16*
Arizona	10	18
Arkansas	12	16*
California	10	18
Colorado	10	18
Connecticut	10	16
Delaware	7	16*
District of Columbia	12	16
Florida	10	18*
Georgia	10	14*
Idaho	10	18
Illinois	10	16
Indiana	n.a.	16
Iowa	10	16
Kansas	10	18
Kentucky	12	16*
Louisiana	12	18*
Maine	10	16*
Maryland	10	16
Massachusetts	10	16
Michigan	10	16
Minnesota	10	18*
Mississippi	10	18*
Missouri	12	18*
Montana	10	18
Nebraska	10	18
Nevada	12	18
New Hampshire	10	16
New Jersey	10	16
New Mexico	10	16
New York	10	18
North Carolina	10	16*
North Dakota	10	18
Ohio	10	16*
Oregon	n.a.	16
Pennsylvania	10	16
Rhode Island	10	16
South Carolina	10	16*
South Dakota	10	18
Tennessee	10	18*
Texas	10	18
Utah	10	18*
Vermont	10	16
Virginia	12	16
Washington	12	18*
West Virginia	12	16
Wisconsin	10	16
Wyoming	10	18

SOURCES: The official legal codes and statutes of the various states; Anthony and Harper, eds., state reports on legislative action and laws, in *History of Woman Suffrage*, 4:465–1011; Pivar, *Purity Crusade*, pp. 141–43; Benjamin DeCosta, "Age of Consent Laws—1886," *Philanthropist*, February 1886, p. 5; Leila Robinson, "Age of Consent Laws—1889," *Woman's Journal*, April 5, 1889, p. 105.
*The law in these states made sexual intercourse with underage females a criminal offense under a statute separate from the rape statute; the offense was typically referred to as "carnal knowledge of female child."

trous; typically they were forced into prostitution or endured a cruel and lonely death. This narrative of seduction had long been popular in nineteenth-century melodrama and romance novels, but reformers adapted it to their own social context and political purposes. The female victim was typically a white working-class daughter in the city, and her male predator a middle-class businessman. The seduction frequently occurred in one of the new places of work and recreation for young women that were emerging in urban areas in the late nineteenth century. . . .

The standard narrative of seduction did not accurately depict the reality of most sexual encounters experienced by young working-class women during this period. They usually formed intimate relationships with young, unmarried men of their own class, not with older, middle-class employers. Though not based on reality, the seduction narrative nevertheless had great power among nineteenth-century audiences because it captured the deep social anxiety about the fundamental changes taking place in the lives of white working-class female youth. . . .

In their leisure time outside of work, young women took part in new commercial amusements that further undermined family influence. Dance halls, movie theaters, cafés, and amusement parks opened in cities throughout the country, offering nightly entertainment to urban youth. These commercial ventures differed in important ways from earlier forms of recreation. Most leisure-time activity throughout the nineteenth century had taken place in family and neighborhood settings and involved all age groups. Small-town families had participated together in picnics, community entertainments, church socials, and dances. Urban workers, too, had enjoyed their leisure in familial and communal contexts as they gathered on street corners and stoops after a day's work, took weekend excursions to the park, or celebrated religious and ethnic holidays in community groups. The few forms of commercial recreation that existed were generally the preserve of men. Male friends and colleagues joined one another in saloons, pool halls, and sports clubs, while women stayed close to home and their local neighborhoods.

The amusement resorts dotting the urban landscape in the late nineteenth and early twentieth centuries departed from these earlier forms of leisure activity by catering primarily to a young, mix-sexed crowd. Adolescent sons and daughters often spent their evenings with their peers at amusement parks, theaters, and dance halls instead of participating in family and neighborhood gatherings. Similar developments had taken place earlier in more developed urban areas, such as New York City, but they became widespread throughout the country during the rapid urban and economic growth of the late nineteenth century.

Urban and economic growth extended new possibilities but also new sexual risks to young working-class women. Increased social autonomy in work and recreation could also expose them to sexual harassment and assault by male employers, coworkers, and companions. Relations with boyfriends sometimes resulted in pregnancy and abandonment. In large cities with highly mobile populations, families could not force a marriage between pregnant daughters and their male partners as effectively as they had in smaller towns and communities.

An out-of-wedlock pregnancy was a difficult, often traumatic experience for young women at this time. They had to bear the economic burden of caring for the child and faced social ostracism and possible family rejection. To escape this shame and financial hardship, young women sometimes resorted to extreme measures, most notably infanticide or illegal and often dangerous abortions to end a pregnancy. The seduction narrative constructed by reformers expressed this sense of sexual vulnerability and danger that young women faced.

By the time Margaret Mead published Coming of Age in Samoa *in 1928, Americans had already become familiar with Freud's ideas about the sexuality of children. Perhaps more than any other, Mead made Americans aware that their own sexual patterns and assumptions were not shared by other societies.*

Coming of Age in Samoa

Margaret Mead

From the Samoans' complete knowledge of sex, its possibilities and its rewards, they are able to count it at its true value. And if they have no preference for reserving sex activity for important relationships, neither do they regard relationships as important because they are productive of sex satisfaction. The Samoan girl who shrugs her shoulder over the excellent technique of some young Lothario is nearer to the recognition of sex as an impersonal force without any intrinsic validity, than is the sheltered American girl who falls in love with the first man who kisses her. From their familiarity with the reverberations which accompany sex excitement comes this recognition of the essential impersonality of sex attraction which we may well envy them; from the too slight, too casual practice comes the disregard of personality which seems to us unlovely.

The fashion in which their sex practice reduces the possibility of neuroses has already been discussed. By discounting our category of perversion, as applied to practice, and reserving it for the occasional psychic pervert, they legislate a whole field of neurotic possibility out of existence. Onanism, homosexuality, statistically unusual forms of heterosexual activity, are neither banned nor institutionalized. The wider range which these practices give prevents the development of obsessions of guilt which are so frequent a cause of maladjustment among us. The more varied practices permitted heterosexually preserve any individual from being penalised for special conditioning. This acceptance of a wider range as "normal" provides a cultural atmosphere in which frigidity and psychic impotence do not occur and in which a satisfactory sex adjustment in marriage can always be established. The acceptance of such an attitude without in any way accepting promiscuity would go a long way towards solving many marital impasses and emptying our park benches and our houses of prostitution.

Among the factors in the Samoan scheme of life which are influential in producing stable, well-adjusted, robust individuals, the organization of the family and the attitude towards sex are undoubtedly the most important.

In his 1948 and 1953 studies of sexuality in men and women, Alfred Kinsey naturalized expressions of childhood sexuality simply by describing their frequency. Here he describes preadolescent sexual responses and also incidents of sexual contact between adults and children. Kinsey believes that for the most part such contact would be harmless "if the child were not culturally conditioned" to respond with fear—a claim that is very much contested today. Kinsey does note that in certain cases an adult can inflict great harm on a child.

Preadolescent Sexuality

Kinsey Institute for Sex Research

Accumulative Incidence of Pre-Adolescent Response

What seem to be sexual responses have been observed in infants immediately at birth, and specifically sexual responses, involving the full display of physiologic changes which are typical of the responses of an adult, have been observed in both female and male infants as young as four months of age, and in infants and pre-adolescent children of every older age.

About one per cent of the older females who have contributed histories to the present study recalled that they were making specifically sexual responses to physical stimuli, and in some instances to psychologic stimuli, when they were as young as three years of age. This, however, must represent only a portion of the children who were responding at that age, for many children would not recognize the sexual nature of their early responses.

About 4 per cent of the females in our sample thought they were responding sexually by five years of age. Nearly 16 per cent recalled such responses by ten years of age. All told, some 27 per cent recalled that they had been aroused erotically—sexually—at some time before the age of adolescence which, for the average female, occurs sometime between her twelfth and thirteenth birthdays. However, the number of pre-adolescent girls who are ever aroused sexually must be much higher than this record indicates.

Comparisons of the records contributed by subjects who had terminated their schooling at the grade school, high school, college, and graduate school levels, indicate that pre-adolescent erotic responses may have occurred in a higher percentage of the groups which subsequently obtained the most extensive schooling; but this may simply reflect a greater capacity of the better educated females to recall their experience.

Nature of Pre-Adolescent Orgasm

Some of the sexual responses of pre-adolescent children, and even those of infants of a few months of age, may terminate in sexual orgasm. There is no essential aspect of the orgasm of an adult which has not been observed in the orgasms which young children may have. This seems to be equally true of the pre-adolescent female and the pre-adolescent male. The pre-adolescent boy does not ejaculate as adult males do when they reach orgasm, but ejaculation depends upon a relatively minor anatomic structure which is not yet developed in the boy; and the absence of ejaculation does not indicate that the boy does not reach orgasm, any more than the absence of ejaculation in the adult female indicates that she does not reach orgasm.

We have previously given a detailed description of orgasm occurring among pre-adolescent boys. We may now extend the record to orgasm among pre-adolescent girls.

Masturbation (self-stimulation) is an essentially normal and quite frequent phenomenon among many children, both female and male. Masturbation is not infrequently the source of orgasm among small girls. . . .

Accumulative Incidence of Pre-Adolescent Orgasm

About 14 per cent of all the females in our sample—nearly half of those who had been erotically aroused before adolescence—recalled that they had reached orgasm either in masturbation or in their sexual contacts with other children or older persons (*i.e.*, in their *socio-sexual* contacts) prior to adolescence. It is not at all impossible that a still higher percentage had actually had such experience without recognizing its nature.

On the basis of the adult recall and the observations which we have just recorded, we can report 4 cases of females under one year of age coming to orgasm, and a total of 23 cases of small girls three years of age or younger reaching orgasm. The incidences, based on our total female sample, show some 0.3 per cent (16 individuals) who recalled that they had reached orgasm by three years of age, 2 per cent by five years, 4 per cent by seven years, 9 per cent by eleven years, and 14 per cent by thirteen years of age. Thus, there had been a slow but steady increase in the number of girls in the sample who had reached orgasm prior to adolescence. In the case of the male, the percentages of those who had reached orgasm also rose steadily through the early pre-adolescent years, but they began to rise more abruptly in the later pre-adolescent years.

Sources of Early Arousal and Orgasm

One per cent of the females in our sample recalled that they were masturbating (in the strict sense of the term) by three years of age, and 13 per cent recalled masturbation by ten years of age. The record does not show what percentage of the early masturbation had brought sexual arousal, but it does show 0.3 per cent of the females in the total sample masturbating to the point of orgasm by three years of age, and 8 per cent by ten years of age.

Psychologic reactions or physical contacts with other girls were, in a few instances, the sources of sexual arousal at three years of age. About 3 per cent had been aroused by other girls by eleven years of age, and 6 per cent by thirteen years of age.

Reactions to or contacts with boys had brought similar arousal in a fraction of one per cent at three years of age, but in about 7 per cent of the sample by eleven, and in 12 per cent of the sample by thirteen years of age.

Out of the 659 females in the sample who had experienced orgasm before they were adolescent, 86 per cent had had their first experience in masturbation, some 7 per cent had discovered it in sexual contacts with other girls, 2 per cent in petting, and 1 per cent in coitus with boys or older males. Interestingly enough, 2 per cent had had their first orgasm in physical contacts with dogs or cats. Some 2 per cent had first reached orgasm under other circumstances, including the climbing of a rope.

Orgasm had been discovered in self-masturbation more often by the girls than by the boys. In earlier pre-adolescence, the boy's first orgasms are frequently the product of physical and emotional situations which brings spontaneous sexual reactions; and although there is a great deal of incidental manipulation of genitalia among younger boys, it rarely brings orgasm. Among the adolescent boys in our sample, masturbation appears to have accounted for only 68 per cent of the first orgasms.

Some sort of finger manipulation of the genitalia, and particularly of the clitoris, seems to have been the commonest technique in the female's early masturbation. The second commonest technique had been one in which the child had lain face down on the bed, with her knees somewhat drawn up while she rhythmically moved her buttocks, building up the neuromuscular tensions which had ultimately led to orgasm. In many instances the genitalia were rubbed against a toy, a bed, a blanket, or some other object on which the child lay face down. In those cases in which the child had failed to reach orgasm, the failure may have been due to lack of a physiologic capacity to respond to that point, but in many instances it may have been due to the child's failure to discover the necessary physical techniques for effective self-stimulation. The acquirement of these masturbatory techniques represents one of the learned aspects of sexual behavior.

The child's initial attempts at self-masturbation had been inspired in some instances by the observation of other children who were engaged in such activity,

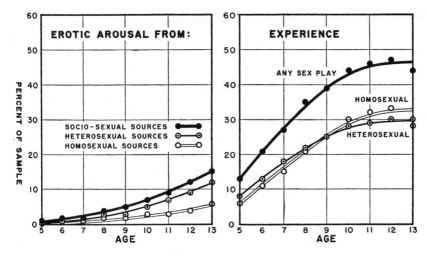

FIGURE 1. Accumulative incidence: pre-adoleseent socio-sexual arousal Including arousal from psychologic stimulation and overt socio-sexual play.

FIGURE 2. Accumulative incidence: pre-adolescent socio-sexual experience Each dot indicates percent of sample with experience by the indicated age.

or through the more deliberate instruction given by some older child or adult. These were quite commonly the first sources of information for most of the males in the sample; but in the great majority of instances females learn to masturbate, both in pre-adolescent and later years, by discovering the possibilities of such activity entirely on their own.

Pre-Adolescent Heterosexual Play

Although 30 per cent of the females in the sample recalled pre-adolescent heterosexual play, and 33 per cent recalled pre-adolescent homosexual play, only 48 per cent recalled any sort of socio-sexual play before adolescence. This means that 15 per cent had had sex play only with boys, 18 per cent had had it only with girls, and another 15 per cent had had it with both boys and girls.

Socio-Sexual Development

For both the females and males in the sample, the earliest sexual contacts with other individuals, either of their own or of the opposite sex, appear to have been the incidental outcome of other play activities, or the imitation of sexual behavior which they had observed among other children or even among adults. The anthropologic record indicates that there is a good deal of this imitative play among children of primitive groups where adult coitus is not as carefully guarded from observation as in our own culture. More of the sex play among children in this country represents the perpetuation of age-old games commonly referred to as "mama and papa," and "doctor." These games were current in the generation which included our oldest subjects, and they still appear under these names in the youngest generation represented in the sample. The specifically sexual nature of these games is not always understood by the child; and even when the small boy lies on top of the small girl and makes what may resemble copulatory movements, there is often no realization that genital contacts might be made, or that there might be an erotic reward in such activity. However, in some communities, and in families where there are several children, it sometimes happens that an older child or some adult may give the girl or boy more extended information, or may even direct the physical contacts so they become specifically sexual.

A considerable portion of the child's pre-adolescent sex play, both with its own and with the opposite sex, is a product of curiosity concerning the playmate's anatomy.

Accumulative Incidence of Heterosexual Play

Our data on the incidence and frequency of sex play among pre-adolescent children are drawn in part from the studies we have made of children of very young ages, but they depend largely upon the recall of the adults who have contributed to the present study. It has been apparent, however, that the adults have recalled only a portion of their pre-adolescent experience, for even children forget a high proportion of their experience within a matter of weeks or months. This is due sometimes to the incidental nature of the sex play, and in some instances to the fact that the child was emotionally disturbed by the experience and blocked psychologically in recalling a taboo activity. But even though the child may not be able to recall its experience, it is possible that it has acquired information and attitudes which will affect its subsequent patterns of behavior. While the records show that 48 per cent of the adult females in the sample had recalled some sort of pre-adolescent sex play, we are inclined to believe, for the above reasons, that a much higher percentage must have had sexual contacts as young children.

About equal numbers of the females recalled contacts with girls and with boys. There is no evidence that their interest in their own sex (the homosexual interest) had developed either before or after their interest in the opposite sex (the heterosexual interest). Freudian hypotheses of psychosexual development proceeding, as a rule, from narcissistic (masturbatory) interests and activities to interests in other individuals whose bodies are similar (the homosexual interests), and finally to interests in individuals who are physically different (the heterosexual interests), are not substantiated by the pre-adolescent or adolescent histories of either the females or the males in the sample.

Because of the restrictions which parents and our total social organization place upon the free intermingling of even small children of the opposite sex, it is not surprising to find that 52 per cent of the females in the sample had had more girls than boys as childhood companions, and that another 33 per cent had had boys and girls in about equal numbers as childhood companions. Only about 15 per cent had had more boys than girls as companions. This lesser significance of boys as the pre-adolescent companions of girls makes it all the more notable that the pre-adolescent sexual activities of the females in the sample were had with boys about as often as with girls. This had undoubtedly depended upon the fact that small boys are usually more aggressive than girls in their physical activities, and even at that age boys are more likely to initiate the sexual activities.

One per cent of the adult females in the sample recalled childhood sex play with boys when they were as young as three, but 8 per cent recalled such play by five, and 18 per cent by seven years of age. All told, some 30 per cent recalled some play with boys before they turned adolescent. The figures differed for the various educational levels represented in the sample: among those females who had never gone beyond high school, some 24 per cent recalled sex play with boys, but 30 per cent of those who had gone on into college, and 36 per cent of those who had gone still further into graduate school, recalled such pre-adolescent play.

The data indicate that the percentage of children engaging in any kind of pre-adolescent sex play had increased in the course of three of the decades represented in the sample. In comparison with the females born before 1900, some 10 per cent more of those born between 1910 and 1919 recalled pre-adolescent sex play. . . .

Techniques of Heterosexual Play

Genital exhibition had occurred in 99 per cent of the pre-adolescent sex play. In perhaps 40 per cent of the histories that was all that was involved.

Anatomic differences are of considerable interest to most children. Their curiosity is whetted by the fact that they have in many instances been forbidden to expose their own nude bodies and have not had the opportunity to see the nude bodies of other children. Their curiosity is especially stimulated by the fact that they have been cautioned not to expose their own genitalia, or to look at the genitalia of other children. The genital explorations often amount to nothing more than comparisons of anatomy, in much the same way that children compare their hands, their noses or mouths, their hair, their clothing, or any of their other possessions. As we have noted in regard to the boy, it is probable that a good deal of the emotional content which such play may have for the small girl is not sexual as often as it is a reaction to the mysterious, to the forbidden, and to the socially dangerous performance.

On the other hand, we have the histories of females who were raised in homes that accepted nudity within the family circle, or who attended nursery schools or summer camps or engaged in other group activities where boys and girls of young, pre-adolescent ages used common toilets and freely bathed and played together without clothing. In such groups the children were still interested in examining the bodies of the other children, although they soon came to accept the nudity as commonplace and did not react as emotionally as they would have if nudity were the unusual thing.

A high proportion of our adult subjects rather precisely recalled the ages at which they had first seen the genitalia of the opposite sex. This emphasizes the importance which such experience has for the child in a culture which goes to such length as our culture does to conceal the anatomic differences between the sexes. Nevertheless, 60 per cent of our adult female subjects believed that they had first seen male genitalia at some very early age, and certainly between the ages of two and five, while another 24 per cent placed their first experience between the ages of five and eleven. By adolescence, about 90 per cent had seen male genitalia.

Something more than a third (possibly 37 per cent) of the females in the sample recalled having seen the genitalia of adult males while they were still pre-adolescent. Another third had seen adult male genitalia first between adolescence and twenty years of age. The first opportunity to observe adult male genitalia in preadolescence had come, in order of frequency, from the following: the child's father (46 per cent), accidental exposure by a male who was not the child's father (19 per cent), deliberate exhibition by an adult male (22 per cent), the observation of relatives other than the father (9 per cent), the observation of the genitalia of the petting or coital partner (2 per cent), and miscellaneous sources (2 per cent). The children raised in homes of the better-educated groups had more often seen adult male genitalia at an earlier age, primarily because of the greater acceptance of nudity in homes of that level.

For 52 per cent of the females who had had any pre-adolescent heterosexual play, the play had involved manual manipulations of genitalia. In a goodly number of instances, these had amounted to nothing more than incidental touching. The heterosexual contacts had been specifically masturbatory in only a small number of cases. There had been mouth-genital contacts among only 2 per cent of the girls, and insertions of various objects (chiefly fingers) into the female vagina in only 3 per cent of the cases.

There had been some sort of coitus in 17 per cent of the cases for which any heterosexual play was reported, but it has been difficult to determine how much of the "coitus" of pre-adolescence involves the actual union of genitalia. In all instances recorded in the sample, there had been some apposition of the genitalia of the two children; and since erections frequently occur among even very young boys, penetrations may have been and certainly were effected in some of the pre-adolescent activity. However, the small size of the male genitalia at that age had usually limited the depth of penetration, and much of the childhood "coitus" had amounted to nothing more than genital apposition.

On the other hand, we have 29 cases of females who had had coitus as pre-adolescents with older boys or adult males with whom there had been complete genital union.

Pre-Adolescent Homosexual Play

Pre-adolescent sex play with other girls was recalled by about the same number of females as had recalled pre-adolescent sex play with boys. Although this sort of play seems not to have been particularly sexual among many of the females in the sample, it had either directly or indirectly taught a number of them how to masturbate. A few (5 per cent) of the girls had had their preadolescent homosexual contacts carry over into adolescence as more mature homosexual activity. . . .

Significance of Pre-Adolescent Sex Play

Significance in Psychosexual Development

In the course of their pre-adolescent sexual contacts with boys and with other girls, many of the females in the sample had acquired their first information about sex. They had acquired factual information about male and female genitalia and sometimes about reproduction, about masturbatory, petting, and coital techniques, and about the significance of adult sexual activities. In fact, many of the contacts had been incidental to and not infrequently the direct outcome of the discussion of such matters. Most of the information so acquired represented a part of the necessary education which most parents carefully avoid giving their daughters at any age.

Effect on Adult Patterns

In the course of their pre-adolescent contacts a significant portion of the females in the sample had discovered what it meant to be aroused erotically, and to be aroused to the point of orgasm. What was still more significant for their ultimate sexual adjustments, many of the females in the sample had learned how to respond in socio-sexual contacts. Some of the pre-adolescent contacts had provided emotional satisfactions which had conditioned the female for the acceptance of later sexual activities.

In not a few instances, guilt reactions had made the childhood experiences traumatic. This was especially true when the children had been discovered by adults, and when reprimands or physical punishment had been meted out to them. These guilt reactions had, in many instances, prevented the female from freely accepting sexual relations in her adult married relationships. When the parents had not become emotionally disturbed when they discovered the child in sex play, there was little evidence that the child's experience had done any damage to its later sexual adjustment. . . .

Nature of Contacts with Adults

The early experiences which the females in the sample had had with adult males had involved the following types of approaches and contacts:

Nature of Contact	Percent
Approach only	9
Exhibition, male genitalia	52
Exhibition, female genitalia	1
Fondling, no genital contact	31
Manipulation of female genitalia	22
Manipulation of male genitalia	5
Oral contact, female genitalia	1
Oral contact, male genitalia	1
Coitus	3
Number of cases with experience	1075

Nearly two-thirds (62 per cent) of these sexual approaches to children were verbal approaches or genital exhibition. In most of these cases the adult male had exhibited his genitalia, but in one per cent of the cases he had persuaded the small girl to exhibit her genitalia. It is difficult, in any given instance, to know the intent of an exhibiting male, but our histories from males who had been involved in such exhibitions and who, in a number of instances, had been prosecuted and given penal sentences for such exhibitions, include many males who would never have attempted any physical contact with a child. The data, therefore, do not warrant the assumption that any high percentage of these males would have proceeded to specifically sexual contacts. It is even more certain that it would have been an exceedingly small proportion of the exhibitionists who would have done any physical damage to the child. In all of the penal record, there are exceedingly few cases of rapists who start out as exhibitionists.

The satisfaction which an adult male secures when he exhibits either to a preadolescent or to an adult, appears to depend, at least in part, upon the emotional excitation which he experiences when he observes the fright or surprise or embarrassment of the female whom he accosts. To an even greater degree, his satisfaction may depend upon the emotional arousal which he experiences when he risks social and legal difficulties by engaging in taboo behavior. In some cases there may be a narcissistic element in his display of his genital capacities. Not infrequently the adult male masturbates before the child. Sometimes, however, his exposure is quite accidental, as in the case of an intoxicated or urinating male, and the child is mistaken in believing that the exhibition is deliberate.

Some 31 per cent of these sexual contacts with adults had involved fondling and petting which, however, still had not involved genital contacts.

In 22 per cent of the cases the adult had touched or more specifically manipulated the genitalia of the child, and in 5 per cent of the cases the child had manipulated the male genitalia. Children, out of curiosity, sometimes initiate the manipulation of male genitalia, even before the male has made any exposure.

In about one per cent of the cases, the male had made oral contacts with the female genitalia, and in about the same percentage of cases the male had persuaded the child to make oral contacts with his genitalia.

Among the children who had had any sort of contact with adults, there were 3 per cent (*i.e.*, 0.7 per cent of the total female sample) who had had coitus with the adult.

Significance of Adult Contacts

There are as yet insufficient data, either in our own or in other studies, for reaching general conclusions on the significance of sexual contacts between children and adults. The females in the sample who had had pre-adolescent contacts with adults had been variously interested, curious, pleased, embarrassed, frightened, terrified, or disturbed with feelings of guilt. The adult contacts are a source of pleasure to some children, and sometimes may arouse the child erotically (5 per cent) and bring it to orgasm (1 per cent). The contacts had often involved considerable affection, and some of the older females in the sample felt that their pre-adolescent experience had contributed favorably to their later socio-sexual development.

On the other hand, some 80 per cent of the children had been emotionally upset or frightened by their contacts with adults. A small portion had been seriously disturbed; but in most instances the reported fright was nearer the level that children will show when they see insects, spiders, or other objects against which they have been adversely conditioned. If a child were not culturally conditioned, it is doubtful if it would be disturbed by sexual approaches of the sort which had usually been involved in these histories. It is difficult to understand why a child, except for its cultural conditioning, should be disturbed at having its genitalia touched, or disturbed at seeing the genitalia of other persons, or disturbed at even more specific sexual contacts. When children are constantly warned by parents and teachers against contacts with adults, and when they receive no explanation of the exact nature of the forbidden contacts, they are ready to become hysterical as soon as any older person approaches, or stops and speaks to them in the street, or fondles them, or proposes to do something for them, even though the adult may have had no sexual objective in mind. Some of the more experienced students of juvenile problems have come to believe that the emotional reactions of the parents, police officers, and other adults who discover that the child has had such a contact, may disturb the child more seriously than the sexual contacts themselves. The current hysteria over sex offenders may very well have serious effects on the ability of many of these children to work out sexual adjustments some years later in their marriages.

There are, of course, instances of adults who have done physical damage to children with whom they have attempted sexual contacts, and we have the histories of a few males who had been responsible for such damage. But these cases are in the minority, and the public should learn to distinguish such serious contacts from other adult contacts which are not likely to do the child any appreciable harm if the child's parents do not become disturbed. The exceedingly small number of cases in which physical harm is ever done the child is to be measured by the fact that among the 4441 females on whom we have data, we have only one clear-cut case of serious injury done to the child, and a very few instances of vaginal bleeding which, however, did not appear to do any appreciable damage.

131

Vladimir Nabokov's novel Lolita *was published in 1955 but was not available in the United States until 1958. In the musings of Humbert Humbert, a confessed child molester, we see a highly sexualized child as an object of adult male desire. The novel and the two films based on it have outraged many.*

Lolita

Vladimir Nabokov

She would be, figuratively speaking, wagging her tiny tail, her whole behind in fact as little bitches do—while some grinning stranger accosted us and began a bright conversation with a comparative study of license plates. "Long way from home!" Inquisitive parents, in order to pump Lo about me, would suggest her going to a movie with their children. We had some close shaves. The waterfall nuisance pursued me of course in all our caravansaries. But I never realized how wafery their wall substance was until one evening, after I had loved too loudly, a neighbor's masculine cough filled the pause as clearly as mine would have done; and next morning as I was having breakfast at the milk bar (Lo was a late sleeper, and I liked to bring her a pot of hot coffee in bed), my neighbor of the eve, an elderly fool wearing plain glasses on his long virtuous nose and a convention badge on his lapel, somehow managed to rig up a conversation with me, in the course of which he inquired, if my misses was like his missus a rather reluctant get-upper when not on the farm; and had not the hideous danger I was skirting almost suffocated me, I might have enjoyed the odd look of surprise on his thin-lipped weather-beaten face when I drily answered, as I slithered off my stool, that I was thank God a widower.

How sweet it was to bring that coffee to her, and then deny it until she had done her morning duty. And I was such a thoughtful friend, such a passionate father, such a good pediatrician, attending to all the wants of my little auburn brunette's body! My only grudge against nature was that I could not turn my Lolita inside out and apply voracious lips to her young matrix, her unknown heart, her nacreous liver, the sea-grapes of her lungs, her comely twin kidneys. On especially tropical afternoons, in the sticky closeness of the siesta, I liked the cool feel of armchair leather against my massive nakedness as I held her in my lap. There she would be, a typical kid picking her nose while engrossed in the lighter sections of a newspaper, as indifferent to my ecstasy as if it were something she had sat upon, a shoe, a doll, the handle of a tennis racket, and was too indolent to remove. Her eyes would follow the adventures of her favorite strip characters: there was one well-drawn sloppy bobby-soxer, with high cheekbones and angular gestures, that I was not above enjoying myself; she studied the photographic results of head-on collisions; she never doubted the reality of place, time and circumstance alleged to match the publicity pictures of naked-thighed beauties; and she was curiously fascinated by the photographs of local brides, some in full wedding apparel, holding bouquets and wearing glasses.

A fly would settle and walk in the vicinity of her navel or explore her tender pale areolas. She tried to catch it in her fist (Charlotte's method) and then would turn to the column Let's Explore Your Mind. . . .

Oh, do not scowl at me, reader, I do not intend to convey the impression that I did not manage to be happy. Reader must understand that in the possession and thralldom of a nymphet the enchanted traveler stands, as it were, *beyond happiness*. For there is no other bliss on earth comparable to that of fondling a nymphet. It is *hors concours*, that bliss, it belongs to another class, another plane of sensitivity. Despite our tiffs, despite her nastiness, despite all the fuss and faces she made, and the vulgarity, and the danger, and the horrible hopelessness of it all, I still dwelled deep in my elected paradise—a paradise whose skies were the color of hell-flames—but still a paradise. . . .

I am now faced with the distasteful task of recording a definite drop in Lolita's morals. If her share in the ardors she kindled had never amounted to much, neither had pure lucre ever come to the fore. But I was weak, I was not wise, my school-girl nymphet had me in thrall. With the human element dwindling, the passion, the tenderness, and the torture only increased; and of this she took advantage.

Her weekly allowance, paid to her under condition she fulfill her basic obligations, was twenty-one cents at the start of the Beardsley era—and went up to one dollar five before its end. This was a more than generous arrangement seeing she constantly received from me all kinds of small presents and had for the asking any sweetmeat or movie under the moon—although, of course, I might fondly demand an additional kiss, or even a whole collection of assorted caresses, when I knew she coveted very badly some item of juvenile amusement. She was, however, not easy to deal with. Only very listlessly did she earn her three pennies—or three nickels—per day; and she proved to be a cruel negotiator whenever it was in her power to deny me certain life wrecking, strange, slow paradisal philters without which I could not live more than a few days in a row, and which, because of the very nature of love's languor, I could not obtain by force. Knowing the magic and might of her own soft mouth, she managed— during one schoolyear!—to raise the bonus price of a fancy embrace to three, and even four bucks. O Reader! Laugh not, as you imagine me, on the very rack of joy noisily emitting dimes and quarters, and great big silver dollars like some sonorous, jingly and wholly demented machine vomiting riches; and in the margin of that leaping epilepsy she would firmly clutch a handful of coins in her little fist, which, anyway, I used to pry open afterwards unless she gave me the slip, scrambling away to hide her loot. And just as every other day I would cruise all around the school area and on comatose feet visit drugstores, and peer into foggy lanes, and listen to receding girl laughter in between my heart throbs and the falling leaves, so every now and then I would burgle her room and scrutinize torn papers in the wastebasket with the painted roses, and look under the pillow of the virginal bed I had just made myself. Once I found eight one-dollar notes in one of her books (fittingly—*Treasure Island*), and once a hole in the wall behind Whistler's Mother yielded as much as twenty-four dollars and some change—say twenty-four sixty—which I quietly removed, upon which, next day, she accused, to my face, honest Mrs. Holigan of being a filthy thief. Eventually, she lived up to her I.Q. by finding a safer hoarding place which I never discovered; but by that time I had brought prices down drastically by having her earn the hard and nauseous way permission to participate in the school's theatrical program; because what I feared most was not that she might ruin me, but that she might accumulate sufficient cash to run away. I believe the poor fierce-eyed child had figured out that with a mere fifty dollars in her purse she might somehow reach Broadway or Hollywood—or the foul kitchen of a diner (Help Wanted) in a dismal ex-prairie state, with the wind blowing, and the stars blinking, and the cars, and the bars, and the barmen, and everything soiled, torn, dead. . . .

"Lo! Lola! Lolita!" I hear myself crying from a doorway into the sun, with the acoustics of time, domed time, endowing my call and its tell-tale hoarseness with such a wealth of anxiety, passion and pain that really it would have been instrumental in wrenching open the zipper of her nylon shroud had she been dead. Lolita! In the middle of a trim turfed terrace I found her at last—she had run out before I was ready. Oh Lolita! There she was playing with a damned dog, not me. The animal, a terrier of sorts, was losing and snapping up again and adjusting between his jaws a wet little red ball; he took rapid chords with his front paws on the resilient turf, and then would bounce away. I had only wanted to see where she was, I could not swim with my heart in that state, but who cared—and there she was, and there was I, in my robe—and so I stopped calling; but suddenly something in the pattern of her motions, as she dashed this way and that in her Aztec Red bathing briefs and bra, struck me . . . there was an ecstasy, a madness about her frolics that was too much of a glad thing. Even the dog seemed puzzled by the extravagance of her reactions. I put a gentle hand to my chest as I surveyed the situation. The turquoise blue swimming pool some distance behind the lawn was no longer behind that lawn, but within my thorax, and my organs swam in it like excrements in the blue sea water in Nice. One of the bathers had left the pool and, half-concealed by the peacocked shade of trees, stood quite still, holding the ends of the towel around his neck and following Lolita with his amber eyes. There he stood, in the camouflage of sun and shade, disfigured by them and masked by his own nakedness, his damp black hair or what was left of it, glued to his round head, his little mustache a humid smear, the wool on his chest spread like a symmetrical trophy, his naval pulsating, his hirsute thighs dripping with bright droplets, his tight wet black bathing trunks bloated and bursting with vigor where his great fat bullybag was pulled up and back like a padded shield over his reversed beasthood. And as I looked at his oval nut-brown face, it dawned upon me that what I had recognized him by was the reflection of my daughter's countenance—the same beatitude and grimace but made hideous by his maleness. And I also knew that the child, my child, knew he was looking, enjoyed the lechery of his look and was putting on a show of gambol and glee, the vile and beloved slut. As she made for the ball and missed it, she fell on her back, with her obscene young legs madly pedalling in the air; I could sense the musk of her excitement from where I stood, and then I saw (petrified with a kind of sacred disgust) the man close his eyes and bare his small, horribly small and even, teeth as he leaned against a tree in which a multitude of dappled Priaps shivered. Immediately afterwards a marvelous transformation took place. He was no longer the satyr but a very good-natured and foolish Swiss cousin, the Gustave Trapp I have mentioned more than once, who used to counteract his "sprees" (he drank beer with milk, the good swine) by feats of weight-lifting—tottering and grunting on a lake beach with his otherwise very complete bathing suit jauntily stripped from one shoulder. *This* Trapp noticed me from afar and working the towel on his nape walked back with false insouciance to the pool. And as if the sun had gone out of the game, Lo slackened and slowly got up ignoring the ball that the terrier placed before her. Who can say what heartbreaks are caused in a dog by our discontinuing a romp? I started to say something, and then sat down on the grass with a quite monstrous pain in my chest and vomited a torrent of browns and greens that I had never remembered eating.

I saw Lolita's eyes, and they seemed to be more calculating than frightened. I heard her saying to a kind lady that her father was having a fit. Then for a long time I lay in a lounge chair swallowing pony upon pony of gin. And next morning I felt strong enough to drive on (which in later years no doctor believed).

132

The communications theorist Neil Postman argues that the childhood we have valued, based on a gradual access to adult knowledge, has been eroded by modern media. By making sexual secrets available to everyone, regardless of age, television has eliminated shame and banished childhood (1982).

The Disappearance of Childhood
The Total Disclosure Medium

Neil Postman

Like alphabetic writing and the printed book, television opens secrets, makes public what has previously been private. But unlike writing and printing, television has no way to close things down. The great paradox of literacy was that as it made secrets accessible, it simultaneously created an obstacle to their availability. One must *qualify* for the deeper mysteries of the printed page by submitting oneself to the rigors of a scholastic education. One must progress slowly, sequentially, even painfully, as the capacity for self-restraint and conceptual thinking is both enriched and expanded. I vividly remember being told as a thirteen-year-old of the existence of a book, Henry Miller's *Tropic of Cancer*, that, I was assured, was required reading for all who wanted to know sexual secrets. But the problems that needed to be solved to have access to it were formidable. For one, it was hard to find. For another, it cost money. For still another, it had to be *read*. Much of it, therefore, was not understandable to me, and even the special passages to which my attention was drawn by a thoughtful previous reader who underlined them required acts of imagination that my experience could not always generate.

Television, by contrast, is an open-admission technology to which there are no physical, economic, cognitive, or imaginative restraints. The six-year-old and the sixty-year-old are equally qualified to experience what television has to offer. Television, in this sense, is the consummate egalitarian medium of communication, surpassing oral language itself. For in speaking, we may always whisper so that the children will not hear. Or we may use words they may not understand. But television cannot whisper, and its pictures are both concrete and self-explanatory. The children see everything it shows.

The most obvious and general effect of this situation is to eliminate the exclusivity of worldly knowledge and, therefore, to eliminate one of the principal differences between childhood and adulthood. This effect follows from a fundamental principle of social structure: A group is largely defined by the exclusivity of the information its members share. If everyone knew what lawyers know, there would be no lawyers. If students knew what their teachers know, there would be no need to differentiate between them. Indeed, if fifth graders knew what eighth graders know, there would be no point to having grades at all. . . .

Civilization cannot exist without the control of impulses, particularly the impulse toward aggression and immediate gratification. We are in constant danger of being possessed by barbarism, of being overrun by violence, promiscuity, instinct, egoism. Shame is the mechanism by which barbarism is held at bay, and much of its power comes, . . . from the mystery and awe that surround various acts. Included among these acts are thoughts and words, all of which are made mysterious and awesome by the fact that they are constantly hidden from public view. By hiding them, we make them mysterious; by making them mysterious, we regulate them. In some cases, adults may not even display their knowledge of such secrets to each other and must find relief in the psychiatrist's office or the Confessional Box. But in all cases it is necessary to control the extent to which children are aware of such matters. Certainly since the Middle Ages it has been commonly believed that the impulse toward violence, sexuality, and egoism is of particular danger to children, who, it is assumed, are not yet sufficiently governed by self-restraint. Therefore, the inculcation of feelings of shame has constituted a rich and delicate part of a child's formal and informal education. Children, in other words, are immersed in a world of secrets, surrounded by mystery and awe; a world that will be made intelligible to them by adults who will teach them, in stages, how shame is transformed into a set of moral directives. From the child's point of view, shame gives power and authority to adulthood. For adults know, whereas children do not, what words are shameful to use, what subjects are shameful to discuss, what acts are deemed necessary to privatize. . . .

In revealing the secrets of sex, television has come close to eliminating the concept of sexual aberration altogether. For example, it is now common enough to see twelve- and thirteen-year-old girls displayed on television commercials as erotic objects. Some adults may have forgotten when such an act was regarded as psychopathic, and they will have to take my word for it that it was. This is not to say that adult males did not until recently covet pubescent girls. They did, but the point is that their desire was kept a carefully guarded secret, especially from the young themselves. Television not only exposes the secret but shows it to be an invidious inhibition and a matter of no special consequence. As in the Middle Ages, playing with the privy parts of children may once again become only a ribald amusement. Or, if that takes the matter too far, perhaps we may say that the explicit, albeit symbolic, *use* of children as material for the satisfaction of adult sexual fantasies has already become entirely acceptable. Indeed, conditioned by such use of children on television, the New York State Court of Appeals ruled in 1981 that no distinction may be made between children and adults in addressing the question of a pornographic film. If a film is judged obscene, the court ruled, then a conviction can be sustained. But if it is not judged obscene, then any law that tries to distinguish between the status of children and adults is invidious. One might say that such a ruling clears the way for continued exploitation of children. Or, from another point of view, that such a ruling merely reflects the realities of our new electric environment. For there are, in fact, very few expressions of human sexuality that television now regards as serious enough to keep private, that is to say, regards as inappropriate for use as a theme for a program or as the focal point of a commercial. From vaginal spray commercials to discussions of male strippers, from programs preoccupied with the display of buttocks and breasts to documentaries on spouse swapping, the secrets unfold one by one, in one form or another. In some cases, to be sure, a subject such as incest, lesbianism, or infidelity is treated with seriousness and even dignity, but this is quite beside the point. . . .

And here we must keep in mind that the stylized murders, rapes, and plunderings that are depicted on weekly fictional programs are much less than half the problem. They are, after all, clearly marked as fiction or pseudo–fairy tales, and we may assume (although not safely) that some children do not take them to be representations of real adult life. Far more impressive are the daily examples of violence and moral degeneracy that are the staple of TV news shows. These are not mitigated by the presence of recognizable and attractive actors and actresses. They are put forward as the stuff of everyday life. These are real murders, real rapes, real plunderings. And the fact that they *are* the stuff of real life makes them all the more powerful. . . .

Not since the Middle Ages have children known so much about adult life as now. Not even the ten-year-old girls working in the mines in England in the eighteenth century were as knowing as our own children. The children of the industrial revolution knew very little beyond the horror of their own lives. Through the miracle of symbols and electricity our own children know everything anyone else knows—the good with the bad. Nothing is mysterious, nothing awesome, nothing is held back from public view. Indeed, it is a common enough observation, particularly favored by television executives when under attack, that whatever else may be said about television's impact on the young, today's children are better informed than any previous group of youngsters. The metaphor usually employed is that television is a window to the world. This observation is entirely correct, but why it should be taken as a sign of progress is a mystery. What does it mean that our children are better informed than ever before? That they know what the elders know? It means that they have become adults, or, at least, adult-like. It means—to use a metaphor of my own—that in having access to the previously hidden fruit of adult information, they are expelled from the garden of childhood.

133

In the 1970s emphasis on children's sexuality began to give way to renewed concern about the sexual exploitation of children. This concern continued to mount throughout the late twentieth century; indeed, the view that children are frequently molested has become a common belief today and underlies issues such as "repressed memory syndrome." According to the psychoanalytic critic Jeffrey Masson, Freud intentionally hid the fact that children were commonly sexually victimized by adults (including parents), and instead argued that children's accounts of sexual molestation were based on fantasy. Masson argues that Freud originally believed his patients stories of abuse, but then retreated to the safer ground of childhood fantasy in order to become more acceptable socially and professionally (1992).

The Assault on Truth
Freud's Suppression of the Seduction Theory

Jeffrey Moussaieff Masson

The objections Freud raises in the letter [to his intimate correspondent Wilhelm Fliess on September 27, 1897] to the reality of the sexual abuse of children sound like those raised earlier by his colleagues, critical of the theory from the beginning. Freud had answered those objections in the three 1896 papers on seduction, . . . papers in which Freud establishes his belief in the reality of childhood seduction, providing evidence and answers to possible objections, the very objections that Freud raises in this letter. The letter symbolizes the beginning of an internal reconciliation with his colleagues and with the whole of nineteenth-century psychiatry. It is as if Freud were standing before his colleagues at the Society for Psychiatry and saying: "You were right, after all—what I thought was true is nothing but a scientific fairy tale."

The idea that Freud made a decisive and permanent decision about seductions, that they were, by and large, unreal, the fantasies of hysterical women, has become standard in psychoanalytic thought. . . .

Freud is saying that whether seduction actually took place or was only a fantasy does not matter. What matters, for Freud, are the psychological effects, and these effects, Freud states, are no different where the event is a real one or imagined. But in actuality there is an essential difference between the effects of an act that took place and one that was imagined.

To tell someone who has suffered the effects of a childhood filled with sexual violence that it does not matter whether his memories are anchored in reality or not is to do further violence to that person and is bound to have a pernicious effect. A real memory demands some form of validation from the outside world—denial of those memories by others can lead to a break with reality, and a psychosis. The lack of interest in a person's store of personal memories does violence to the integrity of that person.

Freud's statement, however, was not taken by psychoanalysts at face value; in fact, psychoanalysts have always shown a greater interest in the fantasy life of a patient than in real events. Freud shifted the interest of psychoanalysis to the pathogenic effects of fantasies, putting less emphasis on the pathogenic effects of real memories in repression. The ideal analytic patient has come to be a person without serious traumas in his childhood. Analysis, it is felt, is not equipped to deal with patients who have suffered real and serious emotional injury in child-hood. This is undoubtedly true, but the more important question is why this has come to be true, and whether it is an inevitable outcome of Freud's shift of interest from real seductions to fantasies. Because these are serious questions, the answers to which make a real difference in the lives of many people, it is important that we be informed of all the possible reasons why Freud made his shift. While I would describe this shift as a loss of courage, I do not believe that this judgment provides an explanation. Perhaps we will never have a single explanation for why Freud shifted his interest from real traumas to fantasies, but I believe that the historical documents allow us to come much closer to an answer than has been possible until now. . . .

Freud suffered emotional and intellectual isolation as long as he held to the reality of seduction. Freud felt his isolation most following the meeting of April 21, 1896, when he first publicly announced the seduction theory. ("I felt as though I were despised and universally shunned.") Freud had hoped that Breuer, after collaborating with him on *Studies on Hysteria*, would gradually alter his views on the sexual etiology of the neuroses. This did not happen. On the contrary, Breuer joined the ranks of those who believed Freud was losing his grip on reality, as we see from an unpublished passage in a letter from Freud to Fliess of March 1, 1896, in which he writes of Breuer that

> our personal relationship, externally reconciled, casts a deep shadow over my existence here. I can do nothing right for him and have given up trying. According to him, I would daily have to ask myself whether I am suffering from moral insanity or *paranoia scientifica*.

Condemnation was not confined to Breuer and Freud's colleagues. Freud had been timid enough in *Studies on Hysteria* when it came to discussing the effects of real seduction. But the book did speak about the importance of sexual life in the origin of the neuroses, and this alone was enough to provoke others to reject Freud's ideas, as is shown by the reviews. The German psychiatrist Adolf van Strümpell, in his review of *Studies on Hysteria* for an influential psychiatric journal, *Deutsche Zeitschrift für Nervenheilkunde*, complains bitterly of Freud's invasion of the private sexual life of the patient. He claims that what Freud and Breuer discovered were only the "fantasies and invented tales" typical of hysterics. Conrad Rieger was even more forceful and unpleasant in his comments on "Further Remarks" in *Centralblatt für Nervenheilkunde Psychiatrie und gerichtliche Psychopathologie*, where he writes:

> I cannot believe that an experienced psychiatrist can read this paper without experiencing genuine outrage. The reason for this outrage is to be found in the fact that Freud takes very seriously what is nothing but paranoid drivel with a sexual content—purely chance events—which are entirely insignificant or entirely invented. All of this can lead to nothing other than a simply deplorable "old wives' psychiatry."

... The strange fact is that no author of this time directly refuted Freud's major contributions relating to the effects of seduction in childhood on a person's later life. Löwenfeld, for example, superior in many respects to his psychiatric colleagues, nevertheless consistently missed the point of Freud's 1896 papers, though he was preoccupied with them and wrote about them seriously. There is no scientific criticism of the thesis, only disavowal and disgust. If Freud found this silence perplexing, he finally decided to identify with it. *Studies on Hysteria* and *The Interpretation of Dreams* are revolutionary books in ways that no subsequent book written by Freud would be. True, he enabled people to speak about their sexual lives in ways that were impossible before his writings. But by shifting the emphasis from an actual world of sadness, misery, and cruelty to an internal stage on which actors performed invented dramas for an invisible audience of their own creation, Freud began a trend away from the real world that, it seems to me, is at the root of the present-day sterility of psychoanalysis and psychiatry throughout the world.

134

As scholars debate whether child sex abuse is rampant and has been covered over since Freud's time, the question of whether children can testify accurately about their sexual abuse has become an urgent legal issue. It was highlighted in the mid-1990s when a town in Washington became the site of a highly publicized child sexual abuse case.

The Unraveling of a Monstrous Secret

Marla Williams and Dee Norton

There is right, and there is wrong.

In Cherie Town's book, it was wrong for her husband to be messing around with other women. So when he started bragging, she picked up the phone and called the Rape Crisis Center.

She told a counselor that her husband, Meredith "Gene" Town, had for years been molesting their two young sons. . . .

So began the painful unraveling of a monstrous secret.

That secret allegedly was shared by at least two dozen adults and some 50 children said to be members of "The Circle." A loosely organized circle of friends consisted of two extended families and a pastor, his wife and a church bus driver—their lives intersecting by chance on the walk to school, at the welfare office, at church and in local taverns.

They were families, police say, in which adults treated children as commodities, "trading them like party favors"—not for financial gain, but for sexual gratification and illusions of power and control . . .

The idea that the same 50 children could be routinely sodomized by the same two dozen adults year after year is so horrific it gives rise to disbelief.

Seeking out and punishing sexual abusers of children has become a national obsession, sometimes with tragic results. Adults, wrongly accused, have lost their jobs, homes, families and all hope of ever leading normal lives. Children, not knowing whether their memories are real, grow up unsure and unhappy—damaged no matter what happened.

Still, the fact remains that more than 400,000 reports of verifiable child abuse are filed nationwide with authorities each year.

Some children were abused in Wenatchee, that much is certain. There is medical evidence to support some charges of sexual molestation. Whether those children were routinely gang-raped, as police and prosecutors say, is another matter.

A kid-swapping, adult-led sex ring such as that alleged in Wenatchee would be "rare indeed," said Dr. Fred Berlin, founder of the Johns Hopkins Sexual Disorders Clinic in Baltimore.

But it wouldn't be impossible.

"Clearly, there is risk of embellishment," Berlin said. "But I believe there is a possibility that people who share such common, aberrant needs could be drawn together because the mainstream of their existence centers on the frequent need to be sexual. "The difficulty in such situations is teasing out the truth."

The official version of what happened in Wenatchee is found at the Chelan County Clerk's Office, on the fifth floor of the Chelan County Courthouse Law and Justice Center.

Reams of legal papers are bound in bright red files, dog-eared and smudged now, from handling by members of the news media.

A second set of files is kept by Chelan County Prosecutor Gary Riesen, whose office is down the hall, just past the Superior Court chambers where the fates of the accused are to be decided.

Four stories below Riesen's office is the Chelan County Jail where the accused—stripped of their shoes, street clothes and freedom—wait for a chance to tell their stories.

From there it's three blocks to the Wenatchee police station, a cramped stone building constructed in the early 1930s. There is no interrogation room, so officers question suspects at their desks, which are arranged in two short rows in a drab gray room. The room's only memorable feature is an oversized Pink Panther that lounges at the desk of Detective Robert Perez, sex-crimes investigator.

Cherie and Meredith Town's former residence, 610 Mission St., is within an easy five-minute walk. The house—a hulking, beige two stories crouched near the curb—is a wreck. Top-floor windows are busted out, the rest covered with plywood. The front walk is overgrown; there's litter where there should be lawn.

The day after Cherie Town called the Rape Crisis Center, Perez stopped by briefly. Before he arrested Meredith Town, he wanted corroborating statements from the boys, then ages 14 and 12.

Perez knew time was short. Word was out that Meredith Town was preparing to skip Wenatchee and take his boys to El Dorado, Kan.

The detective had completed 64 hours of special training in sex-crimes investigation; both he and his superiors were confident of his ability to handle just about any case.

They had no idea, of course, of the difficulties that lay ahead; no hint of conspiracy; no clue that an incestuous ring of pedophiles, the likes of which has never been proved in this country, might be operating in Wenatchee.

Wenatchee was in shock. Many people were horrified, almost grief-stricken by the sex scandal; others were beginning to think police, and Perez in particular, were manufacturing charges.

Kinder critics said police, immersed in wretched detail, had failed to consider the children might be telling tales, exaggerating or even fabricating accounts of sexual abuse. Nearly all the children interviewed by police came from impoverished, troubled homes. Wasn't it possible, some asked, that the children, desperate for attention and approval, hadn't simply said what they thought police wanted to hear?

Others compared the investigation to the Spanish Inquisition.

"It's a witch hunt, pure and simple," said Bob Kinkade, self-appointed leader of the local chapter of Victims of Child Abuse Laws. VOCAL, as the group is more commonly known, is a national organization established to "protect the falsely accused."

Kinkade knows what it feels like to be charged with sexual abuse. He has twice been tried on charges of molesting his stepdaughter. He was found not guilty on two charges; the jury was hung on three others.

A former East Wenatchee cop, Kinkade does not shy from a brawl. In newspapers and on television, he accused Perez of being on a power trip, of leading child witnesses into making false accusations, of trampling on suspects' constitutional rights and bullying adults into signing confessions. . . .

Debate rages in Wenatchee and across the country over whether children are reliable witnesses.

Elizabeth Loftus, a University of Washington professor and nationally noted authority on memory, argues strongly that children, and even some adults, are "highly suggestible" and therefore unreliable. "There are countless suggestive forces," she said. "It is extremely easy for a child, especially when traumatized, to create false memories . . . in an attempt to cope with or explain the experience."

Others argue children do not lie about something as physically and emotionally painful as sexual abuse.

"Children's disclosures may be confusing and inconsistent. A child may misattribute a specific abusive act . . . but, in my 20 years of experience I've found it extremely unusual for a child to fabricate such accusations from whole cloth," said psychiatrist Roland Summit, who has been a consultant on several high-profile sex abuse trials, including the McMartin day-care case in Los Angeles. "The fact is terrible things, unimaginable things, happen to children."

135

Today the sexualization of childhood has become clouded by fears about child sexual exploitation. The Internet is offering new means of access to those who would sexually abuse children. This New York Times *article details one such attempt discovered by investigators in 1996.*

On Prison Computer, Files to Make Parents Shiver

Nina Bernstein

Fertile, Minn.—Anchored to the windswept prairie by a grain elevator and a dead-end railroad track, this town of 900 people seems as remote from the dark side of cyberspace as it is from the lights of Times Square.

Yet 99 of Fertile's children are among thousands whose names were secretly compiled, annotated and stored with a cache of child pornography on a computer used by a convicted pedophile in a Minnesota state prison hundreds of miles away.

The man who managed the computer operation, an inmate with multiple convictions for child sexual assault, remains in prison. He has been the target of a Federal criminal investigation for almost two years, since the Federal Bureau of Investigation seized those files and equipment from a computer programming and telemarketing business run by inmates at the Minnesota Correctional Facility at Lino Lakes, north of Minneapolis.

But at a time when concern over pedophilia has become a flashpoint for national debate over Internet regulation, individual privacy and public safety, most families on the list have no idea that it even exists. Their children appear by name, age and location in dated entries that span six years and include personal details written as "latchkey kids," "speech difficulties," "cute" and "Little Ms. pagent winner." Those on the list range from babies 1 month old to children in their early teens, but most are girls between 3 and 12.

The towns where the children live are alphabetized and coded by map coordinates, as though on a road atlas to the American Midwest. Most are hamlets in northern Minnesota, places born of the railroad in the last century and bypassed by the highway in this one. Now they stand at the threshold of a new information age.

The list of children runs to 52 pages in a computer printout version obtained by The New York Times.

The list has to do with children and sex, the prime suspect has acknowledged to investigators from the Minnesota Department of Corrections, even as he has denied responsibility and cast blame on another inmate. The same computer that hid the list, investigators found, was used to traffic in digital images of nude children and to exchange messages with far-flung pedophiles linked by the Internet to sites like Kid Sex and Ped Net.

State investigators said they feared early on that the list had been compiled for sale to child molesters and sent out to those who could act on it even if its author could not. To this day, they said, they are uncertain whether the list was disseminated; that would have required only a few keystrokes.

Whether the list represents a single criminal's computerized obsession or a kind of nightmare mutation of data-base marketing, the list demonstrates how easily information can lose its innocence in the era of the Internet, a global connection of millions of computers that share messages, data and programs.

Yet the most compelling clues to the list's creation are not in the virtual world, but in the real one. The trail leads to small-town weeklies in which news and photographs of local children have long been a source of community pride. It leads to old court records unavailable on the Internet. It reaches back to evidence purged years ago from any official archive, but indelible in the memory of a police detective, a prosecutor, a defense lawyer and members of a jury whose decision 21 years ago has come back to haunt a new investigation.

Neither the F.B.I. nor the United States Attorney for Minnesota will discuss the case. But from a combination of public records, interviews and confidential documents, the mystery of the list emerges as a case study on the cusp of a new information culture, at the shadowy crossroads of technology and criminal justice.

A wire-mesh fence topped with concertina wire surrounds the medium-security prison at Lino Lakes. But in the fall of 1994, the information superhighway ran right through the walls into a basement office where prisoners sold their computer and telemarketing skills to concerns like Merrill Lynch, 3M and the Mayo Clinic.

The program, known as Insight Inc., dated to the 1970's. Its founders, two inmates of the maximum-security state prison at Stillwater, Minn., started it with help from the Control Data Corporation to raise money for prisoners' college tuition. By 1994, the corporation had a Lino Lakes branch that employed about 40 inmates and boasted a battery of telephones and a state-of-the-art computer system.

Then the success story threatened to become a scandal. A Minneapolis television station, WCCO, ran an exposé on Insight, raising questions of financial abuse. The broadcast disclosed that Insight operated independently of prison authorities and was so lucrative that the murderer at the top of its hierarchy had left prison with $106,000.

Another convicted killer had built a for-profit computer business within the company, never telling some big clients—like the Florida State Lottery, the United States Air Force and the West German Railway—that he was in prison, the station said.

Embarrassed corrections officials suspended Insight and retained an outside computer security company to help in a comprehensive audit. On the computer used by George Gerald Chamberlain, the convicted pedophile who was Insight's manager of computer operations, two computer experts came upon the first example of what they would later call "Minnesota area child research lists." They immediately realized that something was amiss.

A Department of Corrections investigator confronted Mr. Chamberlain, who is serving a 35-year sentence for criminal sexual conduct with four children. "Chamberlain agreed with the investigator that this list had to do with children and sex," an F.B.I. agent wrote later in an affidavit for a Federal search warrant. But Mr. Chamberlain insisted then and in a recent telephone interview with a reporter that he had no idea of where the file had come from. He denied any wrongdoing.

Mr. Chamberlain's computer was one of five in Insight's offices, and other prisoners had easy access to his work area. It was one of two linked by modern to the Internet with equipment specifically designed to capture, manipulate and redistribute images. The other was at the work station of William Arthur Couture, a murderer known even outside the prison as a computer genius. He declined to talk to a reporter.

While Mr. Chamberlain and Mr. Couture tried to implicate each other, the computer auditors followed digital tracks to a startling conclusion: This prison enterprise with a Fortune 500 client list had become a secret site for interstate and international traffic in child pornography, the computer consultants wrote in a confidential report recently obtained by The New York Times.

The link between the pornography and the children's names was unclear to investigators, but the more they learned about Mr. Chamberlain's history, the more sinister the list appeared.

Mr. Chamberlain, 56, has been in prison since 1979, but his adult history of sex-related felonies begins when he was 18 and spans a 20-year period punctuated by prison terms in three states and six failed attempts at treatment, according to court records. His youngest record victim was a 6-year-old girl. State law requires his release from prison in 2002, when he will have served two-thirds of his sentence.

In 1975, Mr. Chamberlain became a suspect in a series of burglaries and sexual assaults on children in the Minneapolis suburbs. In the execution of a search warrant at his home, police detectives seized a green spiral notebook containing a handwritten list of parents' names, addresses and children's names and ages, some marked with a check or an asterisk.

According to a police complaint at the time, three of the marks distinguished homes where children had been sexually assaulted. Detectives eventually concluded that the notebook had been compiled from a set of suburban telephone directories that contained children's names and birthdays, which had been used to hunt and target victims.

To a new set of investigators two decades later, the notebook sounded chillingly like a low-tech version of the computerized list found in Mr. Chamberlain's work-station computer. But there was a problem: Mr. Chamberlain was acquitted by a jury on the 1975 charges, and the notebook was nowhere to be found.

Last year, corrections officials seeking to extend Mr. Chamberlain's prison stay brought him up on prison disciplinary charges in connection with both the pornography and the list. But an administrative hearing board found the case unproved. . . .

There are 67 place names on the printout of the computer list, beginning with Aitkin, Minn., and ending abruptly, 3,000 children later, at Moorhead, Minn. The rest of the alphabet is missing. The largest towns are Fargo, N.D., and Duluth, Minn.; the smallest are like specks in a sea of plowed black earth. Around Thanksgiving 1994, investigators selected a small random sample and started calling.

"We could not tie the list to any current or old crimes," Steven Lydon, chief of investigations, said in a recent interview. "But parents were concerned, as who wouldn't be."

For one mother in Eagle Bend, a farming town of 523, it was as if she had learned that her children had been playing at the edge of a precipice when she had thought they were safe in her own front yard.

"It makes you sick," she said, speaking on the condition that her name not be used.

Her family is one of 35 in Eagle Bend on a list that noted which girls took piano lessons, which child was plump and which 10 entered a small pageant for 6- to 8-year-olds. "Hosted foreign student," it says for her own family, listing a date, June 6, 1988.

That, the woman discovered, was the date of an article and family photograph in the local paper, *The Independent News Herald*, a weekly with a circulation of 2,500 run by her neighbors, Diane and Ernie Silbernagel. Paging through back issues, the Silbernagels found that all the Eagle Bend entries corresponded to articles or photographs.

But how had prison inmates tapped such obscure sources? Access to the Internet, the investigators said. They were wrong—or at least premature.

"Our newspaper was not on the Internet," Mrs. Silbernagel said recently. "In fact, we're just getting on the Internet now."

Later, the Silbernagels notified investigators of another possibility. *The News Herald* exchanged a subscription with *The Prison Mirror*, a paper published by inmates at the Stillwater prison, where Mr. Chamberlain, like Mr. Couture, had been confined for years before his transfer to Lino Lakes.

The Mirror, started by members of the Jesse James gang in 1887, gets up to 70 small-town newspapers. Many are passed on to inmates or to the prison library.

"I believe that's how he got the information," said Mr. Lydon, the chief investigator.

While corrections investigators researched the past, the two digital detectives were probing along an electronic frontier.

The data on Mr. Chamberlain's computer filled more than 8,665 files in 335 directories, according to a confidential report prepared for investigators by Paul D. Porter, chairman of the computer company brought in for the audit, the Security Board.

The report describes how Mr. Porter and an associate retrieved the residue of Mr. Chamberlain's Internet messages, which included references to "Private Collection Teen Nudist" images, cautions about avoiding a law-enforcement sting, instructions on how to make calls that cannot be traced and how to destroy evidence "if busted," and evidence of the transfer of 758 pornographic images, most of children, to an optical disk.

The computer analysts also uncovered several updated versions of the list, including one devoted to children 1 to 7 years old.

Exceptional steps had been taken to protect against disclosure, the computer analysts wrote. A powerful security program had been used to equip Mr. Chamberlain's computer hard drive with the equivalent of a false-bottom drawer. The security program included a self-destruct feature: it would automatically erase data if someone tried to gain access without the right key.

It was Mr. Couture who provided the "Open Sesame" for the secret drive. Details of his interview with investigators come from a Federal affidavit filed later by the F.B.I. for a search warrant. The affidavit refers to Mr. Couture only as an Insight inmate incarcerated for murder, but his identity is clear from the confidential report, which identifies him. "The inmate stated that he had seen images on Chamberlain's computer screen of 'under age nude girls,' " the Federal affidavit said, "and that he had helped Chamberlain set up a computer system to hide the images of 'under age nude girls on his computer,' " The key to unlock the hidden drive was a password phrase: "They cannot commit me."

The phrase had eerie significance. A week earlier, the affidavit said, Mr. Chamberlain had told an investigator who confronted him about the list that he was afraid that the authorities would try to commit him under Minnesota's "psychopathic personality" law when his prison term was up. The law provides for the indefinite civil commitment of dangerous sex offenders to the Department of Human Services for treatment.

A month after Mr. Couture's interview with investigators, he was released on parole, having served 10 years of a 15-year murder sentence.

Mr. Chamberlain insists that Mr. Couture set him up as a fall guy, and he notes that investigators found much digital pornography on Mr. Couture's computer. "I'm innocent," he told a reporter. . . .

In Fertile, people feel so safe they leave their front doors unlocked.

"If people knew, they would be afraid," said Michael Moore, the editor of

The Fertile Journal, a weekly, when he recently learned about the list from a reporter.

They would have "fear for their children," he added, speaking with the certainty of a father who had seen the name of his 7-year-old daughter on the list.

A bear of a man with a salt-and-pepper beard, Mr. Moore was still struggling to understand how information that had seemed moored to one small, safe place had mutated and recombined into something fearful.

"I'm concerned about how it could be perceived," he said. Every name and date on the list, he found, corresponded with a popular annual feature in *The Journal* called "Citizens of Tomorrow." The multipage spread consists of photographs of local children, provided free to the paper by an Iowa photography studio that has been sending itinerant photographers to little towns across the rural Midwest since 1932.

Mr. Moore, who has a telemarketing business on the side, is more aware than most people that the world is full of lists. The prison computer list was apparently created as much from parochial newsprint as from global computer power. But that was no comfort to him.

As it happened, the layout for the 1996 version of "Citizens of Tomorrow" was in his newspaper's three-room office, waiting.

136

Another kind of epidemic — teen pregnancy — has led to a much more lenient at-
titude toward the distribution of contraceptives to adolescents. As a result, despite
the continuing debate about whether parents have the right to know when their
minor children seek contraceptives or abortions, teenagers have increasingly been
freed of parental supervision in these matters. The historian Maris A. Vinovskis dis-
cusses the controversy over parental notification during the Reagan administration.

The Politics of Parental Notification

Maris A. Vinovskis

The provision of federally funded family planning services for adolescents is a
relatively recent phenomenon in our history. Twenty years ago, family planning
providers and policymakers were reluctant to acknowledge publicly that teens
even had access to such services. Yet today the provision of contraceptives to
teenagers, even without their parents' knowledge, seems commonplace and normal to many Americans.

Several factors contributed to this change. For example, the steady expansion
in government provision of contraceptives to all women has led to a greater
tolerance for the provision of contraceptives to unmarried teenagers. A few
outspoken individuals still oppose any government participation in the distribution of contraceptives, but most Americans today see federal involvement as not
only acceptable, but an important government service. Indeed, even many congressmen critical of the current Title X legislation want only to return the control
of the program to states and local governments. As a result, the idea that government should fund contraceptives for unmarried teenagers seems less controversial now because most of us accept and expect federal involvement in providing
family planning services for women.

Strong, negative views of premarital sexual activity were more characteristic
of the 1950s than of the 1960s and 1970s. As our society becomes increasingly
tolerant of premarital sexual activity, providing contraceptives to unmarried
teenagers becomes more acceptable. In fact, premarital activity among teenagers
had become so pervasive that many now accept it as inevitable and focus only
on ways of encouraging sexually active adolescents to use contraceptives effectively. A vocal minority still protests the sexual permissiveness of our society,

but the majority of Americans no longer condemn everyone who engages in premarital sexual activity.

Historically, few have challenged the rights of parents to oversee the behavior of their own children—especially in regard to their sexual development. Only when parents failed to supervise the activities of their children properly was it considered necessary for the church, the schools, or the state to intervene. Colonial and nineteenth-century Americans would have been astonished at the suggestion that unmarried adolescent children should have a right to privacy or contraceptive use. Yet in the 1960s and 1970s a growing contingent acknowledged the rights of children independent of their parents. The rights of unemancipated minors have expanded while parental control over them has contracted.

Certainly one of the most important developments that made parental consent or notification seem unwise was the growing concern among the public and policymakers over the "epidemic" of adolescent pregnancy during the 1970s and 1980s. . . . The emergence of adolescent pregnancy as a major domestic problem in the second half of the 1970s provided an environment conducive to the restriction of parental rights and responsibilities as a means of reducing adolescent pregnancies and abortions. For many adults, concern about curtailing the "epidemic" of adolescent pregnancy took precedence over their desire to involve parents in the contraceptive decisions of their children.

Public opinion polls have shown American adults to be rather evenly split on the wisdom and efficacy of a parental notification requirement. Yet the media and public outcry against the regulations were much more one-sided. In part this reflects the fact that since the late 1960s the number of individuals providing contraceptive services through federally funded family planning programs has increased. As a result, opponents easily alerted and mobilized professionals and volunteers working in these clinics to oppose regulations that they believed would be injurious to their clients. In addition, the great increase in domestic family planning programs during the past twenty years either created or helped to sustain powerful new advocacy organizations (such as AGI, PPFA, and NFPRHA), which played an important part in defeating the Reagan Administration's parental notification regulations. Thus, the development of a domestic family planning profession with its own organizations provided the institutional basis necessary to combat the proposed Title X regulations.

Some of the improvements in the availability of contraceptives for unmarried teenagers are a result of judicial decision in which the courts reaffirmed or even expanded the access of adolescents to federally funded family planning services. The courts often protected unmarried adolescents seeking family planning services from barriers erected by state or federal legislators. The rejection of parental consent for unemancipated minors receiving birth control information and devices, for example, came from the courts, not the legislatures.

Many Americans, especially those who experienced their own teenage years before the 1970s and 1980s, were surprised to discover that emancipated minors could now receive prescription birth control devices from federally funded family planning clinics without their parents' consent or knowledge. The Reagan Administration was determined to reverse this erosion of parental responsibility and authority through the proposed Title X parental notification requirement. This effort forced everyone involved to confront publicly the gradual changes of the past two decades. The strong media opposition, the overwhelming hostility of the public, and the rejection in the federal courts of the proposed regulations have seemingly acknowledged and ratified the gradual and quiet evolution of confidential adolescent access to contraceptive services in family planning clinics.

Judge Stubbs talking to boys in an Indianapolis court, February 5, 1910. *Survey*, vol. 23.

Part Ten

The Child and the State

Traditionally parents, especially fathers, had complete custody and control over their own children. They had the right to their services (or their wages if they worked for others) in return for maintenance and varying degrees of obligation for their education. The child was perceived as an important economic participant in the survival and well-being of the family.

Sometime in the nineteenth century, coinciding with the shift from farm to factory and country to city, the nation began to view children differently: as future contributors to society in an increasingly complicated world. Their nurture and education, not their labor, came to be valued, and the state stepped in to insure that this vision was pursued. In effect, the state became the superparent overseeing the well-being of children. It made the final decisions on how children should be raised and with whom they should live. The state broke the perception of children as workers, imposing child labor laws and compulsory education. It gathered and disseminated information and sought to help in guiding the child's development. And the right to raise one's child without interference could now be severed if the father or mother misused his or her authority in an abusive manner.

In the second half of the twentieth century the role of the state as superparent grew larger as families dissolved and our perception of the world as a dangerous place for children increased. More and more the state as protector was called on to rescue children from family conditions of abuse or neglect. And the state in its judicial role was increasingly called on to settle disputes between parents and others who fought for the custody of the children they had created or parented. By the second half of the twentieth century, what was originally seen as the child's right to protection by the state has evolved to include the right to exercise limited constitutional freedoms: the right to freedom of speech, due process rights in criminal proceedings, the right to vote, the right to contraception and abortion, and the right to be heard in dependency and custody determinations.

137

The government of the Massachusetts Bay Colony, with its largely Puritan population, controlled the behavior of parents as no other colony did. In this seventeenth-century statute we see a preview of what would later become the protective state.

The Family in the Social Order

Colonial Document

Massachusetts Statute, 1642

This Court, taking into consideration the great neglect in many parents and masters in training up their children in learning, and labor, and other employments which may be profitable to the commonwealth, do hereupon order and decree that in every town the chosen men appointed for managing the prudential affairs of the same shall henceforth stand charged with the care of the redress of this evil, so as they shall be liable to be punished or fined for the neglect thereof, upon any presentment of the grand jurors or other information or complaint in any plantations in this jurisdiction.... For this end they, or the greater part of them, shall have power to take account from time to time of [the] parents and masters and of their children, concerning their calling and employment of their children, especially of their ability to read and understand the principles of religion and the capital laws of the country, and to impose fines upon all those who refuse to render such account to them when required.... They shall have power (with consent of any Court or magistrates) to put forth [as] apprentices the children of such as shall not be able and fit to employ and bring them up, nor shall take course to dispose of them.... They are to take care that such as are set to keep cattle be set to some other employment withal, as spinning... knitting, weaving tape, etc.; and that boys and girls be not suffered to converse together so as may occasion any wanton, dishonest, or immodest behavior.... For their better performance of this trust committed to them, they may divide the town amongst them, appoint to every of the said townsmen a certain number of families to have special oversight of. They are also to provide that a sufficient quantity of materials as hemp, flax, etc., may be raised in their several towns, and tools and implements provided for working out the same.... For their assistance in this so needful and beneficial employment, if they meet with any difficulty or opposition which they cannot well master by their own power, they may have recourse to some of the magistrates, who shall take such course for their help and encouragement as the occasion shall require, according to justice. ... The said townsmen, at the next Court in those limits after the end of their year, shall give a brief account in writing of their proceedings herein. Provided, that they have been so required by some Court or magistrate a month at least before. ... This order to continue for two years and till the Court shall take further order.

138

In the second half of the nineteenth century organizations to protect children developed out of the various societies for the prevention of cruelty to animals. Jacob A. Riis describes the case of "Little Mary Ellen Wilson," found beaten in a closet in New York City (1892). Her plight was a catalyst to the "child-saving" movement.

The Child-Saving Movement

Jacob A. Riis

On a thriving farm up in Central New York a happy young wife goes singing about her household work to-day who once as a helpless, wretched waif in the great city through her very helplessness and misery stirred up a social revolution whose waves beat literally upon the farthest shores. The story of little Mary Ellen moved New York eighteen years ago as it had scarce ever been stirred by news of disaster or distress before. In the simple but eloquent language of the public record it is thus told: "In the summer of 1874 a poor woman lay dying in the last stages of consumption in a miserable little room on the top floor of a big tenement in this city. A Methodist missionary, visiting among the poor, found her there and asked what she could do to soothe her sufferings. 'My time is short,' said the sick woman, 'but I cannot die in peace while the miserable little girl whom they call Mary Ellen is being beaten day and night by her stepmother next door to my room.' She told how the screams of the child were heard at all hours. She was locked in the room, she understood. It had been so for months, while she had been lying ill there. Prompted by the natural instinct of humanity, the missionary sought the aid of the police, but she was told that it was necessary to furnish evidence before an arrest could be made. 'Unless you can prove that an offence has been committed we cannot interfere, and all you know is hearsay.' She next went to several benevolent societies in the city whose object it was to care for children, and asked their interference in behalf of the child. The reply was: 'If the child is legally brought to us, and is a proper subject, we will take it; otherwise we cannot act in the matter.' In turn then she consulted several excellent charitable citizens as to what she should do. They replied: 'It is a dangerous thing to interfere between parent and child, and you might get yourself into trouble if you did so, as parents are proverbially the best guardians of their own children.' Finally, in despair, with the piteous appeals of the dying woman ringing in her ears, she said: 'I will make one more effort to save this child. There is one man in this city who has never turned a deaf ear to the cry of the helpless, and who has spent his life in just this work for the benefit of unoffending animals. I will go to Henry Bergh.'

"She went, and the great friend of the dumb brute found a way. 'The child is an animal,' he said, 'if there is no justice for it as a human being, it shall at least have the rights of the stray cur in the street. It shall not be abused.' " And thus was written the first bill of rights for the friendless waif the world over. The appearance of the starved, half-naked, and bruised child when it was brought into court wrapped in a horse-blanket caused a sensation that stirred the public conscience to its very depths. Complaints poured in upon Mr. Bergh; so many cases of child-beating and fiendish cruelty came to light in a little while, so many little savages were hauled forth from their dens of misery, that the community stood aghast. A meeting of citizens was called and an association for the defence of outraged childhood was formed, out of which grew the Society for the Prevention of Cruelty to Children that was formally incorporated in the following year. By that time Mary Ellen was safe in a good home. She never saw her tormentor again. The woman, whose name was Connolly, was not her mother. She steadily refused to tell where she got the child, and the mystery of its descent was never solved. The wretched woman was sent to the Island and forgotten.

John D. Wright, a venerable Quaker merchant, was chosen the first President of the Society. Upon the original call for the first meeting, preserved in the archives of the Society, may still be read a foot-note in his handwriting, quaintly amending the date to read, Quaker fashion, "12th mo. 15th 1874." A year later, in his first review of the work that was before the young society, he wrote, "Ample laws have been passed by the Legislature of this State for the protection of and prevention of cruelty to little children. The trouble seems to be that it is nobody's business to enforce them. Existing societies have as much, nay more to do than they can attend to in providing for those entrusted to their care. The Society for the Prevention of Cruelty to Children proposes to enforce by lawful means and with energy those laws, not vindictively, not to gain public applause, but to convince those who cruelly ill-treat and shamefully neglect little children that the time has passed when this can be done, in this State at least, with impunity."

The promise has been faithfully kept. The old Quaker is dead, but his work goes on. The good that he did lives after him, and will live forever. The applause of the crowd his Society has not always won; but it has merited the confidence and approval of all right-thinking and right-feeling men. Its aggressive advocacy of defenceless childhood, always and everywhere, is to-day reflected from the statute-books of every State in the American Union, and well-nigh every civilized government abroad, in laws that sprang directly from its fearless crusade.

In theory it had always been the duty of the State to protect the child "in person, and property, and in its opportunity for life, liberty, and happiness," even against a worthless parent; in practice it held to the convenient view that, after all, the parent had the first right to the child and knew what was best for it. The result in many cases was thus described in the tenth annual report of the Society by President Elbridge T. Gerry, who in 1879 had succeeded Mr. Wright and has ever since been so closely identified with its work that it is as often spoken of nowadays as Mr. Gerry's Society as under its corporate name:

> "Impecunious parents drove them from their miserable homes at all hours of the day and night to beg and steal. They were trained as acrobats at the risk of life and limb, and beaten cruelly if they failed. They were sent at night to procure liquor for parents too drunk to venture themselves into the streets. They were drilled in juvenile operas and song-and-dance variety business until their voices were cracked, their growth stunted, and their health permanently ruined by exposure and want of rest. Numbers of young Italians were imported by *padroni* under promises of a speedy return, and then sent out on the streets to play on musical instruments, to peddle flowers and small wares to the passers-by, and too often as a cover for immorality. Their surroundings were those of vice, profanity, and obscenity. Their only amusements were the dance-halls, the cheap theatres and museums, and the saloons. Their acquaintances were those hardened in sin, and both boys and girls soon became adepts in crime, and entered unhesitatingly on the downward path. Beaten and abused at home, treated worse than animals, no other result could be expected. In the prisons, to which sooner or later these unhappy children gravitated, there was no separation of them from hardened criminals. Their previous education in vice rendered them apt scholars in the school of crime, and they ripened into criminals as they advanced in years."

All that has not been changed in the seventeen years that have passed; to remodel depraved human nature has been beyond the power of the Society; but step by step under its prompting the law has been changed and strengthened; step by step life has been breathed into its dead letter, until now it is as able and willing to protect the child against violence or absolute cruelty as the Society is to enforce its protection. . . . In the past year (1891) it investigated 7,695 complaints and rescued 3,683 children from pernicious surroundings, some of them from a worse fate than death. "But let it not be supposed from this," writes the Superintendent, "that crimes of and against children are on the increase. As a matter of fact wrongs to children have been materially lessened in New York by the Society's action and influence during the past seventeen years. Some have entirely disappeared, . . . and an influence for good has been felt by the children themselves, as shown by the great diminution in juvenile delinquency from 1875, . . . the figures indicating a decrease of fully fifty per cent."

Other charitable efforts, working along the same line, contributed their share, perhaps the greater, to the latter result, but the Society's influence upon the environment that shapes the childish mind and character, as well as upon the child itself, is undoubted. It is seen in the hot haste with which a general cleaning up and setting to rights is begun in a block of tenement barracks the moment the "cruelty man" heaves in sight; in the "holy horror" the child-beater has of him and his mission, and in the altered attitude of his victim, who not rarely nowadays confronts his tormentor with the threat, "if you do that I will go to the

Children's Society," always effective except when drink blinds the wretch to consequences.

The Society had hardly been in existence four years when it came into collision with the padrone and his abominable system of child slavery. These traders in human misery, adventurers of the worst type, made a practice of hiring the children of the poorest peasants in the Neapolitan mountain districts, to serve them begging, singing, and playing in the streets of American cities. The contract was for a term of years at the end of which they were to return the child and pay a fixed sum, a miserable pittance, to the parents for its use, but, practically, the bargain amounted to a sale, except that the money was never paid. The children left their homes never to return. They were shipped from Naples to Marseilles, and made to walk all the way through France, singing, playing, and dancing in the towns and villages through which they passed, to a seaport where they embarked for America. Upon their arrival here they were brought to a rendezvous in some out-of-the-way slum and taken in hand by the padrone, the partner of the one who had hired them abroad. He sent them out to play in the streets by day, singing and dancing in tune to their alleged music, and by night made them perform in the lowest dens in the city. All the money they made the padrone took from them, beating and starving them if they did not bring home enough. None of it ever reached their parents. Under this treatment the boys grew up thieves— the girls worse. The life soon wore them out, and the Potter's Field claimed them before their term of slavery was at an end, according to the contract. In far-off Italy the simple peasants waited anxiously for the return of little Tomaso or Antonia with the coveted American gold. No word ever came of them. . . .

To-day there are a hundred societies for the prevention of cruelty to children in this country, independent of each other but owning the New York Society as their common parent, and nearly twice as many abroad, in England, France, Italy, Spain, the West Indies, South America, Canada, Australia, etc. The old link that bound the dumb brute with the helpless child in a common bond of humane sympathy has never been broken. Many of them include both in their efforts, and all the American societies, whether their care be children or animals, are united in an association for annual conference and co-operation, called the American Humane Association.

In seventeen years the Society has investigated 61,749 complaints of cruelty to children, involving 185,247 children, prosecuted 21,282 offenders, and obtained 20,697 convictions. The children it has saved and released numbered at the end of the year 1891 no less than 32,633. Whenever it has been charged with erring it has been on the side of mercy for the helpless child. It follows its charges into the police courts, seeing to it that, if possible, no record of crime is made against the offending child and that it is placed at once where better environment may help bring out the better side of its nature. It follows them into the institutions to which they are committed through its care, and fights their battles there, if need be, or the battles of their guardians under the law, against the greed of parents that would sacrifice the child's prospects in life for the sake of the few pennies it could earn at home. And it generally wins the fight.

139

The historian Linda Gordon describes the Massachusetts Society for the Prevention of Cruelty to Children and its early efforts to address the problem of abused and neglected children and their parents. She also suggests that poverty was a major factor in the cases the society took on (1988).

The Progressive-Era Transformation of Child Protection, 1900–1920

Linda Gordon

A stenographer hired at the MSPCC [Massachusetts Society for the Prevention of Cruelty to Children] in 1908, and remaining until 1947, left a vivid memoir of the appearance of that agency when she first arrived.

> We started at the top in the Children's Home where Miss Wilson a typical key-ring-bunch matron, with dyed hair and a compelling voice conducted us on a tour of the Home. . . . the children arose and sing-songed the Lord's prayer which they followed with a rendition of the National Anthem, as their eyes rolled about in restless fashion and their hands were tightly folded. One sprightly little girl wanted to be hospitable but was advised by the Matron not to be a clatter-mouth. . . . Coming down to the next floor below we found a segregated group of older girls, so-called "moral delinquents." They . . . were kept apart lest they contaminate those who were said to be, as the Matron said, the "more wholesome type."
>   . . . we had seven special agents to cover the entire state. They were Benjamin Loring, a Civil War veteran. . . . Accustomed as he had been to fight the battles of the Civil War while in it, and re-fight them verbally after it in the halls of the Grand Army of the Republic, he believed in action. Packing his telescope bag, he would go to the western part of the state to clean up situations reported there. . . . He would recount as follows. . . . "I put the fear of God into them. I took the children, where I thought it best, to the court, and the judge had a special sitting, and I brought them right back to Boston with me. I spread them out . . ." Mr. William R. Critcherson had joined the staff coming from the Boston Police Department. Through the passage of years his word became to be relied upon to the extent that some judges took it as evidence without following certain recognized court procedures . . . he brought many a wayward apprentice around to see the light of better days. . . . James S. Carter, the remaining special agent, had been a newspaper reporter. To him all cases appeared

like "hot stuff" and he just itched to give them great publicity which of course was forbidden. All of these seven special agents carried police badges on the reverse of their coat lapel. . . . If the occasion demanded they exposed that badge to clients and then they report "all was clear sailing."

In 1908, the MSPCC was not very different than it had been several decades previously. The rigid treatment of children was the same, as was the agency's orientation to law enforcement. The agents had no special experience with family problems and lacked critical perspective on their authority and power over the poor.

In the next two decades, this agency, and child-protection work in general, underwent major transformations. The principles and practices developed during this "Progressive" period remained the basic system of regulation of child-raising in place today. Child protection became integrated into the developing social-work profession, specifically into the new field called child welfare, changing both who the workers were and their conception of the problem. Child-protection work became professionalized and secularized, ending the influence of religiously motivated charity volunteers. While the organization's official agents had always been men, the female Christian volunteers had had considerable influence; now the workers became mainly female, although authority and leadership remained in the hands of men. The very definition of their cause changed fundamentally. While they did not desert the title "cruelty to children," the child protectors now saw the problem as family violence. Within this rubric they emphasized child neglect rather than child abuse; and they made out the characteristic villain no longer as a drunken immigrant father but rather as an incompetent, insensitive, and possibly untrained mother in need of professional guidance. They adopted environmentalist rather than moralistic explanations for family violence; they preached a preventive rather than punitive set of solutions.

These transformations were not only fundamental but lasting. In most respects, though certainly not all, the perspective and structures that child-protection work developed by 1920 remain today. The field is still dominated by secular, professional, private agencies using a casework method, although it is often psychiatric as well. The personnel are overwhelmingly female, and the management overwhelmingly male. Environmentalism and prevention remain key slogans for basic policy orientation. Neglect remains the characteristic problem, and mothers are held primarily responsible. . . . A discussion of the Progressive era transformation of this work is essential because it was so enduring. . . .

The professionalization of social work had its roots in the late-nineteenth-century "charity organization" movement. "Charity organization" emerged, in England in the 1860s and in the United States in the 1870s, out of a self-critique by charity workers who denounced the wasteful "sentimentality" of indiscriminate giving. They planned a new "scientific charity" with the eradication of poverty, rather than its temporary amelioration, as their goal. Although they did not anticipate professionalization of charity work, the women volunteers who began the movement were using the idea that social helping should become "scientific" to upgrade their own status. Contesting the demeaning Victorian stereotype of "ladies bountiful" meddling among the poor to while away their leisure, they wanted to transform their charity into skilled labor (like other reformers who tried to reinterpret women's domestic occupations—housewifery and child-raising—as skilled labor). In Boston a group of women charity leaders, particularly Annie Adams Fields, began the Cooperative Society of Visitors in 1875 with the goal of investigating every application for help and providing workrooms and jobs rather than money or goods. This effort gave rise to Associated Charities (AC), Boston's charity organization agency, in 1879. Both the MSPCC and the Children's Aid Society (predecessor of BCSA) were active in the AC.

The most important concept in the charity organization vocabulary was *pauperism*. Poverty was lack of resources; pauperism was permanent, hereditary poverty caused by the loss of will, work ethic, thrift, responsibility, and honesty. Emphasizing the old distinction between the deserving and the undeserving poor, the scientific charity workers believed that alms-giving was counterproductive, because it could weaken independence and the sense of responsibility to provide for oneself and one's family.

The "scientific" approach to clients' needs later became "casework," the first methodology of the new professional social work. Casework began with the collection of the most complete information possible about any individual or family, with the aim of long-term independence, not merely immediate survival, and the conviction that each case required an individual approach. For child-protection agencies, the merits of the casework approach were readily apparent, for looking at each act of child abuse or each desertion as a separate crime had been evidently futile and wasteful, and child-protection workers had quickly learned to look at long-term family patterns. Although the casework method allowed reform-minded social workers to identify environmental causes of clients' problems, and to seek public remedies, in the 1880s the dominant motivation among its organizers was to prevent the undeserving from receiving relief. To put it in modern language, the charity organization societies (COSs) wanted to stop welfare chiselers. To this end COS organizers created a central registry of aid recipients. Agencies were asked to report the names of all those applying to them, and to check the file before offering help. This system worked to prevent duplication of effort, contradictory policies, and clients' cheating. . . .

By the end of World War I, the child-saving establishment in Boston had changed substantially. It was more unified as a result of interagency communication and division of labor. Most agencies were staffed primarily by professionals, and shared professional assumptions about the importance of expertise and the necessity to have only trained personnel handle child welfare problems. In rhetoric all agencies agreed on the limited value of prosecution, and if their actual treatment of cases did not hold back from recourse to the courts, the rhetoric did serve to offer yet another justification for their own informal power in families. Judge Baker [Guidance Center] clinicians led the way in presenting their conclusions as expert, scientific evaluations upon which judges should base their decisions. MSPCC caseworkers already had a tradition of making recommendations to court officers; now they too sought a more "scientific" basis for these recommendations.

The transformed child protectors in turn transformed the definition of the problem they were addressing. Four closely related new approaches grew in this period: an emphasis on neglect as opposed to abuse, environmentalist explanations, a sense that the major problem was familial, and a preference for professional guidance rather than criminal prosecution as a remedy. . . .

The conception of cruelty to children with which the MSPCC began was mainly a vision of vicious and extreme mistreatment of children. The cruelty they saw was shocking, stark, and offensive to a standard they perceived as universal. Today that "cruelty" is usually categorized as child *abuse*, and is distinguished from child *neglect*, the failure of caretakers to meet certain minimal standards of child care, which comprises by far the largest share of the caseload of children's protective agencies. . . . Carstens pioneered in the recognition of neglect, in the rhetoric of environmentalism and alarm about erosion of the family, and in the sloganeering of "prevention." Prevention became a euphemism for a social work rather than a judicial approach, a method that gave greater leeway and autonomous power to social workers and relied less on prosecution or court orders.

It would be wrong, however, to imagine that these changes arose from actual changes in the mistreatment of children. For example, there were a majority of neglect cases even in the Society's earliest records, although they were not identified as such. Consider the following list of new cases, the first fifteen from a randomly chosen monthly list, that of January 1881:

1. Orphan. Abused by dissipated aunt. Sent to Marcella Street Home.
2. Poor, need looking after. Case given to . . . Sub.Agent.
3. Neglect, cause dissipation. Made papers for guardianship.
4. Drunken father—Mother wished to rescue children. 3 of them sent to Alms House to be transferred to Marcella Street.
5. Father was soldier—Mother asks aid. Gave her a letter to Associated Charities.
6. Inquiry as to disposition of an infant. Referred to Mass. Infant Asylum.
7. Acrobat. Performing at the "Howard." Interviewed Proprietor & Parents.
8. Boy ran away from home. Wrote to parents, boy would be likely to visit, no information.
9. Cruel whipping of oldest girl. Investigated. Mother promised not to whip again.
10. Lame. One of its feet turned under. Will take it to Dr. Cabot, on his return.
11. Neglected and whip'd by father, who is dissipated. Mother sober and industrious. House and children cleanly.
12. Father dissipated. Mother sick & destitute. Took case to Dr. Wheelwright, State House.

13. Father and mother separated—former having custody—alleged to be growing up under bad influences. [illegible]
14. Alleged cruelty by mother . . . is willing to place child. Gave Mother letter to Children's Friend Society.
15. Abuse by stepmother. Advised sister to find some one to become Guardian.

Only five of these cases, one third, mentioned actual whipping, cruelty, or abuse. A decade later, the preponderance of neglect cases was even greater:

1. Boy 17 disobedient and untruthful. Advised Navy or arrest as stubborn child.
2. Mother left baby 4 mos and disappeared. Gave letter to Chardon St. to take child.
3. Father does not support. Seen and cautioned.
4. Father has spells of insanity and takes child 2½ away. Advised mother to take guardianship.
5. Father away. Mother dead. Gave advice as to care of children.
6. Wife complained. Man does not support. He claims he has a bad arm and cannot work. Both intemperate.
7. Father colored. Mother white. Man not supporting. $50 rent due. Party will report further. Referred to Overseers of the Poor.
8. Stepfather blind. Two older children will provide for mother if husband can be provided for.
9. Father intemperate. Mother dead. Four older children live away from home. Younger ones not regular at school.
10. Illegitimacy. Mother and J . . . M . . . are living together. The judge discharged . . . [illegible]
11. Girl 10 kept from school by stepmother. Seen and warned.
12. Marriage forced. Parents live apart, child sick. Grandmother is caring for it.
13. Father dead. Mother intemperate. Boy 11 don't know much about her. Has been with an aunt.
14. Mother dead. Party wish to adopt girl. I made the papers.
15. Boy 10 was made to lead a dangerous bull. In correspondence.

In these 1891 cases . . . there was no assault, nor any images of the kind of cruelty that awakened the passions of child-saving and dominated MSPCC publicity. These might be vignettes of ordinary daily life among the very poor.

Their new sensitivity to neglect in the early twentieth century made MSPCC agents believe that their caseload had actually changed, but they were wrong. Rather a different generation of agents was viewing their cases with new assumptions regarding the nature of child development and societal problems. For example, "Children may soon recover from a whipping, while their suffering from the various deprivations is continued for years." Systemic family problems such as desertion and non-support, rather than cruelty, were seen as causal. The state was responsible for improving individual family upbringing. "The city that does not provide adequate playgrounds or wholesome recreations and amusements . . . airy, sunny and sanitary dwellings, that does not enforce its laws dealing with school attendance and child labor . . . will be constantly creating the supply which will make the stream of neglect conditions perpetual." Behind these new assumptions were the complex attitudes usually characterized as Progressive: in this case, particularly the view that crime and violence were caused by the social environment, by structural problems of the society; and that state action could compensate for and correct negative environmental features.

Like many reformers of the Progressive era, child protectors adopted the rhetoric of "prevention." "This is an age of prevention," an MSPCC annual report informed its readers. "In medicine, sanitation and the conservation of natural resources, the theories of prevention are rapidly gaining precedence over the theories of cure." A medical model was adopted: child neglect was "a preventable social disease."

. . . The new conception of neglect was diagnosed in terms of *family* pathology. Although this pathology might be seen to be rooted in poverty, racial, or ethnic inferiority, and the degradation of urban life, the Progressive-era child protectors were mainly drawn to the opposite causal conclusion: that family weakness was at the root of larger social problems. Ameliorative proposals were always aimed at reforming families, not society. In this context, prevention meant protecting children from harm by disciplining parents. As a result, child-protection policy did not significantly move away from its law-enforcement emphasis. The substantive emphasis on family was paralleled by the casework record-keeping system. The family became the definition of the "case"—and notes on dealings with different siblings, even with different generations, were incorporated into the same case records. (By contrast, the pre-casework recording system, notations in ledger books, gave each incident or allegation of child mistreatment a separate case number.)

140

The state, which increasingly meant the federal government, began to take on the role of superparent in the early twentieth century. As the protector of children the state passed child labor laws, established juvenile courts, and began to support children in their families rather than sending them to orphanages (1994).

The State as Superparent

Mary Ann Mason

The rich cannot say to the lowly "You are poor and have many children. I am rich and have none. You are unlearned and live in a cabin. I am learned and live in a mansion. Let the State take one of your children and give it a better home with me. I will rear it better than you can." . . . The deepest, the tenderest, the most unswerving and unfaltering thing on earth is the love of a mother for her child. The love of a good mother is the holiest thing this side of heaven. The natural ties of motherhood are not to be destroyed or disregarded save for some sound reason. Even a sinning and erring woman still clings to the child of her shame, and though bartering her own honor, will rarely fail to fight for that of her daughter.

With this reasoning the appellate court of Georgia reversed the trial court, which had awarded the custody of Mrs. Moore's three illegitimate children all under age twelve to an orphanage. The trial court had relied upon a Georgia statute that declared that any child under age twelve could be removed to an orphan asylum or other charitable institution if it "is being reared up under immoral obscene or indecent influences likely to degrade its moral character and devote it to a vicious life." Without questioning the statute, the court of appeals determined that the trial court had failed to prove that Mrs. Moore was "of an immoral character, unsuitable and unable to rear the children."

In this case the court struggled with two powerful, sometimes contradictory principles. One was a belief in the importance of preserving the family, no matter how poor. The other was the conviction that the state must intervene into families in order to protect children from abusive, neglectful, or immoral parents. These two principles had a profound effect on child custody decisions in the first two decades of the twentieth century. They prompted state courts like Georgia's to abandon the common law doctrine allowing the exploitation of children.

Instead, both courts and legislatures formulated new rules aimed at protecting children.

For example, the concept of the child's best interest was extended to poor children. Originally this concept was developed in the late nineteenth century by judges to determine private custody disputes between divorcing parents. Now, it was applied to poor children generally, not just to the children of divorcing parents. In a radical departure from traditional poor law principles, the state made a tentative commitment to allow poor but "worthy" mothers to maintain custody of their children. Poor children who would have been "bound out" to a master in return for labor in the colonial years, and "placed out" to labor on a midwestern farm or sent to an almshouse or orphan asylum in the nineteenth century, were now more frequently supported in their mothers' home. (Rarely was support provided if the father were present.) If that failed, or if they had no suitable parent, children were increasingly placed in a foster home, which was considered a substitute family rather than an orphanage, or put up for adoption by a new family.

State legislatures also acted to protect children in other important ways during this era, adopting a huge amount of child welfare legislation. The hours and the workplaces where children could labor were closely regulated; other laws dictated the establishment of public schools and required attendance of all children. A juvenile court system was put in place in many states. State legislatures diluted judicial discretion in dealing with the welfare of children, confining it within an elaborate statutory scheme.

At the same time, the divorce rate was exploding, and both courts and legislatures were concerned about the impact that this social change might have on the future of the family. . . . Courts responded by pursuing a new trend in child custody following divorce. The decided trend favored mothers, who were seen as the more nurturing parent, even if the mother was not entirely above moral reproach. Legislatures, meanwhile, passed strict laws, often buttressed with severe criminal penalties, to compel child support from all fathers, including those who lost their children by judicial decree following divorce. Overall, both courts and legislators paid far less deference to fathers, virtually ignoring their common law rights to the custody and control of their children.

In effect, the state became the superparent, generous and nurturing, but judgmental. It made the final decisions on how children should be raised and with whom they should live. In assuming this role, the state finally shattered the common law relationship between parents and children. That relationship once had assumed that a father (and sometimes widowed mother) had complete custody and authority over his children, including absolute right to their services or wages if they worked for others, in return for maintenance and varying degrees of obligation for their education. Child labor legislation now severely restricted the right to the child's services. The right to custody, once absolute, could now be severed if the father or mother misused their authority in an abusive or neglectful manner. Furthermore, both legislators and judges decided that maintenance and custody were no longer mutually dependent rights. A father must support a child even if he lost custody. Finally, the obligation to educate passed from the parent to the state. The public school teacher, not the father or mother, would control the child's education and a good deal of the child's socialization.

The new concern for the welfare of the children was part of the larger, broader reformist movement placed historically in the "Progressive" era. During this era states intruded into the privacy of families in a manner not seen since the selectmen of Massachusetts visited homes to determine whether children were behaving well and receiving religious and civic training. "Childsavers," as they were called, were originally a large and very active coalition of volunteer philanthropists, Women's Club members, and assorted urban-based professionals who rallied against the mistreatment of poor and abused children toward the end of the nineteenth century. In the Progressive era the child-saving movement was increasingly dominated by the developing profession of social work. In contrast to the volunteer childsavers, social workers were trained, paid, and career minded. Social workers focused more on providing services to support a child within his or her family, rather than simply removing a child from a cruel environment.

While men still outnumbered women in early child welfare social work activity, a high proportion of women entered the field, and many reached the top of the profession. These were the women who had benefited from the efforts of the first wave of feminism and from the growing wealth of the middle class. They were college graduates who did not need to marry immediately in order to attain financial security. In ever larger numbers they gravitated to settlement houses, set up to help urban poor, mainly immigrants, and began to train at the growing number of institutions, such as the University of Chicago, that offered training courses in conjunction with a social service agency.

Julia Lathrop, the first chief of the Children's Bureau, created by President Willian H. Taft in 1912, is an example of this second wave of feminists. A child of middle-class abolitionist reformists, who provided encouragement and financial support, Lathrop rode on the victories of the first wave of feminists. Because of their efforts to open up education to women, she acquired a first-class education at Vassar and went on to read law. However, her career choices were severely limited; child saving was one of the few fields where she could use her talents and education on an equal footing with men. She was appointed as the first woman member of the Illinois Board of Public Charities in 1892, the organization responsible for orphaned, abandoned, and neglected children, and in 1899 helped found the Chicago Juvenile Court, the first in the country and the model for the nation. Thereafter, her career soared with the rapidly evolving child welfare movement. Her commitment to children was deeply felt. "Sooner or later," she declared, "as we choose, by our interest, or its lack, the child will win."

Referred to as social feminists (as opposed to pure women's rights advocates), this dedicated group, led by such remarkable women as Jane Addams, Florence Kelley, Lillian Wald, and Julia Lathrop, forced a significant ideological shift in the women's movement. The social feminists . . . turned away from the nine-teenth-century feminists' focus on individual property and civil rights for mid-dle-class women, as expressed in the seminal feminist manifesto, the 1848 Seneca Falls Declaration of Rights and Sentiments, and instead focused their attention on poor children and their families. In so doing the social feminists conformed to the nineteenth-century stereotype of the family as women's sphere and the world as men's sphere. For this reason, historians and modern-day feminists have criticized social feminists as backsliders who relinquished the goal of equal-ity with men and retreated into family concerns. . . .

Still, by supporting rather than challenging the family and the role of women within it, social feminists achieved important political gains, including suffrage and equal custodial rights for mothers—goals that had eluded their more indi-vidualistic nineteenth-century predecessors. Most of the leading social feminists of the early twentieth century supported women's suffrage but based their ar-gument on family welfare rather than individual rights. Jane Addams, in a speech entitled "Why Women Should Vote," argued that women "bring the cultural forces to bear upon our materialistic civilization; and if she would do it all with the dignity and directness fitting one who carries on her immemorial duties, then she must bring herself to the use of the ballot—that latest implement for self government. May we not fairly say that American women need this implement in order to preserve the home?" The nonthreatening argument that the vote was a means for mothers to promote the family, not their own political interests, proved to be the winning strategy in persuading all-male legislatures to grant female suffrage.

This same argument in favor of mothers promoting their children's interests permitted the passage of legislation giving mothers equal custody rights to fathers—a victory not attainable by the first wave of feminists, who fought for equal rights for married women. The arguments of earlier feminists, focusing on the individual rights of women, not those of children or the family, threatened the all-male legislators who feared that equal custody rights would encourage women to leave their husbands. Social feminists, on the other hand, allied with philanthropists, juvenile court advocates, and other reform-minded groups, pushed for a broad program of child protection and support legislation that often benefited their mothers as well. Legislative emphasis on children's rights rather than those of their parents was a winning approach. As Florence Kelley remarked in regard to the common law as interpreted by Blackstone, "Nowhere in the Commentaries is there a hint that the common law regarded the child as an individual with a distinctive legal status." However, she believed that the Pro-gressive era began by recognizing "the child's welfare as a direct object of legislation."

Social feminists promoted family interests while redefining the relationship between children, parents, and the state. They abandoned the nineteenth-century policy of family privacy, which effectively gave parents or, most often, fathers, the right to complete control of their children, as long as they supported them. Instead, the social work profession recognized the role of the state as parent as well. In fact, the state, as represented by its agents, child welfare workers, became the superparent, determining the conditions under which natural parents could raise their children. Critics of the newly developing "helping profession" of social work claim that social workers set out to undermine the family culture of poor immigrants and replace it with their own middle-class values. Historian Christopher Lasch maintains that social workers, through children's aid societies, juvenile courts, and family visits, "sought to counteract the widespread 'lack of wisdom and understanding on the part of parents, teachers, and others,' while reassuring the mother who feared, with good reason, that the social worker meant to take her place in the home."

Still, the new social work philosophy emphasized maintaining poor children in their families, if fit. This commitment represented a major shift in American poor law philosophy regarding the custody of children, probably the most significant change since the Elizabethan Poor Laws of 1601 mandated the apprenticing of poor, idle, or vagrant children. Propelling this ideological shift was the emerging belief that poverty did not necessarily reflect moral weakness; social conditions could force otherwise worthy people into a state of poverty. A good part of the child-saving debate during the Progressive era focused on when and how to support parents so that they would not be forced to give up their children. The first White House Conference on the Care of Dependent Children, called by President Theodore Roosevelt in 1909, offered this agenda:

> Should children of parents of worthy character, but suffering from temporary misfortune, and the children of widows of worthy character and reasonable efficiency, be kept with their parents—aid being given to parents to enable them to maintain suitable homes for the rearing of the children? Should the breaking of a home be permitted for reasons of poverty, or only for reasons of inefficiency or immorality?

Reformers at the conference quickly adopted the position that poverty alone should not justify the removal of a child from his or her parents; only severe physical abuse or neglect or lack of moral fitness would provide sufficient grounds. Far more divisive was the question of how to support a family in poverty. The majority leaned toward private charity rather than government relief as a means of accomplishing this goal. There was widespread concern within the social welfare community that public aid would produce a "dependent" personality and would discourage relatives and charities from carrying their share of the burden. Social feminists, who uniformly agreed upon the family as the best institution for child raising, reflected this split within their own ranks. Jane Addams, Florence Kelley, Julia Lathrop, and Grace and Edith Abbot, all prominent leaders of the settlement house movement, concurred that private charity could not reach far enough to solve the problems of poor families, while others, particularly those associated with well-established charities, including Josephine Lowell Shaw, of the New York Charity Organization Society, and Mary Richmond, who headed the Philadelphia Society for Organizing Charity, strongly opposed the demoralizing factor of state aid. As one Mary Wilcox Glenn of the Brooklyn Bureau of State Charities characterized it, it would encourage "pathological parasitism"

In spite of strong opposition, the shift to state support occurred rapidly at the end of the Progressive era; public law mandating the juvenile court to order support for "worthy" parents unable to maintain their children passed the Illinois legislature in 1911. This law was officially known as the "Funds to Parents," and used gender-neutral language in describing parents.

> If the parent or parents of such dependent or neglected child are poor and unable to properly care for the said child, but are other wise proper guardians and it is for the welfare of such child to remain at home, the court may enter an order finding such facts and fixing the amount of money necessary to enable the parent or parents to properly care for such child.

By 1919 funds for dependent children in their own homes had been provided by thirty-nine states and the territories of Alaska and Hawaii.

141

The federal government's entrance into the business of protecting children began with the creation of the Children's Bureau in 1909. Florence Kelley and Lillian Wald were instrumental in the bureau's formation.

The Children's Bureau

Government Documents

Florence Kelley, "The Federal Government and the Working Children" (1906)

For more than a generation we have had a so-called Department of Education. It has published information so inconclusive and so belated that it is the laughing stock of Europeans interested in our educational institutions; so belated, moreover, that it is worthless for our own uses in obtaining improved legislation in this country.

Meanwhile it is left to a feeble volunteer society to collect a few hundred dollars, here and there, and publish in January, every year, the new statutes which have taken effect in the twelve months next preceding. Why does not the Department of Education do this? Why has not the Department of Labor always done this? Why have they not made it a joint undertaking? What are these departments for, if they are not to furnish to the people information concerning the working children at a time when it can be used?

So far as I have been able to learn by studying the reports of these two departments, the hieroglyphics on the pyramid of Cheops are not more remote from the life of to-day than their statistics are remote from the life of the working children of Georgia and Pennsylvania. . . .

Surely it is more important that the American people should know what is really happening to its young children in industry than that we should learn at brief intervals how the young lobsters are faring on the coast of Maine and the young trout in the remote streams of Northern Wisconsin.

At last, there is a proposal that we should rise from our low position among the nations when we are ranked according to our care of our children. We are not, when graded according to our care and education of our working children, in the same class of enlightened and humane nations as England, France, Germany, Holland, Switzerland and Scandinavia. . . .

It is now proposed that we should limp haltingly after those nations, though

Congress may be by no means ready to legislate in a unified way for the children as it does, for instance, for the textile industry, the glass industry and the interests of agriculture.

It is proposed that there should be devoted to the children one bureau of our government, by means of which the people should be able to obtain, from month to month, recent trustworthy information concerning everything that enters into the lives of the children; everything that makes for or against their vital efficiency, their educational opportunity, their future industrial and civic value.

A bill will be presented to Congress, with the hope that there may be established a bureau of research and publicity in the interests of all the children in the Republic.

"Children Bureau Bill Again Before Congress" (1909)

The bill to establish a federal children's bureau has been introduced in the special session of Congress by Representative Herbert Parsons of New York and Senator Frank P. Flint of California. . . .

For the benefit of new members of Congress and of others who may not have followed discussion of the proposed children's bureau, it will not be amiss to repeat the reasons for establishing this new agency, admirably summarized by Florence Kelley:

"We want the federal children's bureau to furnish trustworthy current data in answer to the following questions, among others:

"1. Blind Children. How many blind children are there in the United States? Where are they? What provision for their education is made? How many of them are receiving training for self-support? What are the causes of their blindness? What steps are taken to prevent blindness?

"2. Subnormal. How many mentally subnormal children are there in the United States including idiots, imbeciles and children sufficiently self-directing to profit by special classes in school? Where are these children? What provision is made for their education? What does it cost? How many of them are receiving training for self-support?

"3. Fatherless Children. How many fatherless children are there in the United States? Of these, how many fathers are dead? How many are illegitimate? How many are deserters? In cases in which the father is dead, what killed him? It should be known how much orphanage is due to tuberculosis, how much to industrial accidents, etc. Such knowledge is needful for the removal of preventable causes of orphanage.

"4. Illiteracy. We now know something about juvenile illiteracy once in ten years. This subject should be followed up every year. It is not a matter of immigrant children, but of a permanent, sodden failure of the republic to educate a half million children of native English-speaking citizens. Current details are now unattainable.

"5. Crimes against Children. Experience in Chicago under the only effective law on this subject in this country, indicates that grave crimes against children are far more common than is generally known. There is no official source of wider information upon which other states may base improved legislation or administration.

"6. Child Labor. How many children are working under ground in mines? How many at the mine's mouth? Where are these children? What are the mine labor laws applicable to children? We need a complete annual directory of state officials whose duty it is to enforce child labor laws. This for the purpose of stimulating to imitation those states which have no such officials, as well as for arousing public interest in the work of the existing officials.

"7. Juvenile Courts. We need current information as to juvenile courts, and they need to be standardized. For instance, no juvenile court keeps a record of the various occupations pursued by the child before its appearance in court beyond (in some cases) the actual occupation at the time of the offense committed. Certain occupations are known to be demoralizing to children but the statistics which would prove this are not now kept. It is reasonable to hope that persistent, recurrent enquiries from the federal children's bureau may induce local authorities to keep their records in such form as to make them valuable both to the children concerned and to children in parts of the country which have no similar institutions.

"8. Efficient Truancy Service. There is no accepted standard of truancy work. In some places truant officers report daily, in others weekly, in some monthly, in others, never. Some truant officers do no work whatever in return for their salaries. There should be some standard of efficiency for work of this sort, but first we need to know the facts.

"9. Registration of Births and Deaths. Finally, and by far the most important. We do not know how many children are born each year or how many die, or why they die. We need statistics of nativity and mortality of children. What Dr. Goler has done for Rochester should be made known to all the health authorities in the United States, and the success or failure of the others in reaching his standards should be published with ceaseless reiteration."

Lillian Wald, The House on Henry Street (1915)

Experience in Henry Street, and a conviction that intelligent interest in the welfare of children was becoming universal, gradually focused my mind on the necessity for a Federal Children's Bureau. Every day brought to the settlement, by mail and personal call,—as it must have brought to other people and agencies known to be interested in children,—the most varied inquiries, appeals for help and guidance, reflecting every social aspect of the question. One well-known judge of a children's court was obliged to employ a clerical staff at his own expense to reply to such inquiries. Those that came to us we answered as best we might out of our own experience or from fragmentary and incomplete data. Even the available information on this important subject was nowhere assembled in complete and practical form. The birth rate, preventable blindness, congenital and preventable disease, infant mortality, physical degeneracy, orphanage, desertion, juvenile delinquency, dangerous occupations and accidents, crimes against children, are questions of enormous national importance concerning some of which reliable information was wholly lacking.

Toward the close of President Roosevelt's administration a colleague and I called upon him to present my plea for the creation of this bureau. On that day the Secretary of Agriculture had gone South to ascertain what danger to the community lurked in the appearance of the boll weevil. This gave point to our argument that nothing that might have happened to the children of the nation could have called forth governmental inquiry.

The Federal Children's Bureau was conceived in the interest of all children; but it was fitting that the National Committee on which I serve, dedicated to working children, should have become sponsor for the necessary propaganda for its creation.

It soon became evident that the suggestion was timely. Sympathy and support came from every part of the country, from Maine to California, and from every section of society. The national sense of humor was aroused by the grim fact that whereas the Federal Government concerned itself with the conservation of material wealth, mines and forests, hogs and lobsters, and had long since established bureaus to supply information concerning them, citizens who desired instruction and guidance for the conservation and protection of the children of the nation had no responsible governmental body to which to appeal.

142

The historian Susan Tiffin describes the context in which juvenile courts were established (1982).

The Establishment of Juvenile Courts

Susan Tiffin

Throughout the nineteenth century, dependent, neglected, and delinquent children were made public wards by a wide variety of courts and social agencies that were often incapable of understanding and dealing with their situations. The courts were frequently restricted in the ways they might dispose of children or forced by monetary conditions and institutional deficiencies to return children to the same detrimental environments from which they had come. Juvenile lawbreakers were particularly unfortunate. In most states, common criminal law did not greatly differentiate between the adult and the minor who had reached the age of criminal responsibility. This varied between seven and twelve years. A child who was caught breaking the law might be arrested by a police officer, deposited in the local cells along with adult offenders, tried in the regular criminal courts, and subsequently fined or committed to the county jail, workhouse, or reformatory. Sporadic attempts had been made to improve these conditions. As early as the 1870s Massachusetts had introduced provision for special court procedures for juveniles. An agent of the State Board of Charities was authorized to attend trials and find homes for those whose behavior did not warrant institutionalization. This incipient probation system slowly gained popularity and, by the 1890s, had become mandatory. In general, however, the criminal courts had failed to deal satisfactorily with juvenile offenders, and more relevant machinery was thought necessary.

Attitudes toward juvenile delinquency at the turn of the century were changing rapidly. The new emphasis on environmental factors in character development made old methods of treatment seem effete. Professional correctional workers and administrators could no longer accept the monolithic explanations of criminal behavior, which attributed delinquent tendencies to biological defects. Cesare Lombroso's theories were losing favor, and more penologists and welfare workers were moving toward the viewpoints of William James, Adolph Meyer, and William A. White. Accepting the fact that deficiencies in character could often be traced to a child's early environment, many came to feel that "the way is open for an attempt to prevent such undesirable traits by an understanding of the child and a modification or elimination of those environmental factors which produce such results." New methods and new machinery were required if this preventive treatment was to succeed policies of retribution and punishment.

A further area in which important changes had taken place was in the courts of equity. . . . Decisions regarding custody of children, guardianship, and administration of the property of minors were reinforcing the idea of *parens patriae*, the belief that the state was responsible for the welfare of the infirm and the helpless. The state's duty toward dependent and neglected children was not a novel idea. Its application to the juvenile offender, however, was a totally new concept. The offender was now looked upon not as a criminal but as a child in need of care. The extension of the parental arm to delinquents, whether valid or not, provided the theoretical foundation for the nonpunitive treatment reformers were seeking.

Establishment

The nation's first juvenile court was established in Cook County, Illinois, in 1899. The story is too well known to need any great elaboration here. Anthony M. Platt and Joseph M. Hawes have presented detailed pictures of its inception. It is only necessary to briefly relate the circumstances surrounding its creation. Although one of the leading agitators admitted that it was "very difficult to say who originated this idea or that," certain groups may be given credit for creating a consensus in favor of a new law. The Chicago Women's Club provided a consistent impetus for reform throughout the 1890s and, in 1895, drew up a bill providing for a separate children's court with probation facilities. Unfortunately the bill was later shelved because of doubts as to the constitutionality of creating a new tribunal with a jurisdiction already assigned to other courts. The dissatisfaction of the Chicago Women's Club was echoed by the discontent of the Illinois Board of Public Charities, whose members condemned the "demoralizing irresponsibility with which juvenile offenders were treated" by the police, the courts, and the reformatories.

The issue was taken to a wider audience when, at the meeting of the Illinois Conference of Charities and Correction in November 1898, papers were presented on the need for reform. Feeling that "all children are children of the state or none are," speakers advocated the creation of "an entirely separate system of courts for children . . . [and] a children's judge who should attend to no other business." Subsequently, the Chicago Bar Association was approached to draft an acceptable bill. A committee of prominent lawyers and executives of charitable organizations, under the chairmanship of Judge Harvey B. Hurd, produced a bill that circumvented earlier problems of unconstitutionality. The proposed legislation conferred jurisdiction on courts already in existence and permitted rather than compelled them to transfer cases to the juvenile court. The act "to regulate the treatment and control of dependent, neglected and delinquent children" was introduced in the Illinois House of Representatives in February 1899 and, despite the reservations of the House Judiciary Committee, was approved. It passed through the Senate in July of the same year.

Other states had reached similar conclusions as to the need for a specifically juvenile court system. In Denver, Colorado, Judge Benjamin Barr Lindsey had independently agitated for a new court and achieved his goal in 1901. Word spread rapidly. Lindsey himself maintained a secretary to answer the thousands of inquiries that came to him from all parts of the globe. Illinois authorities were besieged with requests for copies of their law, and they themselves sent circulars to daily newspapers and journals advocating adoption of their system. The National Conference of Charities and Correction and state conferences took up the question. By 1909 ten states and the District of Columbia had authorized localities to establish juvenile courts. Twelve states followed suit in the next three years. By 1925 only Maine and Wyoming had not made provisions for a children's court. In some states a special court was created to deal with juvenile cases. The majority, however, gave special jurisdiction to courts already in existence.

Scope

Confidence in the benevolence of the state and the absence of other far-reaching public child welfare agencies encouraged the creation of a juvenile court of very broad scope. This sociolegal innovation was given jurisdiction over a wide variety of children's cases. The close connection between dependency, neglect, and delinquency in the minds of reformers had a similar effect. For many welfare workers and philanthropists, there was a definite relationship between the unfortunate, the ill-treated, and the criminal. It was commonly thought that "a child who today is simply neglected may be dependent tomorrow, truant the next day and delinquent the day after that." Wishing to reach children before they had actually committed an offense, they sought to control the behavior of children whose circumstances seemed morally detrimental. Accordingly, they framed laws in which the distinctions between dependency, neglect, and delinquency were conveniently vague and that encompassed all types of youthful misbehavior. In Illinois the definition of delinquency of 1899, which referred to lawbreakers, was later broadened to include nebulous groups of children classified as "incorrigible" or "ungovernable." Their offenses were purely juvenile and often trivial. This loose definition of delinquency, together with definitions of dependency and neglect, gave the court power over a large number of children. . . .

Although delinquency was the court's major concern, it did handle a significant number of dependent and neglected children. Social workers such as Hastings Hornell Hart felt that it was "a great mistake to overlook what can be done by the court for the dependent child." The proportion of children in these categories naturally varied from state to state. In most they comprised an important part of the clientele. In 1915, for example, the Cook County Juvenile Court handled 1,886 cases of dependency, as compared with 3,202 charges of delinquency. All manner of problems were dealt with. Cases of cruelty, failure to protect, desertion, illegitimacy, orphanage, and adoption were regularly brought to court. Problems stemming from destitution of the parents were also handled. Often parents voluntarily came to the court to surrender their children because they were financially unable to cope. In the early days of the court, many hundreds of families were subsequently separated. Following the introduction of mothers' pension legislation in the second decade of the twentieth century, courts were handed another means of confronting the question of poverty. Before 1920, 18 courts were authorized to administer these funds to suitably qualified parents. The scope of the juvenile courts did not stop here. In some states, like Colorado, the juvenile court could bring negligent parents to account under laws prosecuting adults for contributing to the dependency or delinquency of their children. In cities such as Baltimore, an additional service was offered whereby any person might seek aid from the court's probation officers.

Reformers were optimistic that this catch-all legal innovation would solve many youthful problems. It was lauded as "the wisest method yet devised for the care of delinquent and dependent children." Even Theodore Roosevelt, in a message to the U.S. Congress in December 1906, praised the juvenile court for compelling the home to do its duty, for helping unfortunate families, and for building juvenile character.

The guiding principle of this new piece of government apparatus was supposedly the approximation of parental care for children in need of discipline and protection. It was thought that "the juvenile judge has simply the parental and human problem of trying to do just what the child needs to have done for him." For the dependent and neglected, the juvenile court was to offer humane understanding of their misfortunes. A full knowledge of the facts concerning each child's physical, mental, and moral condition and familial and social environment would allow the court to act in that child's best interests. To the parents the court might be a friend or foe. It they were adjudged morally fit and willing to cooperate, it would be "an elder brother, offering encouragement and helpful advice as to how the home may be improved and the environment of the children and of the family generally sweetened and purified." If it was proven that they had neglected the child, the court would be a stern reckoner.

The Judges

A crucial part of this individualized treatment was thought to be the personality and ability of the juvenile court judge. Because of the responsibility that rested upon this person, it was felt that he or she should be specially equipped. In the opinion of corporate lawyer Bernard Flexner, the judge should be not only a trained lawyer but also "a student of and deeply interested in the problems of philanthropy and child life. . . . He should be able to understand the child's point of view and his idea of justice." This faith was shared by many of those who were the first to accept positions in the new tribunals. While in some courts the presiding judge was merely one rostered from another court to serve for a few months, in others the judges chose to serve on the juvenile court bench for a longer period. Such was the case with Judge Richard Tuthill, the first appointee to the Chicago court. His attitude was avowedly paternal. Faced with a delinquent boy, his policy was to "talk with the boy, give him a good talk just as I would my own boy." His successor, Merritt W. Pinckney, a serious, determined man, took his role as paternal overseer just as seriously. The most well-known juvenile court judge was Lindsey, guiding light of the Denver court from 1901 to 1927. A devout pragmatist who was afraid of "consulting and studying any sociological works for fear [he] might embibe [sic] some theory," Lindsey attempted to bring the personal touch to his new creation. He established a rapport with delinquents that became almost legendary in welfare circles. Among the local gangs of Denver and the unfortunate children brought before him, he managed to inspire affection and loyalty.

Not all judges were as confident of the ability of one man to control the reformation, reeducation, and rehabilitation of the children brought to court. Julian Mack, who served on the bench of the Cook County Juvenile Court from 1905 to 1907, berated his comrades for endowing juvenile court judges with innate genius. While giving men such as Lindsey their due, he nevertheless believed that "few judges are really temperamentally fitted, and few are so eminently endowed as to be able to do the juvenile court work and the probation work and all the other work that must be done if the court is to be really successful." He preferred the court to rely more on an efficient, trained staff of probation officers.

Probation

Probation was to be one of the foundation stones of the juvenile court. If the court was not to punish but to place children in improved surroundings, preferably in their own homes, it needed an expert supervisory staff. Homer Folks, chairman of the New York State Probation Commission from 1905 to 1906, explained the usefulness of probation to his fellow delegates at the 1906 National Conference of Charities and Correction. Probation, Folks stressed, was by no means a simple act of clemency on the part of the judge, nor a special relationship between the judge and the probationer. Instead it was a way of dealing with moral delinquency. As applied specifically to neglected children, it was, in effect, an effort to reach the parents and change their attitude toward their children. Folks and his colleagues saw probation as a method that recognized the part of the environment in creating and rectifying children's problems. In the eyes of these reformers, it was the only way in which individualized treatment could be carried out. Ideally, the probation officer would be a friend to the child and the family, going into the home, studying the surroundings, and remedying detrimental influences. Men and women with special qualities and training were needed. Chicago social worker Louise de Koven Bowen envisaged them as "endowed with the strength of a Samson and the delicacy of an Ariel," as being "tactful, skillful, firm and patient." Folks preferred to emphasize the need for adequate training, artful selection, and supervision of probation work by an executive officer other than the judge. Folks and Bowen and their fellow social workers were enthusiastic about the possibilities of development. Probation was, to them, "the cord upon which all the pearls of the juvenile court are strung."

Procedures

Untroubled by doubts as to the benefits of the new system, social workers and legal personnel began the process of inquiring into and treating a host of juvenile problems. For many children the machinery was set in motion when petitions were filed by social agencies, parents, relatives, or other individuals to have them declared dependent or neglected. In Chicago these petitions were received by the Complaint Division of the Cook County Probation Department, which attempted to sift out those cases that did not warrant court action. Anonymous complaints were ignored completely, with perhaps unfortunate consequences for some of the children involved. Others were referred to more appropriate welfare agencies. In 1918, of 3,012 petitions considered by the Complaint Division, some 1,282 were adjusted without the cases being brought to court. Those cases thought to be sufficiently serious were investigated by the Probation Department, which tried to assemble a factual account of the child's history and present social environment. If it was thought necessary, the child in question might be removed from his or her home and taken to the court's detention center. Here the child might stay for two to three weeks before a decision on his or her future was made. The number of dependent children who were kept in the detention home was always smaller than the number of delinquents; nevertheless, in 1905 for example, 579 dependent children were admitted to the Detention Home at 625 W. Adams Street. Here they were examined, washed, given new clothing, fed, and taught by teachers provided by the Chicago Board of Education.

In the early years of the Chicago court, dependency and neglect cases were heard on two mornings per week. The staff tried to make the proceedings as informal as possible and to minimize the child's contact with the court. In general the child would be brought before the bench at the beginning of the hearing and then dismissed unless his or her physical condition was to be introduced as evidence. The youngster's own feelings about the situation were not seen as really relevant to the problem; his or her fate was to be decided by "experts." Much attention was given to the creation of a less austere, more intimate atmosphere. A small chamber without any of the legal trappings of adult courts was thought to be more conducive to the solution of children's problems. The clerk would call each case in order, and the probation officer would come forward with the child, the parents, and witnesses. Grouped around the desk, they would listen to the probation officer's statement and give their own testimony.

Dispositions

After hearing the evidence given by the parties involved, the juvenile court judge decided the disposition of the child before him. Normally the judge accepted the recommendation of the probation officer, since there was little time to devote to each case. Reformers might have envisaged a close, friendly relationship between judge and juvenile, but the large number of cases ruled this out. In Chicago, for instance, 25 cases might be heard in one morning, allowing each one perhaps 10 or 15 minutes of the judge's time.

Having decided upon the status of the child before him, the judge had various options. The case might be dismissed or continued for a definite period. If the child were to be permanently removed from the family or had no family, a guardian might be appointed who would later consent to that child's adoption or placement. A more common alternative in Chicago was to commit the boy or girl to one of the four industrial training schools that served the area. Between 1915 and 1919, 40 percent of children coming before the court were sent to these institutions. It is difficult to know whether this large percentage of commitments was warranted. If, as was claimed, most of the less serious cases were handled externally and only the most grievous instances of neglect and the most clear-cut cases of dependency were brought to court, then this figure might be justified.

Unfortunately, the early case records afford little information except for the age of the child, the number of times in court, and the disposition. When causes were listed they were generally simplified to such classifications as "drunkenness of mother" or "immorality of father." Certainly, the industrial training schools remained a popular receptacle for dependent and neglected children throughout the Progressive era.

A smaller number of dependent children were put on probation. During the years between 1915 and 1919, just over one quarter of all dependent children were returned to their own homes under the supervision of the court. Social workers were confident of beneficial results. Hart, for example, was convinced of "the value of the probation system as applied to the dependent child." In the Cook County Court, "the use of the probation officer to guard the interests of the child brought in as dependent and allowed to remain with the parents is just as valuable for the dependent as it is for the delinquent child." Probation officers visited their charges and the families regularly and attempted to remedy the problems they found there. While this rehabilitation was supposedly carried out through a relationship of trust and understanding, it is obvious that coercion was part of the probation officer's armory. Timothy Hurley could advise probation officers to enter a family almost as one member of it and immediately follow this by urging them to use threats if parents refused to cooperate. Probation officers were backed up by the authority of the court, which had the power to remove children from their families. They did not hesitate to use this weapon to force parents to conform to the behavioral norms they themselves accepted.

143

Judge Ben Lindsey of Colorado was an articulate spokesman for the movement to establish separate juvenile courts (1931).

Juvenile Court and the Artistry of Approach

Ben B. Lindsey and Rube Borough

Thus with constructive laws we built the architecture of the state around its best asset, childhood. And for these more than fifty items of legislation and constructive work I have no apology to make.

But I was to find as our work progressed that these laws, however much they were exploited, praised and many of them copied over this country and in other countries, were not the most important things; that, without understanding men to administer them and to develop their implications, they did not get us very far in the fight for the child and the home.

I might illustrate from my own concrete experiences in those early days of the juvenile court. In my earlier visits, especially to some of these courts, I found the old formalities still persisting. I found, for instance, a judge sitting on a bench clad in his robes of office, with all the absurdities of police or criminal court procedure out in front. I witnessed even the calling of juries to try issues concerning the dependency of children that have no place with juries except in the rare case where there is danger of prejudice and therefore the jury might be preserved as a constitutional right.

I have seen mothers and children in these courts herded in with motley crowds and I have heard pronouncements of sentence from the bench followed by the screams of women and children until, instead of being in a court, I seemed to be in Bedlam. This was notably so in the juvenile court of a very large midwestern city I visited in the early part of this century. It was at that time typical of most of the others like it. It was only a division of a regular court and made no pretense to handling every aspect of a child's case as our court did from its very early inception.

A genuine juvenile court should have the jurisdiction and equipment to deal effectively with every aspect of all cases concerning children. That is to say, all those cases concerning their relations to the state or that involve their relations with their parents or others, and in the relations of the state, their parents and others to them. And the juvenile court's jurisdiction as to practically all of such matters should be (as it is mostly in our Denver Juvenile and Family Court) special, separate and exclusive.

This work cannot so well function or come to its ultimate proper fruition and purpose except through the separate special court of exclusive jurisdiction like that at Denver, Colorado. This is the only way to keep it free from the difficulties, handicaps and abuses of the old-time formal courts, that were never intended to serve the welfare of children, but of which the so-called juvenile court is often mistakenly a part.

Responsibilities for the child's care as to all cases of adoptions, dependencies, delinquencies, the old-time *habeas corpus* or other actions of every kind as to its custody, support, moral and physical care, as far as the state is called upon to any action or share in it, as well as that of any parent or other person, should be thus focused and centralized in the one single, separate, central authority and court. I have studied this question for thirty years and following this plan in the creation of the first juvenile court of this kind in this country, in Denver, Colorado, I am sure we are on the right track.

Perhaps it is the only juvenile court anywhere, even as yet, where, for example, even a murderer could be tried and dealt with in the juvenile court if the victim were a child. In such criminal cases as contributing to dependency or delinquency or statutory rape, indecent liberties against children, and the like, the advantages to the children witnesses and victims to have the sheltering, different, more psychological and better protection of such a court, as we thus first created in Denver, was demonstrated time and again. Other so-called juvenile courts seem utterly helpless and inefficient beside it for real child care and protection in many such of its angles and aspects.*

Understanding judges are more important than all of these things just mentioned, important as they are.

And just as important as understanding judges are intelligent enforcement agencies.

I recall a type of old-time policeman trained alone in the ways of violence bringing a small boy into our court. As the officer came in he glared at the little fellow as though he wanted to eat him up. The boy glared back as though he wanted to throw a brick.

First and foremost, it was evident that no love was lost between the two. The approach in both cases was one of hostility. There is such a thing as human artistry and the greatest of all human artistry, perhaps, is the artistry of approach.

"He is a bad kid," the policeman blurted out, "and there are fifteen or twenty more like him down there about those tracks that I haven't been able to catch because of this kid. For every time I come in sight he is on the lookout and when he sees me coming, he yells, 'Jigger the Bull!' and everybody scoots and I can't ketch 'em—"

---

*The court jury trials and hearings of cases of adult criminals, where the victims were children, were held at special times so as not to come in contact with any children except those necessarily involved as victims or witnesses.

This last with an air of offended dignity.

"And when I got this kid, I asks him the names of the kids that ran away and he says, 'I dunno 'em. I never saw 'em before.' "

And then as he glared at the boy: "The little liar, he knows every one of 'em."

Of course, there is no artistry in that method of approach.

I may say, in justice to policemen, that they are not all alike. I have known officers sent into a neighborhood only to provoke riot while others sent to the same neighborhood evoked respect. One kind helps to enforce the law and the other, because of a different attitude and lack of understanding of human beings, helps to break it.

I have always made it a rule never to call a boy or a girl a liar, if it can be avoided—and it generally can. And yet, in the present case, I had to retain the boy's respect for the policeman as the representative of the law as best I could.

"Jimmie," I said with such warmth of smile and attitude as I was able to command, "I am sure you don't understand the officer and he perhaps doesn't understand you. If you did I don't think you would have run away from him and I doubt if he would think that you were really a liar.

"Now, I don't think you are a liar but I do think that you are afraid. The best boy may be afraid when he doesn't understand things. Then when he is afraid he may say things that are not what we call true.

"But that isn't because he wants to lie. It's because he's afraid and thus he doesn't know what else to do. Now don't you think that is true in this case?"

And presently our little prisoner half smiles through his tears and becomes as garrulous as he has been dumb under the menacing glances of his captor.

"It's jest like ye said, Jedge. I ain't no liar and I don't mean to do nothin' wrong but I'm jest plumb scared."

"Oh, yes," I tell him, "I knew you would admit that. You thought you were going to get in jail or the reform school, didn't you? Well, you are not going to get in any such place. You are just going to tell me the truth, for I know you are a truthful boy. We are going to help the policeman and the neighborhood and everybody."

"Sure," he says, "I'll tell ye how it was, Jedge. I live down there by the railroad tracks, I do, where those kids live. And they said there was watermelons in those box cars and we got in the box cars but we didn't find no watermelons.

"But one of de kids sez he bets there is sumpin good in those boxes 'cause it's got sumpin on 'em about figs and we thinks it is figs.

"So we gets open a box and finds a lot of bottles with sumpin on 'em about figs and we thinks it is sumpin good. So we drinks a whole bottle full—"

And then pausing, he blurts out through his tears: "And I thinks we've done suffered enough."

"Well," I said, "I think so, too, for fig syrup is not recommended in bottle doses."

The policeman doesn't see the humor in this episode that spread about my room and brought titters from the few spectators. Instead, he proceeds to gloat over the boy's confession as evidence of the truth of his charge that the boy was a liar, instead of just a frightened kid.

"I told you he was a liar, Judge," he exploded as he turned on the tearful youngster. "Now you know you told me you didn't know anything about any of those kids and you didn't even know their names, but now you tell the judge that you know them all.

"Now, you tell the judge their names—I want their names, see!"

And the little prisoner, hesitating, appeals from the policeman to the judge, where somehow he thinks he finds sympathy and understanding, not for his sin but for himself. (For we are dealing much more with him, with what he is than what he did and perhaps why he did it.)

I see the tears come to his eyes again, but he is backed now by a certain confidence as he stands there pleading his own case.

"Do yuh tink, Jedge, that it's square for a guy to snitch on a kid?" he asks.

In some other age of Boyville, if you told or tattled on a boy, you "squealed" and a "squealer" was ever outlawed by the gang. But now if you told on a boy, in the slang or vernacular of the gang, you "snitched." And that was against the law. Not our law but theirs. The first commandment of the gang was—and I suspect ever has been and ever will be—"Thou salt not snitch (tattle)—you will get your face smashed if you do." The human quality of loyalty was involved here.

And unless I had sympathy and understanding for their law, how could I expect them to have sympathy and understanding for mine?

But did this particular type of policeman have any respect for the fact that he was dealing with two worlds and the people that inhabited them and the laws that governed them?

And did he understand that unless he had sympathy and understanding for one he could not expect, much less exact, respect for the other?

The child world and its laws were just as real to Jimmie and as much to be observed and respected as our laws. For they were based on the finest of human qualities, loyalty and respect for each other, however much sometimes through lack of maturity they seem to us to be misdirected. If they are misdirected, the least that can be expected of us is wise direction and not hostility.

Yet the whole scheme of the courts as they existed when I came to this work in 1899 was, and always had been, as far as legal directions were concerned, one of hostility, ignorance and revenge. I often wondered whether it was to laugh or to cry over the ignorance and stupidity of the shameless state.

144

The Children's Charter, presented at President Hoover's White House Conference on Child Health and Protection in 1930, was one of the first explicit recognitions of the rights of the child. The charter emphasizes children's rights to health care and education.

The Children's Charter

White House Conference Document

PRESIDENT HOOVER'S WHITE HOUSE CONFERENCE ON CHILD HEALTH AND PROTEC-TION, RECOGNIZING THE RIGHTS OF THE CHILD AS THE FIRST RIGHTS OF CITIZENSHIP, PLEDGES ITSELF TO THESE AIMS FOR THE CHILDREN OF AMERICA

For every child spiritual and moral training to help him to stand firm under the pressure of life

II For every child understanding and the guarding of his personality as his most precious right

III For every child a home and that love and security which a home provides; and for that child who must receive foster care, the nearest substitute for his own home

IV For every child full preparation for his birth, his mother receiving prenatal, natal, and postnatal care; and the establishment of such protective measures as will make childbearing safer

V For every child health protection from birth through adolescence, including: periodical health examinations and, where needed, care of specialists and hospital treatment; regular dental examinations and care of the teeth; protective and preventive measures against communicable diseases; the insuring of pure food, pure milk, and pure water

VI For every child from birth through adolescence, promotion of health, including health instruction and a health program, wholesome physical and mental recreation, with teachers and leaders adequately trained

VII For every child a dwelling-place safe, sanitary, and wholesome, with reasonable provisions for privacy; free from conditions which tend to thwart his development; and a home environment harmonious and enriching

VIII For every child a school which is safe from hazards, sanitary, properly equipped, lighted, and ventilated. For younger children nursery schools and kindergartens to supplement home care

IX For every child a community which recognizes and plans for his needs, protects him against physical dangers, moral hazards, and disease; provides him with safe and wholesome places for play and recreation; and makes provision for his cultural and social needs

X For every child an education which, through the discovery and development of his individual abilities, prepares him for life; and through training and vocational guidance prepares him for a living which will yield him the maximum of satisfaction

XI For every child such teaching and training as will prepare him for successful parenthood, home-making, and the rights of citizenship; and, for parents, supplementary training to fit them to deal wisely with the problems of parenthood

XII For every child education for safety and protection against accidents to which modern conditions subject him—those to which he is directly exposed and those which, through loss or maiming of his parents, affect him indirectly

XIII For every child who is blind, deaf, crippled, or otherwise physically handicapped, and for the child who is mentally handicapped, such measures as will early discover and diagnose his handicap, provide care and treatment, and so train him that he may become an asset to society rather than a liability. Expenses of these services should be borne publicly where they cannot be privately met

XIV For every child who is in conflict with society the right to be dealt with intelligently as society's charge, not society's outcast; with the home, the school, the church, the court and the institution when needed, shaped to return him whenever possible to the normal stream of life

XV For every child the right to grow up in a family with an adequate standard of living and the security of a stable income as the surest safeguard against social handicaps

XVI For every child protection against labor that stunts growth, either physical or mental, that limits education, that deprives children of the right of comradeship, of play, and of joy

XVII For every rural child as satisfactory schooling and health services as for the city child, and an extension to rural families of social, recreational, and cultural facilities

XVIII To supplement the home and the school in the training of youth, and to return to them those interests of which modern life tends to cheat children, every stimulation and encouragement should be given to the extension and development of the voluntary youth organizations

XIX To make everywhere available these minimum protections of the health and welfare of children, there should be a district, county, or community organization for health, education, and welfare, with full-time officials, coördinating with a state-wide program which will be responsive to a nationwide service of general information, statistics, and scientific research. This should include:

(a) Trained, full-time public health officials, with public health nurses, sanitary inspection, and laboratory workers
(b) Available hospital beds
(c) Full-time public welfare service for the relief, aid, and guidance of children in special need due to poverty, misfortune, or behavior difficulties, and for the protection of children from abuse, neglect, exploitation, or moral hazard

FOR EVERY CHILD THESE RIGHTS, REGARDLESS OF RACE, OR COLOR, OR SITUATION, WHEREVER HE MAY LIVE UNDER THE PROTECTION OF THE AMERICAN FLAG

145

In a series of decisions in the 1960s, the U.S. Supreme Court articulated certain constitutional rights for children independent of their parents. In Tinker v. Des Moines *(1965), Justice Abe Fortas argued for the right of young people to exercise freedom of speech in school antiwar demonstrations.*

The First Amendment in School

U.S. Supreme Court

Tinker v. Des Moines Independent Community School District
393 U.S. 503 (1969)

Mr. Justice Fortas delivered the opinion of the Court.

Petitioner John F. Tinker, 15 years old, and petitioner Christopher Eckhardt, 16 years old, attended high schools in Des Moines, Iowa. Petitioner Mary Beth Tinker, John's sister, was a 13-year-old student in junior high school.

In December 1965, a group of adults and students in Des Moines held a meeting at the Eckhardt home. The group determined to publicize their objections to the hostilities in Vietnam and their support for a truce by wearing black armbands during the holiday season and by fasting on December 16 and New Year's Eve. Petitioners and their parents had previously engaged in similar activities, and they decided to participate in the program.

The principals of the Des Moines schools became aware of the plan to wear armbands. On December 14, 1965, they met and adopted a policy that any student wearing an armband to school would be asked to remove it, and if he refused he would be suspended until he returned without the armband. Petitioners were aware of the regulation that the school authorities adopted.

On December 16, Mary Beth and Christopher wore black armbands to their schools. John Tinker wore his armband the next day. They were all sent home and suspended from school until they would come back without their armbands. They did not return to school until after the planned period for wearing armbands had expired—that is, until after New Year's Day.

This complaint was filed in the United States District Court by petitioners, through their fathers, under §1983 of Title 42 of the United States Code. It prayed for an injunction restraining the respondent school officials and the respondent members of the board of directors of the school district from disciplining the petitioners, and it sought nominal damages. After an evidentiary hearing the District Court dismissed the complaint. It upheld the constitutionality of the school authorities' action on the ground that it was reasonable in order to prevent disturbance of school discipline. 258 F. Supp. 971 (1966). The court referred to but expressly declined to follow the Fifth Circuit's holding in a similar case that the wearing of symbols like the armbands cannot be prohibited unless it "materially and substantially interfere[s] with the requirements of appropriate discipline in the operation of the school." Burnside v. Byars, 363 F.2d 744, 749 (1966)....

The District Court recognized that the wearing of an armband for the purpose of expressing certain views is the type of symbolic act that is within the Free Speech Clause of the First Amendment.... As we shall discuss, the wearing of armbands in the circumstances of this case was entirely divorced from actually or potentially disruptive conduct by those participating in it. It was closely akin to "pure speech" which, we have repeatedly held, is entitled to comprehensive protection under the First Amendment. Cf. Cox v. Louisiana, 379 U.S. 536, 555 (1965); Adderley v. Florida, 385 U.S. 39 (1966).

First Amendment rights, applied in light of the special characteristics of the school environment, are available to teachers and students. It can hardly be argued that either students or teachers shed their constitutional rights to freedom of speech or expression at the schoolhouse gate. This has been the unmistakable holding of this Court for almost 50 years....

On the other hand, the Court has repeatedly emphasized the need for affirming the comprehensive authority of the States and of school officials, consistent with fundamental constitutional safeguards, to prescribe and control conduct in the schools. See Epperson v. Arkansas ... [393 U.S. 104 (1968)]; Meyer v. Nebraska, ... [262 U.S. 390, 402 (1923)]. Our problem lies in the area where students in the exercise of First Amendment rights collide with the rules of the school authorities....

It does not concern aggressive, disruptive action or even group demonstrations. Our problem involves direct, primary First Amendment rights akin to "pure speech."

The school officials banned and sought to punish petitioners for a silent, passive expression of opinion, unaccompanied by any disorder or disturbance on the part of petitioners. There is here no evidence whatever of petitioners' interference, actual or nascent, with the schools' work or of collision with the rights of other students to be secure and to be let alone. Accordingly, this case does not concern speech or action that intrudes upon the work of the schools or the rights of other students.

Only a few of the 18,000 students in the school system wore the black armbands. Only five students were suspended for wearing them. There is no indication that the work of the schools or any class was disrupted. Outside the classrooms, a few students made hostile remarks to the children wearing armbands, but there were no threats or acts of violence on school premises.

The District Court concluded that the action of the school authorities was reasonable because it was based upon their fear of a disturbance from the wearing of the armbands. But, in our system, undifferentiated fear or apprehension of disturbance is not enough to overcome the right to freedom of expression. Any departure from absolute regimentation may cause trouble. Any variation from the majority's opinion may inspire fear. Any word spoken, in class, in the lunchroom, or on the campus, that deviates from the views of another person may start an argument or cause a disturbance. But our Constitution says we must take this risk, and our history says that it is this sort of hazardous freedom—this kind of openness—that is the basis of our national strength and of the independence and vigor of Americans who grow up and live in this relatively permissive, often disputatious, society.

In order for the State in the person of school officials to justify prohibition of a particular expression of opinion, it must be able to show that its action was caused by something more than a mere desire to avoid the discomfort and unpleasantness that always accompany an unpopular viewpoint. Certainly where there is no finding and no showing that engaging in the forbidden conduct would "materially and substantially interfere with the requirements of appropriate discipline in the operation of the school," the prohibition cannot be sustained. Burnside v. Byars, supra, 363 F.2d at 749.

In the present case, the District Court made no such finding, and our independent examination of the record fails to yield evidence that the school authorities had reason to anticipate that the wearing of the armbands would substantially interfere with the work of the school or impinge upon the rights of other students. Even an official memorandum prepared after the suspension that listed the reasons for the ban on wearing the armbands made no reference to the anticipation of such disruption.

On the contrary, the action of the school authorities appears to have been based upon an urgent wish to avoid the controversy which might result from the expression, even by the silent symbol of armbands, of opposition to this Nation's part in the conflagration in Vietnam. It is revealing, in this respect, that the meeting at which the school principals decided to issue the contested regulation was called in response to a student's statement to the journalism teacher in one of the schools that he wanted to write an article on Vietnam and have it published in the school paper. (The student was dissuaded.)

It is also relevant that the school authorities did not purport to prohibit the wearing of all symbols of political or controversial significance. The record shows that students in some of the schools wore buttons relating to national political campaigns, and some even wore the Iron Cross, traditionally a symbol of Nazism. The order prohibiting the wearing of armbands did not extend to these. Instead, a particular symbol—black armbands worn to exhibit opposition to this Nation's involvement in Vietnam—was singled out for prohibition. Clearly, the prohibition of expression of one particular opinion, at least without evidence that it is necessary to avoid material and substantial interference with schoolwork or discipline, is not constitutionally permissible.

In our system, state-operated schools may not be enclaves of totalitarianism.

School officials do not possess absolute authority over their students. Students in school as well as out of school are "persons" under our Constitution. They are possessed of fundamental rights which the State must respect, just as they themselves must respect their obligations to the State. In our system, students may not be regarded as closed-circuit recipients of only that which the State chooses to communicate. They may not be confined to the expression of those sentiments that are officially approved. In the absence of a specific showing of constitutionally valid reasons to regulate their speech, students are entitled to freedom of expression of their views. . . .

The classroom is peculiarly the "marketplace of ideas." The Nation's future depends upon leaders trained through wide exposure to that robust exchange of ideas which discovers truth "out of a multitude of tongues, [rather] than through any kind of authoritative selection."

The principle of these cases is not confined to the supervised and ordained discussion which takes place in the classroom. The principal use to which the schools are dedicated is to accommodate students during prescribed hours for the purpose of certain types of activities. Among those activities is personal intercommunication among the students. This is not only an inevitable part of the process of attending school; it is also an important part of the educational process. A student's rights, therefore, do not embrace merely the classroom hours. When he is in the cafeteria, or on the playing field, or on the campus during the authorized hours, he may express his opinions, even on controversial subjects like the conflict in Vietnam, if he does so without "materially and substantially interfer[ing] with the requirements of appropriate discipline in the operation of the school" and without colliding with the rights of others. Burnside v. Byars, supra, 363 F.2d at 749. But conduct by the student, in class or out of it, which for any reason—whether it stems from time, place, or type of behavior—materially disrupts classwork or involves substantial disorder or invasion of the rights of others is, of course, not immunized by the constitutional guarantee of freedom of speech. . . .

As we have discussed, the record does not demonstrate any facts which might reasonably have led school authorities to forecast substantial disruption of or material interference with school activities, and no disturbances or disorders on the school premises in fact occurred. These petitioners merely went about their ordained rounds in school. Their deviation consisted only in wearing on their sleeve a band of black cloth, not more than two inches wide. They wore it to exhibit their disapproval of the Vietnam hostilities and their advocacy of a truce, to make their views known, and, by their example, to influence others to adopt them. They neither interrupted school activities nor sought to intrude in the school affairs or the lives of others. They caused discussion outside of the classrooms, but no interference with work and no disorder. In the circumstances, our Constitution does not permit officials of the State to deny their form of expression. . . .

Reversed and remanded. . . .

*

Mr. Justice Harlan, dissenting.

I certainly agree that state public school authorities in the discharge of their responsibilities are not wholly exempt from the requirements of the Fourteenth Amendment respecting the freedoms of expression and association. At the same time I am reluctant to believe that there is any disagreement between the majority and myself on the proposition that school officials should be accorded the widest authority in maintaining discipline and good order in their institutions. To translate that proposition into a workable constitutional rule, I would, in cases like this, cast upon those complaining the burden of showing that a particular school measure was motivated by other than legitimate school concerns—for example, a desire to prohibit the expression of an unpopular point of view, while permitting expression of the dominant opinion.

Finding nothing in this record which impugns the good faith of respondents in promulgating the armband regulation, I would affirm the judgment below.

146

Constitutional rights to due process in juvenile court were introduced and expanded in the 1960s and 1970s. In the landmark case In re Gault *(1967), the Supreme Court reversed the paternalistic concept on which the juvenile court was based, and moved it toward an adult model of justice.*

Juveniles' Right to Due Process

U.S. Supreme Court

In re Gault
387 U.S. 1 (1967)

Mr. Justice Fortas delivered the opinion of the Court.

This is an appeal under 28 U.S.C. §1257(2) from a judgment of the Supreme Court of Arizona affirming the dismissal of a petition for a writ of habeas corpus. 99 Ariz. 181, 407 P.2d 760 (1965). The petition sought the release of Gerald Francis Gault, appellants' 15-year-old son, who had been committed as a juvenile delinquent to the State Industrial School by the Juvenile Court of Gila County, Arizona. The Supreme Court of Arizona affirmed dismissal of the writ. . . . We do not agree, and we reverse. . . .

On Monday, June 8, 1964, at about 10 a.m., Gerald Francis Gault and a friend, Ronald Lewis, were taken into custody by the Sheriff of Gila County. Gerald was then still subject to a six months' probation order which had been entered on February 25, 1964, as a result of his having been in the company of another boy who had stolen a wallet from a lady's purse. The police action on June 8 was taken as the result of a verbal complaint by a neighbor of the boys, Mrs. Cook, about a telephone call made to her in which the caller or callers made lewd or indecent remarks . . . of the irritatingly offensive, adolescent, sex variety.

At the time Gerald was picked up, his mother and father were both at work. No notice that Gerald was being taken into custody was left at the home. No other steps were taken to advise them that their son had, in effect, been arrested. Gerald was taken to the Children's Detention Home. When his mother arrived home at about 6 o'clock, Gerald was not there. Gerald's older brother was sent to look for him at the trailer home of the Lewis family. He apparently learned then that Gerald was in custody. He so informed his mother. The two of them went to the Detention Home. The deputy probation officer, Flagg, who was also superintendent of the Detention Home, told Mrs. Gault "why Jerry was there" and said that a hearing would be held in Juvenile Court at 3 o'clock the following day, June 9.

Officer Flagg filed a petition with the court on the hearing day, June 9, 1964. It was not served on the Gaults. Indeed, none of them saw this petition until the habeas corpus hearing on August 17, 1964. The petition . . . made no reference to any factual basis for the judicial action which it initiated. It recited only that "said minor is under the age of eighteen years, . . . [and that] said minor is a delinquent minor." It prayed for a hearing and an order regarding "the care and custody of said minor." . . .

On June 9, Gerald, his mother, his older brother, and Probation Officers Flagg and Henderson appeared before the juvenile judge in chambers. . . . Mrs. Cook, the complainant, was not there. No one was sworn at this hearing. No transcript or recording was made. . . . Our information about the proceedings and the subsequent hearing on June 15, derives entirely from the testimony of the Juvenile Court Judge, Mr. and Mrs. Gault and Officer Flagg at the habeas corpus proceeding conducted two months later. From this, it appears that at the June 9 hearing Gerald was questioned by the judge about the telephone call. There was conflict as to what he said. His mother recalled that Gerald said he only dialed Mrs. Cook's number and handed the telephone to his friend, Ronald. Officer Flagg recalled that Gerald had admitted making the lewd remarks. Judge McGhee testified that Gerald "admitted making one of these [lewd] statements." . . . Gerald was taken back to the Detention Home. . . . On June 11 or 12, after having been detained since June 8, Gerald was released. . . . There is no explanation in the record as to why he was kept in the Detention Home or why he was released. At 5 p.m. on the day of Gerald's release, Mrs. Gault received a note signed by Officer Flagg. It was on plain paper, not letterhead. Its entire text was as follows:

Mrs. Gault:
    Judge McGhee has set Monday, June 15, 1964 at 1100 A.M. as the date and time for further Hearings on Gerald's delinquency.

/s/ Flagg

At the appointed time on Monday, June 15, Gerald, his father and mother, Ronald Lewis and his father, and Officers Flagg and Henderson were present before Judge McGhee. Witnesses at the habeas corpus proceeding differed in their recollections of Gerald's testimony at the June 15 hearing. Mr. and Mrs. Gault recalled that Gerald again testified that he had only dialed the number and that the other boy had made the remarks. Officer Flagg agreed that at this hearing Gerald did not admit making the lewd remarks. But Judge McGhee recalled that "there was some admission again of some of the lewd statements. He—he didn't admit any of the more serious lewd statements." Again, the complainant, Mrs. Cook, was not present. Mrs. Gault asked that Mrs. Cook be present. . . . The juvenile judge said "she didn't have to be present at that hearing." The judge did not speak to Mrs. Cook or communicate with her at any time. Probation Officer Flagg had talked to her once—over the telephone on June 9.

At this June 15 hearing a "referral report" made by the probation officers was filed with the court, although not disclosed to Gerald or his parents. This listed the charge as "Lewd Phone Calls." At the conclusion of the hearing, the judge committed Gerald as a juvenile delinquent to the State Industrial School "for the period of his minority [that is, until 21], unless sooner discharged by due process of law." . . .

No appeal is permitted by Arizona law in juvenile cases. On August 3, 1964, a petition for a writ of habeas corpus was filed with the Supreme Court of Arizona and referred by it to the Superior Court for hearing.

At the habeas corpus hearing on August 17, Judge McGhee was vigorously cross-examined as to the basis for his actions. He testified that he had taken into account the fact that Gerald was on probation. He was asked "under what section of . . . the code you found the boy delinquent?"

. . . In substance, he concluded that Gerald came within ARS §8–201, subsec. 6(a), which specifies that a "delinquent child" includes one "who has violated a law of the state or an ordinance. . . ." The law which Gerald was found to have violated is ARS §13–377 [which] provides that a person who "in the presence or hearing of any woman or child . . . uses vulgar, abusive or obscene language, is guilty of a misdemeanor. . . ." The penalty specified in the Criminal Code, which would apply to an adult, is $5 to $50, or imprisonment for not more than two months. The judge also testified that he acted under ARS §8–201, subsec. 6(d) which includes in the definition of a "delinquent child" one who, as the judge phrased it, is "habitually involved in immoral matters."

Asked about the basis for his conclusion that Gerald was "habitually involved in immoral matters," the judge testified, somewhat vaguely, that two years earlier, on July 2, 1962, a "referral" was made concerning Gerald, "where the boy had stolen a baseball glove from another boy and lied to the Police Department about it." The judge said there was "no hearing, . . . because of lack of material foundation." But it seems to have remained in his mind as a relevant factor. The judge also testified that Gerald had admitted making other nuisance phone calls in the past which, as the judge recalled the boy's testimony, were "silly calls, or funny calls, or something like that."

The Superior Court dismissed the writ, and appellants sought review in the Arizona Supreme Court. . . .

The Supreme Court handed down an . . . opinion affirming dismissal of the writ. [A]ppellants do not urge upon us all of the points passed upon by the Supreme Court of Arizona. They urge that we hold the Juvenile Code of Arizona invalid on its face or as applied in this case because . . . the following basic rights are denied:

1. Notice of the charges;
2. Right to counsel;
3. Right to confrontation and cross-examination;

4. Privilege against self-incrimination;
5. Right to a transcript of the proceedings; and
6. Right to appellate review. . . .

We do not in this opinion . . . consider the entire process relating to juvenile "delinquents." For example, we are not here concerned with the procedures or constitutional rights applicable to the pre-judicial stages of the juvenile process, nor do we direct our attention to the post-adjudicative or dispositional process. . . . We consider only . . . proceedings by which a determination is made as to whether a juvenile is a "delinquent" as a result of alleged misconduct on his part, with the consequence that he may be committed to a state institution. As to these proceedings, . . . the Due Process Clause has a role to play. The problem is to ascertain the precise impact of the due process requirement upon such proceedings.

From the inception of the juvenile court system, wide differences have been tolerated—indeed insisted upon—between the procedural rights accorded to adults and those of juveniles. In practically all jurisdictions, there are rights granted to adults which are withheld from juveniles. [F]or example, it has been held that the juvenile is not entitled to bail, to indictment by grand jury, to a public trial or to trial by jury. It is frequent practice that rules governing the arrest and interrogation of adults by the police are not observed in the case of juveniles.

The history and theory underlying this development are well-known. . . .

The early reformers were appalled by adult procedures and penalties, and by the fact that children could be given long prison sentences and mixed in jails with hardened criminals. . . . They believed that society's role was not to ascertain whether the child was "guilty" or "innocent," but "What is he, how has he become what he is, and what had best be done in his interest and in the interest of the state to save him from a downward career." The child—essentially good, as they saw it—was to be made "to feel that he is the object of [the state's] care and solicitude," not that he was under arrest or on trial. The rules of criminal procedure were therefore altogether inapplicable. The apparent rigidities, technicalities, and harshness which they observed in both substantive and procedural criminal law were therefore to be discarded. The idea of crime and punishment was to be abandoned. The child was to be "treated" and "rehabilitated" and the procedures, from apprehension through institutionalization, were to be "clinical" rather than punitive.

These results were to be achieved . . . by insisting that the proceedings were not adversary, but that the state was proceeding as *parens patriae*. The Latin phrase proved to be a great help to those who sought to rationalize the exclusion of juveniles from the constitutional scheme; but its meaning is murky. . . . The phrase was taken from chancery practice, where, however, it was used to describe the power of the state to act in loco parentis for the purpose of protecting the property interests and the person of the child. . . .

The right of the state, as *parens patriae*, to deny to the child procedural rights available to his elders was elaborated by the assertion that a child, unlike an adult, has a right "not to liberty but to custody." He can be made to attorn to his parents, to go to school, etc. If his parents default in effectively performing their custodial functions—that is, if the child is "delinquent"—the state may intervene. In doing so, it does not deprive the child of any rights, because he has none. It merely provides the "custody" to which the child is entitled. On this basis, proceedings involving juveniles were described as "civil" not "criminal" and therefore not subject to the requirements which restrict the state when it seeks to deprive a person of his liberty.

Accordingly, the highest motives and most enlightened impulses led to a peculiar system for juveniles, unknown to our law in any comparable context. The constitutional and theoretical basis for this peculiar system is—to say the least—debatable. And in practice, . . . the results have not been entirely satisfactory. Juvenile Court history has again demonstrated that unbridled discretion, however benevolently motivated, is frequently a poor substitute for principle and procedure. . . .

Failure to observe the fundamental requirements of due process has resulted in instances, which might have been avoided, of unfairness to individuals and inadequate or inaccurate findings of fact and unfortunate prescriptions of remedy. Due process of law is the primary and indispensable foundation of individual freedom. It is the basic and essential term in the social compact which defines the rights of the individual and delimits the powers which the state may exercise. . . . But, in addition, the procedural rules which have been fashioned from the generality of due process . . . enhance the possibility that truth will emerge from the confrontation of opposing versions and conflicting data. . . .

It is claimed that juveniles obtain benefits from the special procedures applicable to them which more than offset the disadvantages of denial of the substance of normal due process. [I]t is important, we think, that the claimed benefits of the juvenile process should be candidly appraised. . . .

[T]he high crime rates among juveniles . . . could not lead us to conclude that the absence of constitutional protections reduces crime, or that the juvenile system, functioning free of constitutional inhibitions as it has largely done, is effective to reduce crime or rehabilitate offenders. We do not mean by this to denigrate the juvenile court process or to suggest that there are not aspects of the juvenile system relating to offenders which are valuable. But the features of the juvenile system which its proponents have asserted are of unique benefit will not be impaired by constitutional domestication. For example, the commendable principles relating to the processing and treatment of juveniles separately from adults are in no way involved or affected by the procedural issues under discussion. Further, we are told that one of the important benefits of the special juvenile court procedures is that they avoid classifying the juvenile as a "criminal." The juvenile offender is now classed as a "delinquent." There is, of course, no reason why this should not continue. . . .

Beyond this, it is frequently said that juveniles are protected by the process from disclosure of their deviational behavior. As the Supreme Court of Arizona phrased it in the present case, the summary procedures of Juvenile Courts are sometimes defended by a statement that it is the law's policy "to hide youthful errors from the full gaze of the public and bury them in the graveyard of the forgotten past." This claim of secrecy, however, is more rhetoric than reality. Disclosure of court records is discretionary with the judge in most jurisdictions. . . .

Further, it is urged that the juvenile benefits from informal proceedings in the court. The early conception of the Juvenile Court proceeding was one in which a fatherly judge touched the heart and conscience of the erring youth by talking over his problems, by paternal advice and admonition, and in which, in extreme situations, benevolent and wise institutions of the State provided guidance and help "to save him from a downward career." [R]ecent studies have, with surprising unanimity, entered sharp dissent as to the validity of this gentle conception. They suggest that the appearance as well as the actuality of fairness, impartiality and orderliness—in short, the essentials of due process—may be a more impressive and more therapeutic attitude so far as the juvenile is concerned. For example, in a recent study, the sociologists Wheeler and Cottrell observe that when the procedural laxness of the "parens patriae" attitude is followed by stern disciplining, the contrast may have an adverse effect upon the child, who feels that he has been deceived or enticed. They conclude as follows: "Unless appropriate due process of law is followed, even the juvenile who has violated the law may not feel that he is being fairly treated and may therefore resist the rehabilitative efforts of court personnel." . . . While due process requirements will, in some instances, introduce a degree of order and regularity to Juvenile Court proceedings to determine delinquency, and in contested cases will introduce some elements of the adversary system, nothing will require that the conception of the kindly juvenile judge be replaced by its opposite. . . .

Ultimately, however, we confront the reality of that portion of the Juvenile Court process with which we deal in this case. A boy is charged with misconduct. The boy is committed to an institution where he may be restrained of liberty for years. It is of no constitutional consequence—and of limited practical meaning—that the institution to which he is committed is called an Industrial School. The fact of the matter is that, however euphemistic the title . . . an "industrial school" for juveniles is an institution of confinement. . . . His world becomes "a building with whitewashed walls, regimented routine and institutional hours. . . ." Instead of mother and father and sisters and brothers and friends and classmates, his world is peopled by guards, custodians, state employees, and "delinquents" confined with him for anything from waywardness to rape and homicide.

In view of this, it would be extraordinary if our Constitution did not require the procedural regularity and the exercise of care implied in the phrase "due process." Under our Constitution, the condition of being a boy does not justify a kangaroo court. The traditional ideas of Juvenile Court procedure, indeed, contemplated that time would be available and care would be used to establish precisely what the juvenile did and why he did it—was it a prank of adolescence or a brutal act threatening serious consequences to himself or society unless corrected? Under traditional notions, one would assume that in a case like that of Gerald Gault, where the juvenile appears to have a home, a working mother and father, and an older brother, the juvenile judge would have made a careful inquiry and judgment as to the possibility that the boy could be disciplined and dealt with at home, despite his previous transgressions. Indeed, so far as appears in the record before us, except for some conversation with Gerald about his school work and his "wanting to go to . . . Grand Canyon with his father," the points to which the judge directed his attention were little different from those that would be involved in determining any charge of violation of a penal statute. The essential difference between Gerald's case and a normal criminal case is that safeguards available to adults were discarded in Gerald's case. The summary procedure as well as the long commitment was possible because Gerald was 15 years of age instead of over 18.

If Gerald had been over 18, he would not have been subject to Juvenile Court proceedings. For the particular offense immediately involved, the maximum punishment would have been a fine of $5 to $50, or imprisonment in jail for not more than two months. Instead, he was committed to custody for a maximum of six years. If he had been over 18 and had committed an offense to which such a sentence might apply, he would have been entitled to substantial rights under the Constitution of the United States as well as under Arizona's laws and constitution. The United States Constitution would guarantee him rights and protections with respect to arrest, search, and seizure, and pretrial interrogation. It would assure him of specific notice of the charges and adequate time to decide his course of action and to prepare his defense. He would be entitled to clear advice that he could be represented by counsel, and, at least if a felony were involved, the State would be required to provide counsel if his parents were unable to afford it. If the court acted on the basis of his confession, careful procedures would be required to assure its voluntariness. If the case went to trial, confrontation and opportunity for cross-examination would be guaranteed. So wide a gulf between the State's treatment of the adult and of the child requires a bridge sturdier than mere verbiage, and reasons more persuasive than cliche can provide.

147

In recent times, as the public has been exposed to serious crimes committed by ever younger children, the laws to protect young children have been consistently contracted. In most states thirteen-year-olds can be tried as adults. In this Richmond, California, case, a six-year-old was charged with attempted murder (1996).

Punishing Very Young Criminals

Peter Fimrite

A 6-year-old Richmond [California] boy who was jailed for allegedly attempting to beat a baby to death has focused nationwide attention on a juvenile justice system that is unequipped to meet the long-term needs of young children who commit violent crimes.

The boy was charged with attempted murder for entering a Richmond apartment with 8-year-old twin brothers last week, dumping 4-week-old Ignacio Bermudez out of a bassinet and punching, kicking and beating the child with a stick before stealing a Big Wheel–style tricycle.

When the three boys were placed in juvenile hall in Martinez, workers had to scramble to find small-sized clothing, toys, teddy bears and educational material appropriate for little children.

"One of the first things the boys asked was, 'Do you have any toys around here?'" said Terrance Starr, the chief probation officer for Contra Costa County. "It's very rare to see a kid under 11 in juvenile hall. We're geared for junior high or high school kids."

Starr said all three boys are under constant supervision and must follow the strict regimen at juvenile hall, including bedtimes, wake-up times and chores. They sleep in rooms with a bed, desk and toilet, but spend most of their time in common areas with the 20 teenagers in the unit.

The county office of education has provided a lesson plan for the 6-year-old, who spends several hours daily with a tutor. Starr said the staff attempts to provide guidance, but it is difficult to meet the needs of a 6-year-old in an environment designed for older boys.

"There's all kinds of stuff in the unit—games, pingpong, checkers, Pac Man machines—we even have teddy bears if he wants one," Starr said. "But the bottom line is he's just a little, teeny kid. I imagine he is somewhat overwhelmed."

The boy may be the youngest person in the nation to be charged with attempted murder. Children under 14 are rarely charged with serious crimes. California law presumes they cannot understand right from wrong.

A guilty verdict against the 6-year-old would create a problem for prosecutors because state law prohibits holding a child under age 11 in the California Youth Authority. County social services agencies are also prohibited from holding dependent children against their will.

Deputy District Attorney Harold Jewett wants to keep the child in a locked facility, and said some sort of accommodation will have to be made until he is 11. What that would entail is unclear, but it would mark a new era for the state juvenile justice system.

"It is not our intention to lock this child up and throw away the key," Jewett said. "We are very much aware of the need for support and intervention, but we also need to protect the public. If there are problems finding adequate facilities to accommodate this boy, then perhaps the juvenile system has to adjust a little bit."

The boy's mother, Lisa Toliver, insists that her son is not violent and criticized the media for depicting her as an uncaring person.

All three defendants are scheduled to return to court Friday for a pretrial hearing.

The twins were charged with burglary and remained in custody yesterday even though a juvenile court referee said they could be released. Probation officials want to make sure the 8-year-olds are not released into a hostile or dangerous environment.

148

In 1970 the U.S. Supreme Court decided that Congress did not need a constitutional amendment to lower the voting age from twenty-one to eighteen in federal (but not state and local) elections.

Vote for Eighteen-Year-Olds
What Justices Said on Both Sides

U.S. News & World Report

Legal scholars and political scientists are still analyzing the historic Supreme Court decision of December 21 upholding the 1970 Voting Rights Act.

By a 5-to-4 opinion, the Court held that Congress could, by statute, lower the voting age to 18 in federal elections, without amending the Constitution.

In another 5-to-4 vote, the Court found that Congress does not have the power under the Constitution to fix the voting age in State and local elections.

Four Justices—including Chief Justice Warren E. Burger, John M. Harlan, Potter Stewart and Harry A. Blackmun—held that the qualification of voters in all elections is a matter reserved to the States under the Constitution.

Four others—Justices William O. Douglas, William J. Brennan, Byron R. White and Thurgood Marshall—found that Congress could, under the Fourteenth Amendment, set the voting age in all elections.

The swing man—Justice Hugo L. Black—voted that Congress could lower the voting age in federal elections but not in State and local balloting. Both of these conclusions are matters of continuing debate.

What follows are key excerpts from the opinions—

Justice Black, for the Court:

"In summary, it is the judgment of the Court that the 18-year-old-vote provisions of the Voting Rights Act Amendments of 1970 are constitutional and enforceable insofar as they pertain to federal elections, and unconstitutional and unenforceable insofar as they pertain to State and local elections. . . .

"In the very beginning, the responsibility of the States for setting the qualifications of voters in congressional elections was made subject to the power of Congress to make or alter such regulations as it deemed advisable. . . .

"Congress has ultimate supervisory power over congressional elections. Similarly, it is the prerogative of Congress to oversee the conduct of presidential and vice-presidential elections and to set the qualifications for voters for electors for those offices. . . .

"On the other hand, the Constitution was also intended to preserve to the States the power that even the Colonies had to establish and maintain their own separate and independent governments, except insofar as the Constitution itself commands otherwise. . . .

"It is a plain fact of history that the Framers never imagined that the National Congress would set the qualifications for voters in every election from President to local constable or village alderman. It is obvious that the whole Constitution reserves to the States the power to set voter qualifications in State and local elections, except to the limited extent that the people through constitutional amendments have specifically narrowed the powers of the States."

Mr. Black based his findings on Article I, sections 2 and 4 of the Constitution. The Justice denied arguments based on what he called "generalities of the equal-protection clause the Fourteenth Amendment."

Three Justices who voted to extend the vote to 18-year-olds in both federal and State elections called it a "valid exercise of congressional power" under the Fourteenth Amendment.

Justices Brennan, White and Marshall cited arguments such as that 18-year-olds are subject to military service, come under the criminal laws in most States, are permitted to marry in every State, are not required to attend school beyond age 18, and many are in the working force.

Justice Brennan, writing for the three, observed:

"Every State in the union has conceded by statute that citizens over the age of 21 are capable of intelligent and responsible exercise of the right to vote. The single, narrow question presented by these cases is whether Congress was empowered to conclude, as it did, that citizens 18 to 21 years of age are not substantially less able. . . .

"In sum, Congress had ample evidence upon which it could have based the conclusion that exclusion of citizens 18 to 21 years of age from the franchise is wholly unnecessary to promote any legitimate interest the States may have in assuring intelligent and responsible voting."

The trio suggested that denial of the right to vote might be banned on grounds of "discrimination" under the Fourteenth Amendment.

Justice Douglas, in a separate opinion, wrote:

"It is said, why draw the line at 18? Why not 17? Congress can draw lines, and I see no reason why it cannot conclude that 18-year-olds have that degree of maturity which entitles them to the franchise."

The four "strict constructionists" held that neither Article I nor the Fourteenth Amendment gives Congress the right to fix the voting age by law in either federal or State elections.

Justice Stewart, joined by the Chief Justice and Justice Blackmun:

A casual reader could easily get the impression that what we are being asked in these cases is whether or not we think allowing people 18 years old to vote is a good idea. Nothing could be wider of the mark. My brothers to the contrary, there is no question here as to the 'judgment' of Congress; there are questions only of Congress' constitutional power. . . .

Contrary to the submission of my brother Black, Article I, section 4 does not create in the federal legislature the power to alter the constitutionally established qualifications to vote in congressional elections. That section provides that the legislatures in each State shall prescribe the times, places and manner of holding elections for Senators and Representatives,' but reserves in Congress the power to 'make or alter such regulations, except as to the place of choosing Senators.'

"The 'manner' of holding elections can hardly be read to mean the *qualifications* for voters, when it is remembered that section 2 of the same Article I explicitly speaks of the qualifications' for voters in elections to choose Representatives.

"It is plain, in short, that when the Framers meant qualifications they said 'qualifications.' That word does not appear in Article I, section 4.

"Moreover, section 4 does not give Congress the power to do anything that a State might not have done, and no State may establish distinct qualifications for congressional elections. . . .

"The States are not free to prescribe qualifications for voters in federal elections which differ from those prescribed for the most numerous branch of the State legislature. And the power of Congress to do so cannot, therefore, be found in Article I, section 4. . . .

"Although it was found necessary to amend the Constitution in order to confer a federal right to vote upon Negroes [Fifteenth Amendment] and upon females [Nineteenth Amendment], the Government asserts that a federal right to vote can be conferred upon people between 18 and 21 years of age simply by this Act of Congress. . . .

"It is obvious that the whole Constitution reserves to the States the power to set voter qualifications in State and local elections, except to the limited extent that the people, through constitutional amendments, have specifically narrowed the power of the States. . . .

"The Constitution just as completely withholds from Congress the power to alter by legislation qualifications for voters in federal elections, in view of the explicit provisions of Article I, Article II and the Seventeenth Amendment."

Justice Harlan, speaking for himself, criticized the Supreme Court for what he called "an era of constitutional revision in the field of suffrage, ushered in eight years ago in *Baker v. Carr*." In that case, the Court issued its historic edict declaring that federal courts have the power to decide on legislative apportionment cases.

Wrote Mr. Harlan:

"I am of the opinion that the Fourteenth Amendment was never intended to restrict the authority of the States to allocate their political power as they see fit, and therefore that it does not authorize Congress to set voter qualifications, in either State or federal elections.

"I find no other source of congressional power to lower the voting age as fixed by State laws, or to alter State laws on residency, registration and absentee voting, with respect to either State or federal elections. . . .

"All the evidence indicates that Congress—led on by recent decisions of this Court—thought simply that 18-year-olds were fairly entitled to the vote, and that Congress could give it to them by legislation. . . .

"Congress exceeded its delegated powers."

Thus, there emerged in the judicial opinions on the Voting Rights Act a split on the Court of 4 to 4 on the basic constitutional question, with Justice Black as a swing man.

Observers suggested that if President Nixon has an opportunity to appoint one more "strict constructionist" to the bench, the High Court will have a firm majority that most legal experts believe would cast their key votes on the side of judicial restraint.

Justice Harlan stated: "In the annals of this Court, few developments in the march of events have so imperatively called upon us to take a fresh hard look at past decisions" as those in the electoral-process area.

Expressing his own view that "such decisions cannot withstand constitutional scrutiny," Mr. Harlan served notice that he would not be bound by recent precedents if new cases affecting voting rights are brought up for review.

The right of eighteen-year-olds to vote in any election was guaranteed by the Twenty-sixth Amendment to the Constitution, ratified in 1971.

The Right to Vote

U.S. Constitution

Twenty-sixth Amendment

SECTION 1. The right of citizens of the United States, who are eighteen years of age or older, to vote shall not be denied or abridged by the United States or by any State on account of age.

U.S. News & World Report also considered the potential impact of the newly enfranchised young voters.

Now That the Voting Age Is Lower . . .

U.S. News & World Report

A possible key element in next year's elections, now being analyzed by political leaders and potential candidates for office, is this:

> Out of each 100 Americans old enough to vote, 18 will be youths aged 18 through 24, eligible for their first trip to the polls.

Never before has the potential youth vote in a presidential-election year been so high. Reason for the boost: ratification on June 30 of the 26th Amendment to the U.S. Constitution, giving extended voting rights to youths over 18. Ohio, the 38th State to ratify, put the amendment across.

When the number of newly franchised young people aged 18 to 21 are added to those who turned 21 since 1968, the total of possible new voters in federal, State and local elections reaches 25.1 million. . . .

What effect? Just what this new factor will mean in 1972 is still largely a matter of guesswork. But some points that are being made—

- The "potential" impact is high, nearly equaling the 31.8 million votes that President Nixon got in 1968.
- In many areas, particularly college and military towns, young people will make up the largest percentage of any age group in the voting-age population. South Carolina and Utah will have the highest percentage of young voters.

But analysts point out that youths who have had the vote have so far not used it as much as their elders. A congressional race in rural Maryland last spring gave 18-year-olds their first chance under the 1970 Voting Rights Act. Fewer than 2 per cent of the 47,000 eligibles turned out.

In four States which have long given young people the right to vote, only 26 per cent balloted in 1970, compared with a 55 per cent turnout for those over 21.

State voter-residency laws may also tend to keep youths, more mobile than older generations, from voting in non-federal races.

Registration drives. Despite this record, a coalition of nonprofit organizations and labor unions is mounting voter-registration campaigns in the 20 States with the most 18-to-25-year-olds now eligible to vote.

The Democratic Party already is involved with current drives. Republicans say they hope to get a campaign under way in December.

Around the nation, "U.S. News & World Report" correspondents checked sentiment in their areas about the effect of the youth vote. Some samplings—

From the South. "Don't look for long lines of newly enfranchised young Americans at the polls come next Election Day"—that's the prevailing view. But a Tennessee Republican leader says the young could have "tremendous impact" in urban areas.

In South Carolina last spring, the 18-to-21 set stayed away from the polls in droves, declining to involve themselves in primary elections for a congressional seat.

From the Midwest. The youth vote has not been a catalyst for political activity in this region so far. Few young people are registering—but the registration drives have not gotten under way.

Most experts seem convinced the youth vote will be small, and young people will vote generally as their parents do.

In Illinois, legislation was defeated that would have prevented university students from voting in communities where they attend school. Sponsor of the bill said the youth vote could mean a "disaster" in which university towns would be "taken over by teen-agers."

From the West. The influence of the youth vote has been proclaimed in California, where students working with blacks are credited with electing Ronald Dellums to Congress last November.

California is one of the few States with some concrete figures on registrations by party. In 14 of the States's largest counties, a tally of youth registrations went this way: 59 per cent Democratic, 20 per cent Republican, the remainder independent or "other."

One registration official said:

"This youth vote is a real time bomb no matter how they register. They're obviously an independent force, and every party and politician has got to come to grips with it."

151

Reproductive rights for adolescents became the controversial focus of the courts in the 1970s and 1980s. In Carey v. Population Services (1977) the U.S. Supreme Court determined that children fourteen to sixteen had a right to contraception.

Contraception

U.S. Supreme Court

Carey v. Population Services International
431 U.S. 678 (1977)

Mr. Justice Brennan delivered the opinion of the Court (Parts I, II, III, and V), together with an opinion (Part IV), in which Mr. Justice Stewart, Mr. Justice Marshall, and Mr. Justice Blackmun joined.

Under New York Educ. Law § 6811 (8) (McKinney 1972) it is a crime (1) for any person to sell or distribute any contraceptive of any kind to a minor under the age of 16 years; (2) for anyone other than a licensed pharmacist to distribute contraceptives to persons 16 or over; and (3) for anyone, including licensed pharmacists, to advertise or display contraceptives. A three-judge District Court for the Southern District of New York declared § 6811 (8) unconstitutional in its entirety under the First and Fourteenth Amendments of the Federal Constitution insofar as it applies to nonprescription contraceptives, and enjoined its enforcement as so applied. 398 F. Supp. 321 (1975). We noted probable jurisdiction, 426 U.S. 918 (1976). We affirm. . . .

Although "[t]he Constitution does not explicitly mention any right of privacy," the Court has recognized that one aspect of the "liberty" protected by the Due Process Clause of the Fourteenth Amendment is "a right of personal privacy, or a guarantee of certain areas or zones of privacy." *Roe v. Wade*, 410 U.S. 113, 152 (1973). This right of personal privacy includes "the interest in independence in making certain kinds of important decisions." . . .

Opinion of Brennan, J.

Of particular significance to the decision of this case, the right to privacy in connection with decisions affecting procreation extends to minors as well as to adults. *Planned Parenthood of Central Missouri v. Danforth, supra*, held that a State "may not impose a blanket provision . . . requiring the consent of a parent or person *in loco parentis* as a condition for abortion of an unmarried minor during the first 12 weeks of her pregnancy." 428 U.S., at 74. As in the case of the spousal-consent requirement struck down in the same case, *id.*, at 67–72, "the State does not have the constitutional authority to give a third party an absolute, and possibly arbitrary, veto," *id.*, at 74, " 'which the state itself is absolutely and totally prohibited from exercising.' " *Id.*, at 69. State restrictions inhibiting privacy rights of minors are valid only if they serve "any significant state interest . . . that is not present in the case of an adult." *Id.*, at 75. *Planned Parenthood* found that no such interest justified a state requirement of parental consent.

Since the State may not impose a blanket prohibition, or even a blanket requirement of parental consent, on the choice of a minor to terminate her pregnancy, the constitutionality of a blanket prohibition of the distribution of contraceptives to minors is a *fortiori* foreclosed. The State's interests in protection of the mental and physical health of the pregnant minor, and in protection of potential life are clearly more implicated by the abortion decision than by the decision to use a nonhazardous contraceptive.

Appellants argue, however, that significant state interests are served by restricting minors' access to contraceptives, because free availability to minors of contraceptives would lead to increased sexual activity among the young, in violation of the policy of New York to discourage such behavior. The argument is that minors' sexual activity may be deterred by increasing the hazards attendant on it. The same argument, however, would support a ban on abortions for minors, or indeed support a prohibition on abortions, or access to contraceptives, for the unmarried, whose sexual activity is also against the public policy of many States. Yet, in each of these areas, the Court has rejected the argument, noting in *Roe v. Wade*, that "no court or commentator has taken the argument seriously." . . . It is enough that we again confirm the principle that when a State, as here, burdens the exercise of a fundamental right, its attempt to justify that burden as a rational means for the accomplishment of some significant state policy requires more than a bare assertion, based on a conceded complete absence of supporting evidence, that the burden is connected to such a policy.

152

In Bellotti v. Baird *(1979) the U.S. Supreme Court ruled that although a minor had the right to an abortion, the state could impose some limitations on that right.*

Abortion

U.S. Supreme Court

Bellotti v. Baird
443 U.S. 622 (1979)

Mr. Justice Powell announced the judgment of the Court and delivered an opinion, in which The Chief Justice, Mr. Justice Stewart, and Mr. Justice Rehnquist joined.

These appeals present a challenge to the constitutionality of a state statute regulating the access of minors to abortions. They require us to continue the inquiry we began in Planned Parenthood of Central Missouri v. Danforth, 428 U.S. 52 (1976), and Bellotti v. Baird, 428 U.S. 132 (1976).

On August 2, 1974, the Legislature of the Commonwealth of Massachusetts passed . . . an Act pertaining to abortions. . . . 1974 Mass. Acts, ch. 706. According to its title, the statute was intended to regulate abortions "within present constitutional limits." Shortly before the Act was to go into effect, [a] class action . . . was commenced in the District Court to enjoin, as unconstitutional, the provision of the Act now codified as Mass. Gen. Laws Ann., ch. 112, 12S (West Supp. 1979).

Section 12S provides in part:

> If the mother [who seeks an abortion] is less than eighteen years of age and has not married, the consent of both the mother and her parents is required. If one or both of the mother's parents refuse such consent, consent may be obtained by order of a judge of the superior court for good cause shown, after such hearing as he deems necessary. . . . If one of the parents has died or has deserted his or her family, consent by the remaining parent is sufficient. If both parents have died or have deserted their family, consent of the mother's guardian or other person having duties similar to a guardian, or any person who had assumed the care and custody of the mother is sufficient. The commissioner of public health shall prescribe a written form [to] be signed by the proper person or persons and given to the physician performing the abortion. . . .

... Plaintiffs in the suit, appellees in both the cases before us now, were William Baird; Parents Aid Society, Inc. (Parents Aid), of which Baird is founder and director; Gerald Zupnick, M.D., who regularly performs abortions at the Parents Aid clinic; and an unmarried minor, identified by the pseudonym "Mary Moe," who, at the commencement of the suit, was pregnant, residing at home with her parents, and desirous of obtaining an abortion without informing them.

Mary Moe was permitted to represent the "class of unmarried minors in Massachusetts who have adequate capacity to give a valid and informed consent [to abortion], and who do not wish to involve their parents." Baird v. Bellotti, 393 F. Supp. 847, 850 (Mass. 1975) (*Baird* I).

The pregnant minor's options are much different from those facing a minor in other situations, such as deciding whether to marry. A minor not permitted to marry before the age of majority is required simply to postpone her decision. ... A pregnant adolescent, however, cannot preserve for long the possibility of aborting, which effectively expires in a matter of weeks from the onset of pregnancy.

Moreover, the potentially severe detriment facing a pregnant woman is not mitigated by the minority. Indeed, considering her probable education, employment skills, financial resources, and emotional maturity, unwanted motherhood may be exceptionally burdensome for a minor. In addition, the fact of having a child brings with it adult legal responsibility, for parenthood, like attainment of the age of majority, is one of the traditional criteria for the termination of the legal disabilities of minority. In sum, there are few situations in which denying a minor the right to make an important decision will have consequences so grave and indelible. ...

For these reasons, as we held in Planned Parenthood of Central Missouri v. Danforth, 428 U.S., at 74, "the State may not impose a blanket provision ... requiring the consent of a parent or person in loco parentis as a condition for abortion of an unmarried minor during the first 12 weeks of her pregnancy." Although ... such deference to parents may be permissible with respect to other choices facing a minor, the unique nature and consequences of the abortion decision make it inappropriate "to give a third party an absolute, and possibly arbitrary, veto over the decision of the physician and his patient to terminate the patient's pregnancy, regardless of the reason for withholding the consent." 428 U.S., at 74. We therefore conclude that if the State decides to require a pregnant minor to obtain one or both parents' consent to an abortion, it also must provide an alternative procedure whereby authorization for the abortion can be obtained. ...

We conclude, therefore, that under state regulation such as that undertaken by Massachusetts, every minor must have the opportunity—if she so desires—to go directly to a court without first consulting or notifying her parents. If she satisfies the court that she is mature and well enough informed to make intelligently the abortion decision on her own, the court must authorize her to act without parental consultation or consent. If she fails to satisfy the court that she is competent to make this decision independently, she must be permitted to show that an abortion nevertheless would be in her best interests. If the court is persuaded that it is, the court must authorize the abortion. If, however, the court is not persuaded by the minor that she is mature or that the abortion would be in her best interests, it may decline to sanction the operation.

There is, however, an important state interest in encouraging a family rather than a judicial resolution of a minor's abortion decision. Also, as we have observed above, parents naturally take an interest in the welfare of their children—an interest that is particularly strong where a normal family relationship exists and where the child is living with one or both parents. These factors properly may be taken into account by a court called upon to determine whether an abortion in fact is in a minor's best interests. If, all things considered, the court determines that an abortion is in the minor's best interests, she is entitled to court authorization without any parental involvement. On the other hand, the court may deny the abortion request of an immature minor in the absence of parental consultation if it concludes that her best interests would be served thereby, or the court may in such a case defer decision until there is parental consultation in which the court may participate. But this is the full extent to which parental involvement may be required. For the reasons stated above, the constitutional right to seek an abortion may not be unduly burdened by state-imposed conditions upon initial access to court.

153

In 1979 the U.S. Supreme Court affirmed the right of parents to commit their children to psychiatric hospitals.

Mental Health and the Rights of the Child

U.S. Supreme Court

Parham v. J. R.
442 U.S. 548 (1979)

Mr. Chief Justice Burger delivered the opinion of the Court.

The question presented in this appeal is what process is constitutionally due a minor child whose parents or guardian seek state administered institutional mental health care for the child and specifically whether an adversary proceeding is required prior to or after the commitment.

Appellee J. R., a child being treated in a Georgia state mental hospital, was a plaintiff in this class action based on 42 U.S.C. §1983, in the District Court for the Middle District of Georgia. Appellants are the State's Commissioner of the Department of Human Resources, the Director of the Mental Health Division of the Department of Human Resources, and the Chief Medical Officer at the hospital where appellee was being treated. Appellee sought a declaratory judgment that Georgia's voluntary commitment procedures for children under the age of 18, Ga. Code §§88–503.1, 88–503.2 (1975), violated the Due Process Clause of the Fourteenth Amendment and requested an injunction against their future enforcement. . . .

J. L., a plaintiff before the District Court who is now deceased, was admitted in 1970 at the age of 6 years to Central State Regional Hospital in Milledgeville, Ga. Prior to his admission, J. L. had received out-patient treatment at the hospital for over two months. J. L.'s mother then requested the hospital to admit him indefinitely. The admitting physician interviewed J. L. and his parents. He learned that J. L.'s natural parents had divorced and his mother had remarried. He also learned that J. L. had been expelled from school because he was uncontrollable. He accepted the parents' representation that the boy had been extremely aggressive and diagnosed the child as having a "hyperkinetic reaction of childhood."

J. L.'s mother and stepfather agreed to participate in family therapy during the time their son was hospitalized. Under this program, J. L. was permitted to go home for short stays. Apparently his behavior during these visits was erratic. After several months, the parents requested discontinuance of the program.

In 1972, the child was returned to his mother and stepfather on a furlough basis, i.e., he would live at home but go to school at the hospital. The parents found they were unable to control J. L. to their satisfaction, and this created family stress. Within the two months, they requested his readmission to Central State. J. L.'s parents relinquished their parental rights to the county in 1974.

Although several hospital employees recommended that J. L. should be placed in a special foster home with "a warm, supported [sic], truly involved couple," the Department of Family and Children Services was unable to place him in such a setting. On October 24, 1975, J. L. (with J. R.) filed this suit requesting an order of the court placing him in a less drastic environment suitable to his needs.

Appellee J. R. was declared a neglected child by the county and removed from his natural parents when he was three months old. He was placed in seven different foster homes in succession prior to his admission to Central State Hospital at the age of 7.

Immediately preceding his hospitalization, J. R. received outpatient treatment at a county mental health center for several months. He then began attending school where he was so disruptive and incorrigible that he could not conform to normal behavior patterns. Because of his abnormal behavior, J. R.'s seventh set of foster parents requested his removal from their home. The Department of Family and Children Services then sought his admission at Central State. The agency provided the hospital with a complete sociomedical history at the time of his admission. In addition, three separate interviews were conducted with J. R. by the admission team of the hospital.

It was determined that he was borderline retarded, and suffered an "unsocialized, aggressive reaction of childhood." It was recommended unanimously that he would "benefit from the structured environment" of the hospital and would "enjoy living and playing with boys of the same age."

J. R.'s progress was re-examined periodically. In addition, unsuccessful efforts were made by the Department of Family and Children Services during his stay at the hospital to place J. R. in various foster homes. On October 24, 1975, J. R. (with J. L.) filed this suit requesting an order of the court placing him in a less drastic environment suitable to his needs. . . .

It is not disputed that a child, in common with adults, has a substantial liberty interest in not being confined unnecessarily for medical treatment and that the state's involvement in the commitment decision constitutes state action under the Fourteenth Amendment. . . . We also recognize that commitment sometimes produces adverse social consequences for the child because of the reaction of some to the discovery that the child has received psychiatric care. . . . For purposes of this decision, we assume that a child has a protectible interest not only in being free of unnecessary bodily restraints but also in not being labeled erroneously by some persons because of an improper decision by the state hospital superintendent.

We next deal with the interests of the parents who have decided, on the basis of their observations and independent professional recommendations, that their child needs institutional care. Appellees argue that the constitutional rights of the child are of such magnitude and the likelihood of parental abuse is so great that the parents' traditional interests in and responsibility for the upbringing of their child must be subordinated at least to the extent of providing a formal adversary hearing prior to a voluntary commitment.

Our jurisprudence historically has reflected Western civilization concepts of the family as a unit with broad parental authority over minor children. Our cases have consistently followed that course [and] asserted that parents generally "have the right, coupled with the high duty, to recognize and prepare [their children] for additional obligations." Pierce v. Society of Sisters, 268 U.S. 510, 535 (1925). See also Wisconsin v. Yoder, 406 U.S. 205, 213 (1972); Prince v. Massachusetts, 321 U.S. 158, 166 (1944); Meyer v. Nebraska, 262 U.S. 390, 400 (1923). Surely, this includes a "high duty" to recognize symptoms of illness and to seek and follow medical advice. The law's concept of the family rests on a presumption that parents possess what a child lacks in maturity, experience, and capacity for judgment required for making life's difficult decisions. More important, historically it has recognized that natural bonds of affection lead parents to act in the best interests of their children. 1 W. Blackstone, Commentaries *447; 2 J. Kent, Commentaries on American Law *190.

As with so many other legal presumptions, experience and reality may rebut what the law accepts as a starting point. . . . That some parents "may at times be acting against the interests of their children" as was stated in Bartley v. Kremens, 402 F. Supp. 1039, 1047–1048 (E. D. Pa. 1975), vacated and remanded, 431 U.S. 119 (1977), creates a basis for caution, but is hardly a reason to discard wholesale those pages of human experience that teach that parents generally do act in the child's best interests. . . .

Nonetheless, we have recognized that a state is not without constitutional control over parental discretion in dealing with children when their physical or mental health is jeopardized. See Wisconsin v. Yoder, supra, 406 U.S., at 230; Prince v. Massachusetts, supra, 321 U.S., at 166. . . . Appellees urge that these precedents limiting the traditional rights of parents, if viewed in the context of the liberty interest of the child and the likelihood of parental abuse, require us to hold that the parents' decision to have a child admitted to a mental hospital must be subjected to an exacting constitutional scrutiny, including a formal, adversary, pre-admission hearing.

Appellees' argument, however, sweeps too broadly. Simply because the decision of a parent is not agreeable to a child or because it involves risks does not automatically transfer the power to make that decision from the parents to some agency or officer of the state. The same characterizations can be made for a tonsillectomy, appendectomy, or other medical procedure. Most children, even in adolescence, simply are not able to make sound judgments concerning many decisions, including their need for medical care or treatment. Parents can and must make those judgments. Here, there is no finding by the District Court of even a single instance of bad faith by any parent of any member of appellees' class. . . . The fact that a child may balk at hospitalization . . . does not diminish the parents' authority to decide what is best for the child. . . . Neither state officials nor federal courts are equipped to review such parental decisions. . . .

In defining the respective rights and prerogatives of the child and parent in the voluntary commitment setting, we conclude that our precedents permit the parents to retain a substantial, if not the dominant, role in the decision, absent a finding of neglect or abuse, and that the traditional presumption that the parents act in the best interests of their child should apply. We also conclude, however, that the child's rights and the nature of the commitment decision are such that parents cannot always have absolute and unreviewable discretion to decide whether to have a child institutionalized. They, of course, retain plenary authority to seek such care for their children, subject to a physician's independent examination and medical judgment.

154

The child who is the focus of a custody or visitation dispute is sometimes given no voice in the court proceedings.

Visitation Rights

Illinois Appellate Court

In re Marriage of Marshall and Nussbaum
278 Ill.App.3d 1071, 215 Ill.Dec. 599 (1996)

Mother filed petition to modify father's visitation rights, and father's action for contempt was transferred from other state. The 12th Judicial Circuit Court, Will County, Ludwig J. Kuhar, J., denied mother's petition, found mother to be in contempt, ordered children to comply with visitation, and found children to be in contempt when they refused to go with father. Mother and children via guardian ad litem appealed. The Appellate Court, Lytton, J., stayed contempt judgment, consolidated action, and held that: (1) finding that father did not pose danger to children was supported by sufficient evidence; (2) children were bound by visitation order; (3) summary disposition of direct contempt did not violate due process; but (4) trial court was required to consider appropriate alternatives before confining minor to juvenile detention facility.

Affirmed in part, reversed in part, and remanded.

Justice Lytton delivered the opinion of the court:

These consolidated appeals arise from a dispute over child visitation. The mother, Kathy Marshall, appeals from the denial of her petition to modify the visitation rights of the father, Sheldon Nussbaum. Kathy and Sheldon's minor children, Heidi and Rachel, appeal a circuit court finding that they were in direct civil contempt for refusing to go to North Carolina to visit Sheldon. For the reasons stated below, we affirm the ruling denying modification of visitation, affirm the finding of contempt against the minors, but reverse the sanctions imposed and remand for further proceedings.

Facts

Kathy and Sheldon were married in January 1982, and resided in North Carolina. The couple had two children. Heidi was born in December 1982, and

Rachel was born in December 1986. In February 1990, the couple separated and Kathy commenced dissolution proceedings.

The record shows that, from the onset, the litigation between Kathy and Sheldon was acrimonious. Each party alleged that the other was guilty of physical and psychological abuse. In three separate pleadings—filed in May 1990, April 1991 and December 1991—Sheldon alleged that Kathy was improperly denying him visitation.

Kathy moved with the children to Illinois in November 1991. A judgment of dissolution of marriage was entered in North Carolina in 1992. In a separate order, entered in April 1993, Kathy was awarded custody of the children. Under the visitation schedule, Sheldon was to have the children in North Carolina for five to six weeks in the summer, every Christmas and every other spring break.

The girls visited their father during the summer of 1993 and for about a week at Christmas; however, Kathy did not send the girls for their spring break visit in April 1994. Sheldon brought a contempt action in North Carolina. In May 1994, Kathy filed a petition in the circuit court of Will County, Illinois, seeking to enroll the North Carolina judgment and restrict Sheldon's visitation rights. Sheldon brought another contempt action when the girls did not come to North Carolina for their summer visitation in 1994.

On September 28, 1994, the North Carolina court declined to exercise further jurisdiction and transferred Sheldon's contempt actions to Illinois to be heard with Kathy's petition to modify.

In late February and early March 1995, an extended hearing was held in the circuit court of Will County. Kathy presented the testimony of a psychologist, Dr. Eleanore A. Ryan. Ryan testified that she was contacted by Kathy in February 1994. Kathy told her that Heidi had been experiencing behavioral problems both at home and at school in the past month. Kathy also reported that Heidi had recently run away from home.

Ryan met with Heidi on February 26, 1994. Heidi said that during the recent Christmas visitation in North Carolina, her father woke her up every night and said that it was father/daughter time. Heidi told Ryan that her father would keep her up until 4:00 in the morning. Heidi said that her father also kept her up nights during the summer visitation in 1993. Heidi also told Ryan she had received a rifle from her father for Christmas, and they went hunting. She claimed that her father forced her to shoot a bird. Heidi told Ryan that she began hearing voices after this visit with her father.

Ryan met with Heidi a second time on March 12, 1994. At this meeting, Heidi said that she was afraid of her father and she was concerned about the upcoming spring break visit. Heidi expressed the fear that if she went to North Carolina, her father would not allow her to return to Illinois. Based on Heidi's fears, Dr. Ryan recommended to Kathy that neither child go to North Carolina for the visit scheduled to start April 1, 1994.

In the meantime, Sheldon had mailed airline tickets to Kathy. Kathy did not call Sheldon until the morning the children were to leave for North Carolina. Sheldon had already gone to the airport.

Ryan met with Heidi nine more times between April 1994 and the hearing in February 1995. During these meetings, Heidi claimed that her father repeatedly stated that her mother and maternal grandparents were evil. He said things would be better if she came and lived with him. Heidi related that her father made her repeat things over and over. Heidi also told Ryan that she had run away from home on February 19, 1994, because her father had told her to do so.

At the hearing, Ryan opined that Heidi was suffering from post-traumatic stress disorder resulting from contacts with her father. Ryan testified at the hearing, "I feel that to schedule any kind of visitation at this point would be very threatening for Heidi, would reduce the feelings of security that she currently has." Ryan testified she interviewed Rachel on three occasions in late 1994 and early 1995. She diagnosed Rachel as suffering "adjustment disorder with mixed emotional features." Ryan opined there should be no visitation with the father at that time.

Kathy Marshall testified that she noted behavioral differences in Heidi following the Christmas visit in 1993. After the February 19, 1994, incident in which Heidi ran away from home for several hours, Heidi began telling her mother that she was hearing voices. Kathy decided to seek professional help and contacted Dr. Ryan.

Kathy also testified that Heidi had told her about an incident, during the 1993 Christmas visit, when Sheldon was going to spank Rachel for crying for her mother. Heidi said that she grabbed her father's arm and told him not to spank Rachel. Heidi stated that her father chased her until she hid behind a waterbed, where he tried to hit her with a stick.

Heidi asked Kathy not to send her back to North Carolina. Heidi stated that she was afraid of her father and he said she would not be allowed to return to Chicago.

On cross-examination, Kathy conceded that just prior to Heidi running away, Heidi had been grounded by her mother for failing to give Kathy a note from Heidi's gym teacher. Kathy also conceded that it made no sense for Heidi to run away to be with her father if she was afraid of him.

Sheldon Nussbaum testified to events surrounding the girls' visitation in the summer of 1993 and at Christmas. Sheldon testified he took each of the girls hunting during their Christmas visit. He took the girls out separately; when he went with seven-year-old Rachel, they did not take any guns. Sheldon denied giving Heidi a rifle, although he did let her use one of his guns. He said it was Heidi's idea to shoot the bird.

He admitted waking Heidi up, but testified that this was at Heidi's request because she wanted to stay up later than Rachel. Therefore, after Rachel would fall asleep, Heidi would get up. Heidi and he would eat popcorn, watch videos and "shoot the bull." Sheldon said that they may have discussed Kathy Marshall, but he denied telling Heidi that her mother and grandparents were evil.

Sheldon also confirmed the incident where he went to spank Heidi and she hid behind the waterbed. He stated that he tried to get her to come out from behind the headboard by "[laying] a guilt trip on her."

He testified that he spoke with Heidi on either February 18 or February 19, 1994. Heidi told him that she planned to run away from home. She was upset because she had been grounded. Heidi went into detail about her plans to run away, but Sheldon did not consider it a serious threat since she said she only planned to hide in the shed or go to a friend's house. He advised her that if she was going to leave she should go to her friend's house. He then tried calling the next day and got no answer. Sheldon further testified that after February 19, he noted a change in Heidi's attitude toward him.

The court interviewed Rachel and Heidi *in camera*. Rachel stated that she "kind of missed" seeing her dad. She spoke of being spanked when she cried for her mother. Rachel also stated that her father said he was going to keep them in North Carolina and not let them see their mother again.

Heidi told the judge that she did not want to see her father. She said that she ran away in February 1994 because her father told her to run away. She claimed to be afraid of her father. She described how her father spanked Rachel for crying. Heidi stated that when she tried to prevent her father from spanking Rachel, her father backhanded her and she got a black eye.

Heidi spoke about the late-night conversations in which her father said that her mother and grandparents were wicked and everyone on her mother's side of the family molested each other. Heidi claimed that she began hearing voices after her summer visit in 1993. She did not tell her mother about the voices because she was afraid her mother would think she was crazy. Heidi told the court she would run away if ordered to go to North Carolina.

On May 10, 1995, the circuit court issued an order denying Kathy's petition to modify visitation. The court found there was no evidence that visitation with Sheldon would seriously endanger the children's physical or moral health. The court noted that visitation had been going on for more than a year prior to 1994 with no complaints from either girl. The court found Dr. Ryan's testimony "nonsensical" and "less than credible." The court ordered that Dr. Ryan have no further input with respect to the counseling of the children.

The court believed that Heidi made up stories at the time she ran away to place blame on her father. The court ordered the parties to seek further counseling for the children. If the parties could not agree on a counselor, the court would appoint one. The court also found Kathy in contempt on the motions initially filed in North Carolina in 1994.

The parties were unable to agree to a counselor to help facilitate visitation. On June 5, 1995, the court appointed Dr. Patricia Miller. Kathy filed a motion to reconsider or, in the alternative, to modify or vacate the order denying modification and holding her in contempt.

On June 13, 1995, the court entered an order which directed Kathy to send the children to North Carolina that day. The children did not go. Sheldon then filed a petition for rule to show cause why Kathy should not be held in criminal contempt.

At a status call held on Kathy's motion to reconsider and Sheldon's petition for criminal contempt, the judge noted he had spoken with Dr. Miller. The parties agreed that Sheldon would travel to Illinois to meet with the children in Miller's office on July 12, 1995. The court stated that it was the court's intention that, at the conclusion of this meeting, the children would leave with Sheldon for their summer visitation in North Carolina.

Dr. Miller's report, filed on July 13, 1995, recommended that the girls not leave on their summer visit until a specific plan was fully established and agreed to by the parties. On that date, the court ordered the parties to cooperate with Miller to obtain additional counseling sessions through July 17, 1995, to facilitate the children's visitation with their father.

On July 18, 1995, the court again interviewed the children *in camera*. Both children were adamant that they were not going. They strongly expressed their beliefs that the court was wrong. Heidi stated that she would "pitch a fit" if forced to go to North Carolina. Rachel told the judge, "I think you must have a very sick sense of humor." After the court indicated that the girls must go with their father, Rachel responded, "You *** just made the biggest mistake probably ever you could have made." When the judge reiterated his decision, Heidi added, "It's not that simple."

At the conclusion of the hearing, the court ordered the children placed in the custody of their father for purposes of going to North Carolina. The order further stated that if the girls refused to cooperate, the Department of Children and Family Services was ordered to take the children into custody and bring them back to the court. The children did not go with their father, and DCFS took custody.

The next day, July 19, 1995, during a hearing on an emergency motion filed by Kathy, the court returned the children to the custody of their mother. The court appointed a guardian *ad litem*. In addition, the court *sua sponte* ordered a hearing be held to determine whether the children should be held in direct civil contempt of court.

On July 21, 1995, the circuit court denied Kathy's motion to reconsider. On July 24, 1995, Sheldon filed a petition asking the court to find Kathy in contempt for failing to pay certain monies over to Sheldon and his attorney.

Also on July 24, 1995, a hearing was held on whether Heidi and Rachel should be held in direct civil contempt. Dr. Miller recommended further counseling. Also, in an attempt to allay the girls' fears about being alone with their father for the summer, Miller proposed contacts with counselors and/or family members while the girls were in North Carolina. The court questioned Heidi and Rachel about their counseling sessions and contacts with their father in the previous week. When the court asked the girls if they were going to cooperate and go to North Carolina, both girls responded that they refused to go.

The court found both Rachel and Heidi to be in direct civil contempt. The court "grounded" Rachel, and ordered that she not leave her mother's home. Rachel could not watch television or have friends over to the house, but she could read and do crafts. The court ordered Kathy to enforce these measures. The court placed Heidi in a juvenile detention facility until she agreed to go to North Carolina. The judge indicated that the girls' conduct arose from the efforts of adults to manipulate the system.

155

While children have gained some rights in regard to free speech and contraception and in criminal proceedings, their rights in custody disputes have yet to be adequately addressed.

A Voice for the Child?

Mary Ann Mason

Consider these facts: A child who steals a candy bar at a Seven Eleven can request a lawyer. A child of fourteen whose parents are dead may choose his own guardian. A girl is entitled to an abortion without notifying her parents in most states. Yet a child who is the object of a brutal tug-of-war between adults is powerless.

In the center of most child custody disputes is a large black hole representing the absence of the voice of the child. There are many ways in which the actual child is not attended to. The wishes and feelings of the child, even a teenager, may not be considered or even sought. The developmental requirements of an individual child may not be presented at trial. And in our typical one-size-fits-all-ages custody legislation the developing needs of children in general may not be considered in drafting legislation that determines custody. Toddlers and teens usually are lumped together in laws that either pose a general best interests standard or suggest a presumption in favor of joint custody without regard to the age of the child—and the custody order issued for a toddler will not be modified as the child's needs grow and change.

Finally, the legal rights of the child (such as they are) are usually not represented. Whether the proceeding is a mediation or a judicial hearing, the focus is too often on the rights of the adults rather than on those of the child. In some custody actions the child's best interests are not even a factor. Such an action may be a contempt hearing for the violation of a custody arrangement or a bid for custody by a biological parent against a ''biological stranger'' who serves as a parent, such as a stepparent. In these instances the only factor considered is whether contact with the biological parent will actually be harmful to the child, not whether it is in the child's best interests.

A recent Illinois court dispute over visitation between Kathy Marshall and Sheldon Nussbaum illustrates the invisibility and powerlessness of children in the legal process. In this case involving two young girls ages eight and twelve, one child was actually ordered to be imprisoned for violating a civil visitation order. Moreover, the children were given no voice to influence the determination of their very lives. The wishes and feelings of the children, expressed directly to the court and to a trained expert, were completely ignored.

Heidi Nussbaum, twelve, and her sister Rachel, eight, refused to visit their father in North Carolina in the summer of 1995, in violation of a court-ordered agreement between Sheldon Nussbaum and Kathy Marshall. When the judge asked the girls if they were going to cooperate and go to North Carolina, both girls responded that they refused to go. The judge found both Rachel and Heidi to be in direct civil contempt. . . .

In this case the only issue the judge considered was whether the mother could prove that the father was endangering the girls' welfare. Since this was technically a contempt hearing for violating a court order, not a custody hearing, the concept of the "best interests" of the child was never introduced. In cases alleging contempt, as with custody disputes involving nonbiological parents, a detriment standard is imposed. This means that a party must prove by the high standard of clear and convincing evidence that the children will actually suffer harm from the contact, not merely that it is against their best interests. The custody agreement is treated like a contract for an exchange of property. The children are the subject of the contract, the property to be exchanged. Like a recalcitrant mule, the property must be forcefully delivered no matter the circumstances. Under these conditions the world-famous due process rights theoretically granted to all Americans under the Constitution are not available to the children.

In the *Nussbaum* case it appeared at first that the children might have a voice. The judge asked them to explain their failure to comply. Initially, too, he permitted their therapist to testify, but ultimately their voices had no bearing on the outcome. Since the children themselves had no legal rights, they became nothing more than the objects of the dispute. The judge could and did choose to ignore them. This is not just an example of one bad judge or one bad jurisdiction; it represents the state of American law in dealing with children's rights.

The idea of legal rights for children apart from those of their parents is relatively new and still very controversial for Americans. Thus far progress toward recognizing children's rights has been jagged and uneven. The Supreme Court first introduced children's rights in the 1960s, the decade that celebrated individual liberties. In a 1965 freedom of speech case in which Quaker school children had protested the Vietnam War in the classroom, the Supreme Court boldly proclaimed that children "did not leave their constitutional rights at the school house door." Yet that same court in the more conservative 1970s allowed censorship of school newspapers and gave school authorities wide discretion to search student lockers.

It is in the arena of juvenile justice that courts have most seriously considered rights for children. In 1965 fifteen-year-old Gerald Gault allegedly made an anonymous obscene phone call to an elderly neighbor. Without the benefit of a lawyer or trial Gerald was sentenced to incarceration in a Boys' Correctional Institution until age twenty-one. The ensuing landmark Supreme Court decision, *In Re Gault*, expanded by several subsequent decisions, gave children who were defendants in juvenile court criminal actions nearly all the due process protections that adult defendants receive in the regular criminal courts, including lawyers and the right against self-incrimination.

In a vicious, ironic turn of events in the 1990s, however, state legislatures, responding to increased juvenile crime, grew eager to throw juveniles into adult courts at ever younger ages and to apply adult punishments to children. Today in most states a fourteen-year-old can be tried for murder as an adult, and a sixteen-year-old can be sentenced to execution.

While the Supreme Court has been willing to recognize some limited rights for children with regard to schools, courts, and other governmental institutions, it has been reluctant to grant children rights that might interfere with those of their parents. Much of this concern has focused on abortion. Soon after *Roe v. Wade* the Court conceded that an adult woman's right to abortion extended to adolescent girls as well, but it also carved out plenty of room for parents' rights. The Court decided that individual states could pass parental consent laws. However, with the ambivalence typical of its earlier decisions on children's rights issues, the Court also held that a girl could bypass her parents by going to a judge. If the judge declared that she was a mature minor, the decision was hers alone.

A minor's consent to abortion is an agonizing issue for parents, and it crosses dangerous battle lines into the raging abortion wars. States are seriously divided on the issue, and the battles continue. Yet there has been some progress on the somewhat less controversial issue of adolescent consent to other sensitive medical procedures, such as the treatment of sexually transmitted diseases and drug and alcohol abuse. In many states now a doctor who cannot give an adolescent an aspirin without parental consent can treat the minor for a venereal disease.

156

The issue of children's rights has been internationalized in the United Nations Convention on the Rights of the Child (1989), signed by all Western powers but not yet ratified by the United States.

United Nations Convention on the Rights of the Child

UN Document

Preamble

The States Parties to the present Convention,

Considering that, in accordance with the principles proclaimed in the Charter of the United Nations, recognition of the inherent dignity and of the equal and inalienable rights of all members of the human family is the foundation of freedom, justice and peace in the world,

Bearing in mind that the peoples of the United Nations have, in the Charter, reaffirmed their faith in fundamental human rights and in the dignity and worth of the human person, and have determined to promote social progress and better standards of life in larger freedom,

Recognizing that the United Nations has, in the Universal Declaration of Human Rights and in the International Covenants on Human Rights, proclaimed and agreed that everyone is entitled to all the rights and freedoms set forth therein, without distinction of any kind, such as race, colour, sex, language, religion, political or other opinion, national or social origin, property, birth or other status,

Recalling that, in the Universal Declaration of Human Rights, the United Nations has proclaimed that childhood is entitled to special care and assistance,

Convinced that the family, as the fundamental group of society and the natural environment for the growth and well-being of all its members and particularly children, should be afforded the necessary protection and assistance so that it can fully assume its responsibilities within the community,

Recognizing that the child, for the full and harmonious development of his or her personality, should grow up in a family environment, in an atmosphere of happiness, love and understanding,

Considering that the child should be fully prepared to live an individual life in society, and brought up in the spirit of the ideals proclaimed in the Charter of the United Nations, and in particular in the spirit of peace, dignity, tolerance, freedom, equality and solidarity,

Bearing in mind that the need to extend particular care to the child has been stated in the Geneva Declaration of the Rights of the Child of 1924 and in the Declaration of the Rights of the Child adopted by the United Nations on 20 November 1959 and recognized in the Universal Declaration of Human Rights, in the International Covenant on Civil and Political Rights (in particular in articles 23 and 24), in the International Covenant on Economic, Social and Cultural Rights (in particular in article ten) and in the statutes and relevant instruments of specialized agencies and international organizations concerned with the welfare of children,

Bearing in mind that, as indicated in the Declaration of the Rights of the Child, "the child, by reason of his physical and mental immaturity, needs special safeguards and care, including appropriate legal protection, before as well as after birth,"

Recalling the provisions of the Declaration on Social and Legal Principles relating to the Protection and Welfare of Children, with Special Reference to Foster Placement and Adoption Nationally and Internationally; the United Nations Standard Minimum Rules for the Administration of Juvenile Justice ("The Beijing Rules"); and the Declaration on the Protection of Women and Children in Emergency and Armed Conflict,

Recognizing that, in all countries in the world, there are children living in exceptionally difficult conditions, and that such children need special consideration,

Taking due account of the importance of the traditions and cultural values of each people for the protection and harmonious development of the child,

Recognizing the importance of international cooperation for improving the living conditions of children in every country, in particular in the developing countries,

Have agreed as follows:

Part I: Substantive Provisions

Article 1

For the purposes of the present Convention, a child means every human being below the age of 18 years unless, under the law applicable to the child, majority is attained earlier.

Article 2

1. States Parties shall respect and ensure the rights set forth in the present Convention to each child within their jurisdiction without discrimination of any kind, irrespective of the child's or his or her parent's or legal guardian's race, colour, sex, language, religion, political or other opinion, national, ethnic or social origin, property, disability, birth or other status.

2. States Parties shall take all appropriate measures to ensure that the child is protected against all forms of discrimination or punishment on the basis of the status, activities, expressed opinions, or beliefs of the child's parents, legal guardians, or family members.

Article 3

1. In all actions concerning children, whether undertaken by public or private social welfare institutions, courts of law, administrative authorities or legislative bodies, the best interests of the child shall be a primary consideration.

2. States Parties undertake to ensure the child such protection and care as is necessary for his or her well-being, taking into account the rights and duties of his or her parents, legal guardians, or other individuals legally responsible for him or her, and, to this end, shall take all appropriate legislative and administrative measures.

3. States Parties shall ensure that the institutions, services and facilities responsible for the care or protection of children shall conform with the standards established by competent authorities, particularly in the areas of safety, health, in the number and suitability of their staff, as well as competent supervision.

Article 4

States Parties shall undertake all appropriate legislative, administrative, and other measures for the implementation of the rights recognized in the present Convention. With regard to economic, social and cultural rights, States Parties shall undertake such measures to the maximum extent of their available resources and, where needed, within the framework of international cooperation.

Article 5

States Parties shall respect the responsibilities, rights and duties of parents or, where applicable, the members of the extended family or community as provided for by local custom, legal guardians or other persons legally responsible for the child, to provide, in a manner consistent with the evolving capacities of the child, appropriate direction and guidance in the exercise by the child of the rights recognized in the present Convention.

Article 6

1. States Parties recognize that every child has the inherent right to life.

2. States Parties shall ensure to the maximum extent possible the survival and development of the child.

Article 7

1. The child shall be registered immediately after birth and shall have the right from birth to a name, the right to acquire a nationality and, as far as possible, the right to know and be cared for by his or her parents.

2. States Parties shall ensure the implementation of these rights in accordance with their national law and their obligations under the relevant international instruments in this field, in particular where the child would otherwise be stateless.

Article 8

1. States Parties undertake to respect the right of the child to preserve his or her identity, including nationality, name and family relations as recognized by law without unlawful interference.

2. Where a child is illegally deprived of some or all of the elements of his or her identity, States Parties shall provide appropriate assistance and protection, with a view to speedily re-establishing his or her identity.

a

b

c

d

e

f

g

a. E. W. Kemble, frontispiece for the first edition of *The Adventures of Huckleberry Finn*, 1884. *b*. Beth Timmons: all-American swimmer in athletic pose. From Joan Jacobs Brumbert, *The Body Project*. Courtesy of Beth Timmons. *c*. Peter Pluntky, Basket of the Canadian Dionne Quintuplets, c. 1935. Courtesy of Peter Pluntky, Stockholm, Sweden. *d*. Photo from the documentary film *Beauty Leaves the Bricks,* by Allen Mondell and Cynthia Salzman Mondell. Courtesy of Media Projects, Inc., 5215 Homer Street, Dallas, TX, 75206, 214-826-3863, www.mediaprojects.org. *e*. Alexander Cross, Teenage Mutant Ninja Turtles. Courtesy of Gary Cross, *Kids' Stuff: Toys and the Changing World of American Childhood. f*. Lewis Hine, Playground in a mill village, 1909. Acquired through exchange with George Eastman House, 1959.860. Courtesy of the Art Institute of Chicago. *g*. Arnold Genthe, *Basket Kid*. Courtesy of the California Historical Society, FN-02332.

Part Eleven

The Child's World

Most children's institutions and beliefs about childhood are constructed by adults. The lived experience of children, though difficult to capture, has left a historical residue in material artifacts, autobiographical reminiscences, and children's stories. There is no typical childhood and never has been. To get a sense of how various children perceived and understood their world, we range broadly over time and space to cull insight from history, memoirs, novels, and children's books.

157

There are very few aspects of infant life in the seventeenth and eighteenth centuries that we can reconstruct with certainty, but the historian Karin Calvert provides an excellent discussion of the swaddling of infants (probably a common if not universal practice), as well as some of their minimal furnishings and other accoutrements (1992). When an infant was swaddled, it was securely bound by long strips of cloth, the upper torso with one, the lower with another. This prevented any movement of the arms or legs and kept the infant straight and immobile.

The Material Culture of Early Childhood
Karin Calvert

The Upright Child

Infants remained completely swaddled for at least the first three months. After that, if the weather was not too cold, their arms were freed, but their legs remained bound. At anywhere from six to nine months of age, swaddling stopped and children went into their first long petticoats. Exactly when a mother decided to modify or give up swaddling depended on the health and physical shape of the child, the work schedule of the mother, and the time of the year, since physicians urged that swaddling be continued through the winter months and that any change wait for warmer weather.

Swaddling was popularly practiced because it served several useful functions. By making it impossible for a child to kick off the bedclothes, it kept a baby warm when the bitterly cold winter air seeped into ill-heated or unheated rooms. It eliminated the risk of chilblains or cracked and bleeding skin that occurred when a child's hands became wet in the normal course of sucking its fingers or thumbs. There was no need to get up in the night to check on babies; they remained covered in the morning precisely as they had been when put to bed the night before. Of course, very tightly bound swaddling could interfere with the child's circulation and cause considerable suffering.

Swaddling bands also made an infant easily and safely portable. The primary responsibilities of seventeenth-century women were managing the household and childbearing, not childrearing. It was their task to effectively and smoothly preserve, conserve, and manage all of the family resources, and it was their lot, as the Daughters of Eve, to bear the risks and pain of childbirth, producing on average a new baby approximately every two years over a span of about twenty years. Since most women continued to bear children until menopause, many still had young children at home when they died. An industrious and thrifty wife was essential for a family's comfort and survival. With so many other priorities, many women had little time or attention to spare for their infants, whose care had to be turned over to others, often servants or older siblings who may have given rather perfunctory attention to the task. But, since infants were considered insensible creatures, who "seem only to live and grow, as plants," needing only rudimentary servicing, not much was actually expected of a caretaker. In such a situation, swaddling helped protect the child. Virtually anyone could safely tend or carry a swaddled baby, since, regardless of how it was held, the child would remain straight, secure, and fully supported within its wrappings. Physicians, in fact, recommended picking up an infant by placing one hand on its chest and another on its back. There was no need to give special support to the head or neck, for the necessary bracing came from the costume, not the attendant. A swaddled baby, like a little turtle in its shell, could be looked after by another, only slightly older child without too much fear of injury, since the practice of swaddling made basic child care virtually idiot proof. Little harm could come to the infant, barring actually dropping it, of course. Unfortunately, dropping did occur all too frequently, since tossing the baby up in the air or from one person to another was a common form of amusement, and accidents happened. Whether through a false confidence in the invulnerability of the child encouraged by swaddling or through common indifference, babies often met with cavalier treatment from those around them. Swaddling, therefore, offered them some useful protection. And when there was no time or person to spare to watch the child, the swaddled baby could be laid anywhere—on a bed, table, or shelf, on the ground in the fields, or even hung from a peg for safekeeping—and be just as comfortable as a native American baby fastened to its cradle board.

A very important rationale for swaddling was to ensure that a child would grow straight and tall, that the dubious lump of infant flesh would be properly molded into the shape of an erect adult. One of the primary justifications for swaddling was the pervasive fear that without such external aid children would never learn to stand erect, would, so the French physician François Mauriceau warned in 1675, "crawl on all fours like little animals for the rest of their lives." Swaddling was considered imperative to form the bent limbs of the newborn into the straight limbs of the adult. Sleeping in the bent fetal position was routinely blamed as a major cause of rickets. A very common and much-feared disease of children in the seventeenth century, rickets was actually due to a calcium deficiency from lack of sufficient milk and sunshine that left young bones too soft to support the weight of the child without bending. Unaware of the real cause of the malady, parents focused on stretching and straightening tiny limbs. Without swaddling, parents and physicians believed, a child might grow bent and misshapen, would certainly never learn to walk, and could never become a whole human being.

While supposedly training the tiny bones in the direction they were to grow, swaddling served a more immediate cosmetic function. The cloth bands and the long mantle that usually covered them actually extended some distance below the infant's feet, visually elongating the tiny figure to more adult proportions. In "The Birth Feast," for example, painted by Jan Steen in 1664, the young mother lies in state in childbed while friends and relatives who have come to admire the new baby and to offer congratulations mill about the room. Near the center of the painting the new father holds up the swaddled child, its body held erect and straight, visually elongated by the linen bands and red mantle. Newborn and newly bound, the child "stands" encircled by the proud father's arm, a tiny upright man. Swaddling not only ensured the future form of infants but endowed them with the desired mature posture right from birth, making them more attractive to contemporary eyes.

This need to express the adult potentiality of the infant suggests an underlying ambivalence about the actual position of the young child in the universal scheme of things. The seventeenth- and early eighteenth-century conceptualization of the organization of life was of a great, unchanging, and perfect chain of being extending from the lowliest organism through the increasingly complex species of the animal kingdom to mankind. Humanity was further ordered by race, from the Hottentot, inevitably placed at the bottom, to European man, inevitably placed at the top. Above the various races stood a multitude of celestial beings, rising upward toward the ultimate perfection of the Holy Trinity. In all of this, mankind stood at a crucial point on the chain—at once the lowest form of thinking creatures, and yet also the finest achievement of earthly creation. Humanity's claim to earthly supremacy rested primarily on its possession of a soul and three characteristics that set it apart from the animal kingdom: the ability to reason, to speak, and to stand and walk erect. An individual's proficiency in these activities further indicated his relative position within the hierarchy of mankind. A European gentleman was admired for the soundness of his reason, the artistry of his conversation, and the grace and dignity of his bearing. On the other hand, the French naturalist Buffon assured his readers that a Hottentot, when pressed, would take to all fours for greater speed of escape or pursuit. Each subspecies of humankind had its allotted place in the scheme of creation. It was all very satisfying to a society that found itself so coincidentally well placed in the grand scheme of things. . . .

Once the mother or nurse had thoroughly and firmly swaddled the infant, she laid it in a cradle upon a mattress of folded cloth, "hard and pricking straw, feather, or dried oak leaves." While cradles had existed since the time of ancient Greece and Rome, seventeenth-century authorities distinguished between "purposely made" cradles and other, presumably improvised beds for young children, suggesting that a specially made baby's bed was still considered a comparative luxury.

Very few cradles have survived from the seventeenth and early eighteenth centuries; but then, very few adult-sized beds survive from the eighteenth century, and virtually none from the seventeenth. Occasionally, probate inventories include a cradle listed among the household effects. That they appear less often than many other common forms of home furnishings is not all that surprising, considering that most inventories represented the estates of mature men or women whose children had already outgrown the need of a cradle. Any baby furniture that might have existed in such households could have worn out over long years of use or could have already been passed on to grandchildren. To further complicate the issue, written references to "cradles" do not necessarily specify whether the term is being used to refer to a specifically constructed infant's bed on rockers or to a baby's bed fashioned from whatever came to hand. The term "cradle" commonly meant any of a large number of possible containers or supports found about the farm and in the house—from a cradle scythe to an iron grate to numerous types of baskets. An infant's cradle referred to the baby's place of lodging, whether in a wicker basket, old box, old chest, or specially designed bed. What really mattered was that any sort of separate bed was better for an infant than being put to sleep with its mother, nurse, or some other older person. Adults, drugged by exhausting physical work, or perhaps by the common daily consumption of ale, all too often rolled over on an infant in the night and smothered it. "Laying over" was a common and worrisome cause of infant mortality, and (to what extent we cannot know) at least sometimes a convenient cover for infanticide. The baby who slept alone slept most safely.

Traditionally, a "purposely made" cradle was a piece of furniture of board construction or wicker, affixed to wooden rockers, and often hooded at one end. Regularly spaced holes or pegs along the upper edge of the sides of many cradles were used to lace a swaddled infant securely in place. Other cradles were made deep enough that the baby could be restrained by firmly tucking the bedclothes under the mattress. The physician Felix Wurtz, writing in the middle of the seventeenth century, describes caretakers who bound their charges with tapes laced "from hole to hole in the Cradle which they tie very hard; for should they not do so, they believe their Child would not stay in the Cradle . . . whereby the inlaid Child is packed up like a pack of Wares." Attendants placed the cradle near the fireplace, both to keep the baby warm and to keep an eye on the child while the daily work of the house progressed. If loosely tied, the restraints kept babies safe from any accidental bump against their rocking beds that might tip them out onto the floor among the bustling activity around them. As in every-thing else concerning infant care, attendants worried more about immediate safety and future growth than about the child's comfort. Overzealous or indiffer-ent attendants could easily lash the child down far too tightly. Felix Wurtz had observed many such cases during his practice; he concluded, "I am assured that by such hard binding, great and anguishing pain is caused." . . .

When infants finally gained their freedom from swaddling bands, their first clothes consisted of a bodice and long petticoats very similar to the costume of their mothers, except that the "long coats" of infancy extended a foot or so longer than the child. The portrait of Mrs. Freake and her daughter Mary painted in Massachusetts in 1674 depicts Mary at about the age of six months dressed in the long coats of infancy. Her stiff, doll-like pose was not the result of an inexperienced or ill-trained artist's inability to adequately portray a lifelike baby.

Mary's little figure looks hard and rigid because, like most children her age, she was probably wearing a stiff corset under her bodice. A young child's corset or stays closely resembled those worn by adult women, except children's stays were corded or quilted for stiffness, rather than boned. Some children wore stays in conjunction with swaddling; others received their first corset when they were long-coated. The stays held Mary's body straight and stiff, giving her the desirable appearance of an erect and mature posture while training her body to grow straight and tall. The artist, however, may have depicted Mary as stiff and upright whether she actually was or not in order to present her with the dignity befitting any civilized person. To make Mary suitably appealing to his seventeenth-century audience, the artist eliminated or glossed over most of her babyish characteristics, which were commonly perceived as the shortcomings and inadequacies of infancy. In an age that considered children by nature disconcertingly animalistic, the artist would have attempted to make Mary look as adult as possible in order to make her image pleasing to his patrons, who in this case were the child's parents—no small consideration.

Long petticoats, however, served more than the cosmetic function of creating the illusion that a baby was proportioned like an adult. The long, entangling skirts helped to keep the child covered and warm, and, most important, utterly foiled any attempt the infant made to move about by crawling. Parents and physicians alike viewed crawling, not as a natural stage in the process of learning to walk, but as a bad habit that, if not suppressed, would remain the child's primary form of locomotion for the rest of its life. The seventeenth-century physician Mauriceau warned that, if not properly swaddled or gowned, children would never learn to walk, but would forever "crawl on all fours like little animals." In the eighteenth century, Dr. William Buchan in his books on child-rearing pointed out to mothers the long-term risks of letting their babies creep. He cited evidence from the narratives of the French naturalist Buffon, who observed that unrestrained African babies readily learned to "shuffle along on their hands and knees; an exercise that gives them ever after a facility of running almost as swift in that manner as on their feet." As late as 1839, when babyish behavior had gained considerable acceptance, the American childrearing authority William Alcott complained that American mothers who wanted their infants to be admired decked them out in excessive finery, forced them to sit up straight, and still prohibited their creeping. As a form of locomotion connected with animals, crawling raised too many fears and negative associations in parents. It further emphasized the differences between children and adults, and it seemed to be development in decidedly the wrong direction. Parents wanted their children to become more like them, not less. Most babies born into middle-class homes before 1800 did not learn to crawl before they learned to walk. It simply was not allowed, or at least was actively discouraged.

American colonists regarded crawling as a demeaning, animalistic form of locomotion beneath the dignity of any human being. Moving about on all fours was fit only for beasts, savages, wild men, the insane, and the subjugated as a token of their subjection. Stories and illustrations abounded of madmen who, when they lost their reason, lost the other distinctly human characteristics of speech and erect posture as well. Examples of the popular association of insanity and crawling extended from the mad Nebuchadnezzar becoming one with the beasts of the field to William Hogarth's rake who ended his days grovelling on the floor of Bedlam. The defeated crawled before the conqueror, as the serpent was doomed to crawl in the dust of the earth as punishment for his mischief in Eden. In fact, a common iconographic expression of the natural order of the universe overturned was a depiction of the learned Aristotle, made mad by love, submitting to the degrading whims of the enchantress Phyllis by sinking to his hands and knees to willingly become her beast of burden. Western culture inculcated a very powerful symbolic language of the hierarchy of things, from Hell below to Heaven above, from the crawling of beasts to the marching of kings. Children, if they were to assume their rightful place in the divine order, had to do so on their feet, not on their hands and knees. Crawling was too distasteful and unsettling to be accepted, even in the very young.

Not surprisingly then, most of the handful of traditional furniture forms designed expressly for children encouraged early standing or walking and prevented crawling. Parents pushed children to stand at as early an age as possible, partly to strengthen their leg muscles to ensure early walking and partly from the common belief that it was unlucky for a child to learn to speak before it had begun to walk. At about the same time that mothers freed their children completely from swaddling bands, they began to make use of the standing stool. Essentially, it looked like any normal wooden stool, with somewhat shorter legs and a round hole in the top into which the child was placed. The device, which fitted rather snugly around the child's waist, supported babies just finding their feet, but did not allow them the respite of sitting or crawling. Unlike somewhat similar products of today, the seventeenth-century standing stool had no attached seat. A child could not get out of the stool or sit down in it. The simplest, and probably most common, versions of the standing stool were homemade. Parents fashioned them of willow rods, narrow wooden boxes, or simply a floor-to-ceiling wooden pole with an attached willow ring that fastened about the little waist and kept the child on its feet. Even simpler was a hollowed-out tree trunk: "The inside and upper edge are smoothed, and a child just able to stand is put into it, while its mother is at work by its side, or going after the business of the house."

158

Jacob Stroyer recalls the violence to which slave children were exposed (1898). Note that Jacob's parents could intervene on his behalf with other blacks, but were powerless to protect him against whites.

My Life in the South

Jacob Stroyer

Gilbert was a cruel [slave] boy. He used to strip his fellow Negroes while in the woods, and whip them two or three times a week, so that their backs were all scarred, and threatened them with severer punishments if they told; this state of things had been going on for quite a while. As I was a favorite with Gilbert, I always managed to escape a whipping, with the promise of keeping the secret of the punishment of the rest. . . . But finally, one day, Gilbert said to me, "Jake," as he used to call me, "you am a good boy, but I'm gwine to wip you some to-day, as I wip dem toder boys." Of course I was required to strip off my only garment, which was an Osnaburg linen shirt, worn by both sexes of the Negro children in the summer. As I stood trembling before my merciless superior, who had a switch in his hand, thousands of thoughts went through my little mind as to how to get rid of the whipping. I finally fell upon a plan which I hoped would save me from a punishment that was near at hand. . . . I commenced reluctantly to take off my shirt, at the same time pleading with Gilbert, who paid no attention to my prayer. . . . Having satisfied myself that no mercy was to be found with Gilbert, I drew my shirt off and threw it over his head, and bounded forward on a run in the direction of the sound of the [nearby] carpenters. By the time he got from the entanglement of my garment, I had quite a little start of him. . . . As I got near to the carpenters, one of them ran and met me, into whose arms I jumped. The man into whose arms I ran was Uncle Benjamin, my mother's uncle. . . . I told him that Gilbert had been in the habit of stripping the boys and whipping them two or three times a week, when we went into the woods, and threatened them with greater punishment if they told. . . . Gilbert was brought to trial, severely whipped, and they made him beg all the children to pardon him for his treatment to them.

[My] father . . . used to take care of horses and mules. I was around with him in the barn yard when but a very small boy; of course that gave me an early relish for the occupation of hostler, and I soon made known my preference to

Col. Singleton, who was a sportsman, and an owner of fine horses. And, although I was too small to work, the Colonel granted my request; hence I was allowed to be numbered among those who took care of the fine horses and learned to ride. But I soon found that my new occupation demanded a little more than I cared for. It was not long after I had entered my new work before they put me upon the back of a horse which threw me to the ground almost as soon as I had reached his back. It hurt me a little, but that was not the worst of it, for when I got up there was a man standing near with a switch in hand, and he immediately began to beat me. Although I was a very bad boy, this was the first time I had been whipped by anyone except father and mother, so I cried out in a tone of voice as if I would say, this is the first and last whipping you will give me when father gets hold of you.

When I had got away from him I ran to father with all my might, but soon found my expectation blasted, as father very coolly said to me, "Go back to your work and be a good boy, for I cannot do anything for you." But that did not satisfy me, so on I went to mother with my complaint and she came out to the man who had whipped me; he was a groom, a white man master had hired to train the horses. Mother and he began to talk, then he took a whip and started for her, and she ran from him, talking all the time. I ran back and forth between mother and him until he stopped beating her. After the fight between the groom and mother, he took me back to the stable yard and gave me a severe flogging. And, although mother failed to help me at first, still I had faith that when he had taken me back to the stable yard, and commenced whipping me, she would come and stop him, but I looked in vain, for she did not come.

Then the idea first came to me that I, with my dear father and mother and the rest of my fellow Negroes, were doomed to cruel treatment through life, and was defenseless. But when I found that father and mother could not save me from punishment, as they themselves had to submit to the same treatment, I concluded to appeal to the sympathy of the groom, who seemed to have full control over me; but my pitiful cries never touched his sympathy. . . .

One day, about two weeks after Boney Young [the white man who trained horses for Col. Singleton] and mother had the conflict, he called me to him. . . . When I got to him he said, "Go and bring me the switch, sir." I answered, "yes, sir," and off I went and brought him one . . . [and] . . . he gave me a first-class flogging. . . .

When I went home to father and mother, I said to them, "Mr. Young is whipping me too much now, I shall not stand it, I shall fight him." Father said to me, "You must not do that, because if you do he will say that your mother and I advised you to do it, and it will make it hard for your mother and me, as well as for yourself. You must do as I told you, my son: do your work the best you can, and do not say anything." I said to father, "But I don't know what I have done that he should whip me; he does not tell me what wrong I have done, he simply calls me to him and whips me when he gets ready." Father said, "I can do nothing more than to pray to the Lord to hasten the time when these things shall be done away; that is all I can do."

159

As a young girl Rose Cohen immigrated to the United States from a small shtetl in Russia. Here she describes her experiences on the ship and, later, her shock when her father forgoes aspects of their Jewish traditions in this new country (1918).

A Russian Jewish Girlhood on the Lower East Side

Rose Cohen

When our names were called I rose quickly and followed Aunt Masha. The clerk who always came to the door, which he opened only a little, looked at us and asked our names. Then he let Aunt Masha go in and pushing me away roughly without a word he shut the heavy door in my face.

I stood nearby waiting, until my feet ached. When Aunt Masha came out at last her face was flushed and there were tears in her eyes. Immediately she went over to her friends (she had many friends by that time) and began to talk to them excitedly. I followed her but she stopped talking when she saw me. I understood that I was not to listen. And so I went away.

This went on for almost a week. Each day her face looked more worried and perplexed.

One afternoon the door of the office opened wider than usual and a different clerk came out holding a paper in his hand. He told us that the English steamer for which we had been waiting was in. And then he read the names of those who were to go on it.

I'll never forget Aunt Masha's joy when she heard that we were to sail the next day. She ran from one to the other of her friends, crying and laughing at once.

"The scoundrel," she kept on saying, "he threatened to send us home. He said he had the power to send us home!" Then she ran over to me and in her joy almost smothered me in her embrace.

I don't remember whether it was on this same day or when we were already on the steamer that our clothes were taken away to be "steamed." As my little underwaist, which still had some money in it, was also taken, we spent some anxious hours. The money was not touched. But when I looked at my pretty little slippers I wept bitter tears. They looked old, and wrinkled, and two of the buttons were off.

On the following evening we sailed off in a small white boat. We all sat on the floor of the deck. I dreaded crossing the ocean for I had heard that the water was rough. The boat rocked fearfully, and there was sickness and even death. But when some time passed and I saw how smoothly and steadily the boat went along over quiet water, I felt relieved. Then came something of gladness. I sat quietly in back of Aunt Masha, watching the full moon appearing and disappearing behind the clouds, and listening to our fellow travellers. Their faces, so worried and excited for weeks, looked peaceful and contented as they sat gazing at the moon and talking quietly and hopefully of the future in the new world.

"How beautiful," I thought. "This is the way the rest of our journey will be." For in my ignorance I thought that we would sail all the way across in this little white boat and that the water would always be calm, and the wind gentle. When I whispered my thought to Aunt Masha she smiled at me over her shoulder, a queer, meaning little smile, which puzzled me. In the morning when we came to an enormous black and white steamer I remembered Aunt Masha's smile and understood its meaning.

We were deathly seasick the first three days. During that period I was conscious, it seems to me, only part of the time. I remember that once when I opened my eyes I seemed to see the steamer turn to one side and then disappear under water. Then I heard voices screaming, entreating, praying. I thought we were drowning, but I did not care. Nothing mattered now. On the fourth day, I became again interested in life. I heard Aunt Masha moaning. A long time seemed to have passed since I saw her face. I tried to lift my head. Finding it impossible, I lay quietly listening, but it hurt me to hear her moaning. At last it became so pitiful that I could not stand it.

"I'll die if I don't get a drop of water," she moaned, "just one drop to wet my throat."

And so as I lay flat on my face I felt about for my tin cup till I found it. Then I began to slip downward feet first until I reached the berth underneath. From there I swung down to the floor. As I stood up the boat lunged to one side and I went flying to the door and fell in a heap, striking my head against the door post. I don't know how long I had been lying there, when I heard the cabin door open and a man's strong voice call out, "Up on deck." I opened my eyes and saw an enormous pair of black boots and the lower part of white trousers.

The man stooped down, looked at me and gently brushed the hair away from my eyes. As I was used now to being pushed about and yelled at, the kind touch brought tears to my eyes. For the first time since I left home I covered my face with my hands and wept heartily.

For a minute or so he stood looking down at me. Then he picked up my cup, which I had dropped in falling, and brought me water. I drank some, and pointed to Aunt Masha. He handed the cup to a woman who came tumbling out of her berth to go up on deck. Then picking me up as if I were a little infant, he again shouted, "Up on deck!" and carried me off.

I had heard that those who were very sick on the steamer and those who died were thrown into the ocean. There was no doubt in my mind, therefore, that that was where I was being carried. I clasped my arms tightly about the man's neck. I felt sick with fear. He climbed up a white staircase and propped me up in a corner on the floor. Then he went away, to fetch a rope, I thought. He returned in a few minutes. But instead of a rope there was half an orange in his hand. He kneeled down in front of me, raised my chin, showed me how to open my mouth and squeezed a few drops of juice into it. A good-natured smile played about his lips as he watched me swallow. Three times between his work he went and came with the half orange, until it was dry.

After a while Aunt Masha came creeping up the steps on all fours, hugging our little bag of zwieback.

From that hour we improved quickly. All day we sat or walked about in the sun. Soon Aunt Masha's little round nose was covered with freckles and my hair was bleached a half dozen shades.

Sometimes while walking about on deck we passed the man who had fed me with orange juice. He always touched his cap and smiled to us.

A week passed.

One day, it was the first of July, Aunt Masha and I stood in Castle Garden. With fluttering hearts yet patiently we stood scanning the faces of a group of Americans divided from us by iron gates.

"My father could never be among those wonderfully dressed people," I thought. Suddenly it seemed to me as if I must shout. I caught sight of a familiar smile.

"Aunt Masha, do you see that man in the light tan suit? The one who is smiling and waving his hand?"

"Why, you little goose," she cried, "don't you see? It's father!" She gave a laugh and a sob, and hid her face in her hands.

A little while later the three of us stood clinging to one another. . . .

One night father came home from work a little earlier than usual and took us to Grand Street. I was dazzled by the lights, the display in the jewelry shops and dry goods store windows. But nothing surprised me so much as the figures in the hair dresser's window. One was a blonde, the other a brunette. One was in pink, the other in blue. Their hair was beautifully curled and dressed, each one with a mirror in one hand and the other held daintily on the back of the hair, went slowly turning around and around and smiling into the mirror.

At first I could not believe that they were not alive until father and Aunt Masha laughed at me. It seemed to me nothing short of a miracle to see how perfect the features were, the smile. And I thought, "Oh, America is truly wonderful! People are not shovelling gold in the streets, as I had heard, but still it is wonderful." When I told it to father he laughed. "Wait," he said. And then he took us to "Silver Smith Charlie's saloon" and I saw the floor studded with half dollars!

From Mrs. Felesberg we learned at once the more serious side of life in America. Mrs. Felesberg was the woman with whom we were rooming. A door from our room opened into her tiny bedroom and then led into the only other room where she sat a great part of the day finishing pants which she brought in big bundles from a shop, and rocking the cradle with one foot. She always made us draw our chairs quite close to her and she spoke in a whisper scarcely ever lifting her weak peering eyes from her work. When she asked us how we liked America, and we spoke of it with praise, she smiled a queer smile. "Life here is not all that it appears to the 'green horn,' " she said. She told us that her husband was a presser on coats and earned twelve dollars when he worked a full week. Aunt Masha thought twelve dollars a good deal. Again Mrs. Felesberg smiled. "No doubt it would be," she said, "where you used to live. You had your own house, and most of the food came from the garden. Here you will have to pay for everything; the rent!" she sighed, "for the light, for every potato, every grain of barley. You see these three rooms, including yours? Would they be too much for my family of five?" We had to admit they would not. "And even from these," she said, "I have to rent one out."

Perhaps it was due to these talks that I soon noticed how late my father worked. When he went away in the morning it was still dark, and when he came home at night the lights in the halls were out. It was after ten o'clock. I thought that if mother and the children were here they would scarcely see him.

One night when he came home and as he sat at the table eating his rice soup, which he and Aunt Masha had taught me to cook, I sat down on the cot and asked timidly, knowing that he was impatient of questions, "Father, does everybody in America live like this? Go to work early, come home late, eat and go to sleep? And the next day again work, eat, and sleep? Will I have to do that too? Always?"

Father looked thoughtful and ate two or three mouthfuls before he answered. "No," he said smiling. "You will get married."

So, almost a week passed and though life was so interesting, still no matter where I went, what I saw, mother and home were always present in my mind. Often in the happiest moments a pain would rise in my throat and my eyes burned with the tears held back. At these moments I would manage to be near Aunt Masha so that I could lean against her, touch her dress.

How Aunt Masha felt I never knew but once. Father brought each of us a black patent leather belt. One day she put hers on and came over to me. "Close your eyes, Rahel," she said, "and feel the belt on me." I did. And as I passed my hand around her waist, I said, "This is how grandmother used to see when we put on something new." When I opened my eyes I saw that Aunt Masha's face was wet with tears. . . .

When Saturday came I felt happy because father stayed at home. After dinner we went out into the street. I walked beside father, clasping his hand tightly. I looked about and wondered how people could find their way without seeming to think about it. All the streets, all the houses, seemed so very much alike.

Father stopped at a fruitstand and told me to choose what I wanted. There was nothing strange to me in that. At home when we sold fruit, as we did sometimes during the summer, Jewish people came on Saturday to eat apples or pears for which they paid the following week. So I thought it was the same here.

I looked and looked at the fruit: "What shall I take?" Apples, oranges, plums, pears—all were arranged in neat pyramids, all looked good and very tempting, surrounded by fresh green leaves, glistening with drops of water. I looked at the strange fruits also. I saw long finger like things with smooth yellow skins, and grapes which I knew by name only. In a glass case on a square of ice there were some slices of watermelon.

"What shall I take?" I asked, turning to father. "Anything you like," he smiled encouragingly. I decided on a slice of melon. I looked up into father's face. I felt proud of him that he had credit at so beautiful a fruit-stand.

As I received the melon in my fingers I saw father take his hand out of his pocket and hold out a coin. I felt the blood rush to my face. I stood staring at him for a moment. Then I dropped the melon on the pavement and ran. Before I had taken many steps I realised that I was running away from home and turned back. In passing the stand I did not look to see if father was still there but ran on.

"My father has touched coin on the Sabbath!"

These words rang in my ears. I was almost knocked over by people into whom I ran but I paid no attention. Others stopped to watch me curiously as I ran by. It seemed to me that it was because they knew what I had just seen and I ran on with my cheeks flaming.

Suddenly it seemed to me that I had been running a long while and I felt that I should be near home. I stopped and looked about, but I could not see the house anywhere. I ran further, looking about wildly and trying to remember things so as to locate myself. Suddenly I came upon a dressmaker's sign which I recognised. I hurried into my room, closed the door carefully, and threw myself down on the cot, burying my face into the pillow.

"Father carries money about with him on the Sabbath. Oh, the sin! Oh, poor grandmother," I thought, "how would she feel if she knew. Brother is only seven years old and already he is so pious that he wishes to remain with a learned Jew in Russia, after mother goes to America, that he may become a great Rabbi. How would he feel? How would they all feel?"

Then I remembered Yanna, who, on hearing that father was in America, and feeling that perhaps we were too happy over it, came one day to torment grandmother.

"The first thing men do in America," she had said, "is cut their beards and the first thing the women do is to leave off their wigs. And you," she had said, turning to me venomously, "you who will not break a thread on the Sabbath now, will eat swine in America."

"Oh, God," I thought, "will it really come to that? shall I eat swine?"

After what I had just seen nothing seemed impossible. In utter misery I turned and felt about with my burning cheek for a cooler place on the pillow. As I did so I remembered that the pillow was one which mother gave me from home. I slipped my arms under it and pressing my lips to it I wept. "No, I shall not eat swine, indeed I shall not!"

160

Mary Paik Lee recalls her life as a Korean immigrant child in a California mining town of the early twentieth century, when transient laborers from various countries did most of the dirty and dangerous work (1990).

Quiet Odyssey
A Pioneer Korean Woman in America

Mary Paik Lee

We were told that there were only a few quicksilver mines in the United States, the largest of which was in Idria. On the way to Idria, we had to stop in Sacramento, because Mother became very ill. We stayed at a boardinghouse owned by a Mr. and Mrs. Lee, where another brother, Young Sun, was born February 26, 1914. Mother was so weary and ill she almost died that night giving birth. Young Sun, also named (but never called) Lawrence, was born more dead than alive, a blue baby. Father and I had to place him in hot and cold water alternately and massage him vigorously. It took a long time to get his circulation going.

After a day or two of rest, we continued to Tres Piños, a very small village some distance south of San Jose, to catch a wagon to Idria. It was a big haywagon with benches on both sides, hitched to four large horses, which took us up the mountains. It took half a day to reach the place. We crossed several creeks and stopped to move big rocks that had rolled down the road from the mountain. The scenery was beautiful—tall pine trees and hilly country—with very few houses along the way. Every time we moved, we came to a different kind of world. This was the best so far. The pine trees smelled good, and the cool air made us feel refreshed.

Mr. Lee had found an old house for us. It had four small rooms, and a shack in the back served as a kitchen and dining area. There was a big oven in the shack and a picnic-style board table with benches on both sides. The house had a small wood stove for heat. The mines, the company buildings, the hotel, the store, the houses of a few Caucasian families, and the boardinghouse for Caucasian workers all had electricity, but there was no electricity in the shacks for the rest of the workers—mainly Mexicans, with a few Koreans. We were back to our old way of living, but we felt happy to be in such a beautiful, wild country. Meung and I had to hunt for firewood again. There was a water pump outside the house, and the outhouse was halfway down the hill.

Mr. Lee took Father to the company office and asked if he could work there. He was accepted and was given a card to record the supplies from the company store which we bought on credit. Father bought kerosene lamps, a sack of rice—and a big ham. It was the first time we children had ever seen such a luxury. The ham tasted wonderful, and we enjoyed it very much for several weeks. . . .

Around the house of every Mexican family in Idria were two or three burros, one or two pigs, and some chickens. We found that burros were a necessity of life in those mountains. They were the only means of getting around because of the numerous rattlesnakes. We needed two of them to bring the firewood down from the mountains, so Father and I went to a neighbor who had several and asked if we could buy two. He brought the burros out to us and told them in Spanish that this man was to be their new owner, that they should go with him and should stay at his house and not come back. The burros just blinked their eyes and stood waiting while Father paid for them. The owner patted their backs and told them to go with us. I asked if we should tie them up. He said that was not necessary, that they knew what to do. Also, he said there was no need to feed them, that they would go up the mountains at night to feed on the grass there. I didn't believe him but waited to see what would happen. The burros followed us home. All my brothers were so excited and happy to see them. They brought water for them to drink and played with them all day. I thought the burros would run away at night and not come back, but the next morning I looked out the window and there they were, standing meekly by the kitchen shack. It was a wonderful surprise to see them there.

Meung and I took the burros up the mountains to look for firewood. There was plenty everywhere. We had to chop the wood into shorter lengths so we could pack bundles on both sides of the burros. We first put down a layer of sacks to protect the burros' bodies; then we tied the bundles of firewood tightly. The burros knelt down to let us tie the bundles with ropes around their bodies, but they would not get up when ordered. We were told this might happen, so we just left them there and returned home. They came home later when they felt like it. They must have received harsh treatment from others and expected the same from us. They were showing their feelings in the only way they knew. When they got home, we took off the loads, and the boys brought water for them and petted them. They seemed to enjoy the attention and love shown to them. After this happened a few times, they decided not to be so stubborn. They stood up after the loads were tied and walked home with us. It was a joy to have such cooperation from them. On weekends we made as many trips as possible to gather wood. We had to pile up a lot of wood by August, because our neighbors had told us that the winter might bring snow storms and that sometimes it might be impossible to get wood. We made a shelter for the woodpile so it would not be covered with snow or get soaked with rain.

The Paik family in Idria, 1915. Left to right, Ernest, Meung Sun, Mrs. Paik, Ralph (in front of mother), Kuang Sun, Stanford, Young (in father's arms), Mr. Paik, and Arthur.

Father worked in the furnace area of the mining company, stirring the rocks so they would burn evenly. He had to wear a piece of cloth over his nose so he would not breathe the poisonous fumes whenever the lid was opened. It was a hard, nasty job that few men wanted to do, even though the pay was five dollars a day, an unheard of amount in those times. But Father was desperate and felt compelled to take it.

The fumes from the furnace were poisonous not only to humans but to plant life as well. Nothing grew where the fumes went. Because quicksilver was used to make explosives, soldiers guarded the entrance to the mines. When the quicksilver was being shipped out, several soldiers accompanied the cargo to its destination. No one was allowed to walk around the mining areas or furnaces. . . .

When we were fairly settled, we looked around for the schoolhouse. It was on top of a low hill not far from our place. Meung and I discovered it was another one-room schoolhouse with a teacher who taught all eight grades. We registered and started going to school the next day. There were about thirty Mexican children at that school, mostly little ones, though some were big boys who looked about twelve to sixteen years old. They had never been to school before and spoke very little English. They were so noisy the teacher had a hard time. She didn't have time for Meung and me. She was forced to tell the boys to go home, but they couldn't understand what she said. I had picked up a few words of Spanish, so I told them what she had said. They were so startled to hear me speak Spanish that they got up and left. After that, the rest of us could learn our lessons.

There was a wood stove in the middle of the schoolroom. The teacher built a fire at noon and heated something in a small pot which smelled so good I asked her what it was. She said it was a can of Campbell's soup that she had bought at the store. That was my first introduction to Campbell's soups. I told Mother about the soup, and she bought one can at the store. She said it was good but that we couldn't afford to buy enough for the whole family.

I noticed that there was no one to sweep out the schoolroom, so I went to the company office and talked to the supervisor. He was a kindly man who listened to my story. I told him that I wanted to earn enough money to buy my books when I got to high school. He decided to hire me. My job was to clean the blackboards, sweep out the room, chop the wood for the stove, keep the outhouse clean, and ring the school bell at 8:30 A.M. so the children would know it was time for school. He would pay me twenty-five cents a day.

I had also been helping in the boardinghouse kitchen every evening. A couple there cooked and served about forty men every day. The wife paid me twenty-five cents every night and gave me leftover roast meat and rolls, which my family enjoyed. One evening while we were all busy in the kitchen, the couple started to argue about something. The wife said something that made her husband so angry he picked up a small can of lard and threw it at her. She screamed and fell to the floor. I was so frightened, I dropped everything and ran home. Father told me not to go there anymore.

Instead, he wanted me to do something for him. He told me to look for two stones of a certain size and thickness. He said he wanted to make a millstone to grind beans, so we could make our kind of food to eat. There were lots of big boulders around, but very few small ones of the size he wanted. It took me several days to find the right kind. When I did, I loaded them on the burros and brought them home. Every day after work, Father would chip away at the stones with a hammer and chisel. He made a beautiful two-piece mill. The top stone had a small oblong hole on one side and a handle inserted on the other side. On its bottom was a small hole, exactly in the middle. The bottom stone had a metal bolt, which fitted into the hole of the top stone. When the two stones were put together and the beans were put into the hole, the upper stone was turned around. It ground the beans into powder—a very ingenious machine. It must have been invented by someone like my father in the ancient days. He was always thinking up ways to improve our living conditions, always making things out of materials other people had discarded. We never had much, but he always tried to make our lives as comfortable as possible—even though harsh circumstances made that difficult most of the time.

Life in Idria was exciting; we had something new to learn every day. In the fall, when the cones on the pine trees were large and ripe, the boys climbed up with hatchets and cut them down. They buried them in hot ashes. The cones opened up in the heat, exposing the big nuts. They tasted better than peanuts and were very delicious. Then the bright red holly berries and small trees made everything look like Christmas. We cut lots of berries and pine tree branches to decorate the schoolroom and make it smell good. Meung cut a small tree for our house, and I went to the company store and bought bright tinsel and decorations for the tree with the money I had earned as a janitor. What a difference from our last Christmas in Colusa!

About two weeks after Christmas, Meung and I walked through the alleys in town to select the best tree that had been put out for the trash man. We picked out one that had some tinsel on it. We took it home and decorated it with strips of colored crepe paper. Our little brothers were happy to see it. Our parents never said a word; they just looked at us with sad faces. I was too young at that time to realize how they must have felt to see such a pitiful sight.

161

Few novels have been altogether successful in recapturing the sense of a child developing within a specific social milieu. One notable exception is Henry Roth's autobiographical novel Call It Sleep *(1934), which conveys the wonder, language, and anxieties of a Jewish immigrant childhood. Here the main character, David, is forced by several local bullies to witness the enormous surge of energy released from a third rail, which he mistakes for the presence of God.*

Call It Sleep

Henry Roth

With one on either side of him and one behind, David climbed up the junk heap and threaded his way cautiously over the savage iron morraine. Only one hope sustained him—that was to find a man on the other side to run to. Before him the soft, impartial April sunlight spilt over a hill of shattered stoves, splintered wheels, cracked drain pipes, potsherds, marine engines split along cruel and jagged edges. Eagerly, he looked beyond—only the suddenly alien, empty street and the glittering cartracks, branching off at the end.

"Peugh! Wadda stink!" Pedey spat. "Who opened his hole?"

From somewhere in the filth and ruin, the stench of mouldering flesh fouled the nostrils. A dead cat.

"C'mon, hurry up!"

As they neared the street, a rusty wire, tough root of a brutal soil, tripped David who had quickened his pace, and he fell against the sword bending it.

"He pissed in his w'iskers," guffawed the second lieutenant.

Pedey grinned. Only Weasel kept his features immobile. He seemed to take pride in never laughing.

"Hol' it, yuh dumb bassid," he barked, "yuh bent it!"

"Waid a secon'," Pedey warned them when they had reached the edge of the junk-heap. "Lemme lay putso." He slid down, and after a furtive glance toward Avenue D, "Come on! Shake! Nobody's aroun'."

They followed him.

"Now we're gonna show yiz de magic."

"Waid'll ye sees it," Weasel chimed in significantly.

"Yea, better'n movin' pitchiz!"

"Wadda yuh wan' I shul do?" Their growing excitement added to his terror.

"Hurry up an' take dat sword an' go to dem tracks and t'row it in—See like dis. In de middle."

"I don't wanna go." He began to weep.

"G'wan yuh blubber-mout'." Weasel's fist tightened.

"G'wan!" The other lieutenant's face screwed up. " 'Fore we kick de piss ouda yiz."

"G'wan, an' we'll letchiz go," promised Pedey. "G'wan! Shake!"

"If I jost pud id in?"

"Yea. Like I showed yuh."

"An' den yuh'll led me go?"

"Sure. G'wan. Id ain' gonna hoitcha. Ye'll see all de movies in de woil! An' vawderville too! G'wan before a car comes."

"Sure, an' all de angels."

"G'wan!" Their fists were drawn back.

Imploringly, his eyes darted to the west. The people on Avenue D seemed miles away. The saloon-door in the middle of the block was closed. East. No none! Not a soul! Beyond the tarry rocks of the river-shore, the wind had scattered the silver plain into rippling scales. He was trapped.

"G'wan!" Their faces were cruel, their bodies stiff with expectancy.

He turned toward the tracks. The long dark grooves between each pair looked as harmless as they had always looked. He had stepped over them hundreds of times without a thought. What was there about them now that made the others watch him so? Just drop it, they said, and they would let him go. Just drop it. He edged closer, stood tip-toe on the cobbles. The point of the sheet-zinc sword wavered before him, clicked on the stone as he fumbled, then finding the slot at last, rasped part way down the wide grinning lips like a tongue in an iron mouth. He stepped back. From open fingers, the blade plunged into darkness.

Power!

Like a paw ripping through all the stable fibres of the earth, power, gigantic, fetterless, thudded into day! And light, unleashed, terrific light bellowed out of iron lips. The street quaked and roared, and like a tortured thing, the sheet zinc sword, leapt writhing, fell back, consumed with radiance. Blinded, stunned by the brunt of brilliance, David staggered back. A moment later, he was spurting madly toward Avenue D.

When he looked behind him again, the light was gone, the roaring stilled. Pedey and his mates had fled. At the crossing, several people had stopped and were staring toward the river. Eyes shifted to David as he neared Avenue D, but since no one tried to block his way, he twisted around the corner and fled toward Ninth Street. His father's milk wagon was standing beside the curb. His father was home. He might guess that something had gone wrong. He'd better not go up. He slunk past his house, cut across the street and broke into a run. At the cheder [Jewish religious school] entrance he turned, scurried through the sheltering doorway, and came out into the sunlit and empty yard. The cheder door was closed. He had come far too early. Trembling in every limb, weak with fright, he looked about for a place to rest. The wide wooden doors that covered a cellar sloped gently into the sun. A new, brass padlock gleamed at their seam—too many of the rabbi's pupils had been banging them on their subterranean way into the cheder yard. He dragged himself over, dropped down on one of the wooden wings and shut his eyes. In the red sea of sun-lit eyelids his spirit sickeningly rolled and dipped. Though the planks were warm and the sun was warm, his teeth chattered and he shivered as if an icy gale were blowing. With a groan of anguish, he turned on his side hardly feeling the warm padlock under his cheek. Deep, shaking sobs caught on the snag of his throat. The hot tears crowded through his sealed eyelids, trickled unheeded across his cheek and nostril. He wept silently.

How long he lay there he did not know. But little by little the anguish lifted, his blood thawed, the sobbing calmed. Empty and nerveless, he opened his eyes; the rough-walled familiar houses, the leaning fences, the motley washing, washpoles, sunlight, the cramped and cluttered patch of blue above him were good. A mottled, yellow cat crept carefully out upon a fire-escape, leapt down behind a fence. Realities warm and palpable. From open windows, the sound of voices, rattling of pots, rush of water in a sink, laughter shearing away loud snatches of familiar speech. It was good. In the veering of the light wind, the odors of cooking, strong and savory, hung and drifted. From somewhere up above a steady chop-chopping began. Meat or fish or perhaps the bitter herbs of the Passover. The limp, vacant body expanded, filled with certainties.

Chop. Chop. The sound was secure. His thoughts took the rhythm of the sound. Something within him chanted. Words flowed out of him of their own accord. Chop. Chop. Showed him, showed. In the river, showed him, showed. Chop. Chop. Showed him, showed. If He wants. Showed him, showed.

—In the dark, chop, chop. In the river, showed him, showed. In the dark, in the river was there. Came out if He wanted, was there. Stayed in if He wanted, was there. Came out if He wanted, stayed in if He wanted, came out if He wanted, was there . . .

—Could break it in his hands if He wanted. Could hold it in His hands if He wanted. Could break it, could hold it, could break it, could hold it, could break it, could hold it, was there.

—In the dark, in the hallways, was there. In the dark, in the cellars was there. Where cellars is locked, where cellars is coal, where cellars is coal, is

—Coal!

—Coal!

He sat bolt upright.

"Rabbi!" his startled cry rang out over the yard. "Rabbi! Is coal under! White in cellars!" He sprang to his feet in exaltation, stared about him wildly. On all the multi-colored walls that hemmed him in, one single vision was written. "Is coal under! White!" Dazedly, he lurched toward the door. "Rabbi!" He rattled it; it held. "Rabbi!" He had to get in. He had to. He raced around the corner of the cheder. The window! He clawed at it. Loose, unbolted, it squealed up easily. There was no hesitation. There could be none. An enormous hand was shoving him forward. He leapt up, abdomen landing on the sill, teetered half in, half out, sprawled into the cheder, hands forward.

That closet! Where all of them were! He ran to it. It was just out of reach. He dragged the rabbi's chair over, stood up, flung open the door. The blue one! The blue one! Feverishly he pried among them—found it. He leapt down, already turning the pages. Page sixty-eight it was—twenty-six—forty—seventy-two—sixty-nine—sixty-eight! On top! With all your might! He wriggled over the bench.

"Beshnas mos hamelech Uziyahu vawere es adonoi yoshav al kesai rum venesaw, vshulav malaiim es hahahol. Serafim omidim memal lo shash kanowfayim, sash kanowfayim lawehhad, beshtayim yahase fanav uvishtayim yahase raglov uvishtayim yaofaif."

All his senses dissolved into the sound. The lines, unknown, dimly surmised, thundered in his heart with limitless meaning, rolled out and flooded the last shores of his being. Unmoored in space, he saw one walking on impalpable pavements that rose with the rising trees. Or were they trees or telegraph-poles, each crossed and leafy, none could say, but forms stood there with footholds in unmitigated light. And their faces shone because the light in their midst was luminous laughter. He read on.

The book returned. The table hardened . . . Behind him the sound of a key probing a keyhole screeked across infinite space. The lock snapped open— suddenly near at hand. Realization struck like an icy gust. With a start of dismay, he spun around over the bench, threw himself at the window. Too late! The rabbi, long black coat and derby, stepped into the light of the open door. He drew back with a groan of fright, but recognizing who it was, his eyes opened wrathfully and he came forward, head cocked sideways.

"How did you get in?" he demanded fiercely, "Ha?" The open window caught his eye. He stared at it, disbelief wrangling with ire. "You crawled in?"

"The book!" David stammered. "The book! I wanted it."

"You broke into my cheder!" The rabbi seemed not to have heard a single syllable. "You opened the window? You climbed in? You dared do this?"

"No! No!"

"Hush!" He paid no heed to his outcry. "I understand." And before David could budge, the rabbi's heavy hands had fallen on his neck and he was being dragged toward the cat-o-nine on the floor. "Fearful bastard!" he roared. "You crawled in to steal my pointers!"

"I didn't! I didn't touch them!"

"You it was took them before!" the rabbi drowned him out. "Sly one! You! Different I thought you were! Hi! Will you scoop!" He reached down for the scourge.

"I didn't! I came for the book! The blue book with the coal in it! The man and the coal!"

His iron grip still unrelenting, the rabbi lowered the cat-o-nine. "The man! The coal! You try to gull *me!*" But uncertainty had crept into his voice. "Stop your screeching!" And haling David after him, he yanked out the drawer of the reading table in which he kept his pointers. One glance was enough. Savagely, he thrust it back. "What man? And what coal?"

"Here in the book! The man the angel touched—Mendel read it! Isaiah!" The name suddenly returned to him. "Isaiah!"

The rabbi glared at the book as if he meant to burn it with his eyes, then his gaze rose slowly to David's face. In the silence, his clogged, apoplectic breathing was as loud as snoring. "Tell me, did you climb in only to read this book." His fingers uncurled from David's shoulder.

"Y-es! About th-that Isaiah."

"But what do you want of it?" His open palms barely sustained the weight of his question. "Can you read a word of chumish?"

"No, but I remembered, and I—I wanted to read it."

"Why?" From under his derby, pushed back by aimless fingers, his black skull-cap peeped out. "Are you mad or what? Couldn't you wait until I came? I would have let you read a belly-full."

"I didn't know when you—you were coming."

"But why did you want to read it? And why with such black haste?"

"Because I went and I saw a coal like—like Isaiah."

"What kind of a coal? Where?"

"Where the car-tracks run I saw it. On Tenth Street."

"Car tracks? You saw a coal?" He shut his eyes like one completely befuddled.

"Yes. It gave a big light in the middle, between the crack!"

"A what—! A—! Between a crack? You saw a light between a crack? A black year befall you!" Suddenly he stopped. His brow darkened. His beard rose. His head rolled back. "Chah! Chah! Chah! Chah!" Splitting salvoes of laughter suddenly burst from the cavern behind the whiskers. "Chah! Chah! Chah! Oy! Chah! Chah! Chah! This must be told." A hasty hand plugged back his slipping derby. "He saw a light! Oy! Chah! Chah! In the crack! Oy! Chah! Chah! Chah! I'll split like a herring! Yesterday, he heard a bed in the thunder! Today he sees a vision in a crack. Oy! Chah! Chah! Chah!" Minutes seemed to pass before he sobered. "Fool!" he gasped at length. "Go beat your head on a wall! God's light is not between car-tracks."

Ashamed, yet immensely relieved, David stood mute, eyes staring at the floor. The rabbi didn't know as he knew what the light was, what it meant, what it had done to him. But he would reveal no more. It was enough that the light had saved him from being whipped.

162

At the same time Roth was re-creating the life of a sensitive Jewish boy in New York, James T. Farrell was re-creating the harsh life of an Irish Catholic boy in Chicago (1932).

Young Lonigan

James T. Farrell

That night when Studs was ready to go out, he walked into the parlor. The old man and the old lady were sitting there, and the old boy was in his slippers sucking on a stogy; and the two of them were enjoying a conversation about the latest rape case in the newspapers in which the rapist was named Gogarty. Studs noticed that when he entered they shut up. He wondered what the hell did they think he was. Did they think he was born yesterday, and still believed in Santa Claus, the Easter Rabbit and storks? He wanted to tell them so, tell them in words that would show how much of a pain they gave him when they treated him as if he was only a baby. But the words wouldn't come; they almost never came to him when he wanted them to. He stood swallowing his resentment.

The old man said:

"You know, Bill, a fellow ought to come home some time. Now when I was your age, when I was your age, I know I liked to get out with the fellows, and that's why I can understand how you feel about bein' a regular guy, and bein' with the bunch, and I don't want you to think I'm always pickin' on you, or preachin' to you, or tryin' to make you into a mollycoddle, because I ain't. I know a kid wants a little liberty, because I was your age once . . . BUT . . ."

Studs got Goddamn sore. He knew what was coming. The old man always worked the same damn gag.

"You see, Bill, you're stayin' out pretty late, and you know, well, it's as your mother says, the neighbors will be thinkin' things, wonderin' if we, the landlords here, set a good example for our children, and live decently, an' if we are takin' the right sort of care of our children. I'm the owner of this here building, you see, and I got to have a family that sets the right kind of an example. Now what do you think they'll think if they see you comin' in so late every evenin', comin' in night after night after most respectable people have gone to bed?"

"But what is it their business?" asked Studs.

"And, William, you know you have to look out for your health. Now what will you do if you go on getting little sleep like you do? You know you should get to bed early. Why, this very day in the newspapers, there was an article saying that sleep gotten before twelve o'clock was better and healthier sleep than sleep gotten after midnight. You're wearing yourself out, and you're wearin' out me, your mother, because I worry over you, because I can't let my baby get tuberculosis," the mother said.

"I'm all right; I'm healthy," Studs said.

"Well, I think, Bill, I think a fellow could get enough play all day and until ten o'clock at night. You always want to remember that there'll be another day," the old man said oracularly.

Studs said that all kids stayed out, sitting on someone's porch, or in the grass in front of someone's house, talking, and there wasn't anything wrong with it, because it was so nice in the evening. And the other kids' fathers didn't care. Mr. O'Brien never kicked about Johnny being out, and Johnny O'Brien was younger than he was.

"If Johnny O'Brien jumps in the river, do you have to?"

That was the way his old man always was!

Studs just stood there. The old man told him to save something for another day. Studs sulked, and told himself there wasn't any use arguing with his old man and old lady. They just didn't understand.

The old man brought out a Lefty Locke baseball book, which he had bought for Studs and forgotten to give him. He said it would be a good thing if Studs stayed in and read it. Studs ought to do more reading anyway, because reading always improved a person's mind. Studs sat down, pouted, and read the book for about ten minutes. But Lefty Locke wasn't anything at all like Rube Waddell; it was a goofy book. He fidgeted. Then he said hesitantly that he'd like to take a little walk, and the old man, disappointed, said all right.

When Studs met the guys, he told them that he'd won a scrap with the old man. That evening they played tin-tin with the girls, and Studs kissed Lucy. It made him forget that his old man and his old lady and home weren't what sisters and priests made them out to be at school and at Mass on Sundays. . . .

STUDS LOVES LUCY . . . LUCY IS CRAZY ABOUT STUDS. . . . . I LIKE TO KISS LUCY—STUDS . . . STUDS KISSED LUCY A MILLION TIMES . . .

Studs saw chalked writings like these all over Indiana Avenue, on sidewalks, fences, buildings. It was two mornings after he and Lucy had been in the park. On the previous day, he had cleaned out the basement for his old man, and he had been too tired at night to wash up and come around. When he read the scrawlings all over, his face got red as a tomato, and he got so sore he cursed everybody and everything. He promised himself that a lot of guys were going to get smacked. He was so sore that he didn't take the trouble to examine the childish writings, a scrawl quite like that of his sister Loretta and her girl-chum, June Reilley.

Danny O'Neill came along, and stopped at Studs' side. He read the words aloud, and laughed. Studs socked him. Danny, in a temper, stuck his tongue out at Studs, called him a bully, and said, mimicking:

"I'm gonna tell Lucy!"

Studs cracked Danny in the jaw with all his might, and the punk, holding his mush in his hands, bawled.

Most of the guys saw Danny's swollen jaw, so they didn't try to kid Studs. The older guys sat on the grass, talking, blaming the punks, planning how they would swoop down on them and get even by taking their pants off and hanging them on trees, making them eat dirt, giving them a dose of it that they wouldn't forget until kingdom come. But the punks had all smelled trouble, and they were gone. The bunch sat around and talked about revenges. Studs didn't say much; he didn't even look anybody in the eye. Suddenly, he got up and left, and the guys said that when Studs walked away from his friends like that, without saying a word, he was pretty Goddamn sore, and when he was pretty Goddamn sore, he wasn't the kind of a guy you'd want to meet in a dark alley. He walked for blocks, not recognizing where he was going, feeling disgraced, feeling that everybody was against him, blaming everybody, blaming that little runt, Danny O'Neill. He felt that he was a goddamn clown. He blamed himself for getting soft and goofy about a skirt. He planned how he would get even, and kept telling himself that no matter what happened, it couldn't really affect him, because STUDS LONIGAN was an iron man, and when anybody laughed at the iron man, well, the iron man would knock the laugh off the face of Mr. Anybody with the sweetest paste in the mush that Mr. Anybody ever got. He vowed this, and felt his iron muscle for assurance. But he didn't really feel like an iron man. He felt like a clown that the world was laughing at. He walked, getting sorer and sorer and filling his mind with the determination to get back at . . . Indiana Avenue, the whole damn street. As far as he was concerned, it could go plumb to hell. He was through hanging around with the Indiana Avenue mopes, and as for O'Neill, well, Studs Lonigan hadn't even begun to pay that little droopy-drawers back yet.

When Studs got home, Martin, speaking like he had been coached, said:

"How's Lucy?"

"I seen Lucy today; she looked nice, like she was looking for someone . . . and she had paint on her lips," Fritzie said.

Frances asked him if he was going over to see Lucy after supper. If he was, she'd walk over with him . . . and she said if he was he had better wash himself clean and shine his shoes.

The old man sang monotonously:

Goodbye, boys . . .
For I . . . get . . . married . . . tomorrow . . .

Mrs. Lonigan seriously warned him that he was still a little young and he would have plenty of time later on for girls, and girls would make a fool of him, and he should not be thinking of them, but he should be praying and meditating to see if he had a vocation or not.

Studs walked out of the room, saying that they could all go to hell.

He heard them laughing after him. Even the walls and the furniture seemed to laugh, to jibe and jeer. He went out for a walk without eating, and he met Helen Borax on Fifty-eighth Street. She asked him how Lucy's gentleman was, and said that she heard he was a specialist in osculation; she said she would never have believed it, but she couldn't doubt all the proof she had seen around the neighborhood in the last few days. And she would never be able to understand how Lucy mistook him for Francis X. Bushman; but then everyone had his or her right to like people. She said she knew Lucy needed a sort of roughneck to carry her books when she went to high school, because Lucy was going to St. Elizabeth's, and it was in a nigger neighborhood, and he could protect her, and walk home with her through the nigger neighborhood. Helen spoke so swiftly and cattishly that Studs couldn't get in a word edgewise. She didn't stop for over five minutes, and then she only paused for breath. After she had talked a blue streak, they stood making faces at each other.

He said, sore as a boil:

"Kiss my . . ."

She blushed, gulped, swallowed, looked shocked and horror-stricken. He turned his back on her, and walked away.

"Lucy's gentleman!" Helen called after him.

He turned and thumbed his nose.

163

The Native American poet Simon Ortiz describes the role of the Acoma and English languages in his formation as an artist (1987).

Growing Up Native American
The Language We Know

Simon Ortiz

I don't remember a world without language. From the time of my earliest child-hood, there was language. Always language, and imagination, speculation, utters of sound. Words, beginnings of words. What would I be without language? My existence has been determined by language, not only the spoken but the unspoken, the language of speech and the language of motion. I can't remember a world without memory. Memory, immediate and far away in the past, something in the sinew, blood, ageless cell. Although I don't recall the exact moment I spoke or tried to speak, I know the feeling of something tugging at the core of the mind, something unutterable uttered into existence. It is language that brings us into being in order to know life.

My childhood was the oral tradition of the Acoma Pueblo people—Aaquumeh hano—which included my immediate family of three older sisters, two younger sisters, two younger brothers, and my mother and father. My world was our world of the Aaquumeh in McCartys, one of the two villages descended from the ageless mother pueblo of Acoma. My world was our Eagle clan-people among other clans. I grew up in Deetziyamah, which is the Aaquumeh name for McCartys, which is posted at the exit off the present interstate highway in western New Mexico. I grew up within a people who farmed small garden plots and fields, who were mostly poor and not well schooled in the American sys-tem's education. The language I spoke was that of a struggling people who held ferociously to a heritage, culture, language, and land despite the odds posed them by the forces surrounding them since 1540 A.D., the advent of Euro-American colonization. When I began school in 1948 at the BIA (Bureau of Indian Affairs) day school in our village, I was armed with the basic ABC's and the phrases "Good morning, Miss Oleman" and "May I please be excused to go to the bathroom," but it was an older language that was my fundamental strength.

In my childhood, the language we all spoke was Acoma, and it was a struggle to maintain it against the outright threats of corporal punishment, ostracism, and the invocation that it would impede our progress towards Americanization. Children in school were punished and looked upon with disdain if they did not speak and learn English quickly and smoothly, and so I learned it. It has occurred to me that I learned English simply because I was forced to, as so many other Indian children were. But I know, also, there was another reason, and this was that I loved language, the sound, meaning, and magic of language. Language opened up vistas of the world around me, and it allowed me to discover knowledge that would not be possible for me to know without the use of language. Later, when I began to experiment with and explore language in poetry and fiction, I allowed that a portion of that impetus was because I had come to know English through forceful acculturation. Nevertheless, the underlying force was the beauty and poetic power of language in its many forms that instilled in me the desire to become a user of language as a writer, singer, and storyteller. Significantly, it was the Acoma language, which I don't use enough of today, that inspired me to become a writer. The concepts, values, and philosophy contained in my original language and the struggle it has faced have determined my life and vision as a writer.

In Deetziyamah, I discovered the world of the Acoma land and people firsthand through my parents, sisters and brothers, and my own perceptions, voiced through all that encompasses the oral tradition, which is ageless for any culture. It is a small village, even smaller years ago, and like other Indian communities it is wealthy with its knowledge of daily event, history, and social system, all that make up a people who have a many-dimensioned heritage. Our family lived in a two-room home (built by my grandfather some years after he and my grandmother moved with their daughters from Old Acoma), which my father added rooms to later. I remember my father's work at enlarging our home for our growing family. He was a skilled stoneworker, like many other men of an older Pueblo generation who worked with sandstone and mud mortar to build their homes and pueblos. It takes time, persistence, patience, and the belief that the walls that come to stand will do so for a long, long time, perhaps even forever. I like to think that by helping to mix mud and carry stone for my father and other elders I managed to bring that influence into my consciousness as a writer.

Both my mother and my father were good storytellers and singers (as my mother is to this day—my father died in 1978), and for their generation, which was born soon after the turn of the century, they were relatively educated in the American system. Catholic missionaries had taken both of them as children to a parochial boarding school far from Acoma, and they imparted their discipline for study and quest for education to us children when we started school. But it was their indigenous sense of gaining knowledge that was most meaningful to me. Acquiring knowledge about life was above all the most important item; it was a value that one had to have in order to be fulfilled personally and on behalf of his community. And this they insisted upon imparting through the oral tradition as they told their children about our native history and our community and culture and our "stories." These stories were common knowledge of act, event, and behavior in a close-knit pueblo. It was knowledge about how one was to make a living through work that benefited his family and everyone else.

Because we were a subsistence farming people, or at least tried to be, I learned to plant, hoe weeds, irrigate and cultivate corn, chili, pumpkins, beans. Through counsel and advice I came to know that the rain which provided water was a blessing, gift, and symbol and that it was the land which provided for our lives. It was the stories and songs which provided the knowledge that I was woven into the intricate web that was my Acoma life. In our garden and our cornfields I learned about the seasons, growth cycles of cultivated plants, what one had to think and feel about the land; and at home I became aware of how we must care for each other: all of this was encompassed in an intricate relationship which had to be maintained in order that life continue. After supper on many occasions my father would bring out his drum and sing as we, the children, danced to themes about the rain, hunting, land, and people. It was all that is contained within the language of oral tradition that made me explicitly aware of a yet unarticulated urge to write, to tell what I had learned and was learning and what it all meant to me.

My grandfather was old already when I came to know him. I was only one of his many grandchildren, but I would go with him to get wood for our households, to the garden to chop weeds, and to his sheep camp to help care for his sheep. I don't remember his exact words, but I know they were about how we must sacredly concern ourselves with the people and the holy earth. I know his words were about how we must regard ourselves and others with compassion and love; I know that his knowledge was vast, as a medicine man and an elder of his kiva, and I listened as a boy should. My grandfather represented for me a link to the past that is important for me to hold in my memory because it is not only memory but knowledge that substantiates my present existence. He and the grandmothers and grandfathers before him thought about us as they lived, confirmed in their belief of a continuing life, and they brought our present beings into existence by the beliefs they held. The consciousness of that belief is what informs my present concerns with language, poetry, and fiction.

164

Piri Thomas's memoir recounts the dangers and enticements of Spanish Harlem and the life of a sensitive Puerto Rican adolescent struggling with issues of identity and masculinity (1969).

Down These Mean Streets

Piri Thomas

I got to my stoop, and made it into the dark gloomy hallway. I cut up the stairs and pushed the door on Apartment 3 and slammed it shut behind me with a blast.

"Hey, what's the matter with you?" my mother called from the kitchen. She came to see for herself. "*Qué muchacho!* You would think you never learned how to shut a door. Listen, go outside and come in again like people."

"Aw, Moms, everything bothers you."

"You heard me."

"Okay, okay, Moms."

I walked out the door, stood outside for a moment, and then opened the door. I looked at fat little Moms standing there with a very serious look on her face. I turned and very deliberately, an inch at a time, slowly closed the door, my face all screwed up with gentle effort and my fingers curled around the doorknob. I took a long few minutes to get the door turned around and sweet Momma was shaking all over with laughter. "What a funny *morenito*," she said.

I joined her and we just laughed and laughed. I kissed her and went into the back room feeling her full-of-love words floating after me.

"Hey, Moms," I called out from the back room. "How come you're so pretty, eh? How come, huh?"

"*Ai, qué negrito.*"

I felt happy. I could hear her softly laughing to herself.

"*Qué bueno* to have a Moms like my Moms . . . umm, *qué eso?* What's smelling so great?"

I walked out in my shorts and came into the kitchen, my face screwed up in a funny face, my nose twitching like a rabbit sniffing. I made like I was floating in the air toward the pots. Ah, I lifted the cover and rolled my eyeballs. I looked out of the corner of my eyes to dig Momma. She was holding her sides, my fat little Momma, tears rolling out of her eyes. *Caramba*, it was great to see Momma happy. I'd go through the rest of my life making like funnies if I was sure Momma would be happy. I stuck my finger in that sweet-smelling pot.

"*Vete! Vete!* Get away from that food with your dirty hands. *Dios mio*, you smell bad, all full of sweat and—"

"Gimme a kiss, Moms; come on, *vente*—a big *jalumbo* kiss."

"Get away, you smell bad, all full of sweat. Go, get in that bathtub and let the water and soap make you soft so the dirt has a chance to come off."

"Aw, Moms, you love me any way I am, clean or dirty, white or black, pretty or ugly."

"*Sí*, you're right, and, my son, I have to love you because only your mother could love you, *un negrito* and ugly. And to make it badder, you're dirty and smelly from your sweat!"

"Aw, look at her." I made a look of disbelief. "Trying to make like I'm not your big love. Ain't I your firstborn, the oldest, the biggest, the strongest?"

"*Sí, sí*," Momma came back at me, "and the baddest. *Vete*, soak for a long time or no dinner."

The water in the bathtub was hot and I looked at my fourteen-year-old frame, naked. I was pretty skinny. I should get fatter. Maybe weightlifting would help, like that ad in the funny book about a 97-pound weakling before and after. Man, the water felt good. I ducked under and held my breath as long as I could. It seemed like hours. I was already bursting my lungs when somebody grabbed my hair and pulled me up.

"Hey, whatta ya think you're doing?" I shouted. I could make out my brother James's face through the water in my eyes.

"Whatta ya think, mopey? I thought you were drowning."

I threw some water at him. "Ah, ha," he said. "So you wanna play, eh?" He ducked and turned on the cold water in the sink, filling the glass we used for gargling.

"Cool, cool, James, I was only kidding. Hold that water, man; I can catch a cold. Be nice, James." He held the freezing water over my head. "Come on, man," I added. "Don't play around. Hey, Moms, tell James to stop farting around."

A little drop of cold water hit my back. I crawled under the water and the rest of the cold water came down. Brrr, I almost left the bathtub in one jump.

"James, I'm gonna punch you in the mouth."

"Sez who?"

"Sez me, you little runt." James filled the glass again. "Whatta ya gonna do?" he said. I couldn't help laughing.

"Nothing, brother dear, I ain't gonna do nothing."

"You cop out?"

"Yeah, I cop out."

"You cop a plea?"

"Yeah, man, I cop a plea. Now will you get the fuck outta here?"

"Moms, Piri's cursing again."

"Why, you stoolpigeon," I said hurt-like, "you Puerto Rican squealer."

"Piri," said Momma from the kitchen, "this is a Christian home. I don't want no bad things said inside a house that belongs to God."

"Moms, I didn't say nothing to James."

"You did so say a curse," she said.

"You heard wrong. I said *buck*, get the *buck* outta here."

"You didn't," James piped in. "I heard you say 'Will you get the *fuck* outta here.' "

"Hey, Moms," I yelled out, "did you hear James, huh? Did you hear him? Go on, stoolpigeon," I said to James. "Whatta ya got to say now, huh? Look in the mirror! Hey Moms," I shouted. "Ain't you gonna holler at him too?"

"What for?"

"What *for*, Moms? Didn't you hear him?"

"I didn't hear nothing."

"Moms, you're deaf. James said, 'Will you get the fuck outta here.' "

"Piri, if you going to keep cursing, when your father comes home you're going to get a strap across your skinny behind."

"My God, there ain't no justice!"

I started to climb out of the bathtub to belt my brother. He didn't back away an inch. He held that damn cold glass of water, and we just looked at each other and burst out laughing.

"Okay, man, we call it a draw," I said, and I eased back into the tub. James started to wash his face and hands. "Say, James," I said half-minded.

"Yeah," came a soap-flubbed answer.

"Did you ever notice how when you're in the bathtub and you lay a fart, little bubbles come up and, *blueeee*, they burst and, man, what a stink? Look, look, there's one, two, three, four, five of them coming up."

"Mowoo, whew, Piri, you're rotten, what a stinking smell, let me outta here."

I said nothing. I just looked at his retreat and smiled an I-got-even-anyhow smile. Then I heard all the kids running to meet Poppa at the door. I wanted to run to meet him too, but I couldn't somehow, and it wasn't because I was in the tub. Even when I did run to meet him, I was like a stranger, outta place, like I wasn't supposed to share in the "Poppy, Poppy" routine.

"Piri, have you finished yet?" Momma called. "Your *padre's* home and he has to take a bath."

Pops, I wondered, how come me and you is always on the outs? Is it something we don't know nothing about? I wonder if it's something I done, or something I am. Why do I feel so left outta things with you — like Moms is both of you to me, like if you and me was just an accident around here? I dig when you holler at the other kids for doing something wrong. How come it sounds so different when you holler at me? Why does it sound harder and meaner? Maybe I'm wrong, Pops. I know we all get the same food and clothes, anything and everything — except there's this feeling between you and me. Like it's not the same for me. How come when we all play with you, I can't really enjoy it like the rest? How come when we all get hit for doing something wrong, I feel it the hardest? Maybe 'cause I'm the biggest, huh? Or maybe it's 'cause I'm the darkest in this family. Pops, you ain't like Herby's father, are you? I mean, you love us all the same, right?

My mind kept up the reverie; my fingers absent-mindedly pulling my floating pee-pee into a long string, like a toy balloon when it's empty, and let it snap back.

Pops, you're the best and greatest Pops in the whole world. It's just that I don't dig why I feel this way. Like I can't get next to you. Jesus, wouldn't it be a bitch if Poppa really didn't love me, I thought. But I doubted it. I mean, you didn't have to dig each other to love each other. Maybe that was it. We didn't dig each other so it made me think he didn't love me. But how come he called Miriam "honey" and the rest of those sweet names and me hardly ever? *Miriam gets treated like a princess. I'd like to punch her in her straight nose. I don't care if Pops don't love me a lot. It just don't mean a thing . . .*

The door opened and Poppa walked in. I looked at him and he smiled at me and swooped down and scooped a handful of water into my face.

Jesus, Pops, you really love me like all the rest, eh? Don't you? Poppa pulled the chain as he took a long, long leak.

"Look, Pops, I can stay under water a long, long time. Watch," I said. And under I went. I held my breath as long as I could. I felt my lungs bursting, like they were on fire, but I hadda show Poppa. I couldn't hold out much longer, but I hadda show Poppa. The lights in my head started to spin and I couldn't stay under any more. I exploded up out of the water, sputtering but happy.

"You see me, Pops?" I gasped, screwing the water out of my eyes. "Did you see me, Pops? I musta stayed under five minutes." I looked up happily, but there was no one there. The bathroom was empty. I felt like I lost something, something more, and I couldn't tell the salty tears from the bath water.

I dried myself off, put on my clean clothes, and walked out into the kitchen. Poppa was standing by the icebox. I didn't look at him as I walked toward the back room. If I wasn't there for him, he wasn't there for me.

"Hey, son," he called. I stopped and my back stayed toward him. "I heard you when you exploded out of that water, you sure got a lot of lung power. I bet you could be a great swimmer."

"You mean it, Pops?" I lit up like a bomb. Poppa *had* noticed my show. "You really think so, huh, Pops? I mean I got good lungs. I'm a little skinny but I'm going to lift weights."

Pops was turning away, losing interest, but who cared? I mean, he had a right to be tired; he needed some rest after working for a wife and kids. I couldn't expect him to be mushy over me all the time. Sure, it was all right for the other kids; they were small and they needed more kisses and stuff. But I was the oldest, the firstborn, and besides, I was *hombre*.

165

Maya Angelou writes movingly of her experiences as a California girl shipped back to Arkansas to live with her father's family after her parents separated. In this passage from I Know Why the Caged Bird Sings *(1969), Angelou recounts how the habits and manners carefully instilled by her grandmother (Momma) were flouted by the poor white children in the neighborhood, whose intention was to humiliate the black neighbor. It was a lesson in racial manners and self-restraint.*

I Know Why the Caged Bird Sings

Maya Angelou

"Thou shall not be dirty" and "Thou shall not be impudent" were the two commandments of Grandmother Henderson upon which hung our total salvation.

Each night in the bitterest winter we were forced to wash faces, arms, necks, legs and feet before going to bed. She used to add, with a smirk that unprofane people can't control when venturing into profanity, "and wash as far as possible, then wash possible."

We would go to the well and wash in the ice-cold, clear water, grease our legs with the equally cold stiff Vaseline, then tiptoe into the house. We wiped the dust from our toes and settled down for schoolwork, cornbread, clabbered milk, prayers and bed, always in that order. Momma was famous for pulling the quilts off after we had fallen asleep to examine our feet. If they weren't clean enough for her, she took the switch (she kept one behind the bedroom door for emergencies) and woke up the offender with a few aptly placed burning reminders.

The area around the well at night was dark and slick, and boys told about how snakes love water, so that anyone who had to draw water at night and then stand there alone and wash knew that moccasins and rattlers, puff adders and boa constrictors were winding their way to the well and would arrive just as the person washing got soap in her eyes. But Momma convinced us that not only was cleanliness next to Godliness, dirtiness was the inventor of misery.

The impudent child was detested by God and a shame to its parents and could bring destruction to its house and line. All adults had to be addressed as Mister, Missus, Miss, Auntie, Cousin, Unk, Uncle, Buhbah, Sister, Brother and a thousand other appellations indicating familial relationship and the lowliness of the addressor.

Everyone I knew respected these customary laws, except for the powhitetrash children.

Some families of powhitetrash lived on Momma's farm land behind the school. Sometimes a gaggle of them came to the Store, filling the whole room, chasing out the air and even changing the well-known scents. The children crawled over the shelves and into the potato and onion bins, twanging all the time in their sharp voices like cigar-box guitars. They took liberties in my Store that I would never dare. Since Momma told us that the less you say to whitefolks (or even powhitetrash) the better, Bailey and I would stand, solemn, quiet, in the displaced air. But if one of the playful apparitions got close to us, I pinched it. Partly out of angry frustration and partly because I didn't believe in its flesh reality.

They called my uncle by his first name and ordered him around the Store. He, to my crying shame, obeyed them in his limping dip-straight-dip fashion.

My grandmother, too, followed their orders, except that she didn't seem to be servile because she anticipated their needs.

"Here's sugar, Miz Potter, and here's baking powder. You didn't buy soda last month, you'll probably be needing some."

Momma always directed her statements to the adults, but sometimes, Oh painful sometimes, the grimy, snotty-nosed girls would answer her.

"Naw, Annie . . ."—to Momma? Who owned the land they lived on? Who forgot more than they would ever learn? If there was any justice in the world, God should strike them dumb at once!—"Just give us some extry sody crackers, and some more mackerel."

At least they never looked in her face, or I never caught them doing so. Nobody with a smidgen of training, not even the worst roustabout, would look right in a grown person's face. It meant the person was trying to take the words out before they were formed. The dirty little children didn't do that, but they threw their orders around the Store like lashes from a cat-o'-nine-tails.

When I was around ten years old, those scruffy children caused me the most painful and confusing experience I had ever had with my grandmother.

One summer morning, after I had swept the dirt yard of leaves, spearmint-gum wrappers and Vienna-sausage labels, I raked the yellow-red dirt, and made half-moons carefully, so that the design stood out clearly and mask-like. I put the rake behind the Store and came through the back of the house to find Grandmother on the front porch in her big, wide white apron. The apron was so stiff by virtue of the starch that it could have stood alone. Momma was admiring the yard, so I joined her. It truly looked like a flat redhead that had been raked with a big-toothed comb. Momma didn't say anything but I knew she liked it. She looked over toward the school principal's house and to the right at Mr. McElroy's. She was hoping one of those community pillars would see the design before the day's business wiped it out. Then she looked upward to the school. My head had swung with hers, so at just about the same time we saw a troop of the powhitetrash kids marching over the hill and down by the side of the school.

I looked to Momma for direction. She did an excellent job of sagging from her waist down, but from the waist up she seemed to be pulling for the top of the oak tree across the road. Then she began to moan a hymn. Maybe not to moan, but the tune was so slow and the meter so strange that she could have been moaning. She didn't look at me again. When the children reached halfway down the hill, halfway to the Store, she said without turning, "Sister, go on inside."

I wanted to beg her, "Momma, don't wait for them. Come on inside with me. If they come in the Store, you go to the bedroom and let me wait on them. They only frighten me if you're around. Alone I know how to handle them." But of course I couldn't say anything, so I went in and stood behind the screen door.

Before the girls got to the porch I heard their laughter crackling and popping like pine logs in a cooking stove. I suppose my lifelong paranoia was born in those cold, molasses-slow minutes. They came finally to stand on the ground in front of Momma. At first they pretended seriousness. Then one of them wrapped her right arm in the crook of her left, pushed out her mouth and started to hum. I realized that she was aping my grandmother. Another said, "Naw, Helen, you ain't standing like her. This here's it." Then she lifted her chest, folded her arms and mocked that strange carriage that was Annie Henderson. Another laughed, "Naw, you can't do it. Your mouth ain't pooched out enough. It's like this."

I thought about the rifle behind the door, but I knew I'd never be able to hold it straight, and the .410, our sawed-off shotgun, which stayed loaded and was fired every New Year's night, was locked in the trunk and Uncle Willie had the key on his chain. Through the fly-specked screen-door, I could see that the arms of Momma's apron jiggled from the vibrations of her humming. But her knees seemed to have locked as if they would never bend again.

She sang on. No louder than before, but no softer either. No slower or faster.

The dirt of the girls' cotton dresses continued on their legs, feet, arms and faces to make them all of a piece. Their greasy uncolored hair hung down, uncombed, with a grim finality. I knelt to see them better, to remember them for all time. The tears that had slipped down my dress left unsurprising dark spots, and made the front yard blurry and even more unreal. The world had taken a deep breath and was having doubts about continuing to revolve.

The girls had tired of mocking Momma and turned to other means of agitation. One crossed her eyes, stuck her thumbs in both sides of her mouth and said, "Look here, Annie." Grandmother hummed on and the apron strings trembled. I wanted to throw a handful of black pepper in their faces, to throw lye on them, to scream that they were dirty, scummy peckerwoods, but I knew I was as clearly imprisoned behind the scene as the actors outside were confined to their roles. . . .

Momma never turned her head or unfolded her arms, but she stopped singing and said, "Bye, Miz Helen, 'bye, Miz Ruth, 'bye, Miz Eloise."

I burst. A firecracker July-the-Fourth burst. How could Momma call them Miz? The mean nasty things. Why couldn't she have come inside the sweet, cool store when we saw them breasting the hill? What did she prove? And then if they were dirty, mean and impudent, why did Momma have to call them Miz?

She stood another whole song through and then opened the screen door to look down on me crying in rage. She looked until I looked up. Her face was a brown moon that shone on me. She was beautiful. Something had happened out there, which I couldn't completely understand, but I could see that she was happy. Then she bent down and touched me as mothers of the church "lay hands on the sick and afflicted" and I quieted.

"Go wash your face, Sister." And she went behind the candy counter and hummed, "Glory, glory, hallelujah, when I lay my burden down."

I threw the well water on my face and used the weekday handkerchief to blow my nose. Whatever the contest had been out front, I knew Momma had won.

166

China Boy

Gus Lee

Gus Lee's novel China Boy *(1991) centers on San Francisco and its extraordinary mix of people in the second half of the twentieth century. For many new immigrants, older immigrants or outsiders like African Americans often served as guides to American life.*

A rail-thin nine-year-old named Toussaint LaRue looked on during these beatings and only hit me once. I therefore assumed that he occupied some lower social niche than mine. Like a snail's.

He took no pleasure in the China Boy rituals. He instead talked to me. I suspected that he had devised a new method of pain infliction.

"Toussaint," he said, offering his hand. "Ya'lls supposed ta shake it." He grinned when I put my hand out with the same enthusiasm with which I would pet Mr. Carter's bulldog. Toussaint, like Evil, had a big gap between his front teeth.

Toussaint would become my guide to American boyhood.

My primary bond to him was for the things he did not do. He did not pound or trap me. He never cut me down. Or laughed with knives in his eyes. Then he opened his heart by explaining things to me, giving me his learning, and taking me into his home.

"China. Don be cryin no mo'. Don work on dis here block, no sir, Cap'n! Give 'er up. When ya'll cry, hol' it inside yo'self. Shif' yo' feet an air-out, go park-side. Preten ya'll gone fishin. Don run, now. Ain't cool."

"Fish in park?" I asked.

"Cheez! Ya'll don colly nothin! Ferget da fish, China. Dry yo' tears."

He told me about the theory of fights. That kids did it because it was how you became a man later on.

"Momma tole me," he said, "in ole days, no Negro man kin hit or fight. We belongs to da whites, like hosses.

"Man fight 'notha man, be damagin white man goods. So he get whipped. An I mean *whipped*." He shook his head and rubbed the top of it, easing the pain of the thought.

"Now, ain't no mo' dat," he said, smiling. "We kin fights, like men." He was speaking very seriously. Fighting was a measure of citizenship. Of civilization. I didn't think so.

"China, stan up."

"Why?" I whined.

"Putchur fists up. Make a fist! Right. Bof han's.

"Dis one—," he said, holding my left. "It fo' guardin yo' face. Dis here one—dat's fo' poundin da fool who call ya out. Here come a punch, and ya'll block it. China—you listenin ta me?"

"No fight, no reason!" I said hotly.

"No reason!?" he yelled. "You can fight wif no *reason*? Boy! Whatchu *talkin* about?"

Uh-oh, I thought. Toussaint's hands were on his hips.

"Evera kid on dis here block like ta knock you upside da head and make you *bleed* and ya'll got no *reason*? China. Ain't no dude in da Handle got mo' cause fo' fightin *evera* day den *you*!"

"Too many boy fight," I said, drawing back from his heat.

"Uh-*uh*! No sir, Cap'n! Big-time nossir! Lissen. Some kids, dey fight *hard*. But ain't *never* gonna be no gangin up on one kid. *Dat* ain't cool." He shook his head. "Kid stan on his feet. No one else feet. Ain't *nobody* gonna stan inaway a dat. An youse best colly dat."

"Hittin' long," I tried.

"Say what?" he said.

"Long. Not light!"

"Wrong? Ya'll sayin fightin's *wrong*?"

"Light," I said.

"Howzat?"

"Bad yuing chi," I explained.

"Say *what*?"

"Bad, uh, karma!" I said, finding the East Indian word often used by my sisters.

"Well, China, ya'll thinks awful funny. Don have nothin ta do wif no *caramels*. No matta Big Willie take yo' candies. Ain't *candies*. It not bein *chicken*. Not bein yella. Ya'll don havta like it. Sakes, China, no one like ta Fist City. Well, maybe Big Willie, he like it. But like it or don like it, no matter none. Ya'll jus *do* it."

He invited me to play in his house. Many of the games involved capturing cockroaches. "Ya'll ready?" he would ask, and I would nod, nervously. Toos would kick the wall next to the sink, and roaches would slither out of the dust and the cracked plaster. Toos would use his plastic cup, smacking it quickly onto the floor, smiling as he watched the captured roach's antennae struggle to escape, its hard body clicking angrily against the plastic.

He made his closest buddies tolerate me. His mother took me to the church of Reverend Jones on Sundays until Edna changed my religion. The simple presence of his company, and that of his pals, saved me from innumerable trashings and gave me time to breathe.

I had never had a friend before, and I cared for him as few lads have for another. My heart fills now when I think of him. That will never change. . . .

Toos's home was on the cross-'hoods thoroughfare. It was Indian Country; trouble came calling with the rising sun.

Toos was skinny and occasionally got picked. He would stand up straight, like an older boy, and roll his shoulders back, like a grown man. He would measure the challenge, giving the Handle crosser a chance to move on. Sometimes his quiet, unfearing gaze was as articulate as my mother's face. When parley failed, he met aggression with his own fury. He was never called out twice by the same youth.

The Haight, six blocks south, was bogeymanland. Boys carried knives, men had zip guns, and women looked more dangerous than twenty San Juan street-fighters with switchblades. Some of the Haight boys wore old-skinned Big Ben coveralls and carried barber shaving razors in the cup of the hand, hiding the flash of steel inside their arm-swaying struts. They could punch a guy and move on. It took a moment to realize that the face had been opened, blood everywhere, the searing pain following long moments after the incision.

"Ya'll stay outa dere," said Toussaint, pointing with a long and skinny thumb at our rival 'hood. "Be boogeymen, big-time."

Until I learned English, I understood it as The Hate.

The Panhandle lay between our 'hoods like no-man's-land, a DMZ that operated without U.N. intervention. Panhandle boys entered the park with great care and only in daylight. It was a jungle of thick eucalyptus, corpses, tangled azalea, and memories of aimless nocturnal screams. Men gathered there at night to smoke and drink and discuss this new land of California. When they disagreed, people died.

The Haight was largely populated by trekkers from Alabama and Louisiana. Mrs. LaRue said their heartaches came from not having a minister. Reverend M. Stamina Jones had followed the LaRues, the Joneses, the Scotts, and the Williamses—the Panhandle families—from Georgia. Others in the neighborhood hailed from Mississippi, Maryland, and Tennessee. I thought they were names of streets.

"No ministers in the Haight, just knife fighters," she said. "They'se lost. Toussaint LaRue and Kai Ting, you listen to Momma! Don't be goin into the Haight, no how and no way. Now. *That* be gospel."

Toussaint taught me about music. He tried to translate the words of the chorus in the church of Reverend Jones, but I always suspected that he lacked certainty in his explanations. But he knew that the chorus moved me, and would rub the hair on my head whenever I found myself weeping in time with its singing. I did not have to be an Imperial Scholar to know that crying in this temple house was accepted; the congregation's choral majesty was salted with tears and accented by open weeping. Sobs often served as confirmation of the truth of Reverend Jones's ministry. A dry-eyed assembly meant that his delivery was off the mark.

Toos also introduced me to Mr. Carter, who owned Evil the bulldog. Mr. Carter was a shipyard worker at Hunters Point who lived across the street from us, with the LaRue home around the corner. He had a platoon of exwives, no prospects of any more, two radios and a record player, and everyone on the block liked him while hating his dog.

Evil was moody. Somedays he raised his black-and-white head to you on a loose leash, anxious for a pat, his eyes half-closed, his teeth looking sadly over-used and brownishly old.

Other days he growled, the fangs angry and huge and brightly wet. He would run around like a broken top with his jaws open, all the kids screaming as they scattered. Evil never caught me; I was the flight expert. He would clamp his maws around a kid's leg and throw his neck back and forth and Mr. Carter would blow that whistle in Evil's ear until he let go. He would then use a fat clothes-hanger dowel to beat the starch out of the dog, and I was the only one who felt sorry for him. . . .

I tried to explain yuing chi, the responsibility of the future, God's ever-watchful scorecard, to Toussaint, but the concept exceeded my vocabulary. I had understood the idea so easily when it was conveyed by the dark, shimmering, expressive eyes of my mother. I was so anxious to explain that fighting was wrong, and would cause later pain, but winning this inarticulate debate was as difficult as prevailing in its subject matter.

I thought desperately about fighting but could not figure it out. I would be noticed, cut down, called horrific names, shoulder-bumped or shoved into the soft tar of the old streets of the Handle. A kid would challenge me and fear would rise inside my stomach like fog on the Bay and swamp me. My lights would get punched out and I would bawl like a newborn.

Flight always overcame Fight.

The very best I could do was control my tears, to a point. It was my only victory over the weakness of my body, the paucity of my combat power, the horror of fighting.

"China, I need yo' help someday too," said Toos.

I looked at him, confused.

"Say dude from da Haight strut here wif a razor, break mah bones and bleed me. Hustle to yo' door, ya'll lemme in. Right?"

I thought of Edna. Edna wouldn't let *me* in.

"Hmm," I said.

Toussaint was a preacher of the handshake. He already knew at this tender age that people got by because they gave each other the biggest gift in the book: time. His momma provided it for him whenever he wanted it. They had a handshake on it, and it gave him the strength of angels.

"You'all lookin at me kinda strange, Kai. Whatcha thinkin?" said his momma, as Toos went out the door.

"Toos ask fo' wata. You *give* wata."

She studied me for a bit, passing me a sad little cup of water, as well. I drank. "Say that again?" she said. So I did.

"Kai. I love my son. Now look here. *Everybody* love their kids. Yo' daddy and his wife, they surely love you, too. Jus' everabody don't know *how*.

"If the Good Lord took my boy from me I would curl up and die; I truly would," she said very solemnly. "He sent me Toussaint LaRue so's I could *love* him, give him my life, my heart." She smiled. "I have the Lord Jesus and I have Toussaint, and they'se my joys.

"Kai. You 'member this, chile. Someday you'all gonna have yo' own little Kai, a little Janie Ting. When yo' child want yo' time, you *give* it. That's our—our *callin*. I *love* my boy, but sometime he want ta play the cockroach game and I'm jes sick of it? Oh, Lord, *really sick of it*." She looked down at the old floor, clicking her tongue. "Or, he tell me the mos' *borin*, stop-your-mind stuff *ever*? My little man, Toussaint, he tell the longest and mos' unfunniest jokes in the world! But I *listen*, and I laugh fo' his joy, and I play him roaches, cuz I'm his momma, and he's my son. It's my God-given duty."

She dried her hands on a rag, and exhaled, looking away from me. "Toussaint's daddy got killed in truck acciden' in Benning," she said softly. "He was an officer. He went inta the army a private, and came back a cap'n, two bright silver railroad tracks on his collar. Lord, what a man he was! Well. The war, it was over, and he made it back from overseas, a pure hero, and he gave me Toussaint, and then we lost him. . . ." Her voice faded.

"He was a good man, Little Kai, and I miss him *evera day*." Her voice was choked. She stopped to blow her nose, shaking her head, hot tears coursing down her cheeks. "God wanted him bad, and took him." She looked toward the door. "Oh, Lord. What a price You exact. . . .

"John LaRue made a promise to me. I think his son done made one to you. Promises be powerful things. I take care of my son's wants. Then he give water to other men when they need it. And we'll have another John LaRue in the world. You want some more water?"

That was yuing chi, karma! And she let Missus Hall and the rats live on the stairs, and roaches in the wall. Mrs. LaRue was Chinese! She just didn't *look* it.

Could you give water to children who asked for it *and* beat the stuffing out of them if a fight was offered? I frowned with the difficulty of the riddle. She was offering me more water.

I took the plastic cup from Mrs. LaRue again, looking at the liquid within it as I drew it to my mouth. The plastic was old and scarred, with a history probably longer than mine. Innumerable scratches and half-cracks made it look tired, as if the serving of its masters and the catching of roaches had somehow cost too much. The water inside the cup sloshed, like the surf in the ocean, and for a transcendent moment all the scale and sense of proportion in the world dissolved, and I could see my mother placing her feet in the roaring waters of the cup. She was communicating with Na-Gung, an ocean away, and with me, from another world. My eardrums tickled, making me shudder, with her reaching for me. The cup was against my lip, and I stared inside it, cross-eyed. I could not drink this water.

"Tank you. Momma," I said. "I keep wata?"

"You want ta take it on home?" she asked.

"No. Want keep here, on sink. Same wata," I said. "Special. Uh, big-time, special."

"You can take it, chile."

"No," I said, shaking my head. "Mo' betta here." I heard Toos come in. Mrs. LaRue took the cup and placed it on the sink.

"China. Ya'll wanna be mah fren'?" asked Toos. Mrs. LaRue smiled and moved away from my field of vision. Maybe three feet.

"Chure, yep," I said. I sensed something weighing in the balance, an unasked question, a favor awaiting fulfillment.

"Den shake on it," he said, extending his hand. Again? I wondered. He took my hand and molded it into his. His was so hard, so rough.

"Squeeze, squeeze hard, China," he said, "like milk'd come out if ya squoze hard. You'se gotta know how." I gripped, and he smiled.

"Now. We'se frens, fo' sure," he said.

"An you can ask him yo' question, honey," said Momma.

"China," said Toos.

"Toos?" I said.

"China. Tell me 'bout yo' daddy."

I frowned. "Tell what?" I asked.

"Anythin, China. Jes *talk* 'bout him."

I began breathing heavily, not knowing what to say.

"I think yo' daddy was in the war, right?" said Mrs. LaRue. I nodded. "He in China army, for war," I said. "He fry airprane wif guns, bomb. He—" I made motions with my hands—"fall in pallashoot. Shoot gun. Save my ma-ma." I was licking my lips. "He very smart. Read books. Pray catch wif me. . . ."

There was a long silence.

"Thanks, chile," said Momma. "Listen. You share yo' daddy with Toussaint, here? Dat's what frens do."

Toussaint was all smiles, and I halfway grinned at him, trying to hide my teeth so the Teeth God would not want them.

167

In her memoir Lydia Yuri Minatoya describes her early schooling and her family's decision to give her a non-Japanese name (1992).

Talking to High Monks in the Snow
An Asian American Odyssey

Lydia Yuri Minatoya

Perhaps it begins with my naming. During her pregnancy, my mother was reading Dr. Spock. "Children need to belong," he cautioned. "An unusual name can make them the subject of ridicule." My father frowned when he heard this. He stole a worried glance at my sister. Burdened by her Japanese name, Misa played unsuspectingly on the kitchen floor.

The Japanese know full well the dangers of conspicuousness. "The nail that sticks out gets pounded down," cautions an old maxim. In America, Relocation was all the proof they needed.

And so it was, with great earnestness, my parents searched for a conventional name. They wanted me to have the full true promise of America.

"I will ask my colleague Froilan," said my father. "He is the smartest man I know."

"And he has poetic soul," said my mother, who cared about such things.

In due course, Father consulted Froilan. He gave Froilan his conditions for suitability.

"First, if possible, the full name should be alliterative," said my father. "Like Misa Minatoya." He closed his eyes and sang my sister's name. "Second, if not an alliteration, at least the name should have assonantal rhyme."

"Like Misa Minatoya?" said Froilan with a teasing grin.

"Exactly," my father intoned. He gave an emphatic nod. "Finally, most importantly, the name must be readily recognizable as conventional." He peered at Froilan with hope. "Do you have any suggestions or ideas?"

Froilan, whose own American child was named Ricardito, thought a while.

"We already have selected the name for a boy," offered my Father. "Eugene."

"Eugene?" wondered Froilan. "But it meets none of your conditions!"

"Eugene is a special case," said my father, "after Eugene, Oregon, and Eugene O'Neill. The beauty of the Pacific Northwest, the power of a great writer."

"I see," said Froilan, who did not but who realized that this naming business would be more complex than he had anticipated. "How about Maria?"

"Too common," said my father. "We want a *conventional* name, not a common one."

"Hmmm," said Froilan, wondering what the distinction was. He thought some more and then brightened. "Lydia!" he declared. He rhymed the name with media. "Lydia for *la bonita infanta!*"

And so I received my uncommon conventional name. It really did not provide the camouflage my parents had anticipated. I remained unalterably alien. For Dr. Spock had been addressing *American* families, and in those days, everyone knew all real American families were white.

Call it denial, but many Japanese Americans never quite understood that the promise of America was not truly meant for them. They lived in horse stalls at the Santa Anita racetrack and said the Pledge of Allegiance daily. They rode to Relocation Camps under armed guard, labeled with numbered tags, and sang "The Star-Spangled Banner." . . .

My mother's camp was the third most populous city in the entire state of Wyoming. Across the barren lands, behind barbed wire, bloomed these little oases of democracy. The older generation bore the humiliation with pride. "*Kodomo no tame ni,*" they said. For the sake of the children. They thought that if their dignity was great, then their children would be spared. Call it valor. Call it bathos. Perhaps it was closer to slapstick: a sweet and bitter lunacy.

Call it adaptive behavior. Coming from a land swept by savage typhoons, ravaged by earthquakes and volcanoes, the Japanese have evolved a view of the world: a cooperative, stoic, almost magical way of thinking. Get along, work hard, and never quite see the things that can bring you pain. Against the tyranny of nature, of feudal lords, of wartime hysteria, the charm works equally well.

And so my parents gave me an American name and hoped that I could pass. They nourished me with the American dream: Opportunity, Will, Transformation. . . .

When we lived in Albany, I always was the teachers' pet. "So tiny, so precocious, so prettily dressed!" They thought I was a living doll and this was fine with me.

My father knew that the effusive praise would die. He had been through this with my sister. After five years of being a perfect darling, Misa had reached the age where students were tracked by ability. Then, the anger started. Misa had tested into the advanced track. It was impossible, the community declared. Misa was forbidden entry into advanced classes as long as there were white children being placed below her. In her defense, before an angry rabble, my father made a presentation to the Board of Education.

But I was too young to know of this. I knew only that my teachers praised and petted me. They took me to other classes as an example. "Watch now, as Lydia demonstrates attentive behavior," they would croon as I was led to an empty desk at the head of the class. I had a routine. I would sit carefully, spreading my petticoated skirt neatly beneath me. I would pull my chair close to the desk, crossing my swinging legs at my snowy white anklets. I would fold my hands carefully on the desk before me and stare pensively at the blackboard.

This routine won me few friends, The sixth-grade boys threw rocks at me. They danced around me in a tight circle, pulling at the corners of their eyes. "Ching Chong Chinaman," they chanted. But teachers loved me. When I was in first grade, a third-grade teacher went weeping to the principal. She begged to have me skipped. She was leaving to get married and wanted her turn with the dolly.

168

Americans have been writing children's literature since the nineteenth century; many of those works are still enjoyed today. The Adventures of Tom Sawyer *(1876), probably the best-loved boys' story in American history, is justly famous for its humor and its portrayal of boys' lives in a small town.*

The Adventures of Tom Sawyer

Mark Twain

But Tom's energy did not last. He began to think of the fun he had planned for this day, and his sorrows multiplied. Soon the free boys would come tripping along on all sorts of delicious expeditions, and they would make a world of fun of him for having to work—the very thought of it burned him like fire. He got out his worldly wealth and examined it—bits of toys, marbles, and trash; enough to buy an exchange of *work*, maybe, but not half enough to buy so much as half an hour of pure freedom. So he returned his straightened means to his pocket, and gave up the idea of trying to buy the boys. At this dark and hopeless moment an inspiration burst upon him! Nothing less than a great, magnificent inspiration.

He took up his brush and went tranquilly to work. Ben Rogers hove in sight presently—the very boy, of all boys, whose ridicule he had been dreading. Ben's gait was the hop-skip-and-jump—proof enough that his heart was light and his anticipations high. He was eating an apple, and giving a long, melodious whoop, at intervals, followed by a deep-toned ding-dong-dong, ding-dong-dong, for he was personating a steamboat. As he drew near, he slackened speed, took the middle of the street, leaned far over to starboard and rounded to ponderously and with laborious pomp and circumstance—for he was personating the *Big Missouri*, and considered himself to be drawing nine feet of water. He was boat, and captain, and engine bells combined, so he had to imagine himself standing on his own hurricane deck giving the orders and executing them: "Stop her, sir! Ting-a-ling-ling!" The headway ran almost out and he drew up slowly toward the sidewalk.

"Ship up to back! Ting-a-ling-ling!" His arms straightened and stiffened down his sides.

"Set her back on the stabboard! Ting-a-ling-ling! Chow! Ch-chow-wow!

Chow!" His right hand, meantime, describing stately circles—for it was representing a forty-foot wheel.

"Let her go back on the labboard! Ting-a-ling-ling! Chow-ch-chow-chow!" The left hand began to describe circles.

"Stop the stabboard! Ting-a-ling-ling! Stop the labbord! Come ahead on the stabboard! Stop her! Let your outside turn over slow! Ting-a-ling-ling! Chow-ow-ow! Get out that head-line! *Lively* now! Come—out with your spring-line— what're you about there! Take a turn round that stump with the bight of it! Stand by that stage, now—let her go! Done with the engines, sir! Ting-a-ling-ling! *Sh't! s'h't! sh't!"* (trying the gauge-cocks.)

Tom went on whitewashing—paid no attention to the steamboat. Ben stared a moment and then said: "Hi-*yi!* You're up a stump, ain't you!"

No answer. Tom surveyed his last touch with the eye of an artist; then he gave his brush another gentle sweep and surveyed the result, as before. Ben ranged up alongside of him. Tom's mouth watered for the apple, but he stuck to his work. Ben said: "Hello, old chap, you got to work, hey?"

Tom wheeled suddenly and said: "Why it's you Ben! I warn't noticing."

"Say—I'm going in a swimming, *I* am. Don't you wish you could? But of course you'd druther *work*—wouldn't you? Course you would!"

Tom contemplated the boy a bit, and said: "What do you call work?"

"Why ain't *that* work?"

Tom resumed his whitewashing, and answered carelessly: "Well, maybe it is, and maybe it aint. All I know is, it suits Tom Sawyer."

"Oh come, now, you don't mean to let on that you *like* it?"

The brush continued to move.

"Like it? Well I don't see why I oughtn't to like it. Does a boy get a chance to whitewash a fence every day?"

That put the thing in a new light. Ben stopped nibbling his apple. Tom swept his brush daintily back and forth—stepped back to note the effect—added a touch here and there—criticized the effect again—Ben watching every move and getting more and more interested, more and more absorbed. Presently he said: "Say, Tom, let *me* whitewash a little."

Tom considered, was about to consent; but he altered his mind: "No—no—I reckon it wouldn't hardly do, Ben. You see, Aunt Polly's awful particular about this fence—right here on the street, you know—but if it was the back fence I wouldn't mind and *she* wouldn't. Yes, she's awful particular about this fence; it's got to be done very careful; I reckon there ain't one boy in a thousand, maybe two thousand, that can do it the way it's got to be done."

"No—is that so? Oh come, now—lemme just try. Only just a little—I'd let *you*, if you was me, Tom."

"Ben, I'd like to, honest injun; but Aunt Polly—well Jim wanted to do it, but she wouldn't let him; Sid wanted to do it, and she wouldn't let Sid. Now don't you see how I'm fixed? If you was to tackle this fence and anything was to happen to it—"

"Oh, shucks, I'll be just as careful. Now lemme try. Say—I'll give you the core of my apple."

"Well, here—. No, Ben, now don't. I'm afeard—"

"I'll give you *all* of it!"

Tom gave up the brush with reluctance in his face but alacrity in his heart. And while the late steamer *Big Missouri* worked and sweated in the sun, the retired artist sat on a barrel in the shade close by, dangled his legs, munched his apple, and planned the slaughter of more innocents. There was no lack of material; boys happened along every little while; they came to jeer, but remained to whitewash. By the time Ben was fagged out, Tom had traded the next chance to Billy Fisher for a kite, in good repair; and when *he* played out, Johnny Miller bought in for a dead rat and a string to swing it with—and so on, and so on, hour after hour. And when the middle of the afternoon came, from being a poor poverty-stricken boy in the morning, Tom was literally rolling in wealth. He had beside the things before mentioned, twelve marbles, part of a Jew's-harp, a piece of blue bottle-glass to look through, a spool cannon, a key that wouldn't unlock anything, a fragment of chalk, a glass stopper of a decanter, a tin soldier, a couple of tadpoles, six fire-crackers, a kitten with only one eye, a brass doorknob, a dog collar—but no dog—the handle of a knife, four pieces of orange peel, and a dilapidated old window sash.

He had had a nice, good, idle time all the while—plenty of company—and the fence had three coats of whitewash on it! If he hadn't run out of whitewash, he would have bankrupted every boy in the village.

Tom said to himself that it was not such a hollow world, after all. He had discovered a great law of human action, without knowing it—namely, that in order to make a man or a boy covet a thing, it is only necessary to make the thing difficult to attain. If he had been a great and wise philosopher, like the writer of this book, he would now have comprehended that Work consists of whatever a body is *obliged* to do, and that Play consists of whatever a body is not obliged to do. And this would help him to understand why constructing artificial flowers or performing on a treadmill is work, while rolling tenpins or climbing Mont Blanc is only amusement. There are wealthy gentlemen in England who drive four-horse passenger coaches twenty or thirty miles on a daily line, in the summer, because the privilege costs them considerable money; but if they were offered wages for the service, that would turn it into work and then they would resign.

The verses of James Whitcomb Riley, the "Hoosier poet," were widely read by young people at the turn of the century. Riley portrays idyllic scenes and innocent children who are often acquainted with ghosts and fairies. His work reflects the nostalgia-tinged view of children's playfulness and closeness to nature (1905).

The Days Gone By

James Whitcomb Riley

O the days gone by! O the days gone by!
The apples in the orchard, and the pathway through the rye;
The chirrup of the robin, and the whistle of the quail
As he piped across the meadows sweet as any nightingale;
When the bloom was on the clover, and the blue was in the sky,
And my happy heart brimmed over, in the days gone by.

In the days gone by, when my naked feet were tripped
By the honeysuckle tangles where the water-lilies dipped,
And the ripples of the river lipped the moss along the brink,
Where the placid-eyed and lazy-footed cattle came to drink,
And the tilting snipe stood fearless of the truant's wayward cry
And the splashing of the swimmer, in the days gone by.

O the days gone by! O the days gone by!
The music of the laughing lip, the lustre of the eye;
The childish faith in fairies, and Aladdin's magic ring—
The simple, soul-reposing, glad belief in everything,—
When life was like a story, holding neither sob nor sigh,
In the golden olden glory of the days gone by.

Dorothy's adventures in Oz have become a staple of child life and a deeply in-grained part of American folklore and the American imagination. The passage we reprint is less well known than other parts of the book (because it was not part of the famous film), but it conveys L. Frank Baum's inversions of reality and the way inanimate objects are brought to life in a fanciful land (1900).

The Wizard of Oz

L. Frank Baum

They began walking through the country of the china people, and the first thing they came to was a china milk-maid milking a china cow. As they drew near the cow suddenly gave a kick and kicked over the stool, the pail, and even the milk-maid herself, all falling on the china ground with a great clatter.

Dorothy was shocked to see that the cow had broken her leg short off, and that the pail was lying in several small pieces, while the poor milk-maid had a nick in her left elbow.

"There!" cried the milk-maid, angrily; "see what you have done! My cow has broken her leg, and I must take her to the mender's shop and have it glued on again. What do you mean by coming here and frightening my cow?"

"I'm very sorry," returned Dorothy; "please forgive us."

But the pretty milk-maid was much too vexed to make any answer. She picked up the leg sulkily and led her cow away, the poor animal limping on three legs. As she left them the milk-maid cast many reproachful glances over her shoulder at the clumsy strangers, holding her nicked elbow close to her side.

Dorothy was quite grieved at this mishap.

"We must be very careful here," said the kind-hearted Woodman, "or we may hurt these pretty little people so they will never get over it."

A little farther on Dorothy met a most beautifully dressed young princess, who stopped short as she saw the strangers and started to run away.

Dorothy wanted to see more of the princess, so she ran after her; but the china girl cried out,

"Don't chase me! don't chase me!"

She had such a frightened little voice that Dorothy stopped and said,

"Why not?"

"Because," answered the princess, also stopping, a safe distance away, "if I run I may fall down and break myself."

"But couldn't you be mended?" asked the girl.

"Oh, yes; but one is never so pretty after being mended, you know," replied the princess.

"I suppose not," said Dorothy.

"Now there is Mr. Joker, one of our clowns," continued the china lady, "who is always trying to stand upon his head. He has broken himself so often that he is mended in a hundred places, and doesn't look at all pretty. Here he comes now, so you can see for yourself."

Indeed, a jolly little Clown now came walking toward them, and Dorothy could see that in spite of his pretty clothes of red and yellow and green he was completely covered with cracks, running every which way and showing plainly that he had been mended in many places.

The Clown put his hands in his pockets, and after puffing out his cheeks and nodding his head at them saucily he said,

> "My lady fair,
> Why do you stare
> At poor old Mr. Joker?
> You're quite as stiff
> And prim as if
> You'd eaten up a poker!"

"Be quiet, sir!" said the princess; "can't you see these are strangers, and should be treated with respect?"

"Well, that's respect, I expect," declared the Clown, and immediately stood upon his head.

"Don't mind Mr. Joker," said the princess to Dorothy; "he is considerably cracked in his head, and that makes him foolish."

"Oh, I don't mind him a bit," said Dorothy. "But you are so beautiful," she continued, "that I am sure I could love you dearly. Won't you let me carry you back to Kansas and stand you on Aunt Em's mantle-shelf? I could carry you in my basket."

"That would make me very unhappy," answered the china princess. "You see, here in our own country we live contentedly, and can talk and move around as we please. But whenever any of us are taken away our joints at once stiffen, and we can only stand straight and look pretty. Of course that is all that is expected of us when we are on mantle-shelves and cabinets and drawing-room tables, but our lives are much pleasanter here in our own country."

"I would not make you unhappy for all the world!" exclaimed Dorothy; "so I'll just say good-bye."

"Good-bye," replied the princess.

They walked carefully through the china country. The little animals and all the people scampered out of their way, fearing the strangers would break them, and after an hour or so the travellers reached the other side of the country and came to another china wall.

It was not as high as the first, however, and by standing upon the Lion's back they all managed to scramble to the top. Then the Lion gathered his legs under him and jumped on the wall; but just as he jumped he upset a china church with his tail and smashed it all to pieces.

"That was too bad," said Dorothy, "but really I think we were lucky in not doing these little people more harm than breaking a cow's leg and a church. They are all so brittle!"

"They are, indeed," said the Scarecrow, "and I am thankful I am made of straw and cannot be easily damaged. There are worse things in the world than being a Scarecrow."

Since 1908 L. M. Montgomery's stories about Anne, the orphaned child who is placed out on a farm, have been favorites of American girls. Anne's exuberance and energy make her lovable but also get her into trouble.

Anne of Green Gables

L. M. Montgomery

Anne had been a fortnight at Green Gables before Mrs. Lynde arrived to inspect her. Mrs. Rachel, to do her justice, was not to blame for this. A severe and unseasonable attack of grippe had confined that good lady to her house ever since the occasion of her last visit to Green Gables. Mrs. Rachel was not often sick and had a well-defined contempt for people who were; but grippe, she asserted, was like no other illness on earth and could only be interpreted as one of the special visitations of Providence. As soon as her doctor allowed her to put her foot out-of-doors she hurried up to Green Gables, bursting with curiosity to see Matthew's and Marilla's orphan, concerning whom all sorts of stories and suppositions had gone abroad in Avonlea.

Anne had made good use of every waking moment of that fortnight. Already she was acquainted with every tree and shrub about the place. She had discovered that a lane opened out below the apple orchard and ran up through a belt of woodland; and she had explored it to its furthest end in all its delicious vagaries of brook and bridge, fir coppice and wild cherry arch, corners thick with fern, and branching byways of maple and mountain ash.

She had made friends with the spring down in the hollow—that wonderful deep, clear icy-cold spring; it was set about with smooth red sandstones and rimmed in by great palm-like clumps of water fern; and beyond it was a log bridge over the brook.

That bridge led Anne's dancing feet up over a wooded hill beyond, where perpetual twilight reigned under the straight, thick-growing firs and spruces; the only flowers there were myriads of delicate "June bells," those shyest and sweetest of woodland blooms, and a few pale, aerial starflowers, like the spirits of last year's blossoms. Gossamers glimmered like threads of silver among the trees and the fir boughs and tassels seemed to utter friendly speech.

All these raptured voyages of exploration were made in the odd half hours which she was allowed for play, and Anne talked Matthew and Marilla half-deaf over her discoveries. Not that Matthew complained, to be sure; he listened to it all with a wordless smile of enjoyment on his face; Marilla permitted the "chatter" until she found herself becoming too interested in it, whereupon she always promptly quenched Anne by a curt command to hold her tongue.

Anne was out in the orchard when Mrs. Rachel came, wandering at her own sweet will through the lush, tremulous grasses splashed with ruddy evening sunshine; so that good lady had an excellent chance to talk her illness fully over, describing every ache and pulse beat with such evident enjoyment that Marilla thought even grippe must bring its compensations. When details were exhausted Mrs. Rachel introduced the real reason of her call.

"I've been hearing some surprising things about you and Matthew."

"I don't suppose you are any more surprised than I am myself," said Marilla. "I'm getting over my surprise now."

"It was too bad there was such a mistake," said Mrs. Rachel sympathetically. "Couldn't you have sent her back?"

"I suppose we could, but we decided not to. Matthew took a fancy to her. And I must say I like her myself—although I admit she has her faults. The house seems a different place already. She's a real bright little thing."

Marilla said more than she had intended to say when she began, for she read disapproval in Mrs. Rachel's expression.

"It's a great responsibility you've taken on yourself," said that lady gloomily, "especially when you've never had any experience with children. You don't know much about her or her real disposition, I suppose, and there's no guessing how a child like that will turn out. But I don't want to discourage you I'm sure, Marilla."

"I'm not feeling discouraged," was Marilla's dry response. "When I make up my mind to do a thing it stays made up. I suppose you'd like to see Anne. I'll call her in."

Anne came running in presently, her face sparkling with the delight of her orchard rovings; but, abashed at finding herself in the unexpected presence of a stranger, she halted confusedly inside the door. She certainly was an odd-looking little creature in the short tight wincey dress she had worn from the asylum, below which her thin legs seemed ungracefully long. Her freckles were more numerous and obtrusive than ever; the wind had ruffled her hatless hair into over-brilliant disorder; it had never looked redder than at that moment.

"Well, they didn't pick you for your looks, that's sure and certain," was Mrs. Rachel Lynde's emphatic comment. Mrs. Rachel was one of those delightful and popular people who pride themselves on speaking their mind without fear or favor. "She's terrible skinny and homely, Marilla. Come here, child, and let me have a look at you. Lawful heart, did any one ever see such freckles? And hair as red as carrots! Come here, child, I say."

Anne "came there," but not exactly as Mrs. Rachel expected. With one bound she crossed the kitchen floor and stood before Mrs. Rachel, her face scarlet with anger, her lips quivering, and her whole slender form trembling from head to foot.

"I hate you," she cried in a choked voice, stamping her foot on the floor. "I hate you—I hate you—I hate you—" a louder stamp with each assertion of hatred. "How dare you call me skinny and ugly? How dare you say I'm freckled and redheaded? You are a rude, impolite, unfeeling woman!"

"Anne!" exclaimed Marilla in consternation.

But Anne continued to face Mrs. Rachel undauntedly, head up, eyes blazing, hands clenched, passionate indignation exhaling from her like an atmosphere.

"How dare you say such things about me?" she repeated vehemently. "How would you like to have such things said about you? How would you like to be told that you are fat and clumsy and probably hadn't a spark of imagination in you? I don't care if I do hurt your feelings by saying so! I hope I hurt them. You have hurt mine worse than they were ever hurt before even by Mrs. Thomas' intoxicated husband. And I'll *never* forgive you for it, never, never!"

Stamp! Stamp!

"Did anybody ever see such a temper!" exclaimed the horrified Mrs. Rachel.

"Anne, go to your room and stay there until I come up," said Marilla, recovering her powers of speech with difficulty.

Anne, bursting into tears, rushed to the hall door, slammed it until the tins on the porch wall outside rattled in sympathy, and fled through the hall and up the stairs like a whirlwind. A subdued slam above told that the door of the east gable had been shut with equal vehemence.

"Well, I don't envy you your job bringing *that* up, Marilla," said Mrs. Rachel with unspeakable solemnity.

172

Since the 1950s the stories of Dr. Seuss (Theodore Geisel) have been a dominant presence in child life, as much for his easy-to-remember rhymed prose as for his extraordinary illustrations. Despite the fanciful names and places, however, Dr. Seuss often deals with important and painful subjects confronting children. In The Sneetches *(1961) he portrays the problems of exclusionism, prejudice, and conformity.*

The Sneetches

Dr. Seuss

When the Star-Belly children went out to play ball,
Could a Plain Belly get in the game . . . ? Not at all.
You only could play if your bellies had stars
And the Plain-Belly children had none upon thars.
When the Star-Belly Sneetches had frankfurter roasts
Or picnics or parties or marshmallow toasts,
They never invited the Plain-Belly Sneetches.
They left them out cold, in the dark of the beaches.
They kept them away. Never let them come near.
And that's how they treated them year after year.

173

What Dr. Seuss is for young children Roald Dahl has become for older ones. His books about the emotional travails of growing up, though they may seem cruel at times, provide a certain sense of solace. In The BFG *(1982), one of Dahl's most popular stories, the* Big Friendly Giant *does not* eat *children.*

Snozzcumbers

Roald Dahl

"But if you don't eat people like all the others," Sophie said, "then what *do* you live on?"

"That is a squelching tricky problem around here," the BFG answered. "In this sloshflunking Giant Country, happy eats like pineapples and pigwinkles is simply not growing. Nothing is growing except for one extremely icky-poo vegetable. It is called the snozzcumber."

"The snozzcumber!" cried Sophie. "There's no such thing."

The BFG looked at Sophie and smiled, showing about twenty of his square white teeth. "Yesterday," he said, "we was not believing in giants, was we? Today we is not believing in snozzcumbers. Just because we happen not to have actually *seen* something with our own two little winkles, we think it is not existing. What about for instance the great squizzly scotch-hopper?"

"I beg your pardon?" Sophie said.

"And the humplecrimp?"

"What's that?" Sophie said.

"And the wraprascal?"

"The what?" Sophie said.

"And the crumpscoddle?"

"Are they animals?" Sophie asked.

"They is *common* animals," said the BFG contemptuously. "I is not a very know-all giant myself, but it seems to me that you is an absolutely know-nothing human bean. Your brain is full of rotten-wool."

"You mean cotton-wool," Sophie said.

"What I mean and what I say is two different things," the BFG announced rather grandly. "I will now show you a snozzcumber."

The BFG flung open a massive cupboard and took out the weirdest-looking thing Sophie had ever seen. It was about half as long again as an ordinary man

but was much thicker. It was as thick around its girth as a perambulator. It was black with white stripes along its length. And it was covered all over with coarse knobbles.

"Here is the repulsant snozzcumber!" cried the BFG, waving it about. "I squoggle it! I mispise it! I dispunge it! But because I is refusing to gobble up human beans like the other giants, I must spend my life guzzling up icky-poo snozzcumbers instead. If I don't, I will be nothing but skin and groans."

"You mean skin and *bones*," Sophie said.

"I *know* it is bones," the BFG said. "But please understand that I cannot be helping it if I sometimes is saying things a little squiggly. I is trying my very best all the time." The Big Friendly Giant looked suddenly so forlorn that Sophie got quite upset.

"I'm sorry," she said. "I didn't mean to be rude."

"There never was any schools to teach me talking in Giant Country," the BFG said sadly.

"But couldn't your mother have taught you?" Sophie asked.

"My *mother*!" cried the BFG. "Giants don't have mothers! Surely you is knowing *that*."

"I did *not* know that," Sophie said.

"Whoever heard of a *woman* giant!" shouted the BFG, waving the snozzcumber around his head like a lasso. "There never was a woman giant! And there never will be one. Giants is always men!"

Sophie felt herself getting a little muddled. "In that case," she said, "how were you born?"

"Giants isn't born," the BFG answered. "Giants *appears* and that's all there is to it. They simply *appears*, the same way as the sun and the stars."

"And when did you appear?" Sophie asked.

"Now how on earth could I be knowing a thing like that?" said the BFG. "It was so long ago I couldn't count."

"You mean you don't even know how *old* you are?"

"No giant is knowing that," the BFG said. "All I is knowing about myself is that I is very old, very very old and crumply. Perhaps as old as the earth."

"What happens when a giant dies?" Sophie asked.

"Giants is never dying," the BFG answered. "Sometimes and quite suddenly, a giant is disappearing and nobody is ever knowing where he goes to. But mostly us giants is simply going on and on like whiffsy time-twiddlers."

The BFG was still holding the awesome snozzcumber in his right hand, and now he put one end into his mouth and bit off a huge hunk of it. He started crunching it up and the noise he made was like the crunching of lumps of ice.

"It's filthing!" he spluttered, speaking with his mouth full and spraying large pieces of snozzcumber like bullets in Sophie's direction. Sophie hopped around on the table-top, ducking out of the way.

"It's disgusterous!" the BFG gurgled. "It's sickable! It's rotsome! It's maggot-wise! Try it yourself, this foulsome snozzcumber!"

"No, thank you," Sophie said, backing away.

"It's all you're going to be guzzling around here from now on so you might as well get used to it," said the BFG. "Go on, you snipsy little winkle, have a go!"

Sophie took a small nibble. "Uggggggggh!" she spluttered. "Oh no! Oh gosh! Oh help!" She spat it out quickly. "It tastes of frogskins!" she gasped. "And rotten fish!"

"Worse than that!" cried the BFG, roaring with laughter. "To me it is tasting of clockcoaches and slime-wanglers!"

"Do we really have to eat it?" Sophie said.

"You do unless you is wanting to become so thin you will be disappearing into a thick ear."

"Into *thin air*," Sophie said. "A thick ear is something quite different."

Once again that sad winsome look came into the BFG's eyes. "Words," he said, "is oh such a twitch-tickling problem to me all my life. So you must simply try to be patient and stop squibbling. As I am telling you before, I know exactly what words I am wanting to say, but somehow or other they is always getting squiff-squiddled around."

"That happens to everyone," Sophie said.

"Not like it happens to me," the BFG said. "I is speaking the most terrible wigglish."

"I think you speak beautifully," Sophie said.

"You do?" cried the BFG, suddenly brightening. "You really do?"

"Simply beautifully," Sophie repeated.

"Well, that is the nicest present anybody is ever giving me in my whole life!" cried the BFG. "Are you sure you is not twiddling my leg?"

"Of course not," Sophie said. "I just love the way you talk."

"How wondercrump!" cried the BFG, still beaming. "How whoopsey-splunkers! How absolutely squiffling! I is all of a stutter."

"Listen," Sophie said. "We don't *have* to eat snozzcumbers. In the fields around our village there are all sorts of lovely vegetables like cauliflowers and carrots. Why don't you get some of those next time you go visiting?"

The BFG raised his great head proudly in the air. "I is a very honourable giant," he said. "I would rather be chewing up rotsome snozzcumbers than snitching things from other people."

"You stole *me*," Sophie said.

"I did not steal you very much," said the BFG, smiling gently. "After all, you is only a tiny little girl."

174

According to the literary scholar Gillian Avery, American children's literature drew heavily on English and continental works, though by the middle of the nineteenth century there was a growing indigenous tradition. Despite an early resistance to fanciful tales, Americans eventually succumbed to fairy stories and other kinds of unrealistic fiction.

American Children and Their Books

Gillian Avery

The 1820s also saw the advent of Samuel Goodrich's Peter Parley books, in which the narrator, Parley, dispenses information in a manner that was to become immensely popular with his readers. The Parley style was didactic, but more informal than the turgid little compilations of facts that hack writers in England were producing about this time, and other American writers took it up. Goodrich also conducted a fierce ideological war against fairy-tales and nursery rhymes. A true child of the New World, he felt that a rational, properly educated generation should have no dealings with these relics of a credulous past. And the great nineteenth-century educator Jacob Abbott, though never as vehement as Goodrich, was also dismissive of fairy-tales. His Rollo, who idly wishes for an Aladdin's lamp, is convinced by his father's calm reasoning that it would not make him any happier, and that one's own honest toil brings the greatest reward.

It is interesting that the same years that saw the emergence of Peter Parley also saw the development of the Father Christmas legend. Early New York publishers might not know how to spell the Santa Claus that the Dutch settlers had brought over with them but, judging by the ferocity with which one of them attacked "old Santa-Claw" in 1814 as a preposterous lie, he was a well known figure even then—the only "fairy" that immigrants were to bring over from the Old World. The first Christmas book featuring Santa Claus with his flying sleigh and reindeer was published in New York in 1821, a year before Clement C. Moore wrote his poem "A Visit from St Nicholas." After that, the idea of the Christmas Eve descent down the chimney to fill children's stockings was ineradicable, whatever the rationalists might say.

The rational approach favoured by Goodrich and Abbott and their kind had been characteristic of English writing for the young in the eighteenth century; it is to be found in works as various as *Little Goody Two-Shoes* and the educational

"NOW TO FILL THE STOCKINGS AS QUIETLY AS POSSIBLE."

Santa Claus — an American contribution to fairy legend. From A Christmas Alphabet. Published by the McLoughlin firm c. 1900.

treatises composed by Richard Lovell Edgeworth and his daughter, the great Maria. But by the middle years of the next century the pendulum in England was swinging back. Fairy-tales had been rediscovered. For a century or more they had been associated with the ignorant, the foolish, those who knew no better. But the scholarly compilations of the Grimm brothers—a translation of some of the stories appeared in England in 1823—seemed to make the genre respectable in a way that the previous century's translations of Charles Perrault's fairy-stories did not. (This may in part have been due to the fact that the English traditionally equate the French with frivolity, the Germans with high serious-ness.) Further respectability was bestowed on fairy-tales by the writings of Hans Andersen, first translated in 1846. The bittersweet flavor of the Andersen tales, strongly infused with moral reflection, was very much to Victorian taste, and he had many imitators.

Andersen had American admirers too, notably Horace Scudder who in the 1860s succeeded in persuading him to contribute to the *Riverside Magazine for Young People*, which Scudder edited. But one is conscious through most of the century of many authors' and publishers' misgivings about fairy-stories. Though there were occasional ventures into fantasy, some of them of great distinction, like James Kirke Paulding's *A Christmas Gift from Fairyland* in 1838 and Christopher Cranch's *The Last of the Huggermuggers* in 1855, these were to disappear unremembered, and the genre did not become popular until Frank Baum wrote *The Wonderful Wizard of Oz* in 1900.

The place of fantasy in American juvenile fiction was to some extent taken by humour. Comic supermen of the Davy Crockett and Paul Bunyan sort had greater appeal than romantic heroes. George Wilbur Peck's "Bad Boy", uproari-ously funny to 1880s readers, could be considered a version of Crockett—who according to the *Crockett Almanac* of 1837 told Congress complacently, "I'm a leetle the savagest crittur you ever did see", then proceeded to hurl all manner of abuse at the Members. Joel Chandler Harris's *Uncle Remus*, the first collection of American popular legends to make any mark, was originally marketed as humour, and America took more readily to Mother Goose's nursery rhymes than to fairy-tales. For fairies to be popular, it seems they had to be comical, like Palmer Cox's Brownies, and it is the humorous verse, such as John Trowbridge's "Darius Green and his Flying Machine", that stands out in anthologies. (Some thirty years before the Wright brothers succeeded in launching themselves into the air, young Darius tries to fly and comes a cropper. As he picks himself up he says, "Wal, I like flyin' well enough, but the' ain't sich a thunderin' sight/ O' fun in't when yo' come to light.") . . .

Samuel Goodrich . . . was outraged at an early age by the violence and terror in fairy-tales. He condemned them as "monstrous, false and pestilential" and pronounced that just as no one would feed children with blood and poison, so no one should administer "cruelty and violence, terror and impurity." Others raised different objections: fairy-tales were not useful, they stood in the way of progress, and they were ungenteel. All these arguments are advanced in *The Fairy Tale*, a little tract published in Providence, Rhode Island, in 1831.

> "I wonder what makes Pa dislike Fairy Tales so much, mother; I am sure they can do us no harm, while we know they are all false."
>
> "Is there no harm in wasting your time in the perusal of nonsensical, and often wicked stories, Julia?"
>
> "Wicked, mother?"

Children learning that stories about fabulous creatures are all lies.

"Yes, Julia, often wicked, though you are not old enough to understand their
coarse allusion to sacred things; besides, my child, time is too precious to waste
it on that which will neither make us wiser or better. Remember, that life is but
a span—a moment—a flash—and I am sure you will think with regret of your
wasted hours."

Julia's mother does not object to outdoor play since this is exercise necessary
to health, but in a purposeful life fairy-tales can have no part. They are sweet-
meats (as Richard Edgeworth saw them), possibly poisonous ones (as was Goodrich's view). But she added an objection of her own: they were not genteel. Julia's
mother, though uncertain of her grammar, is very conscious of the low standing
of such tales, which no doubt she associated with the crudely printed little

versions of such stories as *Sinbad, Blue Beard* and *Cinderella* sold by pedlars to people who knew no better: "Few people of talents, at the present day, write fairy tales; and such nonsense as you was reading, Julia, is never read by well-educated people." And to show her daughter what fiction should be like she reads her an allegory about Intemperance and Luxury and Licentiousness, where Holiness and Prayer triumph, and Industry and Invention make "a black powder which blows rock away very easy," this powder representing "the force of industry accomplishing any desirable object."

The Fairy-Book of 1836 . . . is a pioneer work that includes, as well as eight tales from Perrault's *Histoires*, stories by Mme d'Aulnoy, Mme Leprince de Beaumont and other French writers. Its editor, Verplanck, who unlike Goodrich had been reared in a tradition of fairy-tales, saw them as stimulating courage and daring in boys, gentleness and compassion in girls. Washington, he averred, must have been formed by them: "At any rate, I feel quite positive that he would not have been the first and greatest President of the United States, had he never read "Whittington and his Cat." " And, he pointed out with great truth, the stories of Miss Edgeworth "are but the histories of Giles Gingerbread and Goody Two-Shoes grown up and living among the people of our own days."

In his mock-serious championship of the traditional tales Verplanck speaks passionately of their antiquity, their influence on Shakespeare and the poets, and rejects "the sage opinion that they are not true, and that children ought not to be allowed to read anything but the truth." They have, he insists, an essential moral truth; indeed, history itself "as commonly taught to the young in dry chronological tables and meager catalogues of musty names [does not] contain one quarter so much of living reality."

There was another prevalent objection: "Many worthy people think that this kind of literature is suited only to the old countries, and of course that our American children have nothing to do with such knowledge." William Cardell, who in *The Story of Jack Halyard* set out to write a story with "doctrines and sentiments intended to be American," said as much about nursery rhymes: "[*Mother Goose's Melody*] was a parcel of silly rhymes, made by some ignorant people in England about a hundred years ago. The book was written in bad English, and full of plumping long stories from beginning to end." His hero feels the same: "It is strange," says Jack, who has just read "Hey Diddle Diddle" with much contempt, "that a child of common sense can take delight in reading such falsehoods, and believe that dishes can hop, and dogs laugh, and cows jump higher than eagles can fly."

Samuel Goodrich, who, as we have seen, felt that children should be presented with rational ideas rather than nonsensical verse, spoke with grief about English efforts to revive the rhymes: "A quaint, quiet, scholarly gentleman, called Mr Felix Summerly—a dear lover of children—was invented to preside over the enterprise, to rap the knuckles of Peter Parley, and woo back the erring generation of children to the good old orthodox rhymes and jingles of England." He was thankful to add that the enterprise went bankrupt (this was wishful thinking), though regrettably it did not stop James Orchard Halliwell, the English antiquarian, from devoting the weight of his scholarship to these same foolish rhymes. Goodrich's sorrow at this insensate folly was expressed in his magazine *Merry's Museum* in August 1846, in a dialogue between a boy and his mother, who realizes too late that "these foolish rhymes stick like burrs . . . and the coarsest and vilest seem to be best remembered." She recommends her son to learn "good, sensible things" instead. But these turn out to be Watts' hymns— "I hate 'em," says Timothy tersely, and goes on shouting the jingle he has composed:

> Higglety, pigglety, pop!
> The dog has eat the mop;
> The pig's in a hurry,
> The cat's in a flurry—
> Higglety, pigglety—pop!

. . . Despite Peter Parleyism, Mother Goose rhymes seemed to settle easily in America. Other publishers took over *Mother Goose's Melody* from Isaiah Thomas. In an abridged chapbook version, printed in Windsor, Vermont, in 1814, a verse of "Yankee Doodle" has been added—a rare topical touch:

> Father and I went down to Camp
> Along with Captain Goodwin,
> And there we saw the men and boys
> As thick as hasty pudding.
> With fire ribbons in their hats,
> They look'd so taring fine O,
> I wish I had just such a one
> To give to my Jemimo.

Then, about 1825 Edmund Munroe and David Francis, Boston booksellers and publishers, put out *Mother Goose's Quarto, or Melodies Complete*, and though it was only a small book (about 128 pages) it was the largest collection of rhymes that had yet appeared. It contained most of the *Mother Goose's Melody* rhymes that Isaiah Thomas had reprinted from Newbery, but added others, some from the English *Songs for the Nursery* (Benjamin Tabart, 1805). It included a pedlar's song which gives a glimpse of children's toys of the time—"babies," pipes, "trunks to fill with weekly pence," plumed horses, windmills, toy soldiers, guns and horses.

175

We too often imagine that children's literature is completely distinct from adult literature, but in the late nineteenth century there was great overlap between the two. Children read adult books, and adults were enchanted by children's stories. According to the historian Anne Scott MacLeod, this was a form of romantic escapism typical of its time, but the observation remains true today. Many parents are great admirers of Dr. Seuss, Maurice Sendak, A. A. Milne, Beatrix Potter, and others (1994).

Children in Fiction and Fact

Anne Scott MacLeod

What they read was a great grab bag of material, good, bad, and mediocre, adult and juvenile, books and magazines. Children of the time read, as reading children always do, whatever they could put their hands on, mixing levels and qualities entirely without prejudice. Edna Ferber, for example: "Our reading was undirected, haphazard. . . . By the time I was nine I had read all of Dickens, but I also adored the Five Little Pepper books, the St. Nicholas magazine, all of Louisa May Alcott, and the bound copies of Harper's Bazaar, *Hans Brinker and the Silver Skates*, the novels of The Duchess [a popular romance writer of the day]. . . . Good and bad, adult or infantile, I read all the books in the house, all the books in the store stock, all the books in the very inadequate public library." Another avid reader found her way into the public library stacks. "I went through the juveniles in a few weeks and started on the adult books. I began neatly with A. . . . I read all of Thomas Bailey Aldrich, and through a lot of A's to the B's and started with Cousin Bette. . . . the head librarian called on Mama to see what should be done."

The list of authors grows familiar: Shakespeare, Thackeray, George Eliot, Alcott, Dickens and the Brontës, Hawthorne, Cooper, and Robert Louis Stevenson. So does the eclectic approach: "I do not remember," wrote Mary Ellen Chase, "that I was conscious of any difference in treatment between *Bleak House* and *Little Women*, between George Eliot and Sophie May, that I regarded one as duller than the other [or] more difficult to 'get into.' They were all stories. If they took me into a different world . . . I gloried in the . . . transference; if they related experiences I had had, I felt a . . . sense of companionship and sympathy." . . .

It is not difficult to know why children read adult books. They read them because they were there to be read, because they told stories, because they opened windows on a world of fact and fantasy that transcended daily life—all the reasons people read in any time. That so many adults read children's books, not just to children but for their own pleasure, is more surprising. To understand the widespread adult interest in children's literature one must look at the cultural mood of the late nineteenth century, when that interest was one part of a more general view of child and adult life.

The era was the high point in American romanticization of childhood. Conventional opinion idealized childhood as a free, golden period when children were close to God and nature, when "the real business of life . . . [was] play." At the popular level, the romantic outlook was sentimental, dwelling on children's beauty and innocence. At the aesthetic level, romanticism went farther, surrounding childhood with an aura of myth, seeing in children the elemental qualities of nature unspoiled.

The view of adult life was darker. The twilight of Victorianism found many Americans weary of unbridled materialism and political corruption. The affluent classes feared that their cushioned lives insulated them from "real" experience and that the strictures of Victorian mores flattened emotional life. They hated industrial ugliness. Even more; in spite of exuberant economic success, late nineteenth-century America was beset by social strains: poverty, slums, exploited labor, destitute children, urban crime, and growing class conflict. By the 1890s, consciousness of all these ills was high. Reaction and reform efforts marked American society to the eve of World War I.

Reaction included a cultural outlook widely shared in the middle and upper classes that has been characterized by one historian as "antimodernism," by others as anti-Victorianism. Either term suggests the rising criticism of American society, a criticism that had much to do with shaping cultural tastes in the late nineteenth century. Edith Wharton's autobiography speaks of the "impoverished emotional atmosphere" of old New York. "The average well-to-do New Yorker of my childhood," she wrote, "was . . . starved for a sight of the high gods. Beauty, passion and danger were automatically excluded from . . . life." In search of "beauty, passion and danger," American literary taste turned from the present to the distant past, from complexity to simplicity. Readers deserted domestic realism for myth, folktale, and historical romance, where they hoped to find "the childhood of the race." They admired heroic action, moral grandeur, and emotional openness. Blackmore's *Lorna Doone* was an example, recommended for what one critic called its "manly hero . . . of brawn and heart equally well tempered." Medievalism had a great vogue as late Victorians, looking for the virtues they believed lost in their own time, constructed a highly idealized (and highly inaccurate) idea of medieval society as simple and direct, childlike in its robust emotions and love of action. Medieval myth and legend, reshaped to nineteenth-century sensibilities, came in floods: *The Song of Roland, Robin Hood, King Arthur, Tristan and Isolde*; as epic poetry in *Idylls of the King*, as opera in Wagner's *Ring Cycle*, as children's fare in Howard Pyle's buoyant versions of Malory and the Robin Hood legends, and Sidney Lanier's *Boys' King Arthur*, dense with Victorian renderings of medieval English. "Damsel, as for to tell thee my name, I take no great force: truly, my name is Sir Lancelot du Lake." A good many critics suggested that such literature had a therapeutic effect. G. Stanley Hall, the psychologist often credited with "inventing" adolescence, believed that medieval legends and folk literature would elevate the adolescent imagination. . . .

Families could read together because different generations enjoyed the same literature; they shared an aesthetic. For a decade or so on either side of the turn of the century, there was a community of literary tastes among adults and children greater than ever before or since. Adults and children alike took pleasure in strong narratives, romantic characters, high adventure, and an idealized picture of the world, both contemporary and historical. Many of the best-known authors of the time wrote for both adults and children. The *St. Nicholas Magazine*, a spectacularly successful periodical for children, asked for and got contributions from the most respected writers of the period: Kipling, Twain, Burnett, and Cable, to name but a few.

A romantic view of childhood made adults susceptible to books about children as well. Adults willingly read novels with children as main characters if the children were lovable and the story sentimental. *Rebecca of Sunnybrook Farm, Little Lord Fauntleroy*, and *Captain January* were as familiar to adults as to children. It was surely adult taste that raised *Little Lord Fauntleroy* to the status of a classic; the Burnett book that passed from child to child, now as then, is not *Fauntleroy* but *The Secret Garden*. No doubt children—some children, anyway—enjoyed *Peter Pan*, but it was adults who flocked to the theaters to see the play (with children, of course, but also without them), and it was adults who thought it said something true about childhood. When the play was first produced in London, in 1904, the *Daily Telegraph* proclaimed it "so true, so natural, so touching that it brought the audience to the writer's feet." The response, like much of the literature, was entirely transatlantic. When the play reached America, there was an equal outburst of enthusiasm. The American magazine, *Outlook*, called *Peter Pan* "a breath of fresh air . . . by the writer who . . . has most truly kept the heart and mind of a child."

The *Outlook*'s words go to the core of late nineteenth-century feeling about childhood. In a better world, the crystalline qualities of childhood would not disappear with maturity; adults would be as spontaneous and as innocently joyful as children. It is not easy to imagine Robin Hood in nineteenth-century dress, but he represented the ideal: a boyish heart and mind in manly form. The romantic view held, not only that the best adults retained much of the child in them, but that the truest literary taste was interchangeable with a child's; the best books for children were also good for adults. "Older people," wrote Kate Douglas Wiggin, "can always read with pleasure the best children's books. . . . It would not bore you . . . to be shut up for a day or two with nothing but *Robinson Crusoe, Aesop's Fables, Arabian Nights*, Kingsley's *Water Babies, Alice in Wonderland*, Hawthorne's *Wonder Book* and *Tanglewood Tales*, Andersen's and Grimm's Fairy Tales, *Two Years Before the Mast* . . . the simpler poems of Scott, Lowell, Whittier, or Longfellow, and a sheaf of songs from the Elizabethan poets. If, indeed, you would be dreadfully bored, it is conceivable that you are a bit pedantic, stiff, and academic in your tastes, or a bit given to literary game of very high and 'gamy' flavor, so that French 'made dishes' have spoiled you for Anglo-Saxon roast beef." Like her list of titles, Wiggin's sentiments in this passage are characteristic of her time and class, including the preference for hearty, Anglo-Saxon influences and the slight scorn for those who could not share the tastes of childhood.

176

Some parents would be pleased if their children read anything at all. Children today are inundated with commercial toys and entertainments that can outshine the fantasies provided by books. The historian Gary Cross discusses the crossover between toys and media events that often defines the world of childhood today (1997).

Kids' Stuff

Toys and the Changing World of American Childhood

Gary Cross

No American child in the years between 1977 and 1983 could have avoided George Lucas's *Star Wars* trilogy. American boys, especially, were inundated with toy figures, vehicles, and playsets built around the rivalry of Darth Vader and Luke Skywalker. By 1987 some ninety-four figures and sixty accessories had been manufactured by Kenner, Lucasfilm's exclusive toy licensee. The first two Star Wars movies earned $870 million by 1983 when the final one was released. But the licensed products raked in $2 billion. While delays in production prevented most eager buyers from getting their Star Wars figures in time for the holidays in 1977, a full range of licensed products were already in stores by the time *The Return of the Jedi* appeared in May 1983. Jedi drinking glasses, toothbrushes, and cookies as well as Darth Vader telephones made Star Wars characters ubiquitous. And although these licensed products were in effect free commercials for Star Wars toys, Kenner still spent $12 million in an advertising campaign in 1983. In an effort to revive the sales magic of the movie, Lucas reran *Star Wars* and *The Empire Strikes Back* on TV in early 1984. Each film featured new "toyetic" personalities, vehicles, and other gadgets—easily converted into molded plastic. The first film produced toy robots (R2-D2 and C-3PO), bad guy "Storm Troopers," and, of course, heroic Luke Skywalker and Princess Leia. Later films added TIE Fighters, Scout Walkers, and Ewoks. These toys gave a generation of American youth the opportunity to reenact their favorite scenes from the movie. Star Wars surely set the pace as fantasymakers rushed to invent knockoffs of this science fiction classic, each with accompanying lines of toys.

The impact of *Star Wars* is best seen in the transformation of Hasbro's G. I. Joe line. After years of seeking an answer to antimilitarism, Hasbro discontinued Joe in 1978. But the success of Kenner's Star Wars toys and a political climate after

Ronald Reagan's victory in 1980 more sympathetic to military spending gave Hasbro the opportunity to reintroduce G. I. Joe in 1982. Luckily, they relaunched Joe in the lull between the second and third Star Wars movies. But this time he was neither a soldier doll nor an adventurer but part of a team of fantastic fighters in a Mobile Strike Force. These characters with charming names like Flash and Grunt faced COBRA, an equally determined cadre of bad guys, in futuristic battle gear and settings. No longer was Joe an individual. G. I. Joe was only a trademark, covering a number of constantly evolving matched teams of foes, each with their own accessories of firepower and vehicles. And the Joes had shrunk to the 3¾-inch height made standard by Kenner's Star Wars figures. They were cheap to make, easy to collect, and appropriate for "miniworld" play.

The new G.I. Joe became the bestselling toy of the 1982 holiday season. No wonder. Hasbro had launched a $4 million advertising campaign for the 1982 holidays designed to reach 95 percent of the country's five- to eight-year-old boys fifty times. By 1983 Joe had a TV show. In 1984 G. I. Joe logos appeared on fifty licensed products. By 1988 Hasbro claimed that two-thirds of American boys between the ages of five and eleven owned Joes. . . .

Star Wars and G. I. Joe were just the beginning. Mattel's He-Man and Masters of the Universe, appearing in 1982, closely paralleled the Star Wars formula: the youthful, blond, and muscular He-Man and his team of good guys (Man-At-Arms, Man-E-Faces, Ram Man, the fighting falcon, Zoar, and Teela, a warrior goddess) fought the aged, bony, and evil Skeletor and his horde (Beastman, Trapjaw, Tri-Klops, the "feathered fiend," Screech, and Evil-Lyn, another goddess warrior). A major feature of Mattel's line was Castle Grayskull, shaped like a mountain with a dungeon tower, a landing platform for a "Fright Fighter" vehicle, and a "Viper Tower" (with a "vicious serpent head" that children could spin). Grayskull was the center of the fray in a "fantastic universe beyond all time." "Who will control its hidden secrets and mystical power?" Mattel asked children. "You decide!" He-Man reached the pinnacle of *Toys and Hobby World*'s "Top TV Toys" list in June 1983 (even beating Star Wars). That year Mattel sold 23 million Masters of the Universe action figures. But Mattel went much further when, in the fall of 1983, it delivered a daily syndicated cartoon starring He-Man.

There were many imitations. The best known were based on a Japanese toy novelty—a die-cast vehicle that turned into a semi-human robot warrior with a few deft tugs on wheels and other parts. The first of these was Hasbro's Transformer line, appearing in 1984. The back story, the adventure that gave the toy characters their roles and situations for children to reenact in play, has a familiar ring to it. The citizens of Cybertron were divided into the "good" Autobots and the "evil" Decepticons who, having landed on earth, made war on each other. The Autobots naturally took the shape of cars and the Decepticons, airplanes. Each transformer came with a "Tec Spec Chart" detailing its amazing capacities and a "Bio Card" featuring its "personality." . . .

Drawing upon the action-figure formula, toymakers also shaped little girls' play around licensed characters and fairytale story lines. In 1980 a studio at

American Greeting Cards (known as Those Characters from Cleveland) developed the image of a cute red-headed girl in old-fashioned clothes called Strawberry Shortcake. This was something of a specialty at American Greetings. In 1967 this company featured the homespun image of Holly Hobbie on greeting cards. It was so successful that in 1973 Holly became a licensed character for dolls and plush toys. Strawberry Shortcake similarly exploited a sentimental theme of innocent girlhood. But the new image was a far more sophisticated product. Those Characters from Cleveland used the strawberry theme after survey research showed that little girls identified with strawberries. The character was designed to convey emotions of "security and affection."

More important, from the beginning Strawberry Shortcake was created not merely as a greeting card theme but as a licensing property to be used in toys, dolls, and juvenile furniture. Those Characters from Cleveland charted a three- to five-year product-development cycle. They recognized the synergy created in multiple licenses. In a 1984 publicity brochure they bragged: "The cumulative effect of advertising by *all* licensees and the licensor creates an overall impression that $1 + 1 = 3$." Strawberry Shortcake also differed from Holly Hobbie in other ways. She quickly found "friends": Lime Chiffon and Raspberry Tart joined her in the magical realm of Strawberryland. Kenner won the license to re-create all of these characters in injection mold plastic. And in 1980 Strawberry Shortcake and her pals appeared on TV. In 1983 the line was freshened up with six new friends, including Crepe Suzette with her French poodle and Almond Tea with her pet Marza Panda. As minidolls and playsets, Strawberry Shortcake became a girls' version of Star Wars—a miniworld of playacting fantasy stories.

Following on this success came American Greeting's Care Bears, again in association with Kenner toys. In 1982 Those Characters from Cleveland tested a number of prototypes before finding the perfect look for Kenner's array of hard plastic minidolls. Licensees and American Greetings spent $122.5 million to launch a wide-ranging product line (everything from school supplies to plush animals) for 1983. Although in the teddy bear tradition, Care Bears had more in common with the new G.I. Joe. The Care Bears were a collection of twelve figures with moveable limbs. Each was distinguished by a symbol on the belly signifying a different positive emotion. A child could hardly play with just one or two. Like the action figures, the bears were to work as a team to overcome the killjoy Vovocaine Numb and other grinch-like figures. In the spring of 1986 a Care Bear movie was released, supplementing the six TV specials that had appeared by the previous fall. Each reinforced the story of the bears that cared enough to bring love to the world. A major competitor to the bears was Hasbro's My Little Pony line of pastel minifigures. These diminutive horses with their long and colorful manes combined "friendship" and grooming play. Forty million units were sold between 1983 and 1986. In hopes of extending the line, Hasbro produced a movie in June 1986 and a new secondary line, Flutter Ponies (Pegasus-like winged figures).

177

Children today are enmeshed in the visual media to a much greater degree than ever before as television re-creates the child's imagination. In this Philadelphia Inquirer *(1998) article Don Steinberg discusses how the children's network Nickelodeon uses intensive marketing research on children to achieve its phenomenal success.*

What Makes Nick Tick

Nickelodeon Is a Sensibility, a World, an All-Empowering Club: It's CNN for Children

Don Steinberg

So, sure, *Titanic* has reaped more than half a billion dollars at the box office for Paramount Studios and its mothership, Viacom Inc., transforming the most expensive movie in history into the highest grossing. And that's before *Titanic* reaches the shelves of Viacom's 4,300 Blockbuster Video stores in 20 countries (supposedly there's a Blockbuster within a 10-minute drive of every major neighborhood in the United States).

Still, if you want to understand where this $13 billion media conglomerate is pinning its hopes for the future, it helps to be at the edge of New York's financial district, sitting on the floor at the All-Day Nursery preschool where Jonathan and Alexa, both 4, are surrounded by three researchers.

A video camera draws a bead on the preschoolers to record their responses for later analysis, while a pair of 20something research assistants pull out clipboards to take notes. They're here to road test a forthcoming episode of *Blue's Clues*, television's most popular show with 2- to 5-year-olds.

Since its September 1996 debut on Viacom's Nickelodeon cable network, *Blue's Clues* has soared in the ratings to regularly whip mainstays like PBS's *Sesame Street*, *Barney* and *Mr. Rogers*. The show has been universally lauded by parents and educators as a breakthrough in preschool programming. . . .

It's no surprise that *Blue's Clues* is popular with these kids and millions like them. It's engaging, it's smart and the show's colorful characters—Blue, Gingerbread Boy, Tickety Tock and even Steve—are cuter than a guy in a dinosaur suit.

But the show is more than popular: It exemplifies the two practices that have helped Nickelodeon explode into prominence—not merely as the most-watched children's television programmer, not merely as the leader in advertising revenue among cable channels (having just passed ESPN), but as one of the hottest emerging consumer brands in the world.

What Nick does so successfully is combine obsessive research (knowing its audience) with relentless brand-building (seizing its audience). Nickelodeon's explorations into kids' culture—their values, habits, fears, favorite products—make Margaret Mead's fieldwork for *Coming of Age in Samoa* seem lackadaisical.

Each episode of *Blue's Clues*, for example, is tested for preschooler responses at four different stages during production—unprecedented in the annals of childrens' programming. Then the shows' producers actually incorporate the findings into episodes. In hundreds of organized research sessions a year, kids of all ages tell it all to Nick, on subjects ranging from specific shows and promotions to what they wear and read and buy, and what their parents let them—or don't let them—do.

When, in the early days, children said they wanted a show featuring crazy sports, Nick created *Guts*—kids slam-dunking baskets while bouncing from bungee cords. In another "ideation" session, kids requested a show that was scary—but not so creepy that it would frighten their "little brothers." This evolved into *Are You Afraid of the Dark*? When panelists previewing early *Clarissa Explains It All* episodes said the father character didn't talk like a real one, Nick not only rewrote scripts, but replaced the actor.

"It's amazing what they'll tell us, without even thinking that we might tell their parents," whispers Bruce Friend, Nickelodeon's vice president for research, shaking his head behind a two-way mirror at a session where a roomful of 9-year-old boys are boasting that they watch Comedy Central's foul-mouthed cartoon *South Park*.

The aim of the research is to convert juvenile brainwaves into TV airwaves as faithfully as possible. And Nickelodeon seems to have found the right frequency. The research process has helped the network produce one gem after another: *Rugrats*, which depicts the bemusement of toddlers in a ridiculous adult world; *Doug*, conveying the animated angst of a thoughtful preteen; *Clarissa Explains It All*, the world of a bright and funny girl; *Ren & Stimpy*, a visually arresting cartoon gross-out; *Hey Arnold*!, more animated angst of a thoughtful preteen. And *Kenan & Kel, Pete & Pete, Angry Beavers, All That!* and *Kablam*!

Nick knows what appeals to its audience—sympathetic, familiar characters, hip design, authority-tweaking attitude—well enough to lock in its viewers, confidently enough to go, on occasion, right up to the edge of parental acceptance without ever crossing that line.

But besides helping Nick create shows that work, the intimate knowledge of its audience has allowed the network to define itself masterfully and develop an intensely loyal following as a brand—as trustworthy a name to its viewers as Betty Crocker was to Mom's mom.

Now, when I refer to Nickelodeon as a brand, I don't really mean the more than 2,000 licensed Nickelodeon products: the Rugrats bedroom sets and leisure wear, the Rugrats Oral-B toothpaste, the Rugrats Kraft Macaroni and Cheese.

Neither am I referring to the three Nickelodeon retail stores that have opened so far to sell Nick merchandise (100 more stores are planned), nor the theme-park attractions around the world, such as U Pick Nick at Dollywood and the Nickelodeon TV Machine at Sega World in Australia. Because merchandising is nothing new. Sesame Street has so many licensed products, the Count would lose count, and Warner Bros. has Looney Tunes stores wherever more expensive T-shirts are sold, and Disney is theme parks—but not any of that gives kids the feeling of ownership and membership they get from Nick.

By the Nickelodeon brand, I mean more than just a program lineup and a bunch of characters on T-shirts. What Nickelodeon has been able to accomplish by probing children's heads is to become a sensibility, a world, a subversive and empowering club. The name Nickelodeon promises kids something—about the next show or contest or off-air Nick project—that Disney and PBS and other TV programmers don't come close to approaching. Small wonder that last year Nickelodeon was inducted into the Marketing Hall of Fame, billed as "the highest honor a brand can receive." Nick was enshrined with Kodak, which began its marketing efforts in 1885.

178

Merlyn's Pen *is a bimonthly magazine featuring young people's essays, short stories, and poems; there are different editions for middle school and high school. The three selections here give a sense of the impressive literary talent and range of concerns of middle schoolers.*

Children's Literary Voices

Merlyn's Pen

Bluma Lesch, "Rain"

Our '86 Honda swishes through a puddle, spraying tiny drops of water into the bushes by the road. Green bushes turned black by heavy dark clouds, dark dark just like the negative space on a photocopy, like spilt ink you can't rub off. The clouds have come down to Earth today, wrapped in the dark as if they need protection.

We drive down the street, the one I don't know the name of, past the doctor's office, to I don't know where. And I don't care. The light from cars and street-lights streaks out in the rain like a washed-out painting, and the water runs down our windshield in short little dashes. Watching the raindrops race, I can lose myself. Watching the raindrops race, I can go away and dream of a place under a tree where the sun shines, like in a fairy tale. The grass is soft and green but silvery white too, like olive leaves. The wind is strong but not cold. And the sound of rain in the background makes me happy.

I am always dreaming of Somewhere Else, a place where I am the hero of a great adventure. But really—I am glad that I'm here, even if my brother is too, even if the days come and go with no more adventure than that yellow Post-it on the dashboard. Because someday something will happen, something great and big and important, and then I will think back and dream of a place where nothing ever did.

Bluma Lesch,
Eighth grade, Head-Royce School,
Oakland, California

Stephanie Tesch, "Wonderful"

Sometimes I wonder
if you hold
in your hands
imaginary strings
that are attached to
my lips,
because every time
I see you,
I smile.

— *Stephanie Tesch,*
Ninth grade, Bishop Guertin High School,
Nashua, New Hampshire

Stephanie Grant, "Popularity: An Outsider's View"

"Why do people want to be popular?" I ask myself, staring at my bedroom ceiling. Why do the grades someone receives have such a big influence over whether people like them or not? Why is it that because I'm smart, I'm considered a nerd and consequently I have had trouble making friends? Sitting there trying to answer these questions, a voice keeps saying, deep down inside me, "That's just the way it is." Over and over and over again.

It all started when I was five years old. Back in my old school I had many friends, people I had known as long as I could remember. I joined the kindergarten class at my new school during the fourth quarter. In addition to not knowing anyone, I was a year younger than everyone in the class. The kids in my class that year didn't really bother with me during the last three months of school. In fact, the only time they ever said anything to me was when a few got mad because I had taken a seat at "their" snack table one day. They told me that I couldn't sit with them because I wasn't their friend. I silently wondered why they wouldn't want me as a friend because they didn't even know me. At the time, I thought it was acceptable for kids to ignore the newcomer. After all, I wouldn't have wanted some newcomer stealing my friends away from me, either.

My experiences with those people didn't end there. By fifth grade the very same kids that snubbed me in kindergarten were considered to be popular by the majority of our class. This meant that most, but not all, the fifth-grade students wanted to be their friends. Those who didn't want to be their friend still knew better than to publicly go against the wishes of anyone who was thought of as popular. If they did, they'd be considered "different," which also meant unlikable to most of my classmates. This became a problem because that year the zoning districts for our schools were changed, and I found myself going to a newly built school. Again it was my turn to be the new kid because I had left all of my friends back at the old school. This time around, though, my experience with the popular crowd was something that I'll never forget.

The first couple weeks at my new school were very routine, or as routine as things can be at a new school. I hadn't made friends with any of my new classmates yet. I had found a couple of them to be pretty nice during the first few weeks of school. The two people I was a little shy about meeting in my class were absolutely the most popular girls in my whole grade. In addition to being the most popular girls in the grade, they were also best friends, and they were learning how to manipulate others with their popularity.

One day in October, while my class was standing in line waiting to go outside for recess, the two girls were standing next to me. They were talking about the usual things that were on the mind of an eleven-year-old at the time.

"School's such a pain. I got a C on the math test from last week," said one girl.

The other replied, "Oh, I know. It was so unfair. Hey, when is our next soccer game?"

"Next Saturday, like usual. Hey, did you see that ugly outfit on Michelle today? It was so ugly. It seemed to suit her looks, though."

This conversation was carried on for several minutes, and I gradually became less and less interested in it. I began to ask myself why they had the power to determine who should have friends and who shouldn't. While I was searching in my mind for a rational answer, one of the pair turned to me and asked me what grade I had received on the latest math test.

I reluctantly replied, "An A."

While they gawked at my response, the same girl said to me, "Hey, did you know you're fat?"

The other girl laughed at this comment and others joined in; they were all laughing at her statement. I stood there dumbfounded. I didn't know how to respond to such a needlessly cruel comment. As I thought over what the girl had just asked me, I realized they had started talking about who they thought of as nerds and who should be added to the category. My response to her question about the grade had sealed my fate for the next two years of school.

That day I had been added to the popular person's category of geeks. The laughter continued around me as my self-confidence turned to slush and melted away on the floor beneath their mocking gazes. My thoughts then turned to, "What did I do to them to deserve such a comment? Did I wear something that looks bad today, like Michelle did?" Eventually I started thinking that I might truly be fat, like they had said.

My world changed overnight as I realized that from that day on I would never be really good friends with anyone who was friends with the two girls or anyone who wanted to be friends with them. I had been deemed "unlikable" by those girls, and because of their popularity, I would have very few friends for the rest of fifth grade.

That year I ended up with two friends—a girl and a boy. The boy was smarter than I and was ridiculed just as much as I was that year. "Oh, look," they'd say, "it's the dork and his girlfriend." They didn't understand the truth: he was one of the few people who would listen to me. The three of us and a few others were thought of as the brains in our class. We were the first done with all of our work, and we were always the high scorers on the tests. I suppose that information alone was enough to classify us as outcasts. I never understood why they didn't want to be our friends. What they did to me was make me think there really *was* something wrong with me. What other reason did they have for not liking me? They didn't take the time to get to know me, just like in kindergarten.

It still bothers me when I look back on it all, like now while I'm lying in my bed trying to go to sleep. For the most part, I believe I have grown as a person after my experiences with those people. My self-confidence improved greatly by the time sixth grade had started. By then I realized that those people had no reason to say what they did; I was not fat, and there's nothing bad about being smart. I learned what really mattered was what I thought of myself. When I switched schools again at the beginning of seventh grade, I grew even more because there was a whole new group of people and I could have a fresh new start with them. I made new friends around whom I could act like myself, without feeling like an outcast. Everything has been improving since then because high school is even better than middle school—I have even better friends.

The thing that scares me about how popularity influences people is how cruel it can make them be toward others. People don't seem to think about whom they might be hurting with their words, or how the damage they do might never be erased. The other thing that bothers me is how one day I sat next to one of the two popular girls who gave me such a hard time in fifth grade, and she didn't even recognize me. Though what she did took place four years ago, I still remember her clearly because of it. I find it interesting that I let her change my life so much, and all because of one little laugh. She doesn't realize the reason I am proud of who I am today is because of something she did to me so long ago. She has no clue how much pain she caused me when she laughed at what her friend said to me. She has no idea that because she was popular and the influence she had over people was so great, that by laughing, she made my fifth-grade year in elementary school a year I now want to forget.

Stephanie Grant lives in Oakton, Virginia, and wrote this essay as a ninth-grader at Thomas Jefferson High School for Science and Technology in Alexandria. She is a member of the school varsity softball team and plays alto sax in the marching band. Sometimes in her free time, she states, she takes a flying lesson in preparation for her pilot's license.

Sources

Sources listed here are in the public domain unless otherwise indicated.

Part 1: Childbirth and Infancy

Anne Bradstreet, *The Complete Works of Anne Bradstreet*, ed. Joseph R. McElrath, Jr., and Allan P. Robb (Boston: Twayne Publishers, 1981), 179–80, 196, 206–7. © 1981 by Twayne Publishers.

Catherine M. Scholten, *Childbearing in American Society, 1650–1850* (New York: New York University Press, 1985), 9–13. © 1985 by New York University Press. Reprinted by permission.

Judith Walzer Leavitt, *Brought to Bed: Childbearing in America, 1750–1950* (New York: Oxford University Press, 1986), 98–100, 109–10, 116–17. © 1986 by Judith Walzer Leavitt. Reprinted by permission of Oxford University Press, Inc.

Sally McMillen, ''Mothers' Sacred Duty: Breast-Feeding Patterns among Middle- and Upper-Class Women in the Antebellum South,'' *Journal of Southern History* 51 (August 1985): 338–39, 341–43, 347–48, 355–56. © 1985 by the Southern Historical Association. Reprinted by permission of the Managing Editor.

Lynn Y. Weiner, ''Reconstructing Motherhood: The La Leche League in Postwar America,'' *Journal of American History* 80 (March 1994): 1357–60, 1362–63, 1364–66, 1366, 1367–68. © 1994 by the Journal of American History. Reprinted by permission.

Charles Petit, ''Amazing Births,'' *San Francisco Chronicle*, May 8, 1981, A1. © 1981 by The San Francisco Chronicle. Reprinted by permission.

''Woman Gives Birth to Baby Conceived outside the Body,'' *New York Times*, July 26, 1978, A1. © 1978 by The New York Times. Reprinted by permission.

Melissa Moore Bodin, ''My Turn: The Eggs, Embryos and I,'' *Newsweek*, July 28, 1997, 14–15. © 1997 by Newsweek, Inc. All rights reserved. Reprinted by permission.

Margaret Talbot, ''The Egg Women,'' *New Republic*, March 16, 1998, 42. © 1998 by The New Republic, Inc. Reprinted by permission of The New Republic.

''Three's a Crowd,'' *Newsweek*, September 1, 1986, 68–69, 70. © 1986 by Newsweek, Inc. All rights reserved. Reprinted by permission.

John Locke, *Some Thoughts Concerning Education; and, Of the Conduct of the Understanding*, ed. Ruth Grant and Nathan Tarcov (Indianapolis: Hackett Publishing, 1996), 58–59, 83–84. © 1996 by Hackett Publishing.

Maria Edgeworth, *Works*, vol. 1 (Boston: Samuel Parker, 1825), 19–20, 23, 28–29. © 1825 by Samuel Parker.

L. Emmett Holt, *The Care and Feeding of Children* (New York: D. Appleton, 1923), 192–95. © 1923 by D. Appleton.

John B. Watson, *Psychological Care of Infant and Child* (New York: W. W. Norton, 1928), 79–82. © 1928 by W. W. Norton and Company, Inc. Reprinted by permission of W. W. Norton and Company, Inc.

Nancy Pottishman Weiss, ''The Mother-Child Dyad Revisited: Perceptions of Mothers and Children in Twentieth Century Child-Rearing Manuals,'' *Journal of Social Issues* 34 (1978): 31–33, 35–36, 39–42. © 1978 by Blackwell Publishers. Reprinted by permission.

Joseph M. Hawes, *Children between the Wars: American Childhood, 1920–1940* (New York: Twayne Publishers, 1997), 72–73, 79, 80–81, 81–82. © 1997 by Twayne Publishers. Reprinted by permission of Macmillan Library Reference USA.

Jean Piaget, *The Construction of Reality in the Child*, trans. Margaret Cook (New York: Basic Books, 1954), 101–3, 350–52. © 1954 by Basic Books, Inc. Reprinted by permission of Basic Books, a member of Perseus Books, L.L.C.

Jerome Kagan, *The Nature of the Child* (New York: Basic Books, 1984), 26–31, 70–72. © 1984 by Basic Books. Reprinted by permission of Basic Books, a member of Perseus Books, L.L.C.

T. Berry Brazelton, *Working and Caring* (Reading, MA: Addison-Wesley, 1985), xix–xxiii. © 1995 by T. Berry Brazelton. Reprinted by permission of Perseus Books Publishers, a member of Perseus Books, L.L.C.

Part 2: Boys and Girls

Anne Bradstreet, *The Complete Works of Anne Bradstreet*, ed. Joseph R. McElrath, Jr., and Allan P. Robb (Boston: Twayne Publishers, 1981), 184–86. © 1981 by Twayne Publishers.

A. North, ''Breeching Little Ffrank,'' in *The Penguin Book of Childhood* ed. Michael Rosen (New York: Viking, 1994), 49–50. © 1994 by Viking.

Karin Calvert, *Children in the House: The Material Culture of Early Childhood, 1600–1900* (Boston: Northeastern University Press, 1992), 79–33. © 1992 by Karin Calvert. Reprinted by permission of Northeastern University Press.

Anne Scott MacLeod, ''American Girlhood in the Nineteenth Century: Caddie Woodlawn's Sisters,'' in *American Childhood: Essays on Children's Literature of the Nineteenth and Twentieth Centuries* (Athens: University of Georgia Press, 1994), 7–11. © 1994 by the University of Georgia Press. Reprinted by permission of the Strong Museum, Rochester, New York.

Daniel T. Rodgers, *The Work Ethic in Industrial America, 1850–1920* (Chicago: University of Chicago Press, 1974), 127–28, 132–34, 136, 139–42. © 1974, 1978 by University of Chicago Press. Reprinted by permission.

Brothers Grimm, *Grimms' Fairy Tales* (New York: Grosset and Dunlap, 1945), 101–6. © 1945 by Grosset and Dunlap.

Louisa May Alcott, *Little Women, Good Wives, Wise Men* (London: Octopus Books, 1978), 15–16, 93. © 1978 by Octopus Books.

Carolyn Keene, *The Secret of the Old Clock* (New York: Grosset and Dunlap, 1959), 59–62. © 1930, 1959 by Simon and Schuster, Inc. Reprinted by permission of Pocket Books, a Division of Simon and Schuster, Inc. Nancy Drew is a registered trademark of Simon and Schuster, Inc.

Sigmund Freud, *A General Introduction to Psychoanalysis* (Garden City, NY: Garden City Publishing Company, 1943), 287, 290, 291–93. © 1920, 1935 by Edward L. Bernays. Reprinted by permission of Sigmund Freud © Copyrights, The Institute of Psycho-Analysis and The Hogarth Press.

Karen Horney, *Feminine Psychology* (New York: W. W. Norton, 1967), 57–58, 147–48, 149–50, 155, 160–61. © 1967 by W. W. Norton and Company, Inc. Reprinted by permission of W. W. Norton and Company, Inc.

Margaret Mead, *Male and Female* (New York: William Morrow, 1949), 136–38, 141–42.

© 1949 by Margaret Mead. Reprinted by permission of William Morrow and Company, Inc.

Erik H. Erikson, *Childhood and Society* (New York: W. W. Norton, 1963), 97–100, 101–6, 108. W. Norton and Company, Inc., renewed © 1978, 1991 by Erik H. Erikson. Reprinted by permission of W. W. Norton and Company, Inc.

Carol Gilligan, *In a Different Voice* (Cambridge: Harvard University Press, 1993), 31–33, 35. © 1982, 1993 by Carol Gilligan. Reprinted by permission of the publisher.

How Schools Shortchange Girls (New York: Marlowe and Company, 1995), 25–26, 118–22, 127–28. © 1992 by the American Association of University Women Educational Foundation. Reprinted by permission of the American Association of University Women Educational Foundation, 1111 16th Street, N.W., Washington, D.C. 20036, (202) 785–7700.

Part 3: Adolescence and Youth

Ellen K. Rothman, *Hands and Hearts: A History of Courtship in America* (Cambridge: Harvard University Press, 1987), 90–94. © 1984 by Ellen K. Rothman. Reprinted by permission of Basic Books, a member of Perseus Books, L.L.C.

Emmy E. Werner, *Reluctant Witnesses: Children's Voices from the Civil War* (Boulder: Westview Press, 1998), 8–10, 11–12. © 1998 by Westview Press. Reprinted by permission of Westview Press, a member of Perseus Books, L.L.C.

John Demos and Virginia Demos, "Adolescence in Historical Perspective," *Journal of Marriage and the Family* 31 (November 1969): 632, 632–36, 636–38. © 1969 by the National Council on Family Relations, 3989 Central Ave. NE, Suite 550, Minneapolis, MN 55421. Reprinted by permission.

G. Stanley Hall, *Adolescence* (New York: D. Appleton and Company, 1924), 240–41, 241–42, 250–52, 262–64. © 1904 by D. Appleton and Company.

Stephen A. Lassonde, "Should I Go, or Should I Stay? Adolescence, School Attainment, and Parent-Child Relations in Italian Immigrant Families of New Haven, 1900–1940," first appeared in *History of Education Quarterly* 38 (spring 1998): 37–38, 45–47, 49–50. © 1998 by History of Education Society. Reprinted by permission.

Frederic M. Thrasher, *The Gang* (Chicago: University of Chicago Press, 1927), 23–24, 26–27, 32–33. © 1927 and 1936 by the University of Chicago. All rights reserved. Reprinted by permission.

Margaret Mead, *Coming of Age in Samoa* (New York: William Morrow, 1964), 195–96, 197–98, 200–202, 213–14. © 1928, 1949, 1955, 1961, 1973 by Margaret Mead. Reprinted by permission of William Morrow and Company, Inc.

Erik H. Erikson, *Identity, Youth, and Crisis* (New York: W. W. Norton, 1968), 91–95, 96, 128–134, 135. © 1968 by W. W. Norton and Company, Inc. Reprinted by permission of W. W. Norton and Company, Inc.

Joan Jacobs Brumberg, *Fasting Girls* (New York: Plume, 1989), 27–33. © 1988, 1989 by Joan Jacobs Brumberg. Reprinted by permission of Georges Borchardt, Inc. for the author.

Mary Pipher, *Reviving Ophelia* (New York: Ballantine Books, 1994), 243–46, 247. © 1994 by Mary Pipher. Reprinted by permission of Putnam Berkley, a division of Penguin Putnam Inc.

Jane Mauldon, "Families Started by Teenagers," in *All Our Families: New Policies for a New Century*, ed. Mary Ann Mason, Arlene Skolnick, and Stephen D. Sugarman (New York: Oxford University Press, 1998), 39–43, 43–45, 46–47 39–47. © 1998 by Oxford University Press, Inc. Reprinted by permission of Oxford University Press, Inc.

Sharon Begley, "Why the Young Kill," *Newsweek*, May 3, 1999, 32–35. © 1999 by Newsweek, Inc. All rights reserved. Reprinted by permission.

F. Scott Fitzgerald, *This Side of Paradise* (New York: Charles Scribner's Sons, 1920), 64–66.

Carson McCullers, *The Member of the Wedding*, in *Collected Stories* (Boston: Houghton Mifflin, 1987), 271–74, 275–76. © 1946 by Carson McCullers, © renewed 1974 by Floria V. Lasky. Reprinted by permission of Houghton Mifflin Company. All rights reserved.

Claude Brown, *Manchild in the Promised Land* (New York: Macmillan, 1978), 269–71, 274–76, 278. © 1965 by Claude Brown. Reprinted by permission of Simon and Schuster, Inc.

Paul Monette, *Becoming a Man: Half a Life Story* (New York: Harcourt Brace Jovanovich, 1992), 105–7, 108–9, 129, 132–33. © 1992 by Paul Monette. Reprinted by permission of Harcourt Brace and Company.

D. James Romero, "Adulthood? Later, Dude," *Los Angeles Times*, March 21, 1997, E1. © 1997 by the Los Angeles Times. Reprinted by permission of the Los Angeles Times.

Part 4: Discipline

John Demos, *A Little Commonwealth: Family Life in Plymouth Colony* (New York: Oxford University Press, 1970), 100–103, 104–5. © 1970 by Oxford University Press, Inc. Reprinted by permission of Oxford University Press.

Robert H. Bremner, ed., *Children and Youth in America: A Documentary History*, vol. 1, *1600–1865* (Cambridge: Harvard University Press, 1970), 123–24. © 1970 by the American Public Health Association. Reprinted by permission of the publisher.

John Locke, *Some Thoughts Concerning Education; and, Of the Conduct of the Understanding*, ed. Ruth Grant and Nathan Tarcov (Indianapolis: Hackett Publishing, 1996), 76–79. © 1996 by Hackett Publishing.

Carl N. Degler, *At Odds: Women and the Family in America from the Revolution to the Present* (New York: Oxford University Press, 1980), 86–91. © 1980 by Carl N. Degler. Reprinted by permission of the publisher.

Horace Bushnell, *Christian Nurture* (New Haven: Yale University Press, 1947), 284–86.

Louisa May Alcott, *Little Women, Good Wives, Wise Men* (London: Octopus Books, 1978), 77–79. © 1978 by Octopus Books.

James W. C. Pennington, *The Fugitive Blacksmith or, Events in the History of James W. C. Pennington*, 2d ed. (London, 1849), in *African American Voices: The Life Cycle of Slavery*, ed. Steven Mintz (St. James, NY: Brandywine Press, 1993), 90–91.

Benjamin Spock, *Baby and Child Care* (New York: Simon and Schuster, 1976), 372–75. © 1945, 1946, 1957, 1968, 1976 by Benjamin Spock. Reprinted by permission of Pocket Books, a Division of Simon and Schuster, Inc.

Baker v. Owen, 395 F. Supp. 294 (M.D.N.C.), *aff'd without opinion*, 423 U.S. 907 (1975).

Annette Fuentes, "The Crackdown on Kids," *Nation*, June 15, 1998, 20. © 1998 by The Nation. Reprinted by permission of The Nation.

Part 5: Working Children

Mary Ann Mason, *From Father's Property to Children's Rights* (New York: Columbia University Press, 1994), 30–34. © 1994 by Columbia University Press. Reprinted by permission of the publisher.

Robert H. Bremner, ed., *Children and Youth in America: A Documentary History*, vol. 1, *1600–1865* (Cambridge: Harvard University Press, 1970), 7–8, 107–8, 149–51. © 1970 by the American Public Health Association. Reprinted by permission of the publisher.

Alexander Hamilton, "Report on Manufactures," in *The Annals of America*, vol. 3 (Chicago: Encyclopedia Britannica, 1976), 465–66.

Benjamin Franklin, *Autobiography and Other Writings*, ed. Kenneth Silverman (New York: Penguin, 1986), 12–14.

August Kohn, *The Cotton Mills of South Carolina* (Columbia, SC: Daggett Publishing Company, 1907), 102–3.

David Nasaw, *Children of the City* (New York: Oxford University Press, 1986) 52–57. © 1985 by David Nasaw. Reprinted by permission of Doubleday, a division of Random House, Inc.

Rose Cohen, *Out of the Shadow* (1918; reprint, Ithaca: Cornell University Press, 1995), 81–84, 87–90. © 1918 by George H. Doran Company.

Viviana A. Zelizer, *Pricing the Priceless Child: The Changing Social Value of Children* (New York: Basic Books, 1985), 56–60. © 1985 by Basic Books, Inc. Reprinted by permission of Basic Books, a member of Perseus Books, L.L.C.

Anne Moody, *Coming of Age in Mississippi* (New York: Laurel, 1976), 43–45. © 1968 by Anne Moody. Reprinted by permission of Doubleday, a division of Random House, Inc.

Paula S. Fass, *Outside In: Minorities and the Transformation of American Education* (New York: Oxford University Press, 1989), 122–24, 125–26. © 1989 by Paula S. Fass. Reprinted by permission of Oxford University Press.

Robert William Kirk, *Earning Their Stripes: The Mobilization of American Children in the Second World War* (New York: Peter Lang, 1994), 60–61, 63–65. © 1994 by Robert William Kirk. Reprinted by permission of the publisher.

Prince v. Massachusetts, 321 U.S. 158 (1944).

Samuel G. Freedman, *Small Victories* (New York: Harper Perennial, 1991), 199–200, 201–3. © 1990 by Samuel G. Freedman. Reprinted by permission of HarperCollins Publishers, Inc.

Part 6: Learning

Philippe Ariès, *Centuries of Childhood* (New York: Alfred A. Knopf, 1962), 411–13. © 1962 by Jonathan Cape Ltd. Reprinted by permission of Alfred A. Knopf, Inc.

Robert H. Bremner, ed., *Children and Youth in America: A Documentary History*, vol. 1, *1600–1865* (Cambridge: Harvard University Press, 1970), 40–41. © 1970 by the American Public Health Association. Reprinted by permission of the publisher.

Edmund S. Morgan, *The Puritan Family* (New York: Harper and Row, 1944), 66, 67–68, 87–90. © 1944, 1966 by Edmund Sears Morgan. Reprinted by permission of HarperCollins Publishers, Inc.

Jean-Jacques Rousseau, *Émile* (New York: Dutton, 1963), 132–33.

Carl F. Kaestle, *Pillars of the Republic: Common Schools and American Society, 1780–1860* (New York: Hill and Wang, 1983), 96–98. © 1983 by Carl F. Kaestle. Reprinted by permission of Hill and Wang, a division of Farrar, Straus and Giroux, Inc.

Harvey J. Graff, *Conflicting Paths: Growing Up in America* (Cambridge: Harvard University Press, 1995), 156–57. © 1995 by Harvey J. Graff. Reprinted by permission of the publisher.

Mark Twain, *The Complete Tom Sawyer* (New York: Gramercy Books, 1996), 101–6.

John Dewey, *The Child and the Curriculum* (Chicago: University of Chicago Press, 1902), 11–14, 15–16, 17–19, 30–31. © 1902 by the University of Chicago. All rights reserved. Reprinted by the permission of the publisher.

Paula S. Fass, *Outside In: Minorities and the Transformation of American Education* (New York: Oxford University Press, 1989), 44, 44–47, 49, 49–52. © 1989 by Paula S. Fass. Reprinted by permission of Oxford University Press.

Richard Wright, *Black Boy* (New York: Harper and Row, 1966), 267–74. © 1937, 1942, 1944, 1945 by Richard Wright. © renewed 1973 by Ellen Wright. Reprinted by permission of HarperCollins Publishers, Inc.

Brown v. Board of Education, 347 U.S. 483, 74 S.Ct. 686, 98 L.Ed. 873 (1954).

Diane Ravitch, *The Troubled Crusade: American Education, 1945–1980* (New York: Basic Books, 1983), 228–34. © 1983 by Diane Ravitch. Reprinted by permission of Basic Books, a member of Perseus Books, L.L.C.

Robert Coles, *Children of Crisis: A Study of Courage and Fear* (New York: Dell, 1967), 103, 106–11, 111–13. © 1967 by Robert Coles. Reprinted by permission of the author.

Richard Rodriguez, *Hunger of Memory* (New York: Bantam, 1982), 21–22. © 1982 by Richard Rodriguez. Reprinted by permission of David R. Godine Publisher, Inc.

Jerome S. Bruner, *On Knowing: Essays for the Left Hand* (Cambridge: Harvard University Press, 1962), 118–19, 120–22, 123–24, 124. © 1962 by the President and Fellows of Harvard College. Reprinted by permission of the publisher.

Albert Shanker, "Where We Stand," advertisement in *New Republic*, June 6, 1994, 17. © 1994 by the American Federation of Teachers. Reprinted by permission of the American Federation of Teachers.

Howard Gardner, *Multiple Intelligences* (New York: Basic Books, 1993), 7–10. © 1993 by Howard Gardner. Reprinted by permission of Basic Books, a member of Perseus Books, L.L.C.

"Mother's Little Helper," *Newsweek*, March 18, 1996, 51–53. © 1996 by Newsweek, Inc. All rights reserved. Reprinted by permission.

Part 7: Children without Parents

Abbot Emerson Smith, *Colonists in Bondage: White Servitude and Convict Labor in America* (Gloucester, MA: Peter Smith Publisher, 1965), 71–74. © 1947 by University of North Carolina Press. Reprinted by permission of the publisher.

Aubrey C. Land, Lois Green Carr, and Edward C. Papenfuse, eds., *Law, Society, and Politics in Early Maryland* (Baltimore: Johns Hopkins University Press, 1977), 41–42, 50–52. © 1977 by Hall of Records Commission of the State of Maryland. All rights reserved. Reprinted by permission of the publisher.

David Herbert Donald, *Lincoln* (New York: Simon and Schuster, 1995), 27–28. © 1995 by David Herbert Donald. Reprinted by permission of Simon and Schuster, Inc.

Frederick Douglass, "Narrative of the Life of Frederick Douglass" in *Autobiographies* (New York: Library of America, 1994), 32–34.

Robert H. Bremner, ed., *Children and Youth in America: A Documentary History*, vol. 1, *1600–1865* (Cambridge: Harvard University Press, 1970), 291–93, 298–99, 309–12. © 1970 by the American Public Health Association. Reprinted by permission of the publisher.

Mark Twain, *The Portable Mark Twain*, ed. Bernard DeVoto (New York: Viking, 1946), 213–15, 218–19, 220–21, 222.

Charles S. Johnson, *Shadow of the Plantation* (Chicago: University of Chicago Press, 1969), 61–62, 63, 64–65, 65–66. © 1934 by the University of Chicago. Reprinted by permission of the University of Chicago Press.

Judith S. Wallerstein and Joan Berlin Kelly, *Surviving the Breakup: How Children and Parents Cope with Divorce* (New York: Basic Books, 1980), 55–58, 59–61, 62–63, 64. © 1980 by

Judith S. Wallerstein and Joan Berlin Kelly. Reprinted by permission of Basic Books, a member of Perseus Books, L.L.C.

Arlene Skolnick, "Solomon's Children," in *All Our Families: New Policies for a New Century*, ed. Mary Ann Mason, Arlene Skolnick, and Stephen D. Sugarman (New York: Oxford University Press, 1998), 236–42. © 1998 by Oxford University Press, Inc. Reprinted by permission of Oxford University Press, Inc.

Mary Ann Mason, *The Custody Wars* (New York: Basic Books, 1999), 175–80. © 1999 by Mary Ann Mason. Reprinted by permission of Basic Books, a member of Perseus Books, L.L.C.

Nancy S. v. Michele G., 228 Cal.App.3d 831, 279 Cal.Rptr. 212 (1991).

Johnson v. Calvert, 5 Cal. 4th 84, 851 P.2d 776, 19 Cal.Rptr. 2d 494 (1993).

Al Desetta, ed., *The Heart Knows Something Different: Teenage Voices from the Foster Care System* (New York: Persea Books, 1996), 121–24, 135–38. © 1996 by Youth Communications/New York Center, Inc. Reprinted by permission.

Nanette Schorr, "Foster Care and the Politics of Compassion," *Tikkun* 7:3 (May–June 1992): 19–22, 80–81, 82. Reprinted from TIKKUN MAGAZINE, A BI-MONTHLY JEWISH CRITIQUE OF POLITICS, CULTURE, AND SOCIETY. Information and subscriptions are available from TIKKUN, 26 Fell Street, San Francisco, CA 94102.

Katharine Q. Seelye, "Orphanage Revival Gains Ground," *New York Times*, December 20, 1997, A7. © 1997 by The New York Times. Reprinted by permission.

Part 8: The Vulnerable Child

Jacob A. Riis, *How the Other Half Lives*, ed. Sam Bass Warner, Jr. (Cambridge: Harvard University Press, 1970), 124–29. © 1970 by the President and Fellows of Harvard College. Reprinted by permission of the publisher.

Robert H. Bremner, ed., *Children and Youth in America: A Documentary History*, vol. 1, *1600–1865* (Cambridge: Harvard University Press, 1970), 358–59, 369–70, 388–89. © 1970 by the American Public Health Association. Reprinted by permission of the publisher.

Charles R. King, *Children's Health in America* (New York: Twayne Publishers, 1993), 106–7, 107–9, 109–10, 149–50. © 1993 by Twayne Publishers. Reprinted by permission of Macmillan Library Reference USA.

"If Polio Strikes, What to Do," *U.S. News & World Report*, July 17, 1953, 64. © July 17, 1953, by U.S. News & World Report.

"What the Polio Tests Really Showed," *U.S. News & World Report*, April 22, 1955, 42, 43. © April 22, 1955, by U.S. News & World Report.

Geraldo Rivera, *Willowbrook* (New York: Vintage, 1972), 3, 20–22. © 1972 by Geraldo Rivera. Reprinted by permission of Random House, Inc.

Paula S. Fass, *Kidnapped: Child Abduction in America* (New York: Oxford University Press, 1997), 213–17, 218–21. © 1997 by Paula S. Fass. Reprinted by permission of Oxford University Press.

Suzanne M. Sgroi, "Molestation of Children," *Children Today* 4 (May–June 1975): 19–21, 44.

John Crewdson, *By Silence Betrayed* (Boston: Little, Brown, 1988), 1–5. © 1988 by John Crewdson. Originally published by Little, Brown and Company. Reprinted by permission of the author.

Neil Gilbert, "Miscounting Social Ills," *Society* (March–April 1994): 18, 19–20, 20–21.

© 1994 by Transaction Publishers. Reprinted by permission of Transaction Publishers. All rights reserved.

Sylvia Ann Hewlett, *When the Bough Breaks* (New York: Basic Books, 1991), 124–26, 127. © 1991 by Sylvia Ann Hewlett. Reprinted by permission of Basic Books, a member of Perseus Books, L.L.C.

Todd S. Purdum, "Couple Held in Beating of Daughter," *New York Times*, November 3, 1987, B1. © 1987 by The New York Times. Reprinted by permission.

T. Kuntz, "A Glimpse into a Hell for Helpless Infants," *New York Times*, November 2, 1997, sec. 7, p. 7. © 1997 by The New York Times. Reprinted by permission.

Jan Hoffman, "The Charge Is Murder: An Infant's Death, an Ancient 'Why?'" *New York Times*, December 22, 1996, sec. 4, p. 4. © 1996 by The New York Times. Reprinted by permission.

Hillary Rodham Clinton, "Remarks of the First Lady to Children Now Conference," March 4, 1994.

Al Desetta, ed., *The Heart Knows Something Different: Teenage Voices from the Foster Care System* (New York: Persea Books, 1996), 197–200, 202–3. © 1996 by Youth Communication/New York Center, Inc.

Part 9: Sexuality

Henry James, *The Turn of the Screw*, ed. Robert Kimbrough (New York: W. W. Norton, 1966), 13, 19–20, 52, 53, 83–88.

James R. Kincaid, *Child-Loving: The Erotic Child and Victorian Culture* (New York: Routledge, 1992), 198, 199–200, 201–2. © 1992 by Routledge, Chapman and Hall, Inc. Reprinted by permission of Routledge, Inc.

Sigmund Freud, *A General Introduction to Psychoanalysis* (Garden City, NY: Garden City Publishing Company, 1943), 185–87. © 1920, 1935 by Edward L. Bernays. Reprinted by permission of Sigmund Freud © Copyrights, The Institute of Psycho-Analysis and The Hogarth Press.

Mary E. Odem, *Delinquent Daughters: Protecting and Policing Adolescent Female Sexuality in the United States, 1885–1920* (Chapel Hill: University of North Carolina Press, 1995), 13–17, 20, 22–24. © 1995 by the University of North Carolina Press. Reprinted by permission of the publisher.

Margaret Mead, *Coming of Age in Samoa* (New York: William Morrow, 1964), 222–23. © 1928, 1949, 1955, 1961, 1973 by Margaret Mead. Reprinted by permission of William Morrow and Company, Inc.

Alfred C. Kinsey et al., *Sexual Behavior in the Human Female* (Philadelphia: W. B. Saunders, 1953), 103–4, 105–10, 111–13, 114–15, 119–22. © 1953 by W. B. Saunders Company. Reprinted by permission of the publisher.

Vladimir Nabokov, *Lolita* (New York: Random House, 1989), 164–65, 166, 183–85, 236–38. © 1955 by Vladimir Nabokov. Reprinted by permission of Vintage Books, a division of Random House, Inc.

Neil Postman, *The Disappearance of Childhood* (New York: Delacorte, 1982), 83–85, 85–86, 91–92, 94, 97. © 1982 by Neil Postman. All rights reserved. Reprinted by permission.

Jeffrey Moussaieff Masson, *The Assault on Truth: Freud's Suppression of the Seduction Theory* (New York: Harper Perennial, 1992), 110, 133–34, 134–35, 144. © 1992 by Jeffrey Moussaieff Masson. All rights reserved. Reprinted by permission.

Marla Williams and Dee Norton, "The Unraveling of a Monstrous Secret: Sex Abuse Scandal Has Wenatchee Reeling," *Seattle Times*, June 8, 1995, A1. © 1995 by Seattle Times Company. Reprinted by permission.

Nina Bernstein, "On Prison Computer, Files to Make Parents Shiver," *New York Times*, November 18, 1996, A1. © 1996 by The New York Times. Reprinted by permission.

Maris A. Vinovskis, *An "Epidemic" of Adolescent Pregnancy? Some Historical and Policy Considerations* (New York: Oxford University Press, 1988), 124–26. © 1987 by Maris A. Vinovskis. Reprinted by permission of Oxford University Press, Inc.

Part 10: The Child and the State

Robert H. Bremner, ed., *Children and Youth in America: A Documentary History*, vol. 1, *1600–1865* (Cambridge: Harvard University Press, 1970), 39–40. © 1970 by the American Public Health Association. Reprinted by permission of the publisher.

Jacob A. Riis, *The Children of the Poor* (New York: Scribner's, 1892), 142–52.

Linda Gordon, *Heroes of Their Own Lives* (New York: Penguin, 1988), 59–63, 69–73. © 1988 by Linda Gordon. Reprinted by permission of the author.

Mary Ann Mason, *From Father's Property to Children's Rights* (New York: Columbia University Press, 1994), 85–92. © 1994 by Columbia University Press. Reprinted by permission of the publisher.

Robert H. Bremner, ed., *Children and Youth in America: A Documentary History*, vol. 2 (Cambridge: Harvard University Press, 1971), 757–58. © 1971 by the American Public Health Association. Reprinted by permission of the publisher.

Susan Tiffin, *In Whose Best Interest? Child Welfare Reform in the Progressive Era* (Westport: Greenwood Press, 1982), 216–25. © 1982 by Susan Tiffin. Reprinted by permission of Greenwood Publishing Group, Inc., Westport, CT.

Ben B. Lindsey and Rube Borough, *The Dangerous Life* (New York: Horace Liveright, 1931), 118–24.

"The Children's Charter," in *White House Conference, 1930* (New York: Century, 1930), 45–48.

Tinker v. Des Moines Independent Community School District, 393 U.S. 503 (1969).

In re Gault, 387 U.S. 1 (1967).

Peter Fimrite, "Tiny Suspect Perplexes System," *San Francisco Chronicle*, April 30, 1996, A13. © 1996 by The San Francisco Chronicle. Reprinted by permission.

"Vote for 18-Year-Olds," *U.S. News & World Report*, January 25, 1971, 88–89. © 1971 by U.S. News & World Report. Reprinted by permission.

"Now That the Voting Age Is Lower . . . ," *U.S. News & World Report*, July 12, 1971, 58. © 1971 by U.S. News & World Report. Reprinted by permission.

Carey v. Population Services International, 431 U.S. 678 (1977).

Bellotti v. Baird, 443 U.S. 622 (1979).

Parham v. J. R., 442 U.S. 584 (1979).

In re Marriage of Marshall and Nussbaum, 278 Ill.App.3d 1071, 215 Ill.Dec. 599 (1996).

Mary Ann Mason, *The Custody Wars* (New York: Basic Books, 1999), 65–66, 68–70. © 1999 by Mary Ann Mason. Reprinted by permission of Basic Books, a member of Perseus Books, L.L.C.

United Nations Convention on the Rights of the Child (1989).

Part 11: The Child's World

Karin Calvert, *Children in the House: The Material Culture of Early Childhood, 1600–1900* (Boston: Northeastern University Press, 1992), 22–25, 27–28, 31–33. © 1992 by Karin Calvert. Reprinted by permission of Northeastern University Press.

Jacob Stroyer, *My Life in the South* (Salem, MA, 1898), in *African American Voices: The Life Cycle of Slavery*, ed. Steven Mintz (St. James, NY: Brandywine Press, 1993), 87–89.

Rose Cohen, *Out of the Shadow* (1918; reprint, Ithaca: Cornell University Press, 1995), 61–65, 72–74, 77–80.

Mary Paik Lee, *Quiet Odyssey: A Pioneer Korean Woman in America* (Seattle: University of Washington Press, 1990), 34–35, 35–37, 37–39, 40. © 1990 by the University of Washington Press. Reprinted by permission of University of Washington Press.

Henry Roth, *Call It Sleep* (New York: Avon, 1973), 251–57. © 1934, renewed © 1962 by Henry Roth. Reprinted by permission of Farrar, Straus and Giroux, Inc.

James T. Farrell, *Studs Lonigan* (New York: Vanguard Press, 1935), 102–4, 116–18. © 1932, 1934, 1935 by the Vanguard Press, Inc.

Simon Ortiz, "The Language We Know," in *I Tell You Now: Autobiographical Essays by Native American Writers*, ed. Brian Swann and Arnold Krupat (Lincoln: University of Nebraska Press, 1987), 185–194. © 1987 by the University of Nebraska Press. Reprinted by permission.

Piri Thomas, *Down These Mean Streets* (New York: Alfred A. Knopf, 1969), 18–23. © 1967 by Piri Thomas. Reprinted by permission of Alfred A. Knopf, Inc.

Maya Angelou, *I Know Why the Caged Bird Sings* (New York: Bantam, 1969), 21–25, 26–27. © 1969 and renewed 1997 by Maya Angelou. Reprinted by permission of Random House, Inc.

Gus Lee, *China Boy* (New York: Dutton, 1991), 97–99, 102–3, 107–10. © 1991 by Augustus S. M. S. Lee. Reprinted by permission.

Lydia Yuri Minatoya, *Talking to High Monks in the Snow* (New York: HarperCollins, 1992), 31–32, 33, 34. © 1992 by Lydia Minatoya. Reprinted by permission of HarperCollins Publishers, Inc.

Mark Twain, *The Complete Tom Sawyer* (New York: Gramercy Books, 1996), 12–15.

James Whitcomb Riley, *Child Rhymes* (New York: Grosset and Dunlap, 1905), 60–63.

L. Frank Baum, *The Wizard of Oz* (Garden City, NY: Nelson Doubleday, 1978), 137–40.

L. M. Montgomery, *Anne of Green Gables* (New York: Bantam, 1987), 62–65.

Dr. Seuss, *The Sneetches and Other Stories* (New York: Random House, 1953), 5, 7. TM and © 1961 and © renewed 1989 by Dr. Seuss Enterprises, L. P. Reprinted by permission of Random House, Inc.

Roald Dahl, *The BFG* (New York: Puffin Books, 1987), 48–54. © 1982 by Roald Dahl. Reprinted by permission of Farrar, Straus and Giroux, Inc.

Gillian Avery, *Behold the Child: American Children and Their Books, 1621–1922* (Baltimore: Johns Hopkins University Press, 1994), 2–4, 68–70. © 1994 by Gillian Avery. All rights reserved. Reprinted by permission of the publisher.

Anne Scott MacLeod, *American Childhood: Essays on Children's Literature of the Nineteenth and Twentieth Centuries* (Athens: University of Georgia Press, 1994), 116, 117–20. © 1994 by University of Georgia Press. Reprinted by permission.

Gary Cross, *Kids' Stuff: Toys and the Changing World of American Childhood* (Cambridge: Harvard University Press, 1997), 202–4, 205–6, 207–8. © 1997 by the President and Fellows of Harvard College. Reprinted by permission of the publisher.

Index

The titles of works in the index appear in the way they are used in this volume. For the original titles, the reader is advised to turn to the Sources section.

Abbot, Edith, 553
Abbot, Grace, 553
Abbott, Jacob, 90, 91, 94, 684
"Abortion," 596–598
Acoma Pueblo people, 646–648
Adams, William T. (Oliver Optic), 92–93
Addams, Jane, 551, 552, 553
Adolescence, 4, 6, 7, 123, 125–128, 129–131, 132–138, 139–141, 142–145, 146–148, 149–152, 153–160, 161–165, 166–168, 177–180, 181–182, 183–186, 187–190, 191–195, 196–199, 637–641, 649–652
Adoption, 3, 4, 5, 347, 371–373
African Americans, 2, 3, 6, 187–190, 221–222, 235, 263–264, 313–317, 318–320, 321–325, 326–330, 357–358, 371–373, 625–626, 653–656, 657–662
Age-of-consent campaign, 494–498
Alcott, Louisa May, 90, 98, 218, 690; "Little Women," 98–99; "Learning Self-Control," 218–220
Alcott, William, 623
Alden, Lyman P.: "The Shady Side of the 'Placing-out System,' " 361–362
Alger, Horatio, 90, 93, 94
Alta Bates Hospital (Berkeley, Calif.), 29, 30
Amen, Daniel, 179–180
American Association of University Women, 56, 119; "How Schools Shortchange Girls," 119–121
American Association of University Women Educational Foundation: *How Schools Shortchange Girls*, 119–121
American Federation of Teachers, 337
American High School Today, The (Conant), 323
American Humane Association, 542
American Psychological Association, 308
American Women Suffrage Association, 495
Andersen, Hans Christian, 91, 95, 686
Angelou, Maya, 653; "I Know Why the Caged Bird Sings," 653–656
Anne of Green Gables (Montgomery), 673–675

Anorexia nervosa, 161–165
Anthony, Susan B., 495
"Apprentices, Servants, and Child Labor," 244–246
Ariès, Philippe, 283; "Education and the Concept of Childhood," 283–285
Asian Americans, 3, 275–278, 632–636, 657–662, 663–665
Associated Charities , 545
Attention-Deficit/Hyperactivity Disorder (ADHD), 343–345
Avery, Gillian, 95, 684; "American Children and Their Books," 684–689

Baby Jessica, 381, 382, 383, 384, 385, 386
Baby Richard, 381, 382, 383, 384
Baird, William, 597
Baker, Josephine, 18–19, 427
Baker, Russell Carl, 227–228
Baker v. Carr, 589
Baker v. Owen, 227–228
Ballard, Mary, 125
Barnes, Robert, 22
Bartley v. Kremens, 601
Baum, L. Frank, 670, 686; "The Wizard of Oz," 670–672
Beauvoir, Simone de, 161
Beecher, Henry Ward, 92, 134
Beech Nut Company. See *Happy Mealtimes for Babies*
Begley, Sharon, "Why the Young Kill," 177–180
Bellotti v. Baird, 596–598
Benny, Jack, 254
Berle, Milton, 254
Bermudez, Ignacio, 585
Bernstein, Nina, "On Prison Computer, Files to Make Parents Shiver," 524–529
Best, Joel, 454
Bestor, Arthur, 322
Binet, Alfred, 308
Black, Justice Hugo L., 587, 588, 590
Blackmun, Justice Harry A., 587, 588, 594

Blackstone, William, 231, 494
Blackwell, Henry, 495
Blake, Judith, 42
Blue, Ben, 254
Blue's Clues, 697, 698
Bly, Robert, 198
Bodin, Melissa Moore, 35; "The Eggs, Embryos, and I," 35–37
Bonebright, Sarah, 87, 89
Borough, Rube, "Juvenile Court and the Artistry of Approach," 566–569
Bowen, Louise de Koven, 563–564
Boys' Home, 410–413
Brace, Charles Loring, 359; "Placing Orphan Children with Farm Families," 359–361
Bradstreet, Anne, 4, 11, 44, 79; "Before the Birth of One of Her Children," 11; "In Reference to Her Children, 23 June, 1659," 79–81; "Thoughts on Child Rearing," 44
Brazelton, T. Berry, 9, 72; "Mothers and Fathers and Rearing Children," 72–74
Breast-feeding, 20–22, 23–28
Brennan, Justice William J., 587, 588, 594
Breuer, Joseph, 519–520
Brice, Fanny, 254, 255
Brown, Christine, 449, 450
Brown, Claude, 187; "Manchild in the Promised Land," 187–190
Brown, John, 32, 33
Brown, Lesley, 32, 33, 34
Brown v. Board of Education of Topeka, 318–320
Bruch, Hilde, 161, 162
Brumberg, Joan Jacobs, 161; "Anorexia Nervosa in the 1980s," 161–165
Bruner, Jerome S., 324, 333; "The Quest for Clarity," 333–336
Bunyan, Paul, 686
Bureau of Indian Affairs (BIA), 646
Burger, Chief Justice Warren E., 587, 599
Burkett, Saretta Andrea, "I Won't Abuse My Kids," 473–476
Burns, George, 253, 254, 255
Burnside v. Byars, 574, 575, 576
Bushnell, Horace, 216; "A Milder and Warmer Family Government," 216–217
Byrd, William, 211–212

Cahill, Mary Ann, 28
Calhoun, Arthur, 12
California Court of Appeal. See *Nancy S. v. Michele G.*
California Supreme Court. See *Johnson v. Calvert*
California Youth Authority, 586
Calvert, Crispina, 395–396, 397
Calvert, Karin, 83, 619; "Suits and Frocks," 83–86; "The Material Culture of Early Childhood: The Upright Child," 619–624
Calvert, Mark, 395–396, 397

Cantor, Eddie, 254, 255
Cardell, William, 688
Carey v. Population Services International, 594–595
Carneal, Michael, 180
Carr, Lois Green, 352; "Orphans' Court," 352–354
Catcher in the Rye, The (Salinger), 181
Cattell, James, 307
Center for Surrogate Parenting & Egg Donation, Inc. (Calif.), 39
Chamberlain, George Gerald, 526, 527, 528
Channing, Walter, 19
Charities, 417–421, 424–426, 539–542, 543–548
Charter of the United Nations. *See* United Nations
Chase, Josephine, 310–311
Chase, Mary Ellen, 690
Cherlin, Andrew J., 42
Chern, Chii, 29, 30
Chern, Po-Ying, 29–31
Chernin, Kim, 163
Chicago Juvenile Court, 551
Child, Lydia Maria, 20, 133, 212
Child abduction, 349–351, 438–443, 453–455
Child abuse, 206–207, 359–366, 404–409, 415, 417–421, 436–437, 438–443, 444–448, 449–452, 453–455, 459–461, 462–465, 473–476, 500–510, 511–514, 518–520, 521–523, 524–529, 539–542, 543–548, 555–558, 625–626
Childbirth, 1, 3, 11, 12–15, 16–19, 20–22, 29–31, 32–34
Childbirth without Fear (Read), 27
Child custody, 2, 381–386, 387–390, 391–394, 395–398, 535, 549–554, 603–608, 609–611
Child development, 3, 49–51, 54–55, 56–60, 61–63, 64–66, 67–71, 72–74, 102–103, 104–107, 108–109, 110–115, 116–118, 132–138, 139–141, 303–306, 374–380
Child-Family Digest, 27
Child Find, 453–454
Childhood and Society (Erikson), 110–115
Childhood innocence, 2, 4, 5, 7, 481–487, 488–490, 494–498, 515–517, 669
Child labor, 1, 2, 3, 4, 206–207, 235, 237–240, 241–243, 244–247, 248, 249–250, 251–252, 253–255, 256–259, 260–262, 263–264, 265–268, 269–271, 272–274, 275–278, 347, 349–351, 357–358, 359–366, 535, 549–554, 555–558, 632–636
Childlessness, 41–43
Childrearing, 2, 3, 4, 6, 9, 23–28, 44, 45–48, 49–51, 52–53, 54–55, 56–60, 61–63, 67–71, 72–74, 132–138, 201, 203–205, 208–210, 211–215, 216–217, 218–220, 223–226, 292–293, 619–624
Children's Bureau Bill, 556–557
Children's Aid Society, 359, 545
"Children's Bureau, The," 555–558
Children's Charter, The. *See* White House Conference on Child Health and Protection

Children's Division of the American Humane Association, 444, 445
Children's Hospital (Boston, Mass.), 73
Children's Hospital Medical Center (Oakland, Calif.), 30
"Children's Involuntary Labor," 241–243
Children's literature, 90–94, 95–97, 98–99, 100–101, 218–220, 298–302, 367–370, 666–668, 669, 670–672, 673–675, 676–678, 679–683, 684–689, 690–693, 700–703
Children's rights, 5, 404–409, 535, 570–572, 573–577, 578–584, 587–590, 591, 592–593, 594–595, 596–598, 599–602, 603–608, 609–611, 612–615, 690–693
"Childsavers," 551
"Child-saving" movement, 539
Child welfare, 235, 272–274, 347, 359–366, 404–409, 410–413, 417–421, 422–423, 424–426, 427–431, 539–542, 543–548, 549–554, 555–558
Child Welfare Movement, 424–426
Chinni, Dante: "Mother's Little Helper: Ritalin and Attention Deficit Disorder," 343–345
"Choosing Childlessness," 41–43
Christmas Gift from Fairyland, A (Paulding), 686
Civilian Conservation Corps (CCC), 265, 266, 267
Clausen, Cara, 381
Clinton, Hillary Rodham, 170, 469; "Media Violence and Children," 469–472
Clinton, President Bill, 169, 470
Cohen, Rose, 256, 627; "A Child Worker in the Garment Industry," 256–259; "A Russian Jewish Girlhood on the Lower East Side," 627–631
Coles, Robert, 326; "Children of Crisis," 326–330
Commentaries on the Laws of England (Blackstone), 231
Conant, James B., 322–323
"Contraception," 594–595
"Corporal Punishment," 227–228
Cotton, John, 288, 289, 290, 291
Courtship, 125–128
Couture, William Arthur, 526, 527, 528
Covello, Leonard, 143–144
Cranch, Christopher, 686
Crewdson, John, "By Silence Betrayed: The Sexual Abuse of Children in America," 449–452
Crispell, Diane, 197
Crockett, Davy, 686
Crockett Almanac, 686
Cross, Gary, 694; "Kids' Stuff: Toys and the Changing World of American Culture," 616, 694–696
Cryogenic Laboratories, Inc., 39
Cubberly, Elwood, 308, 311

Dahl, Roald, 679; "Snozzcumbers," 679–683
Darwin: Darwinian, 479; Darwinism, 68, 136

Davis v. Beason, 274
DeBoer, Jan, 381
DeBoer, Roberta, 381
"Declaration by Privy Council of England, 1620," 242–243
Declaration of the Rights of the Child. *See* United Nations
Declaration on Social and Legal Principles relating to the Protection and Welfare of Children . . . , 613
Declaration on the Protection of Women and Children in Emergency and Armed Conflict, 613
DeFrancis, Vincent, 444, 445
Degler, Carl N., 211; "Introducing Children into the Social Order," 211–215
Demos, John, 132, 261; "Adolescence in Historical Perspective," 132–138; A Family Life in Plymouth Colony," 203–205
Demos, Virginia, 132; "Adolescence in Historical Perspective," 132–138
Denver Juvenile and Family Court, 567
Desetta, Al, *The Heart Knows Something Different,* 399–403, 473–476
de Tocqueville, Alexis, 125
Deutsch, Helene, 105
Dewey, John, 62, 303, 307, 310, 333, 334, 335; "The Child and the Curriculum," 303–306
Dickens, Charles, 415
Disabilities, 337–338
Discipline, 4, 6, 9, 45–48, 201, 203–205, 206–207, 208–210, 211–215, 216–217, 218–220, 221–222, 223–226, 227–228, 229–232, 625–626
Disease/health, 415, 417–421
Divorce, 1, 2, 4, 374–380
Domestic Education (Humphrey), 213
Donald, David Herbert, 355; "Abraham Lincoln and Sarah Bush," 355–356
Douglas, Justice William O., 587, 588
Douglass, Frederick, 357; "A Childhood in Slavery," 357–358
Drew, Nancy, 100–101
Drugs, 187–190

Eating Attitudes Test (EAT), 163
Eating Disorders Inventory (EDI), 163
Eckhardt, Christopher, 573
Edgeworth, Maria, 49, 685, 688; "Toys," 49–51
Edgeworth, Richard Lovell, 685, 687
Education, 2, 3, 4, 5, 6, 7, 9, 49–51, 119–121, 142–145, 227–228, 235, 265–268, 275–278, 281, 283–285, 286–287, 288–291, 292–293, 294–295, 296–297, 298–302, 303–306, 307–312, 313–317, 318–320, 321–325, 326–330, 331–332, 333–336, 337–338, 339–342, 343–345, 535, 555–558, 570–572, 573–577, 632–636, 663–665
Edwards, Robert G., 32–33

"Effects of Segregation and the Consequences of Desegregation, The," 319–320
Eisenhower, President Dwight, 321
Elementary and Secondary Education Act (1965), 325
Elizabethan Poor Laws of 1601, 553
Emerson, Ralph Waldo, 126
Epperson v. Arkansas, 574
Erikson, Erik H., 68–69, 110, 153; "Infantile Sexuality," 110–115; "Identity, Youth, and Crisis," 153–160; Eriksonian, 70

Fairy-Book, The (Verplanck, ed.), 688
Fairy Tale, The (1831 tract), 686
Family, 2, 4, 5, 41–43, 72–74, 142–145, 149–152, 166–168, 203–205, 211–215, 216–217, 263–264, 283–285, 288–291, 331–332, 371–373, 374–380, 387–390, 404–409, 422–423, 424–426, 530–532, 535–536
"Family Instruction in Early Massachusetts," 286–287
"Family in the Social Order, The," 537–538
Farrell, James T., 642; "Young Lonigan," 642–645
Fass, Paula S., 307; "Kidnapping in Contemporary America," 438–443; "Children and the New Deal," 265–268; "Testing the IQ of Children," 307–312
Fechner, Robert, 266
Federal Children's Bureau. See *Infant Care* (various editions)
Federal Emergency Relief Administration (FERA), 265
Feldman, Ronald, 412
Ferber, Edna, 690
Fields, Bennie, 254
Fimrite, Peter, "Punishing Very Young Criminals," 585–586
Finkelhor, David, 455
"First Amendment in School, The," 573–577
Fitzgerald, F. Scott, 181; "Petting," 181–182
Five Points House of Industry, 420–421
Five Points Mission, 420–421
Fliess, Wilhelm, 518–519
Folks, Homer, 563–564
Fortas, Justice Abe, 573, 578
Foster care, 3, 5, 347, 399–403, 404–409
Francis, David, 689
Frank, Lawrence K., 61, 62
Franklin, Benjamin, 12, 13, 249–250; "Choosing a Trade," 249–250
Freedman, Samuel G., 275; "Working Children in Contemporary Chinatown," 275–278
Freeman, Frank, 311
Freud, Sigmund, 68, 69, 102, 104, 105, 106, 107, 153, 154, 161, 162, 479, 491, 518–520, 521; Freudian, 57, 108, 161–162; *The Interpretation of Dreams*, 520; "Polymorphous Perversity," 491–

493; "The Sexual Life of the Child," 102–103; *Studies on Hysteria* (with Breuer), 519
Friend, Bruce, 698
Froehlich, Edwina, 25, 28
Fuentes, Annette, "Cracking Down on Kids," 229–232

Gangs, 146–148
Garbarino, James, 179, 180
Gardner, Howard, 339; The Theory of Multiple Intelligences," 339–342
Gardner, John, 323
Garner, David, 163
Gault, Gerald Francis, 578, 579, 580, 584, 610–611
Gays and lesbians, 1, 191–195, 381–386, 387–390, 391–394, 399–403
Geisel, Theodore. See Seuss, Dr.
Gender, 6, 12–15, 77, 79–81, 82, 83–86, 87–89, 90–94, 95–97, 98–99, 100–101, 102–103, 104–107, 108–109, 110–115, 116–118, 119–121, 125–128, 149–152, 161–165, 166–168, 296–297, 494–498, 500–510
Geneva Declaration of the Rights of the Child of 1924, 613
Gerry, Elbridge T., 419, 541
Gesell, Arnold, 58, 62
G.I. Joe, 694, 695, 696
Gilbert, Neil, 453; "Miscounting Social Ills," 453–455
Gilligan, Carol, 116, 163; "Moral Reasoning in Girls and Boys," 116–118
Gilligan, James, 180
Gingrich, Newt, 412
"Glimpse into a Hell for Helpless Infants, A," 462–465
Golden, Andrew, 180, 229
Goldin, Claudia, 261
Goodrich, Samuel, 92–93, 684, 686, 687, 688, 689
Gordon, Linda, 543; "The Progressive-Era Transformation of Child Protection, 1900–1920," 543–548
Gore, Tipper, 166
Government oversight, 2, 3, 5, 6, 201, 203–205, 206–207, 227–228, 229–232, 235, 237–240, 241–243, 244–247, 251–252, 260–262, 265–268, 272–274, 286–287, 294–295, 318–320, 337–338, 347, 349–351, 352–354, 367–370, 381–386, 387–390, 391–394, 395–398, 417–421, 424–426, 535, 537–538, 539–542, 543–548, 549–554, 555–558, 559–565, 566–569, 570–572, 573–577, 578–584, 585–586, 587–590, 594–595, 596–598, 599–602, 603–608, 609–611
GraBois, Stuart, 440
Graff, Harvey J., 296; "The Education of Mary Anna Longstreth," 296–297
Grant, Stephanie, 701–703
Gregory K. *See* K., Gregory

Grimm, Brothers, 95, 685–686; "Briar Rose," 95–97
Grossberg, Amy S., 467, 468
Gutcheon, Beth, 442

Haeckel, Ernst, 68
Hager, Mary, "Mother's Little Helper: Ritalin and Attention Deficit Disorder," 343–345
Haines, Michael, 261
Hall, G. Stanley, 135–136, 138, 139, 149, 153, 692; "The Physiology and Psychology of Adolescence," 139–141
Hamilton, Alexander, 248; "Children and Manufactures," 248–250
Hancock, LynNell, "Mother's Little Helper: Ritalin and Attention Deficit Disorder," 343–345
Happy Mealtimes for Babies (Beech Nut Company), 27
Harlan, John M., 577, 587, 589, 590
Harmon v. Harmon, 389
Harris, Eric, 177
Harris, Joel Chandler, 686
Hawes, Joel, 134
Hawes, Joseph M., 61, 560; "Child Science and the Rise of the Experts," 61–63
Health and illness, 427–431, 432–435, 436–437, 444–448, 555–558, 570–572, 599–602
Henry IV, 211, 213
Hewlett, Sylvia Ann, 456; "Psychiatric Hospitals for Juveniles?," 456–458
Hine, Lewis, 414, 616
Hines, Harlan, 308
Hispanic Americans, 3, 331–332, 649–652
Hoffman, Jan, 466; "An Infant's Death, an Ancient 'Why?,'" 466–468
Hogarth, William, 624
Holt, L. Emmett, 52, 429; "The Cry," 52–53
Home (Sedgwick), 215
Hoover, President Herbert, 570
Hopkins, Harry, 265, 267
Horney, Karen, 104; "Feminine Psychology," 104–107
Howe, Neil, 197–198
Hull, John, 291
Humbert, Humbert, 511
Humphrey, Herman, 213

Ickes, Harold, 265
Illinois Appellate Court. See *In re Marriage of Marshall and Nussbaum*
Illinois Board of Public Charities, 551, 560
Illinois Statute, 1911, 424–426
Immigrants, 3, 6, 142–145, 235, 237–240, 253–255, 256–259, 275–278, 307–312, 331–332, 349–351, 539–542, 627–631, 632–636, 637–641, 649–652, 663–665
Indentures, 2, 237–240, 241–243, 244–247, 347

Individuals with Disabilities Education Act (IDEA), 337–338
Infancy, 3, 9, 56–60, 64–66, 67–71, 72–74, 102–103, 491–493, 619–624
Infant Care (various editions), 27, 56, 57, 58, 59
Infanticide, 466–468
Infant mortality, 417–421, 427–431, 555–558
In loco parentis, 595
In re Gault, 578–584, 611
In re Marriage of Marshall and Nussbaum, 603–608, 610
Insight Inc., 525, 526
Intelligence, 64–66, 72–74, 116–118, 307–312, 333–336, 339–342
International Center for Residential Education, 411
International Childbirth Education Association, 27
Internet, 524–529
IQ (intelligence quotient), 72–74, 307–312, 339, 340

Jacobson v. Massachusetts, 274
Jahoda, Marie, 154
James, Henry, 481; "The Turn of the Screw," 481–487
James, William, 68, 559
Jehovah's Witnesses, 272
Jessel, George, 254
Jewett, Harold, 586
Johnson, Anna, 395–396, 397
Johnson, Charles S., 371; "Shadow of the Plantation: Separation and Adoption," 371–373
Johnson, Mitchell, 180, 229
Johnson v. Calvert, 395–398
Jolson, Al, 254, 255
Jolson, Harry, 254, 255
"Jordan sex case" (Minn.), 449–452
Judge Baker Guidance Center, 545–546
Juvenile court, 549–554, 555–558, 559–565, 566–569, 578–584
Juvenile crime. *See* Juvenile delinquency
Juvenile delinquency, 5, 177–180, 201, 229–232, 359–366, 555–558, 559–565, 566–569, 578–584, 585–586
"Juveniles' Right to Due Process," 578–584

K., Gregory, 381, 383
Kaestle, Carl F., 294; "Moral Education for Citizenship," 294–295
Kagan, Jerome, 67; "Understanding the Infant," 67–71
Kalb, Claudia, "Mother's Little Helper: Ritalin and Attention Deficit Disorder," 343–345
Kath, Judy, 449, 450
Keene, Carolyn, 100; "Nancy Drew and the Secret of the Old Clock," 100–101

Kelley, Florence, 551, 552, 553, 555–556; "The Federal Government and the Working of Children," 555–556

Kelly, Joan Berlin, 374; "Surviving the Breakup: How Children Respond to Divorce," 374–380

Keniston, Kenneth, 137–138, 153

Kennedy, President John F., 324, 325

Keppel, Francis, 324

Kidnapping. *See* Child abduction

Kincaid, James R., "Child-loving: The Erotic Child and Victorian Culture," 488–490

King, Charles R., 427; "Infant Mortality," 427–431

Kinkel, Kipland, 178, 180, 229

Kinsey, Alfred C., 500; "Preadolescent Sexuality," 500–510

Kinsey Institute for Sex Research, 500–510

Kirk, Robert William, 269; "American Children in the Second World War," 269–271

Klebold, Dylan, 177

Klein, Melanie, 69–70

Kohlberg, Lawrence, 116

Kohn, August, 251; "Children in the Mills," 251–252

Kraft, Hy, 253

Kriesberg, Bessie Turner, 253

Kroll, Joe, 412

Kuhar, Ludwig J., 603

La Leche League, 23–28; *The Womanly Art of Breastfeeding*, 23, 25

Larcom, Lucy, 84, 89

Larned, Augusta, 213

Lasch, Christopher, 553

Lassonde, Stephen A., 142; "Compulsory Schooling Parent-Adolescent Relations," 142–145

Last of the Huggermuggers, The (Cranch), 686

Lathrop, Julia, 551, 553

Laura Spelman Rockefeller Memorial, 61

Leavitt, Judith Walzer, 16; "Brought to Bed: Childbearing in America," 16–19

Lectures to Young Men (Beecher), 134

Lee, Gus, 657; "China Boy," 657–662

Lee, Mary Paik, 627; "Quiet Odyssey: A Pioneer Korean Woman in America," 632–636

"Lesbian Parents in Custody Disputes," 391–394

Lesch, Bluma, 700

Lewis, Ronald, 578, 579

Lewis, Ted, 254

Lieberman, Richard, 179

Lincoln, Abraham, 355–356

Lincoln, Sarah Bush, 355–356

Lincoln, Thomas, 355–356

Lindsay v. Lindsay, 388

Lindsey, Ben B., 561, 563, 566; "Juvenile Court and the Artistry of Approach," 566–569

Locke, John, 4–5, 9, 45, 52, 67, 83, 84, 85, 208, 214–215; "Inculcating Self-Discipline," 45–48, 208–210; Lockean, 479; "The Use of Reason in Child Rearing," 45–48

Loftus, Elizabeth, 523

Lombroso, Cesare, 559

Longstreth, Mary Anna, 296–297

Lost Boys: Why Our Sons Turn Violent and How We Can Save Them (Gabarino), 179

Lydon, Steven, 527, 528

Lytton, Justice, 603

MacLeod, Anne Scott, 87, 690; "American Girlhood in the Nineteenth Century," 87–89; "Children in Fiction and Fact," 690–693

Malthus, Thomas, 12

Mann, Horace, 294

Marshall, Kathy, 603–608, 609–610

Marshall, Thurgood, 587, 588, 594

Mason, Abigail, 84

Mason, David, 83

Mason, Joanna, 84

Mason, Mary Ann, 237, 386, 387; "Fathers/Mothers: Children/Servants," 237–240; "The State as Superparent," 549–554; "Fit to Be a Parent," 387–390; "A Voice for the Child," 609–611

Massachusetts Bay Colony, 537

Massachusetts Court Order, 1655, 206–207

Massachusetts Court Record, 1680–85, 207

Massachusetts Society for the Prevention of Cruelty to Children (MSPCC), 543–548

Massachusetts Statute, 1642, 537–538

Massachusetts Statute, 1648, 286–287

Masson, Jeffrey Moussaieff, 518; "The Assault on Truth: Freud's Suppression of the Seduction Theory," 518–520

Mather, Cotton, 14

Mauldon, Jane, 169; "Families Started by Teenagers," 166–168

McCullers, Carson, 183; "The Member of the Wedding," 183–186

McKenzie, Richard, 410, 412

McMartin day-care case, 523

McMillen, Sally, 20; "Mothers' Sacred Duty: Breast-Feeding Patterns among Middle- and Upper-Class Women in the Antebellum South," 20–22

Mead, Margaret, 108, 149, 499; "Adolescent Girls in Samoa and America," 149–152; "Coming of Age in Samoa," 499; "Male and Female: Sex and Temperament," 108–109

Meaney, Michael, 178

Media, 5, 166–168, 177–180, 436–437, 453–455, 469–472, 515–517, 694–696, 697–699

Medicine, 12–15, 29–31, 35–37, 52–53, 343–345, 415, 436–437

"Mental Health and the Rights of the Child," 599–602

Merlyn's Pen, "Children's Literary Voices," 700–703

Merry's Museum, 689

Meyer, Adolph, 559

Meyer v. Nebraska, 273, 274, 574, 601

Middle District, North Carolina Court. See *Baker v. Owen*

Military service, 129–131, 269–271

Milne, A. A., 690

Minatoya, Lydia Yuri, 663; "Talking to High Monks in the Snow: An Asian American Odyssey," 663–665

Minuchin, Salvador, 162

Monette, Paul, 191; "Becoming a Man: Half a Life Story," 191–195

Montgomery, L. M., 673; "Anne of Green Gables," 673–675

Moody, Anne, 263; "Coming of Age in Mississippi," 263–264

Moore, Clement C., 684

Moore, Michael, 528, 529

Mordecai, Ellen, 88, 89

Morgan, Edmund S., 288; "A Puritan Education," 288–291

Morris, Kathleen, 451, 452

Mother Goose, 686, 689

Mother Goose's Melody (Thomas, ed.), 688, 689

Mother Goose's Quarto, or Melodies Complete (Monroe and Francis), 689

Muis, Let Keung, 275, 276

Muis, Sau Ling, 275, 276

Muis, See Wai, 275, 276, 277

Munger, Theodore T., 135

Munroe, Edmund, 689

Nabokov, Vladimir, 511; "Lolita," 511–514

Nader, Laura, 58

NAMBLA (North American Man Boy Love Association), 442

Nancy S. v. Michele G., 391–394

Nasaw, David, 253; "Children at Work in the City," 253–255

National Center for Juvenile Justice, 230

National Center for Lesbian Rights, 388

National Center for Missing and Exploited Children, 454

National Child Labor Committee, 260

National Conference of Charities and Correction, 561, 563

National Congress of Mothers, 26

National Defense Education Act (NDEA), 322

National Intelligence Test, 309–310

National Missing Children Day, 441

National Science Foundation (NSF), 323, 324

National Woman Suffrage Association, 495

National Youth Administration (NYA), 265–267

Native Americans, 646–648

Natural Childbirth Trust Newsletter, 27

Neff, Robert, 29, 30, 31

New Deal, 265–268

New England Girlhood, A (Larcom), 89

New York Catholic Home Bureau for Dependent Children, 422

New York Charity Organization Society, 553

New York City Statute, 1731, 245–246

Nickelodeon, 697–699

Nixon, President Richard M., 590

North, A., "Breeching Little Ffrank" (1679), 82

North American Council on Adoptable Children, 412

Northend, Charles, 294–295

Norton, Dee, "The Unraveling of a Monstrous Secret," 521–523

"Now That the Voting Age Is Lower . . . ," 592–593

Nussbaum, Hedda, 459–461

Nussbaum, Heidi, 603–608, 610

Nussbaum, Rachel, 604–608, 610

Nussbaum, Sheldon, 603–608, 609–910

Odem, Mary E., 494; "Delinquent Daughters: The Age-of-Consent Campaign," 494–498

Oedipus complex, 102, 103

On the Threshold (Munger), 135

Optic, Oliver. See Adams, William T.

Orphanages, 410–413

Orphans, 2, 3, 5, 235, 237–240, 347, 349–351, 352–354, 355–356, 357–358, 359–366, 367–370, 371–373, 399–403, 404–409, 410–413, 417–421, 549–554, 555–558, 673–675

Ortiz, Simon, 646; "Growing Up Native American: The Language We Know," 646–648

Page, Elizabeth, 83, 84

Page, Mann, 83

Painter, Harold, 386

Parens patriae, 560, 583

Parenting, 1, 44, 54–55, 72–74, 79–81, 208–210, 211–215, 218–220, 223–226, 391–394, 395–398, 462–465, 599–602, 603–608

Parents Aid Society, Inc. (Parents Aid), 597

Parham v. J. R., 599–602

Parley, Peter, 684, 688, 689

Parnell, Kenneth, 441, 442

Patri, Angelo, 62–63

Patz, Etan, 438–443

Patz, Julie, 438

Patz, Stanley, 439

Paulding, James Kirke, 686

Peck, George Wilbur, 686

Pedophilia, 438–443, 444–448, 449–452, 453–455, 488–490, 511–514, 521–523, 524–529

Penis envy, 104–107

Pennington, James W. C., 221; "The Life of a Slave Child," 221–222

Perrault, Charles, 95, 686, 688

Perry, Bruce, 178–179

Peterson, Brian C., Jr., 467, 468

Petit, Charles, 29; "Amazing Births: Medical History in 'Miracle' Births," 29–31

Philadelphia Society for Organizing Charity, 553

Piaget, Jean, 64, 68, 69, 116, 340; "The Construction of Reality in the Child," 64–66

Pierce v. Society of Sisters, 274, 601

Pilgrim's Progress (Bunyan), 91

Pipher, Mary, 166; "Reviving Ophelia: Saving the Selves of Adolescent Girls," 166–168

Planned Parenthood of Central Missouri v. Danforth, 595, 596, 597

Platt, Anthony M., 560

Play, 3, 4, 5, 49–51, 83–86, 87–89, 110–115, 694–696, 697–699

Plessy v. Ferguson, 318–319

"Polio," 432–435

Polio vaccine, 430, 432–435; "If Polio Strikes, What to Do," 432–433; "What the Polio Tests Really Showed," 433–435

Postman, Neil, 515; "The Disappearance of Childhood: The Total Disclosure Medium," 515–517

Potter, Beatrix, 690

Poverty, 3, 359–366, 417–421, 422–423, 424–426, 427–431, 539–542, 543–548, 549–554

Powell, Justice Lewis, 596

"Preserving the Home," 422–423

Prince, Sarah, 272–273

Prince v. Massachusetts, 272–274, 601

"Protecting Children from Abusing Masters," 206–207

Prothrow-Smith, Deborah, 179

Psychiatric care, 456–458, 599–602

Psychology, 3, 6, 54–55, 56–60, 61–63, 67–71, 102–103, 104–107, 108–109, 110–115, 116–118, 132–138, 139–141, 153–160, 161–165, 177–180, 307–312, 343–345, 374–380, 491–493, 518–520

Public Works Administration (PWA), 265

Purdum, Todd S.: "Couple Held in Beating of Daughter," 459–461

Pursuit of Excellence, The (Rockefeller Brothers Fund) 322

Ragged Dick (Alger), 93

Ratner, Herbert, 28

Ravitch, Diane, 321; "Education in the Post-Sputnik Era," 321–325

Read, Grantly Dick, 27

Reagan, President Ronald, 441

Reagan Adminstration, 530, 532

Rebel without a Cause (film), 153

Rehnquist, Justice William, 596

Reno, Janet, 229

"Report by Massachusetts Commission on the Support of Dependent Minor Children of Widowed Mothers," 424–426

Reproductive rights, 594–595, 596–598

Reproductive technologies, 1, 3, 9, 29–31, 32–34, 35–37, 38–40, 381–386, 395–398, 427–431

"Request by Virginia Company to Mayor of London, 1619," 241

"Request by Virginia Company to Principal Secretary of James I, 1620," 242

Reynolds v. U.S., 274

Rice, Mary Waterman, 212, 214

Richmond, Mary, 553

"Right to Vote, The," 591

Riis, Jacob A., 417, 539; "The Child-Saving Movement," 539–542; "Waifs of the City's Slums," 417–421

Riley, James Whitcomb, 669; "The Days Gone By," 669

Risen from the Ranks (Alger), 93

Ritalin, 343–345

Rivera, Geraldo, 436; "Welcome to Willowbrook," 436–437

Riverside Magazine for Young People, 686

Rockefeller Brothers' Fund report. See *Pursuit of Excellence, The*

Rodgers, Daniel T., 90; "Nineteenth-Century Boys' Literature," 90–94

Rodriguez, Richard, 331; "Hunger of Memory: The Education of Richard Rodriguez," 331–332

Roe v. Wade, 594, 595, 611

Romero, D. James, 196; "Adulthood? Later, Dude!," 7, 196–199

Roosevelt, President Franklin D., 265, 269

Roosevelt, President Theodore, 553, 558, 562

Ross, William, 125

Rotch, Thomas Morgan, 429

Roth, Henry, 637; "Call It Sleep," 637–641

Rothman, Ellen K., 125; "Courtship and Gender Differences," 125–128

Rousseau, Jean-Jacques, 292; "Émile," 292–293

Rud, James John, 449, 450

Rugrats, The, 698

Russell, Diana, 454–455

Sadker, David, 119, 120

Sadker, Myra, 119, 120

Salinger, J. D., 181

Salk, Jonas E., 430, 432, 433–434

Santa Claus, 684; illustration, 685

SATs, 340

Sawyer, Tom, 299, 666–668

Scapegoat Generation, The: America's War on Adolescents (Males), 197

Schmidt, Dan, 381

Scholten, Catherine M., 12, 41; "Women as Childbearers, 1650–1750," 12–15

School desegregation, 318–320, 326–330

School of Mothercraft, 26

Schorr, Nanette, 404; "Foster Care and the Politics of Compassion," 404–409

Scudder, Horace, 686

Second Sex, The (Beauvoir), 161

Sedgwick, Catharine, 215

Seelye, Katharine Q., 410; "Orphanage Revival Gains Ground," 410–413

Sendak, Maurice, 690

Seuss, Dr. (Theodore Geisel), 676; "The Sneetches," 676–678

Sewall, Samuel, 288

Sexual abuse, 438–443, 444–448, 449–452, 453–455, 500–510, 511–514, 518–520, 521–523, 524–529

Sexuality, 6, 7, 67–71, 102–103, 104–107, 125–128, 139–141, 149–152, 161–165, 166–168, 181–182, 191–195, 479, 481–487, 488–490, 491–493, 494–498, 499, 500–510, 511–514, 515–517, 518–520, 530–532, 594–595, 596–598

Sgroi, Suzanne M., 444; "The Last Frontier in Child Abuse," 444–448

Shanker, Albert, 337; "Children and the Individuals with Disabilities Education Act," 337–338

Sharif, Omar, "How I Lived A Double Life," 399–401

Shaw, Josephine Lowell, 553

Shaw, Ronald M., 391

Sheehy, Gail, 197

Shepherd, Robert, 230, 232

Sherman, Sanford, 30

Sibling Society, The (Bly), 198

Sidney, George, 254

Sigourney, Lydia H., 20

Simmons, Betty M., 272

Skolnick, Arlene, 381; "Solomon's Children: The New Biologism, Psychological Parenthood, Attachment Theory, and the Best Interests Standard," 381–386

Slater, Samuel, 262

Slavery, 2, 3, 6, 221–222, 235, 357–358, 625–626

Smith, Abbot Emerson, 349; "Kidnapping and White Servitude," 349–351

Society for the Prevention of Cruelty to Children, 419, 540–542

Society of St. Vincent de Paul, 422–423

Songs for the Nursery (Tabart), 689

South Carolina Statute, 1740, 246–247

Sphere and Duties of Woman, The, 126

Spock, Benjamin, 9, 27, 28, 58, 59, 227, 663, 664, 223; *Baby and Child Care,* 59; "Managing Young Children," 223–226; *The Pocket Book of Baby and Child Care,* 27

Springen, Karen, "Mother's Little Helper: Ritalin and Attention Deficit Disorder," 343–345

Sputnik, 321, 322, 323

"Standard Form of Indenture for an Apprentice, Virginia, 1659," 244

Stanton, Elizabeth Cady, 495

Star Wars trilogy (film), 694, 695

Stayner, Steven, 441

Steinberg, Don, 697; "What Makes Nick Tick: Nickelodeon Is a Sensibility, a World, an All-Empowering Club: It's CNN for Children," 697–699

Steinberg, Joel Barnet, 459–461

Steinberg, Lisa, 459–461

Stepparents. *See* Lincoln, Sarah Bush

Steptoe, Patrick C., 32–33

Stewart, Justice Potter, 587, 588, 594, 596

Still Missing (Gutcheon), 442

St. Nicholas Magazine, 90, 91, 92

Stone, Lawrence, 211

Stone, Lucy, 495

Story of Jack Halyard, The (Cardell), 688

Stowe, Harriet Beecher, 415

Strawberry Shortcake, 696

Stroyer, Jacob, 625; "My Life in the South," 625–626

Studies on Hysteria (Freud and Breuer), 519

Summit, Roland, 523

"Surrogacy and Child Custody," 395–398

Szmukler, George I., 163–164

Taft, President William Howard, 551

Talbot, Margaret, 38; "The Egg Women," 38–40

Talks with Girls (Larned), 213

Tarkington, Booth, 91

Teacher and the Parent, The (Northend), 294–295

Teenagers, 132–138, 153–160, 166–168

"Teenage Voice from Foster Care," 399–403

"Teenage Voice from Foster Care, A," 473–476

Teen pregnancy, 166–168, 530–532

Terman, Lewis, 308, 311

Tesch, Stephanie, 701

Thomas, Isaiah, 689

Thomas, Piri, 649; "Down These Mean Streets," 649–652

Thorndike, Edward, 310

Thrasher, Frederic M., 146; "The Natural History of the Gang," 146–148

"Three's A Crowd," 41–43

Tiffin, Susan, 559; "The Establishment of Juvenile Court," 559–565

Tinker, John F., 573

Tinker, Mary Beth, 573

Tinker v. Des Moines Independent Community School District, 573

Toliver, Lisa, 586

Tompson, Marian, 25

Town, Cherie, 521–522

Town, Meredith "Gene," 521–522

Toys, 5, 49–51, 83–86, 694–696

Tucker, Sophie, 254

Twain, Mark, 91, 298, 367; "Huckleberry Finn," 367–370, 616; "Tom Sawyer's Examination Day," 298–302; "The Adventures of Tom Sawyer," 666–668
Twenty-sixth Amendment, 591

Ulrich, Laurel Thatcher, 17
Uncle Remus (Harris), 686
Uniform Parentage Act, 391, 392, 393, 396
United Nations: Charter of, 612, 613; "Convention on the Rights of the Child," 612–615; Geneva Declaration of the Rights of the Child, 613; United Nations Standard Minimum Rules for the Administration of Juvenile Justice ("The Beijing Rules"), 613
Universal Declaration of Human Rights, 612, 613
U.S. Children's Bureau, 23, 27, 28, 56, 58, 59, 60, 270, 429, 551, 555, 556, 557, 558
U.S. Office of Education, 266, 269
U.S. Supreme Court, 227, 272, 318, 386, 573, 578, 587, 594, 596, 599, 610–611. *See also by cases*

Vinovskis, Maris A., 530; "The Politics of Parental Notification," 530–532
Violence, 177–180, 201, 206–207, 229–232, 459–461, 469–472, 473–476, 585–586, 625–626, 657–662
Virginia Company, The, 238, 241, 242
"Visitation Rights," 603–608
"Vote for Eighteen-Year-Olds: What Justices Said on Both Sides," 587–590
Voting rights, 587–590, 591, 592–593
Voting Rights Act (1970), 587, 590, 592

Wadsworth, Benjamin, 288, 290
Wald, Lillian, 551, 555, 557; "The House on Henry Street," 557–558
Wallerstein, Judith S., 374; "Surviving the Breakup: How Children Respond to Divorce," 374–380
Ward, Cassey, 387, 388, 390
Ward, John, 387, 390
Ward, Mary, 387, 390
Warner, Charles Dudley, 91
War Production Board, 270
Warren, Chief Justice Earl, 318
Wartime Commission of the National Education Association, 269
Wartime Policies Commission, 269
Watson, John B., 54, 56, 58, 223; "Too Much Mother Love," 54–55
Weiner, Lynn, 23; "Reconstructing Motherhood: The La Leche League in Postwar America," 23–28
Weiss, Nancy Pottishman, 56; "The Mother-Child Dyad Revisited: Perceptions of Mothers and Children in Twentieth-Century Child-Rearing Manuals," 56–60

Werner, Emmy E., 129; "Children's Voices from the Civil War," 129–131
West, Mary, 57, 59
Western Female Seminary, 125
West India Company, 239
West Virginia State Board of Education v. Barnette, 274
White, Francis H., "The Placing-Out System in the Light of Its Results," 363
White, Gregory, 25, 28
White, Justice Byron R., 587, 588
White, Mary, 25, 28
White, Timmy Lee, 441
White, William A., 559
White House Conference on Child Health and Protection, 570; "The Children's Charter," 570–572
White House Conference on Children in a Democracy, 269
White House Conference on the Care of Dependent Children, 422, 553
Wiggin, Kate Douglas, 692, 693
Willard, Frances, 89, 145, 495
Willard, Samuel, 291
Williams, Aubrey, 267
Williams, James, 440
Williams, Marla, "The Unraveling of a Monstrous Secret," 521–523
Williamson, Shameek, "Kicked Out Because I Was Gay," 401–403
Willowbrook (Rivera), 436–437
Willowbrook School, 436–437
Wilson, Mary Ellen, 539
Wingert, Pat, "Mother's Little Helper: Ritalin and Attention Deficit Disorder," 343–345
Wisconsin v. Yoder, 601
Wolfenstein, Martha, 60
Wollaston, John, 83, 84
"Woman Gives Birth to Baby Conceived outside the Body," 32–34
Women's Christian Temperance Union (WTCU), 89, 495
Woodham, Luke, 178, 180
Works Progress Administration (WPA), 265, 266, 267
Wright, John D. , 540, 541
Wright, Richard, 313; "For the Love of Books," 313–317
Wurtz, Feliz, 622

Youth. *See* Adolescence
Youth's Companion, 91

Zelizer, Viviana A., 260; "The Changing Social Value of Children," 260–262
Zuckerman, Michael, 93
Zupnick, Gerald, 597

About the Editors

Paula S. Fass is a professor of history and Chancellor's Professor at the University of California at Berkeley, where she has been on the faculty for twenty-four years. She received her A.B. at Barnard College and an M.A. and Ph.d. in history from Columbia University. An expert on American social and cultural history, she has written extensively on issues of youth, childhood, schooling, family, ethnicity, and the media. Among her most significant works are three major books in the history of childhood and youth, *The Damned and the Beautiful: American Youth in the the 1920s; Outside In: Minorities and the Transformation of American Education; and Kidnapped: Child Abduction in America.*

Professor Fass has been a frequent contributor to professional journals and conferences, and has been widely interviewed in newspapers, on television, and on the radio on matters concerning children and on American culture generally. Most recently she has been interviewed in the *Washington Post*, the *New York Times*, *Chronicle of Higher Education*, ABC News, and National Public Radio. She has served as a consultant for a variety of academic and media projects, including the Aspen Institute for Humanistic Studies, the Poyner Institute for Media Studies, the National Institute for the Humanities, Microsoft's Encarta Encyclopedia, the Spencer Foundation, and the Pulitzer Prizes.

Mary Ann Mason is professor of social welfare at the University of California at Berkeley. Her fields of research include historical and legal issues relating to children and the family. She received her A.B. from Vassar College, her Ph.D. in history from the University of Rochester and her J.D. from the University of San Francisco. She has published several books on children and family issues including *From Father's Property to Children's Rights: A History of Child Custody in America, The Custody Wars: Why Children are Losing the Legal Issues and What We can Do about It,* and *The Equality Trap.* She is the editor of *Debating Children's Lives* and *All Our Families: New Policies for a New Century.* She has also published widely in legal and professional journals.

Professor Mason speaks frequently at national conferences on issues relating to child custody and children's rights. She has written for the *New Republic* and has been frequently interviewed by the media, including the *New York Times, Chronicle of Higher Education*, ABC and NBC News, and National Public Radio. She currently serves on the national board of the Stepfamily Association of America.